The Satisfying Life
Positive Psychology and Personal Growth

Marilyn Hadad
Ryerson University

PEARSON

Toronto

Vice-President, Editorial Director: Gary Bennett
Editor-in-Chief: Michelle Sartor
Acquisitions Editor: Matthew Christian
Marketing Manager: Lisa Gillis
Supervising Developmental Editor: Madhu Ranadive
Project Manager: Ashley Patterson
Manufacturing Manager: Susan Johnson
Production Editor: Sheena Uprety, Cenveo Publisher Services
Copy Editor: Judy Sturrup
Proofreaders: Patricia Jones, Susan Bindernagel
Compositor: Cenveo Publisher Services
Permissions Researcher: Rema Celio
Art Director: Julia Hall
Cover Designer: Anthony Leung
Cover Image: Getty Images

Credits and acknowledgments for material borrowed from other sources and reproduced, with permission, in this textbook appear on the appropriate page within text.

If you purchased this book outside the United States or Canada, you should be aware that it has been imported without the approval of the publisher or the author.

10 9 8 7 6 5 4 3 2 1   [RRD]

Library and Archives Canada Cataloguing in Publication

Hadad, Marilyn, 1950–The Satisfying Life : Positive Psychology and Personal Growth / Marilyn Hadad.

Includes index.
ISBN 978-0-13-208839-8

1. Positive psychology. 2. Self-actualization (Psychology)
I. Title.
BF204.6.H33   2012 150.19'88   C2011-906903-2

ISBN 978-0-13-208839-8

For Milana Drobner. Her life, personal and professional, is based on her faith that life for all of us can and should be meaningful and satisfying. She has been a constant joy and a delight to all who know her, and it is only fitting that a book on positive psychology be dedicated to her.

Contents

Preface

I have taught an upper level psychology course entitled *Models of Personal Growth* for the last 20 years at Ryerson University. In this course, I teach students different, and to them often unimagined, perspectives on what growth and adjustment mean. The students have inevitably responded with enthusiasm to a course which focuses on them and their growth and well-being. It is no wonder, then, that I have watched the development of the field of positive psychology with excitement and joy. Over the years, I have gradually included more and more positive psychology into my course, noting how apt the fit was and how theory benefited from empiricism and empiricism benefited from theory.

Positive psychology courses are proliferating in universities across the world, and as yet there are few textbooks in this area. *The Satisfying Life: Positive Psychology and Personal Growth* emphasizes different conceptions of what constitutes a satisfying, fulfilling life and what research has shown us about how to obtain it. The book discusses the hedonic approach, but is based in the eudaimonic approach (hence the title *The Satisfying Life* rather than, say, *The Good Life*, which has connotations in pop culture of lavish and luxurious lifestyles and an unending stream of pleasurable sensory experiences).

What constitutes a satisfying life differs from individual to individual and from culture to culture. In a multicultural society, this becomes readily apparent. One of the strengths of positive psychology is that its principles may be applied to a multitude of conceptions of a satisfying life, not just those of media-influenced Western society. My aim in writing *The Satisfying Life* was to incorporate as much as I could about what psychology knows regarding how to make one's life as satisfying as possible. To that end, I have not stayed with only the usual topics of positive psychology, but I have expanded my scope to include topics that I teach in my own course, *Models of Personal Growth*, and topics I find trouble many students and interfere with their sense of well-being. Hence, discussions of theoretical and cross-cultural perspectives on adjustment are found here, as well as discussions of stress, procrastination, and loneliness, for example. These discussions may of course be omitted, with no harm done, if an individual instructor so chooses.

My writing style is informal for the most part, although the vocabulary is often more advanced. I choose an informal writing style not only to make the book suitable for lower-level university and college students, but also to engage them. Even on an upper level, we may strive to induce our students to read highly academic writing, but the truth is, they don't like it. And if they don't like it, they may not read it thoroughly, and the likelihood of their retaining the information is lessened. Positive psychology is about what makes life "good," and struggling to read a technical and academic text doesn't make life good. If we admit it, we, the instructors, don't enjoy it very much either (although we may appreciate it as academics). My choice, then, was between a style displaying academic rigour and a style that would have a greater chance of capturing the students' interest. I opted for the students' interest, with the hope of maximizing learning. Most of my previous books have been written in this style, and I have been told on numerous occasions that family and friends of the students have picked up these books to glance at, winding up reading them more fully. Some of my students even said that they had to purchase a second book because they were unable to get the book away from other people! I call that success! That kind of engagement in learning is in keeping with the thrust of positive psychology and seems to me to be more than fitting for this text.

The major problem I had in writing this book was that no sooner had I finished a chapter than new research was published. The research in this area is flourishing, and while I strove to be as current as possible, being completely current was an exercise in futility. For this reason, instructors may wish to assign just-published journal articles to accompany some of the discussions.

Part 1 of *The Satisfying Life* is made up of chapters indicating what has been conceived of as good adjustment leading to a satisfying life in a Western view, an Eastern view, and an Indigenous peoples' (of the Americas, Australia, and Africa) view.

CHAPTER 1: THE SATISFYING LIFE AND HAPPINESS

We all have different conceptions of what constitutes a satisfying life. Even within positive psychology, the satisfying life can be described by the hedonic approach, focusing on pleasurable experiences and sensations, or the eudaimonic approach, focusing on meaning, satisfaction, and fulfillment. These distinctions are discussed, along with a discussion of the typical methods used to study well-being, their strengths, and their limitations (e.g., causality cannot be inferred from correlations). The chapter finishes with a discussion of happiness, what it means, how it is measured, and what correlates with it.

CHAPTER 2: THE SATISFYING LIFE FROM THE PERSPECTIVE OF WESTERN PSYCHOLOGICAL THEORY

Chapter 2 focuses on Western conceptions of the satisfying life. Different psychological theorists have considered optimal adjustment and the satisfying life in different ways. In Chapter 2, some of these differences are explored, giving students a broader perspective on options for examining their own lives. The outlooks of Karen Horney (the real and ideal self, the tyranny of should), Frederick Perls (response–ability), Carl Rogers (the fully functioning person), Abraham Maslow (self-actualization, transcendence), and Rollo May (existentialism, authenticity) are described briefly.

CHAPTER 3: THE SATISFYING LIFE FROM THE PERSPECTIVE OF EASTERN BELIEF SYSTEMS

Chapter 3 broadens the perspective on the satisfying life by discussing Eastern conceptions of this ideal. The satisfying life as conceived of by Yoga, Buddhism, Taoism, Confucianism, Sufism, and Zen are briefly examined.

CHAPTER 4: THE SATISFYING LIFE FROM THE PERSPECTIVE OF INDIGENOUS PEOPLES

Chapter 4 continues exploring conceptions of the satisfying life by examining the views of various Indigenous Peoples, specifically those of Indigenous Peoples of the Americas, of Australia, and of Africa.

Chapters 2, 3, and 4 may be omitted at the instructor's discretion.

Part 2 discusses what science tells us about the inner qualities we need to have a satisfying life, how these qualities impact our lives, and how we can develop them.

CHAPTER 5: OPTIMISM AND HOPE

Chapter 5 covers the area of positive psychology that has received arguably the most attention: optimism. This chapter reviews research on optimism and how to increase it, as well as discussing hope in the framework of hope theory. The relationship between optimism and hope is explored, and the *broaden-and-build theory* of Barbara Frederickson is discussed. The chapter ends with an examination of self-compassion, since the lack of this is a major deterrent to optimism and hope.

CHAPTER 6: SELF-REGULATION

Chapter 6 discusses the research on self-determination theory and the roles of autonomy, competence, and social relatedness in living the satisfying life. Specific topics include self-regulation of both emotion and behaviour and procrastination (as a prime example of a failure to self-regulate). Chapter 6 discusses extrinsic and intrinsic motivation and the effects of high and low motivation on a satisfying life as related to the individual's ability to self-regulate.

CHAPTER 7: CHARACTER STRENGTHS

In Chapter 7, empirical evidence about the role of character strengths and virtues, such as gratitude, forgiveness, courage, and humour, is discussed. The chapter also includes a discussion of wisdom: what it is, how it develops, and how it might be cultivated.

CHAPTER 8: MEANING-MAKING, RELIGION, AND SPIRITUALITY

Meaning-making is found to be a key element in forming a satisfying life and adjusting to the vicissitudes of life. For many people, meaning making is facilitated by religion and spirituality. Indeed, many theoretical orientations contend that a satisfying life is only obtained through transcendence of physical being, belief in "something" beyond oneself, and/or finding a coherence and purpose in human existence. Chapter 8 discusses the roles of meaning-making, religion, and spirituality in living a satisfying life and demonstrates this by examining post-traumatic growth, the growth often shown in the face of pain, loss, and trauma.

CHAPTER 9: STRESS AND RESILIENCE

In twenty-first century society, a common complaint is that life is not satisfying because of the stress that accompanies so much of it. Chapter 9 briefly discusses the way we experience stress, the effects of stress (physical effects, anxiety, depression), and how we can develop hardiness and resilience using positive psychology.

Part 3 examines several environmental influences on the individual that relate to well-being. People are clearly social animals and do not live in a vacuum. How do the environment and our roles in society impact on our ability to live a satisfying life? How can we better deal with the environment in a growing way?

CHAPTER 10: INTERPERSONAL RELATIONSHIPS

High quality social relationships have been found to be part of an array of conditions conducive to a satisfying life. Chapter 10 concentrates on the joys and tribulations of interpersonal relationships and how emotional intelligence plays a part in a satisfying life.

CHAPTER 11: WORK AND LEISURE

The time that we spend awake is occupied either by work or leisure. Both work and leisure can contribute to a satisfying life. Chapter 11 discusses what factors make work and leisure satisfying, as well as balance, savouring, and flow in our experience of the activities that occupy us.

Part 4 examines factors influencing life satisfaction beyond the individual's personal and work life. Besides the relationships we have with friends, family, co-workers, and so on, other external factors can affect our pursuit of the satisfying life and be affected by this pursuit. The effects of our culture and community and the behaviour of ourselves and others within it may impact positively or negatively on our ability to develop a satisfying life. Similarly, the events in our community and the way we relate to the community can have an effect on both our satisfaction and the ability of the community to enhance our satisfaction in life. In Part 4, how positive psychology has been used to increase well-being in real-world examples is discussed as well.

CHAPTER 12: COMMUNITY, MILIEU, AND CULTURE

We are affected by what happens in the communities in which we live; our communities are embedded in a country and culture that influences us, and we may bring a cultural heritage to the way we act and view the world. Chapter 12 examines the effects of community, schools, city, country, and culture on our development of a satisfying life. Particular attention is paid to both the problems and potential growth experienced by people who are newcomers to a country and to the community as a whole as its diversity increases.

CHAPTER 13: APPLIED POSITIVE PSYCHOLOGY

Chapter 13 examines the ways that positive psychology has been used in psychotherapy, schools, colleges and universities, workplaces, and countries and national policies to enhance quality of life, with descriptions of real-world applications.

Each chapter begins with learning objectives to provide a framework for the student. Throughout each chapter are Reflective Exercises. Students may use (or not use) these on their own, or instructors may use them as material for "minute papers" or discussion. The Spotlight on Research boxes describe and critically review a current research project. The chapters include boxed examples to further engage the reader by making the concepts concrete and relevant. Finally, a Comprehensive Summary is provided. At the end of each chapter are Group Discussion Questions which present subjects related to the chapter for debate in class. A glossary with definitions of key terms appears at the end of the book. These pedagogical aids have been useful to me in teaching university for the past 30 years, and will, I hope, be useful to other instructors as well.

Writing this book has been a major undertaking for me over the past year. I seriously doubt that it could have been done without the aid of my dearest friend and colleague, Julia Brandwin-Glait. She read every word and made her comments with humour and insight. It is due to her that tables were added, examples were clarified, and explanations made coherent. I probably could have written a better book if I had listened to her more! She also encouraged me and renewed my own optimism, hope, and self-regulation when they faltered. Julia is the epitome of living positive psychology in her unfailing ability to make meaning and inspire others. "Thank you" is never enough, Julia.

My deepest thanks also go to the incredible publishing team of Pearson Canada. Ky Pruesse, Editor-in-Chief, responded to my initial proposal with enthusiasm and vision, increasing my own excitement and determination. Be well, Ky! Matthew Christian stepped into Ky's enormous shoes for me and has done Ky proud. Thank you, Matthew, you've been an unfailing support. My Developmental Editor, Madhu Ranadive, must surely be the best in the business. She has the knack of spurring one on without nagging and being the world's greatest cheerleader without giving false reassurance. Her comments on the manuscript have been invaluable, and the book would have faltered many times without her. You rock, Madhu! My Pearson Production Manager, Ashley Patterson, has been amazing--the ultimate trouble-shooter, nerve-calmer, and all-round star. I can't thank her enough. I also have appreciation for copy editors, Judy Sturrup, who must have despaired at my total inability to determine when to use "that" and when to use "which" and Susan Bindernagel whose eye is not only eagle-sharp, but sensitive and insightful as well! To all those involved in the production of *The Satisfying Life*, especially the Production Editor, Sheena Uprety, whose work, patience, and tolerance have been outstanding, I give my sincerest appreciation.

The reviewers of this book have shown the highest degree of academic insight, thoroughness, and generosity of spirit in their comments. My thanks go to Mark Holder, University of British Columbia, Okanagan; Andrew Howell, Grant MacEwan University; Deborah Matheson, Vancouver Island University; and John Zelinski, Carleton University.

Finally, my thanks go to you for picking up *The Satisfying Life*. I hope your lives are as satisfying and rich as my life has been in writing this book.

SUPPLEMENTS FOR INSTRUCTORS

Test Item File (ISBN: 978-0-13-291301-0)

This test bank in Microsoft Word includes over 1,000 questions. There are approximately 85 questions per chapter, including multiple choice, true/false, short answer, and essay questions. Each question is accompanied by the correct answer, a page reference where the answer can be found in the book, and a classification of difficulty level (easy, moderate, challenging).

CourseSmart for Instructors (ISBN: 978-0-13-215838-1)

CourseSmart goes beyond traditional expectations, providing instant, online access to the textbooks and course materials you need at a lower cost for students. And even as students save money, you can save time and hassle with a digital *eTextbook* that allows you to search for the most relevant content at the very moment you need it. Whether it's evaluating textbooks or creating lecture notes to help students with difficult concepts, *CourseSmart* can make life a little easier. See how when you visit www.coursesmart.com/instructors.

Pearson Custom Library

For enrollments of at least 25 students, you can create your own textbook by choosing the chapters that best suit your own course needs. To begin building your custom text, visit www.pearsoncustomlibrary.com. You may also work with a dedicated Pearson Custom editor to create your ideal text—publishing your own original content or mixing and matching Pearson content. Contact your local Pearson Representative to get started.

Technology Specialists

Pearson's Technology Specialists work with faculty and campus course designers to ensure that Pearson technology products, assessment tools, and online course materials are tailored to meet your specific needs. This highly qualified team is dedicated to helping schools take full advantage of a wide range of educational resources by assisting in the integration of a variety of instructional materials and media formats. Your local Pearson Education sales representative can provide you with more details on this service program.

SUPPLEMENTS FOR STUDENTS

MySearchLab (ISBN: 978-0-13-290765-1)

MySearchLab offers extensive help to students with their writing and research projects and provides round-the-clock access to credible and reliable source material.

Research

Content on *MySearchLab* includes immediate access to thousands of full-text articles from leading Canadian and international academic journals, and daily news feeds from

The Associated Press. Articles contain the full downloadable text—including abstract and citation information—and can be cut, pasted, emailed, or saved for later use.

Writing

MySearchLab also includes a step-by-step tutorial on writing a research paper. Included are sections on planning a research assignment, finding a topic, creating effective notes, and finding source material. Our exclusive online handbook provides grammar and usage support. Pearson SourceCheck™ offers an easy way to detect accidental plagiarism issues, and our exclusive tutorials teach how to avoid them in the future. And *MySearchLab* also contains AutoCite, which helps to correctly cite sources using MLA, APA, CMS, and CBE documentation styles for both endnotes and bibliographies. To order this book with *MySearchLab* access at no extra charge, use ISBN 0205699421. Take a tour at www.mysearchlab.com.

peerScholar

Firmly grounded in published research, *peerScholar* is a powerful online pedagogical tool that helps develop your students' critical and creative thinking skills. *peerScholar* facilitates this through the process of creation, evaluation, and reflection. Working in stages, students begin by submitting a written assignment. *peerScholar* then circulates their work for others to review, a process that can be anonymous or not depending on your preference. Students receive peer feedback and evaluations immediately, reinforcing their learning and driving the development of higher-order thinking skills. Students can then re-submit revised work, again depending on your preference. Contact your Pearson Representative to learn more about *peerScholar* and the research behind it.

CourseSmart for Students (ISBN: 978-0-13-215838-1)

CourseSmart goes beyond traditional expectations, providing instant, online access to the textbooks and course materials you need at an average savings of 50%. With instant access from any computer and the ability to search your text, you'll find the content you need quickly, no matter where you are. And with online tools like highlighting and note-taking, you can save time and study efficiently. See all the benefits at www.coursesmart.com/students.

About the Author

Marilyn Hadad received her B.Sc. from the University of Toronto and her M.A. and Ph.D. from the Queen's University in Kingston, Ontario. She began her career teaching psychology at the University of Toronto. After 6 years, she found her home at the Ryerson University where she is an associate professor. She specializes in issues surrounding personal growth and other areas of adjustment. She is the author of *The ultimate challenge: Coping with death, dying and bereavement,* published by Nelson Education, Toronto (2009). She coauthored (with Ryerson Professor William Glassman, now retired), the one-semester introductory psychology textbook *Approaches to Psychology,* 5th ed., Open University Press/McGraw-Hill Education, Maidenhead, UK (2009), and is presently working on the sixth edition of that textbook. She is also coauthor, with Ryerson Associate Professor Maureen Reed, of the textbook *The Post-Secondary Learning Experience,* published by Thomson-Nelson, Toronto (2007), to aid students in handling, prospering, and enjoying their postsecondary education. In addition, she has authored the custom publication manuscript *Models of Personal Growth* for her popular and dynamic course of the same name. When not teaching, conducting research, serving on committees, writing, or reviewing textbooks and articles, Marilyn enjoys Canada's art scene and her calico cat, Peaches.

CHAPTER 1

The Satisfying Life and Happiness

Joel says he is a happy man. He savours his food, enjoys the physical delights of life with his partner, gets satisfaction from his work, loves to walk in the woods, and feels that he is becoming better and better as a human being everyday. Yet his life didn't seem to start this way: he came from a home characterized by domestic violence, addiction, and poverty. In the midst of this, Joel kept a bright outlook on life.

Today, Joel isn't rich by common standards and most likely never will be, and he has concerns for the problems he sees in the world around him, including worry about the precarious health of his only child, who has a serious chronic illness.

Nonetheless, he regularly volunteers at a palliative care centre and says, "I'm truly blessed to be able to give this time to people whose lives will soon be over. I may not have a lot of education, but that's OK; there's always something I can give." Far from any of this depressing him, he is a man who wakes up each morning with eager anticipation and gratitude for the opportunities the day will bring.

LEARNING OBJECTIVES

In this chapter, students will learn

- □ What positive psychology is.
- □ How happiness may be defined.
- □ How happiness may be measured.
- □ What makes people happy.
- □ The role of money in happiness.
- □ Whether it is possible to be too happy.

Joel is truly a man to be admired and to inspire others. What's his secret? Psychologists have long been concerned with the problems people encounter in life, the reasons they feel pain, anxiety, and despair, and why they sometimes don't function well. This focus on the unhappy side of life has been worthwhile because it has led to several ways in which this unhappiness can be alleviated. But now, psychology has gone a step further.

POSITIVE PSYCHOLOGY

In 1998, Martin Seligman, the new president of the American Psychological Association, gave his inaugural address calling upon psychologists to begin examining in greater detail the strengths of the human being, how people like Joel can flourish even though his childhood was far from ideal and he has very real worries in his life. The psychologists in the room gave Seligman a standing ovation and, through his guidance, the field of positive psychology was officially recognized.

Positive psychology has itself flourished since that day, with many more psychologists entering into research in the area and new journals devoted to the area being created. **Positive psychology** studies everything that people do that makes them function in an optimal and satisfying way. It includes people's thoughts, feelings, and actions that impact upon themselves, the people in their environment, and their communities. It concentrates on how we, like Joel, can fulfill our potential, give ourselves a happier, more satisfying life, and make our world a better place. It studies our strengths, our values, and our actions that benefit ourselves and others. It is, in a word, positive. The formal definition given by Baumgardner and Crothers (2009) is this:

> Positive psychology is the scientific study of the personal qualities, life choices, life circumstances, and sociocultural conditions that promote a life well-lived, defined by criteria of happiness, physical and mental health, meaningfulness, and virtue. (p. 9)

HAPPINESS

Mother cradles her newborn lovingly as Father stands beside them, with his arms around both. They look at each other and smile. "I just want the baby to be happy," says Father, and Mother nods.

There is a very good chance that a scene such as this was played at your birth, and you may have heard people who love you echo the sentiment since then. You may have said "I just want you to be happy" yourself to someone you care about. That seems to be what we want for ourselves and for others: to be happy, to live a "life above zero" in Baumgardner and Crothers' words (2009, p. 9). Are you happy? Do you live a life above zero? You probably already have a pretty good idea, but take the test in Box 1.1 and find out more about your own happiness.

BOX 1.1

Satisfaction With Life Scale (SWLS)

Diener, E., Emmons, R. A., Larson, R. J., & Griffin, S. (1985). Used with permission.

Below are five statements that you may agree or disagree with. Using the 1–7 scale below, indicate your agreement with each item by placing the appropriate number on the line preceding that item. Please be open and honest in your responding.

- 7 - Strongly agree
- 6 - Agree
- 5 - Slightly agree
- 4 - Neither agree nor disagree
- 3 - Slightly disagree
- 2 - Disagree
- 1 - Strongly disagree

_____ In most ways my life is close to my ideal.

_____ The conditions of my life are excellent.

_____ I am satisfied with my life.

_____ So far I have gotten the important things I want in life.

_____ If I could live my life over, I would change almost nothing.

(Continued)

Understanding Scores on the Satisfaction with Life Scale—Ed Diener

30–35 Very high score; highly satisfied

Respondents who score in this range love their lives and feel that things are going very well. Their lives are not perfect, but they feel that things are about as good as lives get. Furthermore, just because the person is satisfied does not mean she or he is complacent. In fact, growth and challenge might be part of the reason the respondent is satisfied. For most people in this high-scoring range, life is enjoyable, and the major domains of life are going well—work or school, family, friends, leisure, and personal development.

25–29 High score

Individuals who score in this range like their lives and feel that things are going well. Of course their lives are not perfect, but they feel that things are mostly good. Furthermore, just because the person is satisfied does not mean she or he is complacent. In fact, growth and challenge might be part of the reason the respondent is satisfied. For most people in this high-scoring range, life is enjoyable, and the major domains of life are going well–work or school, family, friends, leisure, and personal development. The person may draw motivation from the areas of dissatisfaction.

20–24 Average score

The average of life satisfaction in economically developed nations is in this range—the majority of people are generally satisfied, but have some areas where they very much would like some improvement. Some individuals score in this range because they are mostly satisfied with most areas of their lives but see the need for some improvement in each area. Other respondents score in this range because they are satisfied with most domains of their lives, but have one or two areas where they would like to see large improvements. A person scoring in this range is normal in that they have areas of their lives that need improvement. However, an individual in this range would usually like to move to a higher level by making some life changes.

15–19 Slightly below average in life satisfaction

People who score in this range usually have small but significant problems in several areas of their lives, or have many areas that are doing fine but one area that represents a substantial problem for them. If a person has moved temporarily into this level of life satisfaction from a higher level because of some recent event, things will usually improve over time and satisfaction will generally move back up. On the other hand, if a person is chronically slightly dissatisfied with many areas of life, some changes might be in order. Sometimes the person is simply expecting too much, and sometimes life changes are needed. Thus, although temporary dissatisfaction is common and normal, a chronic level of dissatisfaction across a number of areas of life calls for reflection. Some people can gain motivation from a small level of dissatisfaction, but often dissatisfaction across a number of life domains is a distraction, and unpleasant as well.

10–14 Dissatisfied

People who score in this range are substantially dissatisfied with their lives. People in this range may have a number of domains that are not going well, or one or two

(Continued)

Satisfaction With Life Scale (SWLS), *continued*

domains that are going very badly. If life dissatisfaction is a response to a recent event such as bereavement, divorce, or a significant problem at work, the person will probably return over time to his or her former level of higher satisfaction.

However, if low levels of life satisfaction have been chronic for the person, some changes are in order—both in attitudes and patterns of thinking, and probably in life activities as well. Low levels of life satisfaction in this range, if they persist, can indicate that things are going badly and life alterations are needed. Furthermore, a person with low life satisfaction in this range is sometimes not functioning well because their unhappiness serves as a distraction. Talking to a friend, member of the clergy, counselor, or other specialist can often help the person get moving in the right direction, although positive change will be up the person.

5–9 Extremely Dissatisfied

Individuals who score in this range are usually extremely unhappy with their current life. In some cases this is in reaction to some recent bad event such as widowhood or unemployment. In other cases, it is a response to a chronic problem such as alcoholism or addiction. In yet other cases the extreme dissatisfaction is a reaction due to something bad in life such as recently having lost a loved one. However, dissatisfaction at this level is often due to dissatisfaction in multiple areas of life. Whatever the reason for the low level of life satisfaction, it may be that the help of others are needed—a friend or family member, counseling with a member of the clergy, or help from a psychologist or other counselor. If the dissatisfaction is chronic, the person needs to change, and often others can help.

Were you surprised, or was your score in the range that you thought it would be? Some people may wonder if happiness can actually be measured by asking for ratings on five statements. That's a good question. In reality, studying happiness is more complicated than it may seem. A large part of the problem comes from defining happiness. Try the reflective exercise (on the next page) before you go on.

How Do We Define Happiness?

Hedonism and Eudaimonism

What is "happiness"? Given the quotations in the reflective exercise on the next page, it almost seems that happiness is, like beauty, in the eye of the beholder. Joel defines it in part by the gratitude he feels each day. Traditionally, happiness has been seen from two angles. The first is encompassed by **hedonism**, which involves the pleasure given by objects and experiences. This, of course, can encompass many different things, and the scope of what one may imagine to be pleasurable to different people is boundless. Thus, some people may find that engaging in sensual events such as eating a good meal, drinking fine wine, or engaging in energetic sexual experiences brings them happiness. For others, gaining money, prestige, honour, or power may be the requisites for happiness.

By hedonism, we mean that the person seeks mainly external situations which result in feeling more positive emotions than negative emotions.

Hedonism has been criticized by philosophers for centuries. Aristotle (fourth century BCE, 2003) countered that such pleasures were short-lasting at best and that true happiness could only be found by living a virtuous life. This approach is called **eudaimonia**. A virtuous life, to Aristotle, was a life in which the individual acted in ways that were true to his or her best nature. Only by doing this, he claimed, could lasting happiness be found. In being true to one's nature, Aristotle said that one must live by the **golden mean**, a moderate approach in which one has enough of what one needs and wants, but not too much. Extremism is to be avoided. The eudaimonic approach regards a satisfying life as one in which the individual feels a sense of well-being because of commitment to what is really worthwhile in life, as opposed to pursuit of trivial and temporary sensual pleasures.

REFLECTIVE EXERCISE

What is happiness?

How would you define happiness? An internet search of quotations on happiness yield hundreds, and the variety of definitions for happiness is marked. Do any of these come close to your definition of happiness?

Happiness is nothing more than good health and a bad memory.

—*Albert Schweitzer*

Happiness is having a large, loving, caring, close-knit family in another city.

—*George Burns*

Happiness: a good bank account, a good cook and a good digestion.

—*Jean-Jacques Rousseau*

Happiness is when what you think, what you say, and what you do are in harmony.

—*Mahatma Gandhi*

Happiness lies in the joy of achievement and the thrill of creative effort.

—*Franklin D. Roosevelt*

Happiness is the interval between periods of unhappiness.

—*Don Marquis*

Happiness belongs to the self-sufficient.

—*Aristotle*

Happiness is a Swedish sunset—it is there for all, but most of us look the other way and lose it.

—*Mark Twain*

Happiness is not being pained in body or troubled in mind.

—*Thomas Jefferson*

Happiness is not a goal, it is a by-product.

—*Eleanor Roosevelt*

Happiness is unrepentant pleasure.

—*Socrates*

Happiness is a warm puppy.

—*Charles Schultz*

Contemporary Approaches to Happiness

Researchers who study happiness today are divided on how happiness should be defined, and some lively debates have arisen about this (see, for example, Kashdan, Biswas-Diener, & King, 2008, and Waterman, 2008). All researchers in this area, however, are interested in what makes us feel a sense of well-being, a sense that our lives are going well, and a sense of satisfaction with our existence. Waterman (2008) outlines four conceptualizations of happiness that have been used by different researchers.

Subjective well-being (SWB), studied by a pioneer in this area, Ed Diener (1984, 2000), looks at happiness from the individual's perspective. Diener and his colleagues, as well as others who use this conceptualization, ask first whether the individual has more positive than negative emotions and, second, whether the individual feels satisfied with his or her life. Joel, at the beginning of this chapter, certainly reports that he has subjective well-being.

Hedonic well-being (HWB) has been less well-studied. It is often used synonymously with subjective well-being, but could be seen as referring to experiencing several events that generally give sensual pleasure. Joel's delight in food, drink, and sex indicates that he experiences great satisfaction from these hedonic experiences.

Psychological well-being (PWB), championed by Ryff and her colleagues (e.g., Ryff & Singer, 2008), regards happiness in terms of flourishing in life. Ryff sees a satisfying life as being comprised of an individual's autonomy, environmental mastery, personal growth, positive relations with others, purpose in life, and self-acceptance. These are factors that will be examined in detail in subsequent chapters, but for now we can say that PWB refers to what is psychologically considered to be optimal functioning in life. Our friend Joel seems to have this as well, as witnessed by his good relationship with his partner, his volunteer work that gives his life extra meaning, and his sense of becoming a better person every day.

Eudaimonic well-being (EWB), the approach that Waterman (2008) and Ryan and his colleagues favour (e.g., Ryan, Huta, & Deci, 2008), refers to the extent to which an individual lives in a eudaimonic way, pursuing goals that optimize the individual's personal growth and motivated by internal interest and desire rather than by external gain. Joel's volunteer work at the palliative care centre and his feelings of being blessed seem to be good examples of this.

These four conceptualizations are important in doing research on happiness, but they are not as easy to separate as they may seem. Evidence suggests that eudaimonia and hedonia often exist together (Ryan, Huta, & Deci, 2008; Telfer, 1990). In many cases, it appears that conditions that promote hedonia also promote eudaimonia. Take Joel, for example, who volunteers at a palliative care centre. When asked about how the experience made him feel the first time he did it, his response was "I first volunteered because it seemed like the right thing to do, but you know, it really felt good. I was on a high for the whole week." An action that was motivated by eudaimonia ("the right thing to do") co-existed with a hedonic experience (the physical aspect of volunteering) and an increase in subjective well-being. It can also be said that, for Joel, his behaviour fostered his psychological well-being. This isn't surprising. Many of us feel good about having done something that we believe is ethically right. Aristotle certainly believed that people who lived a virtuous life would get pleasure from it. This, of course, isn't always the case. Sometimes doing "the right thing" brings dissatisfaction and resentment to some people (e.g., whistleblowers who behave ethically, but may lose their jobs), and sometimes the rewards of doing the right thing are slow in coming—we only see them retrospectively (see Martin, 2008).

When Seligman first started the positive psychology movement, he spoke of authentic happiness (in his book of the same name, 2002), but he now feels that this term implies a continually cheerful mood. He says that, upon reflection, he realizes that having a sense of well-being and a feeling of satisfaction with one's life doesn't necessarily involve continual cheeriness. Today, he has expanded his vision of what constitutes real satisfaction or happiness by contending that, to have well-being in life, one must experience positive emotions, be fully engaged in some activities that are done for their own sake, have meaning in life, experience accomplishment or mastery in some areas that are important to the individual, and have positive, supportive relationships with others (Seligman, 2011). We will discuss these elements in detail in the chapters of Part 3 of this book, but for the moment it is interesting to note that Seligman's new formulation has become more eudaimonic and recognizes that the satisfying life is composed of many parts, combining the conceptualizations of happiness that Waterman (2008) has described.

There are many self-help books that claim to be able to give guidelines for increasing hedonic experiences—how to get more attention from the opposite sex, cookbooks, stress reduction through aromatherapy, and so on. In this book, we will concentrate on more long-lasting satisfaction (hence the title of the book, *The Satisfying Life*, rather than *The Good Life* or *The Fun Life*). As a convenience, we will use the terms *happiness*, *well-being*, and *life satisfaction* to include all the definitions that we have discussed.

SPOTLIGHT ON RESEARCH

Self-Help Books

Have you looked at the shelves of self-help books in your local bookstore or library recently? It looks like we will soon have as many self-help books available as fiction books. A quick scan under the category "self-improvement" at Chapters Indigo, Canada's biggest bookseller, indicates listings for thousands of self-help books. It's not difficult to see why such books are popular: they are relatively inexpensive and easily available, they promise results that can be achieved without the aid of professional intervention, and the "secret to success" is revealed quickly, in a few hundred pages at most. Clearly people believe that self-help

books are helpful or there wouldn't be so many of these books published. But are they really helpful?

Do self-help books help, or do they merely pander to Western society's desire for a quick and private answer to what ails us?

Bergsma (2008) reviewed evidence that self-help books that are often recommended by qualified therapists to people with particular psychological problems may be beneficial. That is, a good book on social anxiety for a socially anxious person may be useful, especially if that person is motivated, resourceful, and has a positive attitude toward self-help.

(Continued)

SPOTLIGHT ON RESEARCH

Self-Help Books, *continued*

But the books on general personal growth and personal enhancement may not be so useful. There is little to no scientific evidence about the effectiveness of these books as yet, but there are many reservations. Many books make sweeping and unrealistic claims and lead people to feel inadequate and blameworthy when the claims are not realized. "It must be me," some people might think. "I'm failing again." In some cases books may be written using psychological research, but the authors may not, in fact, be qualified to interpret this research, and so they draw the wrong conclusions from it and give readers erroneous advice.

For example, there are books that advise you to always vent your anger; otherwise it will build up in an internal pressure cooker, eventually doing you harm.

But in fact, psychological research indicates that venting anger is more likely to increase our anger, keeping it fuelled for a longer period of time (e.g., Bushman, 2002).

Perhaps the greatest criticism of many self-help books is that so many of them prescribe a "one-size-fits-all" remedy: if we only follow the path outlined by the author, we will grow, enhance ourselves, become self-actualized, and so on. With the infinite complexity of the human being, it is ridiculous to suppose that "one size" will ever fit all. As a Buddhist expression puts it, there may be one top to the mountain, but there are an infinite number of paths up the mountain to it.

These criticisms and warnings may indeed be valid, but can we conclude that there is no merit to self-help books at all? Bergsma (2008) thinks we need to be aware of the pluses of these books and the active role of the reader. If the reader is aware of the potential problems with self-help books and avoids the more obviously unrealistic ones ("Change your life in one week!"), the books may inspire new perspectives and new possibilities in dealing with life and may give new tools that the reader can put together to design a personal plan of growth, a unique path up the mountain. As Bergsma says, "... the quality of the advice offered in self-help books may be less important than the quality of the reader" (p. 357).

How Do We Measure Happiness?

Happiness or subjective well-being is not a very easy phenomenon to study for the simple reason that it is, well, subjective. We can't get inside people's heads to discover whether they are happy or not and, even if we could, we might not know what to look for, given that different people define happiness in different ways.

Self-Reports

Most research in subjective well-being and in much of positive psychology and personal growth is based on **self-reports**—that is, what people say about themselves, as revealed through asking them to answer open-ended questions or to fill out questionnaires. It seems reasonable that people know what they are thinking and feeling better than anyone else would.

But is that, in fact, true? Have you ever heard someone say "I'm not sure what I'm feeling"? Or have you heard people being urged to "get in touch with their feelings"? Often we find that people say they feel *good* or they feel *bad*. Yet feeling good and feeling bad can encompass many emotions; for example, *good* can mean jubilant, content, infatuated, self-righteous, victorious, vindicated, loved, or respected, and *bad* can mean sad, angry, violated, betrayed, frustrated, annoyed, helpless, unloved, or disrespected. The list goes on to hundreds more adjectives.

While most people can make the distinction between feeling good and feeling bad, many have problems making finer distinctions. This makes some people wonder whether respondents to research questions on happiness really know what they are feeling. Perhaps they are happy and they don't know it. (Think of the person who has lost a loved one—"I was so happy and I didn't even realize it.") Or perhaps they are unhappy, but are unaware of this as well. (Think of the person who responds to the question "How do you like your job?" with confusion and says "Well, it pays the bills." Is he or she happy or unhappy?)

Another concern that many people have with self-reports is whether the individual responding is being honest. Most of us have a tendency to give at least a little bit of a **social desirability** response when we are asked a question regarding our behaviour. That is, we tend to make ourselves and our behaviour seem a little better than reality indicates (Smith, Nolen-Hoeksema, Fredickson, & Loftus, 2003). Would some people, then, be more likely to report being happy when they really aren't? Or a little happier than they really are? This is a consideration, because in North America an admission of being unhappy is often taken as a poor reflection on the individual: in a society in which self-reliance and independence are valued, there may be an idea that unless there is something clearly causing unhappiness, such as the death of a loved one, a person's unhappiness is his or her own fault. Thus, people may be met with the comment "What do you have to be unhappy about?" when they admit to their unhappiness, or "So why don't you do something about it? What's *wrong* with you?" when they discuss their dissatisfaction with life. Sometimes, it may be easier and less problematic for these people to simply say "I'm fine."

Other concerns have to do with facility in communication. If respondents are asked open-ended questions, we can expect that not everyone will be eloquent. Some people simply aren't good at expressing themselves verbally, yet their answers to questions on their subjective well-being are scored alongside the answers of truly eloquent people. Should they be? Will the verbally constrained and the verbally facile people balance each other out in the long run? That is a central point of statistical testing, but statistical testing still leaves us with only probabilities that there has been balance, not with surety.

Correlations

Related to statistics, here's another caution: research done with self-reports, whether they are surveys or interviews, can at best yield only correlations. This refers to the degree of relationship between one factor and another. For example, as we shall see, there is a positive correlation between happiness and lifespan. That means that as the level of happiness increases, the length of the life increases. A negative correlation exists between number of arguments in a marriage and the happiness with the marriage, meaning that as the number of arguments increases, happiness decreases. It is an easy jump, often made by the media, to the conclusion that happiness causes one to live a longer life, or that people fight more in a marriage because they are unhappy in it. Either case may be true, but correlations can't tell us that. Correlations do not imply causality.

Look at the case of the positive relationship between happiness and longevity. Perhaps happiness causes one to live longer. But it's also likely that people who live longer will be happier because of not dying! Or then again, perhaps there is a third factor that can account for both happiness and longevity. People who live longer are probably physically healthy and for the most part feel physically well. Perhaps, as a result of their feelings of physical well-being, these people have an enhanced ability to function independently and participate in activities of their choice. Perhaps this good health accounts for both the happiness and the longevity they experience. Or perhaps there are other factors, or combinations of factors, that account for the relationship between happiness and longevity. The point is that correlations can't tell us anything about the causes of a factor.

Look again at the negative correlation between number of arguments and happiness in a marriage. Does an unhappy marriage cause couples to fight more? Or do high numbers of arguments cause marriages to become unhappy? Or is there another factor, such as basic incompatibility between two people, that causes both arguments to increase and marriages to become progressively less happy?

The Validity of Self-Reports

Naturally, a major source of concern in happiness and positive psychology research is whether the self-report methods used have **validity**—that is, are they measuring what we think they are measuring? Given that there are so many different definitions of happiness, how can we be certain that when we ask two people "Are you happy?" they are thinking about the same emotion with the same definition? Is our question being interpreted in the same way by both people?

Maybe it doesn't matter very much. Happiness is a subjective state, and only the person experiencing it can know what it is he or she is experiencing. It's like colour perception. Can I ever know if you experience blue the same way that I experience blue? Does it matter, as long as we both agree that when we see certain wavelengths of light, we will label them blue? For the most part, researchers in the area of subjective well-being are content to allow subjects to supply their own definitions, recognizing that this is a problem we cannot solve and accepting that we have to live with it and work within its confines.

This non-solution deals with the issue of validity in measurement: does the measurement measure what we think it does? For example, did the Satisfaction with Life Scale presented earlier in the chapter really measure your satisfaction with life? Or did it measure something else, such as how well you can fake happiness or how test-sophisticated you are? Or something else entirely? If the measures that are used in research actually measure happiness, then scores on these measures should relate to more objective measures such as how other people perceive one another, or behaviour such as genuine smiling, or remembering positive events better than negative events. In fact, these measures do. Friends and family members of people who score highly on measures of subjective well-being agree that these are happy people (Sandvik, Diener, & Seidlitz, 1993).

The happier people also remember more positive events than negative events in their lives (Seidlitz, Wyer, & Diener, 1997).

One particularly interesting and oft-cited study suggested that we might be able to predict how happy someone will be later in life by looking at their smiles at an earlier time. Harker and Keltner (2001) examined the pictures of women in their college year-books and noticed that some women showed genuine smiles and some showed fake smiles. Unlike fake smiles, genuine smiles ("Duchenne" smiles) crinkle the corners of the eyes and show bagging under the eyes and raised cheeks. Harker and Keltner followed these women at several points in their lives up to thirty years after they graduated from college. The women who had shown genuine smiles in their college yearbook photographs had different lives and personalities from those who had shown fake smiles. Specifically, the women with genuine smiles reported feeling more positive emotions and few negative emotions, more enjoyment in social interactions, more feelings of competence, and more satisfaction with their lives. They were perceived more favourably by other people, and they had more stable, satisfying, and long-lasting marriages.

Harker and Keltner's results indicate several things: first, there is a relationship between self-reports of happiness and behavioural indicators such as genuine smiling; second, happiness seems to be stable over time; and third, happy people have better social relationships—they are drawn to others and others are drawn to them.

All in all, we seem to be able to trust self-reports for the most part in conducting research on happiness and positive psychology in general. However, this does not mean that we can overlook the potential biases that self-reports may contain. One particular bias may have occurred to you when you took the Satisfaction with Life Scale: you may have been completely honest on your responses, but what kind of mood were you in when you took the scale? There is evidence to indicate that even when we are considering events over a longer period of time (such as evaluating how happy we are generally), our responses tend to be affected by our mood of the moment (Schwarz & Strack, 1999).

Kahneman and his colleagues (see Kahneman, 1999 for a review) also find that the emotional intensity of a single part of an episode affects our evaluation of the entire episode. For example, people undergoing an uncomfortable medical procedure were asked to rate their experience moment-to-moment and then to give an overall rating to the experience. The overall rating people gave was not a simple average of their moment-to-moment evaluations; rather, it was affected by the moment of maximum discomfort and by the final level of discomfort. Kahneman named this the **peak-end rule**, that the maximum intensity and the final intensity of emotion have a disproportionate affect on our evaluations of an experience.

If our present emotional state and the intensity of an experience can affect our recall of events and our answers on self-reports, how can we trust self-reports to tell us how happy people are in general? Despite the correlations between self-reports and other measures, some researchers feel more comfortable using **experience sampling methods** (ESM). These are methods that can be used in real time, in which people are cued by a pager, computer, alarm clock, or other means to record what they are doing and how they are feeling at that precise moment. This can be quite onerous for some people, and at times even impossible. Can you imagine how impractical it would be to leave a test or a business meeting because your beeper says it's time to fill out a questionnaire on how you're feeling? Retrospective ESM asks people to reflect on their experiences and how they felt, usually at the end of each day. The problem that can come up here is that we tend to judge our day by how it ends; events that happened earlier in the day are typically ignored or overshadowed (Stone, Shiffman, & DeVries, 1999).

The best studies of happiness, as well as other emotional states, would be studies that employ several different methods of evaluation: self-reports, reports of others, ESM, behavioural indicators, and so on. Such studies would be laborious and expensive to carry out, and very few have been done. Until more such studies have been conducted, we will have to keep in mind the cautions regarding methodology and recall that the whole area of positive psychology is a work in progress.

Who Are the Happy People?

In general, *we* are! Diener (2000) reports that, on national surveys, North Americans are remarkably happy people (7.89 for Canadians and 7.73 for Americans on a 10-point rating scale). Women seem to be just as happy as men are, if not more so, although the evidence is inconsistent; the occasional finding that women differ from men on their happiness ratings may reflect more on women's general willingness to report their emotional states (Nolen-Hoeksema & Rusting, 1999). Elderly people are just as happy as younger people (Argyle, 1999) although what makes them happy and what decreases their sense of well-being may differ (Gomez, Krings, Bangerter, & Grob, 2009). And when factors such as income, level of education, and occupation are taken into account, race and ethnicity seem to matter very little (Argyle, 1999). Diener, Oishi, and Lucas (2003) conclude that, in all cultures, people's ratings of their subjective well-being depends on how well they believe they are achieving the things that they value. This is conceivably related to the differences between people within cultures as well, an idea we will explore in more detail in later chapters.

Are richer people happier than poorer people? Income level has a complex relationship with happiness, a relationship discussed later in the chapter. What about climate? Wouldn't people living in an idyllic climate be happier than people living under harsher climatic conditions? No, moving to a tropical climate doesn't make people happier either (Argyle, 1987), a finding that is hard to believe as I write this during a February snowstorm.

Are Some People Just Naturally Happy?

We tend to think about happiness or subjective well-being as something we can attain through situations and circumstances in our lives, through particular accomplishments, or through the acquisition of certain objects. That is, we look for happiness as something that the external world gives us. So if we receive love and acceptance from family and friends, respect and admiration from coworkers, high income from grateful employers, the newest and coolest techno-toys, and so on, all the pleasure from these different areas of our lives feeds into our overall emotional state to provide us with a global sensation of happiness. This has been called the **bottom-up model** of subjective well-being (Diener, 1984). This model suggests that you can become happy with the right material goods and personal circumstances.

The **top-down model** of subjective well-being suggests that we have innate predispositions for happiness which then affect our perceptions of the different areas of our lives and make us respond in ways that attract more pleasurable experiences

(Schimmack, 2008). This may be due to cognitive predispositions (Schimmack, 2008) and/or to genetic factors (Lucas, 2008; Lucas & Diener, 2009). Happy people, like Joel from the beginning of this chapter, may view the world in a more positive light, thus making their lives seem rosier than they perhaps really are. It is not the happy circumstances of their lives that are making them happy; rather, it is their happiness that makes the circumstances of their lives seem happy. At the same time, their happiness makes them more likely to engage in more enjoyable situations, makes other people respond to them more favourably, and generally increases the number of pleasurable experiences they have in the course of the day.

Happiness and Genetics? Or Subjective Well-Being and Personality?

Lucas (2008) and Lucas and Diener (2009) suggest that happiness may be regarded as a personality trait, implying that our ability to be happy lies, at least in part, within our genetic structure. What makes them think that happiness has a genetic component? And does this mean that people can't become happier (or sadder) over the course of their lives?

Lucas (2008) and Lucas and Diener (2009) point to four lines of research suggesting that subjective well-being may depend on the personality with which people are born.

1. *The low associations with life circumstances.* While many of us expect that people's levels of happiness will depend on their life circumstances—such as their income, their health, and the quality of their social relationships—the measured associations with such factors are quite small (see, for example, the following section on the impact of money on happiness). Although the data must be interpreted carefully, it appears that even one of the strongest predictors of subjective well-being, marital status, shows a relatively weak association.

2. *Physiological measures.* Behavioural genetic studies comparing monozygotic twins (MZ, identical twins, with identical genes) and dizygotic twins (DZ, fraternal twins, with 50 percent identical genes) find that the correlations between MZ twins on measures that may reflect subjective well-being are higher than the correlations between DZ twins on the same measures. If environment alone accounted for how people score on these measures, we would expect that it wouldn't matter if twins were MZ or DZ if they were raised in the same environment.

    The difference suggests that MZ twins are more similar because of their identical genetic structures (see also Weiss, Bates, & Luciano, 2008). Moreover, studies of twins reared together or apart (i.e., in the same or different environments) indicate that the environment in which the twins are raised contributes very little to their scores on these measures. Studies such as these suggest that propensity for happiness may have a highly heritable component: that 40 percent to 50 percent of the variance in people's scores on these measures may be due to their genetic endowment.

    Also, research on brain activation suggests that people more prone to having positive emotions show more activation in the left hemisphere, while people more prone to having negative emotions have more activation in the right hemisphere. It has been suggested that brain activation may be one of the ways that genes affect feelings of subjective well-being. Perhaps, the idea goes (in a very simplified form), our genes determine which hemisphere of our brain will be more responsive to certain stimuli. If the genes say "left," we may be more prone to happiness, whereas if the genes say "right," we may be more prone to unhappiness, or at least a more neutral emotional state.

3. *Stability over time.* Many studies reviewed by Lucas (2008) and Lucas and Diener (2009) suggest that people seem to report about the same satisfaction with their lives from the time they are children through their late adulthood, despite the life experiences they have had. A happy child usually becomes a happy adult. Also, people who are happy in one area of their lives tend to be happy in other areas of their lives, another finding that seems to remain stable over time. Whatever makes us feel very happy or very sad seems to have a rather temporary effect on us (again, see the impact of money on happiness, following). Within a relatively short period of time, we seem to drift back to our pre-event level of happiness.

4. *Associations with personality traits.* Some personality characteristics, such as extraversion and neuroticism, have a basis in genetic factors. Some studies have found that measures of subjective well-being are significantly correlated with measures of these personality factors. For example, there is a positive correlation between extraversion and happiness and a negative correlation between neuroticism and happiness, correlations that seem stable over time. It does not seem unreasonable to conjecture that a physiological basis for one of these factors may signal a physiological basis for the other factor.

Setpoint theory (Brickman & Campbell, 1971; Brickman, Coates, & Janoff-Bulman, 1978; Headey & Wearing, 1992) suggests that people have a stable point of happiness that they may temporarily stray from, but to which they return in the long run. This biological setpoint for happiness is hypothesized to be an internal mechanism that keeps our emotions balanced. We may experience an event or acquire an object that gives us delight, but our biological tendency is to drift back to our normal level of happiness over time. Research has indicated, however, that some people do become more or less happy over time (see Diener, 2008, for a review), which is an encouraging proposition for many of us!

More questions arise. For example, what makes us happy? What doesn't make us happy?

Will More Money Make Us Happier?

What can make us happy? Most people, when asked that question, think about material goods that money can buy or just say "money"! Certainly money can help us gain hedonic pleasures. A raise in pay, an unexpected bonus, a little extra than expected in a student loan, can reduce stress when we are struggling to make ends meet. Intuitively, then, the idea that money can buy happiness seems to make some sense. But doesn't an old adage also say that "money can't buy happiness"? So what is the truth of the matter?

Anecdotally, we know that many lottery winners report that, after the euphoria of the win wears off, they are no happier than they were before the win. Some cite harassment for a handout by charities, newfound "friends," and supplicant family members as the source of their dissatisfaction. But even when this is not the case, winners still report a return to their usual satisfied or dissatisfied state.

We also recognize that when we ourselves finally attain a material object that we want, our delight in the new acquisition remains only for a short period of time, and then we seem to take the object for granted or even become dissatisfied and start thinking about how much we want something better. The new car seems wonderful for six months, and then we start to plan for our next, even more delightful, car. Our new computer or cell phone satisfies us greatly until we hear of the daily upgrades that we could have if we had a little more money. It appears that money, and the goods that it can provide, only make us happy for a short period of time.

The media pump us full of enticements to spend more money, advertising that the product they supply will bring us success and enjoyment eternally. (That is, until they produce a new item that will make us even happier!) And we seem to listen (Dittmar, 2008). Are we just greedy and incapable of being satisfied? David Myers (2000) refers to our continuing quest for more and better material goods as the **paradox of affluence**: statistical analyses indicate that in the United States, overall, the wealthier the nation becomes, the less its populace seem satisfied with their lives (see also Drakopoulos, 2008).

The relationship between money and life satisfaction is complicated, and so far research has been confusing. Much research found that happiness was only associated with income to a very small degree. It is generally found that the correlation of income and happiness is around .20, a low correlation statistically (see Lucas & Dyrenforth, 2006 for a review). This research typically asks people their income and their degree of subjective well-being and then statistically associates the two. This outcome has been regarded as quite robust and occurs among a number of different groups of people including various income levels.

So, for quite a while, it was taken as a standard that money was not a significant source of happiness for most of us. Joel, for example, would undoubtedly not refuse more money, but it's hard to believe that money would or could make him any happier than he already is. Recently, however, some researchers have examined this data a little more closely and contend that the data has been interpreted incorrectly. Lucas and Schimmick (2009) conclude, after a re-examination of the outcomes of these studies, that the seemingly low correlations actually mean that increased income provides quite a bit of happiness for most of us.

This new analysis appears to be consistent with the results of studies that correlate average income with reported subjective well-being across nations. With only a few exceptions, which we will discuss later, countries whose populace has higher incomes have a happier populace (see Biswas-Diener, 2008; Diener & Biswas-Diener, 2002). People living in nations with very low average incomes have lower levels of satisfaction with life than people living in nations with high incomes, even when purchasing power and the cost of living are taken into account. When a more detailed analysis is performed, looking at people within varying income levels, it is seen that at all levels except the lowest, people in any nation seem to report the same levels of happiness. Rich people, then, are no happier than poor people.

Again, we must pause over these results. In the lowest level of income, it is often the case that people are not able to provide for the basic necessities of life. Not having a roof over one's head or the ability to feed one's children would clearly make anyone unhappy. A rise in income to a level where the necessities, if not the luxuries, of life are obtainable makes these people much happier than they were before.

Additionally, the very, very rich seem to be somewhat happier than their "merely" rich friends. Diener and his colleagues (1985) found that people on the *Forbes* magazine list of the wealthiest Americans score higher in subjective well-being than those whose income is somewhat lower. Does this mean that being rich won't make us happy, but being very rich will? These studies are only suggestive since there are many alternate explanations for the results.

In countries where the average national income is low, there is often a marked lack of the civil liberties and basic freedoms that are taken for granted in richer countries. Additionally, there is typically less effective sanitation and health care. Certainly it is possible that people in nations where average incomes are low may be less satisfied with their lives for any of these reasons. Lack of higher income may be only a side issue for them and a minor factor in their levels of well-being.

Also, can we be sure that in these countries people define happiness the same way that people in other countries do? Perhaps not. Japan, for example, is classified as one of the richest countries in the world, yet the reported level of subjective well-being is less than that of Chile, India, and Brazil, ranked as some of the poorer countries in this study (Diener, 2000). Japan is also a nation known for being reticent to brag or proclaim personal satisfaction or achievement. It may be that the Japanese are just as happy as people in Canada and the United States, but they have a cultural norm which discourages the reporting of this on subjective well-being questionnaires.

By the same token, it may be that people in richer countries feel embarrassed and unsuccessful if they are unhappy or dissatisfied with their lives. As noted above, in nations such as Canada and the United States, there is a strong feeling that the individual is responsible for his or her own happiness, with ample opportunity to make life better. To admit, then, even to oneself that one is not very happy may be seen as an admission of inadequacy, an admission that would make one even more unhappy. I recall a student who insisted she was happy with her new relationship, even while tears flowed down her cheeks as she told me this! "You don't seem happy," I said (gently, I hope). "But I must be," she replied. "He meets all the qualifications on my list for Mr. Right." Had this not been a face-to-face encounter, I wouldn't have seen the tears and I probably would have believed that this young woman was in a state of bliss. While self-reports are seen to correlate well with other measures of people's subjective well-being, they are not perfect, and the same biases may creep into each kind of measure.

Why are we not satisfied with what we have? Why do we start longing for a new television set even before the shine has worn off the one we just bought? Several explanations have been proposed, and they are not necessarily mutually exclusive. The set-point theory suggests that we simply adapt to happiness, that we are on a **hedonic treadmill**: as on a treadmill, we move and we move, but we don't get anywhere. In terms of happiness, we have fluctuations of positive emotions, episodes of happiness, but in the long run, we simply drift back to where we were, with no overall progress (Brickman & Campbell, 1971; Headey & Wearing, 1992). Research bears out that, except for major life changes such as marriage or widowhood, most of us do seem to maintain a stable level of happiness across time (Suh, Diener, & Fujita, 1996; Winter, Lawton, Casten, & Sando, 1999).

Another explanation for our lack of satisfaction is that of **social comparison** (see Baumgardner and Crothers, 2009, for a review of this approach): we feel delight with our new object because we feel that we have something better than other people do—

until we see someone with something even better. We may feel that we are well paid until we find that other people in our company who perform the same job as we do are receiving substantially more money. "Keeping up with the Joneses" is a phenomenon that is very real for many of us.

This sounds bad, but it may not be as bad as we think. Consider this: how do we know how well we are doing in any endeavour? Typically, we know because we compare our achievements to those of other people. Is this not the case when students receive their grades? Which mark gives you more information about how well you know the subject matter, an A in a class in which the average mark is A+ or an A in a class in which the average mark is B–? How can we know if we are receiving appropriate compensation for our work if we do not know what compensation other comparable people are receiving? Such comparisons are reasonable sources of information in areas in which feedback is important if we are to evaluate and possibly improve our performance. The Western tendency, however, is to compare ourselves on areas in which improvement may be impossible or undesirable. "Is she prettier than me?" "Is he taller than I am?" "Is her husband a better cook than mine?" "Is my wife making more money than his wife?" With comparisons such as these, we are doomed to dissatisfaction because there is always someone who is prettier, taller, a better cook, and so on. What can we make of one of my students who, upon receiving a mark of 95 percent, could not evaluate whether he was happy until he determined whether his was the highest mark in the class?

Gardersdottir, Dittmar and Aspinall (2009) suggest that looking for an association between money and happiness will result in incomplete understanding unless we also examine *why* people feel that money will make them happier. In their research, people are asked why they want money: is it for the acquisition of hedonic pleasure for its own sake because it will make them happy, or because acquisition of money is symbolic of their success in areas which they value? The researchers found that people who want money because it will buy them items that they want (not need) find only momentary pleasure in money. But people who want money because of its association with being successful and valued find a more lasting pleasure in it.

Consider the difference between Stan and Oliver, nurses who receive similar raises in pay. For Stan, this means that he can replace last year's car with a new model. For Oliver, it means that he is doing a good job and is valued in his nursing career. It is not surprising that lasting happiness as a result of more money will more likely come to Oliver than to Stan.

Gardersdottir and her colleagues' data are in keeping with the review done by Biswas-Diener (2008): people who have voluntarily given up material luxuries and live a simple life (e.g., the Amish, people who voluntarily simplify their lives) report high levels of happiness with their non-materialistic lives. Materialism (basing one's pursuit of happiness on the acquisition of goods) does not seem to lead to happiness, even if one acquires the goods desired. In fact, it seems to lead to a reduced quality of life (Kasser & Ryan, 1993; Sirgy, 1998). If our goal is money and the objects money can buy, we may always hunger for more, but if our goal is for internal satisfaction and validation of our self-worth, and money symbolizes this for us, money may indeed increase our satisfaction with our lives. It depends on what our goals are and how we interpret or make meaning of objects and events in our lives. As we shall see in upcoming chapters, the role of our individual goals and meaning is very high in our pursuit of happiness.

REFLECTIVE EXERCISE

Then what?

Suppose you won $1 billion (tax free) in a lottery. That should give you enough money to pay off all your debts, provide for your family's present and future, and give you a secure life. What would you do with the rest of the money? Are your plans hedonic or eudaimonic?

Or do they encompass both? After you have done everything you want, let's suppose there is money left over. What would you do with it? How would you live the rest of your life? That is, after all your wants and needs that money can buy have been taken care of, then what?

SPOTLIGHT ON RESEARCH

Children and Happiness

We all want our children to be happy, but what makes them happy? Listening to them, it's hard not to get the impression that a new video game or piece of candy will do the trick. Many parents deprive themselves of material goods or work extra-long hours to be able to afford luxuries for their children because they want them to be happy. But does this really work? Chaplin (2009) studied children of various ages to determine the answer to this question.

The research found that grade three children (about eight years old) reported that their hobbies, people, and pets made them happiest. Children in grades seven and eight (about 12 to 14 years old) reported that material things and people and pets made them happiest, while those in grades eleven and twelve (about 15 to 18 years old) reported that their achievements, as well as people and pets, made them happiest.

The common factor for all age ranges was people and pets: children of all ages get more happiness from contact with their pets and their families, friends, teachers, and coaches than from any other single factor. Even those children who reported that material things made them happiest usually stipulated that this was because the material things they wanted were goods that would, in their minds, enhance their personal relationships through shared enjoyment and increased admiration from others.

The implication of this research is that if parents want to make their children happy, they would be better advised to spend more time with their children instead of working long hours to provide them with material goods. The old saying seems to be true: the most precious thing you can give your kids is your time.

Predicting Our Own Happiness

You may have been sure that more money would make you happy. Similarly, you may have experienced times when getting what you thought would make you happy turned out to be less satisfying than you expected. Predicting how we will react emotionally in given situations is called **affective forecasting**, and it seems that we are not necessarily very good at it.

Wilson and Gilbert (2005) found that people often overestimate the intensity and the duration of the emotions they believe they will experience in future situations. They call this **impact bias**. These researchers believe that one reason impact bias occurs is that people are apt to focus their attention on the specific situation and disregard the outcomes and the context of the situation. They call this **focalism**. So it is not unlikely that when we anticipate a positive event, such as winning a lottery, we ignore the possible problems that may be associated with it while our attention is consumed with all the possible positive outcomes.

Actually, we may be better at forecasting our emotional reactions to positive events than we are to negative events (Van Dijk, 2009; Wilson, & Gilbert, 2005). Remember Joel from the beginning of the chapter? His only child has a chronic serious illness. Although he considers himself a happy man, Joel believes that if his child's health takes a turn for the worse, he will be devastated and may never recover. Of course, in this sad event Joel would be deeply upset, but he is disregarding the fact that a turn for the worse in his child's health may still be overcome and the child will recover.

Wilson and Gilbert (2005) point out that people often overestimate their negative responses to bad situations when they think about them occurring in the future because of focalism and because they underestimate their own resilience and ability to cope with the trials of life. This underestimation is termed **immune neglect** by the researchers. The idea of immune neglect is based on Wilson and Gilbert's (2005) belief that we have a psychological immune system made up of a range of psychological defenses that we use when times are bad, defenses that help us cope with tribulation. We are often unaware of the existence of these defenses, and so in anticipating how we would react to a negative situation, we make our estimation based on how we think we would react without the immune system.

Joel is forgetting about the fact that he has a track record of demonstrating resilience and hope when he confronts problems in life. He is also ignoring the support that he would receive from friends and family and the possibility that even bad experiences can help us grow (read more about this in Chapter 8). Research evidence supporting this is found in an examination of the anticipated emotional responses of athletes contemplating losing a contest (Van Dijk, 2009). Athletes were quite accurate in predicting their levels of happiness at winning a contest, but they believed that they would experience much more unhappiness at a loss than they actually did.

This inaccuracy in predicting our emotions in future situations, especially bad ones, does not imply that we will be unaffected by good and bad life events; it means that we probably will not be as happy or unhappy with these events as we will think we will, and we will cope with the bad events with more hardiness than we realize we have. So even though we may think that we will be ecstatic to just pass a test or tie a game of tennis, we probably won't be quite that happy with these results, and disappointment in a test mark or losing a game of tennis won't be quite as distressing as we fear.

Isn't Just Being Happy Enough?

Although the vast majority of us in the Western world want to be happy for happiness's own sake, there are other positive consequences of being happy—collateral gains, one might say. Oishi and Koo (2008) review the literature and find that, while there is a great deal of variability among people, in general it can be said that happy people are more successful at work, earning higher incomes (but see below!) and better work appraisals from superiors. They are more satisfied with their marriages and have better social interactions with more interest in friendship and social activities, are more involved in collaborative styles of resolving conflict, express more sensitivity to others, and receive more social support in return. Happy people have better health and longer life spans, including improved immunological functioning, all mediated, it is believed, by healthier lifestyles.

Can People Be Too Happy?

Oishi, Diener and Lucas (2009) ask the intriguing question, "Can people be too happy?" Western society seems to be in a search for happiness, but how much? If we are already happy, some of us may feel that we should be happier still, that we should be able to remove all the unpleasant emotions and live in a permanent state of bliss. Most of us, however, would recognize not only the impossibility of this, but the undesirability of it as well. We might wonder how we could know we were happy if we never felt unhappiness. Others might ask if happiness wouldn't get boring after awhile. And some of the more curmudgeonly among us might object to living among a population of eternally happy people, claiming that a state of permanent happiness must be a state of denial, ignorance, or fakery, any of which they would find extremely distasteful. Their thinking is that "if you can stay happy all the time, you just don't get it."

Oishi, Diener and Lucas (2009) point out the arguments that the removal of negative emotions would be a very maladaptive state for us. Fear may be necessary so that we take care not to walk too close to the edge of the cliff or we make sure that we have done the required reading before the exam date; anger may spur us to action of some sort when we have experienced disappointment, failure, injury, or injustice; guilt may ensure that we never steal a candy bar from a store again and we behave ethically in the future. In particular, if we were always happy, if we never experienced dissatisfaction, we would have very little motivation to change anything in our lives. This may mean that we never expose ourselves to the challenges that would help us to fulfill our true potential.

To determine if there are, in fact, optimal levels of happiness, Oishi, Diener and Lucas (2009) analyzed large amounts of data from surveys conducted in various countries around the world. They found that the relationship between level of happiness and various life outcomes was not as straightforward as might be expected. For example, returning to our discussion of money and happiness, income is greater for happier people: the happier people are, the more they tend to earn. That is, up to a point. The happiest people are found to earn less than the moderately happy people! Perhaps they earn less because they spend less time at work—the happiest people are reported to have better relationships and are more likely to do volunteer work in their communities. In addition, the happiest people tend to pursue less education than do those who are moderately happy, perhaps also affecting their subsequent income levels (Oishi & Koo, 2008). Oishi, Diener and Lucas (2009) conclude that the optimal level of happiness varies from individual to individual, depending on what each individual values the most. For those who value relationships and social interaction the most, the highest levels of happiness seem to be attainable. For those who value external measures of achievement (e.g., money, degrees), more moderate levels would appear to be more prevalent. There is a severe lack of research information on the question of how much happiness is actually enough.

In Parts 2, 3, and 4 of this book, we will consider different factors that have been shown to be associated with feelings of happiness. We will also examine some ways to increase our happiness by working with these factors. In the meantime, you might want to explore happiness on your own. A good place to start is Martin Seligman's website, www.authentichappiness.sas.upenn.edu, where you will find emotion questionnaires and a great deal of interesting information.

REFLECTIVE EXERCISE

Do you want to be always happy?

In 1932, Aldous Huxley first published an astounding book called *Brave New World* (Huxley, 1955). In this brave new world, people were always happy, simply by taking the readily available and societally endorsed drug, *soma*. With this drug, and society's acceptance of it, anyone who experienced a state of melancholy or angst and did not consume the drug was judged as pathological. The hero of the book is the man who demands the right to experience his emotions in their raw state, unfiltered by pharmaceuticals, and insists that life without the negative emotions is a life not worth living.

Martin Seligman (2002) reports making a habit of asking his students whether they would accept being hooked up to a machine that would stimulate their brains in ways that would leave them in a state of perpetual happiness. Overwhelmingly, he says, they decline.

Richard Powers' novel *Generosity: An Enhancement* (2009) is about a young woman emerging from some of the worst traumas imaginable, and yet being always happy, optimistic, and glowing with a genuine generosity and bounteousness for life. She never seems to experience any negative emotion: her lows resemble most other people's highs. People around her initially think she must be psychologically ill. Genetic testing, however, claims to reveal that the young woman has a network of genes that predispose her to happiness. Around the world people clamour for the "happiness gene," and offer to buy the young woman's ova to ensure that their children will be happy.

Would you accept *soma* or connection to Seligman's machine? If genetic engineering could allow us to "design" our children, would you use the services of genetic engineers for your own children? What qualities would you select for? Would you include the "happiness gene"? Would you want to live in a society in which artificially induced or genetically enhanced happiness was the norm and considered the only acceptable emotion? Why or why not?

Conclusion

Happiness is not as easy to study as it might appear, and we don't know as much about it yet as we one day will. But the area of positive psychology is really all about what makes us feel good about our lives and what we can do to increase this feeling of well-being. In the next three chapters, we will explore different conceptions of what makes a satisfying life and what a fully-functioning person really is. We will look at perspectives from different theorists in Western culture and then explore the perspectives of Eastern and Middle-Eastern cultures and the Indigenous cultures of North America, Australia, and Africa. There is no right or wrong answer. There is only the answer that makes you feel best.

Summary

- Positive psychology is the scientific study of the personal qualities, life choices, life circumstances, and sociocultural conditions that promote a life well-lived, defined by criteria of happiness, physical and mental health, meaningfulness, and virtue.
- Hedonism involves the pleasure given by objects and experiences. Eudaimonia involves acting in ways that are true to one's best nature.
- Four conceptualizations of happiness include subjective well-being, hedonic well-being, psychological well-being, and eudaimonic well-being.
- In many cases, conditions that promote hedonia also promote eudaimonia.
- Self-reports may be difficult for some people due to a lack of awareness of their emotions, lack of verbal fluency, and the inclination toward social desirability responses. Self-reports also yield only correlations, which do not imply causality. Present emotional state and the intensity of an experience can affect recall of events and answers on self-reports (the peak-end rule).
- Experience sampling methods (ESM) are research methods in which people are cued by a pager, computer, or other means to record what they are doing and how they are feeling at that precise moment.
- Gender, age, race, and ethnicity make little difference in people's ratings of their subjective well-being. In all cultures, these ratings depend on whether people believe they are achieving the things that they value.
- The bottom-up model of subjective well-being suggests that all the pleasure from different areas of life feed into an overall emotional state to provide a global sensation of happiness.
- The top-down model of subjective well-being suggests that there are innate predispositions for happiness that affect perceptions of the different areas of life.
- Happiness may have a genetic component, given the low association between happiness and life circumstances, physiological studies, the stability of happiness over time, and happiness's association with personality traits deemed genetically based.
- Setpoint theory suggests that people have a stable point of happiness that they may temporarily stray from, but to which they return in the long run.
- Whether money makes us happier or not depends on why we want money.

- The wealthier a nation becomes, the less its populace seem satisfied with their lives (the paradox of affluence). Setpoint theory suggests that we adapt to happiness on a hedonic treadmill. Another suggestion is that we believe that more and more material goods will make us happier because of social comparison.

- Affective forecasting is predicting how we will react emotionally in given situations. People often overestimate the intensity and the duration of the emotions they believe they will experience in future situations (impact bias). Impact bias may occur because of focalism or immune neglect.

- Happy people are more successful at work, earning higher incomes and better work appraisals; are more satisfied with their marriages; have better social interactions, with more interest in friendship and social activities, more collaborative styles of resolving conflict, more sensitivity to others, and receive more social support in return; have better health and longer life spans, including improved immunological functioning, all mediated, it is believed, by healthier lifestyles.

Group Discussion Questions

1. Is "happiness" a word that we should abandon altogether in positive psychology since it is so difficult to define and so particular to individual people?

2. When you conclude that someone you know is happy, what factors are you taking into account in saying this? That is, how do you know that someone is happy? What would be the most important factor you could use in making this determination? How often do you think you would be correct?

3. Did any discussion in this chapter surprise you? Do you have reservations about any of the research findings? For example, do you still think that money might bring happiness? Or that a person can't be too happy? Why do you have these reservations? (Remember that you might be right in any of your reservations.)

CHAPTER 2

The Satisfying Life from the Perspective of Western Psychological Theory

As we saw in the last chapter, our conceptions of what constitutes a satisfying life vary from person to person. Similarly, the obstacles that stand in our way are different for each of us. Once we escape from a hedonistic idea of what constitutes satisfaction and fulfillment in life, we are presented with a host of different possibilities. Those who have studied the human mind in the context of the Western world (e.g., Sigmund Freud, Alfred Adler) have mainly been concerned with the difficulties life brings and with the disorders of the mind that can decrease our chances of living a satisfying life. Conversely, some theorists have also tried to determine what makes a healthy personality. Since personality is not observable except through self-reports (which may not be accurate) or behaviour (which may not reflect more than the demands of the situation), it is not surprising that different people have arrived at different conclusions about the mind and different theories regarding its functioning. If you have ever taken a course in the psychology of personality, you may have felt somewhat frustrated in learning about these different theories and wondered which one was right. The answer to this question, for us, is "none of them and all of them."

In this chapter we will briefly examine the theories of some people that you may not have heard much about before. All these theorists have been well respected and have made an impact in the field of personality psychology, but they are not necessarily regarded as completely mainstream. All of these theorists have paid specific attention to the healthy personality and what it takes to make a satisfying life. Their complete theories will not be covered—that is not the purpose of this chapter. The purpose is to present you with diverse ideas about what, in the Western world, has been considered good functioning that leads to fulfillment. Perhaps parts of their theories may resonate with you in your own life or in the lives of people you know or may stimulate you to think about more possibilities. In all the theories presented here, subsequent chapters will show that each of these theorists predicted some of what positive psychology has found empirically to be related to the satisfying life. The premise is that there are many routes to our goals, and we each need to find our own way.

LEARNING OBJECTIVES

In this chapter, students will learn about what constitutes a satisfying life from the Western psychological viewpoints of

- The Humanistic Psychoanalytical Perspective (Karen Horney).
- The Gestalt Perspective (Frederick Perls).
- The Humanistic Perspective (Carl Rogers and Abraham Maslow).
- The Existential Perspective (Rollo May).

THE HUMANISTIC PSYCHOANALYTIC PERSPECTIVE: KAREN HORNEY

Graham tortures himself. He is an excellent student, but he can't tolerate getting anything less than an A in any of his work. If he gets a B+, he feels terrible. "I'm worthless," he thinks. "I'll never amount to anything. I should be able to get As in all my classes. I should be able to study for hours even though I'm working part time to put myself through school and I'm caring for my two little brothers. And speaking of my little brothers, I got impatient with them the other night. I shouldn't do that. I should remember that they're only little kids and I'm the responsible adult. My parents tell me I'm a good brother, but I know they expect me to do better. I expect that of myself. I shouldn't keep thinking about this. I promised my girlfriend that I would help her with her assignment, so I'd better get to it. I'll just stay up later to do my own work." Graham is always tired and he feels trapped. He is in bed at least one day a week because of incapacitating tension headaches. He's only twenty years old.

Graham is a young person who, on the surface, may look like he has the world by the tail, yet inside he's very unhappy. He may be functioning pretty well in the world, but he clearly is not enjoying his life. Why not? It seems obvious that Graham is experiencing anxiety, in much the way we normally use the word in day-to-day conversation. He feels worried and miserable. If we asked Graham if he is anxious, he would undoubtedly say yes. This seems straightforward, but anxiety may be revealed in many different ways; in fact, it may well be that no two people show their anxiety in exactly the same way. And why should they? We know that we are all special, unique individuals; our personalities are all different from one another, so why should we presume that our anxieties will all look alike?

Sigmund Freud first studied where anxiety comes from and how it appears. Following his general guidelines, several theorists modified his approach, noting in particular the individual differences among human beings in their manifestation of anxiety. Karen Horney was one of these theorists.

Karen Horney believed that human beings have a basic tendency to grow and develop their potentialities to the fullest extent. Given a fair chance, she felt that we all will grow toward what she called **self-realization**; that is, we will develop our own unique and special gifts, become attuned to our own thoughts and feelings, express these thoughts and feelings spontaneously, and relate to other people in a free and open manner. This is our birthright, but often something happens to block our development. Horney's position was that we need to uncover and remove the blockages so that all the possibilities of the individual can be manifested.

The Role of Culture

The major culprit in the development of blockages to growth is the environment of the individual. By "the environment," Horney meant two things. First is the overall culture in which the individual is born and raised. Second is the immediate environment of the child's family, most particularly the nuclear family consisting of parents and siblings. Let's look at the role of culture first, since the family behaviour toward a child is affected by the culture in which they live.

Since Horney was practising during the 1920s and the Great Depression of the 1930s, a time of worldwide financial insecurity, it appeared to her that people's anxiety about feeding themselves and their children was pretty logical, and the patients she dealt with exhibited symptoms predominantly related to this.

Her conviction was increased by what she referred to as the **hypercompetitiveness** of American culture (Horney, 1937). American culture was founded on the strength of the individual pioneer, the individual entrepreneur. The conviction that capitalism and the competition bred by a free market was the basis of a strong democracy led to competition in other aspects of the culture. Even today, perhaps few countries in the world are as dedicated to sports events, beauty pageants, television game shows, or success as measured by climbing a corporate ladder as the United States. No wonder, then, that so many of her American patients showed insecurities at not "measuring up," inadequacies at not fulfilling prescribed societal success roles. Instead of being content with their "personal best," or recognizing the impossibility of some goals, Horney found that many people compared themselves to others so much that even their successes were not satisfying to them. Inevitably these people regarded themselves as being personally inadequate because they could not "win the contest."

As a woman, Horney was also concerned with the way culture mandated certain roles and behaviours for people, especially females. If the culture believes that females have certain characteristics, then parents raising daughters will typically encourage these characteristics in their daughters while punishing, or at least discouraging, characteristics that are indicated for the other gender. This, she felt, was a major reason for the lack of female participation in politics, business, economics, and so on (Horney, 1967).

The Role of the Immediate Environment

The human infant is born completely dependent upon caregivers. Besides the physical dependency, there is also an emotional dependency. Many children are born into families that rejoice at their birth and raise the child with love, laughter, discipline, and conscious regard for the child's development of self-esteem.

But other children are not so fortunate. In some cases, they are raised in families that do not really want them and make that known to the child in emotionally destructive ways. This can be seen in families where the child is ignored apart from basic caretaking, or where parents constantly break promises to the child or simply are not warm to the child (take, for example, the real-life case of a child who was bounced on her mother's knee while being called "Mommy's Little Nuisance"). Sometimes children are raised in families in which physical and/or sexual abuse is present, and the child falls victim to that. Sometimes they are raised in families that love them dearly, but because of other external circumstances, the families are constrained from being as mindful of the child as they would like. Such circumstances might include mental or physical illness in the family, addictions, poverty, and family discord.

In some cases, children are raised in families that mean only the best for the child, but through lack of insight or lack of parenting skills, they make errors that have a large impact on the child. For example, Graham's parents may well have believed that they were helping him to fulfill the enormous potential they saw in him by having high expectations of him and by showing disappointment in him when he failed to meet those expectations. But somehow, the message they transmitted to Graham may have been

"If you don't excel, we don't love you." In all these cases and in many more, the child is denied the feeling of complete trust in the caregivers and safety and security in the world. Such is the **basic evil** that lays the groundwork for the blockage of self-realization, said Horney (1945).

How does the child feel under these conditions? Angry, said Horney. The child has what she called **basic hostility**, a resentment and anger against the caregivers who are *supposed* to make the child feel safe and secure and valued and loved, but do not do this. But the child is in a precarious position: no matter how the child feels, there is still the fact of the child's dependency on the caregivers. What is the child to do? The caregivers are the only source of physical support and survival and psychological love that the child has, however meagre this might be. Horney believed that the child feels fear and guilt at being angry with the caretakers, so the child thrusts this away until he or she is no longer aware of it.

But the scarring can still be seen. The child develops (and carries into adulthood) what Horney (1945) called **basic anxiety**. This is a feeling that the whole world cannot be trusted, that there is no real safety anywhere in the world. After all, if Mommy and Daddy (or whoever the primary caretakers were) did not seem to love and value you, who could? If there is no safe haven with the immediate family, safe haven does not exist, goes the reasoning. Out of this basic anxiety, the big blockages to self-realization are formed.

Now it's a pretty safe bet that every one of us can remember times in our own upbringing when our caretakers hurt us: they were not sufficiently sensitive to our developing personalities, they seemed to have their own issues to deal with instead of ours, they forgot about our school play, they did not take us to the zoo when they said they would, and so on. Does this mean that we all have big blockages to growth? No, of course not, said Horney. Caretakers of children are first and foremost people, and as such, they are not perfect. Mistakes will inevitably happen. What produces basic anxiety is the *continued pattern* of such mistakes over the child's formative years, especially when there is no ameliorating force such as an understanding grandparent, aunt or uncle, teacher, or older close family friend who can play a part in demonstrating to the child that there is unconditional love and acceptance for him or her in the world. If the negative early experiences have not been too powerful and intense, later experiences, especially in adolescence, can provide ameliorating effects.

In the end, the more powerful and intense the early experiences of the child, the stronger and more inflexible the child's later thought and behaviour patterns become. This spirals downward: the more inflexible the individual, the less able the individual is to learn from new experiences, and the less the individual learns from new experiences, the more inflexible he or she becomes. Without counteracting influences, the child may well grow up to develop anxieties that can be manifested in many different ways, while never realizing that the root of the problem goes back to those unfortunate early lessons.

The Idealized Self and the Real Self

Since the child has in some way received the message from the parents that he or she is inadequate, the child, in growing up, unconsciously creates a highly flattering image of what he or she is or what he or she ought to be. Horney (1950) called this the **idealized self**. This is the person's dream of what he or she could be or should be or, in some cases, is. The idealized self in a poorly adjusted person is static, inflexible, and always removed from reality in its perfection. But people do not always realize this. They may think that their standards and expectations of themselves are high, but they see this in terms of genuine and realistic ideals that they are proud of. Exactly what the idealized self consists of is determined by the particular individual and his or her environment. For Graham, the idealized self seems to be a perfect student, worker, brother, and boyfriend—someone who always has time to be everything to everybody and who achieves the highest distinctions.

Contrasting this is the perception of the **real self**, what we think we really are. Our appraisals of our real self are not always accurate. Some people may believe that they are far more inadequate than they really are, while others may have an inflated sense of their own adequacy. Graham seems to be one who feels that his real self is "worthless" even though it appears to us that he is a great guy indeed. The problem comes when the gap between what we think we are (our real self) and what we want to be (our idealized self) becomes insurmountably large. We often expend a great deal of energy trying to surmount that gap. The energy that could be put toward self-realization is diverted to the goal of actualizing the idealized self. Horney called this the **search for glory**.

In the search for glory, we feel driven to actualize some artificially-created perfect identity. Since achieving perfection is impossible, we are doomed to failure. Each failure drives us to try harder and harder. "I *should* be able to do A," "I *should* accomplish B," "I *should* feel C," "I *should*, I *should*, I *should* . . ." we think. Our lives are a series of *should*s, to the extent that Horney called this the **tyranny of should**, for tyranny is exactly what it is. In a tyranny, there is no freedom, no compassion, no leeway for spontaneous actions, but there is massive punishment for deviations from what one "should" do. We become constantly terrorized by our set of rules, and two things then happen. First, we become farther and farther removed from the person we really are and can be, an **alienation from self**, in Horney's terms. We do not know what we really think or feel or want anymore. Second, we begin to hate ourselves for not living up to the idealized self we have created. Certainly this seems to be the case for Graham.

In some ways, the idealized self strikes one as helpful. After all, is it not good to try to improve yourself? Yes, said Horney, but improvement means actualizing the wonderful things that you *really* are, not a fantasy image. When anything is based on fantasy rather than reality, it crumbles easily. The person using an idealized self is very vulnerable to any suggestion that the self may be false. Criticism or questioning from the outside world, failure of some sort, or any real insight may be devastating to this person. The biggest drawback of the idealized self, however, is the way that concentration on it pulls a person away from understanding and relating to what he or she really is. Thus, we may not even realize that we have wonderful potential that is crying for development. Our self-hatred has made us blind to our gifts and assets, and our energy is all-consumed in diverting us away from realizing these gifts.

How Do People Show This Problem?

There are many possible ways that people may deal with the anxiety created by the large gap between the real self and the idealized self, Horney (1937, 1945) believed. Some people find their well-being to be dependent on positive interactions with others, through gaining affection or approval, or gaining a partner. In these cases, the individual seems to be coping with anxiety by saying "I need people to be nice to me, to love me, to take care of me. Then they won't hurt me." These are people who are *compliant* or *self-effacing*. Horney also characterized these people **as moving toward other people**. This seems to be the case for Graham who tries to fulfill other people's expectations of him.

For some people, being self-effacing is not the answer. For them, the answer may be found in the opposite attitude. Instead of feeling the need to demonstrate inferiority to others, these individuals feel the need to demonstrate superiority. These individuals take the *hostile* route by **moving against people**. They see the world as a dog-eat-dog competitive jungle in which survival is determined by the ability to fight. Hostile people are determined to fight and to win. To this end, they also demonstrate certain character-istic needs, such as a need for power, admiration, social recognition, perfection, or personal achievement. These needs may be generally acceptable, but in this person, the need has become extreme and the rights of other people are ignored.

Other people choose to be *detached*, or to **move away from people**. For these individuals, the need for independence and to avoid any emotional commitments are paramount. Neither fighting nor belonging seem to be an attractive alternative to the detached person, who feels as if he or she has nothing in common with the rest of the world anyway.

Horney (1937) noted that all of us have experienced some of the feelings described above at different points in our lives, so there is nothing intrinsically abnormal about them. For example, we want affection and approval, but if we do not get it, most of us sadly shrug and move on. We may well get a gleeful delight in an achievement that we have worked hard to attain, and the admiration of others may increase our enjoyment. The difficulty comes when an individual frames his or her life around the attainment of certain needs. The pursuit of these needs becomes all-consuming and haphazard in its target. Whereas a well-adjusted person can flexibly move from need to need as the situation arises and can leave the need behind when the situation passes, the poorly adjusted person is inflexible, stuck in one or a combination of needs, regardless of the situation or its passing.

The Well-Adjusted Person

Well-adjusted people—those who are most likely to have a satisfying life, according to Horney—are those who have a realistic understanding, appraisal, and acceptance of their real selves. The idealized self in such a person is also realistic, with goals and aspirations that the person has a reasonable chance of attaining. These individuals respond to situations and other people in flexible ways, never getting stuck moving toward, against, or away from others, but governing their behaviour in light of the situation at hand.

Graham, Horney would say, needs to understand himself better and get rid of the tyranny of should that he is labouring under. When he appreciates that his real self is much better than he realized, and when he forms a realistic idealized self, he will have a much better chance of achieving a sense of well-being and satisfaction in his life.

Understanding ourselves in commonplace activities

Right at this moment you are reading this book. What can you learn about yourself through what you are doing right now? First, why are you reading this book? Was it assigned to you for course work? Then why did you take the course? Unless the course was compulsory, you must have had some interest in psychology and the area of positive psychology and personal growth in particular. That suggests that you must be willing to look inward and examine yourself, an often courageous move.

What time is it? Where are you? If you are reading this book in the middle of the night because you have a test tomorrow morning, what does that tell you about yourself?

Are you a procrastinator? Have you been abnormally busy with unexpected events recently? Do you feel stressed out right now? How does what you have learned about yourself show up in other areas of your life? For example, if you have discovered that you are introspective, does this reflect the career you have chosen in life? Does it provide a clue to what kind of movies, books, and TV shows you like? If you have discovered that you tend to procrastinate, examine other areas to see exactly where you procrastinate. Is it in studying all courses? Is it in all academic ventures? Do you procrastinate in housecleaning or watering your plants as well? What impact does this have on your life?

THE GESTALT PERSPECTIVE: FREDERICK (FRITZ) PERLS

Tommy is a first-year university student who doesn't seem to enjoy the university experience very much. He isn't involved in much of campus life because he says high school was better. In fact, he keeps all his high school mementoes in his room in the university residence and tells everyone about all the wonderful things he did and the terrific things that occurred in high school.

A couple of his high school buddies attend the same university as Tommy does and they are frankly mystified by what he's saying. By their recollection, Tommy didn't get involved in high school activities and constantly talked about how junior high was much more fun. But then, people who have known Tommy for many years say that he didn't really give any indication of being part of junior high either, preferring to stay on the sidelines and reminisce about elementary school.

This seems consistent to Tommy's female friends too. When it comes to relationships, he compares every girl he dates to the perfect Shauna, the "love of his life" who dumped him in high school. But his high school buddies say that Tommy and Shauna were constantly fighting and making each other's lives miserable. When Tommy thinks about anything except the great times he remembers from the past, he focuses on how wonderful life will be when he finally graduates, when he gets the dream job, when he finds the ultimate life mate. Yes, life today can't compare to the magnificent past, for Tommy, but the future will be even better.

Tommy seems to be having a very difficult time accurately perceiving reality and appreciating what he has. He glorifies the past and future, but in doing so he is losing the present. Tommy is dissatisfied with the way life is at the moment, although he doesn't seem to be taking any time to *experience* life at the moment. He seems to believe that life, or at least something outside of himself, has to bring him the rewards he wants in order for him to be happy. What will happen to him? Chances are that Tommy will never be satisfied with any of the rewards of life that he does attain. Nothing in life at the moment will ever be able to live up to the past that he has glorified or the golden future that he envisions. No flesh-and-blood woman will ever fill the shoes of the ideal woman that he has turned Shauna into in his mind.

Looking at Tommy, we wonder what is wrong with him. He seems to have the potential for some terrific things in his life, but he seems too blind to see it. Our reaction to him is often one of impatience; we want to say "Get with it! Time for a reality check!" There is one school of psychology that might do just that. Gestalt therapy recognized that some people need to be shaken up a little to see the problems that they are creating for themselves and others. Gestalt therapy also based itself on the belief that the human being has the strength and ability to make whatever changes are needed. Fritz Perls, a truly vivid character himself, pioneered this type of therapy and remains the foremost name associated with it. It is not a therapy that the faint-hearted or chronically insecure person might choose in many cases, but it has had a great deal of success and provides us with a path toward personal growth that we might not have anticipated.

Perls' Assumptions

Just as any other theorist or philosopher, Fritz Perls made certain assumptions about the nature of the human being and how to understand him/her. His first assumption was that a holistic approach was needed. The human being, he contended, cannot be understood without looking at all facets of his or her being, not just at isolated portions such as the superego or a particular phobia (1969).

Perls also assumed that the human being is fundamentally healthy and well-adjusted, striving for balance within the body and mind. The problem is that socialization and society get in the way of nature. Left alone, in a natural state, human beings would act in an adaptive way and maintain a balance. We would reach out to the environment to fulfill our needs. If we were hungry, we would go to the kitchen and open the refrigerator, pull out sandwich fixings, and make a sandwich. We would then satisfy our need (eat the sandwich), and when we were full, we would feel the need for food fade away, to be replaced by the next need we experienced. This cycle forms a **gestalt**, a whole, and this process is what we would do in a healthy, adaptive fashion were it not for society, which has coloured our perceptions of what we really need.

Societal expectations have led us away from what we need; instead, we confuse what we *need* with what we *want*. "I need your love," says Romeo. No, says Perls (1947, 1969), you *want* the love of another. "I need money," says Scrooge. No, Scrooge, you *want* money. What we *need* are food, water, air, and shelter. But our environment may have encouraged us to think that we *need* social approval, respect, or a high income, for example. When we get away from what we really need and start to desperately pursue things that we want in the mistaken belief that we need them, we start to get into trouble and we become unhappy. Yet we can become happier. We have the ability within ourselves to re-connect with what we really are.

How can we do that? This involves another one of Perls' strict assumptions: that we can only deal with the present, only *now* is important. Yesterday is past, never to be recaptured. Even our recollections of yesterday are suspect because of the human trick of re-interpreting events of the past. Perls often quoted Nietzsche: "Memory and Pride were fighting. Memory said, 'It was like this' and Pride said, 'It couldn't have been like this'—and Memory gives in." (1969, p. 62). Tomorrow is uncertain and may never come. But today is ours, it is where we live, right here, right now. Poor Tommy, from the beginning of this section, is missing out on his life because he has not learned that. Perhaps tomorrow he will see how wonderful today was, but he cannot seem to see it or enjoy it now, while he is living it.

Perls would particularly feel that Tommy has a problem because he is not *experiencing* his life. Another one of Perls' assumptions is that experience is primary (Perls, 1973). We can listen to lectures, we can sit at the feet of gurus, we can memorize the words of sages or even psychologists, but none of this will make a difference to us or teach us anything unless we actually experience the reality of what has been said. The human being, with a core of health, has a wisdom beyond that which can be put into words. Through our awareness of our lives, through our actual experiencing of our true selves, we develop and get in touch with that wisdom. Again, however, our socialization may have interfered with this. The stress we put on "book-learning" encourages our removal from the act of experiencing first hand what is taught, Perls believed.

What Parents May Do Wrong

While Perls is not an advocate of searching the past in order to fix blame on someone or something, he does say that parents may create conditions that arrest the healthy development of their children, apart from the obviously detrimental conditions of physical, sexual, and/or emotional abuse (Perls, 1969).

Sometimes parents put children in a situation that they are not ready for. Perls calls this an **impasse**, and he gives the example of the "blue baby" who is born unready to breathe on his own. But the child cannot return to the womb. He cannot go farther and he cannot go back. He is stuck, trying to cope with his situation as best he can. A more modern example might be the adolescent whose unhappily married parent makes the child a confidante, revealing intimate details of the parents' marriage. The adolescent may do a wonderful job of being what the parent refers to as a "best friend" but, in truth, the child should not be placed in this position of being pulled apart by love for both parents, but because the child does not immediately show signs of mental disturbance, the parent assumes that he or she is not being psychologically damaged.

The parents are wrong, says Perls. The damage is being done, and for the rest of his or her life, the child may feel undue responsibility for others and fears of being inadequate to the challenge.

On the other hand, there are parents who so desperately wish to make their children's life easy and stress-free that they do everything for their children, acting sometimes like their children's servants. As the children mature, they may get into difficulties in life, but Mommy and Daddy are right there to bail the child out and make the unpleasantness go away. Perls feels that this **overindulgence** cripples the child. How will this child ever function in the world without the parents? Perls says that by depriving the child of the opportunity to make his or her own choices, face the normal stresses of life, and solve his or her own problems, the parents have left the child helpless and mired in self-loathing. Children need to discover the vast capability inside themselves, but over-indulged children may be too afraid to look.

Some parents load their children with **catastrophic expectations**. This means that the parents communicate to the child that if the child does not live up to parental dictates and standards, love and acceptance will be withdrawn. This may be very direct ("Mommy doesn't love bad little boys") or indirect. Sometimes, says Perls, the child mistakenly reaches the conclusion that parental love is contingent on good performance. I recall one student in a business program who wished to be in a social work program. "But my parents will be so disappointed if I switch," she told me tearfully. "They encouraged me in the business program and they've already spent the money for tuition for me for two years." I urged her to talk to her family about the issue, which she fear-fully did. She came back to me with a look of wonderment on her face: "They were happy!" she said. "They said they only encouraged me in the business program because I didn't seem to know what I wanted when I started university and they thought the business program would at least give me a chance to experience university and make up my mind. Now they're just glad I found what I want." This student (today an effective and happy social worker) made assumptions about her parents' acceptance of her that were erroneous. Many of us do, said Perls, and this can lead to a life spent with constant worry about pleasing others to the detriment of our own satisfaction in life.

Still, says Perls, we cannot use a time machine to go back and change what has happened, and if we dwell on the past, we lose today. Let's handle the emotions of the present instead. Note that this may mean dealing with anger or resentment that one still feels toward one's parents because of actions of the past. Deal with those feelings that you have today, says Perls, and finish the business of the past.

What Else Can Go Wrong?

Society! roars Perls. Society is crazy, he says. The expectations and demands put upon people are outrageous. People are not allowed to be open and honest. They are required to put on a false front, to dissemble, and to outright lie. And the society itself is nuts, he says (Perls, 1973, 1992). How can we espouse peace while spending billions of dollars on armaments? How can we pollute the environment and deplete our natural resources, acting as if some fairy godmother were going to repair all the damage we have done and return our world to habitability? Perls shakes his head in disbelief at psychological theories that aim at the goal of functioning adaptively in society. If society is insane, surely the person who smoothly fits into it is insane too.

It's a measure of the potency of the social conditioning we receive that we do not even realize the craziness of the world. This unawareness on our part is a demonstration of the filters that we wear when viewing the world. Wake up, says Perls. Only then can you cope with this insanity and not fall into it. Only through seeing the world and our-selves without these filters can we hope to have satisfying lives and perhaps even reduce the world's insanity.

Anxiety

Anxiety, according to Perls (1969), is an artefact of our not living in the present. Anxiety, he says, is the tension between now and then. Let's take a common example to illustrate what this means. You can't sleep tonight, and you're tossing and turning in bed because you're worried about your oral presentation in class or at work tomorrow. What's going on in your head while you are worrying? You're probably imagining a horrendous failure of some kind that will occur when you give the presentation. But that's tomorrow! Right now, you're safe and warm in bed. If you were living in the present, you would appreciate the comfort of your bed and be aware of your fatigue. You would drift off to sleep. But instead, you're rehearsing a future event that probably will not even occur.

Perls is not advocating never thinking about or planning for the future; clearly, it is advantageous to have goals, plans for achieving those goals, and contingency plans in case something goes wrong with the original plan. If something unpleasant might occur, it would advantageous to have a plan for how to deal with it. But once you have the plan, why continue to dwell on it? "What if?" is not helpful and draws us away from appreciating what we have right now, as well as impeding our ability to formulate reasonable strategies for dealing with life's vicissitudes.

If we're not fully in the present moment, then we're not in contact with our emerging needs. If we're taken in by our conditioning (from parents, friends, society), we're not fully in contact with our authentic selves. We may try desperately to be the person we think someone else wants us to be, ". . . like an elephant who had rather be a rose bush, and a rose bush that tries to be a kangaroo" (Perls, 1970, p. 20). Until each can accept being what they are, both will lead lives filled with dissatisfaction.

Unless we are seriously mentally disturbed, most of us live on two levels, says Perls. One is the level of reality, in which we are very aware of ourselves and our environment. The other level he calls **maya**, which is something like an illusion or a fantasy. It's a level of thinking which Perls believes is mainly rehearsal for future roles and situations. This is where we spend a great deal of our time and energy. Instead of actually living in the world, we tend to live in our minds. One of Perls' most quoted comments is "Lose your mind and come to your senses!"

The only reasonable way to deal with the world is to find the balance between it and our own selves. This balance must be fluid, though. Sometimes we need to give in to society's dictates (e.g., obeying traffic signals) and sometimes we need to resist (e.g., associating with whom we choose rather than only those arbitrarily deemed appropriate).

The Well-Adjusted Person

What is a healthy person, according to Perls' approach? Mentally healthy people are clearly aware of their own needs and the possibilities within their environment as they arise from moment to moment. They may have frustrations in terms of conflicting needs, but they are capable of resolving them without turning them into major crises. They don't allow unfinished business to pile up; rather, they deal with each situation or problem as it arises, and then they let go of it. Their senses are vivid, and their appreciation of the moment and the people in it is intense because of their ability to perceive the world without the baggage of self-serving filters. They respect themselves, they respect others, and they respect their environment. They are authentic—that is, true to what they really are, not trying to be someone else or fit someone else's expectations.

The mentally healthy person has responsibility, which Perls often recasts as *response-ability* (Perls, 1969; Perls, Hefferline, & Goodman, 1994). This means that the individual is able to respond to his or her own needs, expectations, desires, and fantasies, and to shed accountability for the needs, expectations, desires, and fantasies of others.

> ... but this restriction of responsibility in no way implies a lack of caring about the needs of other people nor does it imply an inability to respond to their needs. When people are responsible for themselves, they know that no one else can respond to the world for them. This kind of responsibility derives from self-acceptance, acceptance of the environment as it is, and the maturity to see both self and others in proper perspective.
>
> *(Korb, Gorrell, & Van De Riet, 1989, p. 49)*

The mentally healthy individual is one who is mature. "My formulation is that *maturing is the transcendence from environmental support to self-support*" (Perls, 1969, p. 48, italics in original). What Perls means by *self-support* is the ability of the individual to function independently, without needing the emotional/psychological reassurance or guidance of anyone else.

This is Perls' Gestalt Prayer, a highly controversial and often misunderstood passage in which Perls affirmed the need of all of us to be true to ourselves, unfettered by the expectations of others for us to be what they wish us to be.

> I do my own thing and you do your thing.
>
> I am not in this world to live up to your expectations,
>
> And you are not in this world to live up to mine.
>
> You are you, and I am I,
>
> And if by chance we find each other, it's beautiful.
>
> If not, it can't be helped.
>
> *(Perls, 1969, p. 24)*

REFLECTIVE EXERCISE

Grounding yourself in the present

Perls contended that if a therapist had no other techniques except three questions, that would be enough to help any individual. The questions are "What are you doing?" "What do you feel?" and "What do you want?" Two more questions, extensions of these, may be added: "What do you avoid?" and "What do you expect?" In the individual's quest to become aware of his or her true self, these questions provoke intense self-scrutiny and require being grounded in the present. Try answering these questions for yourself. Are you being honest? Are you saying what you feel or what you think is expected of you or will make you look good? Try answering the questions again. Not easy, is it? Try asking yourself these questions several times a day to keep you aware of your own needs and to ground you in the present.

For Perls, then, Tommy first and foremost must live in the present. He needs to recognize that his dissatisfaction with his life is due more to his distorted glorification of the past and his unrealistic expectations of the present. He lives in maya, and it is time for him to take responsibility for himself and his life.

THE HUMANISTIC PERSPECTIVE: CARL ROGERS AND ABRAHAM MASLOW

Sandeep knew that she was a lucky woman. Her parents had been kind and loving, showing their respect and value for her since she was born. They encouraged her in her interests and applauded when she decided to go to university to pursue her dream of helping to save the oceans by becoming a marine biologist. Her husband shared her interests and was proud of her and her accomplishments. They laughed together often and planned to share their love and joy with the baby that was on the way. Childbirth was a little longer than Sandeep had expected, and more painful, but when the nurse handed her newborn son to her, Sandeep felt her heart expand and she saw the continuation of her ancestors and herself in this "child of the universe," as she called him, in her arms. She felt her strength, she felt her abilities, and she felt her determination to make sure that this child, and all others like him, would have a good world to grow in, and the same love of life that she felt so strongly.

Lucky Sandeep, we may say. Her life appears to be deeply satisfying to her, and she appears to know it and be grateful for it. Most of us would say, with little reservation, that Sandeep is a healthy woman who is functioning at an optimal level. From this albeit brief description, she seems to have no pathologies or "hang-ups" in her life that prevent her from getting the most out of her life.

Psychologists in the past have trained their eyes on the people who have been having problems in life; few have paid much attention to people like Sandeep. Psychologists of the Humanistic approach, however, have.

Carl Rogers

The Fully Functioning Person

Carl Rogers (1951, 1961), one of the founders of the Humanistic approach, insisted that human beings have an innate potential to grow and develop, to become the best that they can possibly be—the **actualizing tendency**, as he called it. The **fully functioning person** he described is fulfilling this tendency to explore and develop. This person uses the actualizing tendency to direct and motivate life in all its facets, leading to love and creativity, as well as happiness and satisfaction in life. The fully functioning person has confidence and high self-esteem and openness to feelings and experiences.

What We Need to Become Fully Functioning

According to Rogers, what the individual needs in order to become fully functioning is threefold: first, we need **unconditional positive regard**. We all need to feel loved, valued, and appreciated. Society is structured so that we can earn some of this by, for example, being kind to others, doing our work to the best of our ability in a responsible fashion, and giving our own love and appreciation to others. Beyond this, however, we also have a need for love and appreciation that we have not earned by any of our actions. Unconditional positive regard refers to the value we are (or should be) given by others because we are members of the human race. While others may not necessarily like our opinions or actions, they owe us basic respect and esteem. A simple way of illustrating this is seen in parents' love for their child: while the child's behaviour may be deplored ("Oh no! He wrote all over the freshly painted walls with his crayons!"), the love for the child himself always remains. Knowing that, while we may make mistakes in many actions of life, the essential "we will not be rejected" provides a platform on which we are able to explore the dimensions of our own beings, with the aim of maximizing our own satisfaction with our lives.

Second, we need **openness**. By openness, Rogers meant the chance to be honest and true to the self, rather than dissembling and playing a false role in order to win approval. Without openness, we move further away from what we really are, becoming progressively enmeshed in role-playing until we don't even know what our true self is any more. Yet many of us, at different points in our lives, may feel compelled to hide the reality of ourselves (especially if that reality conflicts with society's current mores) for fear of punishment, rejection, or other undesirable repercussions. Clearly, becoming a fully functioning person under these conditions is impossible.

Finally, we need **empathy**. Rogers regarded empathy as the ability to see the world through another person's perspective. He believed that we all see the world differently through our own filters, or **phenomenal field**. The absolute reality of a situation is not as important as the way we perceive reality. For example, look back on the case of Sandeep at the beginning of this section. Some people might claim that her life is one that would be highly undesirable for them. "Husband, baby, marine biology? Ugh! I want freedom, excitement, no commitments to any job so that I can take off whenever I want." The point is that it doesn't matter whether Sandeep is objectively right or wrong in her assessment of her life. In this case, there is no right or wrong except insofar as it exists in the individual's eyes. Sandeep perceives her life as a good one, and that's all that matters. Rogers contends that not imposing our own judgments on other people, but trying to view them in their totality, from their own unique viewpoint, allows them the freedom to be themselves without hiding or dissembling, thereby facilitating their own personal growth.

Obviously it is much easier to describe the factors needed for growth than it is to obtain them. When others, perhaps the society in which one lives, dictate what the individual should value and how the individual should behave and think and feel, the self-actualizing tendency may be stifled and becoming a fully functioning person is very difficult.

Abraham Maslow

While the Humanistic Path has been credited as being highly influential in the formation of positive psychology by many psychologists (e.g., Resnick et al., 2001; Strümpfer, 2005), one theorist in particular, Abraham Maslow, has been considered a major pioneer and visionary that inspired much of the work in this area. Maslow felt that, in order to understand the good functioning of the human being, we should study those who function the best and not confine ourselves to the study of people with psychological disorders. In fact, he once said, "To oversimplify the matter somewhat, it is as if Freud supplied to us the sick half of psychology, and we must now fill it out with the healthy half" (Maslow, 1968, p. 5).

The Hierarchy of Needs

In viewing the human being, Maslow saw a growing, developing organism that had the task of fulfilling certain needs. He arranged these needs into a **hierarchy of needs**, with the most basic, life-sustaining needs at the base. Only when the most basic needs were fulfilled could the individual move up the hierarchy to work on fulfilling the next need. Maslow's hierarchy is usually viewed as the pyramid shown below.

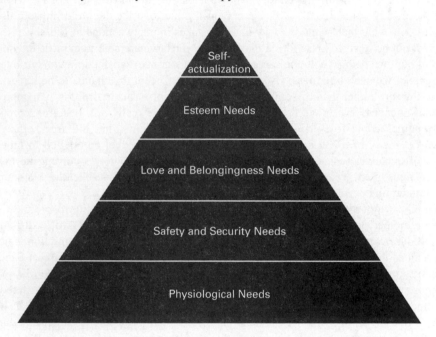

At the base of the pyramid are the **physiological needs** comprised of the elements that are necessary for life (e.g., food, water). The next is the **need for safety and security** in both the physical and psychological senses. We need to feel that we are safe in body and secure in mind and emotion. When these needs are fulfilled, said Maslow, we become concerned with the **need for love and belongingness**. We are social animals who need each other, not only for physical survival, but also for our emotional well-being in feeling ourselves to be cared for and accepted by others and to have a place among them. At the next level are **esteem needs**. Feeling cared for and accepted is wonderful, but when we have that, we also experience the need to be respected by others and by ourselves; we have the need to feel ourselves to be competent and worthwhile and to be viewed in this way by others.

The bottom four needs are what Maslow termed the **deficiency needs** because in fulfilling these needs we attempt to gain that which we lack. The need at the top of the pyramid, **self-actualization**, is the most noteworthy in terms of positive psychology and personal growth. This need, a **growth need** rather than a deficiency need, can never be fully satisfied because there is no limit to how much one can grow. It's felt by few of us. In fact, Maslow (1968) suggested that only about one percent of us ever really experience this need. Let's examine self-actualization further.

Self-Actualization

For Maslow (1970), the term *self-actualization* referred to the state of optimal human functioning. Self-actualized people, said Maslow, have completely or largely fulfilled the lower needs and now experience life in a different way. What are these people like? Here is a list of some of the characteristics self-actualized people are said to possess:

- They make full use of their talents and abilities.
- These people have a clearer and truer view of the world and their place in it.
- They feel a sense of purpose in their dedication to some work or cause that relates to their feeling of connectedness.
- They respond to the world and others with delight and creativity.
- They have a strong sense of right, wrong, virtue, and justice, yet they suspend judgment to listen to other people with an open heart and with respect and humility.
- They feel confident and secure within themselves and want to promote this in others as well.

Sometimes self-actualized people have what Maslow (1964, 1970, 1971) has called **peak experiences**. A peak experience (which can be experienced by those who are not self-actualized, as well) is a situation that seems to take us out of ourselves, giving us a feeling of experiencing life with greater intensity and awareness than normal. This may come when someone hears a particularly stirring piece of music, sees a beautiful nature scene, holds their newborn child for the first time as Sandeep at the beginning of this section did, or in a multitude of different ways. People who have had a peak experience describe it as an almost mystical state of rapture in which they come closer to understanding life more than at any other time. This feeling typically fades rather quickly.

A more enduring, but less intense, experience is the **plateau experience**, in which some situation or event triggers a changed perception of the world and a greater appreciation of life. Some people who have had brushes with death, for example, report that they had such an experience as they realized that they were going to live after all. Now, they may say, they feel more alive and more aware of their lives and the people in them, and they are more grateful for this.

Neither peak nor plateau experiences are necessary for self-actualization, nor does having such an experience indicate that self-actualization is occurring. But people who are self-actualized are more likely to experience further instances of this than are other people. While many of us may have intense moments such as these, few of us actually attain self-actualization. Why is this?

Why Self-Actualization is Rare

The first reason why few of us attain self-actualization is relatively obvious: according to Maslow (1968), we do not experience this need until all the deficiency needs have been fulfilled, and very few of us fulfill all these lower needs. In some famine-stricken parts of the world, for example, it is very difficult to meet the most basic need for the elements to sustain life, right at the bottom of the pyramid. For some of us, safety and security in our environment are difficult to find as war rages around us or as repressive governmental regimes curtail our ability to feel free to express ourselves and create the lives we want for ourselves and our children. In parts of the world with more advantages, such as in most Western nations, we still struggle to find love or a sense of belonging or to find respect in our own eyes and the eyes of others. As long as we still need to search for the means of fulfilling these lower needs, we are not ready to experience the growth need of self-actualization.

In some cultures, the environment that would facilitate self-actualization may be missing. For example, in a culture with strongly prescribed gender roles, individuals may not be able to express their whole selves that probably do not fit artificial roles. In a culture in which men are rejected for not being "macho" enough, a man may find it difficult to self-actualize because the more sensitive, artistic part of his nature, which is crying for development, must be repressed. In a society in which women are not regarded as equals but must remain solely in the domestic sphere, an individual woman with talent and intelligence for mathematics, say, may find self-actualization beyond her reach because her society does not allow her to express her talents.

Another reason we may not self-actualize, even if our deficiency needs have been largely satisfied, is our fear of own potential for greatness. Maslow (1968) called this the **Jonah complex**, after the Biblical story of Jonah who tried to run away from God's command for him to be a prophet and leader of his people. While we may dream of attaining greatness in some endeavour, we may also fear it: greatness brings with it responsibility. If we self-actualize, we will know the truth about ourselves and our potential, and we will need to act on it. Do we really want to take on this work and this role? Will our friends and family still love us when we "rise above them"? If we fulfill our own potential in this way, will this not seem like self-aggrandizement, a socially unacceptable trait? Would it not be safer just to stay small and un-actualized?

Beyond Self-Actualization

Near the end of his life, Maslow (1971) began to voice even more dissatisfaction with the way traditional psychology viewed the human being. Science, he claimed, had become **desacralized**; that is, the sense of awe and wonder in the face of mystery and the unknown had vanished while scientists viewed everything as measurable, quantifiable, and verifiable. The human being, he felt, was more wondrous than that, and he began to conceive of the possibility of human growth beyond that of self-actualization. Self-actualization includes a feeling of being connected to the rest of the world; beyond this, thought Maslow, is the dissolving of the individual self into something much greater and more unified. This has the flavour of what Eastern belief systems have called *nirvana* or *satori*, as we shall see in the next chapter.

The Well-Adjusted Person

According to Maslow, the most satisfying life occurs when a person becomes self-actualized. That means that the deficiency needs have been satisfied and the individual perceives that there is more to life than this. The individual lives in a culture that supports personal growth, is prepared to find out what the "more" is, and is open to experiencing a changed perception of the world. Sandeep, that fortunate woman, seems to be in just the situation in which she has the possibility for self-actualization. Her potential for growth, Maslow would say, is unlimited.

REFLECTIVE EXERCISE

Self-Actualization

Do you know anyone who you think is self-actualized or at least close to it? (This can be a fictional or historical person, or someone whom you do not know personally.) What is this person like? What qualities do you share with this person? What qualities does this person possess that you would like to cultivate in yourself? How can you do this? What holds you back?

Have you fulfilled your deficiency needs? Do you have personal and societal support for your growth? Are you afraid of changing? Talk to the person you feel is self-actualized, if possible. Does he or she think that they are self-actualized? Do you think that self-actualized people claim that they are self-actualized? Or that they are "works-in-progress"?

THE EXISTENTIAL PERSPECTIVE: ROLLO MAY

Deirdre is majoring in computer science in university. She envies her classmates who seem to get such a kick out of designing computer programs and ironing out bugs. It's hard to pry them away from their computers, she thinks, but as for her, she really doesn't care if she ever sees a computer again. It's not that she hates computer science: it's just that she doesn't care. So why doesn't she switch majors? To what? she replies wearily. There's nothing that really interests her; there's nothing she really wants to do; there's nothing she really wants to be.

How did she wind up in computer science in the first place? Deirdre's parents have always guided her in pursuits they think would be best for her. They felt that Deirdre should major in something that would help her get a well-paying job, and computer science seemed to be a good bet. Now in the second year of her program, her marks are adequate but not outstanding. Deirdre doesn't care about that either. She has no close friends and no boyfriend. She doesn't care enough about those around her to attract friends. "People are just sheep, they move about in a mass mindlessly. Why would I want to be close to them?" she says. She spends her time alone in her bedroom, listening to the same music over and over again.

Many mental health practitioners would say that Deirdre is depressed. Certainly it seems that way, and she would probably agree. What she is feeling is all too common, and telling her to "pull up her socks" is not going to help. She would if she could. Why should she be depressed? She has opportunities that she does not seem to realize and conditions that many other people would find blissful. Is she crazy?

There is a school of thought that says no, what she is feeling is really part of the normal human existence. But her unhappiness can be handled in ways to bring contentment, growth, and even joy to her life. This school of thought is called Existential Psychology. It is the result of looking at the human condition using concepts of both psychology and existential philosophy. This approach sees human beings as having common concerns, but unique and individual ways of dealing with them. The focus is put on the way the individual experiences his or her life. Existential Psychology is often regarded as a part of the Humanistic Path, but for our purpose a separate examination of it may be warranted.

Although Existential Psychology, along with existential philosophy, had its start in Europe, its prime proponent has been an American psychologist named Rollo May. He put together his American-influenced upbringing, his own experiences with life and impending death, his traditional training in psychology, and his education in philosophy to form a brand of Existential Psychology that particularly speaks to us living in the world today.

How to Understand the Human Being

Rollo May had enormous respect for the human being. He didn't think that all humans were magnificent creatures, but he believed strongly in the greatness of human potential. He recognized that this potential could be frightening. To maximize your potential, to be all you can be, is an impossibility in life (that would imply that perfection is attainable), but even trying for this involves striving, taking risks, possibly failing. These are all acts of courage (May, 1975). For many of us, not trying, and thereby avoiding the potentially dangerous unknown, is preferable. Many people, therefore, refuse to even acknowledge that there is a potential that could be, at least in part, realized.

May believed that we have to become completely aware of the total human being: the human being must be understood as a total entity, in a place, time, and space (including "psychological space") that is unique to the individual. The person is not to be understood only in terms of past events in his or her life, or only in terms of biological drives or reinforcement contingencies. However, the environment forms part of the individual's reality, in terms of past events impinging on and affecting the human being, drives that can be thought of as the individual's biological environment, and the actual physical environment of the individual's geographical and historical place. The effects of the physical environment on him or her must be included here as well (May, Angel, & Ellenberger, 1958).

The human being is an entity who is becoming—that is, an entity who is growing, striving, developing, who contains his or her own reality and his or her own future, determined by his or her freedom to choose (May, 1983). We must then recognize that we bring our own realities to bear on our interactions with others. This means that we view others through our own being, not through the other's being.

Part of the individual's being is defined by his social interactions. Our social world includes the way we conceive of ourselves in regards to the group or to other individuals. In North America, the rugged individualism that opened up the continent gave way to the strong belief in democracy. The words "all men are created equal" became distorted to mean that all men are the same. Conformism became the hallmark of America, says May (1953). The greatest evil befalling human beings has been seen as ostracism, to be rejected by the group, to be seen as a misfit, as one who does not belong. Instead of choosing to fulfill yourself, you may instead subvert your individuality in favour of being one of the group. Your relationship to the group is part of how you identify yourself.

Authenticity

In the case at the beginning of this section, Deirdre seems to be a woman who is fulfilling a role that she did *not* freely choose. It could be that Deirdre defines herself in terms of conformism to her parents' conception of what she should do. If so, Deirdre is an individual who has cut herself off from growing and developing. She is living by the values and mores put forward by others and not by any values that she has chosen for herself. Indeed, she may not even realize that she has the freedom to choose. In existential terms, Deirdre is not living authentically, or with **authenticity**. No wonder, then, that she feels empty and alienated, detached from herself and others. This is because she has rejected her own basic humanity, along with its greatest characteristic—the freedom of choice. May (1981) stresses that an inclination to reclaim the freedom of choice must come first in a personal growth situation or no change can possibly take place. This would account for why therapy mandated by courts or coerced by others (i.e., therapy not freely chosen by the individual) is so rarely effective.

May (1953) argues that people in Western society have taken science as the ultimate good and have reduced communication to objectively stated fact. In this way, Western people are perhaps not even aware of their subjective state anymore. Thus, for example, we now have researchers who are measuring the symmetry of the human face to quantify what is "beautiful." It is no longer seen as adequate to say "I think she's beautiful." Such subjectivity is seen as invalid.

Yet, May feels, this subjectivity is the basis of the human relationship to the world: how does the world seem to the individual? This is what counts. I remember studying Charles Dickens' novel *Great Expectations* in high school English class. This novel has two endings. The class was required to write an essay on which ending was better and why. The teacher stipulated that it was not appropriate to say that one ending was better than the other "because I like it better; because it satisfies me more."

May would say that the teacher was wrong in her stipulation, that such a manner of education decreases the child's ability to get in touch with how he or she feels. There is no opportunity and no encouragement for the child to find out what brings a good, satisfying feeling of contentment and what brings a bad feeling of distaste, outrage, confusion, ambivalence, or whatever emotion "I don't like" may encompass. May would say that "Because I like it better" is a richer and more valid statement than a discourse on literary merit because it reveals a realism that an objective essay on literature completely neglects.

In the Western world, we find many people who react with confusion when they are asked what emotion they are experiencing. Some of us can say "I feel good" or "I feel bad," but we have trouble pinpointing exactly what *good* and *bad* mean. Are we feeling joy or delight or contentment or pride or love or benevolence? Are we feeling anger or hatred or depression or despondency or shame or guilt? Many of us need training to find out.

The Six Principles of Being

May (1967) puts forth six principles concerning what constitutes the being before us—that is, the individual in the here and now:

1. Every individual is centred in him- or herself. This means, very basically, that the core of the individual is within himself or herself.

2. The individual has a need to preserve this central core. This may be called self-affirmation, the need to say "I am," and it may even be regarded as courage. Without this, the self dies.

3. The individual has the ability to go out from this core of being to participate with others. This involves more courage, however, since it is risky. Not venturing out leaves the human being unconnected and without meaning, but going out too much may lead to over-participation in the world and the conformism that subverts individual identity and choice.

4. The individual has awareness of the world.

    These first four principles are biological truths: they are shared by all living beings. The fifth and sixth principles set human beings apart from other animals.

5. Human beings have self-consciousness. Human beings are aware and *are aware that they are aware*. Human beings are not only aware of events in the world, but they are aware of the effects these events have on them. This means that we have the ability to transcend our immediate situation: we have memory of events no longer present, we can take lessons from past events to help in our interpretation of present events, we can extrapolate to future possibilities. We have developed symbol systems, language being the most powerful, to aid us in this. Because of this, we have freedom of choice. Freedom of choice is the hallmark of humanness to Rollo May. Freedom is part of the fundamental being of the organism, even though many of us may not know it.

6. Anxiety is another fundamental component of the human being. This merits further examination.

Anxiety and Guilt

Anxiety is the feeling we experience in our fight to maintain our being against the threat of nonbeing (May, 1977). At every instant of human existence, there is an awareness that, in making choices, we may choose the self-destructive route. May believes that there is even a temptation in us to do just that. (Have we not all made a few mistakes when we "should have known better"?) Whether we spend time thinking about it or not, we are aware, at every instant, that the choice to live or die is ours.

In all human existence, there are countless temptations and pressures for us to take the easy way out by denying our individuality, fitting in with the crowd, and letting others make the tough decisions about what is right and wrong, what is good and bad. The struggle to be true to ourselves, to not take this easier and ultimately self-destructive route, gives rise to the experience of anxiety. With our self-awareness, we are also aware that our being will end in death, whether we choose it or not. Affirming our values and beliefs and feelings in the face of ultimate annihilation is a struggle in itself and another source of anxiety. May sees anxiety as a reality that cannot be removed, only faced. When this anxiety is not faced, it grows in intensity and manifests itself in maladaptive ways.

Guilt is also seen by May as being inescapable in character. We human beings, in our self-awareness, are aware of our potential, but we are also aware that we can never fully realize this potential, that we will never have enough years of life to reach our full potential. This produces guilt, which, if not faced, can become a source of great distress. Another source of guilt is the awareness that no matter how hard we try, we do not see the absolute being of others because we view them through our own perspectives. Because of this, we do a disservice to others and may not meet their needs. We then feel badly for it.

The lesson for us is that we need to be aware that life and the human condition make demands of us that are scary. We can only deal with this by being aware that this is normal and having the courage to face the tough stuff. And when we interact with others, the most important thing to do is to listen, to try to see the world through the other person's eyes as much as we can, and not to impose our views of the world and what is right and wrong.

Values

One question we must ask ourselves is this: What do we value as being essential to our existence? In other words, what can we not do without? Money? Friends? Honour? Self-respect? Attention? Approval? Challenge? Dignity? Pride? If we strip away all the roles we play, what is left? Whenever one of the values we hold dear is threatened in some way, we feel anxiety.

May (1967) points out that no values are unassailable, and our own values are always being changed or at least modified. Think of how you have changed in the last five or ten years. Have you developed or strengthened some values you did not really think about in the past? Have you mellowed and become more tolerant on some issues? Have you hardened on some other issues? In your own life-long process of growing and developing, have you not changed your mind completely on some issues? Have you not had your "consciousness raised" on some points? This is an inevitable part of the process of growth. Since growth is a life-long process, it is evident that we will always experience threats to our values, and so we will always experience anxiety.

This sounds rather ominous, but actually most of us manage our anxiety in a healthy, growing way and many of us achieve a satisfying life—mainly, according to May (1977), because of our upbringing. The child who has experienced loving, consistent parents who nurture his or her growing autonomy and are realistic in their expectations of him or her is more likely to form a personality that is able to confront threats to its values. Such normal anxiety requires courage in facing it because there is potential for some sort of unknown change in confronting a threat, and the unknown can be scary. But in the normally developing child, this change is regarded more in terms of its potential for challenge and adventure.

Power

Rollo May (1983) believed that the need for power is inherent in the human being. When May says that we are born with a need for power, he means that we need to know that we're able to influence our environment. The infant needs to know that his cries will bring a caretaker with food, warmth, safety. The toddler needs to know that pulling the string will make that toy follow behind her. The schoolchild needs to know that hard work will bring good grades and academic success. And so into adulthood, when we all need to know that our actions are responsible for the outcomes in our environment. This is true power: the knowledge that we can make things happen, that we have significance in this world, even though we can't control every aspect of life.

By our own significance, we bring meaning to our existence. "I affect, therefore I am." This is May's strongest point in his understanding of the human being—that human beings must know that they "count." The greatest harm that can befall a human being is an act that diminishes the person's sense of control. In diminishing the sense of significance the person feels, self-worth and self-esteem are diminished.

When we think of episodes in our lives that have hurt us and have been difficult for us to deal with, the episodes that have sometimes left scars upon us, we see that this element of removing power from us has been a main factor in our trauma. Examples abound. One example reflects a point Fritz Perls made: when parents are overprotective of their children and do not permit the child to develop autonomy, the child is in effect being told "You aren't able to manage the world; others, like Mommy and Daddy, are more powerful than you are, and they will guide you." Such a message may sometimes be necessary for the growing child, but the child who is fed a steady diet of this will never feel that he or she can be effectual in the world. These individuals may become passive, looking for guidance from others, never believing that he or she is "good" enough to direct his or her own life.

> No human being can exist for long without some sense of his own significance. Whether he gets it by shooting a haphazard victim in the street, or by constructive work, or by rebellion, or by psychotic demands in a hospital, or by Walter Mitty fantasies, he must be able to feel this I-count-for-something and be able to live out that felt significance. It is the lack of this sense of significance, and the struggle for it, that underlies much violence.
>
> *(May, 1972, p. 37)*

Wish and Will

Is there anything you wish? Of course. Each individual wishes for things ranging from a new shirt to world peace. **Wish** orients us to the future; wish describes the way we want our lives to be tomorrow or the next day or the next, in at least some small part. At the same time, what we wish for is probably derived to some extent from our past. If we were raised in families or societies that valued appearance, we may wish for items to enhance our appearance. If we were raised in conditions of famine, we may wish for security from hunger.

When we wish, we are pushed from the past and pulled by the future. In many cases our wishes are unattainable. The short person may wish to be tall while the tall person wishes to be shorter. In other cases, the wish is not unattainable, but is not attained. The uneducated person wishes to be educated, but does not return to school even on a part-time or home-study basis. Wish alone is not enough to make our lives what we want them to be.

The element that tries to fulfill our wishes is what May (1969, 1981) terms **will**. Will is the capacity to organize our actions and feelings so that we can actually move toward our goal and fulfill our wish. *Wish* and *will* go together in an ideal situation, with wish providing the imaginative possibility and will providing the practical elements needed to realize the possibility. Herein lies one of the problems of modern life. We wish for much that seems reasonable given the extent of our modern-day achievements, but at the same time these very achievements make us feel small and powerless. It seems that we have a paradox: we desperately need to exert our will but we feel that if we did, it would do little good. For example, many countries, often after much struggle, achieved their desired aim of democracy, and yet, at election time, many people do not vote, feeling that their one vote doesn't count.

Intentionality

When we do decide to exert effort, to exercise our will in the pursuit of some goal, how do we decide what to do? What action do we choose to fulfill our wish? This depends on what May (1969) calls **intentionality**.

Intentionality is the meaning we give to experience and to elements of our environment; it is the orientation to and the perspective we take in viewing the world. May believed that absolute reality is not as important to the individual as is the way he or she perceives reality. Every experience we have had in our lives leads us to form certain characteristics. These characteristics influence how we interpret and react to stimuli we encounter in the world. Thus, when Ms. Jones, the boss, smiles and says "good morning" to two workers, one, who received a compliment for his performance from Ms. Jones yesterday, thinks, "Ms. Jones likes me. I'm moving up in the company." But the other was reprimanded for a careless mistake by Ms. Jones yesterday. In response to the same greeting, he thinks, "Ms. Jones is letting me know that she's watching me. My job is in danger." Since one's career is often very important, the interpretation of the boss' greeting may increase or decrease anxiety. It all depends on how each person interprets the situation.

Intentionality may also change with circumstances. Take the way you interact with this book, for example. If you're reading it for a course you're taking, you're probably making notes or underlining important parts. You're studying. If marks are crucial to you, you're probably concentrating as hard as you can and wishing this book didn't contain so much information. On the other hand, if marks aren't so crucial to you because you're auditing the course, for example, you probably are not doing much studying of the concepts. Rather, you're probably looking for ideas that you can apply to yourself and other people in your life. You're probably enjoying the book a little more than if you were worried about marks.

In either case, when the course is finished, you may be looking at this book with a critical economic eye: How much can you get for this used book? Then again, if you're simply reading this book for interest rather than for a course, you're probably skipping parts that don't seem as applicable to your life as others, and you may be less likely to sell it after you're through. (But you may want to loan it to friends!)

Will, then, is fuelled by wish and directed by intentionality. **Caring** is the source of will (May, 1969). We cannot will, or wish for that matter, if we don't care. Because we're mortal and know that we will one day die, we're hard-wired to care. We have much to do and much to make sense of in a limited amount of time. When we live an inauthentic life, we often lose sight of caring. Since other people have told us what we should do and feel, we no longer know what it is that we care about in an authentic manner. Does this not seem to be the case with Deirdre, whom we met at the beginning of this section? Her well-intentioned parents directed her life so much that Deirdre has lost sight of her caring. But she can get it back, if she recognizes that she has this power and if she chooses to use it. What Deirdre can do is to choose to become passionately committed to her freedom of choice. This doesn't mean that she necessarily needs to become rebellious; it means that she needs to understand her worth by virtue of her humanity.

… man is ontologically constituted by care. It is the refusal to accept emptiness though it face one on every side; the dogged insistence on human dignity, though it be violated on every side; and the stubborn assertion of the self to give content to our activities, routine as these activities may be.

(May, 1969, p. 292)

The Well-Adjusted Person

For May, then, people who have the best chance of achieving a satisfying life are those who know their own values, remain true to themselves, and have the courage to face the inevitable anxiety and guilt of life while committing themselves to acting in an authentic way. They recognize that their interpretations of other people and events are not the only ways of seeing the world, and they are flexible enough to change their interpretations. They exert their ultimate freedom: the freedom of choice in deciding how to interpret and how to react to a situation.

Deirdre, too, must become more aware of herself, her feelings, and her values, and act authentically. She has the freedom to see her education as boring and meaningless or to interpret it as a wonderful opportunity. She can also choose to regard other people as growing, struggling, planning, dreaming individuals, or as puppets. But she has to have the courage to care and the will to act upon her caring.

REFLECTIVE EXERCISE

To recognize our responsibility for our reactions

Think of some episode in your past that had a less-than-desirable outcome. Perhaps it was an argument with a friend or relative. Perhaps it was a low grade on a test or essay. Perhaps it was a conflict with a boss or co-worker or store clerk or police officer or someone else. Think back to how the episode started. What did you do or say? Now think of alternative responses that you could have made. Is there an alternative that might have lead to a more positive outcome? For example, did the argument (no matter who started it) escalate when you yelled? Would a calmer, assertive (rather than aggressive) response have changed the situation, eliciting different responses from the other person? Would the mark on the test or essay possibly have changed if you had started work earlier?

Many people are now responding with "Yeah, but she started it…" "Yeah, but he said…" "Yeah, but I didn't like the course…" "Yeah, but I had other things to do…" If you find yourself justifying your original response to the situation, recognize that there are always *yeah, buts*… and that you have the freedom to choose your reaction. Say to yourself, "The truth is I chose to do what I did. No one forced me. The responsibility for my action is my own, and therefore the responsibility for the outcome is at least partly my own."

Remember that once you take responsibility for your choices, you take control of the choices you will make in the future. No one can "push your buttons" if you take control of your reactions.

Conclusion

In this chapter, we briefly examined four different perspectives on adjustment. All of them seem to stress being true to yourself and being committed to the idea of forming a life in which you respect yourself and others. There are many, many more possible perspectives or paths that one may take for a while, and then switch to another. The object is not necessarily consistency in the path you choose; the object is to find what suits your needs best at each stage you are in. Perhaps a bit of Existentialism and a bit of Humanistic Psychoanalysis? Or a touch of Humanism and a soupçon of Gestalt? Or something entirely different? In the next two chapters, we will see that Western theorists do not have a monopoly on trying to determine what constitutes a satisfying life. You may find that the paths of the Eastern world resonate in you more than those of the Western world (Chapter 3). Or it may be that Aboriginal wisdom and reasoning strike a chord with you (Chapter 4). In any case, we will see in Part 2 of this book that all of these paths have merit, as witnessed by the empirical findings of positive psychology.

Summary

- Karen Horney felt that American culture is marked by hypercompetitiveness. Culture also prescribes roles for people that may inhibit their ability to manifest their true potential. The family of a child may behave in ways that deny the child the feeling of complete trust in the caregivers and of safety and security in the world (basic evil).

- Horney says that the child reacts by developing basic hostility which may develop into basic anxiety, an inability to trust or feel safe in the world.

- Children may create a highly flattering image of what they are or what they ought to be (the idealized self) and an idea of what they think they really are (real self). Problems arise when the gap between the real self and the idealized self are insurmountably large. Trying to surmount that gap is called the search for glory.

- Horney felt that many of us live with the tyranny of should, oppressive beliefs that we must become the idealized self, leading us to become alienated from the self.

- People may deal with their anxiety by moving toward others, against others, or away from others. A poorly adjusted person is inflexible in being stuck in one or a combination of needs, regardless of the situation, said Horney.

- Fritz Perls felt that in a natural state, human beings would maintain a balance by completing a cycle (gestalt) of experiencing a need and satisfying it. Societal expectations have led us to confuse what we *need* with what we *want*.

- Healthy development includes experiencing life in the present. Not doing so is the source of anxiety, said Perls.

- Parents may impede their child's growth by placing demands on the child that he or she is not ready for (placing the child in an impasse), overindulging the child, or communicating catastrophic expectations (failure to live up to parental demands will result in loss of parental love).

- Most of us live in both reality and a level of thinking and illusion (maya) where we rehearse future roles and situations. Instead of living in the world, we tend to live in our minds, said Perls.
- Carl Rogers believed that everyone has an innate tendency to become the best they can be (the actualizing tendency).
- In order to become fully functioning, said Rogers, people need unconditional positive regard, openness, and empathy.
- Abraham Maslow felt that, in order to understand the good functioning of the human being, we should study those who function the best.
- Maslow saw human beings as responding to needs, which he arranged into a hierarchy with the most basic needs at the bottom.
- Peak experiences seem to take us out of ourselves, giving us a feeling of experiencing life with greater intensity and awareness than normal, said Maslow.
- In Maslow's view, we do not all self-actualize because (1) we may not have fulfilled deficiency needs, (2) our culture or society may not support our self-actualization, or (3) we fear our own potential for greatness (the Jonah complex).
- Rollo May believed that human beings have the potential for greatness, but acting on this is risky and takes courage. Each human being contains their own reality and future, determined by the freedom to choose.
- Part of the individual's being is defined by his social interactions, according to May, and society enforces conformism on the individual. Many of us live inauthentically, responding to the demands of others rather than being true to ourselves and our own values.
- In May's view, there are six principles of being: (1) Every individual is centred in himself; (2) The individual has a need to preserve this central core; (3) The individual has the ability to go out from this core of being to participate with others; (4) The individual has awareness of the world; (5) Human beings have self-consciousness, giving them freedom of choice; (6) Anxiety is a fundamental component of the human being.
- According to May, anxiety is the feeling we experience in our fight to maintain our being against the threat of nonbeing. We feel anxiety whenever our values are threatened.
- May believed that the need for power—knowing that we are able to influence our environment—is inherent in the human being. An act that diminishes the person's sense of control is harmful.
- May noted that we *wish* for certain things in the future, but *will* is the capacity to move us toward these goals. Moving toward our goals depends on intentionality, the meaning that we give to experience or elements of our environment.
- May asserted that we have the freedom of choice: we choose what meaning we give to our world, we choose whether to exert our power or not, and we choose whether we will acknowledge our caring and act upon it.

Group Discussion Questions

1. The different approaches described in this chapter will be more or less appealing to different people. What kind of person do you think each approach would resonate with the most?

2. Consider the problem of low self-esteem. Debate how this problem arises and what can be done to increase self-esteem by taking on the roles of one of the theorists discussed in this chapter.

3. Examine each approach individually. What further evidence, discussion, or explanation would you need to become convinced of the correctness of the approach? What would it take to convince you that the approach was incorrect?

CHAPTER 3

The Satisfying Life from the Perspective of Eastern Belief Systems

In the previous chapter, we examined some approaches to becoming well-adjusted and satisfied with life in terms of Western conceptions of what is satisfying, what makes us happy, and what constitutes good adjustment.

LEARNING OBJECTIVES

In this chapter, students will learn about what constitutes a satisfying life from the perspectives of

- Yoga.
- Buddhism.
- Zen Buddhism.
- Sufism.

In psychological terms, we can speak of these approaches as having to do with strong ego development. But there are other ways at looking at personal growth. There are schools of thought that believe that ego development is not what brings satisfaction and meaning to our lives.

These schools of thought believe that the ego must be transcended before we can know true happiness and contentment. Many of these schools of thought come from the East, both the Asia and the Middle East. In this chapter, we shall challenge Western conceptions of growth by examining some Eastern ideas from traditions that are more than one thousand years old.

YOGA

Frank isn't a very happy person. He's in university, but he wants to drop out and get a much-desired job that he just interviewed for. Today, Frank received a failing grade on a test. He thinks negative thoughts about himself ("I'm a stupid loser"), about his professor ("He's an idiot"), about the course ("It's meaningless"), and about his college ("Lousy school, anyway"). He comes home, throws his books against the wall, yells at his little brother, and phones his girlfriend to pick a fight. All these actions have consequences: his books get torn, his brother retaliates by ruining some of Frank's CDs, and his girlfriend breaks their date for the weekend. He can't understand why everyone isn't more tolerant of him since he has just experienced an unpleasant incident and he's worried about whether or not he will get the job he wants. His friend Victoria suggests that he join her in a yoga class to gain some perspective and enlightenment. Frank looks at her in amazement. "Perspective? Enlightenment?" he says mockingly. "What are you talking about? Yoga is only an exercise! You turn into a pretzel to make yourself more flexible!"

Frank has no real idea of what yoga is. We can't blame him; in the Western world in the twenty-first century, yoga is known primarily as a form of stretching exercise. Some people may know that there is more to yoga than just exercise, but typically they are not sure what that is.

Yoga cannot be classified as a religion, although some religions have incorporated yoga into their beliefs. Yoga cannot be classified as a philosophy, although it does contain philosophical elements. Rather, yoga is a whole-world outlook that emphasizes growth and spirituality. Furthermore, it is the oldest systemized path in the world. Yoga has been around for thousands of years and will no doubt be around for thousands more.

The word "yoga" is from the Sanskrit word "yuga" which literally means "yoke," as is used in harnessing horses or oxen to a team. When we harness or yoke animals together, we are joining them to make them united. This relates to the path of yoga since its aim is to help the individual to realize his or her union or oneness with everything. This may sound like a North American New Age idea, but its roots go back to India at least five thousand years ago. Today, there is great diversity in yoga. Many branches have appeared, but all remain faithful to the basic principles set out in the early Yogic literature, such as the *Rig-Veda*, written in ancient Sanskrit around 1500 BCE, the *Bhagavad Gita*, composed about 350 BCE, and *Yoga Sutras*, written by Patanjali in about 150 BCE, (Devereux, 1994; Eliade, 1969; Feuerstein, 1996, 1998; Mascaro, 1962; Nikhilananda, 1953; Varenne, 1976).

The Nature of the Universe

I am I, and you are you. I am sitting on a chair and in front of me is a computer. Maybe you are in a chair too, or maybe you are lying on a bed. I have a cup containing coffee beside me, and my cat is napping in her basket to my left. Look around the room that you are in. Look at all the different objects in the room, one by one. We can do this task easily because we see each distinct object and the boundaries around it. We can see where the cat stops and the basket begins. But according to the beliefs of yoga, we are in error. What we see is **maya**, or delusion. The *true* reality of the universe goes beyond our sense organs. If we could see beyond, we would know that there is only One, that each individual person and object that we see are all One. There really is no boundary between the cat and her basket. Yoga refers to this complete unity as **Brahman**. Brahman is everything. It is every object, every person, every event. It is every molecule, every atom, and every space between every particle. Just as the whole scope of numbers includes zero, so too Brahman, being everything, includes being nothing (Devereux, 1994; Eliade, 1969; Feuerstein, 1996, 1998; Mascaro, 1962; Nikhilananda, 1953; Varenne, 1976).

This provides something of a shock for the Western mind in particular. Western civilization has stressed the search for self, for self identity, self concept, and self esteem. Now we are being told that there is no "self." But I feel like me, a separate individual, and you probably feel like you, too. Yet sometimes we feel a great connectedness with others, when we say that we and another person are "simpatico" or when we feel close to others as we share meaningful experiences. Often we yearn for greater connectedness. The solitude of our individuality is sometimes experienced as a burden when we feel that no one understands us and we feel alienated from our world and our society. Yoga can explain this readily by saying that, when we connect with others, we have a tiny start on seeing past illusion. Likewise, our desire to connect with others is a product of a deep-down realization that we are all One. The only thing that gets in our way of realizing this all the time is the mental filter we use when we view the world. We do not see what we do not look for, and we clutter up our minds with ceaseless chatter that further obscures reality.

Perhaps this should not surprise us too much. After all, we are aware of having filters that affect our perception of the world. We all know we interpret things differently in different situations, such as the way we view a party depending on what our time constraints are, who is going to be at the party, what kind of party it is, and so on. Is it so much of a stretch to suppose that we have even more filters than we realized? The goal of yoga is go beyond the filters that keep us from recognizing the Oneness of the universe and our identity with everything else by quieting the chatter in our minds. This knowledge is within us; it is only veiled by maya. It lies within a true, hidden nature that is called **Atman**. Of course, there is a paradox in this. If everything is Brahman, then Atman must be Brahman as well. True. Therefore, to experience one's Atman is, in fact, to experience Brahman (Devereux, 1994; Eliade, 1969; Feuerstein, 1996, 1998; Mascaro, 1962; Nikhilananda, 1953; Varenne, 1976).

Karma

One of the most important tenets of yoga is the concept of **karma**. Karma is the moral law of cause and effect that is inherent in everything, that is, in Brahman. We have all heard the old sayings "What goes around, comes around," and "You reap what you sow." These sayings reflect karma, but yoga is more rigid about it than our day-to-day philosophy tends to be. While we know that there are consequences to our behaviour, we still hope deep down to get away with some of our less than noble actions. Sometimes it seems that we have done so. But no, says yoga, "The chickens come home to roost," "The piper must be paid." (There are stacks of karmic sayings!) According to yoga beliefs, which include reincarnation, the consequences of every action will be felt, if not in this lifetime, then in another. You can do anything you want: you have complete free will and freedom of action, but you must bear the effects of these actions. This means that you have complete responsibility for your life and the events in it (Devereux, 1994; Eliade, 1969; Feuerstein, 1996, 1998; Mascaro, 1962; Nikhilananda, 1953; Varenne, 1976).

Karma is another difficult concept for the Westerner. This concept is often met with arguments such as "I wasn't responsible for the tornado that devastated my home" or "Winning the lottery is just luck." Wrong, says yoga, everything that happens to you is merited. You set up the conditions, perhaps in a previous life, that caused the tornado to hit you or allowed you to win the lottery (although it must be noted that in the present you are the one who probably chose to live in a tornado-prone area or to buy the lottery ticket!). Sometimes we set up conditions that affect what happens to us without even realizing what we are doing. Here is an area where the yoga masters of thousands of years ago seem similar to modern day psychologists.

Let's take the example of Frank at the beginning of this section. Frank, as you recall, received a failing grade on his test and he had negative thoughts about himself, his professor, the course, and his school. He came home and acted aggressively toward his books, his little brother, and his girlfriend, with negative results. Everyone is probably aware that Frank's actions are not helping him, and we may well think that Frank will learn to behave differently next time. But will he really? Do we not all know people who take out their bad moods on others, regardless of the consequences? Why do they keep doing this? Why do they not learn? Yoga says that the problem is that the law of karma works subtly as well as blatantly. Having acted on his bad mood, Frank has strengthened his tendency to react badly to a disappointment again. Having this tendency, albeit at an unconscious level, he has a further tendency to think those negative thoughts again. When he thinks those negative thoughts, he has a further tendency to act aggressively. And so the cycle goes. According to yoga, acting keeps the cycle going. The answer seems to be "don't act"; if we don't do anything, we can't keep the cycle going. But everyone's life demands that we act on some things, even if only in terms of eating, sleeping, and breathing. How can we not act and yet live?

Let's continue our example to see yoga's response to this. It's a week later, and Frank again receives a failing grade on a test. But in the meantime he has learned about karma. So this time when he starts thinking those negative thoughts, he stops himself and replaces them with other thoughts. Now he thinks, "I need to find out what I did wrong. Maybe I need some help in studying. It's a learning experience." And so he puts his books down carefully when he comes home, says calmly to his little brother, "I didn't do well on a test." His little brother, stunned at Frank's newfound calmness, says, "Hey, Frank, I'll help if I can. Want me to get you some milk and cookies?" Frank phones his girlfriend and confides in her about the test. She responds with love and support. Obviously the outcome of Frank's new behaviour is much more positive than the outcome of his former negative behaviour. But it goes even farther than that. By acting calmly and reasonably, Frank now sets up the tendency to react calmly and reasonably to disappointment in the future. His tendency will be to think more realistic thoughts, and his actions on those thoughts are more likely to be positive and adaptive. What Frank is doing is breaking his old cycle that brings bad consequences and instituting a new cycle that brings good consequences. Karma is not an externally imposed destiny, then. It is the product of our own free choice regarding our actions.

These examples are simplified for illustrative purposes, of course. In reality, Frank cannot break an old cycle that he has repeated many, many times, in one day. But he can weaken the negative tendencies. Each time he acts in a positive way, he weakens the old cycle and strengthens the new until the new cycle is dominant. He then has the habit of reacting in a positive, adaptive way. But there is another catch. It will not work if Frank fakes it. That is, if Frank behaves well toward his books, his brother, and his girlfriend while underneath thinking the same old negative thoughts, the karmic cycle is unchanged. So it will not do Frank any good to think, "I'm a loser, the prof is an idiot, but I'm going to think and act on the idea that this is a learning experience so that I can avoid bad karma." Frank must change his behaviour without regard for what he will gain from it. An analogy for this might be a charitable act. The act is not charitable if the person who performs it is doing it for personal gain, such as being regarded as a wonderful person, or for tax credits, or gaining "good behaviour" points with a deity. Charity is only charity when the person performing the charitable act is selfless, without personal regard.

Selflessness goes beyond renouncing personal gain. It also involves reacting to the world in the here and now, without regard to previous actions or events, and without regard to our egos or personal preferences. This counters the argument that many people voice when thinking about ending the negative cycle. They may be concerned that acting selflessly will attract exploiters. Perhaps it will, says yoga teaching, and that will affect the karma of the exploiters. We must react without worrying about being exploited or even thinking about how we have been exploited in the past. Each event is brand new; the past is irrelevant. This is hard. Very few people are naturally selfless, although most of us have selfless moments. It's going to take training and much practice to learn to do this, but it is part of going beyond the filters that deprive us of seeing Brahman. When we can see that we are all One, acting for personal, individual gain or based on personal, individual history or tendency is impossible. Why? Because there is no such thing as "personal" since there are no individuals.

The Nature of Personality

We cannot see what yoga tells us is reality, that is, Brahman, because we are ignorant. Our ignorance is in mistaking maya, or illusion, for reality. Because we do this, we are slaves to that illusion. We are taught by maya to want the good things that we believe exist and to avoid the bad things that we believe may hurt us in some way. Imagine the very sheltered teenager whose idea of romance comes only from old movies. The teenager will want and expect to find a perfect mate and, in less than two hours, form an ideal union so that he or she will live happily ever after. The adolescent is mistaking the illusion of the old movies for reality and may therefore overlook the very real, but imperfect, possible lovers all around. Or he or she may idealize a love interest, but break off the relationship far too soon because there are problems the movies did not mention. Yoga says that we are like that teenager. We overlook the reality that is before us, and we concentrate on what we *think* the universe is like. No wonder we never feel any real satisfaction for any great length of time!

Because of our ignorance of Brahman, we are ruled by *pleasure* and *aversion* (Feuerstein, 1996, 1998; Nikhilananda, 1953). We seek pleasure by trying to maximize what we feel is good in our lives or what makes us happy, and we have an aversion or a dislike for what we deem to be bad or painful. In fact, we spend our lives chasing pleasure and running from pain. Yet the pleasure, when we find it, is not quite as good as we imagined it to be, and the pain seems unavoidable no matter how fast we run. We buy self-help books to teach us how to chase more effectively or how to run faster without considering that perhaps our concept of what the universe is all about may be flawed. With yoga, we stop the chasing and running. Yoga would have us become free from the desire for pleasure and the aversion of pain. This freedom is not to be achieved by simply denying or repressing our desires and aversions. We cannot just stop wanting pleasure, nor can we suddenly start welcoming pain. First, it would take an immense amount of energy to push our desires and aversions into our unconscious minds. And second, they would probably become stronger and manifest themselves in ways that we might not be able to control so readily.

No, says yoga, refusing to allow oneself desire or aversion is not the answer. The answer is to work with the desires and aversions, to use their energy to understand what they are and where they come from. When we can understand the delusionary nature of our desires and aversions, they lose their intensity and fade away. We can become free of them. Note that this means that we can still enjoy chocolate cheesecake and feel pain when we bump into a door. The difference is that we do not miss the cheesecake when it is not there, nor do we go out of our way to avoid doors.

Consider Frank again, who interviewed for a job he wants. Not only is the salary excellent, but he thinks the job is glamorous and exciting. Moreover, he wants to avoid the failures at school and unemployment. Clearly, he is seeking to maximize his pleasure and minimize his pain. Poor Frank has worked himself into a state of extreme anxiety and feels that he will be stuck at school and the possibility of a "good" life will be over if he doesn't get that job. Yoga would teach Frank to understand why he wants the job, to understand that the glamour and excitement he sees in the job are maya, that there will be many other opportunities to make a living, and that this one job is not the route to ultimate bliss. When Frank can really understand and feel this, he will lessen the intensity of his desire for the job, and his attachment to the job will evaporate. If he gets the job, he is still free to enjoy it, but losing it will cause him no undue pain.

The Goal

Yoga's goal is the quieting of the mind so that the nature of reality, or Brahman, can be realized. We will no longer be ignorant, we will be free of the enslavement of desires and aversions, we will no longer be subjected to the cycle of karma, we will understand ourselves as the One, Brahman. This state, called **samadhi**, is of unimaginable bliss. It is the highest level of consciousness. It defies description and can only really be known and understood by those who experience it (Devereux, 1994; Eliade, 1969; Feuerstein, 1996, 1998; Mascaro, 1962; Nikhilananda, 1953; Varenne, 1976).

The Teacher

We can't do it alone. Yoga beliefs are very clear on this. In order to free oneself from maya and achieve enlightenment, we must have a teacher, a **guru**. The guru is a very special person. He or she must have reached the goal already; otherwise he or she cannot help the seeker find the way. The guru functions as a traditional teacher insofar as he or she determines what type of teaching the student needs, imparts lessons regarding the beliefs of yoga, answers the student's questions, and corrects the student's mistakes. But the guru has to be much more. He or she is a role model. Those who have been fortunate enough to study with true yoga masters report that they could feel the enlightenment radiating from the guru. The guru inspires and motivates them with his or her example.

Sometimes the guru prods and goads the students to shake them from lethargy. The guru is required to have the wisdom that is enlightenment and so can know what the student needs at each point. If the guru has really identified with Brahman, this is natural since the division between teacher and student does not exist for him or her. In addition, because the division between teacher and student no longer exists for the guru, he or she can impart some of his or her own energy directly to the student. This transmission of energy is the initiation process of yoga. It strengthens the student and creates a bond between teacher and student. In this way, the student becomes the latest of a direct lineage that may be centuries old (Eliade, 1969; Feuerstein, 1998).

Schools of Yoga

There is no single prescribed technique of yoga. Rather, yoga teaches that there are many possible routes, and the individual must find the one that is right for him or her. As it is commonly expressed in yoga, there are many paths to the summit of the mountain. Part of the guru's role is to help the person find the individually appropriate path.

Over the centuries, many schools of yoga have developed. Most, however, find their source in the classical yoga taught by Patanjali (Devereux, 1994; Eliade, 1969; Feuerstein, 1996, 1998; Mascaro, 1962; Nikhilananda, 1953; Varenne, 1976). This form of yoga is sometimes known as **Raja-Yoga** (Royal Yoga) or **Ashtanga-Yoga** (Eight-limbed Yoga). Raja-Yoga is made up of eight principles or "limbs." These are not stages in which one must complete the first before going on to the second, but rather all are to be practised throughout. In actuality, it is clear that the student of Raja-Yoga will need to master the first five before going on to the sixth, and the sixth must be mastered before the last two can be accomplished. The first two principles, or limbs, of Raja-Yoga are concerned with moral living and can be considered the "do's and don'ts" of the yoga ethical code (e.g., do act charitably, don't lie). The third and fourth limbs deal with control of the physical body through exercise and breathing techniques. The fifth limb provides a bridge between the physical and the mental states by shutting out distractions from the senses, and the last three concern the alteration of consciousness in a meditative state (Feuerstein, 1998; Nikhilananda, 1953).

Other schools of yoga developed out of Patanjali's Ashtanga-Yoga. Each type emphasizes a particular component of the eight limbs. Different schools will be best for different students (Feuerstein, 1998; Frager & Fadiman, 1998; Nikhilananda, 1953), and we will briefly look at some of these.

Jnana-Yoga is the yoga of wisdom. By the use of contemplative meditation in a wholly detached and rational fashion, the individual pares away what is not real until all that is left is the Ultimate Reality of Brahman. The practitioner of Jnana-Yoga must have a clearly discerning mind and be able to follow a line of reasoning to its conclusion. Once a conclusion is reached (i.e., "X is not real"), the practitioner must act in accordance with the realization.

Karma-Yoga concentrates on acting selflessly, with no thought of reward. This is not an easy path since the requirement is that every action of every day must be selfless. With Karma-Yoga, we can go about our daily lives performing the same activities as anyone else, for the most part. The difference is in the attitude we take toward those activities. While anyone can practice Karma-Yoga, this path may be more appealing to people who have a strong desire to work and act in the service of others.

Bhakti-Yoga is the yoga of love and devotion. It is emotion-based and is said by some to be particularly useful for Western practitioners, given the Western emphasis on emotion. In Bhakti-Yoga, the practitioner focuses on the Divine, in whatever form he or she may conceptualize a deity, as God, Jehovah, Allah, Krishna, The Force, and so on. All actions performed by the individual are dedicated to the Divine who is continuously in the individual's mind. Specific actions, such as chanting, praying, or dancing are often used, but it should also be noted that many people who seem to be practising Karma-Yoga may, in fact, be practising Bhakti-Yoga because they are offering their acts of service to the Deity. This orientation is a little paradoxical in yoga since offering up any action to the Divine implies a separation between the individual and the Deity, whereas yoga is about dispelling the illusion that there are such separations. In Bhakti-Yoga, the individual who finds it difficult to dispel maya strives to become closer and closer to the Deity (which is, of course, Brahman, since Brahman is everything). In becoming closer and closer to Brahman and narrowing the gap between Brahman and the individual, it is felt that eventually the individual will perceive that the gap is not really there.

Hatha-Yoga is the school best known in the Western world. It uses many physical techniques and so may be the path of choice for those who enjoy physicality or for those whose physical being is weak or impaired. Control of the body, most particularly the breathing, results in control of the individual's energy, which can then flow upward through the body, leading to profound physical, mental, and spiritual changes. The practices of Hatha-Yoga are for the sole purpose of giving the individual stability and tranquility in order to better attain enlightenment through meditation. Any other effect (such as having a more graceful-looking body) is secondary and worth little to real yogis.

Mantra-Yoga is not considered to be one of the major schools of yoga, but it is interesting because it forms the basis for Transcendental Meditation, which was popularized by the Beatles and other celebrities in the 1960s and '70s. A **mantra** is a spiritually meaningful phrase or sound that is repeated over and over, aloud or silently, during meditation. The repetition of the mantra helps to focus and calm the mind, stilling the mind's chatter and thereby helping the individual to get in touch with the inner Reality. Mantras can be almost anything that resonates with an individual, but the most famous is *Om*, the symbol for the Absolute.

REFLECTIVE EXERCISE

Karma and Maya

You probably thought of examples of karma in your own life as you read this section. Now try a game. It doesn't matter whether you believe in reincarnation or not, but pretend for a minute that you have lived previous lives. What is there in your present life that might suggest a lesson to be learned from a previous life? For example, the person who is lonely might not have appreciated his or her family and friends in a previous life, so in this life, family and friends are not around. The person who is constantly exploited may have been an exploiter in a former existence. Perhaps the individual who finds it hard to be assertive was overly aggressive last time around!

What are you attached to? What material object would you never lend to anyone? What would you miss the most if you lost it? Why would you miss it? Can't it be replaced? If it has sentimental value to you, doesn't this mean that the object brings back special memories? But would you really forget if the object were gone? So why do you feel so attached to it? Can you see, at least a little, that your level of attachment may be a function of maya? If you were a castaway on a deserted island where food, water, and shelter were readily available, what would you take with you? What would you miss most? What would you fear most? If you think about maya, these questions may become difficult to answer. What do you really need?

What do your reflections about maya indicate about your karma?

Life Stages

Yoga is an intensely practical approach. There is no expectation that everyone will be able to devote the time and energy to meditation, exercises, and so on that will be required to approach enlightenment. Instead, yoga suggests that life be approached in stages that are about 25 years long. The first stage is that of the *Student*. During this first stage of life, the individual's job is to learn. In the second stage, the next 25 years of life, there is a recognition that people must live in society and contribute to the well-being of others. This stage is that of the *Householder*, who creates a family and works to support them. When the children are grown and are ready to become Householders themselves, the individual is able to gradually retire from active family, vocational, and community life. This stage is called that of the *Forest Dweller* because in traditional Hindu times, the individual, with or without the spouse, might retire to a small, secluded cottage in the forest. Even if the individual remains in the family home, the point is that the children now take over the family affairs and the Forest Dwellers, while remaining available for consultation with the younger members of the family, are now freed to pursue their own spiritual advancement. The final stage of life is that of the *Renunciant*. In this stage, the individual removes himself or herself from all contact with other people in order to concentrate completely on spirituality and self-realization (Feuerstein, 1998; Frager & Fadiman, 1998).

For yoga, then, personal growth includes one's duty to the family and the community. Growth is not to be rushed. Rushing implies that the person "desires" growth, but growth cannot be attained until desire is removed. So patience is required, patience along with effort at the right time and in the right way. Enlightenment is not guaranteed in this lifetime, but perhaps there are more lifetimes! In yoga, there is always a second chance.

BUDDHISM

Frank, who we met at the beginning of the discussion on yoga, is, at least a little, affected by what his friend Victoria has told him about gaining perspective and enlightenment from an Eastern approach to life.

Yoga intrigues him, but he wants to sample other possibilities as well. Victoria passes him a poem written by her teacher:

> The snows chill and the sun burns.
>
> Yet I have nothing to teach you.
>
> Yet I have nothing to give you.
>
> You are already complete.

"Huh?" he says, looking to Victoria for some explanation. "This says it all," replies Victoria. "Just be. That's all you have to do."

Whatever her teacher is saying seems to have made an impact on Victoria, but Frank seems to be nothing but confused. What was your reaction when you read this? Did you react the way Victoria did or the way Frank did? This poem reveals Buddhist teaching, especially that of Zen Buddhism. In the following section, we will examine Buddhism and Zen Buddhism. After you read this section, come back to the teacher's poem and read it again. Do you "get it"?

The Life of Buddha

At some time during the fifth or sixth century BCE, a prince was born in northern India to the Gautama family. They named the beautiful, much-welcomed baby Siddhartha. His father, the ruler of an Indian kingdom, called upon sages to foretell what the baby's future would be. They told of greatness: if Siddhartha remained with the world, he would become a great king and conqueror, the unifier of all India. But if he forsook the world, he would become the world redeemer. Siddhartha's father, a worldly man, determined that his child would become the great king, and so he spared no effort and no expense to give Siddhartha a worldly education and experience. The child grew up in luxury. He wore only the finest garments, ate only the finest foods, and was given every material pleasure that the world at that time had to offer. His days were spent mainly in the confines of his father's expansive palaces, where no element of sadness or pain or ugliness would ever touch the treasured son. At the age of sixteen, Siddhartha married a princess of great beauty who quickly gave him a fine son.

In spite of this idyllic existence, Siddhartha, in his twenties, became discontented, asking "Is this all there is?" Although his father had enlisted runners to clear his son's path when he went riding, some say that the gods intervened to give Siddhartha experiences which would change him forever. On one ride, he encountered an old, decrepit man, and so he learned of the inevitability of old age. On the next ride, he encountered a man riddled with illness, and so he learned of disease. A corpse was in his path on the next ride, teaching him about death. And on the fourth ride, he met a monk with a shaven head, possessing only a robe and a bowl, and so he learned that withdrawal from the world was possible. After these lessons, Siddhartha could not return to the luxury of his father's palaces. One night, when he was twenty-eight years old, he silently stole away from his home and his family, exchanged clothes with a poor person, shaved his head, and entered the forest, seeking enlightenment.

First he sought two renowned yogis who taught him the philosophy and practices of Raja-Yoga. But enlightenment did not come. Then he joined a band of ascetics who believed that attachment to the body was the impediment to enlightenment. Siddhartha adhered to their teachings, fasting, exposing himself to the elements, not sleeping and not washing. Instead of reaching enlightenment, though, he almost died. Severe asceticism was not the route to enlightenment, he decided, any more than the indulgence in luxury in his father's house had been.

Tired, fighting despair, he sat beneath a fig tree, determined to remain there in meditation until enlightenment came to him. Despite temptations from a jealous god, and challenges to his right to claim enlightenment, Siddhartha persevered. And it happened. The veils of the material world lifted, and the whole of existence and non-existence was revealed. Siddhartha was now Buddha, the Enlightened One. And the fig tree has been known ever since as the Bo tree, short for *Bodhi*, or enlightenment. The temptation to remain where he was, in the bliss of enlightenment, was great, but Buddha committed himself to telling others what he had found and how he had found it. His mission was to help others achieve the enlightenment that he had found. He followed this mission for forty-five years until he finally died at the age of eighty after accidentally eating some poisoned mushrooms. Even on his deathbed, he sought to relieve the cook of any guilt for serving the mushrooms and conveyed the message that he was grateful for the meal which finally released him to Nirvana, or ultimate bliss.

Such is the story of Siddhartha Gautama, who became Buddha (Frager & Fadiman, 1998; Kit, 1998; Shaku, 1993). How much of this tale is true is unknown and for our purposes doesn't matter. What matters is that this great man asked the same questions that we still ask. He gave us a new perspective, a new path to help us grow and find peace and satisfaction in our lives. His messages have been interpreted in many ways, and his practices have been adopted even while denying belief in his teachings. What did he find out in his meditation that has made such a difference to so many people over so many centuries in so many different places?

The Four Noble Truths

Buddha preached a belief system that was not, in the strictest sense, any kind of belief system at all. On the contrary, he saw no purpose in tradition, ritual, or orthodoxy. He did not even see himself as an authority of any kind. Rather, he said, each individual must learn for himself or herself. The only way to come to enlightenment is to experience it. Many may suggest methods to encourage or to prepare oneself for this experience, but in the final analysis, these are only suggestions. The truth is within you and can only be reached by you. Nonetheless, at the urgings of his followers, Buddha put into words his deepest convictions about the nature of the life we all lead. These have been called the **Four Noble Truths** (Frager & Fadiman, 1998; Kapleau, 1989; Kit, 1998; Shaku, 1993).

The First Noble Truth is that life consists of suffering. In Western society, we have been taught to believe that suffering in life is an indication that something is wrong and needs correcting, not that suffering is normal. But Buddha, who had experienced luxury and had known every material pleasure, knew that the enjoyment he had felt was superficial and temporary. None of the wonders of his father's home had been able to bring him the bliss of his experience under the Bo tree. No matter how much pleasure we might derive from the joys of the earth, the reality of life, as we experience it, is that we are born in pain, we fall ill, our bodies fail us as we age, and still we fear death. In between birth and death, we may be tied to situations that we would rather avoid, and we may be separated from that which we love. At the very least, we experience the pain of trying, futilely, to be continually happy. Why is this so? Why does life contain such pain? Buddha's answer is the Second Noble Truth.

The Second Noble Truth reveals the cause of the suffering in life. The cause is *desire*, a specific kind of desire. We suffer in life, said Buddha, because we long for those elements of life that enhance the ego, believing that the ego is the fundamental "me." "I want, I want, I want!" we insist. From "I want a fancy new car" to "I want to be loved" to "I want to avoid anything that will hurt or diminish my sense of myself," we are concentrating on finding that external something that we think will make us feel fulfilled and satisfied. The more we concentrate on this, the less likely we are to feel satisfied and fulfilled. Does this have to be? Now that we know the cause of our suffering, can we eliminate it?

Yes, says Buddha, we can eliminate our suffering. This is the *Third Noble Truth,* which says that our travail can be removed and we can overcome the self-absorbed craving that has made us so dissatisfied and frustrated. How do we overcome it? Through the Fourth Noble Truth.

The Fourth Noble Truth was Buddha's advice on how to remove the cause of suffering in our lives. It is a prescription for living that we will examine further: the *Eightfold Path*.

The Eightfold Path

In the **Eightfold Path**, Buddha suggested a way in which people could rid themselves of habits that were enslaving them and develop habits that would free them of their selfish cravings. This encompasses a whole change in lifestyle for most people, and as such, it typically does not occur overnight. Rather, the individual must practise the Eightfold Path being aware that, just as in learning anything else, there will be pitfalls and setbacks, but persistence will pay off (Frager & Fadiman, 1998; Kapleau, 1989; Kit, 1998; Shaku, 1993).

Right association is the preliminary step in the Eightfold Path and one that may have already been taken by anyone attempting to follow Buddha's precepts. *Right association* means that one must align oneself with those who are also following the path. We are social animals and we fare best in the company of others, although periods of solitude are healthy and welcome. Our journey along the Eightfold Path will be eased and we will be supported along the way when we have fellow travellers. The journey will be much more difficult if we surround ourselves with those who live a very different lifestyle and who may even scoff at our attempts. You probably already know this if you have ever tried to study for college courses while having a roommate whose idea of the college experience consists only of partying! With right association, the Eightfold Path may be begun (Frager & Fadiman, 1998; Kapleau, 1989; Kit, 1998; Shaku, 1993).

1. *Right Knowledge.* The first element of the Eightfold Path is *right knowledge*. The knowledge that is needed is the Four Noble Truths. Once we understand these, we can direct our lives in a manner consistent with them.

2. *Right Aspiration.* The second element of the Eightfold Path is *right aspiration*. Simply knowing the Four Noble Truths with our minds is not enough. We must also know them with our hearts. Do we believe them? Do we feel a commitment to live with them? Are we really sure that this is what is right for us? Are we ready to give up attachment to the things that we may have been taught all our lives to want and strive for? The path will be arduous, so anyone without such certainty may wish to rethink the whole notion of starting down the path in the first place until they are ready to embrace it completely.

3. *Right Speech.* If our hearts and minds are ready, we can start with the third element of the Eightfold Path: *right speech*. Language is powerful. What we speak reveals what and who we are. The first step in this element of the path is to become aware of what we say. Do our words display unfailing truth? Or outright dishonesty? Or do they contain dishonest rationalizations concerning ourselves? Or overt or implied put-downs of others? If we detect any of these in ourselves, we need to become aware of why we do these things. Typically, it is because we are still acting in the service of

our constrained, selfish egos, in the vain attempt to preserve our pride or to enhance ourselves by diminishing others. When we recognize this, we can change. First, we can make sure that what we speak is the truth. Then we can learn to speak with charity. This does not mean to engage in meaningless flattery or to put ourselves down in order to gain the approval of others. It means to avoid idle chatter, gossip, and even the more insidious sarcasm or tactlessness in truth-telling, which is so often a smoke-screen for cruelty.

4. *Right Behaviour.* Right speech is a good in and of itself, but it must be combined with the fourth element of the Eightfold Path, which is *right behaviour*. In this case, we reflect on the things we have done and on our motivation in doing them. Were our motives self-seeking? Were we "out for ourselves"? Even when we do what appears to be a charitable act, we must sometimes wonder whether we did it for the charity of the act itself or so that others would see our action and admire us and be grateful to us. Would we have performed the charitable act anonymously? Clearly, the path calls for us to move ever in the direction of greater charity and selflessness. Included in the call for right behaviour are the Five Precepts:

   i.   Do not kill.
   ii. Do not steal.
   iii. Do not lie.
   iv. Do not be unchaste.
   v.   Do not drink intoxicants.

5. *Right Livelihood.* Right behaviour extends into the fifth element of the Eightfold Path, which is *right livelihood*. What do you do, or what will you do, for a living? Is it possible to gain spiritual progress if our occupations pull us in the other direction? It is plain to see that we are not following the Eightfold Path if we make a living by working for Murder Incorporated, but Buddha went much farther than this. He said that on the Eightfold Path, we cannot engage in any occupation which destroys life instead of promoting it. He named occupations such as slave trader, prostitute, and armament maker. Today he would undoubtedly add drug dealer and fraudulent television evangelist to the list of occupations to be avoided.

6. *Right Effort.* In this element, Buddha was talking about the human will. Since the Eightfold Path is a difficult one, the individual must be prepared to exert self-discipline and to work at it tirelessly and steadfastly. Buddha recognized our tendency to want to progress quickly, but he cautioned that the quick sprint was not as successful as the steady jog. As Æsop taught us, slow and steady wins the race.

7. *Right Mindfulness.* The next element is *right mindfulness*. The reason that we are living such unsatisfying lives is because we have deluded ourselves into believing that gaining material or psychological goods from the external world will make us happy. This ignorance on our part must be counteracted if we are to aspire to enlightenment. And so our minds must be ever attuned to the reality of life around us and to the truth of our own motivations. We must be constantly vigilant and mindful of our tendencies to slip off the Eightfold Path. We must ensure that we are in control of our senses and our emotions, rather than having them control us. For example, if we see something that frightens or disgusts us, we must meditate on it until we have

mastered the emotion. If we feel anger or hatred, we must discover their roots and transmute the negative emotions into loving kindness for all. This element of the Eightfold Path is very difficult for most of us. We need a great deal of practice at it. Buddha recommended not only working at this all the time, in whatever endeavour we are engaged, but also setting aside some time, during the day or in days of withdrawal, to work (i.e., meditate) on this in silence and solitude.

8. *Right Absorption.* The final element of the Eightfold Path is *right absorption.* This is the ultimate element in which all others come to fruition. With right absorption, our minds become completely enmeshed in Truth and Reality. We fully recognize the deception we have lived with in our lives, and ego, understanding, and thought itself are annihilated in our immersion in All. This is the true state of the mind, said Buddha, the state when all unreality has been stripped away. And this is where we, in Truth, rest. This is the state of **Nirvana**, which literally means extinction. In this state, the boundary between ourselves and all the rest of the Cosmos is extinguished. Rightly so, for it was never really there to begin with.

REFLECTIVE EXERCISE

To Explore the Eightfold Path

In this exercise, examine the elements of the Eightfold Path. How many of these elements do you already live by? Many, no doubt. Which of the others do you think you could adopt with relative ease? Which would give you trouble?

Are there elements that you think you could never adhere to? If so, why? Does this reflect an attachment on your part, or a continuing desire to avoid any suffering? Is that really so bad? There's no right or wrong answer to this, only the truth within you.

The Further Development of Buddhism

Like other philosophies and religions, the teachings of Buddha came to be the centre of controversy (Chan, 1963; Kit, 1998, Shaku, 1993). After his death, Buddha's followers found that there were several issues on which Buddha had remained silent (or that they had forgotten to ask him!). And there were other issues that he did speak about, but different followers interpreted what he said in different ways. Divisions appeared. The *Theravada* school remained a somewhat fundamentalist division in Buddhism, while the *Mahayana* school was more interpretive and open to more divisions within itself. At the risk of being overly simplistic, let's summarize the differences between the two main schools of Buddhism.

The Theravada school sees the human being as an individual, alone in the universe. The Mahayana school regards the human being as always connected to all others. In the Theravada school, the greatest good is to gain wisdom, while the Mahayana school views compassion as the prime virtue. Buddha is revered as a saint by adherents of the Theravada school, while the Mahayana school views him as a saviour.

In the Theravada school, the ideal is for a person to withdraw from the world, becoming a monk or nun, spending his or her life in meditation on the path to enlightenment. Gaining enlightenment, the individual is known as an **arhat** who remains withdrawn from the world. But in the Mahayana school, religion is part of everyday life, and withdrawal to a monastery is unnecessary. In this conception, the individual goes about his or her daily life, including ritual and prayer as well as meditation in whatever he or she does. When enlightenment is reached, the individual is encouraged to follow Buddha's footsteps, staying in the world and helping others on their path to enlightenment. This enlightened individual is known as a **bodhisattva**. (These differences are summarized in Table 3.1). Not surprisingly, the Mahayana school is the more popular division, winning more adherents throughout Mongolia, Tibet, China, Korea, and Japan, than the more rigorous Theravada school, which is found mainly in Sri Lanka, Burma, Thailand, and Cambodia (Frager & Fadiman, 1998; Kit, 1998; Shaku, 1986).

Table 3.1	Differences between Theravada and Mahayana Buddhism	
	Theravada	**Mahayana**
The human being	an individual, alone in the universe	always connected to all others
The prime virtue	gaining wisdom	compassion
Buddha	saint	saviour
Ideal life	arhat	bodhisattva

ZEN BUDDHISM

So many people, authorities all, tell us what to do and how to do it. "But which formula is the one that will work for me?" we ask. "How will I know what's right for me?" Good questions. Zen Buddhism is an approach that leads to the shedding of all questions.

The Origins of Zen

When the Mahayana school of Buddhism spread to China, it combined with belief systems already in existence there, namely Taoism and Confucianism (see Box 3.1 for a brief description of Taoism and Confucianism). In this combination form, it developed into a highly intuitive brand of Buddhism, that is, Zen.

Zen Buddhism is considered by some to be the purest form of spirituality, and it is this form that has spread widely in North America. The name itself reveals the core of the belief. The word *zen* is the Japanese form of the Chinese word *ch'an*, which is derived from the Sanskrit word *dhyana*. Dhyana means meditation, which leads to insight (Kit, 1998; Shaku, 1986). And indeed, as we shall see, meditation is the key to personal growth along the Zen Buddhist path. Get ready for some confusion, because Zen cannot be captured in words. In fact, the belief is that words will distort the essence of Zen. In his Flower Sermon, some say, Buddha simply stood on a hillside and held a golden lotus flower in the air, saying nothing. Only one of his followers understood that this was the essence of Buddhism, and this follower was designated Buddha's successor.

When I was a young professor first called upon to teach an eager class about Zen Buddhism, I asked a Zen **roshi** (a practitioner who has progressed to the point where he/she can be called a master and is permitted to teach) what to say. The answer was "Say nothing. Enter your classroom, sit on a desk, and kindly look at your class until the end of the period. This is Zen." Well, yes, it is, but that's not likely to be very helpful to the class. Or would it have been?

A Brief Note on Taoism and Confucianism

Taoism (pronounced *Dow-ism*) is said by many to be founded by Lao Tzu who lived in the fifth century BCE. It started as a philosophy and became a religion in China in about the fourth century BCE. China was in a continual state of warfare, and Lao Tzu sought a way to end this and bring peace and stability to the country. His book, *Tao Te-Ching* (Lao Tzu, 1988), highlights the concept of *Tao*, or the Way. Tao cannot be explained in words, but it is generally thought to be the life force of the universe. It flows through everyone and everything. It is not considered to be a deity, but it is considered to be responsible for creation. Human beings have drifted away from this force, which constantly changes and moves. Instead of being responsive to the flow and movement of the Tao, we seek to manipulate it, trying to make it flow in the way we want, or to stop flowing when we want to avoid change. This is a mistake that brings us unhappiness because we are doomed to failure in this enterprise. Our aim should be non-interference, to flow with the Tao, thereby bringing harmony, peace, and health to ourselves. In doing this, we should cultivate compassion, moderation, and humility (Chan, 1963; Weber, 1968; Wong, 1997).

Taoism says that the universe is a balance of opposites that move together. The well-known symbol, *yin-yang*, demonstrates this. The symbol indicates that there is yin within yang and yang within yin, and the two are inextricably connected as they revolve together. Yin represents everything that is soft, introspective, and healing, while yang is hard, energetic and sometimes even aggressive. Yin has been used to represent everything that is feminine and yang everything that is masculine. The polarities exist together, and human efforts to separate them are both futile and dangerous.

Confucius is believed to have lived concurrently with Lao Tzu, and he too sought a better way than warfare for China. The philosophy and religion he espoused is contained most particularly in his book *The Analects* (Confucius, 2008). Confucius believed in a God, though not in an afterlife. Life at present was his main concern, and he believed that the best possible life could be obtained through adherence to strict moral values that he laid down. Some of these values include obeying and respecting parents, doing no harm to another in word or deed, avoiding hypocrisy, being loyal to friends, and working for the common good in one's community and country (Chan, 1963; Confucius, 2008; Weber, 1968).

Taoism and Confucianism were the main belief systems in China when Buddhism was introduced. The Taoist concepts of constant change and non-interference with the natural flow of the universe and the Confucian concept of service towards others were incorporated more fully into Buddhist beliefs, resulting in Zen Buddhism (Chan, 1963).

Words and Experience

Zen is completely experiential. Words cannot encompass it because words distort and minimize experience. Imagine for a moment that you are called upon to explain the colour red to a person who has never had the gift of sight. How could you do it? Are there any words you could use to make this person experience red the way you have? Maybe even more to the point, have you ever had an experience that defied description? Can you convey the feeling of falling in love and knowing that you are loved in return, for example? Trying to put this feeling into words does the emotion an injustice. Worse still, words may become replacements for experience.

Take another example. Jack is a brilliant psychologist in terms of conducting research and formulating theories about how people's minds work, yet his personal life is a disaster. His ex-wife contends that he was completely insensitive to her, and his children feel that they have no relationship with him at all. How is it that this accomplished scientist of human behaviour is unable to apply what he knows to his own life? According to Zen Buddhism, it is because Jack has the words, not the experience. But Jack doesn't realize this; he thinks his intellectual understanding is the ultimate form of understanding. Zen Buddhists might suggest that instead of trying to "understand" his children, for example, Jack might try just being with them. Jack's children might agree.

So many experiences in day-to-day life transcend words, that we might expect that we would be unable to verbalize spiritual experiences. This does not mean that Zen Buddhism disregards language totally, though. Zen is a very practical belief system. Words are necessary in day-to-day functioning; after all, we still have to pay the rent. But we must be ever aware of the profound limitations of language. In a well-known Zen saying, words, teachings, any methodology is a finger pointing at the moon. Only a finger. Not the moon. Yet we often confuse the two. We must keep in mind that the goal is the moon. So what is the finger? And what is the moon?

Zen Methods

Let's start by looking at what, in the Zen saying, is the finger. (It is unfortunate that in North America, "the finger" has such different connotations. Try to transcend this.) Zen uses three techniques, stressing that these are only suggestions for what might be helpful. If they don't help you, forget about them. After all, they have no real substance; they are not the moon.

One technique is called **zazen** (Kapleau, 1989; Kit, 1998). Zazen is literally "seated meditation." One sits in a comfortable, but upright position (the yoga lotus position is often used, but it is not required) and meditates. In one variation, one empties one's mind of any thoughts. This is not easy to do, even for a few seconds.

An alternate method is to meditate on sentences suggested by a roshi (Kapleau, 1989; Kit, 1998). This is a technique that is widely misunderstood and derided. The sentences that are suggested by the roshi are, at first glance, nonsensical and paradoxical. They are called **koans**. The following are examples of koans:

What is the sound of one hand clapping?

What was the appearance of your face before your ancestors were born?

The horse sits on top of the tree and the fish walk.

If you speak, I will give you 100 blows; if you are silent, I will give you 100 blows.

The typical response of those who are unacquainted with Zen is to either wonder if this is a put-on of some sort or to search for a deep philosophical meaning to the koan. Both responses are incorrect. The reason the koan looks nonsensical is because it *is* non-sensical! That's the point! The idea is to force our minds to go beyond logic. Logic is wonderful in its place in the day-to-day world, but it is based on words that are not to be trusted completely, as we have seen. When the mind is broken of its reliance on logic and reason, the way may be cleared for intuitive experience. When we can fully realize that we can stand in the rain and not get wet, we can experience reality through a completely different perspective than we have ever known. This is not a guarantee that intuitive experience will occur, only a suggestion of what might help or encourage the intuitive leap.

It should be clear thus far that the individual is on his or her own in "studying" Zen. There are no classes or seminars or group discussions. No team projects. There is only the one lone person trying to gain intuitive experience. There is one person that the seek-er can talk to, though, and that is the roshi or Zen master who is overseeing the path of the aspirant. The aspirant is allowed a brief consultation with the roshi, usually twice a day in a Zen monastery. This is called **sanzen**, or consultation about meditation (Kapleau, 1989; Kit, 1998). At this time, the individual presents the roshi with what he/she has come up with as an understanding or answer to a koan or to whatever the individual has focussed upon during meditation. Sometimes the individual has come up with the "right" answer and the roshi confirms this. But the individual really does not need this confirmation: when the right answer comes, it is so powerful that the individual knows it without being told. On most occasions, though, the roshi tells the individual that he or she is "wrong." This is typically not done in a gentle fashion. The roshi's task is to vehemently reject the individual's incorrect answer because it reveals a continuing reliance on logic and reason, or it is the attempt of the individual to use someone else's answer (even Zen aspirants cheat sometimes!). This violent rejection is thought to fur-ther push the individual's mind into a state of confusion, a state where reason is threat-ened. Great, says the roshi, the more confused you are, the greater the chances that you will get over this reliance on reason in the first place and leave yourself open to intuitive experience.

Zazen, koans, and sanzen are the three techniques often used in Zen practice, but, as we have discussed, they are only the finger pointing at the moon. There are other ways of pointing at the moon too, and the individual must use what works for him or her. The larger question that we must now address is, what is the moon? What is this "intuitive experience" that has been mentioned? What are we really after?

Satori

Maybe after years of practice in meditation, maybe after only moments, all perception and so all life suddenly changes in a blinding flash. You know you are one with all the universe, you feel more alive and more *you* and real than ever before, more than you could ever imagine. And you feel complete joy, the ultimate happiness. This is a descrip-tion of the experience of **satori**, an enlightenment that cannot be encompassed in words

---

Zazen

Sit comfortably in a chair or on a cushion, with a straight but not stiff or tense back. Gently close your eyes and become aware of your breathing. Don't try to control your breath, just be aware of each inhalation and exhalation. When you feel at ease, become aware of your thoughts. Again, don't try to control them, just observe them as they pass through your mind. Now, very gently, let those thoughts pass away completely. Let your mind empty of any thoughts or feelings. Just be. Don't worry if you can't do this in the beginning—it takes practice. If you can empty your mind, you may find that this state only lasts for a few seconds. That's all right; with practice it will last longer. Do this twice a day, and you will find yourself getting calmer and more effective in your everyday life. You may even find enlightenment!

(Frager & Fadiman, 1998; Kapleau, 1989; Kit, 1998). Yet this is only the beginning. One isolated experience is not enough. You continue to meditate, now with a new perspective, and more satoris occur. There are many episodes of enlightenment, each bringing more joy and more feeling of oneness with all creation. This still is not enough, according to Zen beliefs. Now the task is to bring this enlightenment into day-to-day life. With more practice, this sense of enlightenment can be felt in the most mundane of daily tasks. You can feel the wonder and the bliss while washing the dishes, even while studying for an exam!

Remember that Zen is derived from the Mahayana school of Buddhism, in which the individual, once enlightened, may become a *bodhisattva*, one who stays in the world to bring enlightenment to it and to help other seekers attain enlightenment too. But with enlightenment, you do not see yourself helping me to attain enlightenment. With enlightenment, you help yourself because you recognize that you and I are one. With enlightenment, you have infinite love because you see the transcendent beauty that is life. You know that you are not just inextricably connected to the life and the beauty, you *are* the life and the beauty. You now realize that all the opposites and polarities that you thought existed were just figments of your obstinate tendency to use reason. Now you know that there is no you and me, no give and take, no acceptance and rejection, even no life and death: all are One. And you are amazed that you did not know this before. As the Zen masters say, we are like starving people sitting next to a bag of rice; we have been searching for the ox that never strayed. The food, the ox, were always right there, but we didn't know it.

North America has seen an increase in interest in Zen Buddhism, and several Zen roshis have tried to make the practices of Zen more aligned with the Western perspective. Notable among these are Charlotte Joko Beck and Pema Chodron who have both written highly readable and enjoyable books on various aspects of Zen. For example, Charlotte Joko Beck's book *Everyday Zen* (1989, HarperCollins) and Pema Chodron's book *When Things Fall Apart* (2000, Shambhala Publications) and her CD *How to Meditate with Pema Chodron* (2008, Sounds True) are favourites with many people.

Now read the poem excerpt from the beginning of this section again.

The snows chill and the sun burns.

Yet I have nothing to teach you.

Yet I have nothing to give you.

You are already complete.

What does it mean to you now?

SUFISM

What is Sufism?

This is not an easy question to answer. Many people firmly say that Sufism is the mystical sect of Islam (e.g., Lings, 1975), but many others disagree, claiming that Sufism predates Islam and is fundamental to all belief systems (e.g., Shah, 1964). Many of the great sages and revered teachers of Sufism came from an Islamic background and so many of the terms and practices used are Islamic, but several Sufis contend that their belief system is the core belief system of all religions, so Sufism should not be classified as a branch of Islam any more than it should be classified as a branch of Christianity or Buddhism. All religions have the same ultimate goal, a goal that is inherent in the basic humanity of our species, and that is union with the Divine (Marcus, 2008; Shah, 1964).

It doesn't matter whether you call the Divine God, Brahman, Allah, Jehovah, or The Force: it is the Divine, it is All, the only reality. Everything we see, everything we feel, everything we do is, in Sufi reality, the Divine. But we do not realize that. We think we are separate entities; we think that the material world is the absolute world; we think we walk alone in the world. We're wrong, say the Sufis. We have veils before our eyes, so we cannot see the reality of our Oneness with the Divine; we use filters in perceiving and interpreting the world, filters that we have acquired through learning from the environment since we were born, filters that distort reality and further obscure the only reality, that of the Divine.

In order to see this reality, we must tear away the veils and shed the filters; we must focus completely on the Divine through thought, action, prayer—and most of all, through love. Love is the greatest characteristic of the Divine, and therefore must be our greatest characteristic too. After all, if the Divine is All, then we are also the Divine, so we too must be filled with love. So where is it? we may ask. The answer is that it is underneath the veils and filters. In bringing forth our love, our divinity, we must truly examine ourselves and understand our veils and filters. Only then can we remove them and focus, with absolute love, on the Divinity. And then, perhaps, we will transcend our egos and understand that we are One with the Divine, the only reality. Gaining this would confer the greatest bliss and satisfaction to a person, the bliss and satisfaction of the Divine. This may sound like achieving nirvana or satori in yoga or Buddhism. Yes, say the Sufis, we told you that all religions have the same ultimate goal! The goal is union, but the route, says Sufism, is love.

Love is not something that can be taught, nor can one gain an intellectual union with the Divine. Sufism stresses the experience of the individual. Only by actually experiencing the love and the Divine can one know it and be One with it (Marcus, 2008; Shah, 1964).

The Four Stages of Sufism

The Sufi **sheikh** (spiritual leader or teacher) Ibn 'Arabi delineates four stages of practice and understanding in the Sufi belief system (Frager & Fadiman, 1998; Marcus, 2008; Shah, 1964). The first and basic stage, upon which the other three rest, is **sharia**. Sharia is the moral code that people should live by. It is not necessarily reflected in law: some actions may be legal, but ethically offensive (for example, it may not be illegal to lie to one's friend, but it is unethical). With sharia in place, one may then enter the stage of **tariqa**. In this stage, the person practices Sufism specifically. Sufi practices may encompass many, many things, such as prayer, meditation, fasting, reading, listening to stories, parables and jokes, or dancing. Although different orders of Sufism may emphasize particular practices, no one set of practices is applied to all students; rather, the teacher has the responsibility of choosing the practices that are most suitable for the student. By continuing to maintain sharia and tariqa, the individual may enter the third stage, **haqiqa**. Understanding of the truth comes to the person in this stage: now the person fully understands what sharia and tariqa have really been about, why ethics specify certain do's and don'ts, why certain practices may be utilized. The teachings of sharia and tariqa are fully internalized. The final stage of growth is **marifa**, the definitive knowing of the truth, the union with the Divine, and the ultimate goal of Sufism. This is a stage that many may aspire to, but few realize.

Stages of Growth for the Individual

The great Sufi master Al-Ghazali described the human personality and its struggle to grow (for example, see Ad-Dab'bagh, 2008; Ali, 2007). From this, various writers have deduced stages of growth for the human being (e.g., Frager & Fadiman, 1998; Shah, 1964). The stages outlined by Frager and Fadiman (1998) are perhaps most detailed in terms of personal growth. They are not fixed in their sequence; rather, each unique individual may experience them in a unique order or may experience more than one at a time. These stages are:

1. *Initial Awakening.* This can be quite a dramatic stage. Initial awakening occurs as the individual realizes that the world that he or she has known is not sufficient or satisfying. This awakening may come after a crisis or simply as a growing dissatisfaction with the life the person has been living.

2. *Patience and Gratitude.* This is an immensely important stage in the Sufi tradition. Now the individual recognizes that growth does not come overnight and is content with that knowledge. No growth can be achieved until one is patient and content to live in the present, giving up ceaseless striving for future gain. He or she also is grateful that there is enough time in life to grow and develop, so impatience is not necessary or useful. This gratitude extends to everything that one is given, the good and the bad, for all things come from the Divine, and the Divine's plan is for the individual to grow.

3. *Fear and Hope.* On the Sufi path of personal growth, the individual experiences the fear that he or she will lose the path, that he or she will not enter into further stages of growth. Hope exists, however, that even though the individual may stumble on the path, the Divine will accept whatever small steps are made.

4. *Self-Denial and Poverty.* Self-denial refers to placing one's own self-interest aside while one serves others. This service is done because it pleases the Divine, not because it will chalk up points for the individual in the eyes of the Divine or because the individual will be perceived in a favourable light by others. Poverty may be actual poverty in terms of having few or no material goods, but this is not necessary. Even the rich person may practice poverty if he or she is not attached to material wealth. The person who is unattached to the material world is better prepared to be attached to the Divine.

5. *Trust in God.* This is an active time when the individual acts for himself or herself, but puts faith in the Divine that all is good and in accordance with the Divine plan. In this stage there is a recognition that the only will is that of the Divine and that all things come from the Divine, so whatever happens and whatever one does is part of the larger plan. But people are still required to do their part: "Trust God, but tie your camel first," said Muhammad (Frager & Fadiman, 1998, p. 567).

6. *Love, Yearning, Intimacy, and Satisfaction.* In this stage, when the person recognizes that all things come from the Divine, the only desire is to be close to the Divine and to achieve an intimacy with the Divine. The person realizes that this is the only real desire there is, and satisfaction comes from knowing that all the good and bad of life is Divine. How can one then rebel against or be dissatisfied with life in the physical world?

7. *Intent, Sincerity, and Truthfulness.* There is a recognition in this stage that intent is more important than actual actions. People at this stage see that, even though they may fail or be unable to do many things that they want to do, their sincere desire to do these things is paramount. So, for example, if you genuinely want to relieve famine in the world but are unable to do so, your intent is more important that your inability to make the kind of difference you want to make. Whether you can accomplish your aim is in the hands of the Divine: that you want to accomplish the aim is the significant part.

8. *Contemplation and Self-Examination.* In order to become one with the Divine, one must look deeply and honestly within oneself. This is a difficult task, and many obstacles may appear. Part of the Sufi method includes ways of ridding oneself of these obstacles, ways such as meditation.

9. *The Recollection of Death.* While Western culture often fears and avoids the topic of death, the question "What would you do if this were the last day of your life?" is not an uncommon one for people to muse upon. Such a question, if regarded seriously, often changes one's perspective on life and makes one more aware of the richness of present experience. Al-Ghazali suggests engraving this idea upon one's mind so that one never takes the moment for granted or is heedless of the joy and Divinity of life. This stage is, for some people, the beginning of the journey of the Sufi path, for it may bring about the dissatisfaction with life as it is presently experienced, a hallmark of the first stage.

REFLECTIVE EXERCISE

Stages of Growth

Look at the "stages" or qualities that an individual must accomplish on the Sufi path of growth: patience, gratitude, trust, hope, self-denial, and so on. If you were choosing to follow this path, which of the stages do you think might be hard for you?

Which might be easier? Even if this is not the right path for you, can you see ways that adding or increasing some of these qualities in your personality might make you more satisfied with your life? Which ones? How might you add or increase some of these qualities?

The Role of the Teacher

Having a teacher or guide along the Sufi path is mandatory. There are many places on the road where one can make a misstep if not properly guided, and that could be a greater impediment to growth than not starting the journey at all. The teacher (or *sheikh*) must have reached the ultimate goal already, for how can one guide another if one has not successfully walked the path? Finding the teacher is more complicated than simply looking up "Sufis" on the internet, although one certainly can find Sufi centres by surfing the web (try www.haqq.com.au/~salam/sufilinks/).

Sufis very much believe in the old saying "When the student is ready, the teacher will come." When a person decides to explore beyond his or her ego, a teacher will come along, one that the student's heart says is the right teacher. Both the student and the teacher will feel a resonance between them, and neither will doubt that this relationship, which will be lifelong, is one ordained by the Divine. There is a real fear among would-be students, though, that in their ignorance and innocence, they may be duped into a relationship with a bogus sheikh. In his work *The Book of Knowledge,* Al-Ghazali (Faris, 2007) lists the eight duties of the teacher, making the importance of having such a guide very clear and giving students indications of what might suggest that the teacher is genuine.

First, the teacher must regard students and treat them as if the students were his or her own children. That means that the teacher and his or her students are like a family in their relationships with each other. The relationship between a teacher and a student is characterized by the teacher's love and respect for the student, even with the knowledge and understanding of all the student's flaws and shortcomings. Such support maximizes the student's potential for change.

Second, the teacher must teach for love, not for any remuneration or praise. Thus, the teacher's work is free to the student on the premise that the connection to the Divine is not for sale, but is available to all who have the ability and wish to study. A teacher who asks for anything from the student beyond the student's love, trust, and obedience may not be genuine. Genuine sheikhs usually hold regular jobs, sometimes even jobs that are considered to be menial by many people—after all, sheikhs have rents that must be paid too!

The third duty is to advise the student, making sure that the overly ambitious student is not working at a level too high for his or her present capacity. A teacher who promises quick results or demands too much of the student may not be genuine. In giving advice and correcting a student's flaws and mistakes, the teacher's fourth duty is to use indirect methods rather than direct criticism that may embarrass the student or make the student defensive. For example, the teacher may tell a parable in the hope that the erring student will identify with and make the necessary changes.

The teacher's fifth duty is to never belittle or say anything negative about any other teacher or any other tradition of growth. The Sufi teacher must demonstrate tolerance and understanding for all belief traditions. Those who proselytize or urge a student to join him or her rather than any other sheikh is unlikely to be genuine.

A good teacher is aware that students may become easily discouraged if they are presented with information and tasks that are beyond their present capability. So as a sixth duty, Al-Ghazali admonishes the teacher to make sure that what he or she is teaching is appropriate to the student's level of understanding. Sufism is well aware that people see the world through the filters that they have been raised with and these filters have built up over the years. The seventh duty of the teacher is to be aware of the filters that the students are using and to gently guide them away from the filters so that they may perceive reality.

Finally, the eighth duty is that Sufi teachers must practise what they preach. It is not enough to simply "talk the talk"; they must also "walk the walk." This is often the clue that someone is not the teacher he or she claims to be; his or her personal and professional lives must be pure. The "sheikh" who professes to have no attachment to material goods but proudly owns five luxury cars and two palatial homes is not showing the consistency that a real sheikh would.

Social Relationships

The family relationship that exists between a teacher and students is very special in growth on the Sufi path, but other social relationships are also important. Sufism stresses the importance of associating with like-minded people, those who are on the same path, because this helps to open our hearts to others and, ultimately, to the Divine. Al-Ghazali (1975) says that real friends make sure that the other is not lacking in money or food or anything else that might be needed for survival and development. They loyally refrain from criticizing their friends to other people; they let their friends know that they care for them, praying for them and their development with the same fervour and sincerity as they pray for their own. They never give advice that they know cannot be followed; they make sure they never create difficult situations for their friends and do not burden their friends. Moreover, since all people are created by and contain the Divine, all people must be treated with compassion and tolerance.

Roadblocks on the Sufi Path

Growth along the Sufi Path is clearly not easy. Some people are simply not capable of a full understanding of Sufi teachings. Even with the greatest motivation to learn, a person may not be ready. Whether or not the person is ready is the judgment of the teacher. This is not the greatest of the roadblocks on the Sufi Path, however. Within the human being there are several impediments to growth, factors that must be overcome in order to progress. The greatest impediment is *heedlessness*. In our day-to-day state, we are like sleepwalkers who are not aware of what we really are. We forget that we come from the Divine and see ourselves and our environments as being concrete and separate realities. Because of our heedlessness, we may not even realize that the Sufi Path is a possibility, and so we never take a step down that path.

Another problem that stands in our way is the tendency of human beings to possess some qualities that may be positive and others that may be far from positive or growth-stimulating—qualities such as anger, greed, pride, and jealousy. The tendency to have these human qualities within us is referred to in Sufi terminology as the **nafs**. As long as people identify themselves as "I" and prize their egos, nafs (the product of our self-centered consciousness) will dominate people, affecting their reason and judgment negatively. One goal of Sufism is to bring the nafs under control so that they no longer dominate.

In Sufism, the nafs are considered to have different manifestations or categories, the lower ones called **animal nafs** by Al-Ghazali and the higher ones called **human nafs**. The animal nafs are irrational and respond only to base wants and needs, but these can be controlled by the human nafs, which are concerned with reason and rationality (Ad-Dab'bagh, 2008). Sometimes the nafs are considered levels in the personality (Frager and Fadiman, 1998):

1. The **Commanding Nafs**. This is the nafs that incites us to evil. It controls our thoughts and dominates our actions. It has no morality, no conscience, no sense of mercy or understanding. At this level, a person is unaware that there is any good except in fulfilling personal desires. Thus, people at this level who feel they have been wronged might seek revenge, returning the hurt a hundred times over, seeing this as the appropriate means of dealing with the wrong they have endured. People who covet the belongings or achievements of another might steal or damage what the envied person has. The credo seems to be "Do unto others before they do unto you."

2. The **Accusatory Nafs**. As understanding and faith grow, the individual might be plagued by self-recrimination and guilt for the deeds committed by the commanding nafs. At this level, a person may still commit the wrongs, but feel remorse and try to do better, with little success. Alternatively, the person may try to justify his or her actions, a reaction that still speaks to a burgeoning awareness that the actions have been wrong. While still dominated by the commanding nafs and the accusatory nafs, the person is not able to follow the Sufi path. At this level, it would seem that the person is now starting to use the human nafs to deal with the animal nafs.

3. The **Inspired Nafs**. Coming to this level, the individual can start on the Sufi path. At this level, people have a greater understanding of the wrongs they do under the rule of the commanding nafs and the accusatory nafs, but they gain real motivation to make changes in their lives. They now temper their actions with compassion and morality. Spiritual activities prescribed by the Sufi path can now be undertaken with pleasure, and the power of the commanding nafs and the accusatory nafs is significantly diminished. The individual at this level seems to be psychologically healthy and mature, receiving respect from others and according them respect as well. This, according to a more Western conception, appears to be the level that people should strive for, but in Sufi thought, it is a level that includes danger. At this level, people may become smug in their development and take a great deal of pride in themselves, thereby sabotaging their further development, and leaving them vulnerable to the temptation to go astray.

The need for a teacher or master to keep the person grounded and on the Sufi track is evident here.

4. The **Contented Nafs**. At this level, the person has surmounted the difficulties posed by the previous nafs and feels great peace. There is a surrender of the old desires and attachments; the old angsts are replaced by trust, gratitude, and love. There is even the beginning of a surrender of the ego or sense of self, as the individual prepares to come closer to the Divine All.

5. The **Pleased Nafs**. The person at this level has come even farther, and now both the good and the bad in life are accepted and appreciated. There is realization that all things come from the Divine, both the good and the bad, so even the tribulations of life must be somehow "good," and as such, are welcomed with gratitude.

6. The **Nafs Pleasing to God**. Further realization of the Divine comes at this level as the individual now recognizes the omnipotence of the Divine. All things come from the Divine, and the individual is powerless without the Divine. People at this level have no fears and no wants; they feel complete and whole. Frager and Fadiman (1998) use this analogy:

> A broken mirror creates a thousand different reflections of a single image. If the mirror could be made whole again, it would then reflect the single, unified image. Healing the multiplicity within themselves enables people to experience the world as a whole and unified. (page 573)

7. The **Pure Nafs**. This is the final level, at which the ego is completely transcended and the person is in complete union with the Divine. The enlightened individual recognizes that there is nothing but the Divine—that all else and especially the sense of separation or selfhood has been an illusion.

Even in examining the obstacle of the nafs, Sufism regards the potential for progress toward the Divine. Whether Sufis describe roadblocks, stages of growth in general, or stages for the individual personality, the path puts an emphasis on the positive, and on the potential for growth. Hope, trust, love are hallmarks of this approach.

There is a love of laughter among Sufis. Often Sufism is taught to followers by means of stories, parables, and jokes. It seems fitting, therefore, to end this section with a couple of well-known Sufi jokes that also contain a Sufi lesson:

> Hodja wanted to learn how to play the lute. So he approached a music teacher and asked him, "How much do you charge for private lute lessons?"
>
> "Three silver pieces for the first month; then after that, one silver piece a month."
>
> "Oh, that's very fair," exclaimed Hodja. "I'll start with the second month."
>
> *(Fadiman & Frager, 1997, p.165)*

> One day a friend visited Hodja and said, "Hodja, I want to borrow your donkey."
>
> "I'm sorry," replied Hodja, "but I've already lent it out to someone else."
>
> As soon as he said this, the donkey brayed.
>
> "But Hodja, I can hear the donkey! It's in the stable."
>
> Shutting the door in this friend's face, Hodja told him with dignity, "A man who believes the word of a donkey above my own doesn't deserve to be lent anything!"
>
> *(Fadiman & Frager, 1997, pp. 168–169)*

Conclusion

The Eastern approaches to personal growth and a satisfying life are well within the domain of the eudaimonic conception of happiness. The satisfying life, to these approaches, involves rising above the material world's delights and above the overwhelming concern many people have with their own circumscribed selves. These pathways involve a recognition of the human being's true essence as being one with an all-encompassing Force, Entity, or Power. This is the only truth, the only reality; all else is illusion.

This is a premise that is often difficult for the Western mind to accept. In the West, the dominant ideal has been that of the individualist who succeeds in creating, building, and acquiring more, bigger, and better material objects. The concrete side of life is the side that has been emphasized in the West, with extra value placed on science and technology rather than on arts or spirituality. Eastern conceptions of personal growth and what constitutes a satisfying life challenge the conceptions that many Westerners have been raised with. Whether an approach is right or wrong is not the issue: the issue is whether an approach incites us to consider possibilities we had not considered before and to come to a better understanding of what *we* really want for our lives, as opposed to what we have been taught we *should* want. Exposure to Eastern approaches very often forces Westerners to think in different categories and, as we shall see in subsequent chapters, has opened up new therapeutic and life-enhancing interventions for us all.

Summary

- Yoga is a whole-world outlook that emphasizes growth and spirituality.
- What we see around us is maya, or delusion. The *true* reality of the universe is that there is only One, referred to as Brahman. Within us lies a true, hidden nature that is called Atman. If everything is Brahman, then Atman must be Brahman as well.
- The goal of yoga is go beyond the filter that keeps us from recognizing the Oneness of the universe and our identity with everything else by quieting the chatter in our minds.
- Karma is the moral law of cause and effect that is inherent in everything.
- Because of our ignorance, we are ruled by pleasure and aversion.
- When we realize the true nature of reality, Brahman, we reach enlightenment or samadhi.
- In order to free oneself from maya and achieve enlightenment, we must have a guru.
- Raja-Yoga is made up of eight principles and is the form of yoga from which other schools are derived. Jnana-Yoga is the yoga of wisdom, using contemplative meditation in a wholly detached and rational fashion. Karma-Yoga concentrates on acting selflessly, with no thought for reward. Bhakti-Yoga is the emotion-based yoga of love and devotion. Hatha-Yoga uses many physical techniques, for the purpose of giving the individual stability and tranquility in order to better attain enlightenment through meditation. Mantra-Yoga involves the use of a spiritually meaningful phrase or sound that is repeated over and over, aloud or silently, during meditation.
- Buddhism is the product of the enlightenment of Siddhartha Gautama and his convictions about the nature of the life called The Four Noble Truths.

- The Mahayana school spread to China, combined with Taoism and Confucianism, and developed into Zen Buddhism.
- Zen is completely experiential. Words distort and minimize experience.
- Zen techniques include zazen (seated meditation), koans (paradoxical riddles used as a meditative focus), and sanzen (consultations about meditation with a roshi).
- Enlightenment, or satori, brings joy and a feeling of oneness with all creation. This enlightenment is then brought into day-to-day life.
- The centre of Sufi belief is the belief that everything is, in reality, the Divine.
- The goal of Sufism is to transcend our egos and understand that we are One with the Divine.
- The four stages of Sufism include sharia, the moral code; tariqa, the specific practices; haqiqa, in which the person fully understands sharia and tariqa; and marifa, the definitive union with the Divine.
- In growing, the individual must go through stages of initial awakening; patience and gratitude; fear and hope; self-denial and poverty; trust in God; love, yearning, intimacy, and satisfaction; intent, sincerity, and truthfulness; contemplation and self-examination; and the recollection of death.
- Having a teacher or guide (sheikh) is mandatory.
- Sufism values social interaction, especially with like-minded people, and stresses the need for tolerance and compassion toward all.
- The greatest impediment in growth is heedlessness. Another impediment may be our human qualities, called nafs.

Group Discussion Questions

1. Some people have proposed that yoga be included as an event at the Olympics. What is your view of this? How would yogis react to this? If you were on an Olympic committee given the responsibility to make the decision, how would you vote?

2. Is the poem (in the section on Buddhism) trite or profound? Does it convey something meaningful about life and how to live it? Or is it a rather depressive viewpoint about life?

3. Is the message of Sufism really any different from that of yoga or Buddhism? If you think it is, what makes it different? If you think it isn't different, what are the similarities and how can you account for them?

CHAPTER 4

The Satisfying Life from the Perspective of Indigenous Peoples

Simon is a Canadian of Cree extraction. He has always lived with his parents in the city, and they have grown away from their roots and their heritage. Simon, in fact, knows almost nothing about his people's traditions and worldview, but he has felt a growing discomfort with his lack of information and understanding. He has developed a pervasive feeling that there must be more than the view he gets of his heritage from the media. He's lucky, though: his great-uncle is an elder who lives on a nearby reserve, and he has invited Simon to stay with him on his reserve for the summer to learn about Cree beliefs. Simon is eagerly and expectantly looking forward to this.

Simon is not alone in his feelings and in his lack of knowledge. Many indigenous people, and many non-native citizens in all countries, exhibit the same unfamiliarity with their roots. Simon's family, like many, has adopted a mainstream North American viewpoint and lifestyle and, until Simon's unrest, has been content with this. In fact, they have friends who feel that there is no place for the "old ways" in today's world. They disagree and are highly supportive of Simon's summer plans.

LEARNING OBJECTIVES

In this chapter, students will learn about what constitutes a satisfying life from the perspectives of

☐ The Indigenous Peoples of the Americas.

☐ Australian Indigene.

☐ The Indigenous Peoples of Africa.

In technologically advanced societies from New York to Hong Kong, there is a tacit understanding that technological advancement marks the level of development of a culture, with less technological cultures labelled primitive. But is technology a measure of true civilization? Is this a valid assumption? Or is this an assumption based solely upon a technological perspective of the world?

Why did some cultures not choose to pursue technological development? Certainly not because of a lack of intelligence or initiative or even resources in many cases. The very survival of people such as the Inuit of northern Canada or Indigene in the Outback of Australia, under the severest of weather conditions, argues for their intelligence, industry, and creativity. The inescapable conclusion is that some people of the earth have not regarded technological development as the litmus test of their culture. For many cultures, progress and development have been seen in very different terms, perhaps in terms of spiritual or artistic development, or in terms of harmony and balance with the cosmos. As with the other perspectives we have examined in Chapters 2 and 3, the issue is not whether we "agree" or not: it is whether we can understand and appreciate another approach. It is only recently that those persons who are not of indigenous populations have even attempted such an understanding. It's long overdue, for Simon and for the rest of us.

Most of this chapter is about the indigenous peoples of the Americas because most of the literature on these groups concentrates in this area. In fact, many of the best scholars of indigenous traditions and beliefs are Indigenous People themselves, and they have written with both knowledge and deep insight, as well as with formal study. Smaller sections of the chapter will examine the traditions and worldviews of Australian Indigenes and indigenous Africans.

INDIGENOUS PEOPLES OF THE AMERICAS

A Note on Terminology

What do we call these first settlers of the American continents? This is something of a sensitive question. Traditionally, they have been called (and many call themselves) *Indians*. While many find this acceptable, others point out with righteous distaste that this misnomer is the legacy of Christopher Columbus, who assumed he had reached India on his voyage and hence was greeted by people who must be *Indians*. The terms *native* and *indigenous* have been used, but both of these words seem to refer to something or someone that has arisen spontaneously in the land and, as we will see, it is unclear whether these people did originate in the Americas or whether they were the earliest immigrants.

Others of these people prefer the term *First Nations Peoples* (for those inhabiting Canada) and *Native Americans* (for those inhabiting the United States), but this is an artificial division since many of these people belong to the same groups. Should they be called something different simply because of a politically inspired dividing line between Canada and the United States? In addition, many descendents of immigrants arriving in the New World after 1492 feel themselves to be "native" Canadians, Americans, and Mexicans, for example. These are just some of the arguments that have been used in the dispute over the appropriate form of reference to use.

Generally, it is appropriate to call anyone by the name that he or she prefers, but the absence of consensus about the correct term of reference makes this very difficult. For the purpose of this book, we will refer to the first settlers of the American continents as *The People*. Why? Because that is what they first called themselves. Almost every name of a band or tribe meant *the people* or some variant of this in the original language. For example, the Sioux called themselves *Lakota*, meaning *the allies*; the Navajo called themselves *Dine*, meaning *the people*; the Chippewa called themselves *anish insubag*, meaning *spontaneous men* (Deloria, 1994). In the absence of an agreed-upon alternative, The People as a form of address seems to meet with our intentions to be respectful.

Another note: groups that are called bands in Canada are called tribes in the United States. Similarly, in Canada, land set aside for First Nations use by the government is called a reserve while in the United States, it is called a reservation.

Who Are The People?

People occupied the Americas many thousands of years before either the Norse explorers or Christopher Columbus even dreamed that there might be a land mass across the ocean. Where did they come from? There is no definitive answer to that question. Besides the accounts of The People themselves, there have been many theories, including the idea that they were the remnant of the lost tribe of Israel, and the idea that they were the descendants of the survivors of the lost continent of Atlantis. Most archaeologists today accept the theory that The People are Asian in origin, having crossed a land bridge spanning the Bering Strait or sailed across the Pacific Ocean about 12,000 years ago during the Pleistocene Epoch. Yet today, even these "generally accepted" theories are in doubt. Human artifacts from areas ranging from Alaska to near the tip of South America have been dated as being far, far older than 12,000 years, perhaps even 100,000 years. The nature of many of the artifacts has led several scientists to suspect that there were many migrations of people from Asia. Linguists tell us that the languages of The People fall into several groups—that is, they may not be all related to each other. This makes many people wonder if perhaps there were not several migrations of people of different Asian cultures who first settled the Americas. It may even be that the Americas were the original sites of the development of The People (Wilson, 1998).

As you can see, there is quite a lively debate going on in the scientific community regarding the origins of the first people to populate the Americas, and as more artifacts and better methods of dating are found, we can expect this debate to continue. But this is of little importance to many of The People themselves. Listen to the words of Alfonso Ortiz, an American university-trained social scientist:

> My world is the Tewa world. It is different from your world... Archaeologists will tell you that we came at least 12,000 years ago from Asia, crossing the Bering land bridge, then spreading over the two American continents... But a Tewa is not so interested in the work of archaeologists.
>
> A Tewa is interested in our own story of our origins, for it holds all that we need to know about our people, and how one should live as a human. The story defines our society. It tells me who I am, where I came from, the boundaries of our world, what kind of order exists within it; how suffering, evil and death came into this world; and what is likely to happen to me when I die...
>
> *(as quoted by Wilson, 1998, p. 12)*

It seems that traditional scientists and The People have different ideas about what is important in determining their roots. The worldview of The People is not the same as the worldview typically taught in Western schools, as Simon will learn.

The People are not a single, homogeneous group of individuals sharing a culture, nor have they been such for an unknown amount of time, if ever. On the contrary, there are rich and profound differences to be found among the beliefs and perspectives of different bands and groups. This chapter cannot begin to encompass the great diversity that is found; however, there is also a core of commonality among the differing beliefs. In this section, we shall examine those commonalities of themes, worldviews, and beliefs as they pertain to a satisfying life without pretending to be all-inclusive.

Change

On Simon's first day of his stay with his great-uncle, Herbert Long Deer, his uncle takes him on a tour of the reserve, and talks about commonplace matters, such as how the large tree was small many years ago and how different it looked in the winter. He introduces Simon to some of his friends and comments on how he watched them grow from babies to toddlers to young adults. He notes that Simon once was happy to be a typical teenager in the city, and how, now in his young adult years, he has left many of his younger pastimes behind and is seeking to learn more about his heritage. "Everything changes," he says mildly. "I wonder what you will be tomorrow."

Uncle Herbert has given Simon a lesson, but not through direct teaching. His comments throughout the tour of the reserve have made Simon realize that it is clear that change is part of the universal pattern. The idea of change is important to The People, change as a necessary and vital component of life. The individual can and does change, the society can and does change, the universe can and does change. What remains the same are the basic belief system and the values of the community (Coyhis & Simonelli, 2008; Highwater, 1982). In one of the stories Uncle Herbert tells, there is a character (also in the legends of almost all groups of The People), the Trickster, that points this out.

Sometimes known as Coyote or Raven, the Trickster exists only to disrupt the person's comfortable view of life. The Trickster throws a monkey wrench into life as a means of demonstrating that life is unpredictable and that change is the only constant. Highlighting this is the fact that the many languages of The People contain few nouns but many verbs. This indicates that The People regard even inanimate objects as dynamic and changing rather than static. Thus, a wooden chair is regarded as the tree that once was and the kindling that one day will be (Ross, 1996).

Most of the groups of The People find it rather amazing that other cultures insist on a single, consistent identity for any individual across his or her life span. We often say "I'm not the same person that I was," but except in extreme cases, we expect people to behave in a constant and predictable (for them) fashion. We encourage people to "find themselves," with the implication that once this has been accomplished, the individual can rest easily knowing who or what he or she is. But this isn't logical to The People. After all, as we get older our bodies alter, our thinking becomes more sophisticated, our social relationships change, we mature emotionally, our responsibilities and tasks become different. And tellingly, Simon's viewpoint is changing. Of course the "I" of today is not the same as the "I" of yesterday, nor will it be the same as the "I" of tomorrow. Why pretend or demand a consistency that not only isn't there, but *shouldn't* be there?

The People incorporate change into their belief system. On the individual level, there are ceremonies of change at different points in the individual's life. Often a physical or social change is marked by a change in name. This change usually reflects a particularly meaningful and life-altering event in the person's life, including the passage to adulthood (Highwater, 1982). In some cases, the individual may change gender. This is not to suggest that sex-reassignment surgery is regularly carried out. But almost all groups of The People recognize the "two-spirited person" who is thought to encompass elements of both male and female within one individual. In some cases, the two-spirited person takes on the dress and role of the opposite sex, and such a change is accepted and respected by The People (for example, see Jacobs, Thomas, & Lang, 1997, for a collection of some interesting stories).

On a wider level, the family constellation of The People may change, not only through the cycles of birth and death, but also by the deliberate and ceremonial addition of family members. He or she who was a close friend, one whose spirit is on the same path, may literally become a brother or sister. In so becoming, the new sibling takes on the responsibilities and the place of a brother or sister in the family (Brown, 1989).

Within the band or tribe, changes may occur because of the new visions given to individuals, or because decisions must be made in view of different environmental or social conditions. For example, the elders of the group may suggest (not order!) that the group forego its traditional yearly trip to a certain hunting area because of weather conditions. Certainly the acceptance of living on reserves and reservations came as a result of changing political and social factors. Some changes will be seen as good, some will not. But change is inevitable.

Many groups believe that civilizations rise and fall as time goes on. Today there is a belief shared by many that the time of The People had waned and is now returning in a new and rejuvenated form (e.g., McGaa, 1990). Old ceremonies and rituals are being restored, but there are many who say that the old ways have been forgotten. The People have traditionally not written down their histories or their beliefs, let alone formulae for their rituals. How, then, can the old ways be brought back? The People have retained their history and understanding of the universe in an oral tradition, stories passed by word of mouth by those, like Simon's Uncle Herbert, trained and committed to the transmission of the culture.

But, many will protest, doesn't an oral tradition bring about change in the story? Doesn't the teller subtly emphasize and reinterpret that which he or she has learned so that the message transmitted today is not the same as the message transmitted many years ago? Of course, reply The People, but you sound as if you think this is a bad thing. On the contrary, goes the reasoning, the *strength* of the oral tradition is that the message can be altered to fit the times. The belief system, then, is always relevant to the situation in which The People find themselves. As long as the fundamentals remain, change is expected and welcomed. What, then, are the fundamentals?

The World, An Ecosystem

After nearly destroying our planet (and we may do it yet!), human beings are starting to recognize that the world is not simply a supply of raw materials, but is, in fact, a highly interdependent ecosystem. If we cut down the trees, we have done more than ravage a forest. We have upset the balance of countless species of plants and animals, and the effects will be felt across the globe, even influencing the quality of the air we breathe.

The People have known this for millennia. A fundamental part of the worldview of The People is that human beings exist within a vast and complex set of relationships of nature. Note the terminology—we are *of* nature, not just *in* nature. These relationships connect us and make us a part of the workings of entire Creation. We are part of the ecosystem, part of the delicate and wondrous balance and harmony of the universe. The People find humility in this belief. You have no right to be arrogant as a human being; your assumption of a special place and special rights within nature is flawed, they say. You are an element just as every other animal species, every plant, every feature of the geological landscape, rivers, hills, oceans are elements of Creation. Each has a role to play, and there are no leading players. No one role is more important than another, for none can exist without the harmonious blending of others (Carmody & Carmody, 1993; Deloria, 1994; Forbes, 2001; Quispe, 2009).

As human beings, we may, in fact, be less significant in many ways than other elements of the biosphere because, while we are dependent on other elements for our survival, it is difficult to imagine other elements' dependency on us. If plants don't provide food and oxygen, we die. This means that insects and wind, for example, are necessary for our survival since the survival of plants depends on them, among other constituents. But if human beings are eradicated from the earth, isn't it likely that the other elements will not only survive, but thrive? Don't we have an indication of this when we look at pieces of land, sidewalks, and summer homes that have been left to their own devices? Grasses have grown up, weeds flourish, wildflowers bloom, insects buzz, and perhaps even certain small animals have taken up residence. Our presence may be missed in providing what we have come to accept as "order," but the forces of nature seem unimpressed with our desire to mow lawns and clear away spider webs.

Relationships

Simon understands why Uncle Herbert is a conservationist who recycles as much as he can and watches out for unnecessary waste. "When we hurt the environment, we hurt ourselves," says Uncle Herbert. But Simon is a little puzzled when he thanks Uncle Herbert again for inviting him to stay for the summer and Uncle Herbert replies, "No need for thanks. This is for me and for all of us as much as for you."

What Simon will learn is that The People say that they *are* relationships, not that they *have* relationships. And these relationships are with all the various parts of nature, seen and unseen, human or non-human, animate or inanimate. The People, then, are all related or connected to one another in some way. They are also all related or connected to other components of the physical world, including both animate life forms and inanimate geophysical features. The entire biosphere is a vast and complex web of relationships, and it is within these relationships that we find our place and purpose in life (Carmody & Carmody, 1993; Coyhis & Simonelli, 2008; Deloria, 1992, 1999; Verluis, 1997).

The social organization of The People is based on the family unit. But the definition of the family unit is very extended. Thus, all the men and women in the band or tribe may be regarded as being in the relationship of siblings, parent/child, grandparent/grandchild, cousins, and so on. Among the Sioux, when the actual family relationship becomes too nebulous (e.g., second cousin once-removed), the relationship is redefined as a sibling connection (Deloria, 1992). So instead of worrying about exactly what to call Fred, who is the grandson of your mother's first cousin, you would simply call him "brother." In addition, the majority of groups have special ceremonies of adoption to formally include new members of the family. As a further type of connection, in some groups an individual may be born into a clan within the group. This is a unit that has certain individual duties and obligations to the rest of The People in terms of providing food, healing, and leadership, for example. To be born into a clan in one group makes a person related to members of the same clan in other groups. Thus, the family is extended beyond the band boundaries.

To The People, there is another element of life that is equally connected to that which can be seen. This is the unseen spirit world. The People believe that the spirit world, comprised of forces of nature, greater and lesser deities, and the souls of those who have died, is a vibrant part of the world in which we live. There is no division of a spirit world and a physical world; they are all connected. To pray does not require going to a church, synagogue, mosque, or temple. All one must do to speak to the spirits is simply to speak. They will hear for they are all around. The web of life is extended, then, to include the spiritual. The People are indivisibly connected to all the possibilities of the cosmos, whether seen or unseen, inanimate or animate, ethereal or corporeal (Carmody & Carmody, 1993; Deloria, 1994; Highwater, 1982; Hultkrantz, 1967; Renault & Freke, 1996; Verluis, 1997).

REFLECTIVE EXERCISE

Interconnectedness

All of us have felt alone now and again. But are we really alone? Are we really unconnected to anything else in life, or are we simply not used to recognizing our connections? Take a few moments right now to examine yourself in this regard. For example, what are you wearing? Someone made those clothes. Someone wove that fabric; someone grew or manufactured the raw materials that made the fabric. Those people have contributed to your welfare, and you, in buying the clothes, have contributed to theirs. Have you eaten today? What did you eat? Did you recognize the gifts of the plants and animals that made up your food? Did you see your role as a conservator and respectful user of these gifts? Did you realize that when you smiled at your professor and looked attentive that your professor's lectures were actually a little more enthusiastic and dynamic than they would have been had you not smiled? In your giving, you are also getting.

Religion

Uncle Herbert's friend, George, is not one of The People and has not been raised in their ways. He was raised in a strong Catholic family, and he faithfully attends Mass and goes to confession every month. And every year, he tries to cheat on his income tax. Certainly most Catholics, and countless others of any religious/moral/ethical nature, would be disgusted by George's hypocrisy, but they would all have to admit that his behaviour is not uncommon in a society that separates church and state. In Canada and the United States, this separation is even legislated. It is not surprising that many people see no contradiction in maintaining religious convictions while behaving unethically in secular matters. But to The People, this is a matter of great puzzlement. Since the spirit world is completely connected with the physical world, how can there be such a separation? There is no single word in any of The People's languages that means *religion* (Deloria, 1992; McGaa, 1990; Renault and Freke, 1996). That's because there is no separation between religion and other parts of life. All acts are spiritual acts and spirituality is part of everything we do. This is why Uncle Herbert pauses a moment before eating the blueberry he has picked. Picking a blueberry and eating it must be accompanied by an appreciation and a message of thanks for the gift of the berry, the elements of nature that have aided the berry to grow, the spirits that have directed the elements of nature, and the Creator who first started the whole process. In a way, all day-to-day life for The People is a prayer, and blasphemy is just as possible in brushing your teeth as in showing disregard for ceremonies. The People, then, live and breathe in an atmosphere of the spirit as much as in a literal biosphere.

This does not mean that ceremonies or religious rituals are any less important for The People. It means that ceremonies and rituals are not the only expressions of spirituality: all behaviour expresses spirituality. One thoughtless act does not upset the harmony of life. The forces of life are stronger than that. But a continued disregard, a series of many thoughtless acts, will have ramifications, and then restoring the harmony of the cosmos may be more difficult.

The spirituality of life is an ongoing process, as well. The revelations and insights of religion are just as likely to occur today, in The People's view, as they were thousands of years ago. This provides another reason why religion must be seen as a vital component of everyday life, since spiritual truths may be experienced by anyone at any time. Again, change is seen as a normal component of life. While respect is given to the insights of ancestors from a dimly remembered past and guidance is sought from these ancestors, the prime focus is on the experiences of the individual in the present. What has the individual experienced that has given him or her a new, fresh, and/or deepened understanding of the web of life? This is deeply personal. The "truth" that one person has experienced is not preached to others on the understanding that if the spirits or ancestors had wanted to reveal this insight to others, they would have done so. If an individual does tell of an experience that had meaning for him or her, the individual does not discuss his or her interpretation of that experience. Rather, the tale is told and the listeners are left to form their own meaning (or not) from the tale. From this, they may decide whether or not to incorporate the message into their own belief framework (Deloria, 1999; Highwater, 1982).

The Land

When we view nature as a whole with each part equally important in its role, it becomes clear that "ownership" of any element is illogical. Not only do human beings have no right to own other elements, but such ownership would be impossible since each element has its own individual part to play. The People have been greatly troubled since the coming of Europeans to the Americas by their demands for land. Treaties were made in which The People were required to cede "their" land. This was a meaningless request in many respects. The People replied that they didn't own the land, so how could they cede it? The land, however, was given to them for their use, for their homes, for their inspiration and insights. In this way, and in many other ways, it was sacred to them. It is still sacred. It will always be sacred. The People have had thousands of years to serve and interact with the sanctity of the land. They have had thousands of years to accumulate special sacred areas. Removing The People from the sacred land is a terrible kind of disruption since it pulls them away from what has defined them in their relationships, and perhaps just as troubling, it opens the possibility that those individuals who take the land not meant for them are profaning it and disrupting the balances even more.

Vine Deloria (1994, 1999) and others (e.g., Basso, 1996) make the case that the land serves as the basis for the identity of The People. They feel that the European mode of understanding life is through time, placing historical events in a clear chronology. But for The People, life is understood through space: not *when* it happened, but *where* it happened.

The structure of their religious traditions is taken directly from the world around them, from their relationships with other forms of life. Context is therefore all-important for both practice and the understanding of reality. The places where revelations were experienced were remembered and set aside as locations where, through rituals and ceremonials, the people could once again communicate with the spirits. Thousands of years of occupancy on their lands taught tribal peoples the sacred landscapes for which they were responsible and gradually the structure of ceremonial reality became clear. It was not what people believed to be true that was important but what they experienced as true. Hence revelation was seen as a continuous process of adjustment to the natural surroundings and not as a specific message valid for all times and places.

(Deloria, 1994, pp. 66–67)

REFLECTIVE EXERCISE

Your Personal Geography

Take a walk in your neighbourhood. Is this the neighbourhood you grew up in? If so, really look at the places you pass, connecting them with some event in your life. See, there's the place where you first learned to ride a bicycle. And over there is where you and the other kids used to play field hockey. And that's where you went to temple every week. Isn't that the path you and your first girlfriend walked down when you shared your first kiss? If you are now living away from the neighbourhood of your childhood, take the walk in your mind. If you can, in either case, collect some photographs of the meaningful places of your life. Are there any particular spots that are especially important or sacred to you?

What about your life today? Are you aware of the space around you today, or do you rush past with your mind elsewhere and without noting where you are? Find a sacred space for yourself. Even in the largest and most congested cities, it is possible to find a garden, a park, a museum, a place of worship, which can be the place of inner peace for you. When you are tired, stressed, and feeling perhaps a little down and discouraged, a trip to your sacred place may be rejuvenating and bring you back to the realization of what is truly meaningful in your life, even if the trip is only in your mind. If you can, try to find out about the special places of your parents' and grandparents' lives. These too are your roots.

Volition

The People believe in free will. No one is forced to do anything. The individual is seen as making his or her own choices, not controlled by destiny, spirits, or society at large. It is considered acceptable to give counsel or make suggestions when asked, but the individual is under no compulsion to follow through on these suggestions (Sams, 1999). So when Simon asks Uncle Herbert what chores around the house he would like Simon to take on for the summer, Uncle Herbert raises his eyebrows and answers "What needs to be done? What do you want to do?"

How does one regulate society, then? What guarantee is there that the necessary work for survival will be done? What about the law breakers? Each community of The

People was typically small, and people depended on each other for the continued survival of the group and for life satisfaction and well-being. All children were raised by the community with an understanding of what their place was and what duties and responsibilities they have in the present and will have in the future. They were expected to fulfill these. If they did not, the whole community knew, and the individual was shamed. The community wanted to know *why* the individual chose not to fulfill his or her obligations. The assumption was that something had gone wrong with the individual, and the community attempted to help the individual find his or her way back to the path. The emphasis was not on punishment or coercion, but on healing (Coyhis & Simonelli, 2008; Ross, 1992, 1996).

Such an orientation was used traditionally and is now being restored in many areas. This orientation is also being applied to the legal system in some cases. In Canada, for example, there are programs of what has been termed *native justice* which rely on a *healing circle*. The healing circle consists of victims and perpetrators of wrongdoings, their families, people from the community who have knowledge of the individuals most intimately involved, people who have particular experience with the type of wrongdoing under discussion, and representatives of the wider judicial system. The goals are fourfold. The first is to show the perpetrator of the wrongdoing that his or her actions have had injurious consequences for both the victim and the community as a whole. The second is to find out why the perpetrator chose to act as he or she did. The third is to devise a program by which the perpetrator may decide to make different choices in the future. And the fourth is to allow the victim and the community to grow and be strengthened, even by an injurious act.

Ross (1996) reports extensively on the example of how a healing circle may deal with the crime of child molestation. The molester is seen as having used his own volition to make the choice to molest a child, but the healing circle wants to know why he made this choice. Does he understand the feelings of children? Was he molested himself as a child and was never healed of this trauma? Is his molestation triggered by an indulgence in drugs or alcohol? The child and his or her family tell the molester what his actions have done to them and how they feel now. Within the circle are trained molestation survivors who have been healed or are on their way to such healing. In relating their own experiences, without bitterness or anger, they help the victim and the community deal with the wrongdoing that has occurred, and they devise a plan for the perpetrator to change. This may include alcohol or drug counselling, what might be termed "sensitivity training" to gain empathy for the feelings of others, and parenting classes. This plan, of course, requires that the perpetrator make the choice to change. But The People believe that anyone can make this choice, and help will be provided in carrying out the decision to change. Ross (1996) further reports that the preliminary results of such healing circles are very positive, with a large reduction in recidivism and a strengthened feeling of community relationships. The wrongdoer is more likely to grow, make restitution, and choose differently in the future.

Responsibility

The People have not paid much attention to their "rights" within their relationships. Rather, they concentrate on their responsibilities and duties. To live a good life means, in part at least, to fulfill one's obligations in all of one's relationships with life. The ultimate responsibility is to maintain the balance and the harmony of the vast interconnectedness of the cosmos, starting with the family/group, extending to other species of life, including elements of the landscape, and culminating in reverence and respect for the spirit world (Coyhis & Simonelli, 2008).

Groups usually see all members as being of a single family, with connections to all other families as well. As in a family, each individual has responsibilities for the care and well-being of other members of the family. To work for personal goals that are not in the service of the whole is unthinkable (Deloria, 1994). As we have seen, The People feel that any member who does not look out for the good of the whole, or who actually commits harm to some members of the group, needs to be guided back to the path of harmony. Punishment is not considered. Rather, as in the healing circle, finding a way to help the wrongdoer make restitution, regain harmony, and become rehabilitated so that he or she offends no more is seen to be the responsibility of the community. This is a responsibility to the victim, to the perpetrator of the wrongdoing, to the community, and to the Universe as a whole (Ross, 1992, 1996).

Most of The People have always been hunters, depending on other animals and fish for meat. The People feel that human beings should be deeply grateful for the sacrifice that these of their brothers and sisters are making in giving up their lives to serve as sustenance for The People. So, hunting is not a sport. An animal is killed with reverence, often with a ceremony of gratitude. In most cases, there is an obvious repayment of some sort to the great web of nature for the taking of a life. This may be something overt, such as throwing part of the animal back to nature or leaving a gift of tobacco where the animal was killed. To maintain balance and respect, as well as to act with responsibility, the food that is acquired is shared with other human beings or elements of nature for which The People are responsible (e.g., dogs, horses). It is clear, then, that people should take only what they need and give back what they can, even if this means something as abstract as a rededication of themselves to be responsible and aware of their place in the universe (Versluis, 1997). This, of course, is the ideal. Individuals among The People, like individuals in every group everywhere, do not always live up to the ideals of their culture or belief system.

In summary, what has Simon learned of human beings' role in the Universe? The People believe that our role is one of responsibility. Human beings must work to maintain the balance and the harmony of Creation. We must not destroy heedlessly; we must not take without giving back; we must show respect and protectiveness for the other elements of nature, for they are, in a very real sense, our brothers and sisters. A disturbance to them means a disturbance to us, just as a pebble thrown in a pond ripples out to all parts of the pond, disturbing all of the water. The ceremonies and rituals of The People are to this end: to help to maintain, or sometimes to restore, the harmony of the components of the cosmos (Versluis, 1997). This is the case for Rain Dances, which seek to restore a balance so that the rains may come, if they will. This is the case for the individual Vision Quest, in which the single person is asking the forces of the cosmos to indicate what his or her special relationship to these forces really is and how the individual should live in this relationship to promote harmony. Maintaining the harmony and balance of the universe is vital to having a satisfying life.

The Medicine Wheel

Most groups of The People have an ancient circular symbol known as the Medicine Wheel. In some cases, the Medicine Wheel has been given physical form, the symbol of the relationship to the land and geography being clear. The best known of these are the Moose Mountain Medicine Wheel in Saskatchewan, Canada and the Big Horn Medicine Wheel in Wyoming, United States. The Medicine Wheel, like the circular symbols of so many cultures, shows the interconnectedness of life and the possibilities and potentialities of life. Typically the Medicine Wheel is divided into four parts, corresponding with the four major directions, north, south, east, and west. We start in the east, as in the rising of the sun, and we travel around the Wheel in a clockwise direction, to the south, the west, and finally to the north. Each direction has its own lessons to teach and its own spiritual, emotional, physical, and mental gifts to bestow. Should anyone manage in this lifetime to reach north, the journey continues, going from north to east, as further deeper lessons are taught and further gifts are attained. There are some guidelines for what is encompassed by the Medicine Wheel, but much is individual. The Medicine Wheel is often referred to as a mirror, indicating that what one person sees is not what another person sees. The lessons are both universal and individual (Bopp, Bopp, Brown, & Lane, 1989; Coyhis & Simonelli, 2008; Sams, 1999).

The east, the beginning, is where we learn to perceive and appreciate the here and now. We focus our attention on what is before us and around us, rather than thinking and dreaming about what once was or what we hope will be in the future or how we wish things were right now. Here we use the qualities of a child in finding delight in the world, in loving unreservedly and spontaneously, and in seeing through artifice and pretension. The People say that one cannot continue on any path or take any journey without fully realizing where one is right now.

In the south, we find the heat, the passion, and the romance of summer. We learn to love one significant other, but at the same time we recognize that we must gain control of ourselves and our emotions. If we do not, our love may become obsessive and possessive, and we will lose that one special person while diminishing ourselves. As we learn this self-discipline, we also learn that self-discipline must extend to other areas of our lives. We must curb our appetites so that we retain self-control, and we must form goals and learn how to work toward them. Now the focused attention that we learned in the east becomes a passionate involvement in the world. Our emotions and passions lead us to idealism, with a desire for the welfare of the universe, with the capacity for generosity, compassion, and kindness, and with a righteous indignation at injustice. While these feelings are worthy, they too must be controlled. These passions must be expressed freely, but in ways that do not hurt others. Righteous indignation at injustice, for example, is harmful when it erupts into violence but beneficial if it is used to bring comfort and solace to those who have been wronged and to right the wrong that has been done.

In the west comes sunset, or darkness. Here we learn the power of meditation or prayer, and we learn to manage that power. Here we will be tested. By meditation or prayer, we travel to the centre of our being and we experience the connection between our spirit and the rest of the cosmos. Spiritual insight will only come if we exercise the self-discipline that we have learned in the south to set aside time for prayer, meditation, and personal reflection daily. Some of us will say that we don't have enough time in our day for this. Some of us become uncomfortable if we are alone in silence with ourselves.

The sound of other people, the TV, or music is much more comforting. These reactions suggest that we have much work to do to learn the lessons of the west. Perhaps we haven't learned the lessons of the south well enough yet. We may need to go back.

The People say that the greatest lesson to be learned through the self-reflection in the west is to understand and accept ourselves as we are, to understand that we are both physical and spiritual beings, and to understand the need for sacrifice. Sacrifice means that nothing must be taken from the universe without giving something back. As we deepen our understanding of our role in the universe, we come to comprehend that this is not really *sacrifice* on our part, but a just and valid, freely given return for the cosmos' lessons and gifts.

The north is the direction of true wisdom, the direction of completion. We learn to finish what we started, and we learn that all things have an end. We learn how to stand apart from our emotions and our knowledge, not to discard them, but to gain a clear and unbiased perspective. And now we learn balance, the harmony by which all the universe resonates together. Part of the wisdom we gain is that we know nothing, and we start the journey in the east again, going through all the directions as many times as needed to gain further lessons and gifts. We cannot stay in any one of the four directions, for each is incomplete without the other three. The ultimate home, reached after all the lessons of the four directions have been learned, is the centre of the Medicine Wheel (Bopp, Bopp, Brown, & Lane, 1989).

In learning about the Medicine Wheel, Simon comes to understand that the most important lesson is the process. The journey, the quest, is more important than ultimately reaching some state of perfection. All of life is interconnected, all of life is cyclical, all of life is a journey. Satisfaction in life is about making the journey an enriching one for oneself and for others.

The Sacred Tree

The story and symbol of the Sacred Tree are used in some variation among most of the groups of The People. According to the story Uncle Herbert tells, with its rich symbolic content, the Creator of All planted a Sacred Tree under which all the people of the earth could gather to learn, to gain wisdom and personal empowerment, and to be healed. The Tree is rooted in the earth, the Mother of us all, and its branches reach to the sky, our Father. The Tree bears fruit in the form of lessons showing the way to become more loving, compassionate, just, patient, wise, courageous, respectful, humble, and giving and to develop many other valued characteristics.

The Tree is the heart of the people. If people forget its teachings, or choose not to follow its path, or, worse still, wantonly ravage it, they will destroy the quality of their lives. They will cease to dream the dreams of wisdom and empowerment; they will quarrel over trivia; they will lose the ability to be truthful and deal with each other with candour and honesty; they will become filled with pain and rage and depression. In many groups of The People, it was prophesied that this would indeed come to pass. But the Tree will not die. It will live, and one day the people will awaken and search again for it.

Many of The People believe that this prophecy has come to pass and that we live in a time of reawakening, when there is a renewed respect and longing for the wisdom that was perhaps misplaced for many reasons, for many years. This respect and belief that the traditional ways of The People contain truths of great benefit is shared by many of those who are not of The People but who nonetheless recognize that wisdom and the path to a meaningful life may be revealed in ways that are not necessarily of their own heritage. Some of The People feel that the traditional teachings are for all the creatures of the earth since we are all made by the same Creator (e.g., McGaa, 1990). Others of The People are not so sure. Their feeling is that there may be different messages for each group of people, that if the Creator wanted others to have the particular message given to The People, He would have given it to them as well (e.g., Deloria, 1994, 1999).

In 1982, a conference was held in Lethbridge, Alberta in which elders of The People from various communities and groups in North America participated. In their commitment to help their communities to continue to develop meaningful lives and restore the belief systems of The People, they formed the Four Worlds Development Project. One of the endeavours of this project was the publication of the book *The Sacred Tree*, in which they attempted to synthesize common principles of The People across the continent. Here are the twelve basic principles that emerged from their work (Bopp, Bopp, Brown, & Lane, 1984, pp. 26–30):

1. *Wholeness.* All things are interrelated. Everything in the universe is a part of a single whole. Everything is connected in some way to everything else. It is therefore possible to understand something only if we can understand how it is connected to everything else.

2. *Change.* All of creation is in a state of constant change. Nothing stays the same except the presence of cycle upon cycle. One season falls upon the other. Human beings are born, live their lives, die, and enter the spirit world. All things change. There are two kinds of change, the coming together of things (development) and the coming apart of things (disintegration). Both of these kinds of change are necessary and are always connected to each other.

3. *Cycles and Patterns.* Changes occur in cycles or patterns. They are not random or accidental. Sometimes it is difficult to see how a particular change is connected to everything else. This usually means that our standpoint (the situation from which we are viewing the change) is limiting our ability to see clearly.

4. *The seen and the unseen.* The physical world is real. The spiritual world is real. These two are aspects of one reality, yet there are separate laws which govern each of them. Violation of spiritual laws can affect the physical world. Violation of physical laws can affect the spiritual world. A balanced life is one that honours the laws of both of these dimensions of reality.

5. *Human beings are spiritual as well as physical.*

6. *Human beings can always acquire new gifts, but they must struggle to do so.* The timid may become courageous, the weak may become bold and strong, the insensitive may learn to care for the feelings of others, and the materialistic person can acquire the capacity to look within and to listen to his or her inner voice. The process human beings use to develop new qualities may be called *true learning.*

7. *There are four dimensions of "true learning."* These four aspects of every person's nature are reflected in the four cardinal points of the medicine wheel. The four aspects of our being (physical, mental, emotional, spiritual) are developed through the use of our volition. It cannot be said that a person has totally learned in a whole

and balanced manner unless all four dimensions of his or her being have been involved in the process.

8. *The spiritual dimension of human development may be understood in terms of four related capacities*:

> First, the capacity to have and to respond to realities that exist in a non-material way such as dreams, visions, ideals, spiritual teachings, goals, and theories.

> Second, the capacity to accept those realities as a reflection (in the form of symbolic representation) of unknown or unrealized potential to do or be something more or different than we are now.

> Third, the capacity to express these nonmaterial realities using symbols such as speech, art, or mathematics.

> Fourth, the capacity to use this symbolic expression to guide future action—action directed toward making what was only seen as a possibility into a living reality.

9. *Human beings must be active participants in the unfolding of their own potentialities.*

10. *Volition.* The doorway through which all must pass if they wish to become more or different than they are now is the doorway of the will (volition). A person must *decide* to take the journey. The path has infinite patience. It will always be there for those who decide to travel it.

11. *Aid will be given.* Anyone who sets out (i.e., makes a commitment and then acts on that commitment) on a journey of self-development will be aided. There will be guides and teachers who will appear and spiritual protectors to watch over the traveller. No test will be given that the traveller does not already have the strength to meet.

12. *Failure.* The only source of failure on a journey will be the traveller's own failure to follow the teachings of the *Sacred Tree.*

The teachings of the Sacred Tree are concerned with many things, including the nature of the universe and the human being's place in it. From these teachings emerges what the Four Worlds Development Project participants have abstracted as a code of ethics: behavioural guidelines that are universal to all groups of The People. The goal is to move toward harmony and balance in the cosmos. This is the definition of *good.* "What should I do to live a good life?" asks Simon. "You must do as you wish," answers Uncle Herbert. "But many of us live by the guidelines of the Sacred Tree."

The first guideline is to be appreciative. We give thanks for all the good things of life, every morning and every evening. At this time, while giving thanks, we also review our own feelings and actions of the day. The purpose of this is not to gloat over our successes, nor to lay a guilt trip on ourselves for our failings. This is a learning experience. What did we do well? We remember to do that again. What could we have done better? We resolve to improve in that area.

The next guideline is to show respect for all the creations of the earth. Each piece of creation, from the most powerful human being to the smallest grain of sand, is part of the wholeness of creation and must therefore be honoured. Respect is not "earned," according to The People; it is the *right* of every element of the cosmos. Very specific principles can be derived from this, many of which are encompassed by being ecologically aware and involved in preventing pollution and guarding the different species of creatures that share the planet. Other principles can be seen as simple courtesy toward other human beings—*all* other human beings. Respect does not imply liking or agreeing with everyone. We respect others even if we don't like them, even if we think that what they are saying is nonsense and what they have done offends us. Attention must be paid to others simply because they are our fellow creatures. Strangers and outsiders must be treated the same way that friends and family are treated.

We respect the privacy of others. Specifically this means that we must not intrude on people's personal space or touch their possessions without their permission. We do not gossip. The People believe that we must not ask others about personal matters, but by the same token, if we wish to discuss personal matters with others, we should not wait to be asked or coaxed, we should ask if the other person is willing to listen. "May I discuss this with you?" is a question which not only must be asked, but must be answered honestly. If the response is "I would rather you didn't," we need to understand that this is not necessarily a personal rejection, but may be because the other person is busy, preoccupied, troubled, or uncomfortable and cannot give us the attention (i.e., respect) that he or she would like to be able to give at that moment. We respect the other person's desire not to become involved in our story at that moment, if that is his or her wish.

In the view of The People, respect especially needs to be shown when we are working in a group, a committee, or a council. Have you ever been working with others on a project and one person in the group becomes very angry if his or her idea is not adopted? It often ruins the group, doesn't it? The ethical guideline of the Sacred Tree states that when we give our idea in the group, it is no longer our possession. It is now the possession of the group. When all the ideas are the possession of the group, it becomes possible for the group to discuss them objectively and choose which to act on or how to modify an option. If an option is rejected, it is not a rejection of the person who had the idea. After all, without his or her idea, other ideas may not have been conceived. Respect, then, is paid to all in the group. And let's not forget respect for the group as a whole. When the group decides on an option, this decision must be respected. People must not undermine any chance of the decision working well by speaking against the decision outside the group.

Another guideline of respect in the view of The People concerns hospitality. If we have a guest, it is required that the guest be given the best that we have. If we do not have adequate resources or the ability at a particular time to give our best (whether it be food, accommodation, or attention), or if we aren't willing to show respect in this way, we shouldn't entertain. Respect means that we are willing to put ourselves out for the comfort of our guest.

Since a key principle of The People is the unity of creation, it is not surprising that one of the ethical guidelines of the Sacred Tree is that disrespect to one person is disrespect to everyone, including oneself. If one person is hurt, all people are hurt. Injure another and we injure all of us, including ourselves.

In order to have a happy, meaningful life, we need to know ourselves too. We need to know what helps us and what harms us. If we find that, after we listen to alternative music, our mind is refreshed and we feel relaxed and energized, we must, by all means, listen to alternative music. But if listening to alternative music sets our teeth on edge, we must avoid it. "Different strokes for different folks" is a truism for a reason. We must not be swayed by what other people tell us "should" do us good or contribute to our development. They may be right or they may be wrong. We may receive guidance, help, and inspiration from a variety of sources, some of which may be unexpected. But we must not be fooled into believing just what we want to believe. We must listen to what our hearts are *really* telling us. We need to practise moderation and balance in all things. Extremes are never good for us because they limit us, make us obsessive, and isolate us from the wider world of possibilities and relationships within the universe.

And finally, our most important task on earth is to be of service. We must reach out to other elements of creation, to make their existence better. Happiness comes not from what we get, but from what we give.

BOX 4.1

The Twelve Teachings from the Wellbriety Movement

The Wellbriety Movement is a modern Native American approach to wellness and sobriety. It is a unique approach to conquering addiction, formed by Native Americans, that provides twelve teachings with applicability to everyone who wishes to learn from The People's perspective.

1. The honor of one is the honor of all; the pain of one is the pain of all.

2. In order for anything to grow, it must struggle to do so first.

3. All permanent and lasting change starts on the inside, then works its way out.

4. Conflict precedes clarity.

5. Healing takes place when we want it to, choose to, like it, and love it.

6. We move toward and become that which we think about. If we move toward and become like that which we think about, then isn't it time to begin thinking about what we are thinking about?

7. We can be in one of two states of mind: (1) I don't know what I don't know. (2) Now I know what I don't know. If we can get from (1) to (2) we can begin to solve our problems.

8. The leadership systems currently in place to often look at us as our *doing*, and they say *do* differently in order to change. But the Indian way says were [*sic*] not human doings, were [*sic*] human *beings*. If we want to change the *doing* in leadership, I need to change my being. And the way to change my being is to change my intent.

9. They need our love the most when they deserve it the least.

10. Declare healing, not war, on alcohol and drugs. It is not a war on drugs; it is a healing journey!

11. Inside of every human being is the innate knowledge of his or her own well being.

12. The Creator doesn't so much expect you to be successful as he expects you to be faithful.

Source: Coyhis & Simonelli, 2008, p. 1944

The "Psychology" of The People

The scientific world, of which psychology is a part, is basically a reductionist world. We look at the smallest parts and later put them together to see the larger aggregation of parts. That is, we start with the smallest and work our way up to the largest. In botany, for example, we look at the pistil, the stamen, the corolla, the photosynthetic mechanism of the plant, and we hope that this will help us see the place of the plant in the ecosystem. In psychology, we look at the lateral hypothalamus, the ability to recognize the letter A, the behaviour of an organism when the amount of reinforcement is varied, the efficacy of group decision making as compared to individual decision making. And we hope this will help us to understand the whole working of the individual human being. How then do we understand the perspective of The People, who understand the whole and then use this understanding to help determine the position of the smaller parts?

This fundamental difference in worldviews makes it difficult to relate the beliefs of The People to a psychology of personal growth when "personal growth" is regarded as the growth of one person. If you say to a typical psychologist that you are related to a wheat sheaf, he or she will think that you are delusional. If you say to a shaman (a wise and healing person of The People) that you are *not* related to a wheat sheaf, he or she will think that you are delusional!

While the Western view of personal growth implies a *personal gain to the individual* in terms of feeling and functioning within oneself, The People's view of personal growth implies a *cosmic gain to the entire universe* in terms of feeling and functioning better. The individual can only grow and develop in relationship to the universe. Growth means finding better ways to fulfill obligations to others within the universe by becoming better and better at playing one's part in maintaining and enhancing harmony and balance. And this will lead the individual to a personally satisfying life.

Simon, as one of The People, has a rich and fulfilling heritage in the worldview traditionally held by his people. His native heritage is not alone in its richness and differing perspective from that of technological cultures. Let us briefly examine two other perspectives held by indigenous peoples.

AUSTRALIAN INDIGENES

The case of an urban young person such as Simon returning to a traditional environment to learn about his roots is not confined to the Americas. Simon's story could have happened in Australia just as easily. There, too, Indigenous people raised and living in urban environments have sought to understand the fundamental beliefs of their culture. If Simon were an Australian Indigene and his great-uncle Herbert an elder of an Indigenous group, what would he learn?

Origins

Australian Indigenous culture is one of the oldest cultures in the world, some scholars even say the oldest (e.g., Flood, 2006). It dates back at least 40,000 years, but the precise dating is uncertain: it may have been more like 50,000 to 100,000 years (Goosen, 1999). The stories told by the Indigenes say that these people have always been in Australia, that they did not come from some place else, but archaeological evidence makes it fairly certain that settlers from Africa (and perhaps Asia, say some archaeologists such as Thorne and Birdsell, as cited by Flood, 2006) took the first sea voyage to Australia in primitive boats that would probably not withstand a two-way trip.

The earliest Australians had little choice but to settle on the new land since Australia was generally lacking in the materials needed to build watercraft to take them back where they came from (Flood, 2006). They spread across Australia in groups, sometimes maintaining a connection with some groups, but often losing touch with others. Moving inland from the more fertile and hospitable shores, they found a country vastly different from that of their original home: the interior of Australia (the Outback) is generally characterized as arid and desert-like. Even the animals they encountered were strange to them. Who had ever seen the ancestors of a kangaroo or an emu before? Surviving in this land would take intelligence, courage, and hard work. Indigenous development of sustainable land use, many techniques of which have been brought back for use in Australia today, testify to the ability of the people (Gostin & Chong, 2006).

A Caveat

Like the The People of the Americas, Australian Indigenes have an oral tradition, not a written one, so there are no records of earliest cultural traditions. What is known comes from the stories told by Indigenes today who live in traditional groups and settings and from what anthropologists have been able to piece together through talking to these people during their research and through finding artifacts. Very little has been written by Indigenes themselves who study the traditional culture of their people. Moreover, as is the case among The People of the Americas, there is great diversity among groups of Indigenes, yet core beliefs exist among all groups. In this section of the chapter, we will examine what has been generally accepted by scholars today as reflecting the traditional Indigenous worldview and beliefs.

The Dreaming

To understand Indigenous culture, it is necessary to understand the *Dreaming* (or, as sometimes known, the Dreamtime). This is the story of the creation of the world and the story of the world as it exists today and in all time periods.

In the beginning there was matter, perhaps mud-like, perhaps like a flat, featureless plain. Beneath this matter lay dormant the Ancestral Beings or Spirit Beings. They awoke and rose to the surface, taking on forms that were combinations of human, animal, and/or plant. On the surface, they lived very human-like lives, eating, drinking, dancing, hunting, and so on. They created tools and left artifacts. They moved across the plain, leaving traces of their existence in their wake. By their deliberate creation or just by leaving their traces, the Ancestral Beings created the features of the land, such as mountains, streams, rocks, caves, sandhills, and stars. By their activities and their words they also created the model for life, the structure of society, and its rules and rituals. The products of the Dreaming dominate all aspects of traditional Indigenous life (Edwards, 2006; Flood, 2006; Swain, 1995).

The Ancestral Beings are said to be the ancestors of Indigenes and of other species as well, sometimes at the same time. Thus Kangaroo-man is thought to be the progenitor of both one group of Indigenes and of kangaroos. The Ancestral Beings eventually went back into the earth, often through death. But they are still present in the land and in the people, animals, and plants that they spawned. The Dreaming occurred in the distant past, and it occurred in the recent past, and it is occurring today, and it will occur in the future. In fact, the events of the Dreaming are timeless. In Indigenous thought, there is no past, present, or future.

Time

Indigenes do not measure time in a linear fashion. That is, they do not use the concepts of past, present, and future. Life consists of events that may be rhythmical in nature, but are not regarded according to when they took place. The day may contain many changing elements that the people are aware of, but they are not ordered in terms of their occurrence (Swain, 1995).

The Dreaming, say Indigenes, took place in the past, but it is possible to enter into the ongoing reality of those events by performing rituals today. What was in the past is still present, but we may need to invoke spiritual powers to experience it (Edwards, 2006; Flood, 2006; Swain, 1995). If the past is still in the present, that means that the Ancestral Beings are still among us, the features of the land are still being formed, and the "old ways" are not old ways at all, but are as fresh and vibrant as a new creation. The Dreaming is completely relevant to the present because it *is* the present (and what others would call the past and the future).

To the Western mind, the present is this moment that we living right now, but to the Indigene, the present is greatly extended and expanded to include the past. To the Western mind, what we do in the present may influence the future, but the past is immutable. To the Indigene, though, because the present is so greatly extended, actions in the present can influence events in the past. For example, Goosen (1999) relates the brief anecdote concerning a sacred object that was believed to be an artifact of the body of an Ancestral Being. The object was accidentally chipped but no one was allowed to repair it. The reason was that the object had been created from the body of the Ancestral Being, and when the chipping occurred, the Ancestral Being's body was changed. Repairing the object would cause the Ancestral Being's body to be changed yet again, an undesirable state of affairs. Confused? It seems very apparent to Indigenes. Let's put this into more concrete terms; let's say that the Ancestral Being's arm, A^1, became a specific tool, B^1. In Indigenous beliefs, A^1 can *only* produce B^1 and B^1 can *only* be produced by A^1. In becoming chipped, that specific tool B^1 was changed to specific tool B^2. Since B^2 now exists, it must have come from something different from A^1. That means that the Ancestral Being's arm, which became tool B^2, must be different from Ancestral Being's arm A^1. It must be A^2. Chipping the tool in the present must have changed the arm from which it came in the past. Correcting the chip will result in B^3 which would involve changing the arm to A^3 since A^2 can only produce B^2.

The Land

The Ancestral Being came from the precursor of the land and created the features of the land along with the people, the animals, and the plants. In any geographical area, the same Ancestral Being created and continues to create all that is contained in that area: the people, the animals, the plants, and the land itself. In this creation, elements of the

Ancestral Being itself were passed into the creation. Thus, there is something spiritually the same within each part of creation in that area (Edwards, 2006).

Not surprisingly, Indigenes feel a special respect for nature and elements of the Ancestral Being's creation because of their identification with it (deSouza & Rymarz, 2007). While there is deep reverence for all land and all the elements of the earth, there is a special relationship with the elements of the local geographical community. The inseparability of the Indigene from others in his or her community and the other elements of the community mean that the local land and all that it contains are considered sacred. The Indigenes identify with all other elements that were created along with them: according to them, they *are* the land and all the other elements within that land.

The land lives, and direct contact with the earth is spiritually important (Goosen, 1999). The primary duty of the Indigene is to replenish and balance the life-energy of the land that is identified with them. This is done through rituals that ensure the continued existence of the world and all the elements with it. During these rituals, the Indigene becomes linked with the actual experience of the Ancestral Being in the Dreaming (Edwards, 2006).

The idea of the identification of the person with the land and all elements within it also mandates an understanding that other people *are* the land that they live on as well. Archaeologists and anthropologists have yet to find any evidence in the artifacts of the past or the stories of the people that there was ever violence committed because one group of Indigenes wanted to acquire the land (or the power of the land) from another group of Indigenes. This, in fact, would have worked against the would-be conquerors because they would not be able to properly renew the land that was not *them*. The only two known instances of Indigenous groups going to war over territory were clearly affected by colonialization and not by the traditional beliefs of the Indigenes (Swain, 1995).

REFLECTIVE EXERCISE

What if you could change the past?

We know in psychology that our memories of the past are not completely accurate, that we reconstruct events in ways that may or may not reflect what actually happened (see Loftus, 2003, for example). We all imagine sometimes that if certain elements of our past had been different, we might have different outcomes today. For example, one person might remember being raised in a dysfunctional family and bitterly blame that for his or her lack of education today. But if he or she managed to obtain a good education and a fulfilling career, he or she might remember the past more kindly.

Perform a thought experiment: imagine that you could change one element of your past, something no greater than one event or one decision. What difference would it make to your life now? Can you make that difference today? If you can, would it change how you regard the past? Have you "changed" the past in remembering it in a different way? Even if the past isn't changed, does it make you happier to remember it with a different interpretation?

Spirituality and the Self

Similar to The People of the Americas, Australian Indigenes have no word for religion, yet is clear that their traditional belief system is highly spiritual (Goosen, 1999). In fact, like The People of the Americas, there is no division between the spiritual and the secular worlds. The Dreaming occurs in the present, the Ancestral Beings move among and within the people, the living and the dead move in spheres without apparent separation (Cox, 2009). Some people, medicine men and shamans, are believed to possess great psychic and magical abilities, but these abilities are, to some extent at least, possessed by everyone: the medicine men and shamans have only developed their abilities further. Indigenousness, say some Indigenes, *is* spirituality (Cox, 2009).

> The Indigenous world view is essentially *inclusive* or *holistic* [italics in original]. Humans and all natural phenomena, including animals and plants in all their diversity, are seen as equal manifestations of a timeless spiritual or cosmic order.
>
> *(Gostin & Chong, 2006)*

Indigenes' conception of themselves is traditionally different from that of the conception of self held by the Western mind. For people in technological Western cultures, there is a firm and fixed sense of self, separate and different from the body, from the spirit, from other people. For Indigenes, however, the self is part of all other elements of the earth. It has no boundary, nor is it fixed and changeless (Cox, 2009). This expansion of the sense of self is part of the belief that the world is all-inclusive and divisions are false. Thus, Indigenes clearly see the interconnectedness of mind and body and spirit; the living and the dead co-exist; the past is in fact the present; their actions and energy give life to the land, and the land gives back life again to them (Maher, 1999; Swain, 1995; Tse, Lloyd, Petchkovsky, & Manaia, 2005).

The inclusiveness of the sense of self makes it reasonable that Indigenous groups have no leaders, although there are respected elders and individuals who are in charge of some rituals. Hierarchical organization of power would make no sense—"how could you be above me when essentially you are me?" The only way one could gain prestige in this culture might be by deepening one's spiritual understanding and ability. As hunters and gatherers, Indigenes need to travel light, without the burden of anything but bare necessities. Material possessions have little worth beyond their functional value for Indigenes: the accumulation or distribution of material wealth would not be a means of gaining more prestige or power, as it might be in many other cultures (Bourke, 2006; Swain, 1995).

If Simon were an Australian Indigene, he would find that the traditional belief system of his people had similarities with those of The People of the Americas. He would identify himself with something much greater than his singular self—in the Indigenous case, with the land itself and all the elements that spring from the land. He would see the "good life" and his responsibility as a human being to maintain the harmony of the earth, just as he would as a member of The People. Now let's look at what someone like Simon would learn if he were a native African.

THE INDIGENOUS PEOPLES OF AFRICA

When we speak of indigenous peoples, perhaps the only true people who can be said to be indigenous are the natives of Africa. According to anthropologists and archaeologists,

Africa, about three million years ago, was the birthplace of the human race which changed, evolved, and gradually spread from there to other continents (Fortey, 2008). Similar to the native peoples of the Americas and Australia, daily life is not separated from spiritual life. The Supreme Creator, the lesser deities, and the dead are part of everyday life to the African native. There is no division between the seen and the unseen worlds (Asante & Nwadiora, 2007). Religion is primary and all facets of day-to-day life reflect it and are influenced by it (Mulago, 1991).

The Traditional African Worldview

Given the great diversity of African groups, some scholars contend that it is difficult to generalize a traditional African worldview (e.g., Oosthuizen, 1991). Yet some commonalities can be found among the differing beliefs, customs, and rituals.

Primarily, the traditional worldview is that of a holistic universe—the world is really one entity. There is no division made between the seen and the unseen worlds: the unseen world is populated by spirits of the dead and by deities whose aid and intervention take place every day. Nature is also endowed with life and meaning. The beliefs and philosophy are of a practical nature, aimed at maintaining the peace, harmony, and balance of the world so that all the people and other beings of the seen and unseen worlds may survive well and prosper. Individualism is not conducive to survival of the group, so traditional African society revolves around the family, the community, and the rest of the world. Each member of society is valued and is cared for, each member must feel a sense of belonging, and the dignity of the individual is respected because this contributes to the dignity of all beings (Asante & Nwadiora, 2007; Mbiti, 1989; Oosthuizen, 1991; Thomas, 2005).

"In the Western tradition it is taught that 'love is the greatest virtue' but in the African tradition, 'character' seems to be the common virtue accorded that place" (Asante & Nwadiora, 2007, p. 16). The identity or the character of the individual is not an independent inner quality as it is in Western thought. The traditional African viewpoint is that of holism, that the individual and the rest of the cosmos are one. The view of the self in the traditional African worldview, then, is that the self is defined in terms of the relationship or the group that one is in. It extends into the environment and is open to all the elements in the environment. The self is seen as flexible, not static, and changes as the situation or the environment changes. The most satisfying and fulfilling state for the self is to have balance and harmony within the self and between the self and the environment. Maintaining this harmony requires being on good terms with the entire social and spiritual environment (Zuesse, 1991).

Life, in the traditional African worldview, is participation. This includes participation in personal relationships, participation in rituals to the ancestors and the lesser deities, participation in the life of the community, and participation in the maintenance of the balance and harmony of the world.

Since traditional African beliefs include the idea that the entire universe is really one entity, interconnectedness of all things is paramount. Traditional African life is closely tied to nature. Some groups are hunters and gatherers, but many are agriculturalists. In either case, the dependency and understanding of the ways of nature are vitally important to the groups. The earth itself is considered to be a living thing in traditional African belief (Mbiti, 1989; Oosthuizen, 1991; Thomas, 2005; Zuesse, 1991).

Relationships

Relationships, then, are not only important but inevitable. The solitary person who avoids relationships is cut off from all the rest of being and is in danger of diminishing his or her own soul as well as endangering the community (Zuesse, 1991). Clearly, social conflict is to be avoided because this threatens the balance of the world and brings danger to everyone. Good relationships, between people and between people and the deities and ancestors, bring power and order to the world and physical health and prosperity to the group. The fully functioning person is the one who is seen to be well-integrated into society. Objectivity in regarding life and the events in it is not an option (Oosthuizen, 1991; Zuesse, 1991).

The importance of maintaining balance and harmony in the world is so great that to bring discord is considered to be the definition of evil. Every deed must be accompanied by the intention to bring or maintain balance and harmony (Mulago, 1991).

> In this ethical system, individual members of the society had the interest and welfare of the community at heart. They did not go about acting and behaving as though they only lived in the community. They were careful not to do anything that would bring suffering to other members of the society. In that kind of society, it was unthinkable to see the very rich and the very poor co-existing. Such a situation did not arise because the rich were morally expected to share their riches.

(Mbon, 1991, p. 106)

Religion

Religion is part of daily life: it informs the actions and thoughts of the people and regulates the structure of society. Nothing in traditional African belief is *not* religion. (Mbiti, 1989; Thomas, 2005).

According to African tradition, there is one Supreme Creator. The Creator is imbued with immense energy and power, with the ability to restore justice and the balance and harmony of the world. Although the Creator created the laws, ethics, and structure of society before humans were created, he, she, or it (there is no specification of gender, if the term can be applied at all) is not involved in the day-to-day life of mankind. Rather, the Creator retreated from the earth after the creation, leaving lesser deities to manage the affairs of the earth and to assist human beings. The Creator may be called upon by these lesser deities if human beings ask for this, but essentially the Creator remains uninvolved. The Creator, however, is seen to be responsible for major crises, such as devastating thunderstorms. Under these conditions, the Creator may be petitioned directly by the people or by lesser deities or the ancestors to cease interfering in nature, and let the lesser deities, whose purview this is, restore the balance and harmony of the earth (Zuesse, 1991). The lesser deities are not necessarily good or bad—they simply are. Their role is to maintain the balance of the earth, but their involvement in human life depends upon what they are asked for and how they choose to fulfill or deny the wish (Asante & Nwadiora, 2007).

The Ancestors

Of primary importance to the African native are the ancestors. Those who have died remain in touch with their families as long as they are remembered. For this reason, the elderly, who will soon be ancestors, are revered, and having children to remember them is important. The ancestors watch over and protect their families and may be called upon to ask the lesser deities to intercede in the affairs of mankind or ask for special consideration from the Creator. The dead, then, are not removed from the world of the living, but are very much a part of it. Native Africans traditionally pray to (but do not worship) the ancestors, making sacrifices to them of food and material goods as if they were alive, since they are the prime intermediaries to the Divine. Rituals are a highly significant part of traditional African life since it is through ritual that the placation and intercession of the ancestors and the lesser deities are sought. Many of these rituals are officiated by divine kings who gain their divinity by their relationship with the ancestors. Their living humanity and this relationship with the ancestors are believed to make them highly effective as intermediaries between the ancestors and the people (Asante & Nwadiora, 2007; Thomas, 2005).

Rituals

African scholar Douglas E. Thomas (2005) contends that no culture on earth is more ritualized than traditional African culture. It is by rituals that people communicate with the unseen world; it is by rituals that people become members of the society. The fact that rituals are the same each time they are performed adds to the harmony and balance of the earth by their predictability. Their sameness brings a sense of comfort and control to the people and provides the cement that binds the people to each other and to their larger community. We can surmise that these rituals add to the sense of meaning and structure in life, and well-accomplished rituals bring about greater satisfaction and well-being.

Rituals are particularly important in the people's communication with the unseen world. In order to petition or propitiate the deities or the ancestors, rituals must be performed strictly according to the customs of the group, or else the world becomes unbalanced and calamity may strike. If calamity does strike, it may not be to only the individual who did not perform the ritual correctly or who forgot to perform the ritual at all, it may be to the individual's whole community with consequences in perhaps the wider world as well.

If a young man like Simon were to leave an urban dwelling place to reconnect with his African heritage, he would undergo several rituals to cleanse him and to make him part of the group. He would probably spend many years learning the rituals and the proper way to conduct them (Thomas, 2005). His sense of purpose and belonging to something greater than just himself (in the Western view) would be thus enhanced.

Time

The traditional African worldview does not regard time in the linear fashion of past, present, and future as does the Western worldview. Rather, time is measured by event (e.g., the performance of a special ritual for a particular purpose) with a concentration on what has happened and what is happening now. The future is only regarded in a limited sense: all that is important is what will happen in the near, foreseeable future, usually no more than a few months (Mbiti, 1989; Oosthuizen, 1991). Time is not of the urgency typically seen in urban Western cultures and does not control the individual. Thus, to the traditional African, it does not matter if a person is late for an event as long as he or she takes part in it, even for only a short period. The event is vital, not the time one arrives for it (Oosthuizen, 1991).

The traditional African perspective is that of active participation in a vital, dynamic world in which all elements are interconnected. Independence of thought is not an asset in this perspective, but adherence to tradition is more than simply thought to be appropriate: it is critical to the well-being of the individual, the group, and the world. The sense of well-being that an individual strives for is gained by amiable integration and participation in the group and its activities.

REFLECTIVE EXERCISE

To Live in the Present

Life in the Western world seems to be dictated by time. Many people feel almost panicky if they do not know what time it is, and they schedule their lives to the minute. In doing so, they sometimes miss out on the present.

Find a day when you can clear your schedule of the preplanned activities that we all have. Try spending that day fully in the present, without worrying about tomorrow, let alone the more distant future. Take a holiday from time and do what you want, making sure that you stay aware of where you are and what you are doing. This is part of mindfulness, a topic we will pursue in a later chapter because of its relationship with living a satisfying life.

Conclusion

The belief systems and worldviews of the indigenous peoples that we have reviewed in this chapter differ from each other but have much in common. In all these perspectives, the emphasis is on wholeness, the interrelationships between people and between people and the environment. Great respect and care are given to the land, and each element of the environment is considered important and part of each individual's own self and well-being. This may be a logical outcome of groups of people who strive to survive in often unfriendly environmental conditions. The indigenous peoples that we have discussed are not very concerned about their own egos, but they are very concerned about each other and about nature. This is not a completely unknown outlook in the urbanized and technological Western world. Indeed it is an outlook that is coming to be shared more and more by those who are concerned for ecology and who recognize that perhaps the wonderful technological gains that have been made have resulted in our forgetting that there may be more to our worlds than what we can see and possess.

Summary

- To the indigenous peoples of the Americas (The People), change is a necessary and vital component of life.
- To The People, human beings exist within a complex set of relationships with nature. Each element of nature has a role to play and no one role is more important than another.
- The People say that they *are* relationships, not that they *have* relationships. They are also all related or connected to other components of the physical world, including both animate life forms and inanimate geophysical features.
- For The People, there is no separation between religion and other parts of life.
- The land serves as the basis for the identity of The People. Life is understood by *where* it happened, not *when* it happened.
- The People believe in free will.
- For The People, to live a good life means to fulfill one's obligations by maintaining the balance and the harmony of the vast interconnections of the cosmos.
- The journey around the Medicine Wheel symbolizes the journey of life, with lessons and its own spiritual, emotional, physical, and mental gifts at each point along the way.
- The Sacred Tree contains twelve basic principles that are common to The People across North America, providing guidelines for living a fulfilled and satisfying life.
- The People's view of personal growth implies a cosmic gain to the entire universe in terms of feeling and functioning better.
- To Australian Indigenes, the Dreaming (or the Dreamtime) is the story of the creation of the world and the story of the world as it exists today and in all time periods.
- Indigenes do not use the concepts of past, present, and future. Life consists of events that may be rhythmical in nature, but are not regarded according to when they took place.
- To the Australian Indigene, the present is greatly expanded to include the past. Because the present is so greatly extended, actions in the present can influence events in the past.
- The inseparability of the Indigene, from others in his or her community and the other elements of the community means that the local land and all that it contains is considered sacred. They *are* the land and all the other elements within that land.
- The primary duty of the Indigene is to replenish and balance the life-energy of the land that is identified with them.
- For Australian Indigenes, there is no division between the spiritual and the secular worlds.
- Material possessions have little worth beyond their functional value for Indigenes.
- The traditional African worldview is that of a holistic universe. There is no division made between the seen and the unseen worlds.
- Traditional African society revolves around the family, the community, and the rest of the world. Each member of society is valued and is cared for, each member must feel a sense of belonging, and the dignity of the individual is respected.

- Life, in the traditional African worldview, is participation in personal relationships, in rituals to the ancestors and the lesser deities, in the life of the community, and in the maintenance of the balance and harmony of the world.

- The fully functioning person is the one who is seen to be well-integrated into society, in the traditional African worldview.

- Religion is part of daily traditional African life: it informs the actions and thoughts of the people and regulates the structure of society.

- According to African tradition, there is one powerful Supreme Creator who is not involved in the day-to-day life of mankind.

- Day-to-day traditional African life is influenced by lesser deities and the ancestors, the dead relatives of group members.

- It is by rituals that traditional African people communicate with the unseen world and become members of the society.

- By the traditional African worldview, time is measured by events, with a concentration on what has happened and what is happening now. The future is only regarded in a limited sense: all that is important is what will happen in the near, foreseeable future.

- The traditional African perspective is that of active participation in a vital, dynamic world in which all elements are interconnected.

- The emphasis in all these perspectives is on wholeness, the interrelationships between people and between people and the environment. The indigenous peoples of the Americas, Australia, and Africa are not very concerned about their own egos, but they are very concerned about each other and about nature.

Group Discussion Questions

1. In some ways, the beliefs of indigenous peoples of the Americas, Australia, and Africa are reminiscent of Eastern belief systems, such as yoga and Buddhism. What are these similarities? Why do you think such similarities might exist?

2. Some people contend that there is little value in reviving the beliefs and traditions of past traditional cultures, that they have no place in the twenty-first century. What do you think about that? Is there any value in Simon's quest to reconnect with his traditional heritage, for example? What might the value be?

3. To a greater or lesser extent, ritual plays a role in the lives of the groups we have discussed in this chapter. Does ritual play a role in Western life in the twenty-first century? If so, in what ways? Is this of value to Western culture? If not, why not? Should an absence of ritual be mourned in Western culture?

CHAPTER 5

Optimism and Hope

Deep always seems to be smiling. Even when he's working at something difficult, a little smile plays around his lips, as if he were engrossed in something that fascinated him. His marks in university are good, and his professors love him because he looks so attentive and "into" what they are saying. He's certainly the most popular young man in his class: his friends say that just being around him makes them feel better; that he can unfailingly find something positive to say. They like him so much, they try to do nice things for him whenever they can (the surprise birthday party last August was one example). He works hard at his part-time job as a sales clerk, too. His parents aren't well off, and he needs to pay his own way in university, and besides, he says, "Hard work builds character!"

He was surprised that he got the job so easily, but his employer says, "Sales is all about connecting with people, and Deep is the best at that. One look at his smile and the attention he focuses on you and we knew he would be great at this job." Deep plans his day and schedules his activities to make sure he gets done what he needs to get done. He has two or three ideas about every task he undertakes so that if one way doesn't work out, he can move to another with little difficulty. He believes that his life is up to him, and he can "make it" or he can "blow it." He believes he will always make the right choices to "make it." When asked about his plans for the future, Deep says that nursing is the career for him, and he knows if he studies hard enough, he'll be employed at a good hospital and make a difference with his patients.

LEARNING OBJECTIVES

In this chapter, students will learn about

- ☐ The definition of optimism.
- ☐ The differences between optimists and pessimists.
- ☐ The different types of optimism.
- ☐ Tealism and positive illusions.
- ☐ The possible benefits of pessimism.
- ☐ How to increase optimism.
- ☐ The difference between optimism and hope.
- ☐ How hope develops in children.
- ☐ The "broaden-and-build" theory of positive emotions.
- ☐ Self-compassion.

Deep is an optimist and he has hope for his future. More than likely, he will be successful; he already has success in what he does and people are drawn to him. And the more success he has and the more people are drawn to him, the more optimistic and hopeful he feels.

Optimism and hope have been studied by psychologists for several years, and most of the commonsense predictions that can be made seem to be true. If only we could all be as optimistic and hopeful as Deep! In this chapter, we will examine what is known about optimism and hope and determine whether we can increase these qualities in ourselves.

OPTIMISM

The Definition of Optimism

Optimism can be defined as a positive orientation that focuses concentration on the positives of life instead of the negatives. Optimists see the glass as half full, not half empty. For some people, like Deep, optimism is almost a way of life: he concentrates on the positive in all areas of his life. He looks at each event in his life with an eye to how it can teach him something and how he can grow from it. He tackles each task with the belief that he is capable of doing it. He believes that his future may hold disappointments and setbacks but, for the most part, he will have a happy life.

Actually, most of us are at least a little like Deep, especially in individualistic cultures that believe in egalitarianism (Fischer & Chalmers, 2008)—that is, cultures in which the individual's characteristics, needs, and efforts are considered as or more important than those of the group, and each individual is seen as being worth as much and as important as any other. In these cultures, when asked whether we believe that good things will happen to us, most of us answer "yes" (Williams & Gilovich, 2008). In addition, most of us think that we will have more positive things happen to us than will happen to other people (Armor, Massey, & Sackett, 2008; Hoorens, Smits, & Shepperd, 2008; Lench & Ditto, 2008). We make this statement so quickly when asked that it seems that it is an automatic response, occurring without taking factual information into account (Karademas, Kafetsios, & Sideridis, 2007; Lench & Ditto, 2008). We also believe that having an optimistic outlook is the best way to approach life, and we believe that other people should be more optimistic, even if the optimism is unwarranted (Armor, Massey, & Sackett, 2008).

Optimists and Pessimists

It's sometimes taken for granted that pessimism is the opposite of optimism, but this is questionable. There is evidence that optimism and pessimism may be two distinct factors (e.g., Szalma, 2009). That means that one can, conceivably, be both optimistic and pessimistic. For example, Deep may be an optimistic person when it comes to his own life, but when asked about whether he thinks politicians will start to care more about the environment, or whether famine will ever be wiped out, he may answer "Not a chance." Most of us lean more heavily toward optimism or pessimism, though, and we realize that optimists may feel some pessimism, and pessimists may feel some optimism.

Optimists and pessimists differ in another way: optimists are more flexible in allocating their attention than pessimists are. They pick out what is personally useful to attend to rather than spreading their attention in a less efficient manner (Abele & Gendolla, 2007). Greater flexibility is found in their thinking as well, and they expend energy reframing a situation to highlight positive and growth-inducing elements of an unfortunate situation. Deep, for instance, concentrates on ways to be a good student while holding down a part-time job. He doesn't bemoan his fate at having to put himself through school; rather, he views the situation as one that will aid his personal growth. Pessimists, on the other hand, use their energy to distract themselves and deny the failure or disappointment (Scheier, Carver, & Bridges, 2002).

In terms of coping with life, there is a fundamental difference between optimists and pessimists that suggests a major reason why optimists fare better in life than pessimists do. Pessimists concentrate on *avoiding* the situation or task at hand because of their expectation that they will fail. When they conclude that they don't have the resources to achieve a particular goal, rightly or wrongly, they give up (Szalma, 2009). This precludes any possibility of success for them, of course, and reinforces their expectations of failure. They place their attention on coping with their own feelings of failure (**emotion-focused coping**) rather than on coping with the situation or problem at hand (**problem-focused coping**) (Nicholls, Polman, Levy, & Backhouse, 2008; Szalma, 2009).

Optimists, on the other hand, believe that they will succeed and actively approach the situation, looking for different methods of coping with it. They are proactive in their coping, seeking additional information and planning their strategies (Sohl & Moyer, 2009). Because of their expectations of success, they are more motivated to try another strategy if one method of dealing with the situation fails. This utilizes the flexibility in their thinking and activity in putting their thinking into action. Naturally, in doing this they are more likely to experience success than pessimists are, and this success further reinforces their expectations of success (del Valle & Mateos, 2008; Geers, Wellman, Helfer, Fowler, & France, 2008).

Deep is an excellent example of optimistic coping. He looks at the events in his life as challenges that he is capable of dealing with, and he has concrete plans for handling these challenges. Deep even has contingency plans in case his initial plans don't work out! It may look like success comes readily to Deep, but as we come to know him, we realize that success comes because of Deep's actions. He is young man who feels confident and prepared to manage whatever life throws at him. His optimism is not unfounded.

We sometimes think of optimists as being "cock-eyed" and persistent in trying to achieve goals even when it is clear to us that the goal is unattainable. We are wrong in this assumption. Optimists do persist longer than other people, but they adjust their behaviour to the situation at hand and quit trying to complete a task when it is obvious that they are knocking their heads against a stone wall (Weber, Vollman, & Renner, 2007). They also use humour to deal with their failures and disappointments more than pessimists, who tend to focus on their unhappiness with the situation (Scheier, Carver, & Bridges, 2002). All in all, optimists feel better about their lives; they are happier people (Scheier, Carver, & Bridges, 2002), and it has been demonstrated that they are healthier people (Seligman, 2002). Box 5.1 summarizes some of the differences between optimists and pessimists.

Optimism has been studied in various ways, and the first notable distinction that we must make is between dispositional optimism and explanatory optimism.

Dispositional Optimism

When life is not clear-cut, do you expect a good outcome? Are you typically optimistic about your future? Do you expect more good things than bad things to happen to you? These questions are the core of a small, commonly used test of dispositional optimism called the Life Orientation Test (Revised) created by Scheier, Carver, and Bridges (1994). If you answered yes to these questions, you have dispositional optimism.

Dispositional optimism is considered a personality trait that disposes people to see the positives in life more than the negatives. It may be that we are born with a certain biological predisposition that supports the development of optimism (Isen, 2005; Schulman, Keith, & Seligman, 1993; Taylor, Dickerson, & Klein, 2005), but certainly it is affected by the environment in which we grew up and the environment we presently live in (Määttä, Nurmi, & Stattin, 2007; Peterson & Steen, 2009; Segerstrom, 2007). Dispositional optimism is general: it affects all or most aspects of our lives with the tendency to look for the good. This doesn't mean that we can't see the down side of life. Of course we can. But we don't see the negative things in our lives as events or parts of life that will always make us unhappy or that we can't overcome. In fact, people with dispositional optimism feel that many, if not most, of the events of life are within their control, and they can do something to make the negativity go away or avoid it in the future (Grote, Bledsoe, Larkin, Lemay, & Brown, 2007; Ruthig, Hanson, & Marino, 2009). Instead of concentrating on past experiences, they set their sights on future goals and how they will achieve them (Zhang, Fishbach, & Dhar, 2007).

Deep has dispositional optimism. He knows that he must work longer hours than students who have wealthy parents who finance their education, but he believes that his hard work will make him appreciate his education more and give him valuable skills for the future. He knows that if he persists on this route, he won't always have to work such long hours. When he comes home tired from his sales job, but knows that he still needs to put in a couple of hours studying, he says to himself, "You can do this. It will all be worth it. Life is pretty good right now, and it's going to be even better in the future." As we shall see, he's probably right.

BOX 5.1

Differences between Optimists and Pessimists

Optimists:	Pessimists:
see the glass as half full	see the glass as half empty
are more flexible in allocating attention	are more rigid in allocating attention
are more flexible in thinking	are more rigid in thinking
reframe situations to highlight the positive and growth	distract themselves or deny the situation
approach problems	avoid problems
use problem-focused coping	use emotion-focused coping
use humour to deal with setbacks	concentrate on their unhappiness when confronted with setbacks
experience greater feelings of well-being	experience fewer feelings of well-being

---

The Benefits of Dispositional Optimism

Research has found that optimists like Deep have a greater sense of well-being in life (Ho, Cheung, & Cheung, 2010; Karademas, 2007). In addition, they get higher grades in school (Määttä, Nurmi, & Stattin, 2007; Ruthig, Hanson, & Marino, 2009). They also show better athletic performance (Gordon, 2008; Nicholls, Polman, Levy,

& Backhouse, 2008). At work, they earn higher salaries and more job promotions (Segerstrom, 2007). In their personal lives, they have a wider, more supportive social network and more social interest (Barlow, Tobin, & Schmidt, 2009), and they have happier marriages (Batool & Khalid, 2009). They are physically healthier and live longer (Brummett, Helms, Dahlstrom, & Siegler, 2006; Brydon, Walker, Wawrzyniak, Chart, & Steptoe, 2009; Steptoe, O'Donnell, Marmot, & Wardle, 2008), showing more tolerance for pain (Geers, Wellman, Helfer, Fowler, & France, 2008; Rosenberger, Kerns, Jokl, & Ickovics, 2009).

A great deal of research has demonstrated that people with dispositional optimism handle stress more effectively (Baldwin, Kennedy, & Armata, 2008; Brodhagen & Wise, 2008; Lai, 2009; Steptoe, O'Donnell, Marmot, & Wardle, 2008; Tusaie, Puskar, & Sereika, 2007). This may be part of the reason why they tend to have better mental health (Burris, Brechting, Salsman, & Carlson, 2009; Grote, Bledsoe, Larkin, Lemay, & Brown, 2007; Hirsch, Wolford, LaLonde, Brunk, & Morris, 2007).

REFLECTIVE EXERCISE

Can you make good things happen to you?

Now that you know that optimists attract several positive outcomes to themselves because of their optimism, can you take advantage of this in your own life? Even if you aren't an optimist, try reacting as if you were an optimist in one area of your life, and see what happens. For example, take the attitude that you will be able to master the material in one course that you are taking and will do well on the next test. You might find that this makes studying a little easier and it might reduce anxiety at the test, leading to improved performance.

Do you want to lose a few pounds or become physically fit? Find a healthy diet or exercise program (one that your physician approves of for you), and start it with the attitude that the program will work and that you will be able to stick to the program despite daily setbacks. Is it easier to stick with the plan? Is it working? Note that an optimistic attitude isn't enough—you must also plan how you will execute your studying, dieting, exercising, and so on, and consider contingency plans for the setbacks that will inevitably occur. Try acting like an optimist in just one area for a month (maybe a month is too optimistic! How about a week?) and evaluate the results. You may find that the exercise is worth continuing!

Some of the beneficial effects of optimism are, in part, because of a self-fulfilling prophecy. As we have seen with Deep, he gained a part-time job and is successful in it because of his optimism. Without this optimism, Deep might never have even applied for a job as a sales clerk since it is something he had never done before. Without his apparent optimism, his employers might not have hired him since they admit that his sunshine smile and attention to people made him the top candidate for the job. Without his optimism, Deep might get fed up with working at a part-time job while being a full-time student and quit one of these enterprises. Without his optimism, Deep might never finish his nursing training, never attaining the job he wants and making a difference to other people who need him. Without his optimism, Deep might not have such staunch and caring friends. It even seems that part of the reason that optimists like Deep have better health and live longer is because they take better care of themselves, eating better, exercising, sleeping more, and refraining from drugs, alcohol, and smoking (Burris, Brechting, Salsman, & Carlson, 2009; Lai & Cheng, 2004). So it seems that being optimistic makes us believe that good things will happen, and good things happen because we are optimistic!

Explanatory Optimism

If something good happens to you, like getting a good mark on a test or being hired for the job you want, how do you explain it to yourself? Do you say "I worked hard and it paid off," or do you say "Wow, I got lucky on that one!"? What if your car breaks down when you are the way to school? Do you tell yourself that it was "just one of those things" and perhaps you need to maintain the car a little better? Or do you curse and tell yourself that, as usual in your life, whatever can go wrong, will? The way you explain life's occurrences reflects your explanatory style.

Martin Seligman (2002, 2006) conceived of optimism as an explanatory style. He reflected on his own earlier work, which demonstrated that a sense of helplessness could be learned by having many experiences that the individual cannot change or affect in any way. This helplessness can be a forerunner of depression for some people. He also noted the work of cognitive behaviourists who examined the statements that depressed people make to themselves, statements such as "You're so stupid. You never do anything right. Your whole life is a disaster and there's nothing you can do about it." These statements are indicative of faulty thinking and irrational beliefs on the depressed person's part. They omit any reference to the role of the environment in the person's behaviour, they assume that every aspect of life is bad for the person (a situation rarely found in fact), and they suggest that nothing will ever change for the person, whereas one constant in life is that everything changes!

In order to help these depressed people, cognitive behavioural clinicians teach them to replace their faulty thoughts with more logical and upbeat ones. For example, instead of saying to oneself "My whole life is a disaster," the individual would be taught to say "This aspect of my life may not be going so well, but other aspects of my life are really looking good!" (Take a look at Box 5.2 for some more examples of the irrational beliefs that people hold and the more rational beliefs that could replace them.) As people become accustomed to saying more realistic and positive things to themselves, they begin to feel less depressed and less helpless to change their lives and their outlooks. Seligman reasoned, then, that something that looks like optimism can be learned. His book, *Learned Optimism* (2006), made this idea clear and provided people with both an understanding of optimism as an explanatory style and the techniques to increase one's usage of an optimistic explanatory style to create a happier life.

Explanatory optimism is the tendency to explain life's events within a positive framework of expecting life to work out in a constructive way. People with dispositional optimism usually also have explanatory optimism, but not always. For example, Deep might try to learn Latin, a subject that he has never tried before, and find he has no real gift for it. He might then quit, saying to himself, "You are a major loser when it comes to Latin!" Yes, he is saying something negative to himself, but examine how he does this: he narrows his self-condemnation to one single area, one that probably isn't very important to him. His sense of self-worth and his belief in his abilities aren't really affected, but he probably won't waste time trying to master Latin anymore! So it seems that explanatory optimism can be used by people with dispositional optimism to reflect their disposition, but explanatory pessimism might keep them from persisting on a task that can't be done, isn't worth doing, or won't turn out well. Box 5.3 illustrates the possible combinations of dispositional and explanatory optimism and pessimism.

BOX 5.2

Irrational beliefs—do you hold any of these beliefs?

Irrational: Everybody has to like me.

Rational: Nobody is liked by everybody. It's great that I have so many wonderful people in my life who do like me.

Irrational: I have to get an A on every test.

Rational: It's nice to get As on tests, but the important thing is that I do my best and that I value the learning.

Irrational: There's no point in playing a sport if you aren't going to win.

Rational: Sports are fun and good for you; winning is less important.

Irrational: If my boyfriend/girlfriend gets angry with me, I know the relationship will soon be over.

Rational: Every couple disagrees now and then. If we work this out, our relationship could be stronger than ever.

Irrational: If my children are upset with me, it's obvious that I'm not a good parent.

Rational: All children get upset with their parents sometimes. That doesn't reflect on my parenting abilities.

Irrational: If my significant other loved me, he/she would always know when I'm upset and what I'm upset about.

Rational: My significant other isn't a mind reader. He/She is very responsive as long as I tell him/her what's wrong.

Irrational: I deserve to be happy.

Rational: I deserve the chance to pursue happiness.

Irrational: I can't be well-adjusted because I had a rotten childhood.

Rational: I can learn and grow from the childhood I had and become well-adjusted and compassionate because of it. It's my choice.

Irrational: If I got plastic surgery and/or lost weight, I would be completely happy with my life.

Rational: Maybe plastic surgery and/or weight loss would be beneficial, but that wouldn't make me miraculously happy and satisfied with my life. My happiness needs to come from inside me.

The Need to be Realistic

This brings us to a point that Seligman emphasized, and that other researchers, such as Schneider (2001), have found data to support: optimism must be realistic to be useful. It isn't useful to tell oneself that a situation is rosy when it isn't. Doing that would probably mean that we wouldn't take the necessary steps to make things better that need improving. In day-to-day life, we find people saying that they don't need to see the physician for that little lump or that their children would never use illegal substances, for instance, only to find, when it's too late to do anything about it, that they had been like the proverbial ostriches with their heads stuck in the sand and now they must deal with very unpleasant consequences.

BOX 5.3

Dispositional and Explanatory Optimism and Pessimism

	Dispositional	**Explanatory**
Optimist	Sees the world, in general, optimistically and typically uses optimism in explaining both general and particular events.	May or may not have dispositional optimism; uses optimism to explain only select events.
Pessimist	Sees the world, in general, pessimistically and typically uses pessimism in explaining both general and particular events.	May or may not have dispositional pessimism; uses pessimism to explain only select events.

Peterson (2006) reminds us of the American folklore tale of John Henry, a railroad worker who competed in a race with a steam-powered machine to drive spikes. John Henry won, but he died of a heart attack in doing so. **John Henryism** refers to a belief that one can achieve anything if one works hard enough and long enough. Many children are told the John Henry moral (but not the whole story) by their parents, who mean to encourage children to learn persistence and determination. Certainly it reflects optimism because it foretells the successful attainment of any goal based solely on the work the individual puts in, a factor within the individual's control. The problem with the belief is that it isn't true: there are often elements beyond our control that influence whether we will attain certain goals or not. For example, I am 5′3″ have short legs, and a chubby (but cute!) little body. If my dream had been to become a professional basketball player, I could have put all my time and energy into refining my basketball skills at the expense

---

REFLECTIVE EXERCISE

John Henryism

Were you one of the many children who was told that you could "be anything you want"? How do you feel about that statement now? Can you think of occupations that, no matter how much you might want them, would be closed to you for reasons beyond your control? Have you found that perhaps this isn't much of an issue for you because what you want happens to coincide with your talents anyway? (This is likely to occur—we are usually more attracted to areas that we are good at!)

What will you say to your own children? Will you tell them that they can be anything they want in order to encourage and motivate them? Is there a better, more realistic way that children can be encouraged and motivated?

of learning other skills and pursuing other endeavours. My physical being may allow me to become a good player, but never at the level required for a professional team. Even though I can control how much I practise my basketball skills, I can't control my height or the length of my legs, and aiming for something that will depend on elements that I can't control is likely to break my heart. That's the problem with John Henryism: it can lead people to waste their lives chasing something that was always unattainable, while they miss all the potential joys and achievements they could have had pursuing attainable goals.

The bottom line is that optimism is more likely to be beneficial when it is realistic— that is, when we have the reasonable expectation that we have the ability and the resources available to affect a situation that is controllable, optimism is related to our success in attaining a goal and our happiness and fulfillment along the way.

Positive Illusions

Most of us have **positive illusions**. That is, people typically see themselves in a more positive light than is perhaps warranted. Several researchers have examined this phenomenon and confirm that it is found in most psychologically healthy people across most cultures (Fischer & Chalmers, 2008; Gold, 2008). Specifically, we believe our personal attributes and our past behaviour are better than that of most other people (e.g., we are more honest, more generous, a better friend than most other people). We see ourselves through a mist of self-enhancement. Also, we believe that we have more control over events than we really do, especially good events. That is, we believe, unrealistically, that we can make good things happen to us or make bad events better, but we don't believe that we are responsible for bad events occurring. And we believe that the future will be more positive for us than is realistically valid; we believe that other people will have normal futures, with a mix of good and bad events, but that we will experience mainly good events in our futures.

These beliefs begin early in life, with parents modelling and fostering these ideas (Carr, 2007). We don't realize we hold these positive illusions, for the most part, and we encourage other people to be more optimistic, even if the optimism is based on unrealistic beliefs (Armor, Massey, & Sackett, 2008).

Actually, mildly depressed people tend to be more realistic and accurate in their judgments of themselves and life in general than are people who are not depressed: they hold fewer positive illusions. Their more realistic beliefs are called **depressive realism** (Allan, Siegel, & Hannah, 2007; Blanco, Matute, & Vadillo, 2009; Whitton, Larson, & Hauser, 2008; Yeh & Liu, 2007). This means that mildly depressed people don't see themselves or their futures as being better or rosier than other people's, they believe that they will have mix of good and bad experiences in their lives, they don't believe that they have more control over situations in their lives than they really do, and they are more likely to take personal responsibility for any failure they experience. Often these people have been referred to as "sadder but wiser." It seems that this "wisdom," or at least the greater accuracy in perceiving oneself and life in general, comes at quite a cost—sadness. Is it worth it? Before you read more about positive illusions, do the reflective exercise on the next page.

Are positive illusions necessarily a bad thing? Probably not, in general. After all, evaluating ourselves more positively than other people makes us feel good and unique, more comfortable in our own skins. If we feel that we can control events, we will work harder to do so, and in situations that can be controlled, that's very useful. If we feel that we can take bad situations and make them better, we are more likely to be able to find meaning and grow when bad things happen to us (more on this in Chapter 8).

REFLECTIVE EXERCISE

Is accuracy worth it?

Before you read on, consider the question seriously. Is being completely realistic and accurate in our self-appraisals and our appraisals of life really worth the sadness that may accompany it? Have there been times in your life when you were told "the truth" and it had no effect but to hurt you?

(People sometimes do that—hide cruelty behind a smokescreen of "honesty.") Do positive illusions about yourself and life make your life better or worse? In what areas of your life would you like to be completely realistic? In what areas of your life do you think that a few positive illusions might be beneficial?

Optimists have been found to be more effective and more likely to make meaning of bad events, even a diagnosis of cancer (Matthews & Cook, 2009; Pinquart & Fröhlich, 2009), and it has even been suggested that meaning-making is critical for optimism (Ho, Cheung, & Cheung, 2010). Feeling that we have no control over events increases stress and anxiety for us, while feeling that we have control and asserting it decreases stress (Gold, 2008; Nevid & Rathus, 2007). If we believe that our future is bright, we have the courage and the desire to go on in life, and we do better in life (Ruthig, Hanson, & Marino, 2009).

So it sounds like positive illusions benefit us in many ways. In fact, when a crisis hits that shatters our positive illusions, indicating to us that perhaps we are not as great as we think we are, that we can't control life events as much as we think we can, and that the future may not be quite as rosy as we want, we may feel great stress and even depression (Carr, 2007).

But let's not take this too far. The positive illusions that can be helpful to us are not really wildly unrealistic. After all, we're not assuming that we're perfect or that our futures will be perfect, and we recognize that there are some things we can't control. If our positive illusions were completely unrealistic, we would have problems. For example, if we think we are perfect, we have no motivation to correct any flaws and to grow as human beings. If we believe our futures will be perfect, we will impose unrealistic expectations on ourselves and the other people who make up our lives now and will make up our lives in the future. We will also feel very badly, perhaps even cheated or betrayed, when future events turn out to have their ups and downs. If we believe we can control everything, we will feel guilty and responsible when our best efforts fail to make life perfect. So if our positive illusions are extreme and grandiose, they may harm us, but if they are kept within moderation, we can profit from them.

Is Pessimism Ever Good?

Perhaps not "good," but not necessarily so bad. I have a student who says "I know I always do well on tests, but I go into each one expecting to do badly." My student is guarding against disappointment by using **defensive pessimism**, a type of negative thinking that directs anxiety about possible failure into productive action (del Valle & Mateos, 2008; Norem & Chang, 2002).

Defensive pessimists usually do as well at tasks as optimists do (Lim, 2009; Norem & Chang, 2002; Seery, 2008), but they are unlike optimists, who expect good outcomes and worry very little about the possibility of failure. Defensive pessimists expect failure, and they worry about the situation. They feel anxiety and lowered self-esteem, with their focus on everything that could go wrong (Norem & Chang, 2002). Defensive pessimists' expectations of themselves and their abilities are low, but they prepare for a task in a thorough manner.

Defensive pessimism has the effect of making it easier to deal with failure or disappointment, if it does come, because it was anticipated and not a shock: if you expect to fail, success comes as a pleasant surprise. The performance of defensive pessimists on tasks benefits from their defensive pessimism because they harness the energy engendered by the anxiety and channel it into success strategies and planning ways to prevent the worst-case scenario that they fear will arise (Lim, 2009; Norem & Chang, 2002; Seery, 2008). My defensively pessimistic student, for example, says that she studies extra hard so that "when I fail, I'll feel that it was mostly my fault but not *completely* my fault." Of course, with the hard work she puts in, she doesn't fail; she does well. And then she has the reward of a pleasant surprise!

Although pessimism may sometimes work for us, it is wise to remember the words of essayist and poet Ralph Waldo Emerson in his poem "Borrowing":

Some of the hurts you have cured,
And the sharpest you still have survived.
But what torments of grief you endured
From evils that never arrived!

(Ralph Waldo Emerson, 1912)

Can We Become More Optimistic?

Yes, definitely, says Martin Seligman. His books, *Learned Optimism* (2006) and *Authentic Happiness* (2002), outline techniques that any of us can use to increase our optimism. Recall that Seligman concentrates on explanatory optimism. He contends, along with some of those who contributed to the development of cognitive behavioural therapy (e.g., Albert Ellis, Aaron Beck), that our mood states depend greatly on how we explain events to ourselves and what statements we make to ourselves about ourselves and our abilities. Pessimists seem to regularly say negative, defeatist statements to themselves, statements that reflect a belief that bad things will *always* happen to them (i.e., **stable causes**), that bad things will happen in *every* area of their lives (i.e., **global causes**), and that the bad things stem from *traits of the individual* rather than from external factors (i.e., **internal causes**).

The trick to increasing optimism, says Seligman, is to learn to omit those broad negative statements and replace them with ones that are more positive and realistic.

These statements would recognize that having one bad event happen does not mean that bad events will always happen (i.e., replace unrealistic stable causes with the more realistic thought that bad things are temporary and are happening just this once). They would also recognize that bad events are not as pervasive as the pessimist has claimed (i.e., replace global causes with statements that reflect that the bad event has been specific to one area of life), and that sometimes external factors have more to do with the occurrence of bad events than the individual's personality traits (i.e., replace internal causes with external causes).

In order to do this, Seligman (2002, 2007) has devised the **ABCDE technique** to use whenever you find yourself thinking something negative and defeatist. To make this technique clear, let's use the example of Delia, a friend of Deep's and a pessimist. She is a student who failed a test and is now thinking "I'm so stupid. I'm never going to pass this course or get my degree. I'll probably never be able to support myself, let alone a family! What a loser!" Here's how the ABCDE technique works:

A. *Adversity*. First identify what set off this train of thought. That's the event that triggered the pessimistic thought. In Delia's case, the adversity was the failed test.

B. *Belief*. What are the beliefs about the adversity? What do you think caused the adversity? What do you believe the adversity indicates about the rest of your life and your future? Delia believes that the failed test is because of her overall intellectual inadequacy and further proves that she is intellectually inferior. Her belief is that a single failed test indicates that she will fail in all other tests, other courses, in any academic pursuit, and in any job-related pursuit in the future.

C. *Consequences*. What are the results of holding these beliefs? Does this attitude serve you well or ill? For Delia, the consequences of holding these beliefs about one failed test are very negative: she feels badly about herself and her prospects for the future, and her motivation to try harder or to find different study techniques is probably decreased.

D. *Disputation*. Look back on your beliefs. Are they logical? Are they true? If they aren't logical and true, argue with yourself. Seligman suggests practising disputation using the following strategies:

a) Ask yourself if there is any real evidence to support these beliefs. Is there evidence to the contrary? In Delia's case, there is no evidence that one failed test foreshadows complete academic and occupational failure in the future. On the contrary, there are millions of people who fail a test and move on to wonderful achievements. And Delia, herself, has clearly passed tests and done well academically before, since she is now in university.

b) In disputing the beliefs, ask yourself as well whether there are other, better ways of looking at the situation. For example, there are many reasons a person could fail a test, and several reasons could be applicable to each particular case. Pessimists tend to regard the worst possible reason as being the only valid one instead of recognizing that many factors played a part in the situation. Delia, for instance, is regarding the reason for her failure as her lack of intelligence. But she could regard the failed test as an indication that her study methods need changing, that she didn't have enough sleep the night before the test, that the course was more difficult than she had realized, that the professor's questions were of a kind that she was not familiar with, and so on. These factors all probably affected Delia's performance, and these are factors that she can control in the future and that don't need to rob her of her self-esteem and motivation.

c) In your disputation, examine whether the implications of your beliefs are realistic and valid, or whether they are imagining a catastrophe that is unlikely to occur. Delia believes that one failed test means failure forever. Really, Delia? Isn't that a little far-fetched?

d) Seligman also suggests that disputation include a look at how useful the beliefs are. He suggests that even if a belief were true, if it isn't useful, if it doesn't assist you in functioning in day-to-day life or in your personal growth, it isn't worth it. Believing that one failed test dooms her entire future and proves her lack of intelligence is not useful for Delia: it can't bring about any possibility of Delia doing anything to change the situation or even to cope with it. The belief's cost is far greater than any benefit it might have.

E. *Energization.* After you dispute your negative and irrational beliefs, you will undoubtedly find yourself feeling better. You will be more positive and more motivated to try again. Delia will feel the disappointment of a failed test, but she will probably also feel an increased determination to do better in the future, and she will most likely be very active in a search for new study strategies and ways of maximizing her own potential.

Seligman suggests following the ABCDE technique whenever adversity, major or minor, hits you. In the beginning, it may be more useful to write down each step. As you become more practiced, the technique will become habit and you will automatically re-form your beliefs into more reasonable and useful self-statements. You will, in fact, form the habit of explanatory optimism!

To get more information on this and other areas of positive psychology, you might want to register (for free!) at Martin Seligman's website, *Authentic Happiness* (www.authentichappiness.sas.upenn.edu). On this website you will be able to take a number of psychological tests, including an optimism test, which will be scored for you online. At the same time, your scores will be used anonymously in Dr. Seligman's research.

HOPE

It would seem, on the surface, that hope is inextricably tied to optimism. After all, both optimism and hope seem to be about believing that the future is glowing and goals can be achieved. Some researchers feel that this is so (e.g., Rand, 2009; Seligman, 2002, 2006), but most researchers feel that this is not necessarily the case. Hope, as conceptualized by many positive psychologists, contains elements that are not always found in optimism. The two concepts are related, but they are not the same (Barlow, Tobin, & Schmidt, 2009; Hirsch, Wolford, LaLonde, Brunk, & Morris, 2007; Wong & Lim, 2009).

Hope Theory

Snyder (1998, 2002; Bailey & Snyder, 2007; see also Rand & Cheavens, 2009, for a review) formulated *hope theory*, a theory that defines hope as being goal directed and as having two components, **agency** and **pathways**. Agency is the motivational factor that leads the hopeful person to say "I can do this." So Deep, who wants an education, says to himself, "I know it will be a challenge, but I'm going to be able to work part time and be a good student." If that were all Deep did, it probably wouldn't get him very far. It would be like wanting to be physically fit while never exercising! The pathways portion of hope leads Deep to formulate strategies and plans for getting where he wants to go. This is the cognitive and active component that gives Deep a means to achieve his goal. So, according to Snyder, **hope** is "a pattern of thinking in which a person has both the capacities to find routes to desired goals (called pathways thinking) and the motivation to use those routes (called agency thinking)..." (Bailey & Snyder, 2007, p. 234).

The pathways portion of hope makes it unlike optimism: with optimism, we can believe that good things will happen to us, but we don't necessarily have a plan for achieving them. Consider the optimist who believes that an outside force, such as a deity or parents or a mentor, will smooth the way for him or her. This person may never put much effort into any endeavour, may never fulfil his or her potential, and is more likely than not going to be disappointed at some point in life. So, for example, we could optimistically say "I know I'm going to get a good job" without getting a skill or an education or even applying for a job. We may base our belief on faith alone, that "the universe will unfold" for us, and the job of our dreams will be waiting for us as soon as we're ready. We may have the agency, but not the pathways. That means that the optimism may be unrealistic, as in cases we have already seen. Hope may be unrealistic as well if our goals are unachievable and our plans for getting them are inadequate, inappropriate, or we don't implement them. But at least we have a chance!

Similarly, a pessimistic person may still have hope. "I'm pretty sure this isn't going to work, but I'm going to try anyway," the pessimist might say. The pessimist, then, has a goal that he or she finds worthwhile and recognizes that, even if the odds are against him or her, there is a marginal chance of success. If the pessimist has the motivation to try to achieve a goal (agency) and a strategy to use to achieve the goal (pathways), he or she has hope.

The Benefits of Hope

Hope is a vital component of an active and satisfying life and is considered a key psychological strength (Harris & Larsen, 2007; Park & Peterson, 2006; Valle, Huebner, & Suldo, 2006). Without hope, there is no reason to do anything. Hope has been found to be the major factor in motivating goal-oriented behaviour and is highly useful for the achievement of goals and in dealing with events that are within the individual's control (Rand, 2009). Even in small children, hope is positively related to happiness (Park & Peterson, 2006). When people lose hope, depression may follow and even suicidal behaviour can occur (see, for example, O'Connor & Cassidy, 2007). When a person has been given the diagnosis of a terminal illness, hope remains. Perhaps now the hope is not for a miracle cure, but for other important elements in the person's life. For example, many terminally ill people who have accepted that their lives will end soon retain the hope that their deaths will be painless and dignified, that they will be able to finish any uncompleted tasks, that they will have a chance to say what they want to say to their loved ones (see Hadad, 2009 for a review of this). The goals may change, but the hope remains.

Sometimes, helping people increase their hope is an effective way to facilitate their coping with several of life's stresses. Harris and Larsen (2007) at the University of Alberta conducted research on hope and coping with HIV. They reviewed literature that indicates that people with HIV who have hope perceive their health to be better, actually have better health, and adjust better emotionally to their diagnosis than those without hope. Harris and Larsen specifically examined the use of peer counselling in helping people with HIV gain more effective coping strategies and found that fostering hope was an integral part of the effectiveness of the counselling. Those who were counselled explained that their hope had been increased by the acceptance shown them by the counsellors: their future might not hold a cure for HIV, but it would hold social support, they would not be alone, they would not be misunderstood, they would not be uncared for. The peer counsellors, having HIV themselves, were both models and mentors, demonstrating coping techniques and inspiring hope by their own examples. Not only did those being counselled benefit, but the counsellors also reported feeling inspired and worthwhile through their ability to increase the hope in others. Counselling others increased their own hope that they could have meaning in their lives and do something worthwhile for others—their HIV status conferring a benefit in this case rather than a liability.

REFLECTIVE EXERCISE

What role does hope play in your life?

You should have some indication of whether or not you are a hopeful person by now. What do you hope for? Do you have hope in the way that hope theory defines hope? That is, do you have agency and pathways, the motivation and the strategies? Do you have "wish" or "will, " in Rollo May's (1969, 1981) terms?

If you find that you are a little lacking in either agency or pathways, can you think of ways to increase this? Can you find more routes to your goals? If you can, does this make you feel more hopeful? Do you think this increases your chances of attaining your goals?

THE DEVELOPMENT OF OPTIMISM AND HOPE

We have seen how to increase optimism and hope, but how is it that some people seem to be optimistic and hopeful from the time they are small children? What fosters these strengths in children? The answer is that, in general, we can say that optimistic and hopeful parents have optimistic and hopeful children.

Children may not be born with optimism and hope, but they can acquire it. Certainly the most influential people in a child's life are his or her parents. Parents nurture and guide their children and, perhaps most profoundly, they serve as role models for their children. As infants, children form attachments or bonds with their primary caretakers.

Attachment

In classic research, Mary Ainsworth and her colleagues (1978, 1979) described three basic patterns of attachment that might be developed, depending on how the caretaker has interacted with the child. *Securely attached* babies have caretakers who are responsive to them and encourage their babies' exploration. These babies, in turn, are able to leave their caretaker's side happily to explore the surrounding environment, using the caretaker as a home base to which they may return for comfort before venturing forth again. Securely attached babies are rarely angry and are typically cooperative.

Avoidant children have caretakers who are not responsive to their needs and impose a great deal of control over their children. These babies are often angry but don't seek the caretaker for comfort, usually actively avoiding him or her.

Other caretakers are inconsistent in their interactions with their children, sometimes being responsive and encouraging, and sometimes being non-responsive and controlling. These children are often what Ainsworth called *ambivalent* babies, who tend to be anxious, reacting to the caretaker with mixed signals, reaching out for contact while squirming away from it. From these descriptions, we can surmise that children learn different things in the course of their lives about what to expect from relationships.

Securely attached children seem to have learned that it is safe and exciting to explore the world, that there is someone at home base to guard and protect, to comfort and soothe, providing a safe haven to return to and find encouragement and solace. In exploring the world, the child inevitably encounters obstacles and barriers that he or she must find a way to handle. In successfully maneuvering around obstacles and overcoming barriers, the child learns "I can do this!" and "I'm picking up some techniques to use," that is, optimistic thinking and hopeful agency and pathways. It is little wonder that people who were securely attached in childhood become more optimistic and hopeful adults (Shorey, Snyder, Yang, & Lewin, 2003).

As their caretakers control them and are not responsive to their needs on a consistent basis, avoidantly and ambivalently attached children, however, may have learned that help is not always there for them and that the world may be a scary and dangerous place that will hurt them, an orientation that leads to more pessimistic thinking and less hopefulness.

Parenting Styles

Part of the way parents have fostered a secure attachment with their babies is a reflection of their *parenting style*, a style that continues long after the children have left the baby stage. Baumrind's (1971; Baumrind & Black, 1967) categorization of parenting style is well-established, and while very general (e.g., few parents will fall completely within any one category in all areas of their interactions with their children), it provides useful indications about how optimism and hope may be fostered in children.

Authoritarian parents are very strict and controlling of their children. They rarely explain why there are certain rules to be obeyed, but they insist on obedience, with swift and forceful punishment for noncompliance. Their children tend to be distrustful, inhibited, socially withdrawn, and unhappy. It seems reasonable that authoritarian parents foster ambivalently or avoidantly attached children.

Permissive parents have few rules and see themselves as their children's resources rather than their children's role models. Those rules they do have are often negotiated by consulting with the children. Punishment is rare, and children govern themselves as much as possible. Their children are often immature and uncertain: they have received so little guidance that they don't seem sure of themselves and their abilities. Their children may be ambivalently or securely attached.

Authoritative parents provide clear rules and boundaries for their children, explaining the reasons for these rules and boundaries. They set high standards for their children, but encourage the child's unique personality and interests at the same time. They show their love for their children freely, but also make it clear that they are in control. Their children seem to be the most secure, self-reliant, and happiest, and the most likely to be securely attached.

Research evidence indicates that children are more likely to develop optimism when they have had authoritative parents (Jackson, Pratt, Hunsberger, & Pancer, 2005).

In a similar fashion, hope is more likely to develop in children who have received authoritative parenting styles, perhaps because of the sense of safety this style gives the child (Heaven & Ciarrochi, 2008; Heaven, Ciarrochi, & Leeson, 2010; Park & Peterson, 2006).

Authoritative parents may be actively encouraging optimistic and hopeful thinking and actions in their children, and they themselves may be good role models for optimism and hope. In more specific terms, parents whose children hear them use an optimistic explanatory style are teaching their children that bad events sometimes happen because of external causes, not because of inadequacies within the person, and that people can face challenges and setbacks and find ways to cope with them. These parents are teaching their children that a bad action does not make a person bad ("That was a bad thing to do" instead of "You're a bad boy!"), a failure does not make a person a loser, and a tragic event does not make a tragic life. In addition, parents may actively reward and encourage their children for speaking and acting in optimistic ways (Carr, 2007; Seligman, 2002, 2006, 2007).

In addition, as children venture into the world, they have more experiences that affect their optimistic expectations. If children encounter lack of success in school, for example, their optimism about their academic performance decreases (Määttä, Nurmi, & Stattin, 2007). Even as adults, our optimism may change as our resources change, especially our social resources. Segerstrom (2007), for example, studied students in their first year of law school and again ten years later. She found that more optimistic students made more money ten years later, but that didn't make them more optimistic. However, growth of their social network did predict increased optimism, which in turn predicted better mental and physical health.

Similarly, children may view their goals in a positive and hopeful light, but they must learn that *planning* pathways and how to traverse these pathways is critical to attaining their goals. Furthermore, they must learn *how* to plan in the attainment of their goals; they must learn *strategies* for the actual attainment of goals. These skills are typically learned from parents, starting in the earliest years of life. Again, the primary way these skills are taught is through modelling the parents' actions and through parental encouragement and reward for hopeful behaviour.

A Caveat

A warning note must be sounded concerning encouragement and reward, however. Many parents believe that praising and rewarding their children for all their endeavours will build their self-confidence and self-esteem, as well as making them optimistic and hopeful. Besides, parents want their children to be happy, and receiving praise and reward seems to make them happy.

But are these parents really sending their children the message they want to send? In many cases, no, says Seligman (2002, 2007). Children who receive praise and reward unconditionally may become passive. Why should they do anything when reward and praise comes for nothing? Also, they may not be able to understand when they are successful and when they are not: if they receive reward and praise for everything they do ("A for effort"), how will they know when they have actually achieved mastery of a skill or task? In addition, they may come to expect that praise and reward will come to them without their effort, an expectancy that the outside world will not fulfill! This may lead them to feel betrayed, insecure, and mistrustful. As they learn that the world outside their nuclear family does not reward them for simply being, but really expects successful action from them, children may lose trust in their parents as well. After all, Mom and Dad have shown themselves to be unreliable in terms of the feedback they have given the child. Love, not praise and reward, should be unconditional and non-contingent on the child's behaviour, says Seligman. Once more we see that realism, with perhaps a small positive spin, provides the best outcome.

SELF-COMPASSION

It's very difficult to have optimism and hope if you beat yourself up for mistakes you made or for failures and disappointments you have experienced. Many of us become more pessimistic about our abilities and our futures because of this, and we may rob ourselves of hope by decreasing our motivation to set and reach a goal (agency). Deep's friend Delia, for example, told herself that she is a "loser" because of her failure on one test. Because of this, she is likely to face future tests with the attitude that she will probably do poorly on them as well. Most likely, she won't strive for the goal of academic excellence. In fact, she may even give up her goal of earning a degree, and this will make her feel more like a loser than she did before. Delia, with a spiraling-down lack of optimism and hope, has little self-compassion.

Self-compassion entails kindness towards oneself in the face of failure and disappointment. It involves forgiving oneself for mistakes and noting that mistakes are part of the imperfection that all human beings have in common and that one can learn and grow from one's mistakes. It includes the ability to regard the situation as distinct from the person; that is, it regards the mistake, failure, or disappointment as an unfortunate but normal part of life and makes no judgment about the person who experienced it. Self-compassion doesn't try to deny, avoid, or minimize the experience or the emotions accompanying it, nor does it wallow in them or exaggerate them. It accepts them without judgment, simply and forthrightly (Neff, 2009).

Self-compassion is a concept studied by Kristin Neff over the past ten years, in part as a reaction to the modern-day emphasis on developing self-esteem as the route to a satisfying life. The argument has been made that self-esteem can easily slip into self-absorption and narcissism, with people holding distorted views of themselves that lead them to the assumption that they are superior to others (e.g., Baumeister, Campbell, Krueger, & Vohs, 2003). Taking a cue from Buddhism, Neff (2003b) reasoned that being kind to oneself may result in a healthy attitude about oneself in much the same way as self-esteem does, but without the same potential problems.

To study whether this might be so, Neff (2003a) developed a scale to measure self-compassion that she and her colleagues used in a number of research projects. Self-compassion, she found, is positively related to happiness and optimism (Neff, Rude, & Kirkpatrick, 2007). Students who have high levels of self-compassion have less fear of failure and are more effective in coping with the distress of receiving a poor mark (Neff, Hsieh, & Dejitterat, 2005). These students did not lose optimism in the face of a disappointment, but believed they could do better in the future. They concentrated on managing their negative reactions and learning from the situation, indicating their hope by maintaining their goal and seeking better pathways to attain the goal.

People who have compassion for themselves have more life satisfaction (Neff, 2003b) and better psychological health (Neff, Kirkpatrick, & Rude, 2007). They also score higher on measures of emotional intelligence (which we will discuss in Chapter 10) and wisdom (Neff, 2009; Neff, Rude, & Kirkpatrick, 2007). Moreover, high scores on self-compassion are also positively related to stable feelings of self-worth and self-esteem (Neff & Vonk, 2009). That means that for people with self-compassion, the sense of valuing and liking themselves did not depend on other people's opinions or judgments or on the particular situation they were in.

It makes sense to conclude that having the compassion for ourselves that we often show for other people will be advantageous in developing and maintaining our optimism and hope. Perhaps, as well, if we can treat ourselves kindly in recognizing and accepting that we, like everyone else, have human flaws, will make mistakes, and will experience failure and disappointment, we may increase our self-esteem. After all, self-compassion is clearly worth having, and knowing that we have it should make us feel good about ourselves.

THE "BROADEN-AND-BUILD" THEORY

Now for the best part of the positive emotions of optimism and hope: they pave the way for more positive emotions and experiences in the future. Barbara Fredrickson has formulated the very influential **broaden-and-build theory** of positive emotions, with supporting evidence (Burns, Brown, Sachs-Ericsson, Plant, Curtis, Fredrickson, & Joiner, 2008; Fredrickson & Branigan, 2005; Fredrickson & Joiner, 2002; Fredrickson, Mancuso, Branigan, & Tugade, 2000).

Frederickson says that positive emotions lead to **nonspecific action tendencies**, such as a tendency to approach situations in life rather than avoid them, to explore rather than to remain static, to interact rather than remain isolated. Optimistic people, for example, try out new situations and interact more with others. This gives them the opportunity to become aware of a wider world with more possibilities, and to experience more positive situations. In this way, they may also learn more ways of being happy, being satisfied, experiencing a wider variety of positive emotions, and gaining more strategies to use in the future to increase their positive emotions. Fredrickson calls this process learning better **thought-action tendencies**. These people's thinking and experiencing have become broader, and they can now build upon the experiences and learning that have taken place to ensure more satisfaction and positive emotions in the future. They have entered an upward spiral, as one positive quality leads to more positive qualities.

Let's illustrate this by looking back at our friend Deep. He is optimistic and hopeful. Because he is optimistic and hopeful, he sees more possibilities in his life, and this leads him to try more things, many of which work out well and indicate to him that success is possible. So working hard is rewarded by his good marks, his success in his employment, and his popularity with others. His good marks and his success in his employment increase his self-esteem and confidence and motivate him to keep on this path, finding even more ways to become successful. His confidence brings him more success and more friends, potential sources of social support and fulfillment. He may think that good things happen to him, but in truth, his own optimism and hope are putting him in situations in which his positivity makes positive outcomes more likely. He will probably experience more gratitude for his positive outcomes and for the social support he gets in life (and this, in turn, will increase his optimism and hope). As we will see in upcoming chapters, the broaden-and-build theory applies to many more positive emotions than just optimism and hope.

Fredrickson (Fredrickson & Joiner, 2002; Fredrickson, Mancuso, Branigan, & Tugade, 2000) also notes that positive emotions are both psychologically and physically helpful after we have experienced negative emotions. Her **undoing hypothesis** suggests that after we experience negative emotions, having positive emotions helps us regain our balance and flexibility as well as decreasing our physiological responses to stress (see Chapter 9). So Deep, the student nurse, may experience an unhappy shift in his nursing placement, one in which a favourite patient dies. He will, of course, be sad at this, but Deep will also probably experience gratitude that he was able to know this patient and that he was able to perhaps ease some pain and bring some pleasure to the patient. The positive emotion of gratitude will help him cope with the stress and unhappiness he feels at the patient's death.

Conclusion

It's hard to imagine a satisfying life that does not contain optimism and hope. Life is difficult, indeed, for people who believe that their futures hold little but negative events. Of course, these people do little to try to change their outlook or their predicted futures: without optimism and hope, there is no perception that such changes are possible, or if attained, will make any difference. The self-fulfilling prophecy is apparent in their lives. They believe they will have no success, so they don't try very hard; they believe no one cares for them, so there is no point learning social skills or even in caring for others. But the self-fulfilling prophecy works for people who do have optimism and hope as well. Their optimism and hope lead them to try new things and to try harder and to learn from mistakes, all factors that lead to greater success in life. They expect people to be interesting and to be receptive to them, so they seek out people more readily, most likely with a smile and a friendly greeting. And other people are drawn to this and respond positively.

So we can conclude that optimism and hope are important for our personal growth and for our sense of well-being and fulfillment in life. They lead to even more good feelings. But they are not alone. In upcoming chapters in Part 2, we will examine more personal qualities that contribute to the attainment of a satisfying life.

Summary

- Optimists are more flexible in allocating attention, more flexible in thinking, reframe situations to highlight the positive and growth, use problem-focused coping, use humour to deal with setbacks, and experience greater feelings of well-being.

- Pessimists are more rigid in allocating attention and in thinking, distract themselves or deny the situation, avoid problems, use emotion-focused coping, concentrate on their unhappiness when confronted with setbacks, and experience fewer feelings of well-being.

- People with dispositional optimism see the positives in life more than the negatives. They feel that many, if not most, of the events of life are within their control.

- Optimists get higher grades in school, show better athletic performance, earn higher salaries, have more job promotions, have a wider, more supportive social network and more social interest, have happier marriages, handle stress better, have better mental and physical health, show more tolerance for pain, and live longer.

- Some of the beneficial effects of optimism are because of a self-fulfilling prophecy.

- Explanatory optimism is the tendency to explain life's events within a positive frame-work of expecting life to work out in a constructive way. Explanatory optimism must be realistic to be useful.

- We hold positive illusions, seeing ourselves and our futures in a more positive light than is realistically warranted and believing that we have more control over events than we really do. If positive illusions are very unrealistic, they may be harmful, but if they are kept within moderation, they may be beneficial.

- Mildly depressed people tend to be more realistic and accurate in their judgments of themselves and life in general (depressive realism).

- Defensive pessimism directs anxiety about possible failure into productive action. Defensive pessimists usually do as well at tasks as optimists do, but they have lower self-esteem and a lower sense of well-being.

- Pessimists say negative statements to themselves, reflecting stable, global, and internal causes for the negative elements of their lives.

- Optimism can be increased by changing the negative self-statements to more realistic positive self-statements.

- Hope requires having a goal, with the motivation (agency thinking) and the ability to find a way to achieve it (pathways thinking).

- Securely attached children and children with parents who use an authoritative style of parenting are more likely to have optimism and hope.

- Optimism and hope can be fostered in children by parental modelling, encouragement, and praise contingent on the child's mastery of tasks and skills.

- Self-compassion is positively related to happiness, optimism, higher life satisfaction, higher emotional intelligence and wisdom, and better psychological health. It is also positively related to stable feelings of self-worth and self-esteem.
- Fredrickson's broaden-and-build theory contends that positive emotions broaden attention and experience, which increase positive emotions in the future. Furthermore, her undoing hypothesis suggests that positive emotions counteract the psychological and physical effects of negative emotions.

Group Discussion Questions

1. Might it ever be better to be a pessimist than to be an optimist? Under what conditions might it be a better idea to be a pessimist?

2. On a world and historical level, we might wonder whether some moments of history were caused or influenced by the positive illusions of some political and economic leaders. For example, it could be argued that the sound defeat of one political party in a recent Canadian election was because of the party members' positive illusion that the leader, who spent many years living in another country, would be popular to Canadians when he returned to Canada. Can you think of other instances of possible positive illusions that might have influenced historical situations or current events?

3. What would it be like to live in a world in which everyone was a hopeful optimist? Are there problems with this kind of world? What are they? Would you like to live in such a world?

CHAPTER 6

Self-Regulation

Sandy and Duncan are often regarded as an odd couple by their friends because they seem so unalike in many respects. Sandy is organized and controlled and feels a great deal of satisfaction with this. At work, she completes her tasks long before deadlines. At home, she cleans up as soon as she finishes any activity. She always seems poised and calm, taking the greatest problems in her stride. Everyone who knows her agrees that she would definitely be the person they would like to have around in an emergency. Yet she is not emotionless: she is fun and loving with the people she is close to, and she gets angry at the injustices she sees in the world.

Duncan, on the other hand, is a chronic procrastinator whose home looks like a cyclone hit it. He is forever losing his car keys, a fact that, combined with his lack of a sense of time, makes him late for every occasion. "I just can't get organized," he says. He also flies off the handle in anger at each little thing that goes wrong, sometimes to the extent of alarming people around him. He shows remorse for this afterwards, and he reminds people that he shows his love and his joy in intense ways as well. "Whatever Duncan feels, he feels a lot!" say his friends. "That's just the way I am," says Duncan fatalistically.

> ## LEARNING OBJECTIVES
>
> **In this chapter, students will learn about**
> - The benefits of self-regulation.
> - Self-awareness.
> - Self-regulation theory.
> - Intrinsic and extrinsic motivation.
> - Autonomy, competence, and social relatedness as psychological needs.
> - Ego depletion.
> - The causes and effects of procrastination.
> - Emotion regulation.
> - Strategies for regulating emotions and their effectiveness.

Sandy and Duncan are two people who vary greatly in self-regulation. Many of us claim that in some areas of our lives we have no self-discipline, no self-control, and this tends to make us less satisfied with our lives. There is no question that being able to regulate our thoughts, feelings, and actions is a necessary skill in life. Otherwise, we would accomplish almost nothing, from pursuing higher education to maintaining our health. Many people, like Duncan, also claim that they can't help their behaviour, that it is out of their control, suggesting that whatever directs their behaviour is internal, resulting from heredity or a physiological problem. ("It's not my fault. I have a hot temper just like my dad.") While these people may be honest and sincere in their beliefs, in most cases they are simply wrong. In most cases, self-regulation is a learned skill, and it's never too late to learn it.

In this chapter, we will examine self-regulation, but first, let's get rid of the word "discipline." When we say we have no self-discipline, we mean that we have not learned to regulate our behaviour or our emotions. The word "discipline" has such negative connotations that we can defeat ourselves by using the word. If we have no discipline, the implication is that we should receive discipline from an outside source, a throwback to our early days of being scolded, deprived of dessert, or even spanked. At the very least, it implies that we should feel guilty about our "flaw." It will be more productive to talk in terms of self-regulation and self-determination instead. These can and should be regarded as positive skills that we can develop and can use when we choose to.

THE BENEFITS OF SELF-REGULATION

There is no doubt that self-regulation is necessary for us to have a sense of well-being, and there is much research to indicate that this is important for success in life. For example, self-regulation is found to be predictive of academic success (e.g., Obradović, 2010; Waschull, 2005; Wolfe & Johnson, 1995), generally beyond any other factors, including measured intelligence (Duckworth & Seligman, 2005). The ability to self-regulate predicts greater financial success and more success with interpersonal relationships (Tangney, Baumeister, & Boone, 2004). We can deal with our daily stresses more effectively if we are able to monitor and regulate ourselves as well (Compton, Robinson, Ode, Quandt, Fineman, & Carp, 2008). And, not surprisingly, the ability to self-regulate is positively related to mental health (Domes, Schulze, & Herpertz, 2009; Gross & Munoz, 1995; Harrison, Sullivan, Tchanturia, & Treasure, 2009; Yap, Allen, & Ladouceur, 2008). Duncan might be better served to develop more self-regulation, given all the benefits it conveys.

The first step in self-regulating our behaviour and emotions is to become aware of what we are doing and what we are feeling. After all, if we don't know what we're doing or feeling, we have little chance to change these actions and emotions. We will briefly examine self-awareness first.

SELF-AWARENESS

What are you feeling right now? If your answer is "I feel good" or "I feel bad," delve a little deeper. What does it mean when you say this? What does feeling good or feeling bad consist of for you at this moment? Many of us get stymied at this point. What are you doing right now? Yes, you are reading this book, but are you also biting your nails, wiggling your toes, or twirling your hair? Are you engaging in automatic behaviours without even being aware of it? We are so accustomed to thinking about the past or the future and engaging in behaviours that we aren't really aware of until someone tells us to stop that we are often very removed from ourselves. (Fritz Perls and Rollo May talked about this in their theories, as did Buddhism, especially Zen; see Chapters 2 and 3.) Part of the reason Duncan may react so strongly when he gets angry is because he doesn't recognize the cues for the build-up of his anger, so he doesn't know how to stop it or channel it appropriately. Sandy, on the other hand, seems very much aware of her emotions and her behaviour, allowing her to find strategies to regulate her feelings and direct her behaviours in the ways she wishes.

Being aware of yourself, where you are, what you are doing, what you are thinking, and how you feeling has been studied in recent years by looking at *mindfulness*. Mindfulness refers to being aware of present experiences and regarding them without judgment or evaluation. Mindfulness allows us more ability to choose our emotions and our reactions to them (Chambers, Gullone, & Allen, 2009). Being aware and non-judgmental about our emotions alone reduces our physiological reactions to emotion and provides a method of regulating ourselves (Herwig, Kaffenburger, Jäncke, & Brühl, 2010).

Mindfulness has an effect on us psychologically as well. Neuroticism is considered to be a personality trait in which people are more prone to have negative emotional experiences. People who have a great deal of this trait are impulsive and have less ability to self-regulate, probably because they are very low in mindfulness. Not being aware of their feelings and behaviours plays a large part in their inability to control what they are feeling and doing (Fetterman, Robinson, Ode, & Gordon, 2010). It is no wonder that they are more prone to symptoms of anger and depression (Feltman, Robinson, & Ode, 2009).

SELF-DETERMINATION THEORY

Why are you reading this book? Are you reading it because it has been assigned to you for a course you are taking? Are you reading it because you "have to" and maybe you feel a little resentful? Are you reading it because you "have to," but that's OK since you know the information will be helpful in passing a course? Are you reading it because you "have to" but that too is OK since you know how guilty you will feel if you don't get good grades in the course and how great you will feel if do? Are you reading it because you "have to," but that's even more OK because you find the information useful for your own life? Or are you reading it because you want to, given your own interest in the topic? Each of these possibilities reflects different motivations for reading the book. Each one is valid and indicates the reason why you perform this action. That's what **motivation** is—the activation you have towards doing a task.

Motivation has been of great concern to psychologists and philosophers for many years and is of equally great concern to most of us in our daily lives. How often have we felt that we are "not motivated" to do something? In taking on a new role, actors often ask "What's my character's motivation?" These questions suggest that we believe that some internal feeling gives us the drive to do something and we want to know the reasons why we do (or do not) perform the action.

Ryan and Deci (2000a, 2000b) formulated *self-determination theory* to examine motivation and how people use it and control it. This theory encompasses several sub-theories and elements of it have been studied and supported for many years.

Intrinsic and Extrinsic Motivation

In the first place, Ryan and Deci (2000a) distinguish between internal or intrinsic and external or extrinsic motivation. **Intrinsic motivation** is the motivation that comes from inside you. With internal motivation, we perform tasks because of our own interest, curiosity, and satisfaction, without the necessity of any external reward or coercion to perform the task. Tasks that are performed for intrinsic motivation are perceived as more pleasant and typically result in better outcomes (Deci & Ryan, 1995; Nix, Ryan, Manly, & Deci, 1999; Ryan, Deci, & Grolnick, 1995; Sheldon, Ryan, Rawsthorne, & Ilardi, 1997; Stavrou, 2008). For example, students who study because of intrinsic motivation usually enjoy their educational experience more and receive better grades (Archer, Cantwell, & Bourke, 1999; Sheldon & Houser-Marko, 2001). For this reason, teachers and instructors hope to inspire a "love of learning" in students from the earliest grades. Intrinsic motivation has been regarded as the most desirable kind of motivation, the kind that will lead the individual to persist in performing the task, to be more likely to complete the task, and to derive the most pleasure and satisfaction from the task. Ryan and Deci (2000a, 2000b) suggest that we are born with intrinsic motivation and cite the naturally occurring behaviours of exploration in infants as a prime indication of this. As we grow, however, more behaviours and activities are required of us that do not have the same inherent pleasantness and joy attached to them. These behaviours and activities are governed by extrinsic motivation.

Extrinsic motivation refers to performing an action because outside influences say it is desirable or even mandatory. It has been regarded as less desirable and more likely to be less effective in providing people with the persistence and satisfaction that are so often needed to have a fulfilled life (Deci & Ryan, 1995; Nix, Ryan, Manly, & Deci, 1999; Ryan, Deci, & Grolnick, 1995; Sheldon, Ryan, Rawsthorne, & Ilardi, 1997). Ryan and Deci (2000a, 2000b), however, suggest that this is too general a statement of extrinsic motivation and that extrinsic motivation itself can be partitioned into different categories. Their research and theorizing indicates that there are really four different kinds of extrinsic motivation, each of which may lead us to feel differently about performing a particular task and resulting in different outcomes.

If you are reading this book because you "have to" and would probably never pick it up if you didn't have to study for a test on its contents, you probably have what Ryan and Deci (2000a) call **external regulation**. This means that your only reason for reading the book comes from outside forces which will reward you (with good grades) for performing the task or will punish you (with poor grades) for not performing it. Not surprisingly, this form of motivation is often accompanied by resentment, less attention to the task, less persistence in accomplishing it, and more procrastination.

Alternatively, you might be reading this book because you "have to," but you feel that you will experience lowered self-esteem and even guilt if you don't achieve the good grades. This motivation, called **introjected regulation**, is more internal because it focuses on your inner feelings. You may still feel resentment about performing the task, but you are more likely to grudgingly get to work on it and persist in accomplishing it. This kind of motivation is still considered to be extrinsic because it stems from having learned from outside forces, such as parents and teachers, that poor grades are not desirable, resulting in the individual experiencing a reduction in self-esteem if they are not achieved. Essentially, someone beyond yourself has put an emphasis on good grades as a means of gaining personal esteem and satisfaction, and so you strive to attain these by performing tasks that have little or no internal interest to you.

A third possibility is that you are reading this book because you "have to," but you feel that its contents will be beneficial in your personal life and your work. This is **identified regulation**. This form of motivation is still extrinsic because you are not reading for pleasure or for interest (which would indicate intrinsic motivation). Rather you have the conviction that reading the book will have benefits for you in your external life; that is, you have identified the task as having relevance to your own goals. Consequently, you buckle down and tackle the task, even though you anticipate no enjoyment from it.

Finally, you may be reading this book because you "have to," but you know that the information might be useful in helping you to understand yourself and forming a satisfying life. Your motivation is still extrinsic because, again, you might not have freely chosen this book to read; you might have chosen lighter self-help books. Nonetheless, you have willingly complied with your instructor in reading this book because of its potential for greater insight into yourself, something that you value. This is called **integrated regulation**: its source is still external to yourself, but your compliance is based on your own belief system. It is called integrated because you have been taught or have learned in some way that self-insight is desirable, and you fully believe that this teaching is true, so you have integrated the belief into yourself. Your persistence, enjoyment, and success at a task for which you have integrated motivation are typically as great as if you had intrinsic motivation (Grolnick & Ryan, 1987; Ryan & Connell, 1989; Williams, Rodin, Ryan, Grolnick, & Deci, 1998). Sandy, in the case study above, may have this kind of motivation. It is unlikely that she intrinsically enjoys all the tasks she completes, but she does seem to feel some satisfaction for having a well-regulated life.

The different kinds of motivation can be seen as a continuum (Ryan & Connell, 1989; Ryan & Deci, 2000a), with intrinsic motivation at one end, followed by integrated regulation, identified regulation, introjected regulation, and finally external regulation:

Intrinsic ---------- Integrated ---------- Identified ---------- Introjected ---------- External
Motivation   Regulation   Regulation   Regulation   Regulation

As one moves along the continuum from intrinsic motivation to external regulation, the degree of free will in doing a task decreases, as do the pleasure and success one gets from it. Sometimes the motivation will change. In fact, since many of the activities we must attack lack an intrinsically motivating component, the aim for us when we speak of increasing our motivation is to move external regulation as the motivator farther along the continuum to identified or even integrated regulation. For example, I sincerely hope that those of you who may have started reading this book because of external regulation find, in the reading, that your motivation changes to identified or even integrated regulation as you come to realize its relevance to your own life and goals.

The foregoing discussion may imply that intrinsic motivation is good and extrinsic motivation is bad, but that is much too sweeping a generalization. For one thing, as we have seen, identified and integrated regulations function similarly to intrinsic motivation. In addition, Brdar, Rijavec, and Miljković (2010), working in Croatia, remind us that different people and different cultures may view extrinsic motivation differently. While it is true that intrinsic motivation and intrinsic goals are generally related to feelings of subjective well-being, it may take opportunity and money (extrinsic goals) to pursue intrinsic goals.

In countries in which economic conditions are poor, people may have what appears to be the extrinsic motivation for financial success, but closer examination may reveal that people striving for and achieving this goal may have a higher sense of subjective well-being because achieving this goal means that they can accomplish intrinsic goals, such as providing security for their families, pursuing greater education, and having more free choice of their activities. The use of extrinsic motivation may mean survival for the individual and for their family, and it may be used as a means to an intrinsic end rather than as an end in itself. Brdar, Rijavec, and Miljković (2010) also remind us that in collectivist cultures, the needs of the group are often more important to individuals than their own personal needs. That means that group well-being takes priority over individual well-being and may be seen as the higher goal, sometimes achieved through extrinsic motivational goals. So if subjective well-being is not as great in collectivist cultures, this may be fine with the people so long as the group well-being is at an acceptable level.

REFLECTIVE EXERCISE

Motivation

Examine your own motivation in different areas of your life. In what areas are you intrinsically motivated? For example, do you have hobbies that you do purely for the pleasure of doing them and do you find them absorbing? Would you count socializing with your friends as intrinsically motivating? Is socializing *always* intrinsically motivating for you? Or are there times when you would really rather be doing something else? Or feel that you *should* be doing something else? Or you just feel the need for solitude? Then why are you socializing? What is your motivation for this? If it is not strictly your own volition to socialize, what's the external coercion for you? What about other areas of your life? Are you gardening because this is a hobby that refreshes you? Or because you know you will enjoy relaxing in your beautiful garden once the work is done? Or because you know you will feel guilty if the weeds aren't pulled or the grass isn't mowed? Or because the neighbours will disapprove of you if your garden isn't show-worthy? Or because a significant person in your life will reward or punish you if you do or do not accomplish the task? Or are all of these reasons components of your motivation? How do you feel about the motivations you show in different areas of your life?

Autonomy

It seems clear that the continuum of motivation reflects the individual's choice and free will in determining whether he or she will do a task, be successful at it, and feel satisfaction from it. This is the area that Ryan and Deci (2000a, 2000b) call **autonomy**, and they consider it to be one of the basic psychological needs that we all have. We need to feel that our lives are determined by ourselves, for the most part, in order to feel satisfaction and well-being. In fact, when we feel that we "must" do something, our pleasure in it may be undermined. Franklin (2010) relates the (apocryphal) story of a Jewish storekeeper in Nazi Germany who was daily harassed by young thugs who shouted vile racist comments outside his shop. One day he approached them and offered them money to continue the harassment, an offer they accepted with glee. The storekeeper paid them for a few days and then told them that he had no more money, but asked them to continue the harassment. They refused, indignant at the idea that the storekeeper wanted them to work for free!

The Overjustification Effect

The storekeeper was a man ahead of his time. The classic research demonstrating this effect was done by Lepper, Greene, and Nisbett (1973). These researchers selected young children who enjoyed drawing and offered them rewards for doing this activity—that is, they rewarded children for doing what they already enjoyed doing for no other reason but for the pleasure of it. After two weeks, the rewards were withdrawn, and the children stopped drawing. It appears that the children now saw drawing as a means to obtaining rewards, and when the rewards stopped, they ceased to find a reason to draw. The rewards (extrinsic motivation) had undermined the intrinsic pleasure the children had. This has been called the **overjustification effect** and has been found to be quite robust in a number of different situations (Lepper & Greene, 1978).

The overjustification effect can be seen as an instance of decreased autonomy. The children in Lepper, Greene, and Nisbett's (1973) experiment and the young Nazi thugs performed certain activities because they chose to, with no external stimulus to influence them. When an influential external stimulus was provided for them, it came to control their actions to some extent because of the stimulus's desirability. Even though the individuals in question still chose to perform the activity, they came to make the choice based on the external stimulus; they came to have external regulation instead of intrinsic motivation. In a sense, then, the external stimulus was controlling their choices and thereby decreasing their autonomy. With their autonomy reduced, the activities became less pleasurable, and the individuals ceased to perform them when their autonomy was restored with the cessation of the external stimulus.

Autonomy and Self-Regulation

More recent research has indicated that autonomy is an important component in self-regulation. Reeve (2002), for example, reviewed studies in education and found that the evidence strongly suggests that students who are given autonomy support by their teachers fare better in academic settings, with better grades and more enjoyment. Teachers who allow their students some choice in what activities they will tackle at what time and in what manner find that their students thrive in this environment and accomplish more academic work. In a similar fashion, people are more likely to persist in exercise programs if they are allowed to choose the time, place, and type of exercise they will perform, and they are often more likely to report enjoying exercise (Lim & Wang, 2009).

People who are high in autonomy are also more open to new information, which is important for decision-making in a variety of areas (Pavey & Sparks, 2008). Autonomy, then, seems to be a critical component in fostering intrinsic motivation and identified regulation.

Development of Autonomy

Autonomy can be supported by teachers and coaches, but its development starts earlier than that. Kasser, Ryan, Zax, and Sameroff (1995) examined data on children over several years (longitudinal data), and found that warm mothers who support their children's autonomy (e.g., "Hey Sweetie! Which t-shirt do you want to wear today, the red one or the green one? You look really good in both of them!") have children who are more likely to have intrinsic motivations and to be more prosocially oriented. On the other hand, children whose mothers are more controlling (i.e., giving the child less autonomy: "I'm putting your red shirt on you. No discussion!") and are cold or rejecting have children who have lower self-esteem and are more susceptible to extrinsic motivations. (Note that mothers are specified because, in this study, mothers were more likely to be the primary caretakers of the children. It may well be that the same results are found with other primary caretakers, such as fathers or grandparents.) Williams, Cox, Hedberg, and Deci (2000) found that high school students with controlling or rejecting parents were also more likely to have extrinsic rather than intrinsic motivations.

In further support of the role of primary caretakers, a meta-analysis of 41 studies on parenting practices and self-regulation in preschool children found that parental positive control that is characterized by guiding, teaching, and rewarding the child was related to the child's development of self-regulatory behaviour, while negative control characterized by coercive, critical parental strategies was related to a deficit in children's ability to self-regulate (Karreman, van Tuijl, van Aken, & Doković, 2006). Soenens and Vansteenkiste (2010) found that, even cross-culturally, negatively controlling parents impede the development of self-regulation in their children. We are led to wonder what the parents of Duncan in the opening scenario were like: were they over-controlling or under-controlling, or did they have little impact on Duncan's adult lack of self-regulation?

REFLECTIVE EXERCISE

Autonomy

Do you feel like an autonomous person? Do you see your life as controlled by you or by other external forces? Does this pertain to all areas of your life? If not, which areas does it pertain to? Why is this so? How do you feel about it? Consider the possibility that while we are all externally controlled in some manner (e.g., could society exist if there were no laws?), we always have the choice about how we will respond to the control.

We can respond with resentment or rebellion, or with acceptance and resignation, or with humour and good will. Which choice will be more beneficial depends on the situation and your own needs, but the choice is yours. That much autonomy always exists.

If there are areas of your life in which you feel controlled and don't like it, how might you go about gaining personal control? Can you change the situation, or if not, can you change your response to it?

While autonomy is an important part of self-regulation and intrinsic motivation, it is not the only part. Ryan and Deci (2000a) suggest that another basic psychological need that must be fulfilled is that of competence, or self-efficacy.

Competence

A second basic psychological need that Ryan and Deci (2000a) postulated is that of competence. **Competence** is the need to feel that one can be effective in performing a task. It would be very difficult to feel intrinsic motivation for a task if we did not feel that we could master it, even if the task were challenging. In our day-to-day lives, there are many things that we have **amotivation** for (that is, no motivation at all) because we know that we simply don't have the knowledge or ability to perform the task. We probably spend little time bemoaning the fact that we can't become invisible since, as science presently stands, this isn't within the realm of possibility given our own capacities. But there are other tasks we may avoid based on our beliefs about our competence.

Albert Bandura (1977, 1997) studied competence under his term of *self-efficacy*. Self-efficacy theory states that people have beliefs about their own abilities to do things, to make desired changes in the environment, whether it be reducing a carbon footprint or learning to tie one's shoes. These beliefs may or may not be accurate. In fact, many people hesitate to try new activities because of their erroneous beliefs that they will be unable to perform the activity effectively. Our self-efficacy, which may differ from task to task, is instrumental in determining which activities we will undertake, how long we will persist in them, and whether we will even attempt to overcome obstacles in our way.

Effects of Self-Efficacy

When we talk about self-regulation, behaving in ways that will take us to our goals, we first must consider how we choose these goals. We don't choose them simply because they are desirable; we choose them because they are desirable *and* we feel that we have the ability to reach them, albeit sometimes with hard work. This, of course, brings in our beliefs about our self-efficacy on that particular goal and task. Duncan seems to feel that he has little self-efficacy in organizing and regulating his life, while Sandy shows a great deal of confidence in her ability to tackle whatever task comes her way. You may know people who don't pursue higher education because they believe they are incapable of it or at least will not be good students. Or people who won't learn to play tennis, say, because of their contention that they are "not athletically inclined." And you may feel frustration with these people because your judgment indicates that their faith in their own ability is less than reality warrants. In fact, there may be areas in your own life that reveal a lack of self-efficacy, which your friends and family believe is incorrect.

After choosing our goals, self-efficacy beliefs also influence what activities we will undertake to reach those goals (Bandura, 1997; Maddux, 2009). For example, with a sense of self-efficacy for learning, we may set the goal of gaining more education. Assuming that interest and opportunity are equal, some people with a high sense of self-efficacy in this area may choose the activity of taking university courses. For others, this activity may seem too strenuous and beyond their self-efficacy, and the activity chosen is to enrol in a non-credit course for enjoyment.

Self-efficacy beliefs affect how much persistence we will show when we meet obstacles in the activities that we have chosen to pursue our goals (Bandura, 1997; Maddux, 2009). People with a higher self-efficacy persist more when the inevitable obstacles arise, whereas people with lower self-efficacy may decide to quit the activity.

Finally, our beliefs about our self-efficacy have an effect on how we evaluate our own performance (Bandura, 1997; Maddux, 2009). What constitutes "success" in an endeavour is often a subjective judgment. Someone with a higher sense of self-efficacy may feel that just accomplishing a difficult task indicates success, while someone with a lower sense of self-efficacy may regard anything less than an outstanding result as an indication of lack of competence. For people with a higher sense of self-efficacy, progress toward the goal is usually seen as reinforcing their belief in their ability and enhances their persistence, thus leading them to more progress and eventual success (Bandura, 1997; Maddux, 2009).

On a very simple level, we can assume that you feel self-efficacy in your ability to learn about positive psychology and personal growth. If you didn't have this, you undoubtedly would never have started reading this book. To take it further, you have self-efficacy in being able to read or to understand what is read to you. Again, you would not have started this book without that self-efficacy.

There are countless areas in our lives in which we feel self-efficacy but are so accustomed to it, we don't even notice it anymore. For example, many years ago, learning to dress yourself was a major accomplishment, and one that probably required several less-than-successful attempts before you mastered it. Today, dressing yourself is more likely to be automatic, with the only question being "What shall I wear?" This skill will remain automatic, with your discounting the importance of your self-efficacy for the rest of your life, unless you become disabled through an injury. At that point, you may need to relearn the skill, and it will appear more complicated and difficult than you had been aware of since your toddler years.

Without self-efficacy we would not be able to feel self-esteem. Being competent and able to do meaningful things is a large part of what makes us feel worthwhile as human beings and is clearly related to our success in life and our sense of subjective well-being (Sellers, Dochen, & Hodges, 2011). Not surprisingly, people who are depressed have a lower self-efficacy than do people who are not depressed (Bandura, 1997). Part of their depression is their pervasive belief that they are not as competent as other people, and so they feel inadequate as human beings. Dysfunctional anxiety, as well, is attributed to low self-efficacy because of the belief some people have that they cannot deal with stressful or threatening situations (Bandura, 1997). Consequently, they avoid the situations in some manner (e.g., not accepting a promotion at work, not entering university, having an emotional "meltdown" that requires other people to intervene in supporting the person and undertaking the task themselves). This avoidance naturally does nothing to increase people's self-efficacy; it usually lessens it even further despite the short-term relief at avoiding the stress, and it increases anxiety and tendencies to avoid even more in the future.

Lack of self-efficacy is detrimental to our physical health as well (Maddux, 1993; Schwarzer, 2008). Many people maintain a health-endangering overweight condition because of their belief that they can't lose weight, for instance. Or they may not undertake an exercise program because they doubt their ability to do the exercises properly and maintain the program. Similarly, some people may fail to attempt to quit smoking, stop drinking to excess, and engage in many other harmful behaviours because of their lack of self-efficacy in these areas. Lack of self-efficacy can even influence the workings of the body by lowering the effectiveness of the immune system (Bandura, 1997).

Sources of Self-Efficacy

Bandura (1997) asserts that self-efficacy beliefs arise in five ways. The first way is through personal experience. When we experience success in performing an activity, we are given the proof that we are able to accomplish the task. Unless we insist on attributing our success to "luck" or some other external factor, we come face to face with the fact that we have actually been capable of doing the task. We are then more likely to try it again, with greater confidence. If our successes are repeated, our belief in our ability increases, and we persevere at the activity and overcome obstacles more readily with our enhanced self-efficacy. Personal experience is by far the most effective way of gaining self-efficacy, but it's one that demands that the individual attempt the task, something that people with a low sense of self-efficacy may not do. Does Duncan, for example, even try to regulate himself more? It seems more likely that he has given up on this.

The second source of self-efficacy is through watching other people. When we see other people accomplishing a task, we may feel that it is more likely that we can do it too, especially if the people we watch are similar to us (see also Peng, 2008). That's the reason behind testimonials given by "average" people in advertisements for weight loss programs, exercise programs, products touted to relieve unpleasant physical symptoms, and so on. This is a good technique for advertising: research has shown that even children may undertake activities that they have feared (e.g., petting a dog when they fear dogs) if they watch other children happily performing the feared activity.

Another way to gain self-efficacy is to imagine performing the activity. If we imagine ourselves successfully performing the activity, we can increase our actual feelings of self-efficacy about that activity. This is not as powerful as a concrete personal experience of success in an activity, but it has been shown to be an effective tool therapeutically in reducing fears and enhancing performance. This technique is often used by professional athletes before a competition to increase their feelings of competence and thereby increase their chances of success.

We can also gain some self-efficacy through verbal persuasion. Pep talks sometimes work. When someone we like and trust tells us of their faith in our ability to accomplish a task, we may feel more like they are right, and our sense of self-efficacy for that task increases. Pep talks are usually effective only in the short-term, but that may be enough to persuade us to attempt the task and experience some success.

Finally, our own physical and emotional state can help us gain self-efficacy. When we feel physically or emotionally "down," we tend to feel less self-efficacy. Feeling good or even neutral seems to lead us to have more confidence in our abilities.

Self-Efficacy's Effect on Self-Regulation

In support of the effectiveness of self-efficacy on self-regulation and success are several studies in which self-efficacy was related to adherence to medication regimens (Gatti, Jacobson, Gazamararian, Schmotzer, & Kripalani, 2009), the effective management of chronic illnesses such as epilepsy (Robinson, Dilorio, DePadilla, McCarty, Yeager, Henry, Schomer, & Shafer, 2008) and the likelihood of abstinence from drinking in members of Alcoholics Anonymous (Moos, 2008). Several studies have also supported the idea that high self-efficacy is related to achieving higher grades and more satisfaction in the educational experience (e.g., Bembenutty, 2009; Schunk, 1984, 1989; Puzziferro, 2008). Lower self-efficacy, however, is related to higher burnout rates among university students (Bresó, Salanova, & Schaufeli, 2007).

Not only does increasing self-efficacy benefit performance, but in particular one form of self-efficacy should be noted. Deborah Kennett and her colleagues Narnia Worth and Carol Forbes (2009) at Trent University in Ontario studied people who are regular exercisers and those who wish to become regular exercisers. They found that people who are regular exercisers are more likely to have higher self-efficacy not only in their ability to formulate workable schedules, but also in finding ways to overcome obstacles to exercising.

Feeling confident about being able to find ways to overcome obstacles and resist temptation was also found by Moos (2008) to be an important component of self-efficacy among alcoholics. This is a technique that many of us never think of. We may make plans to achieve a goal, and we may even map out our strategy for accomplishing the goal, but we may overlook the roadblocks that inevitably arise. Without a plan for getting around the roadblocks, we may give in to the temptation to just quit. Does the following example of common student behaviour resonate with you? Students often postpone working on an assignment until the weekend before the assignment is due, giving the excuse that they will have an unbroken period of time to concentrate on the task. They are, of course, assuming that they won't get a cold, their best friends won't hit a crisis that needs help and support, their computer won't break down, and so on. Life is full of roadblocks, and a plan for dealing with obstacles seems more and more important.

REFLECTIVE EXERCISE

Self-Efficacy

While you clearly have self-efficacy in countless areas of your life, there may still be areas in which you do not feel such competence. Have you tried to perform any tasks in this area? Or have you simply avoided them because of your conviction that you would not perform to the standards you feel are adequate? Reconsider these areas. Why not find a non-evaluative and non-threatening way to attempt to perform in these areas? Set your standards for adequate performance at a novice level. You may note in this context that you set higher standards for yourself than you would for other people—adjust this to a more reasonable level. Since self-efficacy is best developed by personal experience of success or progress toward success, why not give yourself a chance to experience this? Nothing ventured, nothing gained, as the old saying goes!

Two of the five ways Bandura (1997) suggests that self-efficacy is developed and enhanced involve other people, in modelling them and in hearing their expressions of faith in our abilities. This points to the third basic psychological need that Ryan and Deci (2000a, 2000b) believe is critical in the development of intrinsic motivation and a sense of subjective well-being.

Social Relatedness

The final basic psychological need that Ryan and Deci (2000a, 2000b) postulate is that of social relatedness. In order to function in this world in a satisfying way, we need other people. We need to feel that we belong and that we have the affection and approval of others. It would be extremely difficult to develop the skills needed to self-regulate and have a sense of well-being in an atmosphere of constant rejection and disapproval.

Parenting in the Development of Self-Regulation

Without affection and approval, children are unable to accurately gauge their own performance and their own abilities. After all, the opinions of significant adults are all that children have to go by when they are young. If those opinions say "You are worthwhile and competent," children will incorporate this into their self-belief. On the other hand, a steady diet of "Let me do that, you aren't able to" or "Go away and don't bother me" communicates the message that the child is incompetent and worthless. As we have seen in the section on autonomy, rejecting and controlling parents have children who are less prosocial and are less likely to have intrinsic motivation (Kasser, Ryan, Zax, &

Sameroff, 1995; Williams, Cox, Hedberg, & Deci, 2000). But mothers who provide security and support for their babies' autonomy, as seen by their exploratory behaviour, have babies whose intrinsic motivation is enhanced (Frodi, Bridges, & Grolnick, 1985).

As we grow, more activities come under regulation from the outside world. Have you seen a two-year-old whose reaction to any request is "No!"? In some cases, the child, saying no, will still willingly comply with the task ("Have a cookie." "No!" as the child grabs the cookie and devours it). But in many other cases, the child's refusal indicates that the child doesn't want to do the task; that is, the child has no intrinsic motivation for the task. Getting dressed, going to bed, and picking up toys are all examples of tasks that generally require external regulation for the child to comply. For many children, as time goes on, external regulation changes to introjected regulation as the child comes to know that compliance will earn self-approval. ("I'm a good boy. I picked up all my toys.") Further along, the child may have identified regulation ("It's important to put your toys away.") until perhaps one day the child's motivation is integrated. ("I like having a tidy space to play in and I like having my toys put away somewhere safe.") The motivation is still extrinsic since the task is not being done for pure enjoyment (i.e., the child does not say "It's so much fun to pick up my toys!"), but the identified or integrated motivation gives the child a feeling of satisfaction and well-being. Note that it all started from the social context of a caretaker imposing an external regulation on the child. Without this external regulation, no motivation to pick up toys, for example, may ever have developed.

Ryan and Deci (2000b) propose that the movement from external regulation to integrated regulation is facilitated when the individual feels attached and attracted to the person who imposes the external regulation in the first place. They cite, as evidence, research done by Ryan, Stiller, and Lynch in 1994 in which children who felt more cared for and attached to their parents and teachers showed greater internalization of the regulation of positive school-related behaviours. In addition, Volling, Blandon, and Kolak (2006) found that positive relationships with the mother and the father predicted greater self-regulation in their children. These researchers also found that homes with high marital conflict had children who were low in self-regulation, highlighting the need for a secure and stable environment for the development of children's ability to self-regulate.

The Environment

If our aim is to increase the internal motivation to perform a task, the social context in which we are operating needs to be one in which we feel secure and valued. Intuitively, this makes sense. No matter how much you may like the activities your work involves, it's hard to do your best work or enjoy it if you feel that your instructor or your employer doesn't really like and respect you. Indeed, working in an atmosphere of dislike, disrespect, and distrust seems to sap us of our vitality and our desire to attempt any of the tasks set before us.

Providing a safe and secure environment in which we are more likely to begin to internalize motivation is only one way that social relatedness is a critical component of self-regulation. Another function of the social environment is to validate and value our competence. Ryan and Deci (2000b) note that no matter how supportive and secure the environment, if we are given tasks that are beyond our competence, motivation is unlikely to come under internal control. A child, for example, who is not cognitively ready to master abstract concepts is unlikely to undertake tasks which involve these concepts unless an external regulation is imposed. Part of the reason for this is probably because in undertaking these tasks the child runs into more failure experiences than success experiences, and the child's sense of self-efficacy is diminished. The social environment, then, also needs to set challenging tasks and conditions for the individual that the individual has the competence to meet. Rewarding and valuing the successes that then occur is a way in which social relatedness enhances the individual's perceived self-efficacy.

A third way in which social relatedness enhances intrinsic motivation and the development of integrated regulation is through its support of the individual's autonomy (Ryan & Deci, 2000b). Since autonomy is an important component of self-determination, a social environment that provides threats and punishments for non-compliance will not result in internalizing of motivation, since the individual will always operate with the understanding that there is no choice but to undertake the task. And as we have seen, external coercion undermines internal motivations for action (e.g., see the discussion of the overjustification effect).

Social support helps facilitate self-efficacy and the self-regulation of a number of important activities, such as managing epilepsy (Robinson, Dilorio, DePadilla, McCarty, Yeager, Henry, Schomer, & Shafer, 2008), diabetes (Fortmann, Gallo, Walker, & Philis-Tsimikas, 2010), and HIV/AIDS (Swendeman, Ingram, & Rotheram-Borus, 2009). The support of other people also helps to motivate us to engage in physical exercise (Lim & Wang, 2009). It's no wonder that a common tip given to people who rarely exercise is to join a gym with a supportive buddy!

Social relatedness, then, is a vital component in the facilitation of internalized motivation by its effect of giving the individual the context in which to learn, to safely explore, to develop self-efficacy, and to freely choose to perform activities. We can speculate that Sandy grew up in such an atmosphere. Lucky Sandy! Internalized motivation, whether intrinsic, identified, or integrated, can develop and thrive throughout the lifespan in a socially supportive atmosphere. This is a social environment in which the individual feels safe and valued, autonomy is both permitted and respected, and competence is validated and rewarded. Or, internalized motivation can diminish and even disappear if the environment is rejecting, restrictive, and unrewarding.

Ego Depletion: A Cautionary Note

Have you ever heard it said that, for example, you shouldn't try to lose weight and quit smoking at the same time? The idea is that trying to exert self-regulation in two areas at the same time will spell doom for the ability to regulate in either area. There is some truth to this. Research has demonstrated that the amount of self-control exerted on a second task is reduced if self-control had been exerted on a first task (Bayer, Gollwitzer, & Achtziger, 2010; Baumeister, Gailliot, DeWall, & Oaten, 2006; Zyphur, Warren, Landis, & Thoreson, 2007). For instance, if people are told they can eat from a bowl of radishes, but not from a plate of cookies and chocolate, they subsequently show less persistence in solving a frustrating puzzle. Having exerted self-regulation in managing the frustration of resisting the cookies, people seem to have less ability to deal with the frustration of the puzzle. Baumeister (2002; 2008) calls this **ego depletion**.

Based on findings such as these, Baumeister (2002, 2008; Baumeister, Vohs, & Tice, 2007) devised a model of **self-control** (his term for voluntary and conscious self-regulation) likening self-control to the action of a muscle. Just as the physical body only has a certain amount of strength and energy, so too there is a finite amount of strength and energy available for our minds to make use of our ability to self-regulate. As we use our muscles in some activity, such as playing a game of tennis, we deplete some of our strength and energy so that if we attempt to use our muscles again, in a second game of tennis, we find we are less energetic and vigorous in our playing. If we are given a good reason to summon up extra energy, say a $100 bet riding on the second game, we are able to do it up to the point at which exhaustion sets in and all our energy is depleted. When we exert self-control, says Baumeister, we use energy from a finite store, depleting our resources. If we are called upon to exert self-control again, we have less psychological energy available to us. Baumeister suggests that this is not a question of complete depletion of energy, but of conservation of energy for a future task. We can typically tap our reserve store that we have been conserving if the motivation is great enough, but again, only up to a point before we exhaust the store.

The analogy to a muscle used by Baumeister (2002, 2008) holds up when regarding the replenishment of the energy. Just as exercising a muscle builds up its strength and lengthens the amount of time it can be used, the more a person practises self-control, the more slowly ego depletion takes place (Baumeister, Gailliot, DeWall, & Oaten, 2006). Ego depletion can also be slowed through positive emotions such as humour, cash incentives, and social goals such as the desire to help others or to be a supportive partner (Baumeister, Vohs, & Tice, 2007). Ego depletion can also be reduced by having implementation of "if–then" plans (Baumeister, Voh, & Tice, 2007; Bayer, Gollwitzer, & Achtziger, 2010). When we plan to carry out a task or achieve a goal that requires self-regulation, we are more likely to succeed and less likely to deplete our store of psychological energy if we make concrete plans for how we will go about accomplishing our ends, especially if we have plans for how we will deal with obstacles such as the temptation to quit or be distracted. Making such plans beforehand means that we will not have to expend energy deciding what to do or avoiding roadblocks when we are actually working at the task. All we have to do is to implement our already-made plans.

PROCRASTINATION: A FAILURE OF SELF-REGULATION

"I'll get to work on the essay on the weekend when I have uninterrupted time. It's due on Monday, so I'll really go at it and I'll get it done on time. It may not be the best essay, but at least it will be done." We saw this example above, one of the most common ones that I, as a professor, have heard from my students. Have you ever said this or known someone who said this? Have you ever procrastinated? Almost all of us have procrastinated at some time or other, and the majority of students report that they procrastinate often, with about 50 percent saying that they are chronic procrastinators (Steel, 2007).

How does procrastinating make you feel? For most of us, procrastination brings with it guilt and some anxiety. We put off some tasks, especially if the due date for the task is far off (Schouwenburg & Groenewoud, 2001; Strongman & Burt, 2000) and do something more pleasurable. Sometimes we don't even enjoy the more pleasurable activity because we have a nagging feeling that we should be doing something else. When we finally get busy on the delayed task, we experience more negative emotions—anxiety, agitation, worry, and sometimes resentment. Sure enough and not surprisingly, we don't do the task very well. Why do we do this to ourselves, and often repeatedly? Surely we are only creating more problems for ourselves and making ourselves feel bad as well. It sounds like self-sabotage, and in many ways it is. Certainly it seems to be, as Steel (2007) puts it, the "quintessential self-regulatory failure" (p. 65).

We have a number of excuses for procrastinating. Suddenly something else needs to be done more urgently. "I can't start the essay until my desk is clean." And then we take two hours to clean off a desk that could have been tidied in 10 minutes! Some people who procrastinate claim that they work better at the last minute under time pressure. But then, many people who drink alcohol and drive claim that they drive better after they have had a few drinks! In both cases, the person may actually believe what he or she is saying; the problem is that the person is generally wrong.

For many of us, procrastination is a bad habit we would like to get rid of (but we may not get around to it). In fact, 95 percent of procrastinators say that they wish they could reduce it (O'Brien, as cited by Steel, 2007). To that end, self-help books in abundance are written, complete with ideas about the causes of procrastination and suggestions for ending it. While some self-help books are very good indeed, others are not very accurate. In this section we will examine what research can tell us about procrastination, its causes, and its remedies.

Definition

On the surface, it would seem that there is no problem in defining what procrastination is—we all know what it is, don't we? But perhaps we don't. Is procrastination simply the delay of a task? Some people have defined it that way (e.g., Steel, 2007; Wohl, Pychyl, & Bennett, 2010), but many others insist that this definition is not complete (e.g., Solomon & Rothblum, 1984). For these researchers, the definition of procrastination must include a negative emotional component. For example, imagine that you are watching your favourite television program. It will be over in 10 minutes. But your significant other says "Would you take out the garbage, please?" "Sure," you answer. "In ten minutes when the show is over." Probably you feel no discomfort or distress, no guilt or anxiety, in delaying this task for a brief period of time, and when you do the task, you think little of it. Is this procrastination? By a definition that says procrastination is delaying a task, the answer is yes. Yet few of us would really call this behaviour procrastinating, and few of us would worry about such behaviour. In fact, we might worry more about someone who missed the last 10 minutes of a favourite program to comply with that kind of request immediately!

A better definition, one that fits with our common experience and our intuitive understanding, might be that **procrastination** is the tendency to delay a task to the point of discomfort (Solomon & Rothblum, 1984). This seems to capture the essence of both the behaviour and reaction to it in an understandable way and is the definition we will use in this section of the chapter.

Causes

Why do we procrastinate when we suffer for it? Why do we choose to do something we know will bring us grief in the end? Procrastination is not conducive to a satisfying life. Certainly many of us have good intentions. Many students, for example, start a new semester with the solemn vow that this will be the semester that they don't procrastinate. And they don't procrastinate, for a while. Like New Year's resolutions, however, this often lasts a couple of weeks, and then the old habits return.

Many people have proposed a number of reasons for procrastinating, and probably every individual has his or her own unique set of reasons, but research has indicated that not all of the reasons given may be true or even hold for the majority of people. Before we examine some of the possible causes of procrastination, let's look at the bottom line. In a massive review and meta-analysis of the often conflicting research on procrastination, Piers Steel at the University of Calgary (2007) determined that people procrastinate because the task is aversive to them in some way. It may be an unpleasant chore, or one that is boring (to the individual), or is frustrating, or that contains what someone may perceive as having a great possibility of resulting in failure. The most common reason that people give for procrastinating is that the task is uninteresting or unpleasant. Of course, what is uninteresting or unpleasant is a matter of personal preference, and people vary widely on this. Some people, for example, will procrastinate doing schoolwork to do housework instead (cleaning the desk first), while others will procrastinate doing housework to do schoolwork instead. They also procrastinate when the rewards for doing a task are delayed, and there is little or no immediate punishment for their procrastination.

It seems that some of the usual reasons that researchers have hypothesized to cause procrastination are really reasons that an individual may find a task aversive. Others may not be. Let's examine some of these reasons.

Timing may be cited as a reason to procrastinate. As noted earlier, we tend to procrastinate more when the deadline for completion of the task is far off (Schouwenburg & Groenewoud, 2001; Strongman & Burt, 2000). We procrastinate at this time because we can. There is little pressure to complete the task as yet, "there's always tomorrow," and the aversiveness of the task can be ignored for the present. As the deadline for completion comes closer, procrastination begins to decrease as we feel increasing pressure and anxiety.

We may also procrastinate because of low self-efficacy. As we saw in our discussion of self-efficacy, this is a major component of self-regulation, and as such, it is not surprising that it is related to procrastination (Klassen, Krawchuk, Lynch, & Rajani, 2008; Wolters, 2003). If we feel that we cannot do a task adequately or successfully, we tend to find the task aversive. Who wants to do something they know they will mess up? And so, procrastinators put it off for as long as they can. This explanation is closely related to another common explanation for procrastination, namely, fear of failure (e.g., Alexander & Onwuegbuzie, 2007; Özer, Demir, & Ferrari, 2009; Schouwenburg, 1995). Lack of self-efficacy is a component of fear of failure.

Other components include perfectionism and evaluation anxiety (Solomon & Rothblum, 1984), and as such, include elements of irrational beliefs (i.e., the belief that failing or not performing a task well indicates one's worthlessness as a human being). While fear of failure has been found to be somewhat related to procrastination, it appears that the self-efficacy component is the major contributor to the effect (Wolters, 2003). It should be noted, as well, that some people procrastinate even when their self-efficacy does not play a part in the task. For example, people planning large social gatherings, such as weddings, always seem to have a problem determining how many people will attend the event because a number of invitees have not responded with an acceptance or rejection right up to the last minute. This may not be due to a lack of self-efficacy, but may be due to a lack of decision-making or simple forgetfulness.

Sometimes our procrastination is because of self-handicapping. The idea here is that, fearing failure, people may attempt to save their pride by building into the performance of the task a component that will explain any disappointing results. If one does a task in a very short amount of time, less time than the task required, any poor outcome can be attributed to the lack of time put into the task, not the individual's lack of ability or talent. It's not uncommon to hear these people say to others or themselves "If I'd taken more time with it, it would have been better"—they've given themselves the "out" ahead of time by ensuring they didn't allow themselves enough time. In some cases, self-handicappers may postpone a task until the last minute, but in general it seems that they are more likely to perform other actions of self-handicapping rather than postponement (Lay, Knish, & Zanatta, 1992). Procrastinators are more likely to simply use the delay tactic in approaching a task. Self-handicapping for them, then, may be more of a side effect of procrastination rather than a reason for it.

Many people believe that a major cause of procrastination is laziness. Are procrastinators simply lazy people, as non-procrastinators seem to imply? *Lazy* may be a misleading word. Lazy suggests someone who avoids all effortful activity. Yet procrastinators, as we have seen, may be very industrious indeed; they just direct their energy and efforts to tasks that are not as urgent but are more pleasant. But there is some basis for the belief that laziness may play a part. Wolters (2003) studied undergraduate student procrastinators and found that a work-avoidance orientation to academic studies was a major predictor of procrastination, along with low self-efficacy. A work-avoidance orientation refers to the attitudes of students who wish to put as little time and effort as possible into tasks, who would rather not work too hard, and who prefer tasks that can be accomplished in a short period of time to tasks that require more time expenditure. These specific attitudes seem to fit well with most people's definition of lazy. These students display poor academic achievement, but how much of this is due to procrastination and how much is due to other factors (e.g., lack of attention) is unknown.

REFLECTIVE EXERCISE

Procrastination

Do you procrastinate? Under what conditions do you procrastinate? For example, do you procrastinate on academic tasks, but not on tasks such as getting ready to go out to dinner? Or do you procrastinate on that kind of task too?

Why do you think you do it? How does your procrastination make you feel? Is it something you wish to change about yourself? (If so, read below.) Do you think that people like Duncan who are always late may be procrastinators? Why do you think that?

Personality and Behavioural Correlates of Procrastination

What are people who procrastinate like? First, they are not neurotic, nor are they usually perfectionists, since most perfectionists start work early to achieve the perfection they seek (Steel, 2007). They do, however, seem to have little faith in their own abilities, as seen in their low scores on measures of self-efficacy and self-esteem. In keeping with this, they are more likely to procrastinate when they believe their efforts will be evaluated. Steel's (2007) review of the literature finds that research suggests procrastinators may be rather impulsive people, with greater responsiveness to whether a task is pleasant or not. Unlike non-procrastinators, they tend to start their work with pleasant tasks first and follow with unpleasant tasks, if time permits (which it often doesn't). Their orientation to time is not typically toward the future—that is, they don't seem to spend much time thinking about what will happen in the future if they put off doing tasks. They tend to dislike structure and routine, which implies that boredom might be more aversive to them than to non-procrastinators.

Steel's (2007) review also reveals that procrastinators have been reliably found to prefer short-term goals to long-term goals and that they are easily distracted. They are lacking in organization, a finding that is consistent with their dislike of structure. Howell and his colleagues (2006) find that procrastinators are not very good at keeping promises to themselves in general. Their intent is good, they certainly mean to attack a task with plenty of time to spare, especially when the deadline for completion is distant, but many report being "unable" to stop themselves from procrastinating at this time. As time progresses, however, they usually work harder than non-procrastinators at the last minute.

The Results of Procrastination

Many of the studies reviewed by Steel (2007) found that student procrastinators report that their general feelings of well-being are impaired by their procrastination, but this is not a universal finding. For many, feelings of anxiety as a result of stress are low during the beginning of a semester, but build as the end of semester and deadlines approach. While procrastinators may feel guilty for procrastinating as they reflect on their past behaviour, their overall mood may not be negative as they contemplate this.

A less equivocal finding is the result of procrastination on performance. As Steel puts it, "… procrastination is usually harmful, sometimes harmless, but never helpful." (2007, p. 80). In general, Steel's review indicates that student procrastination is related to lower overall GPA, lower grades in individual courses and assignments, and lower marks on final examinations. In the post-educational world, procrastinators tend to put off saving money and managing their finances, leading them to a reduced state of financial well-being, as compared to non-procrastinators.

More important than grades or finances is the effect of procrastination on health. Steel's (2007) review indicates that procrastinators postpone seeing a physician for health problems, a dangerous tendency that often leads to the worsening of a physical condition.

Is Procrastination Always Bad?

The short answer to this question is that it depends on how you define procrastination. While it is easy to put a negative label on procrastination, Chu and Cho (2005) point out in their research that this may be too much of a generalization. They used the definition of procrastination that does not include a negative emotional component—that is, for them, procrastination is the delaying of a task. Under this definition, there appear to be two different kinds of procrastinators, **active procrastinators** and **passive procrastinators**. We have been talking about passive procrastinators so far, those who feel badly about their procrastination and show poorer performance because of it. Active procrastinators, however, are more like non-procrastinators. They have as high a sense of self-efficacy as non-procrastinators, and they feel almost as much mastery over their time. But they are also very flexible in their use of time. Chu and Choi speculate that active procrastinators may delay doing a task because of their judgments that other tasks should have higher priority and must be dealt with without delay. These people are very responsive to a rapidly changing environment, and they are able to react more immediately and spontaneously. They may prefer the "rush" of last-minute pressure and may even find this stimulates their creative thinking. The product of their last-minute work is of comparable quality with the work of non-procrastinators and substantially better than the work of passive procrastinators. They seem to feel little or no negative emotion as a result of procrastinating, and rather, they function very well since their use of time has a purpose (i.e., they are doing more urgent tasks). For them, procrastination is not a failure of self-regulation, but probably shows that they are very self-regulated. So to a certain extent, whether procrastination is a problem or not is a matter of the definition we use.

Overcoming Procrastination

The ultimate question in this section, of course, is this: how do we stop passive procrastinating? This has been the domain of many self-help books (e.g., Burka & Yuen, 2008), some of which are very helpful. But given what we have discovered in this section, we can make some concrete suggestions based on the research evidence. These ideas may be helpful even if you are not a procrastinator but simply would like some hints about enhancing your self-regulation.

1. *Increase your self-efficacy.* As we noted above, self-efficacy is best enhanced when we have successful experiences with a task, so try to give yourself some. For example, if you find that you procrastinate in writing essays, take a course in writing to make you more proficient. If that isn't possible, write short paragraphs on any topic (perhaps keep a journal?) simply to give yourself the chance to write without being evaluated. You may find that this is actually fun, and it can be a stress-reducer as well as aid in enhancing your self-awareness.

2. *Build in rewards.* Since procrastination is more likely when rewards are distant, give yourself some short-term rewards. This is easier if you break your work into small sections (e.g., write one paragraph, clean only the sink in the kitchen, work for just 10 minutes). The task seems less overwhelming this way, and you can reward yourself after each segment is completed (e.g., a cup of coffee or soft drink, five minutes of playing with the dog, listening to a favourite piece of music). Make sure the rewards

are small (it won't work if your reward for ten minutes of work is an entire evening of relaxation!) and contingent on having accomplished that segment (it won't work if you can have your reward at other times—then it isn't a reward, it's just a pleasurable experience). Some people even find that once they start a small segment of their work, they find it rewarding to continue.

3. *Eliminate distractions.* That means that the television should not be playing (multi-tasking doesn't work, no matter how often or loudly people contend that it does—check out http://news.stanford.edu/news/2009/august24/multitask-research-study-082409.html), nor should work be attempted in the presence of people who are not involved in tasks of their own. Study with a dedicated group or in a location that is designated for study, at your desk where you do not play with the computer or spend time checking your email or having fun on the web, in a quiet library, or some other location where distracting cues can be minimized. You might also consider posting a note to yourself to remind yourself to focus on the task at hand.

4. *Value your task.* Since we tend to procrastinate more on tasks that are aversive to us, find ways to lessen this aversiveness by reminding yourself of the real value of the task. For example, you are not writing the essay because you "have to," but because this will increase your writing skills and your critical thinking, which will be of huge benefit for you in the future. The essay will give you a chance to learn something new and interesting and to express how you feel about the topic. As another example, a clean kitchen will be more hygienic and pleasant to use and will give you a feeling of satisfaction when it is done.

5. *Get organized.* While it is tempting to use organization, such as sharpening every pencil that you can find, as a means of procrastinating, overall organization is essential. If you are writing an essay, organize it first by breaking the task into smaller segments. First, you need to find out what your instructor requires for the essay. Then you need to choose a topic; next comes doing the research necessary for the essay; and then writing an outline, and so on. At this point, you can tackle each segment of the outline and reward yourself for completing each section. Organization breaks what sometimes seems like a long, overwhelming task into smaller, less aversive, manageable segments. It also helps to overcome the frustration procrastinators often feel in doing a large task, a feeling that may lead them to quit working. It makes it easier for you to reward yourself appropriately and it helps to avoid unanticipated roadblocks, such as a printer that has run out of ink.

6. *Set daily goals.* Daily goals are helpful in overcoming procrastination and keeping you focused on what needs to be done without overwhelming you. Accomplishing small segments of a large task on a day-to-day basis is rewarding in itself, and the task will get done without last-minute panic. It also helps to keep a record of your activities. Keep a log of your goals and what you accomplish each day, as well as whatever obstacles you encountered and how you did or did not deal with them. Monitoring your own behaviour will give you more control over it by making you aware of where your strengths are and what may trigger you to avoid your work.

7. *Plan for obstacles.* You have your own individual triggers that tempt you away from your work; become aware of them and plan exactly what you will do to avoid or resist them. For example, if you know that your friends tempt you to use your hour between classes to socialize with them instead of studying, plan how to avoid them at

this time or what you will say to excuse yourself. But socialization is an important daily goal too, so also plan when you socialize and how much time you will spend doing this.

So far we have discussed behavioural regulation, an area in which a great amount of practical and meaningful research has been done. Now we turn to emotion regulation, another area of importance and a large amount of research.

EMOTION REGULATION

Emotion regulation refers to "the set of processes whereby people seek to redirect the spontaneous flow of their emotions" (Koole, 2009, p. 6). There are some people, like Duncan in this chapter's case study, who contend that their emotions are overwhelming and control them, but this is generally not the fact. The truth is that the vast majority of us do control our emotions on a daily basis; otherwise, we would weep in the grocery store as a sad piece of music is played in the background, or we would laugh and dance in the aisle when we see an old friend at a funeral.

The Need for Emotion Regulation

Emotion regulation is a necessary part of life for optimal functioning. In a social sense, we need to maintain a poised and pleasant frame of mind when we meet a new person, even if that person reminds us of someone we intensely dislike; in a potentially confrontational situation, an out-of-control display of anger will make matters worse instead of better; in our romantic lives, continued displays of jealousy, resentment, and indifference tend to be reasons for the object of our affections leaving us (Van Cleef, 2009).

Emotion regulation also plays a large role in psychological health: people with psychological disorders such as anorexia nervosa, depression, and borderline personality disorder show an inability to regulate emotions effectively (respectively, Harrison, Sullivan, Tchanturia, & Treasure, 2009; Yap, Allen, & Ladouceur, 2008; Domes, Schulze, & Herpertz, 2009). In fact, Gross and Munoz (1995) find that inability to regulate emotions is widely found in a variety of psychological disorders. It has even been suggested that lack of emotion regulation may play a large part in the commission of crimes (Day, 2009).

We generally make the assumption, both in our day-to-day lives and in research, that people want to have pleasant emotions and avoid unpleasant emotions, and in truth we do (Volokhov & Demaree, 2010). But Tamir (2009) presents evidence that this is not always the case. In some cases, we may prefer unpleasant emotions if we believe that the unpleasant emotion will be useful to us. For example, a student may wish to feel some fear rather than relaxation and contentment when studying for an imminent examination. A person facing a confrontation with another may wish to feel anger rather than amiable sociability. When a young friend of mine said that she was about to watch a sad movie for the sixth time, I asked her why, since it makes her cry. "But that *is* why!" she answered! Often, Tamir's data says, we are not aware of our preferences or the reasons for them, but the preferences remain. In the following discussion, the emphasis is placed on promoting positive emotions, but we must bear in mind that the same principles may apply to the promotion of negative emotions if we deem them useful in the context in which we find ourselves.

The Development of Emotion Regulation

While it may be that some of us are born more sensitive to emotional arousal than others and some may perhaps have a slight genetic edge over others in ability to regulate emotions (Canki, Ferri, & Duman, 2009), emotion regulation is for the most part influenced by the environment and is learned.

From early years, parents socialize their children in the understanding and regulation of emotions by talking to them about emotions, explaining causes and consequences of emotions, reacting to their emotions, directly teaching them how to self-regulate, and modelling emotions, emotion regulation, and emotional reactions themselves (Denham & Kochanoff, 2002; Lunkenheimer, Shields, & Cortina, 2007; Morris, Silk, Steinberg, Myers, & Robinson, 2007). Clearly, parents who are unemotional, who punish emotions, or who avoid discussion of emotions will not be helpful in the development of emotion regulation.

Even in adolescence, parents who dampen their children's positive moods tend to have children who are deficient in emotion regulation skills (Yap, Allen, & Ladouceur, 2008). As late as the beginning college years, research has found that young adults whose mothers are psychologically controlling (e.g., "You disappoint me so much I hate to get up in the morning") have young adult children who show lower levels of emotion regulation (Manzeske & Stright, 2009). And, as is the case with behaviour self-regulation, secure attachment with parents predicts later ability to emotionally self-regulate (Morris, Silk, Steinberg, Myers, & Robinson, 2007).

How We Regulate Emotions

How do we regulate our emotions? We have a variety of techniques, some more useful than others. Some of our techniques are quite maladaptive. Some people may binge eat, drink alcohol to excess, take mind-altering illegal drugs, shop or gamble with money they don't have or can't afford to spend, or engage in other damaging activities that momentarily make them feel better. While there may be a short-term effect of enhanced positive moods, in the long term these techniques are more harmful than helpful and often leave people feeling worse than they did before.

Looking at more adaptive techniques, Gross (1998, 1999, 2001, 2002) proposes a model of emotion regulation sub-dividing the kinds of strategies we may use. There are **antecedent-focused strategies**, which are strategies that we use to manage an emotion before it is fully activated, and there are **response-focused strategies**, which we use when the emotion is already activated.

Antecedent-Focused Strategies

Antecedent-focused strategies may also take different forms. One form is that of **situation selection**. We may choose the situation we want to be in to enhance or regulate our emotions. So, for example, if we wish to celebrate the end of a semester, we may choose to socialize at a party. The overall mood of the party will, presumably, enhance our own good mood. Or we may feel that the party will cheer us up if we believe that the semester has not gone well.

Sometimes we use **situation modification**. When a situation is not conducive to the emotions we want to feel, we may change the situation. For instance, if we want to cheer up and the music on the radio is downbeat, we may change to a more upbeat station.

We may also use **attentional deployment**. If something occurs during a situation that we can't change and we don't want to leave, we may shift our attention to something else. Imagine you are in a coffee shop with four friends and one friend is in an angry mood that doesn't match yours. You may subtly turn away and start a conversation with another friend in order to avoid dealing with a mood of anger.

Cognitive change may be helpful as well. We use this particularly when we wish to feel better about something. An example of this was given by Seligman (2006) in Chapter 5 (see Box 5.2). When we use cognitive change as a strategy, we change our perceptions and interpretations of a situation. **Reappraisal** is a common strategy in this category and is typically used to change a potentially negative emotion into a more positive one. So, if we feel badly because of a romantic break-up, we may start thinking "I'll never be loved by anyone." With reappraisal, we would change this essentially irrational belief into "This relationship didn't work out for me. The next one will probably be much better after all I learned," a more rational thought and one that would decrease feelings of hopelessness and depression.

Response-Focused Strategies

Maladaptive emotion-regulation strategies are often of the kind described earlier, and take the form of engaging in ultimately destructive activities, such as drinking to excess. These are predominantly response-focused strategies, applied when the negative emotion is already in full swing. This form of response-focused strategy, **response modulation**, is not always so maladaptive. For example, the technique of **suppression** refers to managing an emotion by hiding the expression of it. With this technique, we mask our true emotion, usually in order to get through a situation so that we can feel better afterwards. Thus, the person who is nervous on a first date may hide the nervousness, with the hope that the nervousness will dissipate as the date progresses, and the second date will be more pleasant.

Effectiveness of Emotion-Regulating Strategies

Gross (2001) proposed that strategies that are used before an emotion is completely activated will be more effective in regulating emotions than those used after the emotion is already fully activated, and for the most part, research has indicated that he was right. Most people do use antecedent-focused strategies, especially reappraisal, even when they are not instructed specifically to do so (Volokhov & Demarree, 2010), and reappraisal appears to be the most effective one, followed by attention deployment (Augustine & Hemenover, 2009; Hofmann, Heering, Sayer, & Asnaani, 2009).

Reappraisal has also been found to be more effective in reducing anger than suppression or simple acceptance of emotion (Szasz, Szentagotai, & Hofmann, 2011). In a review of emotion regulation strategies used by people with psychological disorders, Aldao, Nolen-Hoeksema, and Schweizer (2010) found that adaptive strategies such as reappraisal are related to less psychopathology than are maladaptive strategies such as rumination (thinking about a situation unremittingly) or suppression, and for this reason, cognitive behaviour therapy, which includes teaching people how to reappraise their situation, is often very helpful.

We will not discuss emotion regulation any further right now because, in essence, this whole book is about making our feelings about our lives more positive and more satisfying, and this, of course, is mainly achieved through emotion regulation.

SPOTLIGHT ON RESEARCH

Emotion Regulation in Students

A particularly relevant study for many readers of this book is one conducted recently in Italy by Schmidt, Tinti, Levine, and Testa (2010). These researchers surveyed the emotions and emotion-regulating strategies of 610 high school students with questionnaires three weeks before their final diploma examination. They found that the strategies these students used to deal with their emotions depended on the type of emotions they felt. Some students saw the upcoming examination as important, but felt that their ability to cope with it was low. They felt fearful and anxious about the examination, and tended to use drugs more to cope and to focus their thoughts on the examination without being able to distance themselves from it.

Other students also regarded the examination as important and believed that their ability to cope with it was low, and they saw the results of the examination as being out of their control. These students felt frustration and powerlessness, and they often used drugs to cope, but they also distanced themselves from the situation and suppressed thoughts of the examination.

Still other students felt more positively about the examination, feeling confident and in control of the outcome.

These students coped with their emotions by using reappraisal and problem-focused strategies. Certainly the strategies used by these students are the most adaptive because they not only maintain more positive emotions, such as optimism and hope, but they also lead to behaviours, such as increased studying, that are more likely to achieve success and maintain their positive emotions. The researchers note that these students are also building useful resources for the future, in line with Fredrickson's (2001) broaden-and-build theory (see Chapter 5).

Of course, as in any questionnaire research, we must rely on the self-awareness of the students and on their honesty in reporting their emotions and their coping strategies, and we must remember that the results reveal only a correlation, so causality cannot be inferred. Perhaps another factor, such as coming from a dysfunctional home, led to the results of feelings of powerlessness being related to drug use, for example. And we wonder, how did the students fare in their examination three weeks later? The researchers, unfortunately, did not measure the relationship between anticipatory emotions or coping strategies and the outcomes of the examinations.

REFLECTIVE EXERCISE

Emotion Regulation

How do you regulate emotions? Do your techniques seem adequate to you? Which techniques do you use? When do you use them? Are there situations in which you feel that regulating your emotions would be inappropriate or cut down on your fun? What kinds of situations are these? Do they have anything in common? Is there anything about your emotion regulation that you would like to change? Why?

Conclusion

All in all, it seems clear that being able to regulate how we act and how we feel is vital to our achieving a satisfying life. This is not to say that we must regulate everything. What would life be if we couldn't sometimes be unstructured in our actions or explode in love and joy with the people we hold dearest? The key is in finding a balance and being able to determine for ourselves when we need to regulate ourselves and when regulation would simply mean being inhibited and inflexible. Finding that balance is individual and in itself is part of self-regulation.

But what of Sandy and Duncan? Will they make it as a couple? That's unsure. Certainly some odd couples remain happily together for a lifetime, while others leave the relationship in frustration. If they do remain together, it seems obvious that some self-regulation will have to take place: perhaps Duncan will need to learn some emotion regulation (it's frightening and sometimes dangerous to live with someone who has uncontrolled anger) and at least learn to be a little neater and come close to being on time. Sandy, too, will need to become more flexible and learn to let go a bit—the dishes don't really have to be washed the minute she finishes eating, especially if it means leaving a wonderful conversation with a loved one. And a little clutter probably won't kill her. Perhaps she can learn to see Duncan's (modified) lack of self-regulation as a counterbalance to her own way of being and rejoice in the spontaneity that his approach brings.

Summary

- Self-regulation is predictive of academic success, greater financial success, and more success with interpersonal relationships, and is beneficial for dealing with stress.
- Being self-aware is the first step in self-regulation. Mindfulness refers to being aware of present experiences and regarding them without judgment or evaluation. It allows more ability for us to choose our emotions and our reactions to them.
- Self-determination theory examines motivation. With intrinsic motivation, we perform tasks because of our own interest. Tasks that are performed for intrinsic motivation are perceived as more pleasant and typically result in better outcomes.
- Extrinsic motivation refers to performing an action because outside influences say it is desirable or even mandatory. It has been regarded as less desirable and less effective in providing people with persistence and satisfaction.

- There are four kinds of extrinsic motivation: (1) external regulation, from outside forces that will reward or punish for performing a task or for not performing it; (2) introjected regulation, from feelings of guilt or lowered self-esteem for not performing the task or feelings of self-enhancement for successful completion; (3) identified regulation, from a belief that doing a task will further other external goals; and (4) integrated regulation, from beliefs that the task is valuable in itself.
- Autonomy is important in developing intrinsic motivation. Intrinsic motivation may be undermined if we feel that we are being compelled to do something we normally would for pleasure (the overjustification effect).
- A feeling of competence or self-efficacy is important for intrinsic motivation. Without self-efficacy, we would not be able to feel self-esteem.
- Self-efficacy develops through our experience with accomplishing tasks, by watching others perform activities, by imagining successfully performing a task, by verbal persuasion from people, and by our physiological state.
- Social relatedness is a factor in the development of intrinsic motivation and identified regulation.
- Ego depletion occurs when self-control has been exerted on a first task; the amount of self-control available to be exerted on a second task is reduced.
- Severe procrastinators tend to be more impulsive, with greater responsiveness to whether a task is pleasant or not. They start their work with pleasant tasks first and follow with unpleasant tasks, if time permits. They tend to dislike structure and routine, preferring short-term goals to long-term goals. They are easily distracted, lack organization, and are poor at keeping promises to themselves.
- Student procrastination is related to lower overall GPA and lower grades in individual courses, assignments, and final examinations. Post-educationally, procrastinators put off managing their finances, leading to a reduced state of financial well-being. They also postpone seeing a physician for health problems.
- Active procrastinators have as high a sense of self-efficacy as non-procrastinators, and they feel almost as much mastery over their time. They may delay doing a task because of their judgments that other tasks should have higher priority.
- Procrastination may be overcome by (1) increasing self-efficacy, (2) building in rewards, (3) eliminating distractions, (4) valuing the task, (5) becoming more organized, (6) setting daily goals and monitoring behaviour, and (7) planning how to overcome temptations and obstacles.
- Emotion regulation is mainly influenced by the environment and is learned.
- Antecedent-focused strategies are strategies that manage an emotion before it is fully activated. We may use situation selection, situation modification, attentional deployment, or cognitive change, including reappraisal of the situation we are in.
- Response-focused strategies are applied when the negative emotion is already in full swing. It includes response modulation such as suppression or managing an emotion.
- Antecedent-focused strategies are more effective than response-focused strategies. Cognitive change strategies such as reappraisal are often used and can be very effective.

Group Discussion Questions

1. Can there be too much self-awareness? Does the answer to this question really depend on how a person uses and reacts to self-awareness?

2. Is non-conformity a measure of autonomy? What's the difference between non-conformity and autonomy?

3. Some parents praise their children for their efforts to accomplish a task even if they do it incorrectly. Will this build self-efficacy in a child? What are the benefits and pitfalls of "giving an A for effort"?

4. "Never let anyone see you cry." "Bottling up emotions is bad for you." Debate the merits of these two statements.

CHAPTER 7

Character Strengths

"No matter how dreary and gray our homes are, we people of flesh and blood would rather live there than in any other country, be it ever so beautiful. There is no place like home." [Dorothy to the Scarecrow]

– Baum, 1944, p. 29

"Can't you give me brains?" asked the Scarecrow.

"You don't need them. You are learning something every day. A baby has brains, but it doesn't know much. Experience is the only thing that brings knowledge, and the longer you are on earth the more experience you are sure to get... I'm not much of a magician, as I said; but if you will come to me tomorrow morning, I will stuff your head with brains. I cannot tell you how to use them, however; you must find that out for yourself."

... "But how about my courage?" asked the Lion anxiously.

"You have plenty of courage, I am sure," answered Oz. "All you need is confidence in yourself. There is no living thing that is not afraid when it faces danger. True courage is in facing danger when you are afraid, and that kind of courage you have in plenty."

... "How about my heart?" asked the Tin Woodman.

"Why, as for that," answered Oz, "I think you are wrong to want a heart. It makes most people unhappy. If you only knew it, you are in luck not to have a heart."

"That must be a matter of opinion," said the Tin Woodman.

– Baum, 1944, pp.152–154

LEARNING OBJECTIVES

In this chapter, students will learn about
- □ The Values in Action classification system of virtues and strengths.
- □ The effects of character strengths on life satisfaction and well-being.
- □ Gratitude.
- □ Forgiveness.
- □ Courage.
- □ Humour.
- □ Wisdom.

The Wizard of Oz by L. Frank Baum (1944) has been a favourite of both children and adults for over 100 years, in part because of the lessons it conveys about what might be called virtue. Dorothy learns the meaning of gratitude for her home and her family and friends; the Scarecrow wants brains although it is clear that he already possesses wisdom; the Lion wants courage, but he seems to be confusing courage with fearlessness; the Tin Woodman wants a heart, although he has previously revealed his love and forgiveness for others. These are only a few of the positive qualities or character strengths that are demonstrated in the book.

CHARACTER STRENGTHS
The Problem of Definition

Character strengths and virtues have not been studied extensively in the past, probably because of the subjectivity of the value judgment that such study implies. What is a strength or a virtue? Even within a culture, people often have very different opinions about this. The Tin Woodman and the Wizard of Oz disagree about whether having a heart is good or not. In the non-fictional world, to some people, for instance, compassion and mercy are virtues, classified as "good," while to other people, compassion and mercy are more indicative of weakness, classified as "bad."

Another potential stumbling block in studying virtues or character strengths is that each may be context-specific. That is, whether a person demonstrates a character strength depends on the situation he/she is in. For example, are you honest? If you were given twenty dollars more in change at a store than you should have received, would you return it? What if you received twenty cents more? Most students in my classes answer "yes" to both questions, and feel that they have established themselves as honest. Now imagine the following scenario: Aunt Penelope has just had a new haircut that she loves but you think is awful. She asks you what you think. Do you answer honestly and tell her the haircut is terrible? Or do you find other things to say, such as "Wow, that's so different. It takes a little getting used to. I bet it's really going to be easy and comfortable for the summer." In this case, my students feel that honesty is not the best policy; in fact, honesty would be cruel, and they opt for tact and compassion over honesty. What do you think? Is honesty the best policy only in certain circumstances?

Despite these problems, the working definition of **character strength** for us is "a subset of personality traits that are morally valued" in most cultures (Gillham, Adams-Deutsch, Werner, Reivich, Coulter-Heindl, Linkins, et al., 2011, p. 31).

The Values in Action Classification System

Peterson and Seligman (2004), along with colleagues, undertook the mammoth task of developing a classification system for character strengths and virtues, the *Values in Action* (VIA) classification system. They included only those qualities that were found to be valued across cultures and in different historical time periods. With these criteria in mind, they propose that there are six core virtues, each of which includes several more specific character strengths.

1. *Strengths of wisdom and knowledge.* These represent the ability both to acquire information and to use it in beneficial ways. Included are creativity, curiosity, love of learning, open-mindedness, and perspective.

2. *Strengths of courage.* These strengths entail accomplishing goals in the face of obstacles and opposition from the inner or the outer world. They include honesty/authenticity/integrity, bravery, persistence, and zest/vitality.

3. *Strengths of humanity.* These strengths pertain to our ability to be socially connected to other people. They include kindness, love, and social intelligence (the ability to get along well with others).

4. *Strengths of justice*. These strengths are also social in nature, but on a broader level. They refer more to how an individual relates to a group or a community. These strengths are fairness, leadership, and teamwork.

5. *Strengths of temperance*. Strengths of temperance are those qualities that prevent us from going overboard in life. These strengths include forgiveness/mercy, modesty/humility, prudence, and self-regulation.

6. *Strengths of transcendence*. Strengths of transcendence are those qualities that allow us to make meaning in our lives and to become connected to something larger than ourselves, to the wide universe or Cosmos. These transcendent qualities include appreciation of beauty and excellence, gratitude, hope, humour, and religiousness/spirituality.

Effects of Character Strengths

There has been some effort to study the effects of all character strengths on the individual's sense of well-being and satisfaction in life. Lounsbury, Fisher, Levy, and Welsh (2009) measured character strengths on the VIA and found that all of them were positively related to life satisfaction in university students, and most were related to greater college satisfaction and grade point average as well. Similarly, Peterson, Park, and Seligman (2006) studied the VIA measures for 2,087 adults, many of whom had or had recovered from a serious physical illness. The researchers found that the participants who had or had recovered from a serious illness had higher scores on appreciation of beauty, bravery, curiosity, fairness, forgiveness, gratitude, humour, kindness, love of learning, and spirituality. The researchers suggest that some character strengths may ameliorate the stressful effects of illness.

Other research has examined a limited number of character strengths and found positive relationships with life satisfaction as well. Gillham et al. (2011), for example, found that in adolescents, strengths of transcendence predicted future life satisfaction. Lavy and Littman-Ovadia (2011) found that love, zest, gratitude, curiosity, and hope were related to higher life satisfaction in nearly 400 adults.

Still other research has investigated the effects of informing people of their top strengths and teaching them how to strengthen those qualities. Rust, Diessner, and Reade (2009) found that this type of intervention was effective in increasing the life satisfaction of college students. Macaskill and Denovan (2011) were interested in fostering a love of learning in university students and also found a positive effect. An important component of the interventions was informing people of their top strengths. Take the VIA survey for yourself at www.viacharacter.org for free to find out your own top strengths.

The greatest amount of research has focused on the effects of individual character strengths on well-being and life satisfaction. We have already discussed some of the character strengths of the VIA in previous chapters (e.g., hope and optimism in Chapter 5 and self-regulation in Chapter 6). In the rest of this chapter, we will discuss a few more that have received some empirical attention.

GRATITUDE

Gratitude, as it were, is the moral memory of mankind.

—*Georg Simmel (in McCullough, Emmons, & Tsang, 2002)*

The gratitude of most men is but a secret desire of receiving more benefits.

—*La Rochefoucauld (in McCullough, Emmons, & Tsang, 2002)*

Gratitude is not only the greatest of virtues, but the parent of all others.

—*Cicero (in McCullough, Kilpatrick, Emmons, & Larson, 2001)*

If the only prayer you ever say in your entire life is "Thank you," it will be enough.

—*Meister Eckhard (in Froh, Yurkewicz, & Kashdan, 2009)*

Reflect on your present blessings, of which every man has many, not on your past misfortunes, of which all men have some.

—*Charles Dickens (in Emmons & McCullough, 2003)*

Ingratitude! thou marble-hearted fiend, more hideous when thou show'st thee in a child than the sea-monster!

—*Shakespeare's* King Lear *(in Froh, Sefick, & Emmons, 2008)*

Gratitude has been discussed by philosophers, theologians, and scholars for many centuries, as the above quotes indicate. Yet it has received little attention from the world of psychological research until the last decade or so. The research that has been conducted has led to the following quotation from contemporary scientists: "Gratitude is perhaps the quintessential positive psychological trait, as it involves a life orientation toward the positive in the world" (Wood, Maltby, Gillett, Linley, & Joseph, 2008, p. 854). That's a very strong statement, and, as we shall see, there may be truth in it.

What is Gratitude?

Gratitude is a positive emotion that arises when we feel that someone has voluntarily and intentionally done something (or tried to do something) that benefited us, even if it cost the benefactor to do so. Gratitude is an emotion that is found in nearly all cultures and is emphasized in the major religions of the world (McCullough, Kilpatrick, Emmons, & Larson, 2001). It is classified as a strength of transcendence by Peterson and Seligman (2004) because the feeling of gratitude makes us aware of something larger than ourselves, the kindness of others, the gift of life, and so on.

Although some cynics have contended that gratitude is little more than a reflection of the indebtedness we feel when someone has done something beneficial for us, research indicates that indebtedness and gratitude are two different feelings. Indebtedness is an unpleasant emotion; it often carries resentment and aggravation with it. Most of us don't like feeling that we "have to" do something for someone else because society expects or even demands it from us. It makes us feel that we have been a burden to our benefactor, or we are in some way inferior to the benefactor, or that our freedom of choice in what we do has been curtailed. When we feel indebted, but not grateful, it may be that we perceive the benefactor's intentions as selfish ("I'll help you move, but you have to help me next weekend") and we are less likely to feel kindly disposed toward our benefactor and less likely to want to help him/her.

On the other hand, gratitude makes us want to do something nice for our benefactor and even increases our kindness to other people, not just because we are expected to or because the benefactor's actions have put us in an overall good mood (Emmons & McCullough, 2003; Goei & Boster, 2005; Tsang, 2006a; Watkins, Scheer, Ovnicek, & Kolts, 2006). In fact, feeling gratitude causes us to want to help others even when it costs us something to do so (Bartlett & DeSteno, 2006; Tsang, 2006a).

Characteristics of Grateful People

Research has substantiated that gratitude is related to many other positive characteristics that people may possess. For example, grateful people are more agreeable, psychologically stable, and more self-confident without being arrogant than are less grateful people (Watkins, Van Gelder, & Frias, 2009). They interpret events as more positive than do less grateful people (Lambert, Graham, Fineham, & Stillman, 2009) and they remember the good episodes of their lives more (Watkins, Van Gelder, & Frias, 2009). They have more positive thoughts before they go to sleep and they sleep better (Wood, Joseph, Lloyd, & Atkins, 2009). Grateful people have more adaptive coping skills than do less grateful people (Vernon, Dillon, & Steiner, 2009; Wood, Joseph, & Linley, 2007).

Grateful people are more prosocial (McCullough, Emmons, & Tsang, 2002) and are more ready to forgive others for transgressions (Bono & McCullough, 2006; Toussaint & Friedman, 2009). They perceive themselves to have more social support, less stress, and fewer symptoms of depression than do less grateful people (Wood, Maltby, Gillett, Linley, & Joseph, 2008). They see favours that are done as being more valuable and positive and see benefactors as more genuinely helpful and as having paid a larger price for doing the favour than do people with less gratitude (Wood, Maltby, Stewart, Linley, & Joseph, 2008)

Grateful people are less materialistic than are less grateful people (Lambert, Fincham, Stillman, & Dean, 2009; Polak & McCullough, 2006; Tsang, 2002). They are more likely to be spiritual and religious, seeking a closer relationship with the Divine or with the Cosmos, than are less grateful people (Emmons & Kneezel, 2005; McCullough, Emmons, & Tsang, 2002).

The Effects of Gratitude on Well-Being

Gratitude has been found to play a causal role in increasing our feelings of well-being and is even being used as a therapeutic intervention for people with depression and anxiety (Bono & McCullough, 2006). People who feel gratitude in life report more psychological and subjective well-being than do those who feel less gratitude, above and beyond other personality characteristics they may have (Lambert, Fincham, Stillman, & Dean, 2009; Toussaint & Friedman, 2009; Wood, Joseph, & Linley, 2007; Wood, Joseph, & Maltby, 2008, 2009). Indeed, Park, Peterson, and Seligman (2004) found that the only two factors that were more predictive of a sense of well-being were hope and zest.

It seems clear that gratitude plays a large part in life satisfaction and good functioning in life. In fact, gratitude has a large role to play in influencing many parts of our lives. McCullough, Kilpatrick, Emmons, and Larson (2001) proposed that gratitude is a moral state that encompasses three functions. First, it acts as a barometer signalling changes in the relationship between two people, with one having given a kindness and the other having benefited from the kindness. Second, it is a motive that indicates to people that kind acts should be reciprocated to the benefactor and done for other people. Third, it is a moral reinforcer because the expression of gratitude is pleasant for the benefactor, resulting in him/her performing more acts of kindness in the future. While there is evidence that gratitude performs all three functions, it seems that the strongest support is for gratitude as a moral reinforcer (Baumgardner & Crothers, 2009).

With an eye to the research findings, Watkins, Van Gelder, and Frias (2009) suggest five ways in which gratitude contributes to happiness:

1. It enhances happiness directly by making one enjoy the kindnesses more.

2. It leads a person to focus on the good things in his/her life and devote less attention to the bad things and the deficiencies of his/her life. In this way it leads to more optimism about the future and less envy and depression in the present.

3. It is highly beneficial to social relationships. Grateful people are more likely to express their gratitude and to engage in more prosocial acts, thereby making their relationships more pleasant and more likely to be maintained and stable.

4. It may be helpful in coping with adversity because the concentration on the good aspects of life is useful in making meaning of distressing episodes and finding the "silver lining" in the storm cloud.

5. It facilitates remembering the pleasant aspects and memories of one's life.

It is very much worth noting how well the evidence about the benefits of gratitude fits with Frederickson's (Frederickson & Branigan, 2005; Frederickson & Joiner, 2002; Frederickson, Mancuso, Branigan, & Tugade, 2000; Otake, Shimai, Tanaka-Matsumi, Otsui, & Frederickson, 2006) broaden-and-build theory, as discussed in Chapter 5. When someone has done us a kindness, we feel gratitude. This in itself makes us feel better than we felt before. We express our gratitude to our benefactor, and this makes the benefactor feel better than he/she did before. It also makes it more likely that the benefactor will look upon us favourably and be more likely to bestow kindness on us again in the future, making both of us feel better.

As well, both we and the benefactor are more likely to perceive kindness in the world, to interpret people and events in a more positive framework thereby seeing the world as a more benevolent place, and to act more prosocially toward other people. This increases other people's positive feelings and makes them more likely to be well-disposed toward us and others. This will increase our social interactions and perhaps increase the social support we have in times of trouble, again, making all of us feel better. In feeling better, we have more optimism, more hope, and a more satisfying life, as do the recipients of both gratitude and kindness. One act of kindness followed by one act of gratitude can start a spiral upwards of good feelings and positive benefits for us and many other people. That's pretty inspiring!

As we have seen, people who have more gratitude in life also tend to be people who forgive more readily (Bono & McCullough, 2006; Toussaint & Friedman, 2009).

One of the situations in which we usually feel gratitude is when we have committed an act that is less than exemplary and we require forgiveness. When forgiveness is forthcoming, the relief and gratitude we feel increase our overall sense of well-being. Let's turn to a closer examination of forgiveness.

REFLECTIVE EXERCISE

Gratitude

Seligman, Steen, Park, and Peterson (2005) devised exercises that they thought might increase people's happiness. One exercise was very successful in this, at least for a few weeks. Try it yourself: write a letter to someone you are grateful to, telling them why you are grateful and what their action or presence in your life has meant to you. If possible, deliver the letter in person. If you find that this exercise makes you and the recipient happy (and Peterson, 2006, contends that it "works" 100 percent of the time), why not make this exercise part of your life, perhaps on a monthly basis?

FORGIVENESS

Abel and Byron had been best friends since they were in grade school. They learned to read together, skinned their knees together, and went to university and roomed together. They always said that they had each other's back. Then Gillian came along. Abel was smitten with her immediately and confided this to Byron, who helped him plan how to approach her. But Gillian had other ideas—she was taken with Byron and asked him to go out with her. Byron said yes. Abel was crushed. Not only did Gillian seem to prefer Byron to him, but, as he saw it, his best friend betrayed him in accepting a date with Gillian before Abel had a chance to approach her. At first, Abel could only think of resorting to physical violence against Byron, but Abel is a pretty peaceful guy, and hitting people isn't his style. But he thinks about the situation non-stop, and he fantasizes about what he would like to say to Byron, including some very nasty, hurtful things that he knows would wound Byron. Byron is sorry, but puzzled by Abel's reaction. He thinks Abel is over-reacting in saying that his actions were a betrayal. "It's not as if they were already dating and I broke in," he says. He has tried to talk to Abel to defend himself, but Abel won't speak to Byron, who has finally given up.

Abel and Byron seem to have lost a relationship that clearly meant a great deal to both of them. Abel feels betrayed by his best friend in that his trust has been broken, while Byron doesn't think that what he did was a betrayal. He may be sorry for Abel's upset, but he doesn't seem to be sorry for accepting the date with Gillian. What is Abel to do in this situation? Should he deny his feelings of betrayal in order to keep his relationship with Byron? But if he did that, would he be true to himself? Would the relationship ever be the same again? Would Abel ever be able to feel trust for Byron? Should Abel confront Byron the way he fantasizes? Or would that simply cause more long-term hurt and end the relationship with bitterness and more pain? Would it make Abel feel better? Is it possible for both men to talk to each other, to gain some understanding of each other's perspective on the situation and their feelings about it?

Can Byron learn to have more sensitivity to his friend and perhaps regret accepting the date with Gillian? Can Abel forgive Byron?

We all have thousands of episodes in our lives that call for us to forgive others. In the course of a day, we may have our toes stepped on by a stranger in an elevator, we may have a co-worker forget to do work that was promised, we may have a family member look uninterested when we try to tell him/her about the exciting thing that happened to us, we may have the person we love most tell us that he/she loves someone else. Do we forgive these people? As we shall see, that depends on several factors. We will also discuss the even more difficult situation of having to forgive ourselves.

What Is Forgiveness?

One of the contentious issues in the area of forgiveness is deciding exactly what it means (Lawler-Row, Scott, Raines, Edlis-Matityahou, & Moore, 2007). For example, does forgiveness mean simply letting go of the anger one initially feels in a situation? If so, then has one forgiven another if the anger dissipates over time? Does forgiveness mean a complete reconciliation of the relationship, as if the transgression had never occurred? If the transgressor is a stranger who has done wrong, does forgiveness need to be communicated to the stranger? Does forgiveness mean having positive feelings about the transgressor? If so, can parents ever forgive the person who killed their child, even if the death was accidental? Is forgiveness a choice we make or an emotion we experience? And is it necessary in order to have a satisfying life? So many questions for a concept we use every day!

Some researchers (e.g., Peterson & Seligman, 2004; Worthington, 2005) have been very clear on what forgiveness is not: forgiveness is not forgetting about the transgression or denying that it took place, nor is it excusing or condoning the transgression. Forgiveness is not about minimizing the hurt that the transgression has caused. Therefore, **forgiveness** is about acknowledging and accepting the hurt that we feel and finding a way to move past it. Lawler-Row, Karremans, Scott, Edlis-Matityahou, and Edwards (2008) contend that there is consensus that forgiveness involves two processes: (1) releasing negative emotions even though one has the right to them, and (2) fostering positive emotions toward the transgressor, even though he/she has no right to them.

Many of us find the first process, letting go of our own negative emotions, to be easier than the second process, fostering positive emotions toward the transgressor. But it is important to note that fostering positive emotions toward the transgressor doesn't necessarily mean that we have to embrace the person who hurt us with the love we would shower on a non-transgressing best friend or family member. It means that we learn to have some compassion and perhaps even empathy for the person who hurt us. It doesn't mean that we ever forget the hurt or even regain the trust we once had in the transgressor, but we may come to understand (if not agree with) the transgressor's perspective on the situation and feel a measure of generosity toward him/her. In our example above, Abel, while not agreeing with Byron's position, may be able to comprehend that Byron had no intent to betray him; rather, the two men interpreted the situation in different ways. Abel, in forgiving Byron, may come to the point at which he can say "I won't confide anything about my love life to Byron again, but I can see he didn't mean to hurt me and he's upset that he did hurt me. So I guess he and I can still be friends, even if it takes a lot of time to get back to where we were."

The Effects of Forgiveness on Well-Being

Some people wonder if we should even bother trying to forgive those who have hurt us. In terms of positive psychology, the answer is a resounding yes! There is much to gain by forgiving, and much to lose by not forgiving. Forgiveness is associated with better physical health (Lawler, Younger, Piferi, Jobe, Edmondson, & Jones, 2005; Lawler-Row, Karremans, Scott, Edlis-Matityahou, & Edwards, 2008), better psychological health (Burnette, Davis, Green, Worthington Jr., & Bradfield, 2009; Orth, Berking, Walker, Meier, & Znoj, 2008; Tse & Yip, 2009; Ysseldyk, Matheson, & Anisman, 2009), and a more satisfying life (Hill & Allemand, 2010; Lawler-Row & Piferi, 2006; Tse & Yip, 2009).

Obviously, since no one is perfect and we all make mistakes, relationships cannot survive without forgiveness. Without forgiveness, relationships would be impossible, and so the beneficial effects we get from social support would be gone. Certainly, not forgiving a person who has transgressed against us damages the relationship even further. Without forgiveness, in many cases we are left with only anger and resentment, ruminating on the ills that have been done to us. This is hardly the sort of optimistic, positive thought that is associated with a satisfying life, but it is the sort of thinking that is often associated with depression and anxiety (Allemand, Job, Christen, & Keller, 2008; Burnette, Davis, Green, Worthington Jr., & Bradfield, 2009; Tse & Yip, 2009).

Characteristics of Forgiving People

Some of us find it easy to forgive people in some situations but not in others. Other people seem to have a general trait of forgivingness that allows them to forgive more easily across a wide variety of situations. What are forgiving people like? First of all, while we often assume that forgiving others will make us better adjusted, Orth, Berking, Walker, Meier, and Znoj (2008), in studying 347 people, found that while forgiving a transgressor made people feel better in the short term, in the long run forgiveness did not predict better adjustment; on the contrary, being well-adjusted predicted forgivingness. So people who are forgiving seem to be people who have good psychological health to begin with. They are generally low in the personality dimension of neuroticism, which means that they do not have an overall tendency to experience negative emotions such as anxiety and depression.

Hill and Allemand (2010) also found that people who forgive more readily are those who have low levels of distressing emotions in general and also stress the importance of having solid social relationships. Forgiving others, to them, may be necessary in maintaining these relationships. It may also be that these people have valued relationships because they forgive easily. Another possibility (and none of these is mutually exclusive) is that they possess other qualities, such as good adjustment, which leads both to their having and valuing social relationships and to their relative ease in forgiving others. Not surprisingly, these people also have better relationships with others (Lawler-Row & Piferi, 2006).

Other qualities of people who are forgiving have been discovered. People who are forgiving are more likely to accept themselves, feel personal autonomy in their lives, and feel that their lives have meaning (Lawler-Row & Piferi, 2006). For example, when someone disappoints or transgresses against us, we, like Abel, may ruminate about this and keep our sense of having been "sinned against" alive and even increasing (Burnette, Davis, Green, Worthington Jr., & Bradfield, 2009). Allemand, Job, Christen, and Keller (2008) found that people who can stop their rumination and regulate their emotions, especially in reducing negative emotions, are more likely to be forgiving (see Chapter 6 for information on the regulation of emotions).

Being able to regulate emotions is important in forgiveness. When we have been transgressed against, it's easy to fly off the handle and express our very justifiable hurt and outrage, but this is rarely a good strategy. People who forgive transgressions against them tend to take a direct approach to their situation. They take time to calm their anger and understand their feelings, then they assertively, but not aggressively, communicate their feelings to the transgressor. That means that they speak about their own emotional state without raising their voices or using sarcasm or unsavoury language or accusations. Then they attempt to work out a resolution with the offender. Certainly this method is more likely to bring about a reconciliation or at least to end the possibility of hostility in the relationship. It also gives the offender a chance to understand what the other person believes the offender did wrong, the effects the action had on the other person, and provides an opportunity to apologize and make amends. Contrast this to the other common technique that people may use when they feel wronged. Imagine the scene of a couple leaving a party:

"What's wrong?"

"Nothing."

"C'mon, something's wrong, what is it?"

"You know very well what you did."

"No I don't, what did I do?"

"Well if you don't know, I'm certainly not going to tell you."

This situation is unlikely to lead to any resolution and likely to result in more hard feelings, but now on the part of both people involved. The transgressor may not realize what the problem is, or may not realize the impact of his/her actions. And with the "silent treatment" there is no chance of either making amends or not making the mistake in the future. Now both people need forgiveness: the transgressor for whatever it is that he/she has done, and the victim who refuses to deal with the problem in an open and honest fashion.

Most religions emphasize the need for forgiveness, pointing to the forgiveness and mercy of a deity as an example. A deep belief in religion and spirituality also implies feeling a greater sense of connectedness to other people and to the universe. It is not surprising, then, that people who are religious and spiritual are more forgiving (Laufer, Raz-Hamama, Levine, & Solomon, 2009; Lawler-Row & Piferi, 2006).

Being forgiving is found more often in women than in men (Exline & Zell, 2009; Miller, Worthington Jr., & McDaniel, 2008). This is generally attributed to the differing Western gender role socialization and prescriptions given to males and females. Females are traditionally raised to feel that the social domain is more important than any other and that it is their role to facilitate and maintain healthy social relationships. Consistent with this is the fact that women are more likely to be religious, holding more closely to the values, such as forgiveness, that are promoted by religion. It is not uncommon even today to hear some men say that their wives, for example, "take care" of the religion for the family. Males, on the other hand, are traditionally raised to be aggressive and power-ful, with an implied taboo against letting transgressions against them go unpunished. Indeed, a traditionally raised man may be accused of being "a girl" (intended to be an insult) if he forgives too readily! These gender roles are not as predominant any more, and it will be interesting to see if males and females differ on their forgivingness in future generations.

The Transgressor

Normally, one would think that transgressors are repentant for the harm they have caused, especially if harm was not their intent. Similarly, one would think that an apology would be more likely to lead to forgiveness. Both these assumptions are generally found to be correct (e.g., Eaton & Struthers, 2006; Franz & Bennigson, 2005), but not always.

Struthers and his colleagues at York University in Toronto have discovered that sometimes forgiving someone does not induce remorse, and sometimes an apology for a transgression actually impedes forgiveness. In one study (Struthers, Eaton, Shirvani, Georghiou, & Edell, 2008), people who said directly "I forgive you" to an offender were perceived as "holier-than-thou," decreasing remorse in the offender. These researchers suggest that the explicit forgiveness enhanced a sense of shame in the offenders. Experiencing a sense of shame is damaging to the offender's self-image and might motivate them to justify their actions or avoid the person whom they have harmed, thereby making reconciliation unlikely. This suggestion is supported by Exline and Zell (2009), who found that increasing shame in women resulted in their being less likely to forgive. If, on the other hand, the victim merely says "It's OK" or "It's all right" and then continues with a normal conversation, implying forgiveness rather than directly stating "I forgive you," the offender is less likely to feel shame and more likely to feel regret for the action, enhancing the desire for reconciliation.

In another study, Struthers and his colleagues found that when there has been a deliberate intent to harm another person, an apology is less likely to lead to forgiveness: if someone has deliberately hurt us, our reaction to their apology is more likely to be increased mistrust of the offender, an implied reaction of "Oh yeah? Well if you're so sorry, why did you do it in the first place and why are you apologizing now? What's the catch?" (Struthers, Eaton, Santelli, Uchiyama, & Shirvani, 2008). In the case of Abel and Byron, then, unless Abel becomes convinced that Byron did not mean to betray his friend, an apology from Byron might make the situation worse between them. By the same token, if Abel suddenly says to Byron "I forgive you," Byron's reaction may well be indignation since he doesn't feel that he did anything wrong.

It is clear that Abel and Byron see their situation very differently. They need to be able to see each other's perspective, they need to be able to empathize with each other a little more, in order for forgiveness and reconciliation to take place. Empathy is something we try to teach our children when we ask them "How do you think that made him feel?" or "I think you're feeling sad right now. Am I right?" Getting along well in the social world would be very difficult if we couldn't see other people's viewpoints or imagine what it might be like to walk in their shoes. It's not surprising that increased empathy is strongly related to forgiveness (see Exline & Zell, 2009, for a review).

Shame and Guilt

Forgiving oneself is an element of self-compassion, a topic that was discussed in Chapter 5. Forgiving other people may be hard enough, but many of us find it even more difficult to forgive ourselves. Rangganadhan and Todorow (2010) found that people who feel shame for their actions are less likely to forgive themselves than people who do not feel such shame. Interestingly, feeling a sense of guilt did not impede self-forgiveness.

Let's make the distinction between guilt and shame: when we feel guilt, we feel bad about what we have done (the external action), but when we feel shame, we feel bad about ourselves (the internal self-concept). It's easier to get over our guilt (e.g., vow not to repeat an external action in the future) than it is to deal with our shame (e.g., revise our self-concept).

In a study of student procrastination, Wohl, Pychyl and Bennett (2010) found that students who procrastinate feel bad about their actions (or lack of actions), leading them to avoid the task even further, as it increased their negative feelings about themselves. But being able to forgive themselves for procrastinating predicted less procrastination in the future. Although these researchers did not differentiate between guilt and shame in their study, we might speculate that the students who felt guilty about their procrastination found it easier to forgive themselves and change their behaviour in the future, as opposed to students who felt shame about their procrastination (and what they believed that procrastination said about their character) and could not self-forgive.

REFLECTIVE EXERCISE

Forgiveness

What does forgiveness mean to you? Do you feel that it is enough to let go of the negative emotions? Or do you feel that reconciliation and resumption of the pre-transgression relationship must be part of forgiveness?

Do you forgive easily? Have you been in a situation in which you needed forgiveness? Was it given in a way that made you feel better and restored the relationship? Are there situations that you would find unforgivable? What might they be? Or do you believe that every transgression should be forgiven? Are there conditions you would set to forgiveness? Is saying "I'm sorry" enough?

COURAGE

Which of the following acts would you consider to be courageous?

- A middle-aged woman leaves her abusive husband to live on her own for the first time.
- A college student is offered a copy of the final exam but refuses it.
- A previously physically inactive man attempts to climb a mountain.
- A police officer races to the scene of domestic violence.

- A shy child leaves her mother on her first day of school.
- A soldier lays his body on a land mine while shouting for his buddies to leave.
- A teenager goes to the prom bald after losing her hair as a result of chemotherapy.

Why do you consider some or all of these acts to be courageous? What does courage mean?

What Is Courage?

As seen in the above examples, courage can be seen in many different actions, and we don't all agree on what should be considered courageous. Do you realize how courageous you are? Probably not. When we speak of courage and heroism, we tend to think first of examples of war-time exploits, of the amazing men and women who stand ready to fight fires in order to save us, sometimes even without pay, and of the daring rescues we read about in newspapers.

From another point of view, philosophers such as Paul Tillich (1952) contend that we must show courage in order to live. After all, we face each day with the knowledge that we may die at any time or that fate may intervene to bring us misfortune that will affect the rest of our lives; we persist in trying to grow and become the best we can be, even though we know that our whole lifespan will not be long enough to realize our full potential; we tackle each task we are given knowing that whatever the end result, it will not be the product of our "best" efforts, but one that is compromised by the time and resources we have available to us. We live our lives with the faith that good will prevail and justice will triumph, in our lives and in the world at large. Tillich believes that psychological disorders such as anxiety and depression are a failure of courage, but existential psychologists such as Rollo May (1975, 1977) insist that even neuroses reflect people's courageous attempts at coping with the world, even though these attempts are misguided and ultimately self-destructive (see Chapter 2).

In positive psychology, courage has been studied very little and certainly deserves more attention. Recall that Peterson and Seligman (2004) found that courage was one of the virtues that people may possess, a virtue that encompasses bravery, honesty/ authenticity/integrity, persistence, and zest/vitality. People who are courageous in any action may show bravery or valour since their actions may meet with personal or group consequences that are detrimental to the physical or psychological well-being of the individual, yet they commit the act anyway. Their actions reveal their beliefs in spite of possible disapproval or danger. They commit to the action and persist in it, even when warned off. And they put all their energy or vitality into it: courageous actions are rarely half-hearted.

Types of Courage

Since courage is another quality that is subjective, we must note that there are several kinds of courage. The first distinction must be made between general courage and personal courage (Pury & Kowalski, 2007; Pury, Kowalski, & Spearman, 2007). **General courage** reflects actions that the majority of people would find risky and would avoid. For example, the actions of a firefighter in racing into a burning building to rescue people would indicate an act of general courage. **Personal courage**, however, while perhaps no less courageous, reflects actions that are risky for a particular individual, but would not be considered risky for most people. In showing personal courage, the individual must overcome obstacles that are particular to the individual and the situation. An example of this is seen in classrooms every day: a student who is terrified of public speaking swallows his/her fears and enrolls in a non-credit course that will require the student to give presentations to the class. Public speaking may not be enjoyed by everyone, but most students do not find it terrifying. The student who truly fears it (and there are many!) shows personal courage in opting to take the course and face the fear.

Courage can also be classified in other ways. There is **physical courage**, in which an action may result in the person's bodily harm or even death (e.g., the firefighter in the example of general courage above). There is **moral courage**, in which a person stands up for what he/she believes in, even in the face of possible disapproval, rejection, or other negative consequences (e.g., the teenager who refuses to join friends in taking drugs). There is **psychological courage**, in which the person performs an action that may threaten his or her psychological well-being (e.g., the student who fears public speaking in the example of personal courage above) (Putnam, 1997). Other forms of courage have been described, such as **vital courage**, a form of psychological courage in which a person lives and thrives in the face of physical or mental illness (Lopez, O'Byrne, & Peterson, 2003).

General Conceptions of Courage

Identifying an act as courageous is a judgment call. When a person goes bungee-jumping for the first time, some people may call this act courageous, while other people call it foolhardy. In order to define courage, it becomes necessary to examine just how people define courage in their own minds, their general conceptions of courage. Rate, Clarke, Lindsay, and Sternberg (2007) performed a series of studies to determine how people decide whether an action is courageous or not. Their findings indicate that to be judged as courageous, an act must have several components.

The first component is intent: the act must be intentional. If a person performs an act that just happens to save people's lives, it is not considered courageous. An example might be throwing a "piece of junk" away from a crowd and finding out later that it was a hand grenade. This act is considered lucky, but does not involve courage.

The second component is mindful deliberation—that is, people must perform the action with awareness and deliberateness. The act must be the result of decision-making on the part of the person. Acts that are performed without thinking (such as a parent running into the path of oncoming cars to pull a child to safety) are less likely to be considered courageous. On the other hand, an act that has been decided upon with awareness of the risks involved is more likely to be considered courageous (e.g., after seeing another person drown in the attempt to save someone, a person jumps into the water to attempt a rescue anyway).

The action performed must also entail some risk, physical or psychological, to the person to be called courageous. For example, jumping into a swimming pool at the shallow end to pull another person to the pool edge would not be considered courageous—that is, unless the person jumping into the pool was afraid of the water! In applying this criterion for courage, onlookers may not always be aware of the subjective risk that the actor feels and so may not regard the act as courageous while, to the actor, the act was indeed courageous.

Courageous acts are those that people perceive as having a worthy goal. People are less likely to call an act courageous if the goal of the act was not motivated by some desire for a greater good. The motivation for the act must be to make the situation better in some way. Thus, acts that involve sacrificing oneself for others' benefit are more likely to be considered courageous. For instance, coming to the defence of a colleague may entail incurring the wrath of the boss, but the person who does it anyway is more likely to be called courageous.

Fear is a more controversial component. In many cases, the courageous person is one who is seen to feel fear but performs the action in spite of this. While most theorists (e.g., Goud, 2005; Hannah, Sweeney, & Lester, 2007) regard overcoming fear as an essential part of courage, Rate and his colleagues found it to be more marginal, perhaps because as a factor it might have been engulfed by the factor of risk. Pury, Kowalski, and Spearman (2007; see also Woodard & Pury, 2007) found that overcoming fear was a bigger factor in identifying personal courage than in general courage.

The Relationship of Courage to Other Character Strengths

Courage is not unrelated to other character strengths. Common sense indicates that in order to forgive, for example, one must have the courage to overcome one's resentments and hurts. In order to be connected to other people and to be kind, one must have the courage to risk rejection and heartbreak and to stand up for others, even at one's personal expense.

In order to have hope, one must have the courage to continue striving in the face of uncertainty and possible defeat. It is not surprising, then, that Matthews, Eid, Kelly, Bailey, and Peterson (2006) found a relationship between courage and hope in their examination of the characteristics of future military leaders. Pury and Kowalski (2007) found that the strengths of courage were related to the strengths of transcendence, such as hope and spirituality, and to kindness. In fact, in their study, the character strength of persistence (part of the virtue of courage) was so strongly linked to hope that these researchers claim "Hopeful persistence may be the hallmark of courage" (p. 127).

Characteristics of Courageous People

What does it take to be a courageous person? Put another way, what is a courageous mindset comprised of? Hannah, Sweeney, and Lester (2007) speculated on this and, reviewing research evidence, postulate that openness to experience, conscientiousness, resilience, and a high sense of self-esteem and self-efficacy are important. People who are open to experience also tend to be unconventional. They don't necessarily do what most other people would do, such as avoid taking risks to benefit others. Conscientious people feel a strong sense of duty and would be more likely to do what they believe to be the "right" thing, even at a cost to themselves. Resilient people (as we will see in Chapter 9) are able to cope with stress better and show the ability to bounce back after defeats and disappointments. They are more persistent, one of the character strengths associated with courage. People with high self-esteem and a high sense of self-efficacy are more likely to overcome fear in order to behave in a courageous manner.

Hannah, Sweeney, and Lester (2007) also emphasize the need for hope. Without hope, there is little point in being courageous. Courage requires a goal, the ability to think of pathways towards that goal, and the ability to continue towards the goal despite obstacles. Hope (as we saw in Chapter 5), includes these. These theorists also note that a courageous mindset includes internal beliefs and convictions (e.g., that the powerless must be guarded) that prompt people to behave in ways (often courageous ways) that are congruent with these beliefs.

Social pressures and expectations may also encourage one to act in courageous ways. In addition, the way people identify themselves and explain their previous actions may increase their propensity for courageous behaviour. That is, if you believe yourself to be a courageous person based on actions that you have performed and identified as courageous in the past, you will be more likely to act courageously in the future.

Courage and Personal Growth

Goud (2005) points out that although our first inclination is to call only acts that benefit others courageous, courage is a necessary part of personal growth as well. Without personal growth, we obviously stay as we are. To grow means to change, and change can be frightening. We may realize that we can be better than we are, but at least we are functioning, maybe not too badly, without changing. Who knows what will happen if we do change? Will we have to make sacrifices that are very great? Will our friends reject us? Will we have to face things about ourselves that are not pleasant? At least, as we are, we are "the devil we know." Entering therapy is often a very courageous act because it signifies our willingness to learn more about ourselves, our strengths, and our weaknesses and to make changes that, we hope (we don't *know*) will make our lives better. Both Carl Rogers (1971) and Abraham Maslow (1971) contended that lack of courage is why people do not grow and may remain stuck in their present state (see Chapter 2). Again, I ask, based on what you're reading and learning in this book, do you realize how courageous you are?

Increasing Courage

How can we become more courageous? Goud (2005) offers some specific strategies such as increasing your self-efficacy. The more confident you feel in your own abilities, the more likely it is that you will behave in a confident and courageous manner. Bandura (1997) outlined ways to do this (see Chapter 6). You might also make a list of your own strengths and think about them. You may not realize what a wealth of personal resources you already have, and becoming more aware of them will not only increase your confidence, and therefore your courage, but make them more available for your use. Think also about what you truly believe in. What are your values? What will you make sacrifices for? On a more dramatic level, ask yourself what you would die for. The more you keep these values in the front of your mind, the more likely you are to behave in congruence with them.

Another aid in increasing courage is to learn to control your emotions; this, clearly, is vital in overcoming fear. Become connected to your wider environment: by doing this, you affirm the meaningfulness of life and open new opportunities for growth. Becoming more courageous obviously isn't about winning medals for heroism. It's about enriching our lives and making our lives more meaningful (Woodard & Pury, 2007).

REFLECTIVE EXERCISE

Courage

Typically, more than 50 percent of college students report that sometimes they cheat (Staats, Hupp, Wallace, & Gresley, 2009). Note that this is the percentage of students who admit to cheating, not the actual proportion of students who do cheat. Is this shocking to you? If so, is it because you thought more students cheated? Or fewer?

Staats and her colleagues (Staats, Hupp, & Hagley, 2008; Staats, Hupp, Wallace, & Gresley, 2009) consider students who don't cheat to be heroes. They believe that students who don't cheat are showing integrity in remaining true to what they believe to be right, even in the face of temptation and a hundred excuses that their friends may make for cheating. Staats and her colleagues find that students who don't cheat in the present are less likely to cheat in the future and are less prone to discounting the undesirable aspects of cheating.

What do you think about this? Is cheating ever excusable? If so, under what conditions? If not, how do you respond when you see someone cheat? Is your inclination to remain silent or to report this? Why do you choose this response? Are you a hero?

HUMOUR

Naman, Hugo, and Vincent are attending the funeral of their former teacher. After a stirring eulogy by the teacher's son, Naman remarks that he hopes someone one day looks at him in his coffin and says that he was a good friend. Hugo says, "I hope someone looks at me in my coffin and says I was true to my principles." Vincent says, "I hope someone looks at me in my coffin and says, 'Look! He's moving!'"

Naman and Hugo laugh at Vincent's comment and feels that Vincent has, as usual, broken the stress of the moment with his humour. He always seems to be able to do that, but he doesn't play the clown: he just seems to know when people need to laugh. It's no wonder that he's so popular. Vincent contends that his humour is what keeps him functioning in the face of day-to-day life, and he knows that people appreciate his upbeat approach.

Laughter, it is often said, is the best medicine. Certainly there are enough comedies on television and at the movies to make us believe that there is a ready market for humour. Did you find Vincent's joke funny? Some people may not; they may see it as inappropriate given the circumstances. But in this case, with Vincent's personality, it seems to be a joke that is meant well, with no disrespect intended.

Humour is another character strength that Peterson and Seligman (2004) consider to be part of transcendence. Humour has been hypothesized to be based on incongruity in a situation (Moreall, 2010). We see humour when something doesn't "fit," such as in Vincent's joke: moving in a coffin doesn't fit with being in the coffin (i.e., being dead) in the first place. Seeing incongruity in a situation makes us change our perspective and see the situation in a different context, thus helping us to transcend our own view.

Types of Humour

Research indicates that there are basically four types of humour (Martin, Puhlik-Doris, Larson, Gray, & Weir, 2003). **Affiliative humour** is humour that is often used for social purposes to build relationships. It isn't nasty or demeaning to the self or to others. It merely highlights incongruity and is characterized by joking around, telling funny stories, and laughing in social situations. Vincent's joke is of this type, and it seems to be the kind he favours, since his friends say that he uses jokes to break the tension of a situation.

Self-enhancing humour is humour that may also be used to build relationships, but its primary purpose seems to be to protect one's own ego by reframing a potentially threatening situation into one that is not so threatening. It doesn't demean the self or others, and it too is useful in building social relationships. For example, the young lady who trips when getting on a bus, landing in the bus driver's lap, removes the possible embarrassment of the situation by saying, "I always have the good taste to fall for a man in uniform!" Now, instead of seeing herself as clumsy or being self-conscious about what the bus driver and other passengers think about her, she sees herself and others are likely to see her as quick-witted and likeable. Affiliative humour and self-enhancing humour are considered positive forms of humour because their intent is benign and their effects are adaptive.

The remaining two types of humour are considered negative since their effects are malignant and maladaptive. **Self-defeating humour** is humour that is generally well-intended, but it demeans the self. People using this type of humour often intend to build relationships by putting themselves down to get a laugh (maybe before someone else does, they might think). As we shall see, this typically doesn't work. An example of this type of humour might be when someone is praised for doing something, he or she replies "I have my moments. Unfortunately, they're only moments."

Aggressive humour is humour that demeans other people, with the attempt to get a laugh at the expense of others. Jokes that employ negative stereotypes fall into this category (e.g., "dumb blonde" jokes), as does ridicule, teasing, sarcasm, and using humour to manipulate or criticize others. Its effects are destructive to relationships because people get hurt by this form of humour.

Effects of Humour on Well-Being

People who have positive humour are happier and more satisfied with their lives (Erickson & Feldstein, 2007; Kuiper & Borowicz-Sibenik, 2005; Kuiper & McHale, 2009; Peterson, Ruch, Beermann, Park, & Seligman, 2007). But humour does not seem to be a direct cause of happiness; rather it has its beneficial effects through its effects on other factors. For example, humour is also related to and supports optimism and hope (Cann & Etzel, 2008), which in turn are related to happiness and life satisfaction. One way it does this is through benefits in coping with stress.

Humour has mainly been studied with regard to its role in dealing with stress. Many people are like Vincent and claim that only their humour gets them through the tough times. Marziali, McDonald, and Donahue (2008) studied elderly people at Baycrest, a large multi-health centre for elderly people in Toronto, and found this response to be a common one for older people who are dealing with a variety of physical and mental challenges. These researchers, like many others, found that humour is associated with managing stress in an adaptive manner (see also Cann & Etzel, 2008; Capps, 2006; Miczo, 2004; Wanzer, Sparks, & Frymier, 2009).

How does humour help us cope with stress and so affect our sense of well-being? For one thing, it directs our attention away from the threatening situation (Booth-Butterfield, Booth-Butterfield, & Wanzer, 2007). Note the way Vincent's joke diverted his friends' and his own attention away from envisioning their own deaths.

Booth-Butterfield, Booth-Butterfield, and Wanzer (2007) suggest that humour may also make people feel that they have handled or managed the stressful situation and so can move on. Again, Vincent's joke may have done this; it's unlikely that the conversation among the friends resumed a personal and extremely stressful note after his joke. Also, affiliative humour, like Vincent's, attracts people to us, and so it decreases loneliness (Miczo, 2004) and adds to the pool of potential social support when we need it in stressful times (Kuiper & McHale, 2009; Marziali, McDonald, & Donahue, 2008).

Nicholas Kuiper and his colleagues at the University of Western Ontario have done extensive and important work in determining how humour helps us achieve happiness (see, for example, Kuiper & Borowicz-Sibenik, 2005; Kuiper & McHale, 2009). Their research suggests that people evaluate themselves: I am good and people like me, or I am worthless and people don't like me, for example. If they endorse negative statements about themselves, they are more likely to use self-defeating humour (i.e., jokingly putting themselves down) in social situations as a means of ingratiating themselves with others. But this doesn't work: in fact, others draw away from those who use self-defeating humour. If people endorse positive self-statements, however, they are more likely to be open to new experiences and to enjoy the company of others, factors that increase their use of affiliative humour.

This use of affiliative humour attracts more people to them, increasing their encounters with new experiences and heightening their self-esteem, thus contributing to their satisfaction and enjoyment of life. (Notice how the broaden-and-build theory again receives support.) Not surprisingly, a strong sense of humour is also related to fewer symptoms of depression (Capps, 2006; Erickson & Feldstein, 2007; Marziali, McDonald, & Donahue, 2008).

Most researchers, (including Booth-Butterfield, Booth-Butterfield, & Wanzer, 2007; Erickson & Feldstein, 2007; Kuiper & Borowicz-Sibenik, 2005; Marziali, McDonald, & Donahue, 2008; Miczo, 2004; Wanzer, Sparks, & Frymier, 2009) also find that humour is related to **coping efficacy**, that is, to how well we believe we can handle a situation. In a stressful situation, we first appraise the situation to determine how great the threat is, then we evaluate how well we think we can cope with the stress (we will discuss stress in greater detail in Chapter 9). Humour induces us to see the situation in a less severe light. Our appraisal of the situation, then, is not one of high threat. Furthermore, in being able to see the situation with humour, we calm the negative emotions we might feel, allowing us to think more clearly and find ways of dealing with the stress.

Having dealt with the situation in a more positive fashion, we are more likely to think back on this occasion and form the positive self-statement "I can deal with stress well with humour," or, as Vincent says, "Humour keeps me functioning in day-to-day life." This kind of self-statement increases our coping efficacy, so when the next stress-ful situation arises, we feel less stress and more confidence in our ability to cope. Since stressful situations arise continually in everyone's life, the confidence that we can handle the stress adds a great deal to our overall satisfaction with our lives.

On both psychological and philosophical levels, John Moreall (2010) argues that humour is beneficial and vital to a good life for ten reasons:

1. Humour allows us to enjoy incongruity and respond to it with curiosity, awe, and even art, transcending our practical experience.

2. Humour helps us cope with difficult situations, both psychologically and physically, increasing our coping efficacy, lowering physical indicators of stress, and enhancing the immune system.

3. Humour fosters thinking in providing new perspectives that promote critical thought and creativity.

4. Humour helps us to regulate our negative emotions, allowing us to respond to the world more rationally.

5. Humour fosters our personal growth in making us more objectively aware of our own foibles when we laugh at ourselves.

6. Humour makes us more patient and tolerant as the incongruity allows us to see the world through a wider perspective than our own self-interest.

7. Humour reduces social friction when we use affiliative humour and when we show increased tolerance for incongruity. It can also induce other people to forgive us more readily.

8. When not used to extreme, self-defeating humour can keep us humble. Moreall relates the story of John F. Kennedy's response to a child who asked him how he became a war hero: "It was completely involuntary—they sank my boat."

9. When we use humour in regarding our disappointments, we make it more likely that we will not be overcome by frustration and we will persevere.

10. Humour reduces fear and so promotes courage.

No doubt you can think of many more ways that humour facilitates our enjoyment of life. How about this one: It's just plain fun!

REFLECTIVE EXERCISE

Humour

What are some of your favourite jokes? What are some of your best lines? What kind of humour do you like? Think of a comedian, TV show, or movie that you found funny. What kind of humour did it contain? Slapstick? One-liners? Funny stories? Start a collection of jokes, funny lines, funny events, and so on and look at the collection whenever you feel a little down.

Is a similar sense of humour an important factor in making friends for you? Do your friends share your brand of humour?

WISDOM

In Chapter 3, we met a character, Victoria, who found great meaning in a poem written by a practitioner of an Eastern belief system. This is the poem:

> The snows chill and the sun burns.
>
> Yet I have nothing to teach you.
>
> Yet I have nothing to give you.
>
> You are already complete.

After reading the poem, the practitioner said to Victoria, "No matter whether you reach enlightenment or not, the snows will still chill you and the sun will still burn you. Those are useful things to know."

Does this story reflect wisdom to you? It does in Zen thinking (see Chapter 3). If it seems wise to you, what is it that shows wisdom? Before you continue reading, try the reflective exercise below.

REFLECTIVE EXERCISE

What is Wisdom?

Think about someone you know, or know of, who you would consider to be wise. What is it about them that makes them wise in your estimation? What qualities do they have?	Now think about some action of your own in the past that you consider to have been wise. What makes you consider it wise?

What Is Wisdom?

Chances are that you, like most people, described an incident in which you were wise that revolved around one of three themes: situations in which you showed empathy and support for another person, situations in which you showed self-determination and assertiveness, or situations in which your knowledge of other people and the world and your flexibility in dealing with them were at the forefront (Glück, Bluck, Baron, & McAdams, 2005).

As you probably noted, wisdom is a very difficult concept to define. As a first step in explaining it, let's see what qualities people consider to be part of wisdom. Jason et al. (2001) found that people believe wise individuals feel balanced and centred within themselves; they are warm, intelligent, and spiritual, with a love and reverence of nature and a concern for the environment. Of course, many people who are not wise have these qualities as well, so this doesn't get us very far in determining what wisdom is.

Further research and theorizing have lead to a variety of definitions of wisdom, none of which is universally accepted in psychology today. Common elements can be derived from the definitions, indicating that in most people's eyes, wisdom has a cognitive component: wise people handle problems and decisions well. There is also an affective (emotional) component: wise people transcend their own self-interests and feel warmth and compassion for others. And there is a behavioural component: wise people act on their understanding of the world and help others and their environment. Some theorists and researchers, such as Baltes and Sternberg (see Scheibe, Kunzmann, & Baltes, 2009; Sternberg, 1998, 2001) focus on the cognitive and behavioural elements of wisdom; others focus on the affective component, especially that of self-transcendence (e.g., Beaumont, 2009; Le & Levenson, 2005). But most agree that wisdom reflects all of these characteristics.

The definition we shall use is that of Webster (2010): "**Wisdom** is defined as the *competence* in, *intention* to, and *application* of, *critical* life experiences to facilitate the *optimal development* of *self* and *others*" (p. 71, italics in original). This means that a wise person is defined as one who is competent in cognitive activities such as decision-making and problem-solving, and they mean for their actions and advice to be wise; they use what they have learned from important experiences in their lives in their day-to-day functioning, looking to maximize their personal growth, and they share their wisdom with others freely.

Personal and General Wisdom

Some researchers make a distinction between personal wisdom and general wisdom (e.g., Beaumont, 2009; Mickler, & Staudinger, 2008). **Personal wisdom** is about the self and one's own life, while **general wisdom** applies to other people and life in general. While personal wisdom and general wisdom are related to each other (Mickler & Staudinger, 2008), they are not necessarily found together. Some people who seem to have great general wisdom don't apply it to themselves, make bad decisions, and never develop optimal functioning. Likewise, some people who have personal wisdom remain involved only with themselves, never reaching out to their environment to share their wisdom. These people are not necessarily self-involved; they may hold the attitude that others must find their own way in life and so are reluctant to help.

Personal wisdom, say Mickler and Staudinger (2008) is characterized by (1) a deep knowledge of one's own characteristics, strengths and weaknesses, goals, and meaning in life; (2) self-regulation of one's emotions and knowledge about how to express them appropriately; (3) recognition that one does not live in a vacuum, but is interrelated with one's own history and present space, as well as one's relationship to others; (4) recognition of and tolerance for other values besides one's own, with the ability to evaluate one's own values in a critical way without damaging one's self-esteem; and (5) recognition that life is unpredictable in many instances and that complete information about oneself and one's situation is not always available.

The Development of Wisdom

Wisdom develops over time: it is a process, not an end state. It is possible to say "I am wiser than I was before" but not "I am wise" (McGrath, Rashid, Park, & Peterson, 2010). Developing wisdom requires life experience, facing the good and the bad episodes of life and interpreting these events in ways that enhance learning from them (Jennings, Alwin,

Levenson, Spiro III, & Mroczek, 2006; Mickler & Staudinger, 2008; Schiebe, Kunzmann, & Baltes, 2009). This may be one reason why people around the world perceive old age as including increased wisdom (Löckenhoff, De Fruyt, Terracciano, McCrae, De Bolle, et al., 2009). This perception is not always correct (e.g., Jennings, Aldwin, Levenson, Spiro III, & Mroczek, 2006; Mickler & Staudinger, 2008), but clearly people of any age who show wisdom have been through experiences they have learned from. In fact, the foundations for wisdom can be seen in adolescence and early adulthood (Beaumont, 2009; Glück, Bluck, Baron, & McAdams, 2005; Webster, 2010).

The role of experience is seen in an interesting series of interviews, done by Monika Ardelt (2005). She found that elderly people who possess wisdom have managed the obstacles and crises of their lives by certain highly adaptive techniques. First, they distance themselves from the situation by remaining calm and taking a step back to look at the situation from a broader, more objective perspective. They cope with the crisis in an active fashion, by looking for the positive things within the situation, by taking responsibility for their own happiness (i.e., they do not subscribe to the idea that external people, objects, and events "make" them happy or unhappy), and by accepting that they can't control everything in life. They make a point of learning from their experiences; they make sure they don't make the same mistake twice, and they learn to listen to the advice of people who have greater experience and understanding of situations like theirs.

Ardelt (2005) found that elderly people with little wisdom essentially did not deal with the crises and obstacles in their lives at all: they accepted problematic situations, even when they could change them, or they passively looked to God to work things out for them. Their belief was that their happiness or unhappiness was contingent on outside forces. They also focused on themselves and their own well-being, rather than being more concerned with the welfare of others, as the wise people were. Wise people, in describing something pleasant that happened to them, related stories about being able to help someone else, and stories about the gratitude they felt when someone helped them.

Ardelt (2005) cautions that it may not be possible to generalize her results because she only interviewed three wise and three not-so-wise (as pre-determined by testing) people. Nonetheless, these results are very consistent with other studies, such as those of Jennings, Aldwin, Levenson, Spiro III, and Mroczek (2006), who found that military veterans who found positive benefits in even the horrors of combat were wiser.

Characteristics of Wise People

Like the elderly people interviewed by Ardelt (2005), people who have personal wisdom in particular also show self-transcendence (Beaumont, 2009; Le, & Levenson, 2005). *Self-transcendence* is the ability to look at oneself, other people, and life in general without one's ego getting in the way. When we tell a person to "get over yourself," what we are saying is, in fact, transcend your own self-involvement and your own way of seeing things and see reality from a wider perspective, one that includes other people's points of view. We are saying that the person should take into account more than just self-interest and recognize the broader scope of the universe. Wise people appear to do just that.

Wise people also have compassion for themselves (Neff, Rude, & Kirkpatrick, 2007). They recognize their flaws and inadequacies, but they are also kind to them-selves, showing patience and understanding as they attempt to cope with the problem or overcome it. They recognize that their own distress highlights their connection to the rest of humanity, which also suffers and tries to cope. Self-compassion does not mean hiding from, excusing, or rationalizing inadequacies and problems (see Chapter 5): on the contrary, wise people experience the pain without self-pity, exaggeration, or excess drama. They realistically face their distress, but with the same compassion they would show to others.

In 1805, British writer and critic Samuel Johnson said "Love is the wisdom of the fool and the folly of the wise" (in Knowles, 1999). That doesn't seem to be a very positive thought about love. Certainly wise people love—we have seen that in their compassion and caring for others. And this may be the key. Le and Levenson (2005) examined mature and immature love in their relationship to wisdom. Wise people, it seems, love in a non-possessive way, a way that is characterized by a concern and caring for another person's growth and well-being without any strings attached. This is a mature love, a love that transcends concern about the individual's personal welfare. Mature love doesn't keep score; with mature love, we love without asking for anything in return. We don't even ask for our love to be reciprocated. People who are not so wise often love in an immature way: their love is possessive and revolves more around them-selves and what they will get from the other person than it does about the other person's well-being. Again self-transcendence is a critical feature. Not surprisingly, Le and Levenson speculate that wise people with mature love have advantages in establishing and maintaining intimate relationships that people with immature love do not have.

Are wise people happy? That depends on what you mean by "happy." They don't typically have a great number of what many people would call pleasant thoughts and experiences. But then, they aren't looking for that in life (Kunzmann & Baltes, 2003; Webster, 2010). They subscribe to a eudaimonic view of happiness (see Chapter 1) and find satisfaction and fulfillment in understanding themselves and others and in reaching out to connect with their greater environment in a helpful way. Gaining understanding of oneself, other people, and life in general is not always conducive to pleasant thoughts: it often means coming face to face with unpleasant facets of one's own personality and behaviour, the personality and behaviour of other people, and the distresses of life (Scheibe, Kunzmann, & Baltes, 2009). But wise people seem to find this worthwhile, and do not avoid looking at themselves, others, and the world with brutal honesty. In this regard, some theorists define wisdom as the ability to see past the delusion of what we want to believe or have been taught to believe and to evaluate ourselves, others, and life by our own honest reasoning (McKee & Barber, 1999). Since we all have a propensity for self-deception and most of us have an inclination to see the best in ourselves and others, this can make us unhappy. But wise people, as we have seen, have compassion for themselves and for others that allows them to transcend blame and feelings of lack of self-worth, showing instead patience and tolerance and the striving to overcome and help others overcome flaws and obstacles.

Increasing Wisdom

Can we increase our wisdom? Presumably this would be the wish of many people, since wisdom has been called the ultimate hallmark of human development (Baltes & Smith, 2008). In addition, Schwartz and Sharpe (2006) contend that wisdom is necessary for the proper utilization of all the other character strengths and virtues.

Sternberg (2001) believes wisdom can be taught and has implemented a curriculum to specifically foster the cognitive components of wisdom in middle school. The curriculum teaches the required subject matter utilizing critical and creative thought, modelling by the teacher, and integrating subjects with each other. Thus, a book in English literature, say, would be taught with reference to the lives of people who lived at the time of the book's setting, including their history, geography, economic and political climates, and religious and cultural beliefs.

Children would speculate on how they would feel in the situations of the book and would analyze the book in terms of both their own values and the values of the time (promoting flexibility of thought). Children would also read about wise judgments in real life to foster their critical thinking about their own values and decisions. As Sternberg (2001) says, "A fundamental idea in teaching for wisdom is that one teaches children not *what* to think, but, rather, *how* to think" (p. 237, italics in original).

Glück and Baltes (2006) also found that they could increase wise responses in people who had had life experiences that they learned from, were self-regulating, and open to growth. The technique was to merely tell them to give wise answers! Other than that, it seems that the best course is to try to cultivate some of the qualities that wise people demonstrate: increase empathy for others, take multiple perspectives into account when making decisions and viewing the world, and develop tolerance, patience, and compassion for yourself and for others.

Let's take an example. Imagine that Rolf is trying to decide whether to take a new, higher-paying job in another country. His family is not altogether happy about the prospect of uprooting themselves. How can Rolf decide what to do? In an unwise fashion, he might say to himself "I want this job. My family is overreacting. They might not see it now, but this will be better for them." Or, again unwisely, he might say "I want this job. I'm a selfish lout. How can I even consider doing this to my family?" In a wise fashion, he might say "I want this job, but I understand that my family has some real concerns. Just because I'm excited about the job doesn't mean that they will be too. They have a lot going on right here, and they seem happy with their lives here. I had better talk to them so that I can understand their worries better. Maybe I can talk to someone who has been through this kind of change and find out what problems they encountered and how their family dealt with it."

In the latter response, Rolf is showing components of wisdom in having more empathy for his family's feelings and in showing compassion for their perspective. He is not deluding himself into thinking that he knows what's best for everyone. He is also showing flexibility and tolerance in his willingness not to make the decision until he gets more information from his family and advice from someone who has had the same type of experience. He is showing compassion for himself, too, by not denying his own feelings or blaming himself for having them. His final decision can be based on a wise balance between his own interests and the interests of his family who will also be profoundly affected.

Much information has been found about wisdom, even without a universally accepted definition of it, and the research is ongoing. The question is whether we will ever be wise enough to truly understand ourselves.

Conclusion

We have only scratched the surface in examining character strengths. Research on character strengths is in its infancy and is progressing rapidly. It is encouraging, however, that psychologists are tackling this difficult area and are pursuing their studies even though they know that they have undoubtedly not captured the "final truth" in any of these areas and that their definitions and formulations will evolve as more research is done. Note that this takes courage, wisdom, and certainly a great deal of humour!

Summary

- Character strengths are a subset of personality traits that are morally valued in most cultures. Higher levels of character strengths are positively related to a sense of well-being and life satisfaction.
- The core virtues established by Peterson and Seligman (2004) are (1) wisdom and knowledge, (2) courage, (3) humanity, (4) justice, (5) temperance, and (6) transcendence. Each of these includes several character strengths.
- Gratitude makes us want to do something nice for our benefactor and even increases our kindness to other people. It plays a causal role in increasing our feelings of well-being.
- Grateful people are more agreeable, psychologically stable, and more self-confident without being arrogant; they interpret events as more positive; they are more pro-social; they perceive themselves to have more social support, less stress, and fewer symptoms of depression; they have more adaptive coping skills; and they remember the good episodes of their lives more.
- Forgiveness involves releasing negative emotions and fostering positive emotions toward the transgressor.
- Forgiveness is associated with better physical and psychological health and a more satisfying life.
- Forgiving people are more likely to accept themselves, feel personal autonomy in their lives, feel that their lives have meaning, and have the ability to stop rumination and regulate their emotions. People who are religious and spiritual are more forgiving, as are women. Increased empathy is related to forgiveness.
- Sometimes forgiving someone does not induce remorse and sometimes an apology for a transgression actually impedes forgiveness.
- People who feel shame for their actions are less likely to forgive themselves.
- Courage involves intent, mindful deliberation, risk, a worthy goal, and overcoming fear.
- Courage is related to hope, to the strengths of transcendence, and to kindness.
- Openness to experience, conscientiousness, resilience, and a high sense of self-esteem and self-efficacy are important to have a courageous mindset.
- Positive forms of humour are affiliative humour and self-enhancing humour. Negative forms of humour are self-defeating humour and aggressive humour.
- People who have positive humour are happier and more satisfied with their lives.

- Humour is associated with managing stress in an adaptive manner by directing attention away from the threatening situation.
- Affiliative humour attracts people to us, adding to our potential social support.
- Humour is related to coping efficacy, inducing us to see the situation in a less severe light, calming the negative emotions we might feel, and allowing us to think more clearly and find ways of dealing with the stress.
- People believe wise individuals feel balanced and centred and that they are warm, intelligent, and spiritual, with a reverence for nature and the environment.
- To most people, wise people handle problems and decisions well, transcend their own self-interests, feel warmth and compassion for others, act on their understanding of the world, and help others and their environment.
- Personal wisdom is about the self and one's own life, while general wisdom applies to other people and life in general.
- Personal wisdom is characterized by (1) a deep knowledge of one's own characteristics, strengths and weaknesses, goals and meaning in life; (2) self-regulation of one's emotions and knowledge about how to express them; (3) recognition that one is inter-related with one's own history and present space, as well as one's relationship to others; (4) recognition of and tolerance for other values besides one's own, with the ability to evaluate one's own values in a critical way without damaging one's self-esteem; and (5) recognition that life is unpredictable in many instances and that complete information about oneself and one's situation is not always available.
- Developing wisdom requires life experience, facing the good and the bad episodes of life and interpreting these events in ways that enhance learning from them.
- People who have personal wisdom also show self-transcendence, the ability to look at oneself, other people, and life in general without one's ego getting in the way. Wise people have compassion for themselves and love in a non-possessive way, and they subscribe to a eudaimonic view of happiness.
- Components of wisdom may be taught and fostered.

Group Discussion Questions

1. Do you believe that people should seek to enhance their strengths or lessen their weaknesses? Which approach would be more beneficial?
2. Can people be too grateful or too forgiving? What might be the problems in having an abundance of either character strength?
3. Does communication through email and texting reduce our ability to use humour in our encounters with other people? Does the use of "lol" really help?
4. Do you think that the kind of curriculum promoted by Sternberg to teach wisdom will really help? Are there other components that you feel should be added to the curriculum?

CHAPTER 8

Meaning-Making, Religion, and Spirituality

Matt spends most of his days playing video games, although he quickly finds himself feeling bored. Occasionally, he uses recreational drugs and drinks alcohol, but he finds little pleasure in that either. He dropped out of university after one semester even though his grades were adequate, although not as good as he was capable of since he saw little reason to study or attend classes. "The courses are useless. The other students are robots, and the professors are dried-out hulks," he contends. He only started university at his parents' insistence and because he had no other plans. His parents are now urging him to return to school or find a job.

But Matt doesn't have much desire to do either of these; everything seems pointless to him. He doesn't know where the hours of the day go for him, but he knows he gets no satisfaction from his days. His life seems like a series of dreary events and people who are virtually without face or character to him. There's no excitement, no passion in his life, and each day is only a dull repetition of the day before.

LEARNING OBJECTIVES

In this chapter, students will learn about

- Situational and global meaning.
- How meaning is created.
- Extrinsic and intrinsic religiosity.
- The effects of religion and spirituality on well-being.
- How religion facilitates meaning-making.
- Post-traumatic growth and its effects on well-being.

Matt is a fictional character, yet many, if not most, of us have experienced at least a shade of the feelings he has. For Matt, life is without purpose, and he has no place in what he sees as a buzzing world of puppets whose strings are pulled by some nameless force. It is easy to see that Matt has found no meaning in life.

Finding meaning in our lives is a large part of living a satisfying life. Some people, perhaps Matt, seem to be waiting for the meaning in their lives to be revealed to them. Others believe that meaning in life must be created by them through their own endeavours or through finding a path that has a goal or purpose that resonates within them and that they can make their own.

MEANING-MAKING

What Is Meaning-Making?

Existential psychologists, such as Rollo May, have put much emphasis on the role of **meaning-making** in life, noting that our constructions of events, people, and our own roles in life are developed in unique ways by each of us (see Chapter 2). Not surprisingly, even the definition of meaning-making differs from individual to individual.

Perhaps the simplest and most straightforward definition is "the imposition of structure, coherence, and significance on events in our lives" (Hadad, 2009, p. 248). For Steger (2009; Steger, Oishi, & Kashdan, 2009), having meaning in life refers to "the extent to which people comprehend, make sense of, or see significance in their lives, accompanied by the degree to which they perceive themselves to have a purpose, mission, or over-arching aim in life." (p. 682). This seems to be exactly what Matt is lacking: his life has no significance, and the world has no coherence or purpose to him.

Situational and Global Meaning

Meaning is clearly a very large term: it encompasses both the meaning we find in the various events and episodes of our day-to-day life, from rather trivial ones such as missing a bus to larger ones such as dealing with rejection from a loved one (**situational meaning**) and the meaning we find in life in general, the world, the Cosmos (**global** or **cosmic meaning**) (Park & Folkman, 1997; Yalom, 1980).

Situational meaning is very dependent on our own life experiences and the context in which we are interpreting an event, object, or person. For example, consider the numerous ways that someone can interpret the delivery of a bouquet of flowers. "It means he loves me!" says the enamoured young woman. "It means he's done something he knows I'll be angry about!" says the suspicious wife. "It means he feels sorry that I'm sick," says the ailing neighbour. "It means he wants to give me an example of the kind of work he does so that I'll choose him to be our florist for the wedding," says the groom-to-be. Many more possibilities exist, each one possible in a particular context, given the experiences and personalities of the person who is interpreting the event. A more common example for students is derived from the experiences many students have in their first semester of university. Arrival at university generally signifies that a student has done well in high school. How, then, is a poor mark on the first university level test construed? It can be construed as an indication of lack of intelligence and an indication that he/she should drop out by someone whose self-esteem and self-efficacy are not very high. Or it can be construed as a wake-up call to put in more time studying in a more effective way by someone whose self-esteem and self-efficacy are higher.

Global or cosmic meaning is more dependent on belief systems that we have been taught, through our religions, societies, and cultures, as well as our own unique interpretations. Global meaning refers to our understanding of the universe and our place in it. Do we believe that the universe is a tapestry, with each individual contributing a vital thread to its overall pattern? Do we believe that there is a deity whose pattern has been in place since the beginning of time and who has created a role for us to fill? Do we believe that we are purely biological beings, isolated on a small and insignificant planet? Such beliefs may be explicitly taught to us, generally from childhood by our caregivers and teachers. They may be modified in light of our own experiences and philosophical musings, or they may be confirmed to us in the same way. When the events of our lives are large and even traumatic, such as the death of a loved one, situational and global meanings may be entwined. Thus, one person may see the death of a parent in extreme old age as a grievous personal loss that is ameliorated by a belief that the parent has been "called home to God." Another person may also experience this death as a personal loss that is an expected part of the cycle of life, rooting the human being in the natural processes of the biology of life. Global meaning may be regarded as informing the situational meaning in this case.

Exploring Meaning

Imagine the following scenario: You have worked at a new job for three weeks. When you come in to work this morning, your co-worker frowns at you as she says a terse "Good morning." How would you interpret this? What meaning would it have for you? Would you worry? Why? Now create at least two alternative meanings for this event. What other possible interpretations could you put to your co-worker's actions? Are these interpretations likely? As likely as your original interpretation?

Have you ever been in a situation in which you feel you may have been misjudged? Did the person judging you make a valid interpretation of your actions? Why do you think the person chose that particular interpretation? Is it possible that the person made the judgment based only on what he or she saw, not having any knowledge of what was in your mind or the way you regarded the situation?

Have you ever made a judgment about a person in a similar manner—that is, only on the basis of observable behaviour, without knowing what was in another person's mind or how that person regarded the situation? For example, have you ever thought that someone you just met was very unfriendly because he or she said little? Is it possible that the person was actually just shy? Don't feel too guilty. Most of us have done this. The tendency to judge another person's personality, especially a stranger's, by the behaviour you see rather than taking the situation into account, is common and is part of what we call the fundamental attribution error. The only way to avoid it is to become aware that what you see is not always what you get and that people's behaviour is governed by much more than simply their personalities.

The Effect of Making Meaning in Our Lives

In order to cope with the vicissitudes of life and to live a satisfying life, we seem to need a sense of what the world is and where we fit in it. Without it, we have difficulty in determining how to interpret personal events, how to conduct our lives, and how to relate to other people. We need a structure of some sort and an idea that our own existence has consequence and worth within the world. We need a sense of connection with others, valuing them and feeling them value us. The structure and sense of coherence is up to us. The meaning of their lives differs for all people, coming from the individual's unique experiences, society, culture, and religion. Sometimes, meaning is given to people by belief systems, such as religion, as we have seen and will be expanded upon later. But even for these people, their own interpretations and experiences of life inform this meaning. So it can be said that somehow, with the raw materials we have, we create our own meaning. But does this really make a difference in the quality of our lives?

A great deal of research has been done examining the effects of meaning-making on our lives. It seems clear that people who say their lives have meaning experience more happiness and have a greater sense of well-being and life satisfaction (see the work of Steger and his colleagues, 2008, 2009 for a review). They also feel a greater sense of control in their lives and more engagement in their work (Bonebright et al., 2000; Ryff, 1989; Steger, 2009). Moreover, they report feeling depressed and anxious less often, and they are less prone to suicide or substance abuse (Debats et al., 1993; Harlow, Newcomb, & Bentler, 1986). Not surprisingly, they have less need for psychotherapy as well (Battista & Almond, 1973).

One may wonder, however, if possibly these people are well-adjusted and happy, and because of this, they find meaning in their lives. Not so, report Steger and Kashdan (2007). Their research indicates that meaning is independent of other forms of well-being, suggesting strongly that making meaning is one of the elements that goes into developing a satisfying life.

How Is Meaning Created?

Matt in the opening scenario would probably love to create meaning in his life, but for him, this is easier said than done. In fact, theorists suggest that situational meaning is made in a wide variety of ways, sometimes without our even realizing that we are doing it. For example, O'Connor (2002–2003) contends that we can make meaning in isolated situations of our lives in four ways.

First, we may find a purpose in our present state or experiences. We may make meaning by undergoing present suffering or deprivation, recognizing it as a necessary step toward a goal. Students, for instance, may tolerate monetary problems, hard work, lack of time for leisure activities, and frustration because of their desire to obtain an education. Parents may endure sleepless nights, curtailment of their social lives, and large financial expenditures when they have a baby, knowing the joy a child can also bring.

Second, we may construct stories or explanations after an event or action which may have been in some way noteworthy. For example, saying "It was really all for the best" or "I hated it at the time, but now I see that it was all for my own good" helps us cope with disappointments or failures by transforming them into learning experiences that foster our personal growth. Similarly, we may find meaning in our own actions when we convince ourselves that our actions were valid and right. Take the case of the individual who tells a lie ("I'm sorry, I can't go out with you because I have so much work to do.") He may then tell himself a lie to preserve his own sense of self as an honest, caring person: "I didn't want to make her feel bad or embarrass her" when the real truth was less in line with his self-image ("I'm not very assertive.").

In a similar fashion, a third possibility is that we may construct stories about events or actions in order to emphasize how to make the environment more predictable and pleasant in the future by exerting control. An example of this can be seen when we remember a disappointment and recognize how our own actions contributed to it. Knowing our own responsibility for what led to the unfortunate incident helps us modify our own behaviour in ways that facilitate avoiding the problem in the future. Making meaning in this way again transforms the incident from a simple disappointment to a learning experience. For example, the student who loses marks on an essay because of a late submission due to procrastination might remember the episode as having learned what *not* to do. This may lead to a determination to stop procrastinating, with the effect of having a much more satisfying and productive life, as well as higher grades.

Sometimes we construct stories to glorify ourselves, a fourth way of making meaning. When we have done something that we feel rather guilty about, for example, we may create a meaning about this event that removes the negative information about ourselves and becomes more consistent with the positive image we have of ourselves. I once caught a student plagiarising in her essay. I was sure it was plagiarism because the plagiarized author was me! She contended however that she was not a plagiarizer; "all" she did was copy the essay of a student at another university! For her, it was far less threatening to her image of herself and her self-worth if she convinced herself (and me) that she was an honest student who would never commit the academically heinous (and in this case, highly ironic) crime of plagiarizing a published author and that the fault lay with her friend who wrote the essay originally.

In examining their lives on a larger scale than isolated incidents, we can see people creating overall meaning by a further variety of measures. While the choices are many, Compton (2005) notes that there are several common methods. We may create meaning by achieving more consistency and coherence among the various facets of our self-identities and life-goals. Thus, if we identify ourselves with our talent for mathematics, we will have a more meaningful and satisfying life if we engage in activities and pursue careers in which this talent may be utilized.

Or, says, Compton (2005), we may develop a consistent life scheme. This is the story of our lives. Biographies of famous people are very popular, and many of us find the story of someone else's life to be intriguing. Perhaps this is due, in part at least, to the fact that we all construct stories of our lives. In doing this, we may find patterns and connections between events and relationships in our past and in our present. We may even find that by imposing structure and meaning out of the mass of events of our lives in a story, we can make some predictions about the future in terms of what to do (or not do) and what to expect in many situations (see Bosticco & Thompson, 2005).

Another strategy is to strive for overall goals. If what we do today is in service of what we want for tomorrow, our lives will have more meaning and be more satisfying. Often people find that their present activities are not in line with what they want in life. For example, the young woman who dreams of going back to the farm where she was raised and breeding goats may feel empty in university where she is studying accounting. Studying animal husbandry or re-conceptualizing her study of accounting as being a valuable part of her future as a farmer would help her make meaning of her university career.

We also create meaning by being of service to others. Many of us feel that our lives have meaning if we can "make a difference" in the world. Serving others who need help, whether it is raising a child, caring for an elderly relative, entering a service profession such as medicine or social work, or establishing a drop-in centre for troubled youth, reminds us that the world contains more than just our own concerns and connects us to others in a meaningful way. In a similar fashion, working for a cause that we believe in, one that we see as benefiting others and the world at large, aids us in recognizing that our contribution to the world is meaningful and the world may be a little better for our service to it.

Creativity also helps us in making meaning. While perhaps we all are creative in our own ways, some people seem to be more creative than others. Some people find their meaning in the works they create, works that may even outlive them and bear witness that they have contributed to the world.

Life lived as fully and deeply as possible is another meaning-making strategy. This reflects an appreciation for and involvement in life to the greatest extent possible. The person who makes meaning in this way may not engage in a multitude of sensory experiences, but he or she certainly notices the roses and breathes in their scent.

We can even make meaning out of suffering. This seems strange, but as Viktor Frankl noted, we can make even our bad experiences and our pain in life mean something. Viktor Frankl (1984) was a psychiatrist who survived the concentration camps of Nazi Germany. His experiences there indicated to him that the only inmates who survived the camps were those who found a meaning in their existence, such as living to bear witness to the atrocities or to find family members who may have also survived. From suffering, he felt, meaning and growth can be found. Growth can come from our pain when we use it to develop more understanding of ourselves, more compassion for others who experience pain, and more depth in relating to the world. The topic of post-traumatic growth is an interesting one and will be explored more fully later in the chapter. For now, we can note that some religious people even deal with their physical pain by "offering it up": the idea is that perhaps God will note that they bear their pain cheerfully on the understanding that their suffering will do someone else some good, maybe in redeeming their souls or maybe in alleviating their pain.

Spiritual experiences help to create meaning for some people. Some individuals have experiences in which they feel their connection to the universe or that make them stand in awe of the world they live in. Such experiences, reminiscent of what Maslow called "peak experiences" (see Chapter 2), indicate to these people very clearly that they are part of something far larger than themselves. These experiences may be found in a wide variety of situations such as in watching a child being born, in viewing a beautiful sunset, or in having a near-death experience, which we shall discuss later in this chapter.

It's important to note that no matter which method is used to create meaning, the individual exercises choice. We often feel that we have no choice in life, that the events of life crowd upon us without our permission or our will. In fact, there is always choice for us. We may not always be able to dictate what will befall us in life, but as we have seen in previous chapters, many of the events that occur in our lives derive from previous responses that we have made: for example, optimistic people are more likely to have successes that pessimistic people do not have since they expect success and are more persistent in their pursuit of it (see Chapter 5).

Equally important is the choice we make in how to interpret an event. We may not have chosen to lose our job, for instance, but we can choose how to react to it. We may react with despair and feelings of inadequacy or injustice, or we may react with the belief that this was the "kick-in-the-pants" we needed to upgrade our education, find a better job, or change our work habits, for example. In the second case, we are reacting by creating meaning out of a perhaps uncontrollable event. In most cases, then, people who say "I can't help feeling this way" are wrong: they just do not realize that the choice of how to react is theirs. As the Existentialists say, this is where we have ultimate freedom, in the gap between stimulus and response, when we make the choice of what the response will be. Matt, our friend at the beginning of this chapter, seems to be one of the people who does not realize that the gap is there.

A Caveat

It must be noted that there is a difference between *having* meaning in one's life and *searching* for meaning. Steger, Oishu, and Kashdan (2009) conducted research that yielded results indicating that people who are searching for meaning have less life satisfaction than those who have found meaning. This seems quite reasonable: since meaning is more likely to be created than "given" to one, a passive search, waiting for "the light" to be delivered, may be frustrating and fruitless.

REFLECTIVE EXERCISE

The General Life Purpose Scale

The following is a scale devised by Byron and Miller-Perrin (2009) to assess people's general sense of how much purpose their lives have. There are no right or wrong answers; this is only a short quiz to help you identify how high your own life purpose is. Possible scores range from 15 to 105. The higher your total score, the more purpose you feel in your life. (Byron and Miller-Perrin found that the average score of 103 undergraduate students was in the mid 80s.)

Instructions: Please use the following scale to indicate how much you agree with each statement. Write the correct number from the following scale on the blank provided by each item.

1	2	3	4	5	6	7
Strongly disagree	Disagree	Slightly disagree	Neither agree nor disagree	Slightly agree	Agree	Strongly agree

(1)_____ I have goals that I am working toward.

(2)_____ I am confident about who I am.

(3)_____ I am confident about where I am going in life.

(4)_____ I have a well-developed understanding of my gifts and talents.

(5)_____ I have no sense of direction in my life.

(6)_____ I know how I should be using my gifts and talents.

(7)_____ I have a good sense of purpose in life.

(8)_____ I am unsure about what I should do with my life.

(9)_____ I make a difference in the lives of those around me.

(10)_____ My life is valuable and worthwhile.

(11)_____ I have a strong sense of the reasons for my living.

(12)_____ I have identified my mission in life.

(13)_____ My life does not serve any purpose.

(14)_____ I am making a contribution to society.

(15)_____ I am taking actions now that are moving toward my mission in life.

If the search for meaning actually means looking for areas in which to create our own meaning, the search may still be a long and arduous one, but the discomfort felt during this time may be highly worthwhile in the long run. Young people in particular may experience considerable distress in trying to find the areas in which to expend their efforts in creating their own meaning. Without a fully developed sense of identity, they may explore many areas and find them wanting before they hit upon the area in which their own meaning can be made. Some may even give up the search, as Matt at the beginning of this chapter seems to have done. Nonetheless, it is apparent that the search, difficult though it may be, can be amply rewarded in the increased satisfaction that may be ultimately found.

RELIGION AND SPIRITUALITY

Mrs. Caldwell radiates an inner glow. She loves her life and feels deeply connected to all parts of the universe. She was raised in a religious home but, as a child and young person, the love of God always seemed remote from her. She attended church regularly and tried to do her best to follow the tenets of her religion, as she had been taught and was expected to do. When she was in her mid-forties, she "had an experience," as she phrases it, that changed her. Since "the experience," her love of life and her sense of purpose have increased. Every morning she feels a renewed sense of joy in the day, and she eagerly looks forward to what the day will bring. Life is a constant wonder to her. Her certainty that there is a loving deity is profound, and now she says that the world is "swimming in God." Although she has such faith in God, she doesn't feel the need to attend church so regularly, and sometimes her time in quiet prayer seems more like meditation and her relationship with God to be a partnership.

Mrs. Caldwell seems to have achieved what most of us want: a joy in her life and a sense of wonder about the world. She is clearly a highly religious woman. Does this make a difference? Is this what is giving her such life satisfaction?

The twenty-first century seems to be experiencing a paradox in the area of religion and spirituality. On one hand, hundreds of millions of people across the world claim that they adhere to a particular religion, and new denominations and sects seem to be springing up, suggesting that religion has never been more popular. On the other hand, more and more people seem to disparage religion, contending that it's artificially restrictive and authoritarian (Hill et al., 2000). Some people may contend that while they are not religious, they are very spiritual and that their spiritual beliefs give meaning to their lives. In all cases, a mention of religion or spirituality often brings heated and emotional responses from people. One problem is that we are not always clear about what we mean when we speak of religion and spirituality.

What's the Difference Between Religion and Spirituality?

The definitions of religion and spirituality are somewhat controversial. Hill et al. (2000) discuss the problem of defining religion and spirituality in a historical vein. They note that, until the latter part of the twentieth century, these words were used almost synonymously. Thus, if a person was seen as being religious, it was assumed that this person was spiritual as well. Similarly, a spiritual person was assumed to be religious.

Next came the idea that "religious" meant simply belonging to a recognized and organized religion, while "spiritual" embraced more unorthodox and unorganized belief systems, as have been popular in New Age movements of the 1970s and 1980s.

For those studying religion and spirituality and their relationship to well-being, these definitions have not been satisfactory. For example, is the person who attends church because it is helpful to his business to be seen in such a community gathering really to be regarded as religious? Or should we regard the person who has a deep abiding belief in a deity, attends a place of worship, and participates in formalized worship practices while also feeling a strong kinship and connection with all elements of the universe to be considered *only* religious? Differentiations between the terms are still evolving.

Table 8.1 provides an interesting view of the percentage of people in several countries who believe in God and the percentage who claim to have had a religious experience. Clearly, many people who believe in God have not had what they believe to be a personal experience of the Divine. It may be that those who have had such an experience would also classify themselves as spiritual, but that does not mean that this experience is necessary for spirituality to exist. We'll see later whether the "experience" Mrs. Caldwell mysteriously alludes to was religious in nature.

Pargament and Mahoney (2009) define spirituality as "a search for the sacred" (p. 612). Yet he and his colleagues (2005) define religion as "a search for significance in ways related to the sacred" (p. 667). These definitions seem the same. What differentiates religion and spirituality, then? As Pargament and his colleagues explain in several articles (e.g., 1997, 2000, 2002, 2005), the two concepts intertwine. Religion and spirituality both involve an active process in which people strive to find what is, to them, something of worth and value in the universe. The search is within the realms of religion

Table 8-1	Percentage of people who believe in God and have had a religious experience	
Country	**Belief in God (%)**	**Religious Experience (%)**
France	52	24
Russia	52	13
Sweden	54	12
Denmark	57	15
Netherlands	57	22
Norway	59	16
Hungary	65	16
Great Britain	69	16
Spain	82	19
Northern Ireland	92	26
Poland	94	16
Ireland	95	31
United States	95	41
Source: Spilka et al. (2003)		

and spirituality when it involves the sacred. The sacred includes that which people find holy or greater than themselves, such as the belief in a deity or in the sanctity of life.

Religion involves an organized structure, with (usually) given places where adherents to a structured belief system meet to pursue the search for significance together with the same set of assumptions and convictions and given behaviours and practices designed to aid in the search. The adherents of a religion also give validation and support to each other in their search.

Spirituality too refers to a search for significance in the universe, but it may not be attached to a belief in a deity, nor does it necessarily have a formalized structure. People may conceive of themselves as spiritual if they feel themselves to be part of something larger than themselves, such as nature or the entire Cosmos. They may not believe in a Supreme Being or Beings, and they may not believe in universal moral principles that provide values and govern the way life should be lived. They may not attend any groups gathered to share their values; indeed, the spirituality they have may be completely unique to themselves.

If one is religious, is one also, by definition, spiritual? Zinnbauer et al. (1997) found that when asking American respondents whether they were religious or spiritual, 74 percent reported that they were both. Further questioning revealed that most of these people classified themselves as religious because they belonged to a particular organized religious group and they had a belief in a higher power. When calling themselves spiritual, however, they included a description of themselves as having a personal transcendent experience or feeling of relationship with a higher power. For them, "religious" seemed to signify a rather objective state, whereas "spiritual" entered a more subjective realm. Mrs. Caldwell, we would guess, would be much like these people, and would classify herself as both religious and spiritual.

Contrast the data Zinnbauer et al. (1997) found with those in Table 8.1. The data in the table indicates that in the United States, 41 percent of people surveyed said that they had had a religious experience, while in Zinnbauer et al.'s study, 74 percent of respondents claimed to be spiritual. It seems clear, then, that the presence of a religious experience is not the only way that one comes to define oneself as spiritual.

Some (a very few, 4 percent) people in Zinnbauer et al.'s (1997) study, however, identified themselves as religious but not spiritual. Some of these people meant only that they identified themselves as belonging to a particular group and attended a place of worship with more or less regularity. When questioned about their actual belief in the tenets of the group to which they said they belonged, many of these people indicated that they did not believe the tenets or were unsure about them. Several of my students indicated to me that they belonged to a particular religious group, but when asked what they believed, answered "I don't know. It seems a little strange. But I go to church because it pleases my parents" and "Well, it's what I was taught. So I guess I believe it." Should responses such as these qualify as religiousness? Not according to the definition used by Pargament and his colleagues.

Extrinsic and Intrinsic Religiosity

A concept put forward by Gordon Allport in 1950 is useful in distinguishing between types of religiosity. He distinguished between **extrinsic religiosity** and **intrinsic religiosity**. Extrinsically religious people have no clear belief in the tenets of a faith, but follow religious practices because of societal or familial expectations. There doesn't seem to be any quest for significance within the framework of their professed religion.

Extrinsic religiosity is contrasted with *intrinsic religiosity*: in this form of religiosity, people follow the practices of a particular faith because of their profound belief in the truth of the teachings of their faith. These people seem to have examined their faith and internalized its teachings as part of their being. They may or may not follow all the practices laid down within their faith, but they have given their religion thought and have concluded that the tenets of the religion are valid and provide the proper guidelines for life. It seems evident that people with intrinsic religiosity are more likely to be spiritual than those with extrinsic religiosity, although some might not define themselves as such. Typically, people define themselves as religious and spiritual if they both adhere to an organized religion and feel themselves to be part of a whole bigger than themselves.

The personal experience of transcendence of the self into something larger seems to be the hallmark of spirituality, but not necessarily of religiosity. The deep and abiding faith that Mrs. Caldwell seems to have would indicate that her religiosity is of this nature. In exploring the effects of religion and spirituality on a satisfying life, these distinctions turn out to be important.

REFLECTIVE EXERCISE

Religion, Spirituality, and You

Do you identify yourself as belonging to an organized religion? Would you classify yourself as having intrinsic or extrinsic religiosity? If you have religious beliefs, why do you believe? Have you ever thought about your religious beliefs before? Are you comfortable doing so now? If not, why not?

Consider exploring other religions, simply to find out what they believe and why.

Do the beliefs of other religions tell you more about your own beliefs?

Do you consider yourself to be spiritual? What makes you spiritual? Have you had experiences that have increased your spirituality? If not, would you like to have such experiences? If you define yourself as spiritual, is this within the context of an organized religion, or does it stand apart?

Effects of Religion and Spirituality on a Satisfying Life

Does religiousness have a positive effect on attaining a satisfying life? In a word, yes, but the effect is not very large. Early research found inconsistent results regarding the effects of religion on well-being, partly because the distinction between intrinsic and extrinsic religiosity had not been made.

In general, people who claim to be religious are happier and more satisfied with their lives than those who do not claim to be religious (Leondari & Gialamas, 2009; Peterson & Seligman, 2004), and religious involvement is positively related to better mental health (Koenig, McCullough, & Larson, 2001; Laurencelle, Abell, & Schwartz, 2002; Simpson, Newman, & Fuqua, 2007; Vaillant et al., 2008). People who attend a place of worship regularly and believe in an afterlife feel more tranquillity and less anxiety in their lives (Ellison, Burdette, & Hill, 2009), and studies following people over many years indicate that people who attend a place of worship frequently live longer and are healthier than those who do not (Koenig, McCullough, & Larson, 2001; Strawbridge et al., 1997). There are negative effects of holding religious doubt on mental health, but these lessen over the lifespan (Galek et al., 2007). In fact, the positive relationship between religion and happiness is stronger for the elderly than for other age groups (Baumgardner & Crothers, 2009).

Children and adolescents who have high religious involvement are less likely to abuse drugs and alcohol or be involved in delinquent activity or early sexual activity (Baumgardner & Crothers, 2009), and this seems to continue as they reach young adulthood: American students who report being spiritual and healthy are less likely to engage in high-risk behaviours than are students who report less spirituality, and they are more likely to engage in healthy activities such as exercise. This suggests that highly spiritual students seem to integrate their spirituality into the rest of their lives, most especially into their decision-making (Nelms et al., 2007).

People who classify themselves as religious report more life satisfaction if they are living in countries that can be regarded as religious, suggesting that the social dimension of religious activity and the feeling of belongingness may be critical factors (Okulicz-Kozaryn, 2010).

It seems clear that religiosity is related to a greater sense of well-being in life or to factors related to this. We can speculate that this is the case for Mrs. Caldwell, although there may be more involved in her life satisfaction than religiosity. There are a couple of caveats to the research results, however. First, most of the research has been conducted on people espousing a Christian belief. It is generally assumed that the particular faith is not relevant, as long as it includes a belief in a loving and forgiving deity. This assumption may or may not be warranted. A second stipulation is that the results of research are for groups of people, but there is considerable variability among these people. That is, religiosity may be related to well-being for some people in the group, but not all. Indeed, it may be negatively related to well-being for some and not related at all for others.

The Functions of Religion

How does religion actually improve quality of life? After all, religion is made of many components. Compton (2005) reviews some of the factors known to increase satisfaction in life and notes that these factors are particularly found within many religions.

For one thing, he notes, attending religious services puts one in the position of meeting people and gaining social support. Religions also typically encourage altruism and helping others, which has been found to be related to a sense of well-being. (This will be discussed further in Chapter 10.) Many religions actively promote healthy lifestyles, as well. For example, the Mormon faith rejects the use of alcohol and tobacco. (The effects of having good health on life satisfaction were discussed in Chapter 1.)

On a more psychological level, many religions help people resolve conflicts within themselves and find lifelong goals. Religions usually provide their adherents with techniques for coping with stressful situations. For example, the adherent may be encouraged to look at the stress as part of God's plan or a problem that will be resolved in the afterlife. (Coping with stress will be discussed in Chapter 9.)

SPOTLIGHT ON RESEARCH

The Power of Prayer

Almost 84 percent of Canadians claim to belong to an organized religion (Statistics Canada, 2001), and for most of these religions, prayer plays an integral part. We can conclude, then, that probably most Canadians pray on a regular basis. Prayer, it has been found, is positively related to both physical and psychological well-being (e.g., Ai, Peterson, Bolling, & Rodgers, 2006; Salsman, Brown, Brechting, & Carlson, 2005).

But Whittington and Scher (2010) noted that prayer may take several different forms: prayers of adoration ask for nothing and simply worship the deity; prayers of thanksgiving express gratitude to the deity; prayers of supplication ask the deity for intervention in some matter. Then there are prayers of confession in which a person admits to a transgression and asks for forgiveness. Prayers of reception ask for divine guidance. Finally, obligatory prayers are fixed prayers that adherents of some religions are required to recite, usually a fixed number of times per day. Whittington and Scher wondered if all types of prayer were related to well-being or only some of them. They asked 430 participants from several different religions to complete six questionnaires online, measuring their frequency of different types of prayer and their sense of well-being. Their statistical analysis indicated that prayers of thanksgiving were positively related to well-being, self-esteem, and optimism, a finding consistent with the research on the character strength of gratitude (see Chapter 7).

Additionally, prayers of reception were positively related to self-esteem, optimism, and having meaning in life. Prayers of adoration were positively related to both optimism and having meaning in life.

But prayers of confession were related to lower well-being, lower self-esteem, and less optimism. Prayers of supplication were related to lower well-being overall, and obligatory prayers were related to lower optimism. Whittington and Scher feel that these three types of prayer may be more indicative of extrinsic religiosity because they are aimed at either getting something from the deity or avoiding the deity's displeasure. They are also prayers that focus on the self rather than on the deity.

While the researchers note that their results do not imply causality (i.e., it may be that people with less well-being choose more self-related prayers, or a third factor may affect both prayer type and well-being), it seems that when people pray in an egoless manner, in prayers that give something to the deity (love, gratitude, acknowledgment of greater wisdom), well-being is increased.

Religion Facilitates Meaning-Making

In the context of this chapter, the most important function of religion is that it provides a meaning for life. Silberman (2005) notes that religion as a meaning system influences people's beliefs about themselves, other people, and the world in general; it provides expectations about consequences (such as, good people will be rewarded); it encourages goals and prescribes behaviours to meet these goals; and it influences emotions (e.g., religious people, like Mrs. Caldwell, may feel more joy in the world if they believe that all living creatures are loved by God).

Crystal Park (2005) believes that the meaning-making function of religion is the most important one in increasing our feelings of well-being in life, especially in helping us cope with stress. She outlines several ways in which religion may do this. First and foremost, religion in itself attempts to answer many of the "big" questions in life, questions such as "Why am I here?" "Why is there suffering in life?" and "Why do bad things happen to good people?" Religion provides a philosophical framework for understanding the world and, in doing this, usually prescribes a basic plan for living well.

Because of the philosophical understanding of the world that religion provides, people who are religious have ways of interpreting life events that are congruent with the philosophy. When a stressful event occurs, religious people may more readily interpret this event as meaningful and find that, rather than being overwhelmed by the stress, they gain comfort in the belief that this event too is part of a plan and perhaps "God gives a back for every burden." This facilitates their ability to cope with the stressful event because the event is *perceived* as less stressful, and people's belief in having the ability and the help to cope with it reduces their distress and enhances their efficacy.

If the event is one that cannot be ameliorated by any practical means (e.g., a bereavement), religion provides comfort that, in the long run, wrongs will be righted and the deity's plan for the universe will be fulfilled. In some cases, the promise of a glorious afterlife provides comfort and strength for dealing with the problems that life may bring. Park has found in her own research that intrinsically religious people are more likely to experience growth after stress, especially in their feelings of being closer to the deity and believing that they have learned from their distressing experience (Park, 2006, 2005; Park, Cohen, & Murch, 1996; see also Pargament, Koenig, & Perez, 2000; see the discussion of post-traumatic growth later in this chapter).

Emmons (2005) pays particular attention to the way religion as a meaning-making system helps people establish goals, an important part of developing a satisfying life, as we saw in Chapter 6. Goals, he believes, are the concrete expressions of life purpose: they both reflect meaning and are sources of meaning in life. People have goals in terms of their work and/or achievements, their interpersonal relationships, their religion and/or spirituality, and their desire to transcend their self-interests and be of service to others.

Goals in the domain of religion and spirituality are oriented toward forming a relationship with that which the individual considers sacred by transcending the self and becoming integrated into a larger whole. Emmons' research has found that goals in the area of religion/spirituality are consistently related to people's feelings of well-being, both in healthy people and in people with chronic and progressively disabling neuromuscular disease (2005; Emmons, Cheung, & Tehrani, 1998). It seems that even those people who are experiencing continual pain and fatigue have a greater feeling of well-being when they have goals that they believe will bring them closer to their interpretation of the Divine.

What Accounts for the Relationship Between Faith and Well-Being?

Many researchers have wondered if other elements of religiousness or spirituality were really responsible for the relationship between faith and well-being. Steffen and Fearing (2007), for example, noted that Freud contended that religion is an example of people denying reality in order to gain the comfort needed for civilization to exist. This denial, he said, is a form of defensiveness that people use to protect themselves from potentially threatening situations. Steffen and Fearing wondered if Freud might have had a point: are religious people more defensive? Might this account for their tendency to see themselves as well-adjusted and doing fine? As well, the researchers thought, perhaps religion brought about its beneficial effects because religious people might be less willing to admit to having difficulties in their coping with life since this might imply a lack of trust in a deity.

Since most studies have measured well-being and religiousness by self-reports (i.e., simply asking people), this possibility is a very real one. To find out if such defensiveness accounts for the relationship between well-being and religiousness, Steffen and Fearing (2007) gave religious people objective tests to determine further relationships. They found that religiosity was indeed related to higher defensiveness, but defensiveness did not account for the relationship between religiosity and psychosocial adjustment. That means that while many religious people might be more likely to deny harsh realities than others are, this tendency is *not* what determines whether they feel a sense of well-being in their lives. Mrs. Caldwell may strike some of us as being rather naïve in her view of life. "Sometimes life is horrible," we may protest. Perhaps Mrs. Caldwell does deny some of the grim truths about life, but if she is like many people in Steffen and Fearing's study, this does not have a major impact on her life satisfaction, for good or ill.

Byron and Miller-Perrin (2009) also questioned what element of religiousness or spirituality was really responsible for the relationship between faith and well-being. They reasoned that since (1) life purpose is related to feelings of well-being, and (2) religious or spiritual faith contributes to people's sense of purpose in life, so it might be that life purpose is the mediator between faith and well-being. That is, perhaps faith increases feelings of well-being through its enhancement of people's sense of a purpose in life. Their research indicated that this is so. This suggests that a major contribution of religion and spirituality to people's satisfaction in life is in helping them create meaning, especially in their feelings that their lives have a purpose.

Is Religion Always a Positive Influence?

Extrinsic Religiosity

As indicated above, earlier research found inconsistent results regarding the influence of religion on well-being. Understanding the difference between intrinsic and extrinsic religion cleared up some of the confusion, but not all. Pargament (2002) pointed out that some forms of religion are more supportive than others. In order to reap the benefits of religious belief, people must not only be religious, but they must also have internalized their beliefs. This means that they have examined their beliefs rather than simply *think* they believe because they have been taught the tenets of a religion. Such unexamined religious "belief" is, in fact, no real belief at all.

Unexamined "belief" is more like the readily disputed statement "All women want to get married." It is a statement that can be transmitted to people, who may accept it until they stop to think about it. When the statement is attacked, they have no argument to support their claim and often resort to a simple dismissal of the attacker or the contention "Well, everybody *knows* that." In times of distress, people who have not examined their faith may find that their religion has no power to help them make meaning because they have never thought enough about these beliefs to integrate them into the situation they are experiencing. Sometimes, a crisis makes people really think, and at this time, some people who have never examined their religious beliefs may turn away from them altogether. On the other hand, examination may lead them to a different understanding and their new belief, now totally theirs, is one that will aid them in dealing with their distress.

Pargament (2002), from a Christian perspective, also notes that even intrinsic religion may not be helpful: it depends on exactly what the individual believes. Believing in a merciful, forgiving, and loving deity, as Mrs. Caldwell does, is more likely to give comfort in distress than the belief in a punishing and unforgiving deity. Even in day-to-day life, in the absence of a crisis, the belief in a harsh deity who is on the lookout for our transgressions with an eye to punishing us may make our every step uneasy and fraught with potential danger, hardly conducive to feeling a sense of well-being. Furthermore, the feeling of closeness to a forgiving and loving deity provides more reassurance in conducting our lives than the feeling that God, although forgiving and loving, is remote from us and uninvolved in our lives. The degree to which people have integrated the belief in a close, loving, and merciful deity into their daily lives is also a factor in religion's ability to increase a sense of well-being.

Religious Doubt

Murray and Ciarrocchi (2007) investigated another instance in which intrinsic religiosity did not increase an individual's sense of well-being. Students from a small Catholic college in the United States were given measures of shame and guilt, subjective well-being, spirituality, and personality in general. The findings indicated that spirituality is a stronger predictor of life satisfaction than any personality variables, but that students who felt conflicted about their religious beliefs experienced a higher level of shame and guilt, which was related to a decreased life satisfaction. Intuitively this makes sense. Certainly most people feel some guilt if they do something wrong, especially if they feel they are disappointing someone they care about and who cares for them. It is reasonable that a strong intrinsic belief in a loving deity will lead someone to feel shame until there is atonement and presumably forgiveness. But if individuals are conflicted in some way about their belief in a deity, they are much less sure that (1) there is a deity to forgive them, and/or (2) the deity will forgive someone whose faith may be uncertain.

In agreement with this is research by Gauthier and his colleagues (2006) in which a significant negative relationship between life satisfaction and having religious doubts was also found. These researchers suggest that in addition to the shame and guilt experienced for holding these doubts, doubting people may also fear being rejected by what may have been a formally supportive church community. Also, they speculate that the loss of a system of meaning that belief in religious tenets previously gave would cause doubting people distress and additional confusion in times of stress. Interestingly, they found that religious beliefs are more likely to be related to increased well-being in women, but not in men, but religious doubts are more strongly related to decreased life satisfaction in men than in women. Gauthier and his colleagues add another stipulation: religious doubt only seems to be related to decreased life satisfaction in people who are prone to ruminate on their doubts, rather than those who simply hold doubts but give them little thought.

Ciarrocchi, Dy-Liacco, and Deneke (2008) also find religious doubts to be related to decreased life satisfaction. They note that one of the key features of intrinsic religious belief in a loving and merciful deity is the optimism and hope that these beliefs impart. With such a belief, people are more likely to feel that they can endure present distress in the expectation of better times to come and reward for faith and morally good actions. Mrs. Caldwell seems to be a prime example of this. Not surprisingly, these researchers found that religious doubt and/or belief in a punishing and severe deity were related to pessimism and a lack of hope for the future.

Hope as a predictor of life satisfaction in this study was found to be *agency* hope rather than *pathways* hope (see Chapter 5). This means that hope predicts life satisfaction when people use it to act in ways that they believe the deity will approve of and reward in the long run; when people feel that they can actually *do* something to make the future better (with the deity's aid), they experience more life satisfaction as opposed to people who feel that either there is no hope or there is nothing they can do but trust in the deity to make things right in the end. Recall that our happy Mrs. Caldwell has come to see her relationship with God as a partnership. This suggests that she feels that she is an active participant in her life, and she relies on God for help.

The effects of religious doubt seem to be long-lasting. In a longitudinal investigation of older American adults, Krause (2006) found that having greater doubt about religious beliefs is related to a decreasing sense of well-being over time.

Religious Disappointment

Sometimes, religious involvement can be a disappointment. Carleton and his colleagues (2008) found that African-American urban adolescent females who are coping with low income and stressors such as discrimination and racism reveal a beneficial effect of religious coping, such as attending religious services and seeking social support from their religious community. No effect was found for the females' male counterparts, though. In addition, these results were only found for low levels of stress. Carleton and his colleagues suggest that at low levels of stress, religious beliefs may lead females to cope with daily stressors by seeing them as part of a great plan, with relief to come in a better tomorrow. But when the stress becomes higher or chronic, the promise of that better tomorrow seems to be broken, as if the deity had withdrawn support and protection from the individual or should not have let the stress happen in the first place.

This disappointment may give rise to higher levels of depression and overall distress. Furthermore, the effect of religious coping disappeared when the positive effects of social support were removed. It may be, indicated Carleton and his colleagues (2008), that the social support was the most important factor for these adolescent females; its effects disappeared when the stress led the respondents to conclude that the support that was available was not applicable to their situation or useful for it. The moral of this story seems to be that religious coping may or may not be helpful, depending on the particular belief, the situation, and the individuals involved.

Near-Death Experiences

When pressed, Mrs. Caldwell shyly recounts more of her story. She says that she had an experience when she had a serious heart attack that increased her feelings of closeness to God. The doctors reported that she went into cardiac arrest and they resuscitated her with difficulty. During that time, she says, she felt herself leave her body and look down on it and the medical staff working on it. Then she felt herself drawn into a dark tunnel, at the end of which was an incredibly bright light. As she was drawn through the tunnel, her entire life flashed before her, in detail, yet only, it seemed, in a second.

She says she saw it all, the events of her life, their impact on her, what she thought and felt at the time, and the impact she had on others. Her father (long since dead) seemed to step out of the light, shining himself, and told her gently that she had to go back, that her work wasn't finished yet. She protested that she wanted to stay with him, but he insisted, and she felt herself pulled back through the tunnel and slip back into her body through her head. The medical staff says that she made a full recovery from her heart attack, but that she was clinically dead for four minutes. Her life, she says, has not been the same since. She no longer fears death, she feels herself to be connected to all living things, and life is even more meaningful and rich. Ten years later, the experience is just as vivid to her as if it had just happened, and the effects of the experience become more pronounced and more entwined with her life every day.

The discussion so far has centred mainly on religion, with spirituality perhaps intertwined. This is because the research has focused on religion and religiosity. With its connection to organized structures of belief and worship within societies, it is easier to study. But one rather strange phenomenon has become more prevalent and has been studied more in the past thirty years that is more directly applicable to the area of spirituality rather than religion. That phenomenon, reported by Mrs. Caldwell, is the **near-death experience (NDE)**.

Van Lommel (2006) has defined the near-death experience as "the reported memory of the whole of impressions during a special state of consciousness, including a number of special elements such as out-of-body experience, pleasant feelings, seeing a tunnel, a light, deceased relatives, or a life review" (pp. 134–135). Mrs. Caldwell's NDE has these characteristics, but no two individuals have exactly the same experience.

Near-death experiences are occurring more often as medical procedures for the resuscitation of patients become more common and more effective. That they exist is unquestioned. They have been reported in the folklore of numerous cultures for many centuries, and in contemporary times, random surveys in Germany and the United States suggest that perhaps four percent to five percent of people in western society may have experienced NDEs (Gallup, Schmied, et al., as cited by Van Lommel, 2006).

Their existence may be taken as fact, but the source of the experiences and the meaning of them have been hotly debated. Explanations for them include physiological processes, psychological processes, and metaphysical theories, with some of the theories contending that the experience is merely an artifact of physiological or psychological processes, and others contending that it is evidence of an afterlife. None of the theories set forth have won acceptance, each having a lack of supportive evidence and/or valid arguments against them (see Greyson, 2006 and Kastenbaum, 2009 for a review of theories). Note that no matter what the theory or what the evidence, the possibility of an afterlife is still, and probably will always be, a matter of faith, not science.

Components of the Near-Death Experience

In a review of NDEs, Greyson (2006) has grouped the most common features of them into four components. One element is the cognitive component. People having NDEs may report changes in their thought processes, such as extreme speed of thought, lucidity and clarity, distortions of time, detailed memory of the panorama of their lives, and a sense of sudden insight, revelation, or understanding. The second element, the affective component, includes emotions of peace and tranquillity, joy, well-being, unconditional love, and a sense of being connected to the whole universe.

Thought and emotion, the first two components, are typical areas of study for psychology, but the third and fourth components are not. The paranormal component consists of out-of-body experiences, the ability to communicate telepathically, knowledge of the future, and intense physical sensations engendered by stimuli that are not physically present. The transcendental component reflects reports of having left the normal day-to-day world to arrive in another place, inability to fully enter another realm which is often glimpsed but from which one cannot return, and an encounter with a mystical presence and/or a deceased person.

Not all components are experienced by every person who has an NDE, and in some cases, one component is emphasized more than the others.

Effects of Near-Death Experiences

In the context of this chapter, the causes of NDEs are not relevant, nor are interpretations of their actual meaning. What is profoundly relevant, however, is the effect that NDEs have upon their experiencers. While some (few) NDEs may include images of damnation and horror, and some may leave their experiencers with great distress, the large majority of these experiences have very positive effects in terms of life satisfaction and subjective feelings of well-being. Mrs. Caldwell certainly credits her experience as having had a positive effect on her.

The positive effects found by several research studies (e.g., Greyson, 1983, 1992; Noyes, 1980; Ring, 1984; Sutherland, 1990; Van Lommel, 2001) include a highly decreased fear of death, decreased materialism, a decrease in pursuit of social status and prestige, and a desire to be of service to others, along with greater compassion for others. Other common effects are a heightened appreciation of life, decreased competitiveness, greater confidence, and flexibility and confidence in dealing with stressors. Most importantly for this chapter is the finding that people who have NDEs usually report enhanced meaning in life and dramatically increased spirituality.

These factors are all associated with greater life satisfaction and sense of well-being, as we see in greater detail in previous and subsequent chapters. The last two effects are particularly important for this examination of the effects of spirituality on life satisfaction. NDE experiencers report that their lives have increased meaning since their experiences. They find more purpose in their day-to-day lives and more coherence and unity within the universe. This change may not be fully integrated into their lives for several years, but it is long-lasting, perhaps even permanent (Flynn, 1986). In addition, and in conjunction with this, researchers have found that people who have had NDEs report more spirituality than before the experience.

Cherie Sutherland, an Australian sociologist who interviewed NDE experiencers about their changes in spirituality, found that the experiencers described their experiences as spiritual, but not religious (1990). She found that it was common for those she surveyed to turn from the organized religion they had held before and become more globally spiritual, not affiliating with any organized religion. This echoes the results of Ring (1980), who also found that NDE experiencers had a decreased orientation toward religion, with an increased feeling of spirituality, which they described as an *inward* religiosity. Their belief in a higher power may have been intensified, but the traditions and rituals of organized religion seemed to have little appeal for them. Mrs. Caldwell, for example, did not seem to find church attendance or formalized ritual as important after her NDE, yet her feelings of closeness to God were evidently increased. Musgrave's (1997) research supports this: the NDE experiencers she surveyed reported that their new inward religiosity took precedence over adherence to a formalized religious doctrine. The experience was so profound for 73 percent of her respondents that they claimed the NDE had led them to find their life's purpose.

Near-Death Experiencers

NDEs have been found in people of all ages, even children too young to have any expectations about what life after death might bring. People from all backgrounds, cultures, and religions (even atheists) seem to be equally likely to have such experiences. For example, McLaughlin and Mahoney (1984) found no relationship between religious orientation or religious involvement prior to the experience and the depth of the NDE experienced. In fact, as yet, no factors that have been studied (e.g., age, gender, history of mental disorder) have been found to be related to the occurrence of NDEs (Greyson, 2006).

A cross-cultural study of NDEs did find that while a belief system was not related to the *occurrence* of NDEs, it did affect the way the experience was *interpreted* (Osis & Haraldsson, 1977). This indicates that the effect of belief systems was upon meaning-making, not upon the experience itself. Thus, Mrs. Caldwell, a Christian, might interpret her experience as being in accord with her conception of Christianity, while someone with a Buddhist belief might be more likely to interpret the experience as transcending the suffering of life and glimpsing nirvana.

Mrs. Caldwell remembered her experience vividly many years later. This is usual. Over time, the accounts experiencers give of their experiences do not change: Greyson (2007) found that even though it is common for people to change their accounts of both mundane and dramatic events over time, after twenty years, NDE experiencers reported the same story as they had told originally.

Not only do NDEs seem to transform those people who have experienced them in ways that are conducive to their finding more satisfaction and meaning in life, but merely learning about NDEs increases the learner's sense of spirituality and meaning (Ring & Valarino, 1998). A noted psychiatrist of my acquaintance told me that he never had much spiritual feeling and considered himself purely a scientist, explaining the universe in terms of physical processes—that is, until, as a young intern, he witnessed three people have NDEs within the course of a week of his duty on an emergency ward. The psychiatrist, now in his late sixties, contends that this was so compelling for him that, while he still values science greatly, he developed and retained a profound belief that "there is more to life" and that his own life has a profound meaning, even in the face of the many frustrations and trials he has faced. It seems obvious to everyone who knows him that he has an inner peace and lives life with zest and happiness.

REFLECTIVE EXERCISE

Near-Death Experiences

Many people believe that the existence of near-death experiences demonstrate that there is an afterlife. Do you think there is? What do you think the afterlife might be like?

What do you think about near-death experiences? Does knowledge of them make you wonder about the possibilities of an afterlife? Do you think that knowledge of NDEs will make your spirituality increase? Or at least make you question

the possibility of spirituality in yourself a little more? Why or why not?

Does the idea of an afterlife increase your own feelings that life has a meaning? Read more about NDEs and the question of whether there is an afterlife. Which of the theories about NDEs do you find most compelling, if any? If you can, ask a nurse or physician if they have been told of a near-death experience by any of their patients. Did it change their attitudes in any way?

Inducing Spirituality

Near-death experiences may induce spirituality, but they are a rather drastic way of doing so, and there seems to be no way that NDEs themselves can be predictably induced—some people have them, and some people don't. But Saroglou, Buxant, and Tilquin (2008) have found other ways to induce spirituality. These researchers showed Belgian university students videos of beautiful nature scenes, childbirth, comedy, or a neutral film, and then gave them questionnaires about their religious belief and spirituality. They found that when the students had been primed with a video designed to elicit their sense of transcendence and wonder (the nature scenes and childbirth), the students reported more religious beliefs and spirituality than did the students who had seen the neutral film or the comedy. The effect of priming was stronger for spirituality than for religious beliefs. This may be because those students with religious beliefs were already firm in this belief, and the induction of self-transcendent emotions added little to this. Spirituality, however, is more marked by feelings of connection with the universe, and the videos of nature and childbirth may have reminded students of this or even enhanced their spiritual feelings.

Another method of inducing spirituality was investigated by Macavei and Miclea (2008). They studied this by presenting American students with a story of an astronaut stranded on a remote planet. In what they called the "framing" condition, they added that the cause of this situation was in the hands of a loving and merciful deity. This was omitted for the "non-framing" group. Both groups were then asked questions about how worried and sad the astronaut should feel. The "framing" group responded that the astronaut should feel less worried and sad than did the "non-framing" group who indicated that they thought the astronaut's situation was a punishment or a random state of affairs. The researchers concluded that framing the situation in the context of a loving God induced more positive responses and hope, while omitting framing resulted in respondents fearing some sort of chastisement by a severe deity. This suggests that one additional reason why regular attendance at a place of worship is positively related to well-being is that, in some religions, such attendance reminds the individual of the love and forgiveness of God, thus "framing" situations for worshippers.

POST-TRAUMATIC GROWTH

The aftermath of many near-death experiences points to the possibility of personal growth after having undergone a trauma. Indeed, we have often heard it said that "What doesn't kill us makes us stronger," and we have heard others say that their bad experience made them "sadder but wiser." In 1995, Tedeschi and Calhoun explored this phenomenon, naming it post-traumatic growth.

What Is Post-Traumatic Growth?

Post-traumatic growth (PTG) refers to positive changes that people may report after having had aversive experiences. These changes may be in several areas, such as worldviews, interpersonal relationships, and self-concepts. People who have PTG report finding new sources of strength in themselves, having more appreciation for life and for other people, more self-awareness, enhanced spirituality, and a sense of new possibilities for themselves in life. In the years since Tedeschi and Calhoun's (1995) discussion of PTG, a great deal of research and theorizing has been done to find out under what conditions PTG is most likely to occur and how to account for it.

Events Leading to Post-Traumatic Growth

Post-traumatic growth has been found in a variety of situations, from living through stressful environmental events such as disastrous tornadoes or violent events that may occur to victims of crime or people in areas of warfare, to personal experiences such as the illness of a child, parental divorce, or bereavement (e.g., Colville & Cream, 2009; Gerrish, Dyck, & Marsh, 2009; Linley & Joseph, 2004). People who witness traumatic events happening to others may experience PTG as well (Chopko & Schwartz, 2009).

PTG has been found in people who have been given the diagnosis of serious and life-threatening illnesses such as cancer, HIV/AIDS, multiple sclerosis, and so on (see Barskova & Oesterreich, 2009, and Hefferon, Grealy, & Mutrie, 2009, for reviews on the research into the relationship between PTG and medical conditions).

Effects of Post-Traumatic Growth on Well-Being

Many studies examining the effects of PTG on psychological and physical well-being find a positive effect (e.g., Durkin & Joseph, 2009; Morrill et al., 2008). Barskova and Oesterreich (2009) note that the changes accompanying PTG, such as more appreciation of life and other people, as well as more awareness of one's self and its potentials and limitations, are beneficial for people with life-threatening or chronic illnesses and often mean a better quality of life for them. PTG may increase the probability that they will adhere to a medical regime, thus ameliorating their symptoms and sometimes prolonging their lives.

Durkin and Joseph (2009) find that people who experience PTG have an increased sense of psychological well-being, a eudaimonic growth in terms of their outlooks on themselves, other people, and life in general, and not just a return of positive emotions after the traumatic event (Durkin & Joseph, 2009).

But some studies have found inconsistent effects of PTG on well-being, especially when measurements are made at one point in time rather than following individuals over a longer period of time (Zoellner & Maercker, 2006). This may, in part, be due to the fact that research in this area is in its infancy, with definitions of PTG and scales of measurement sometimes varying among researchers (Pat-Horenczyk & Brom, 2007).

Splevins, Cohen, Bowley, and Joseph (2010) also note that more care needs to be taken in studying PTG cross-culturally. For example, what constitutes "personal growth" may vary from culture to culture. Buddhists, they note, don't strive for "happiness" as do many non-Buddhists. For them, well-being includes accepting suffering as part of the nature of life. It may be that post-traumatic growth for a Buddhist means a movement from raging against suffering to accepting the suffering, rather than any enhancement of relationships or changes in views of the self or the world in general. Typically, this would not be captured by Western questionnaires that are meant to measure PTG. In spite of this, the researchers report, a great deal of cross-cultural consistency has been found.

Explaining Post-Traumatic Growth

Several theories of PTG have been put forward (see Zoellner & Maercker, 2006 for a review of these), but two of the most prominent ones are those of Joseph (2004, 2009; Linley & Joseph, 2011) and Tedeschi and Calhoun (1995, 2004). For our purposes in this chapter, we will take special note of the common parts of the explanations given by several of these theories.

Experiencing a trauma upsets our worldview: "This isn't the way the world is *supposed* to be," we say, "This isn't *supposed* to happen to me!" But it has happened. That's reality. All our assumptions about how the world works, how we function in it, what other people are like, and so on have been thrown into a turmoil. We struggle to make sense of it all (i.e., to create meaning). This may take us some time, and the search for meaning, as we have seen, may be distressing as we need to go over the traumatic event repeatedly. But eventually we arrive at a new worldview and a new view of ourselves and others. When people experience post-traumatic growth, their new worldview is one of positive enhancement and greater connectedness to others and to the world, and they may have an increased sense of psychological well-being.

This explanation goes far in clarifying why PTG is more likely to be found after time has passed since the traumatic event (Barskova & Oesterreich, 2009; Gerrish, Dyck, & Marsh, 2009; Pollard & Kennedy, 2007): people need time to process what has happened and to formulate a new worldview. This explanation is supported by studies such as that of Chopko and Schwartz (2009), who found that police officers who regularly witness horrific sights in the course of the work show little PTG when they simply accept that the terrible events they see are part of life. PTG is more likely to be an outcome when they think about what they have seen and reflect on life in general.

It's also generally found that PTG is more likely to occur in people who experience moderate levels of distress at the traumatic event rather than extreme distress (Colville & Cream, 2009; Levine, Laufer, Hamama-Raz, Stein, & Solomon, 2008). This may be in part because the extreme distress impairs the individual's ability to bring coherence to what has happened and to revise his or her worldview. Consistent with this are the results of Ho, Chu, and Yiu's (2008) research which found that people who are optimistic in their explanation of events are more likely to experience PTG after a trauma than are those who explain events pessimistically (recall from Chapter 5 that pessimists have less hope and might be less inclined to formulate a positive post-trauma worldview).

Post-Traumatic Growth and Religion

As we have seen, a belief in a religion is positively related to making meaning. It should come as no surprise, then, that religion and spirituality are usually positively related to post-traumatic growth. Although sometimes a person may turn away from religious beliefs following a traumatic occurrence, feeling that the deity is cruel or uncaring or perhaps doesn't exist at all, usually people find solace in their faith. In a review of eleven studies, Shaw, Joseph, and Linley (2005) concluded that after a traumatic event, people with religious faith were more likely to show PTG and that the trauma led them to develop faith or to deepen their faith. Their growth included positive religious coping, religious openness, religious participation, intrinsic religiousness, and a willingness to face the hard questions of life (e.g., what's the meaning of life? If there is a God, why do we suffer?). This is suggestive of the benefits of religion and spirituality, and it is reinforced by a study by Harris and her colleagues (Harris, Erbes, Engdahl, Tedeschi, Olson, Winskowski, & McMahill, 2010) which finds that after a non-interpersonal trauma (e.g., a natural disaster), people who pray for calm and focus are more likely to experience post-traumatic growth.

But O'Rourke, Tallman and Altmaier (2008) note that measurement scales of post-traumatic growth and religiosity/spirituality typically don't draw distinctions between religiosity and spirituality or between extrinsic and intrinsic religiosity, and that they contain too few items to give an adequate picture of this realm of experience anyway. Clearly this is an important and fertile field for future research.

Conclusion

Achieving the satisfying life is helped by making meaning, which in turn is aided by religion and spirituality. This does not mean that one cannot have a satisfying life if one is not religious or spiritual, but it is questionable whether life can be satisfying if it is felt to have no coherence and no purpose. Meaning-making can be seen in many of the factors that have been found to be related to subjective well-being. For example, the relationship of optimism and hope to life satisfaction, discussed in Chapter 5, can be seen as a reflection of a person's tendency to interpret events in a positive way and to regard painful experiences as conducive to learning about one's self and how to avoid mistakes in the future. Optimism and hope, then, may be considered particular forms of meaning-making.

The role of religion and spirituality in achieving a satisfying life is also clearly related to character virtues and strengths, such as forgiveness and gratitude (Chapter 7), and the meaning-making role in religion and spirituality has been demonstrated. Is meaning-making the real key to living a satisfying life? What do you think?

Summary

- Meaning-making refers to the extent to which people comprehend, make sense of, or see significance in their lives, accompanied by the degree to which they perceive themselves to have a purpose, mission, or over-arching aim in life.

- Meaning-making may be situational or global.

- People who say their lives have meaning are happier and have a greater sense of well-being and life satisfaction. They also feel a greater sense of control in their lives and more engagement in their work; they report feeling depressed and anxious less often, and they are less prone to suicide or substance abuse.

- Meaning in isolated incidents may be made by (1) finding a purpose in our present state, (2) constructing face-saving stories after an event or action, (3) constructing stories about events or actions in order to emphasize how to make the environment more predictable and pleasant in the future by exerting control, or (4) constructing stories which glorify us.

- Meaning of our overall lives is made by (1) achieving more consistency and coherence in our self-identities and life-goals, (2) developing a consistent life scheme, (3) striving for overall goals, (4) providing service to others, (5) dedication to one or more worthy causes, (6) expressing creativity, (7) living life as fully and deeply as possible, (8) attitudes toward personal suffering, and (9) spiritual experiences.

- People who are searching for meaning have less life satisfaction than those who have found meaning.

- Religion may be expressed as a search for significance in ways related to the sacred, usually within an organized structure of belief; spirituality can be conceptualized as a search for the sacred, which may or may not include an organized religion.

- Extrinsically religious people have no clear belief in the tenets of a faith, but follow religious practices because of societal or familial expectations. Intrinsically religious people follow the practices of a particular faith because of their profound belief in the truth of the teachings of their faith.

- People who claim to be religious are happier and more satisfied with their lives than those who do not claim to be religious.

- People who attend a place of worship regularly and believe in an afterlife feel more tranquility and less anxiety in their lives.

- Religious involvement is positively related to better mental health, but there are negative effects of holding religious doubt.

- People who attend a place of worship frequently live longer and are healthier.

- Children and adolescents who have high religious involvement are less likely to abuse drugs and alcohol or be involved in delinquent activity or early sexual activity.

- American students who reported being spiritual and healthy were less likely to engage in high-risk behaviours and were more likely to engage in healthy activities.

- Religion as a meaning system influences people's beliefs about themselves, other people, and the world; it provides expectations about consequences; it encourages goals and prescribes behaviours to meet these goals; and it influences emotions.

- Intrinsically religious people are more likely to experience personal growth after stress.
- In times of distress, people who have not examined their faith may find that their religion has no power to help them make meaning. Or, examination may lead them to a different understanding and their new belief will help in dealing with distress.
- Spirituality is a stronger predictor of life satisfaction than any personality variables.
- Internal conflict about religious beliefs is related to a higher level of shame and guilt, which in turn is related to a decreased life satisfaction.
- Religious doubt and/or belief in a punishing and severe deity are related to pessimism and a lack of hope for the future.
- Hope predicts life satisfaction when people use it to act in ways that they believe the deity will approve of and reward in the long run.
- A near-death experience (NDE) is the reported memory of impressions during a special state of consciousness.
- The large majority of NDEs have very positive effects in terms of life satisfaction and subjective feelings of well-being. Experiencers report a number of factors that lead to an increased meaning in life and dramatically increased spirituality.
- People may feel more spiritual if they are exposed to cues that indicate wonder in life or the presence of a loving God.
- Post-traumatic growth (PTG) refers to positive changes in several areas, such as worldviews, interpersonal relationships, and self-concepts that people may report after having had aversive experiences.
- PTG has a positive effect on psychological and physical well-being.
- PTG is more likely to occur in people who experience moderate levels of distress at the traumatic event rather than extreme distress.
- Religion and spirituality are usually positively related to post-traumatic growth.

Group Discussion Questions

1. Is meaning something that we find, that is given to us, or that we create?
2. Can true religiosity exist without spirituality?
3. How can a person know if he or she is spiritual?
4. Are the effects of near-death experiences merely the result of relief and gratitude that one did not die?

CHAPTER 9

Stress and Resilience

When Mr. Blodgett, the tyrannical boss, calls Katherine into his office and tells her to write a seventy-page report by the end of the week, Katherine feels her stomach rise to her throat. How will she ever do that? It will take hours of overtime work. Her husband is out of town and so can't take care of the kids, who are both under six years of age. Not only that, but her daughter's school play is coming up next week, and Katherine must make a costume for her. Katherine takes five deep breaths and sits at her desk planning her timetable and her strategy for getting everything done. Within a few minutes, she feels more relaxed and energized to begin her tasks. "When the going gets tough, the tough get going," she says.

Mr. Blodgett isn't finished. Next, he calls Poppy into his office and tells her to write a different sixty-page report by the end of the week. Poppy feels sick to her stomach, thinking about how little time that gives her. Her daughter is in the same play as Katherine's daughter, so Poppy, too, has to make a costume, and she hopes her husband can help. Poppy sits at her desk and feels worse and worse as time passes. "I'll never be able to do this," she thinks. "This is Mr. Blodgett's way of finding an excuse to fire me. I should never have taken this job. But where will I ever get another job if he fires me?" Poppy feels so sick that she leaves work early and has an emotional meltdown in her car. By the time she gets home, she is feeling very ill and needs to take the next two days off work.

For Katherine and Poppy, an unexpected early due date for a major report has put an additional load on them, on top of their already-present obligations and tasks. They are both clearly stressed. But the two women handle this stress in very different ways. Katherine tackles the situation head-on, with resilience, while Poppy dissolves into anxiety and illness. In this chapter, we will look at how stress affects these women, and us, and how we can make our lives more satisfying by dealing with stress effectively.

STRESS

No matter how much we try to get rid of it, stress is always a part of our lives. That's the nature of life, and we share a common bond in our experience of it. What is completely individual, however, is exactly what situations we find stressful. For one person, giving a speech in public is highly stressful, while for another person this may be non-stressful or even exhilarating. For each of us, whether we find a situation stressful depends on the situation as well. For example, your roommate's joking may be a welcome relief in many situations, but not at the time you're studying for an exam the next day.

Weiten, Lloyd, Dunn, and Hammer (2009) define **stress** as "any circumstances that threaten or are perceived to threaten one's well-being and thereby tax one's coping abilities" (p. 71). Clearly this covers a wide variety of situations, some occurring outside of ourselves and impacting on us, and some that arise within ourselves and affect our sense of well-being profoundly. The tiger lunging at your throat obviously puts you in a stressful situation, but so does a constant worry about whether you're attractive, smart, personable, and so on. The reports required by Mr. Blodgett are external stresses for Katherine and Poppy, but Poppy also seems to have the inner stress of self-doubt and

---

REFLECTIVE EXERCISE

Stress Vulnerability Scale

Rate each item from 1 (almost always) to 5 (never), according to how much of the time each statement applies to you.

I eat at least one hot, balanced meal a day.	_____
I get 7 to 8 hours sleep at least 4 nights a week.	_____
I give and receive affection regularly.	_____
I have at least one relative within 50 miles on whom I can rely.	_____
I exercise to the point of perspiration at least twice a week.	_____
I smoke less than half a pack of cigarettes a day.	_____
I take fewer than 5 alcoholic drinks a week.	_____
I am the appropriate weight for my height.	_____
I have an income adequate to meet basic expenses.	_____
I get strength from my religious beliefs.	_____
I regularly attend club or social activities.	_____
I have a network of friends to confide in about personal matters.	_____
I have hope and faith in my future.	_____
I am in good health (including eyesight, hearing, teeth).	_____
I am able to speak openly about my feelings when angry or worried.	_____
I have regular conversations with the people I live with about domestic problems, e.g., chores, money and daily living issues.	_____
I do something for fun at least once a week.	_____
I am able to organize my time effectively.	_____
I drink fewer than 3 cups of coffee (or tea or cola drinks) a day.	_____
I take quiet time for myself during the day.	_____
Subtotal	_____
Total (subtotal minus 20)	_____

Total your score and subtract 20. Any number over 30 indicates a vulnerability to stress. A total score between 50 and 75 suggests serious vulnerability, and over 75 means extreme vulnerability.

Source: Susceptibility to Stress scale from the Stress Audit, version 5.0-OS, developed by Lyle H. Miller and Alma Dell Smith. Copyright ©1987, 1994 Biobehavioral Institute of Boston, Brookline, MA 02146.

fear about the consequences of the failure she feels sure will come. Like most of the rest of us, Katherine and Poppy probably wish they had a stress-free life, but, in truth, those periods of time when we are without external stress may be enjoyable for a while, but eventually they may become boring and stressful too.

Western society seems to have a rather ambivalent attitude towards stress. On one hand, we bemoan it and look for ways to get rid of it, but on the other hand, the extremely busy person who seems to be dealing with stress all the time is often regarded with some admiration. One of my students remarked that if he didn't have stress, people would think that he was lazy! The reality, of course, is that we all have stress; the key is how we handle it. Some people, like Katherine, deal with stress better than others. They show **resilience**, the ability to handle stress and bounce back from stressful situations.

Before you go on, take the Stress Vulnerability Scale in the Reflective Exercise box. You can also take Wagnild and Young's (2009) well-documented test of your resilience at www.resiliencescale.com for free.

WHERE DOES STRESS COME FROM?

Change

In the great majority of situations, stress can be seen to come from four major sources (Weiten, Lloyd, Dunn, & Hammer, 2009). The first is *change*. Change is one of life's constants, but it does cause us stress because we have to adapt to it. The change may be pleasant (e.g., graduating from school, getting a new job, getting married, having a child), but it still taxes us. The more changes that occur in a short period of time, the more adapting we must do, and our stress increases (Holmes & Rahe, 1967). This additive effect of stress cannot be overlooked. This is why, at the end of a semester, for example, a student who is successfully coping with having several major assignments due at the same time and is studying for final exams may break down at finding there is no more milk in the refrigerator. (Even this example has change in it: from having no assignments due to having several assignments due, and from having milk available to having none.) Katherine and Poppy experience the change from their normal working day to also having a new long report to write with a short deadline.

Frustration

Frustration is another source of stress. When we feel frustration, it means that one of our goals has been blocked in some way, and this may lead us to react with anger. In the example of our stressed-out student with no milk, frustration is also present: our friend has the goal of drinking some milk but is blocked in this goal by its absence. Katherine and Poppy may feel that their goals of getting reports written are blocked by the short deadline and the obligations they have to their children.

Conflict

Conflict in decision-making is stressful to us as well. We make hundreds of decisions each day, from when to get up in the morning to when to go to bed at night. Many of these decisions are made without much thought, but some of our decisions are more important and require some active thinking. Should I or shouldn't I? In some cases, there are positive benefits to a decision, but there are also problems with it.

For example, staying up all night talking to a friend has the benefit of pleasurable interaction but the problem of functioning well without sleep the next day. This is called an *approach–avoidance conflict*. Another decision may be between two options. Should I do A or B? In some cases, the decision is not very difficult because both options have clear benefits and we feel that we can't go wrong in choosing either: an *approach–approach conflict*. An example of this might be choosing between two movies that we want to see.

Sometimes our options are both negative and we speak of being between a rock and a hard place. An *avoidance–avoidance conflict* such as this might be seen in deciding which of the two domestic chores that we hate we should do first. Generally we delay making this kind of decision for as long as we can, and this causes us the greatest stress. Chances are that this is the kind of conflict Katherine and Poppy feel: they can work on their reports but possibly feel like failures in their maternal roles, or they can fulfill their maternal roles to their satisfaction but fail to complete acceptable reports, possibly resulting in job loss.

Pressure

Pressure can be another source of stress. We feel pressure when we try to handle expectations that are put upon us by other people and/or by ourselves. Sometimes this can be a crushing stress. It feels terrible when we believe we have let other people down, and feeling that we let ourselves down can be a source of low self-esteem, guilt, and depression. We need to be aware, however, that sometimes the pressure we feel from other people may be more our own creation than theirs. A common example is found in the case of young people who believe that their parents expect them to pursue a particular career, one that they really don't want to pursue. In most cases, parents simply want their children to find a career that will support them and satisfy them. The expectations the children think the parents have aren't in the parents' minds at all. But in the case of Katherine and Poppy, the expectations of Mr. Blodgett are very real. It may be that their expectations of themselves in their motherhood roles are somewhat unrealistic, though.

Daily Hassles

Finally, we can't forget another source of stress for us: our *daily hassles* (Kanner, Coyne, Schaefer, & Lazarus, 1981; Lazarus, 1990; Serido, Almeida, & Wethington, 2004). Much of the stress in our lives comes from the basic process of living. There seems to be so much we have to do. Laundry, cooking, grocery shopping, picking up dry cleaning, and the list goes on. Imagine this situation: you jump out of bed, finding that your alarm clock has failed and you are in danger of being late for work. As you land on the floor, your foot tells you that the cat coughed up a hairball during the night. Racing to the shower, you discover that there is no hot water. And chugging the milk right out of the refrigerator, you find that it has gone sour. Still, you persist and run out the door to your car. But the battery is dead. You have been up for 20 minutes, and already you have the start of a bad day. All of these events provide stress for you, but none of them are catastrophic, and when you tell friends about your bad morning, they are more likely to laugh than to commiserate.

These are daily hassles, the little stresses of living that usually include elements of change, frustration, conflict, and/or pressure. Other daily hassles may come from living in an unsafe neighbourhood, having a mild but chronic illness or disorder, feeling unsatisfied with some facet of yourself and your relationships with others, and so on. None of these qualifies for the category "major problem," but they serve to complicate our lives and impair our feelings of well-being, and an accumulation of these may cause us as much or more stress than major events in our lives. For Katherine and Poppy, writing reports, even with a short deadline, is part of the working world, a daily hassle. Similarly, the demands of child-care may be daily hassles as well, even though they both love being mothers. The accumulation of both types of hassles makes their situations stressful.

REFLECTIVE EXERCISE

Your Own Stresses

Think about your own stresses. Do they reveal one or more of the sources of stresses we discussed above? The following are the top 10 stresses that American university students report (Darling, McWey, Howard, & Olmstead, 2007):

1. grades
2. lack of money
3. uncertainty of professional future
4. current world events
5. major course of study
6. lack of study time
7. quantity of homework
8. parental expectations of school performance
9. lack of sleep
10. quality of class instruction

If you are a student, do you agree with this list? Students do carry a great deal of stress, especially in their first year of college or university, a finding that is cross-cultural (Bayram & Bilgel, 2008; Bouteyre, Maurel, & Bernaud, 2007; Darling, McWey, Howard, & Olmstead, 2007; Wong, Cheung, Chan, Ma, & Tang, 2006). Stress is again present in the change that students make after their graduation, when they start their careers (Murphy, Blustein, Bohlig, & Platt, 2010). If you are not a student, what stresses do you experience? Can you describe them in terms of change, frustration, conflict, pressure, and daily hassles?

THE PSYCHOLOGICAL EFFECTS OF STRESS

In a nutshell, stress usually makes us feel miserable (Lazarus & Folkman, 1984; McIntyre, Korn, & Matsuo, 2008). We may feel depression, and the depression we feel brings more stress upon us since, in part, the effects of depression serve to impair our thinking and our interpersonal relationships (Liu & Alloy, 2010). When stressed, we may ruminate and worry, like Poppy. We may feel that the joy of other parts of our lives has been sucked away. Sometimes it seems impossible to think about anything else or to focus on other aspects of our lives.

Indeed, stress does have an effect on our ability to think. Our attention is diverted from tasks at hand, impairing our performance on these tasks. A test-anxious student, for example, may say "I can't even read the test paper; the questions make no sense, and I never heard of any of the topics before." What is really going on is a constant buzz in the student's head: "I'm never going to pass this test. I can't understand this. I'm going to fail the course. Then I'll never get my degree. I won't get a decent job. I'll probably never get any kind of job. I'll wind up dead on the street." and so on. The negative comments engendered by the student's reaction to the test get in the way of focusing attention on the test itself, and the student chokes with the pressure.

This is part of the reason why, at many colleges and universities, students are not allowed to leave an exam room for the first twenty or thirty minutes. Imagine our test-anxious student again. Now he is thinking "I can't pass this test so I'll leave. OK, I can't leave for thirty minutes so I'll just sit here until I can." Having made this decision, the student feels calmer. While waiting with nothing else to do, he glances again at the questions on the test and finds that they actually do make sense and tap topics that the student has studied. And so our test-anxious student may start to write answers and may even finish the test successfully! However, we must note that a little stress might be a good thing. If the student were totally relaxed at the test, he might fall asleep, or at least be too relaxed to be alert. If the task is difficult, as a test might be, a moderate amount of stress seems to yield optimal functioning (Weiten, Lloyd, Dunn, & Hammer, 2009). Poppy, though, is so consumed with negative thoughts about her stresses that she can't think about how to handle them, she can only react with illness and intense emotionality.

Burnout

When stress, extreme or traumatic, has been prolonged, the effects of stress can be much more severe. Stressful events in life even have a high association with suicide attempts (Baca-Garcia et al., 2007). In situations in which stress is prolonged and the individual feels powerless to change it, **burnout** may occur. Burnout has primarily been studied in the working world, but it is not limited to it.

When burnout occurs, the individual feels drained of energy, cynical, and lacking in self-efficacy. The individual's humour seems to dwindle and social relationships are impaired as the individual believes that no one else fully comprehends the problem. This lack of comprehension is mainly in the person's perception rather than reality. It may be plain to onlookers that the person needs to leave or change the situation or change his/her way of regarding it, but the person is resistant to this. The person shows an increased susceptibility to depression (Chen, Siu, Lu, Cooper, & Phillips, 2009) and other subsequent mental disorders (Toppinen-Tanner, Ahola, Koskinen, & Väänänen, 2009), and physically the individual is harmed as well, with an increased risk of cardiovascular disease and other health impairments (Melamed, Shirom, Toker, Berliner, & Shapira, 2006; Toppinen-Tanner, Ahola, Koskinen, & Väänänen, 2009).

Too many people assume that the person who burns out must be "weak" or deficient in some way, but research suggests that the culprit is more likely to be the situation itself. Situations in which the person has little control rob the individual of feeling that he/she has *any* power in the situation; situations in which there is little or no recognition of the individual's efforts leave the individual feeling that perhaps their efforts really are meaningless; situations in which there is too much work and too little time to do it leave the individual feeling that he/she is on a treadmill with no end in sight. If the situation also contains co-workers or other people with whom the individual has a conflict, the person may come to feel nothing but dread at having to confront this day after day.

In these situations, the person experiencing burnout becomes less productive, becomes less committed to the task, and may have more physical illnesses, resulting in increased absenteeism in the workplace (Maslach, 2003). Sadly, this happens more to people who have been highly committed to the task, even idealistic about it, and have dedicated their lives to it at the expense of other facets of life. Burnout often happens to the best people in an area. Many people assume that running their own business will decrease their stress since, they feel, they can make their own rules, but the responsibility, commitment, time obligations, financial pressure, and the stress increase in this situation, and the incidence of burnout is higher in those who are self-employed than in those who are employed by others (Jamal, 2007).

People with burnout on the job bring their exhaustion and their psychological and physical symptoms home with them as well. Burnout in one intimate partner affects the psychological and physical health of the other partner too, and the partner's incidence of burnout is thus increased (Bakker, 2009).

Compassion Fatigue

Less severe is the recently-researched effect of **compassion fatigue**. This is the name given to a condition in which a caregiver feels overwhelmed by his/her exposure to the needs of others. Compassion fatigue is found in situations in which a person is a caregiver who has cared so much that he/she has depleted their own energy and the amount of caring he/she can feel begins to decrease (Sprang, Clark & Whitt-Woosley, 2007; Tehrani, 2007). It has been found in nurses, social workers, and animal care workers, and no doubt future research will find it in many other situations. For example, the stress upon the caregivers, such as family members, of terminally ill patients is often quite profound. After caring for someone, especially in the home, for a lengthy period of time, the caregiver—who is typically not professionally qualified for the task and who is grieving for the debilitation of a loved one—may feel worn out almost to the point of exhaustion (see Hadad, 2009).

Posttraumatic Stress Disorder

More severe is the case of people who have personally experienced or witnessed traumatic events that have placed enormous stress on them. In some cases, they develop **posttraumatic stress disorder**. Posttraumatic stress disorder (PTSD) is a major psychological disorder that can manifest after someone has been involved in an incident in which stress has been extreme. It was originally studied in conjunction with the severe problems displayed by many veterans returning from the Vietnam War, but it has been found in many other situations as well.

PTSD is characterized by symptoms of recurring experiencing of the trauma through flashbacks, dreams and visions, general emotional numbing to day-to-day events, and avoidance of stimuli that might remind the person of the trauma. Accompanying these symptoms are increased arousal and anxiety, impaired social relationships and vulnerability to substance abuse, as well as increased risk of several physical disorders. Although there may be some genetic predisposition making PTSD more likely in some people (see a review by Koenen, 2007), the situation itself seems to be the major factor in developing the disorder. PTSD has been diagnosed in combat veterans, emergency aid and rescue workers (Alvarez & Hunt, 2005), criminal attack survivors, survivors of major disasters, and the clean-up crews of gruesome scenes (Ursano, Fullerton, Vance, & Kao, 1999). The symptoms of PTSD may arise immediately after the trauma, but in some cases do not appear until months or even years later. The symptoms may decrease over time, but in some cases remain for the rest of the person's life (Durand, Barlow, & Stewart, 2007).

REFLECTIVE EXERCISE

Psychological Reactions to Stress

How do you respond to stress in your own life? Do you worry and ruminate? Get angry? Become depressed? Distract yourself in some way to avoid thinking about the stress? Have you ever noticed an impairment in your thinking or decision-making when you feel stressed? Ask your friends and family if they have noticed any particular characteristics about you when you are stressed. The more you know about your own responses, the better able you will be to manage your stress.

The psychological effects of stress may obviously be quite severe, but recall that posttraumatic growth is also possible (see Chapter 8).

THE PHYSIOLOGICAL EFFECTS OF STRESS

Both Katherine and Poppy had an immediate physical reaction to the news that they would be required to write a lengthy report in a short period of time. While most of us are aware of the negative psychological effect that stress has on us, many of us are not aware of the toll stress takes on our bodies. But, as Williams, Suchy, and Rau (2009) say, "...understanding individual differences in stress risk and resilience has been the cornerstone of health psychology and behavioral medicine." (p. 126).

The General Adaptation Syndrome

The physiological effects of stress were first studied by Hans Selye (1956) at McGill University in Montreal. Selye contended that any stress, psychological or physical, provokes the same physiological reaction in our bodies. This point is still being debated by science (see, for example, McEwen & Wingfield, 2010), but his contention provides a starting point in our understanding.

When stress comes upon us, Selye said, we begin the **general adaptation syndrome**. This is comprised of the body's reaction to mobilize itself to deal with the stress. First, we have the **alarm reaction**, a general gearing-up of the body to flee the threat or to fight it. Our muscles tense, our mouths become dry, our heart rate increases, and our stomachs churn.

Such physiological reactions may be highly adaptive if the threat is one that we can fight or flee from, as it might have been for our early ancestors. But today, our stresses tend to be prolonged and sometimes even chronic. In this case, we enter the second stage of the general adaptation syndrome, the **resistance stage**. Our physiological responses start to subside, but they typically don't go back to a normal level. We may not feel that our bodies are running at a higher level than normal, but they are. Selye felt that this was a very dangerous stage for us, because we may think that we are coping with the stress very well and do not seek ways to deal with it further. Like an engine running at a level above its norm, our bodies run the risk of burning out. When this happens, said Selye, we enter the **exhaustion stage** in which our physical resources are now depleted and we fall ill with what he called **diseases of adaptation** which may be severe enough to kill us. These diseases of adaptation are more generally called **psychosomatic disorders** today. Psychosomatic disorders are very real physical problems that are believed to be caused, at least in part, by stress and other psychological factors. For example, time pressure and family conflicts are related to psychosomatic complaints (Höge, 2009).

The Endocrine System

Modern science has investigated the physiological reactions to stress in more detail. Today we know that the major response to stress comes from the endocrine system, the system that secretes hormones into the body. The endocrine system receives information to secrete hormones, first, from the brain. When we perceive threat, a small part in the middle of the brain, the hypothalamus, is activated and sends signals to the pituitary gland which, in turn, signals part of the adrenal glands to release the hormones known as corticosteroids. These corticosteroids stimulate the release of chemicals that serve the function of increasing energy and, in case we are injured during our fight or flight, reducing tissue inflammation. At the same time, the hypothalamus sends signals that result in another part of the adrenal glands releasing other hormones, known as catecholamines, into the bloodstream. Catecholamines target the part of our nervous system that regulates the normal body functions. An increase in catecholamines speeds up our heart rate, quickens our respiration, inhibits digestion (which at the time of threat would be a needless expenditure of energy), and sharpens our eyesight. Our bodies are ready to move in fleeing the threat or in fighting it.

The specific nature of the results of activation of the hypothalamus, pituitary gland, and adrenal glands (the **HPA axis**) is a general finding, but it seems not necessarily a universal one: for example, in people suffering from PTSD, the specific neurochemical patterns are somewhat different, indicating that our physiological response to stress depends on our individual experience and psychological reactions to stress (Miller, Chen, & Zhou, 2007).

The Effects of Stress on Health

These physiological responses were no doubt of great benefit to our ancestors who had to cope with running from or fighting dangerous animals, and they may be of great benefit to us today—if our stress comes from a physical source, such as being threatened by a mugger. But in the normal course of events in North American lives with the stresses we typically encounter, these responses are of less immediate use and may even endanger us. We may make it worse for ourselves since it seems that, when under stress, we engage in less healthy lifestyles, which in turn makes it more difficult for us to physiologically deal with the stress (Roohafza et al., 2007).

The negative effects of stress on health have been seen in many studies (e.g., Kiecolt-Glaser, McGuire, Robles, & Glaser, 2002; Schüler, Job, Fröhlich, & Brandstätter, 2009; Williams, Rau, Cribbet, & Gunn, 2009) and these effects can even be seen in adolescents (Nielsen & Hansson, 2007). But not all studies have the same results. Öhman, Bergdahl, Nyberg, and Nilsson (2007) conducted a longitudinal study that did not indicate long-term health effects as related to prolonged moderate stress. Also, Phillips, Der, and Carroll (2008) found that only health-related stresses were related to mortality. These researchers suggest that different types of stress can have different effects on health.

The effect of stress on the cardiovascular system has received a great deal of research attention. Since the body's response to stress increases blood pressure and heart rate, as well as changing the biochemistry of the blood, it would be expected that deleterious effects would be seen in the cardiovascular system with prolonged stress. This is indeed the case. Long-term stress, such as occupational stress, has been found to be related to hypertension, heart attacks, and strokes (Byrne & Espnes, 2008; Esler, Schwarz, & Alvarenga, 2008a). This may be especially true in the case of people who already have a predisposition to perceive and experience negative emotions, such as hostility (Hughes, 2007; Stanley & Burrows, 2008). In addition, a sudden acute stress can trigger cardiac catastrophes such as heart attacks and death (Esler, Schwarz, & Alvarenga, 2008b). The good news is that positive emotions are beneficial in bringing the cardiovascular system back to normal after a stressful situation (Chida & Hamer, 2008; Souza et al., 2007).

Have you noticed that you or your friends seem to be more prone to colds and flus after a period of prolonged stress (such as at the end of a semester at school)? Once people (such as professors) thought this was a myth, that the rash of ill students that emerged at the end of semester were faking their illnesses in order to complete the work they had put off. Today, we're less skeptical. One particularly deleterious effect that stress can have on us is compromising our immune system. A great deal of research has verified this effect (e.g., Brydon, Walker, Wawrzyniak, Chart, & Steptoe, 2009; Lamkin et al., 2007; McGregor, Antoni, Ceballos, & Blomberg, 2008; Segerstrom & Miller, 2004).

Chronic stress has two possible effects on the immune system: it can suppress the ability of the immune system to keep us safe from factors such as microorganisms, allergens, and improperly functioning tissue; and it can increase the functioning of the immune system to the point that we are attacked by our own bodies. Contemporary research is not so much concerned with establishing this (that's been done) as with discovering exactly how these effects are produced in the immune system and what can be done to ameliorate these effects. As we shall see later in our discussion of coping with stress, changing our psychological response to stress changes our physiological responses too (e.g., Denson, Spanovic, & Miller, 2009; Worthington & Scherer, 2004).

The negative effects of stress can be seen on other areas of bodily functioning as well. For example, stress is related to digestive disorders, as may be the case for Poppy (Armata & Baldwin, 2008), headache and other body pains (Hwang et al., 2008), sleep disruptions (Williams & Moroz, 2009), sexual functioning (Blonna, 2007), premenstrual syndrome (Blonna, 2007), and poor health outcomes in children whose mothers experienced prenatal stress (Beydoun & Saftlas, 2008). Researchers have studied the relationship between stress and several specific disorders and found that stress may be linked to the onset or progress of diseases such as the common cold, asthma, epileptic seizures, and many more (Weiten, Lloyd, Dunn, & Hammer, 2009).

If we already have a physiological disorder, a disease, or have suffered a trauma to our bodies such as surgery, we are already suffering from stress, both on our bodies and on our minds in coping with the stress. Physiologically, stress can make the situation worse, especially if the disease is autoimmune in nature (e.g., rheumatoid arthritis, ulcerative colitis) since stress compromises the workings of the immune system.

While philosophers have long debated the connection, if any, between the mind and the body, the answer seems quite clear to psychologists: the body affects the mind and the mind affects the body. In fact, it sometimes seems unclear where one starts and the other stops, if a separation can be made at all.

REFLECTIVE EXERCISE

Physiological Stress Reactions

How do you respond to stress physically? Have you ever felt your heart race, your mouth go dry, your stomach churn in response to stress? Do you have other reactions of a physical nature? Do you lose your appetite? Or become unable to sleep? Do you fidget?

If you are aware of body responses to stress, how do you deal with them? If you are not aware of body responses, try tuning in to your body a little. Listening to our bodies can give us valuable information about our health and cues about finding coping mechanisms.

RESILIENCE

Primary and Secondary Appraisal

When we are confronted with stress, we first engage in **primary appraisal** (Lazarus & Folkman, 1984). We make a determination of whether the event is, in fact, threatening to us and how threatening. Next we engage in **secondary appraisal** (Lazarus & Folkman, 1984), deciding if we can cope with the stress. These appraisals occur very quickly and often without our awareness, and in both appraisals we see the role of positive emotions.

Determining whether a situation is a threat to us or not is dependent on our past experience and on our personalities. For example, if we have never written a test before or heard anything about tests, we may not consider taking a test to be threatening. After all, we won't die from it, will we? But if we have had tests in the past that we didn't do very well on, with negative consequences, or we have heard that there is a great deal riding on the results of the test, the test may seem threatening indeed. This may be especially the case if academic success is part of the way we gauge our self-worth. If we tend to be optimistic about our lives, a test may seem less threatening. Similarly, if we have studied hard and feel a sense of efficacy about the content of the material the test covers, we may feel less stress and more energized in the situation. Primary appraisal, then, reflects a number of factors that are particular to the individual.

Secondary appraisal is also an individual matter. We estimate the resources we have in dealing with the stress based on our past coping, our sense of self-efficacy, and our own worldview. The person who has had test anxiety in the past may assume that the test situation is very threatening and react with high anxiety in the present situation. Every professor has had students who claimed "I can't do multiple choice (or short answer or essay or…) questions," and who feel threatened by the very thought of a test. Not surprisingly, their anxiety gets in the way of their studying and their performance on the test. But other students may feel that they have demonstrated their competence on tests in the past and feel that, with hard work, they can handle the next test with relative ease. Subsequently, and again not surprisingly, they are able to focus well on the test and perform in a proficient manner.

Emotion-focused and Problem-focused Coping

There are two basic ways of coping with stress, **emotion-focused coping** and **problem-focused coping**. With emotion-focused coping, we concentrate on the emotions that the stress arouses within us and we try to deal with those. With problem-focused coping, we concentrate on the situation which is causing us stress and try to change or avoid the situation.

Let's go back to the stress of taking a test. With emotion-focused coping, the test-anxious student may put effort into calming down and avoiding the anxiety. This might be done by a number of techniques, some adaptive and some not so adaptive. Some students may decide to exercise to the point of exhaustion, for example. Others may drink alcohol until any thoughts of tests (or anything else) are temporarily eradicated. Some others may clean house, shop, gamble, spend time with friends, overeat junk food, and so on. Other students may use meditation, physical relaxation training, or yoga to make themselves feel calmer. There are many possibilities, some adaptive and some maladaptive, but the purpose of all of them is to get rid of the negative feelings.

The purpose of problem-focused coping is to deal with the situation, so our test-anxious student may study hard, drop the course, or actually make himself/herself sick to avoid the test or provide a reason for a less-than-stellar performance. Again, the list of possibilities is long. So problem-focused coping can be adaptive or maladaptive as well.

For both emotion-focused coping and problem-focused coping, the adaptiveness of the technique used depends largely on the situation, although problem-focused coping is used more by people who cope well with stress (e.g., Campbell-Sills, Cohan, & Stein, 2006; Kaiseler, Polman, & Nicholls, 2009). In situations that can't be changed, emotion-focused coping is the only adaptive option. If the situation can be changed, if a problem can be solved, then problem-focused coping seems to be the better alternative. In many, if not most, of the stressful situations of our lives, both forms of coping can be used, by themselves or together. So a student with test anxiety may employ a technique such as deep breathing to calm emotions as well as joining a study group to help tackle the anxiety-causing problem.

It's important to note that we often engage in both adaptive and maladaptive strategies at the same time (Clauss-Ehlers, 2008). Our test-anxious student may employ the adaptive strategies of deep breathing and joining a study group, but while breathing and studying may still gulp down multiple bags of potato chips!

Katherine and Poppy, in their primary appraisal of their situations, clearly felt that there was a potential threat in having to write major reports in such a brief period of time. Katherine, however, used emotion-focused coping by deep breathing to calm herself and then used problem-focused coping in planning how to tackle her responsibilities. This led her to a secondary appraisal that she could manage the situation. Poppy, on the other hand, quickly used secondary appraisal to conclude that she could not manage the situation and used a problem-focused coping of becoming sick, thereby avoiding work and the task at hand.

What Is Resilience?

People like Katherine, who can bounce back from stressful situations relatively quickly, are said to be resilient. But what does "bouncing back" really mean? For some researchers, it means psychological and physical recovery from stress in a short period of time (e.g., Tugade & Fredrickson, 2007). Others would claim that resilient people are those who have ways of coping that prevent reacting to stress at high levels (e.g., Ong, Bergeman, Bisconti, & Wallace, 2006). Other researchers would include growing from the stressful experience as a vital part of resilience (e.g., Clinton, 2008). This lack of agreement has provided a problem in coming to general conclusions about resilience since any conclusions must be based on the results of studies that define resilience in different ways (Almedom & Glandon, 2007; Campbell-Sills, Cohan, & Stein, 2006; Davydov, Stewart, Ritchie, & Chaudieu, 2010).

Another problem in examining resilience is the question of whether or not it is a general personality trait, as assumed by many researchers (e.g., Kwok, Hughes, & Luo, 2007; Tugade & Fredrickson, 2007; Waugh, Fredrickson, & Taylor, 2008). While there are several tests of resilience that claim to measure resilience as a stable and global disposition to bounce back from stress (e.g., the Brief Resilience Scale, by Smith et al., 2008; the Connor-Davidson Resilience Scale, by Connor & Davidson, 2003), Vanderbilt-Adriance and Shaw (2008) reviewed studies indicating that children who experience a great deal of stress may show resilience in only some domains of their lives. For example, they may maintain good grades in school, but internally they may feel distress and upset. This suggests that rather than being a stable trait, resilience depends upon the situation as well.

Characteristics of Resilient People

Assuming that resilience can be seen as a general tendency in some people, we can make some conclusions about what these people are like. Resilient people differ from those who are less resilient in several ways. For one thing, they physiologically and psychologically recover from a negative event (even one that they anticipate but does not occur) faster than do less resilient people. This may be because they summon up positive emotions to counteract the negative feelings of stress by reappraising the situation and/or finding meaning in it (Ablett & Jones, 2007; Ardelt, 2005). They ruminate on the negatives of life less (Philippe, Lecours, & Beaulieu-Pelletier, 2009; Tugade & Fredrickson, 2004; Waugh, Fredrickson, & Taylor, 2008).

Resilient people are more likely to use problem-focused coping processes rather than emotion-focused coping (Campbell-Sills, Cohan, & Stein, 2006; Kaiseler, Polman, & Nicholls, 2009), and they are flexible in their coping: when one strategy is ineffective, they switch to another if they think it will have a greater chance of success (Lam & McBride-Chang, 2007).

Not only do resilient people have better coping techniques, they seem to have personality characteristics that aid them. For example, they are more likely to have an optimistic outlook (Baldwin, Kennedy, & Armata, 2008; Baker, 2007; Brodhagen & Wise, 2008; Grote, Bledsoe, Larkin, Lemay, & Brown, 2007; Lai, 2009; Steptoe, O'Donnell, Marmot, & Wardle, 2008), and they appraise themselves positively (Johnson, Gooding, Wood, & Tarrier, 2010). They have more self-esteem and feelings of personal control in their lives (Mimura, Murrells, & Griffiths, 2009; Windle, Markland, & Woods, 2008), with more personal self-efficacy (Karademas, Kafetsios, & Sideridis, 2007; Martin & Marsh, 2008; Shen, 2009).

Resilient people also feel more meaning in life (Park, 2005, 2010; Van Dyke & Elias, 2007). They are more open to new experiences (Williams, Rau, Cribbet, & Gunn, 2009), and they are more conscientious in terms of controlling their behaviour and emotions in order to fulfill a goal (Williams & Moroz, 2009).

Resilience in Children

A great deal of the research on resilience has centred on children. This is natural since a major aim in raising children is to help them withstand the vicissitudes of life. For children, resilience is related not only to their own personalities, but to the experiences they have within their families and their wider communities. A number of reviewers have noted this (e.g., Dolan, 2008; Masten, Cutuli, Herbers, & Reed, 2009; Vanderbilt-Adriance & Shaw, 2008). Children who are intelligent, feel that control of their lives lies within themselves, can regulate their emotions, and can attend well to stimuli in the environment seem to be more resilient than children without these qualities.

Genetic factors, especially those that are related to an "easy" temperament from birth, seem to be protective. The children who have better coping strategies, possibly because of their temperament or their intelligence, are more resilient.

Protective factors within the family include a warm relationship with a caregiver and parental monitoring of the child's activities and friends (see also Holt, Buckley, & Whelan, 2008 and Iwaiec, Larkin, & Higgins, 2006). Benzies and Mychasiuk (2009, see also Brennan, 2008), concentrating on family resiliency, add to this list: families characterized by a positive outlook on life and a strong sense of purpose, as well as higher self-efficacy, are more resilient. The parents tend to have a higher level of education and income, as well as more family cohesion. These parents provide stimulation and support for the child that increase the child's and the family's ability to deal with stress.

Clinton (2008) notes the importance of open communication within the family. She observes the research findings that indicate that parents who have a self-reflective style, believe they are able to overcome adversity, and are committed to relationships tend to have children with a higher level of resilience. In adolescence, as well, increased perceived family support is related to resilience (Tusaie, Puskar, & Sereika, 2007), while maltreatment as a child is related to decreased resilience in adulthood (Campbell-Sills, Forde, & Stein, 2009).

In the community, the resilient family has access to active involvement in community affairs, peer acceptance, and supportive mentors. A community that is cohesive and contains youth organizations, high-quality schools and constructive after-school activities also fosters resilience in the child. The community that is safe and has available quality health care is additionally important in developing the family's resilience.

Not surprisingly, resilient children are more academically successful (Kwok, Hughes, & Luo, 2007).

Hardiness

Resilience has often been studied in connection with the psychological factor of **hardiness**. Hardy people have been found to be high on three crucial factors of functioning: (1) they view change as challenge rather than threat, (2) they are committed to seeing life and events as purposeful, and (3) they believe they have control over their lives and destinies (Maddi, 2002, 2006). To this triad, researchers who study **mental toughness** in athletes in particular add the fourth factor of confidence: mentally tough athletes are hardy and they have confidence in believing that they can overcome obstacles (Clough, Earle, & Sewell, 2002; Horsburgh, Schermer, Veselka, & Vernon, 2009; Nicholls, Polman, Levy, & Backhouse, 2008).

Katherine, in the case study at the beginning of the chapter, is a hardy, resilient person. She controls her reaction to the situation she finds herself in and views it as a challenge that she, with her self-efficacy, has confidence she can handle. It is likely that her children will learn this approach to stress from watching their mother, and, hopefully, become resilient adults as well. Poppy, though, is less resilient. For her, the situation is fraught with threats that she does not feel she can handle. As she takes refuge in her illness (which we assume is at least in part caused by her stress reactions), she further diminishes her sense of self-efficacy and confidence and provides an example for her daughter that we hope her daughter will not emulate.

A Cross-Cultural Note

Michael Ungar and his colleagues (Ungar et al., 2007) at Dalhousie University in Nova Scotia performed a multi-method study as part of the International Resilience Project. Their findings led to conclusions that we would be wise to note, especially in the multicultural world we live in. In studying young people between the ages of 12 and 23 years, in 11 different countries comprising several different cultures, they found that in every setting the young people had seven areas in which they felt tension and stress that demanded their adaptive coping abilities. These areas were (1) access to material resources, (2) relationships, (3) identity, (4) power and control, (5) cultural adherence, (6) social justice, and (7) cohesion (personal interests balanced with being part of a larger community). The importance of each of these areas and the amount of tension it engendered differed from culture to culture, however. Ungar and his colleagues state

Findings show that *youth who experience themselves as resilient, and are seen by their communities as resilient, are those that successfully navigate their way through these tensions. Resilient youth find a way to resolve all seven tensions simultaneously according to the strengths and resources available to the youth individually, within their family, community, and culture....*

The data reveal no evidence that one way of resolving these tensions is better than another. (p. 294, italics in original)

The cultural context, then, often indicates the relevant and adaptive ways of coping with the stress of life. Too often we assume that there are universally adaptive ways of being resilient and behaving in a way that maximizes our chances of having a satisfying life, but we must remember that we don't live in a vacuum and that factors from the wider world around us must be taken into account. As an example of this, Ungar and his colleagues (2007) quote a Russian boy who indicates that financial tension was a major source of stress for him because, he claims, in Russia, even high school education costs a great deal of money. In another example, a Palestinian boy discussed his search for identity without using the word "I": identity, for him in his cultural milieu, was fully integrated into the Palestinian political movement for an independent state. Clauss-Ehlers (2008) echoes this belief and emphasizes that not only does social support foster resilience, but cultural support is important as well.

REFLECTIVE EXERCISE

Resilience

How well do you cope with stress? Would you consider yourself to be resilient? Recall an event in which you showed resilience and an event in which you didn't. What were the differences between these events? How do you account for your own resilience or lack of resilience? What factors in your personality and your life allow you to bounce back from adversity or decrease your ability to bounce back?

COPING WITH STRESS

It's very comforting to know that we can increase our resilience, and several researchers have investigated the effectiveness of programs designed to do this (e.g., Judkins, Arris, & Keener, 2005; Steinhardt & Dolbier, 2008). Certainly there are calls on many sides to do just that (e.g., Clinton, 2008; Dolan, 2008; Jackson, Firtko, & Edenborough, 2007). In this section we will discuss a few techniques that have been demonstrated to be effective in coping with stress and increasing resilience. There are many techniques (e.g., chewing gum! Smith, 2009a, 2009b), and I encourage you to take a course in stress management and/or read one of the many excellent textbooks available on the topic (e.g., Blonna, 2007; Duffy, Kirsh, & Atwater, 2011; Weiten, Lloyd, Dunn, & Hammer, 2009).

The first point to note is that having only one strategy for reducing stress is not adequate. As we have seen, resilient people are flexible in their use of coping strategies, switching from one to another as the need arises (Lam, & McBride-Chang, 2007). This means that those people who say, for example, "I exercise vigorously to cope with my stress" may be applauded for this, but they need more techniques. What happens if they get ill and can't exercise? What if they find themselves in a situation like that of Katherine and Poppy's? It wouldn't be realistic for them to start exercising vigorously at their desks!

Since we have seen that there is a strong connection between the mind and body, it's necessary to take care of the body, to make sure that it's in the best shape possible to cope with the stresses that will impinge upon it. Regular exercise, adequate sleep, and proper nutrition are all vital to both our physical and psychological well-being. It's a good idea to avoid over-indulgence in alcohol and caffeine and to avoid smoking and using illegal drugs.

Since resilient people have many of the qualities that we have discussed previously, it would be advisable to cultivate these qualities. Resilient people are optimistic, so following Seligman's (2002, 2006, 2007) ABCDE technique that we discussed in Chapter 5 would be a good idea. Resilient people self-regulate their behaviours and emotions and feel a sense of self-efficacy, so perhaps some ideas from Chapter 6 would be relevant. Resilient people feel meaning and purpose in their lives; they are more likely to experience posttraumatic growth if they are faced with extreme stress. So considering related aspects Chapter 8 might be prudent as well.

Physical Relaxation

We also need some general techniques for relaxing so that we can cope with stress more effectively. Part of the physical reaction to stress is to tense the muscles. Since we are

---

SPOTLIGHT ON RESEARCH

Gum-Chewing to Reduce Stress

It's no joke. A great deal of research has indicated that chewing gum increases alertness and improves performance on a variety of tasks (e.g., Smith, 2009a). And now research is finding that anecdotal reports of gum-chewing as a means of dealing with stress are actually valid. Smith (2009b) gave online surveys to over 2200 people in the United Kingdom, asking about their frequency of gum-chewing and the stress they felt at work and in their lives in general, their levels of anxiety and depression, and whether or not they had high blood pressure or high cholesterol levels. His statistical analyses revealed that gum-chewers reported feeling less stress at work (even though they were more likely to experience negative conditions at work) and in life overall, and were less likely to feel depressed or to have high blood pressure or high cholesterol. He concluded that gum-chewing is an effective way of reducing stress, although he admits his data are only correlational and cannot be used to infer causality: it could be that a third unknown factor accounts for why some people both chew gum and feel less stress. Smith reports that his research was supported by the Wrigley Science Institute, part of the company that makes chewing gum. This support seems like a wise investment on the part of the institute and the company!

often under stress that is long-lasting, our muscles may be in a chronically tensed state and we may not really know how to relax them (Nevid & Rathus, 2010). Instructions for a progressive muscle relaxation technique are in Box 9.1. There are also other techniques for physical relaxation: for example, four excellent techniques are given on Dr. Emmet Miller's CD *Letting Go Of* Stress (http://drmiller.pinnaclecart.com).

BOX 9.1

Deep Muscle Relaxation

1. Find a quiet place to sit or to lie down comfortably on your back with your hands at your sides and your eyes closed. Take two or three slow, deep breaths and relax your body as much as you can between each step.

2. Clench the fist of one hand and tense your arm as much as you can and hold this position for five seconds. Concentrate on how this tension feels. Now relax your arm and let your fingers straighten out. Concentrate on how this relaxation feels. Now do the same for the other hand and arm.

3. Raise your shoulders in a shrug until you feel the tension in your shoulders and your neck. Hold this position for five seconds. Concentrate on how this tension feels. Now relax your shoulders. Concentrate on how this relaxation feels.

4. Tighten the muscles in your stomach. Hold them in this position for five seconds, concentrating on how the tension feels. Now relax your stomach muscles and concentrate on the feeling of relaxation in these muscles.

5. Tighten the muscles in your legs and concentrate on the tight feelings in your leg muscles for five seconds. Now relax your legs. Concentrate on how this relaxation feels.

6. Frown and close your eyes as tightly as you can for five seconds, concentrating on the feeling of tension in your face. Now relax your face and eyes. Concentrate on how this relaxation feels.

7. Clench your teeth as hard as you can for five seconds and concentrate on the tension in your jaws. Concentrate on how this tension feels. Now relax and concentrate on how this relaxation feels.

8. Check your whole body: concentrate on relaxing each part of your body and imagine that all tension is flowing out of your body. Stay like this for two or three minutes, then open your eyes and start to gradually look around you. Stretch lightly, and then, when you feel like it, stand up and stretch again. It's a good idea not to jump up quickly since the procedure will have decreased your heart rate and blood pressure and getting up too quickly might make you dizzy.

The greatest benefits of deep muscle relaxation are achieved when you practise the procedure twice a day for about four weeks. Then, you will probably find that, in the course of your normal day, when the stress gets high, that you can simply *think* about a relaxation session, and your body will begin to relax.

Source: Hadad, M. & Reed, M. J. (2007). *The post-secondary learning experience.* Toronto: Nelson Education, p. 62.

Meditation

A particularly effective stress management technique that is receiving much attention today is meditation. There are many specific techniques of meditation, but the main point is to induce a relaxed state by the focused attention on one thing. That one thing could be a word or sound (a **mantra**, in Transcendental Meditation), an object such as an unbroken egg or a candle flame, or one's own breathing. The gentle movements of T'ai Chi require focused concentration on each movement and are a form of meditation as well. Much of Buddhist meditation emphasizes mindfulness. With mindfulness we concentrate on each moment in time without judging or analyzing. We let our thoughts come and go while we simply experience being.

Meditation has been found to increase brain wave patterns related to relaxation, reduce blood pressure and heart rate, and reduce stress and increase positive emotions in healthy people and in people with pre-existing psychological and/or physical disorders (Chiesa, 2009; Chiesa & Serretti, 2009; Coppola & Spector, 2009; Junget al., 2010; Yang, Su, & Huang, 2009). One way of meditating is described in Box 9.2. If this technique doesn't appeal to you, try another. There are a variety of books available to teach you meditation: there is even *Meditation for Dummies* (Bodian, 2006)! The techniques work, but they require more practice than is immediately apparent. In fact, many beginning meditators are astounded to discover for the first time how unfocused their minds have been. Practice is the key. Even if you feel completely unsuccessful in your first attempts, keep at it. You will get better day by day, and even the attempts that you consider unsuccessful are beneficial to you.

BOX 9.2

How to Meditate

1. Find a comfortable place where you will not be disturbed. Sit in a (preferably) straight-backed, comfortable chair and let your muscles relax.

2. Close your eyes and focus on your breathing. Repeat in your mind the word "one" every time you inhale and "two" every time you exhale. Don't try to control your breathing—just let it happen.

3. When your thoughts stray or interrupt your concentration on your breathing, just gently bring your focus back to your breathing without judging or blaming yourself.

4. When you are ready to stop meditating, stop. Open your eyes and gradually return to your normal awareness. Check your watch to see how long you have been meditating (even two minutes is fine in the beginning) and aim to increase the time slowly each day.

5. Aim to meditate for about twenty minutes twice a day. Before breakfast and dinner are good times.

Breathing

In the case study at the beginning of the chapter, Katherine dealt with her stress by first taking a few deep breaths. Part of our physiological reaction to stress is to breathe shallowly, but too much of this can make us feel light-headed or dizzy because the oxygen:carbon dioxide ratio in our blood is out of balance (Nevid & Rathus, 2010). Deep breathing can correct this, especially if the diaphragm is used effectively. Diaphragmatic breathing is breathing in a relaxed way, through the nose, taking the same amount of time to inhale and to exhale. When done correctly, the stomach rises as you inhale and lowers as you exhale, unlike our usual breathing which only expands the chest. You can monitor this by placing your hands on your stomach while lying in bed. With a little practice, monitoring will probably not be necessary, and your handling of stress will be improved (Nevus, & Rathus, 2010).

Note that physical relaxation, meditation, and breathing techniques need practice. The idea is to become proficient in these techniques *before* the stress hits you. Believing that you don't need to perform one of these techniques until you feel stressed is like saying that you don't need to train for a marathon race until the day of the race! If you practise these techniques to proficiency in relatively unstressful times, your body will react less vigorously and debilitatingly to stress when it lands upon you. Poppy, a person who has such detrimental reactions to stress, seems to be a person who very much needs to start one of these techniques as soon as possible.

Reappraisal

People who are resilient use reappraisal when confronting stressful situations. They change their primary appraisal of a situation from one that is threatening to one that is challenging and may have meaning and benefit in the long run. We can use Seligman's (2002, 2006, 2007) ABCDE in this regard as well (see Chapter 5). Let's take Poppy's stressful situation as an example.

Adversity: Requirement to write a lengthy report in a short period of time

Belief: Poppy's belief is "I can't do it, it's all too much for me! I'm going to fail and lose my job!"

Consequences: Poppy has an emotional meltdown and becomes physically ill.

Disputation: This is the time for Poppy to argue with herself: "I've been at this job for a while now, and I've managed to get things done. There must be ways of getting help and handling all this. It won't be the end of the world to ask for help or to hand in a report that isn't as good as the one I could do if I had more time. I need to get organized and creative in handling this, as I've done in the past. After all, it's just another one of the challenges we face in life."

Energization: Poppy will probably feel more confident and energized by this reappraisal and will do a better job at accomplishing her tasks. At least she won't feel so overwhelmed and most likely won't get ill.

Decision-Making

Of course, we also need more specific techniques for dealing with stress. For example, we have seen that one source of stress is in the conflict that comes from decision-making. How can we reduce this stress and make better decisions? Irving Janis and his colleagues (e.g., Janis & Mann, 1977; Herek, Janis, & Huth, 1987, 1989) have spent many years studying how people make decisions and how they can improve their decision-making ability and reduce their stress. He notes that we often make poor decisions because we fail to ask ourselves crucial questions, such as the following:

- *Have I really explored all the available options?* Very often we stop looking for options after we discover one or two. But there may be several and better options available to us if we persist in our search. Brainstorming with a friend can be a good way to come up with more ideas.

- *Will the options I have really accomplish what I want?* For example, will dealing with your stress by shopping to the point that your credit card is maxed out really get rid of your stress? Or will it actually cause you more stress?

- *Have I taken into account the pluses and minuses, for myself and for others, of each option?* No option is perfect and there will be gains and losses associated with each one. In addition, each option may have gains and losses for other people besides ourselves, so we need to take into account the ramifications of our decisions on others. This is a good place to make up a balance sheet of pros and cons.

- *Have I included new information in my decision-making?* We often stop looking for new information too soon in the decision-making process. This new information could change the balance of pros and cons for each option or even change the need for the decision itself, but we might not know this if we cut off our search for information too soon.

- *Do I know how to put my decision into operation? Can I deal with a worst case scenario?* Let's go back to Katherine, our friend who deals with stress well. We can imagine that as she plans how to tackle the tasks that are upon her, she makes decisions on a plan of action that is both realistic and effective. So, for example, she would not plan to stay up all night for three nights in a row to finish the report Mr. Blodgett wants. This would be unworkable (and would result in a very poor report!). She would consider the possibility that further obstacles may arise, and she would make contingency plans for these. "If I don't have all the information I need for the report, I'll get it from Mr. Blodgett's assistant. If I can't get the costume made, maybe my neighbour can do it for me. Or I can purchase a costume from the store downtown."

Dealing With Criticism

One of the stresses in both our personal and our professional lives is criticism. Nobody likes it. But can we learn and grow from it without it causing us too much stress? When we receive criticism, we often react in an automatic fashion, becoming defensive about ourselves, lashing out at the critic, and/or feeling worthless and rejected. None of these reactions will serve us well. This is a good time to stop and think before reacting. We have options for responding, so why not find the option that will optimize our own growth and sense of well-being?

Be aware, first of all, that just because someone criticizes you, it doesn't mean you have to change yourself. You are free to reject the criticism. This might be the case when the critic is someone who finds fault with everyone and everything on a regular basis or is clearly in a bad mood and is striking out at others as a (maladaptive) way of dealing with his/her own stress.

You might also choose to reject criticism that seems incongruent with evaluations from other sources. For example, if one person tells you that the dinner you made was overcooked, while four other people tell you it was perfectly cooked, you probably will want to reject the criticism of the solitary critic. On the other hand, if the criticism you receive is a replay of comments you have heard from others several times before, it would be to your advantage to pay attention and decide whether you want to make changes or not.

Since none of us is perfect, criticism may be valid, and while receiving it may be painful, it may also afford us information that we didn't have before and alert us to the need to change in order to achieve the satisfying life that we want. It's a wise idea to ask a critic to be as specific as possible in their criticism. For instance, it won't be easy to change insensitive behaviour if your critic doesn't tell you in what ways you have been insensitive. So if the criticism is about some personality trait, make sure you ask the critic to specify the behaviour that was objectionable. (Remember this when you're giving criticism, too: attack the behaviour, if you must, but not the individual.) Then you can make a decision about whether you want to make changes in your behaviour.

If you decide that changes would be beneficial to you, formulate a plan for implementing change. You might even consider asking your critic for help in this. Take for example, the case of criticism given by your superior at work. If you listen carefully to the criticism and ask for clarification with the attitude that you want to learn from the criticism, your superior's regard for you will most likely increase. If you formulate a plan and take it to your superior asking if he/she thinks this will be a good way to grow, you are demonstrating your maturity and respect, as well as ensuring that you have heard the criticism accurately and have devised a workable plan. Your superior's regard for you is again likely to increase and he/she may also feel more useful and worthwhile in their professional role. Everybody wins.

Behaviour Modification

Maybe you have decided to change your behaviour in light of the criticism you have received. Or maybe you have a behaviour or habit that you would like to change because of the stress it causes you (smoking, biting nails, chewing hair, overeating, and so on). When you make this decision about a single readily identifiable behaviour, you might find that simply "changing" a habit is not as easy as it seems. After all, you have probably been engaging in this behaviour for quite a while, and often without even being fully aware of it (virtually every smoker has lit a cigarette only to find that he/she already has one lit!). Consider using behaviour modification as a way to make the change a little easier and far more likely to succeed.

Behaviour modification uses the principles of learning to change behaviour and, in many cases, works quickly and with a minimum of distress. Here's how to do it (Hadad & Reed, 2007; Watson & Tharp, 2007): First, identify specifically the behaviour you want to change. For example, if you want to stop procrastinating, phrase it as "I want to stop putting off studying until the night before the test" or "I want to tackle the housework before my home looks like a cyclone hit it."

The next step is to identify what your goal is in specific terms as well. Be realistic! If you want to stop procrastinating, for instance, a goal of "never procrastinating again" is daunting and suggests that you won't settle for anything but perfection (see Chapter 6).

Then, when you fail, you may feel discouraged, with a lowered self-esteem, and you may abandon your efforts altogether. Realistic people recognize that they aren't perfect and don't demand this of themselves. They may strive for excellence and growth, but they don't require absolute perfection.

Now you need to identify specifically the behaviours you need to accomplish your goal. Once more, be realistic! For example, setting a goal of writing all your essays at the beginning of a semester or completing all your housework immediately after you come home from work in order to overcome procrastination isn't feasible. But setting a goal of working on an essay or doing housework for half an hour five days a week, say, will provide you with more flexibility and behaviours that are more manageable and therefore more likely to be accomplished. Likewise, if your goal is to lose weight, as an illustration, a starvation diet and four hours of exercise each day are not only infeasible, they're dangerous! A better idea, then, is to specify behaviours such as cutting out junk food or sugary desserts, and to start exercising for fifteen minutes a day four days a week, gradually working up to one hour a day on six days of the week. If the behaviour you want to adopt is too large, break it into small steps that are more manageable and will still take you to your goal. (An old tip for dieters, as a case in point, is to forget about losing twenty pounds and concentrate on losing one pound at a time.)

Now, collect baseline data. For one or two weeks, don't try to change your behaviour, just monitor it. How many cigarettes do you actually smoke? When do you smoke them? How often and under what conditions do you bite your nails? In most cases, people find that there are specific circumstances under which they engage in their problem behaviour. Knowing this, it becomes easier to avoid the problem situations and to develop strategies to do something else instead.

With goals and behaviours specified and documented, you are ready to plan the program. Having determined what the cues are for your problem behaviour, you can plan how to eliminate the cues or deal with them in a different way. For example, if you find that you overeat when you are with friends, you might want to avoid the situation for a while, or enlist their aid in helping you choose healthier, less caloric food when you're with them. If you bite your nails when you watch television, you can avoid the television or, more realistically, find something else to do with your hands: roll a marble in your palms, stroke a pet, take up knitting.

Reinforce yourself for sticking to the behaviours that will lead to your goal. The reward should be small, but it needs to be frequent, especially in the beginning of the program. Make sure your reward is something that you *only* attain through your program. A good reward for tackling work instead of procrastinating, for instance, might be a cookie, or fifteen minutes of listening to your favourite music or watching television (but you can't have cookies, or listen to the music, or watch television at any other time). You can accumulate your reward if you wish: "If I spend thirty minutes working on my essays for five days in the week, I can spend Saturday night watching television or going out with friends, etc." *Do not punish yourself* if you fail to accomplish the behaviours you wish. Punishment doesn't work. Just start again. Consider writing your program down as a contract, specifying what behaviours will be reinforced and what the rewards will be. The more specific you are, the better.

Finally you are ready to implement the program. You may find that you need to make some changes to your program because your planned steps were too large or your rewards too small or too infrequent. Give yourself some time on the program. After two or three weeks, you will probably find that your behaviour is changing and you are less dependent on the rewards. At this point you can increase your steps and make the conditions under which you obtain your rewards a little more strict.

When you reach your goal, you can gradually taper off the rewards, making them less and less frequent. Weaning yourself off the program is a better idea than abruptly discontinuing the program because it increases the probability that your new behaviours will not disappear.

Social Support

Let's not forget the people who are dear to us as a source of coping. A moderating effect of stress is social support, which may decrease stress and enhance coping (Chen, Siu, Lu, Cooper, & Phillips, 2009; Haslam, Jetten, & Waghorn, 2009; Jonker & Greeff, 2009; Shen, 2009). It makes sense, then, to foster our social networks and maximize the benefits we give and receive in social interactions. We will discuss social networks in greater detail in Chapter 10, as well as examining some specific techniques that can be used to enhance our interactions with others and minimize any misunderstanding, thereby increasing our chances of having a satisfying life.

Conclusion

There is no question that stress is a major component in preventing us from having satisfying lives. The connection between the mind and the body is profound, and the types of stress that we have in the twenty-first century play on both our bodies and our minds. There is no way to get rid of stress completely, and, in fact, we wouldn't want to. After all, stress occurs when we graduate from school, get a highly desired job, buy a new car or a house, have a child, and so on. The high moments of our lives are stressful because they bring about change, with new decisions and responsibilities. But who among us would wish to forego this stress? For many of us, life with no stress at all would be a dull and colourless existence. No highs and no lows. One might even say that life without any stress would be stressful in its boredom! The trick is in dealing with stress. If we can become more resilient, tackling our stresses as challenges and finding meaning and growth in the inevitable tragedies that befall us and the wonderful things that happen to us, we will go a long way to maximizing our chances of being fulfilled in life. And it doesn't get better than that.

Summary

- Stress is any circumstance that threatens or is perceived to threaten one's well-being and thereby taxes one's coping abilities.
- One general source of stress is change because it taxes our abilities to adapt.
- Another source of stress is the frustration that arises when a goal meets with an obstacle.
- A third source of stress is in the conflict of decision-making.
- Pressure causes us stress because we feel that we have to meet expectations.

- Daily hassles, the little chores and problems of our day-to-day lives, are stressful as well.
- Psychologically, stress can cause anxiety, worry, and depression, impairing our ability to think and increasing negative self-statements.
- Burnout can result from prolonged exposure to situations that people feel powerless to change. People who burn out are more susceptible to physical and psychological disorders.
- Compassion fatigue occurs when a caregiver feels overwhelmed by the needs of others.
- Posttraumatic stress disorder (PTSD) may arise after someone has been involved in an incident in which stress has been extreme. Symptoms include recurring experiencing of the trauma through flashbacks, dreams, and visions; general emotional numbing to day-to-day events; and avoidance of stimuli that might remind the person of the trauma. There may also be increased arousal and anxiety, impaired social relationships, and vulnerability to substance abuse, as well as increased risk of several physical disorders.
- The General Adaptation Syndrome is the body's response to threat. It is comprised of the alarm stage, the resistance stage, and the exhaustion stage.
- The major physiological response to stress comes from the endocrine system of the body.
- Stress decreases health in its effect on the cardiovascular system, the immune system, and in a variety of other ways.
- Resilience is the individual's ability to cope with and bounce back from stress.
- Primary appraisal involves determining whether an event is threatening and how threatening it is. Secondary appraisal involves deciding whether we can cope with the stress.
- Emotion-focused coping concentrates on the emotions that the stress arouses. Problem-focused coping concentrates on the stressful situation and changing or avoiding the situation. Problem-focused coping is used more by people who cope with stress well.
- Resilient people physiologically and psychologically recover from stress faster.
- Resilient people feel more meaning in life, ruminate on the negatives of life less, are more likely to use problem-focused coping processes, and are flexible in their coping. They are optimistic and feel more personal self-efficacy. They have more self-esteem and feeling of personal control. They are more open to new experiences, and they are more conscientious in terms of controlling their behaviour and emotions.
- Hardy people (1) view change as challenge rather than threat, (2) are committed to seeing life and events as purposeful, and (3) believe they have control over their destinies.
- The cultural context of a person's life often indicates the relevant and adaptive ways of coping with the stress of life.
- People can learn strategies for decreasing their stress and increasing their resilience. Several techniques are needed in order to have the flexibility required to cope with stress.

Group Discussion Questions

1. Does the mind–body connection seem plausible to you? Why do you think so many medical doctors still seem to be resisting the notion that the mind can affect the body?

2. Some schools are specifically teaching children stress-management techniques, such as meditation (as we will see in Chapter 13). Is this a valid way to spend class time? Or does such teaching belong in the hands of the family?

3. Many people feel that we experience more stress and have less resilience in the twenty-first century than we had in previous ages. Do you agree with this? If so, why do you think this might be the case?

CHAPTER 10

Interpersonal Relationships

The scene is a playground. Several small children are playing happily in a sandbox, occasionally running over to a group of parents who are chatting and laughing among themselves while watching their kids. One woman, Angela, seems to be at the heart of the group of parents. Everyone gravitates to Angela—she listens, she cares, she always knows what to say, she's a real friend, other people say. As far as Angela is concerned, nothing is more important to her than people, her family and her friends. "They make me so happy," she says.

On a nearby bench sits a solitary woman, Naomi, whose little boy is playing with his blocks at her feet. They don't interact much. Every once in a while, they look over wistfully at the groups of children and parents, but they don't approach them. Naomi and her son are new in town and feel quite isolated, not knowing anyone. They both feel lonely and unhappy, wishing they could be part of the happy groups they see. Naomi watches Angela, in particular, and envies her relaxed style and her social aplomb.

LEARNING OBJECTIVES

In this chapter, students will learn about

- ☐ Factors influencing first impressions.
- ☐ Factors influencing friendships.
- ☐ Maintaining a friendship.
- ☐ Types and styles of love.
- ☐ The conditions that give rise to falling in love.
- ☐ The causes and effects of romantic breakups.
- ☐ The causes and effects of loneliness.
- ☐ What emotional intelligence is and the abilities it entails.
- ☐ The benefits of emotional intelligence.

The scenario above can be seen in playgrounds and parks in cities and towns across the world. Interacting with others is an important part of our lives, and the lack of interaction may leave us lonely and distressed. From the evidence presented in previous chapters, it seems quite apparent that our life satisfaction is closely tied to our social lives. Self-described happy people and those who have high self-esteem report having satisfying relationships with others (Bagwell et al., 2005; Harker & Keltner, 2001; Holder & Coleman, 2008; Murray, 2005). Because the data is correlational in nature, it is not possible to determine whether happiness in people like Angela causes them to create better social relationships or whether they are happy because they have satisfying relationships. Or perhaps happy people have another characteristic, such as optimism, that creates better social relationships. The chances are that all of these possibilities are true and many factors work together to give us the enrichment of the company of other people in a fulfilling way. Certainly we can say that social relationships play a large part in our experience of life satisfaction.

How happy do other people make us? Powdhavee (2008), a social economist, conducted research to determine this, using a statistical analysis called the shadow pricing method. With this method, Powdhavee found that, in Great Britain, increases in social relationships and social involvement are worth up to £85,000 (roughly $135,000 in Canadian currency in 2010)! It's difficult to determine if giving people that much money would make them just as happy as having fulfilling social relationships (recall in Chapter 1 we saw that, after a certain point, money doesn't bring us happiness), but it clearly supports the notion that our social lives are very important to us in terms of life satisfaction. Abraham Maslow (see Chapter 2) considered the need for belonging to be a physical need, only less pressing than the need for food, water, air, and the need for safety, and as we shall see, social relationships do have an impact on our health.

In this chapter, we will start right at the beginning in first meeting a person and following the development of the relationship.

FIRST IMPRESSIONS

They say that first impressions are important, and there is truth in this. Based on a first impression, we may make a decision whether to pursue a relationship with another person. Obviously, when we first meet someone, we have little information to go on, so we make use of whatever small bits of information are present. Sometimes we are very wrong in our assessment. Let's examine the factors that lead to the first impressions and the errors we can make.

Physical Appearance

One piece of information that we find very important is physical appearance. Even though it is dangerous to base one's complete opinion of another person on how that person looks, we find a certain utility in this that is undeniable. For example, while there may be corrupt police officers or people posing as police officers illicitly, running to someone wearing a police uniform is probably our best course of action if we are in trouble. The utility of physical appearance is very limited in ascertaining a person's character, though, and may even feed into bigotry. If we're interviewing potential baby-sitters, we may assume that the young lady with numerous tattoos and body piercings would not be a suitable or responsible person to take care of our child, as compared to the preppy looking young lady. Be careful! Some murderers such as Paul Bernardo and Ted Bundy looked very respectable and conservative, a front they used to lure their victims. So physical appearance can sometimes give us clues about another person, but is not necessarily to be solely relied upon.

Physical appearance has been found to be very influential, however, in our assumptions about what that person is like. One finding in psychology has been called the **beautiful is good** phenomenon. Research has found that people who are attractive by their culture's standards are assumed to have a host of other positive qualities, such as greater sociability, intelligence, poise, and mental health, and more success in their relationships, academic performance, and occupations (Langlois et al., 2000; Olson & Marshuetz, 2005). This is a rather discouraging finding for those of us who don't have movie-star good looks.

But there is some indication that the judgmental reliance on physical appearance may be changing a bit in the research done recently by Steven Dayan and his colleagues (Dayan, Lieberman, Thakkar, Larimer, & Anstead, 2008). They examined the evaluations given to before and after photographs of women who had been given injections of botulinum toxin A (Botox) to smooth facial wrinkles. Evaluators who saw only the after photographs rated the women higher on attractiveness, dating success, and athletic success, but not on academic performance or occupational success. To these respondents, beauty was not necessarily linked to brains. Adding comfort to this is the finding that, when asked about desirable qualities in a mate, physical attractiveness was ranked eighth by men and thirteenth by women, well below qualities such as dependability and maturity (Buss, Shackelford, Kirkpatrick, & Larsen, 2001).

Reputation

Another factor in our initial perceptions of people is what, if anything, we have heard about the individual—their reputation (Sleebos, Ellemers, & de Gilder, 2006). If we are meeting someone that we have heard positive statements about, we are more inclined to be open to the person. But if we have heard negative statements, it may be that we don't give the individual much chance to correct or confirm these statements. Have you ever avoided taking a class because you heard the instructor was terrible? Maybe the instructor *is* terrible, but maybe you are needlessly avoiding a situation you might have enjoyed based on simply the subjective opinion of other people who might have biases.

Communication Style

In meeting a person, there are forms of verbal and nonverbal communication. If the person speaks and acts in what is typically regarded as a societally unacceptable manner, we tend to form a negative opinion of that person and may not wish to pursue a relationship with him/her. Take, for example, the case of meeting a person who doesn't smile, make eye contact with us, say hello, or shake hands when introduced. This person seems to be sending the message that he/she doesn't really want to meet us. The person who stands relatively straight, makes eye contact, is articulate, and seems poised and confident is usually regarded more favourably than the person who slouches, seems unsure, and has trouble finding words, even if the person's behaviour is well within societal norms (Duffy, Kirsh, & Atwater, 2011).

Stereotyping

We obviously can make some serious mistakes in our first impression, especially if we are relying on stereotypes of people based on a group they belong to (Duffy, Kirsh, & Atwater, 2011). While some stereotypes may contain some truth (e.g., most nurses are caring people), there is wide variability among members of any group, and our preconceptions may lead us to avoid them without regard for their individuality.

A member of a group may be stigmatized because of the group he/she belongs to, as well. For example, even though signs of the disease are not visibly apparent, people are less likely to develop relationships with others who are HIV positive. We must assume that this is part of the stereotyped stigma that is attached to HIV since people don't show the same disinclination to have relationships with others who have cancer (Horan et al., 2009). This is a sad case of a stereotype leading us astray. (Since we're talking about stereotypes, for the record, most professors are *not* eggheads who can only talk about their own subject matter and do so until the listener is asleep. Nor do most walk into walls because they are so distracted by their intellectual musings. And we try not to be badly dressed and covered with chalk dust.)

The Fundamental Attribution Error

We also make mistakes if we allow ourselves to fall victim to the **fundamental attribution error** (we mentioned this in Chapter 8) when we do not take account of the situation people are in and conclude that their behaviour is caused by their personalities. (Once more for the record, maybe the professor isn't smiling on the first day of class because of the towering headache he/she has with the chaos of the first week of classes, not because he/she hates teaching and students!)

Global Judgments

Another problem we have is in making **global judgments** about people. This means that when we see one positive trait or action by another person, we tend to attribute many more positive qualities to the person (the **halo effect**). By the same token, if we see one negative trait or action, we tend to attribute many more negative qualities to the person (the **devil effect**). Imagine that you are starting a new job and meet a co-worker for the first time. If that person smiles warmly and greets you with enthusiasm, you tend to suppose that the person is honest, hard-working, intelligent, and so on, but if the person greets you in an offhand or even rude manner, you are more likely to assume that the person is also stupid, lazy, dishonest, and so on (Duffy, Kirsh, & Atwater, 2011; Palmer & Loveland, 2008). We seem to pay more attention to the unexpected negative greeting than we do to the socially expected positive greeting, which may indicate nothing more than a social rote response.

REFLECTIVE EXERCISE

First Impressions

Test yourself. The next time you are at a restaurant, waiting in line at the grocery store, or riding the bus or subway, look at the people around you. Are you making judgments about their personalities from their appearance? Are there some that you would be more likely to feel comfortable talking to than others? Why?

Think back on the first time you met a friend of yours. What was your first impression? What factors led you to that first impression? Were you right? Have there been times when you found that your first impression of someone was wrong?

Do you worry about your own first impression? On a job interview, for example, it pays to worry about it and make sure it's as positive as possible. What kind of first impression do you think you make? Ask other people what their first impression of you was. Ask your friends and family how they think you come across at a first meeting (siblings can be particularly honest and brutal in answering this). What is it about you that leads to the particular first impression you make. Do you want to change it? How can you do that?

All in all, first impressions are important, and while we may change our minds about a person who makes a good first impression, we may not give the person who makes a bad first impression the chance to show us we were wrong in jumping to conclusions. Let's look back at Angela and Naomi in the scenario at the beginning of the chapter. To Naomi, Angela looks happy and engaged. The group of people around Angela suggests to Naomi that Angela is well-regarded and communicates appropriately with others. Angela appears to have no stigmatizing factors associated with her, at least none that Naomi can see, and Naomi reaches the conclusion that Angela's personality must be sparkling and she must have an all-around wonderful life. Naomi may or may not be correct in her assessment of Angela, but she clearly wishes she were part of Angela's social group. If Angela were to look at Naomi, she might conclude that Naomi, being alone with her son and not approaching the group, is antisocial and probably has several negative traits. Angela might not be drawn to her based on this conclusion. (But, as we shall see later in the chapter, Angela has a quality that might lead her to question this first impression.)

FRIENDSHIPS

We assume now that the first impression has been good enough for us to decide that we won't avoid the person in the future. We are still a long way from becoming friends with the person, though.

Factors Influencing Friendships

Propinquity

The first factor that influences whether we will become friends is **propinquity** or how physically near we are to the person. We are more likely to make friends with the person who lives next door to us than the person who lives a block away; we are more likely to make friends with the person whose office is across the hall from us than the one whose office is two floors above us (Kubitschck & Hallinan, 1998; McPherson, Smith-Lovin, & Cook, 2001). This makes sense: there are more chances to interact with a person who is physically nearby, more chances to learn more about the person and for him/her to learn about us, and more chances to overcome any negative impressions that might have been given at the first meeting. If we know that we will be in close proximity to the person for large periods of time, we are more motivated to develop a friendly relationship. Even with the twenty-first century's addiction to email and texting, it is still easier to keep up with a person's daily life and to allow them to keep up with ours when they are close at hand.

Similarity

Similarity is another important factor in whether we will pursue a friendship or not (Kubitschek & Hallinan, 1998; McPherson, Smith-Lovin, & Cook, 2001). In the beginning, a shared interest or experience may give us something to talk about to get the friendship started. Fraley and Aron (2004) even found that strangers who shared a humorous experience in a research laboratory found each other more likeable than strangers who didn't share such an experience. This doesn't mean that our friends have to be just like us in every way—on the contrary, we may be enlightened, enriched, and amused by the differences between us and our friends. In general, though, we tend to like people who are like us, especially in terms of fundamental values and basic worldviews. It may not matter if you are a dockworker and your friend is a dentist, but it may matter if you value education, say, and the other person thinks it's a waste of time. How likely is it that a social activist will choose a staunch conservative for a close friend?

Self-Disclosure

Friendships proceed by mutual **self-disclosure**. As the relationship progresses, the individuals gradually reveal more and more about themselves to each other. Emotional self-disclosure, that is, revealing what one is feeling, breeds intimacy between two people; self-disclosure of only factual information, such as what one had for breakfast, won't be effective (Laurenceau, Barrett, & Rovine, 2005).

Self-disclosure can be tricky for many people. There are some people who feel uncomfortable telling anyone their feelings, hopes, and fears, no matter how long they have known the person or how much they like the person. This is unfortunate since no one can enter their world if they won't reveal what their world is like, but we must at least understand these people because self-disclosure really can be risky. They may be rejected for what they disclose, or their deeply-held thoughts and feelings may be minimized by the other person. That means it's wise to be very careful about whom you disclose to. Then there are other people who reveal too much too soon, before any intimacy has started to develop. They strike us as inappropriate; not only does their self-disclosure go beyond what is socially acceptable, it may also seem that they are forcing intimacy on us that we may not be ready for. Then again, we may think, these people may be indiscriminate in revealing personal feelings, thoughts, and events to anyone at all. That doesn't make us feel very valued.

Maintaining a Friendship

The Role of Attachment

Maintaining a friendship calls for care as well. Our early attachments form a basis for future interactions with the world. Starting from a secure attachment to a caregiver, we typically continue to view the world as an interesting place to explore because we know that there are other people available to help us if we need it and to give help and support if they need it (Feeney, 2004; Hart, Shaver, & Goldenberg, 2005; Park, Crocker, & Mickelson, 2004). With an early secure attachment, we learn to view ourselves and others optimistically, yet realistically (Fraley, Fazzari, Bonanno, & Dekel, 2006; Kim, 2005). We are in a better position to form good relationships with other people, and we do just that (Feeney, 2006). In fact, Noftle and Shaver (2006) found that secure attachment predicts good interpersonal relationships even more than personality factors do. As Feeney (2004) discusses, a good relationship with another person implies that the other will provide us with a safe haven from the stresses of the world and a secure base from which we can venture forth to explore the world and our opportunities in it. We, having a secure attachment ourselves, will in turn provide the same for the other person (Mikulincer, Shaver, Gillath, & Nitzberg, 2005).

Social Support

In providing us with this safe haven and the secure base, we receive social support. Social support includes responsiveness to our needs, but not all responsiveness is helpful or supportive. Responsiveness that is perceived as intrusive, for example, may be appreciated in the short term if the interference solves an immediate problem, but in the long run it undermines our sense of self-efficacy.

A common source of disagreement between people arises when one person wants to "vent" about the events of the day or a problem that arose, while the other person responds with instructions on how to deal with the situation. "I don't need you to solve my problems. I just need you to listen!" is a common complaint that one partner of a relationship may have about the well-intentioned responses of the other partner. This highlights the fact that real responsiveness must be in accordance with what the individual *needs*, not what the other *assumes* he/she needs. The most obvious way to avoid this problem is to simply ask "What do you need?"

We usually think about safe havens, secure bases, and responsiveness in terms of distressing life events, but Gable, Gonzaga, and Strachman (2006) have demonstrated that among people with intimate relationships, the response to positive life events may be even more important. These researchers identify four different types of response to a person relating good news:

1. "That's terrific! You really deserve this! Let's celebrate!"
2. "That's nice."
3. "Don't get too worked up. It won't be as good as it sounds."
4. "Uh." If that.

It's not surprising that the first response is the one that makes us feel good about a relationship and makes us feel supported. This is independent of how the other person responds to a distressing life event. The person may be warm, helpful, and supportive when things go wrong, but then, that's expected. The first response to good news may be more telling in a relationship, making one feel understood and valued, that one's efforts have been noticed and applauded, and that our joy is reasonable and shared. The other three responses leave us feeling that the other person either doesn't know or doesn't care how important the event was to us. The third and fourth, in particular, cross the line into being cruel.

Active Listening

In order to be responsive, we need to listen to the other person. Really listen. Typically, when another person is talking to us, we are only partly listening. We are thinking instead, usually about how to respond. That means we still seem to be focusing on ourselves rather than on the other person. The technique of active listening is meant to avoid this (Verderber, Verderber, & Berryman-Fink, 2008) and has been taught in communication training programs in a wide variety of settings (see Weger, Castle, & Emmett, 2010, for a review). In active listening, we stop thinking and focus on the person who is talking, paying attention to what the person is saying, how the person is saying it, and any nonverbal signals that may accompany the speech.

It often happens that people are unclear or leave out details when they are telling us something, especially if they are distressed. In active listening, we ask for clarification with open-ended questions. We paraphrase what the person has been saying to make sure that we understand and to let the other person know he/she is being heard correctly. This also gives the person a chance to correct us in our understanding and/or to correct the statement or impression that was made. At the end, we summarize what we have heard, including the emotions, and we reflect meaning, if possible. Here's an example of active listening:

Joan: I feel so rotten. I didn't get the job. And I know I was qualified. This isn't fair!

Mary: You sound really disappointed that you didn't get the job.

Joan: I am disappointed. But more, I'm mad! I did everything I was supposed to and it still didn't work out.

Mary: It's frustrating when you try your best with little success.

Joan: Yeah. Well, maybe I could have taken that extra course. But I shouldn't have to! How can they think I'm not good enough!

Mary: It sounds like you feel diminished by the turn-down.

Joan: Yeah, it really hits the self-esteem! I know that's crazy.

Mary: What makes you think it's crazy?

Joan: Well, it probably wasn't me. They probably had a lot of great applicants.

Mary: So maybe the rejection wasn't personal?

Joan: No, it probably wasn't. I need to figure out what the others had that I don't have.

Mary: You mentioned an extra course. Is that something you would consider?

Joan: I think I should. It's a rough job market and I need all the extras I can get.

Mary: It's been disappointing and maddening, but you know it wasn't a personal rejection and there's something you can do to get extra qualifications. Sounds good!

Joan: Yeah. Thanks, Mary. I feel better.

Mary paraphrased what Joan said, asked clarifying questions, and summarized Joan's feelings and decision. She didn't preach to Joan about what she "should" do, or try to analyze her (e.g., "You always take things personally!"), nor did she minimize Joan's feelings. Rather, she acknowledged them and allowed Joan to examine herself. Mary didn't try to solve Joan's problem for her, which would have further reduced Joan's already shaky sense of self-efficacy, but she provided an accepting and empathetic environment for Joan to come to her own conclusions, which will strengthen her sense of self-efficacy. Joan is grateful to Mary because of this, and no doubt regards her as a good friend. The paraphrasing in particular is an element that increases Joan's liking for Mary (Weger, Castle, & Emmett, 2010).

Note, however, that the efficacy of active listening is somewhat in dispute (see Hafen & Crane, 2003 for a discussion of this controversy). It's not a guarantee that you will be regarded more positively, nor that it will improve relationships. What it may do, however, is remind you to be more attentive to others and give them the social support that they need and want.

REFLECTIVE EXERCISE

Active Listening

Do you use active listening? Specify an example of it the best you can recall. Has it been effective for you? Does anyone you know use it when you talk with them? If so, how does that make you feel? If you haven't used active listening before, first of all note whether you really are giving your full attention to a person talking to you or whether you are thinking about how to respond. Try being mindful of a conversation, attending wholly to the person that is with you. Now practise active listening techniques. You will be surprised at how quickly you get the hang of it and develop your own style. You may also be touched at how appreciative other people are of your attention and responses to them.

LOVE

Ah, love. Is it really what makes the world go round? Many would say yes, and research in positive psychology has revealed that it is certainly a large part of what leads to a satisfying life. We use the word *love* on a continual basis, referring to everything from a life partner or our children to a piece of dark chocolate. Let's stick to love for human beings in this chapter, though. But what exactly *is* love? It's hard to say, and many people might prefer not to even try. In 1982, U.S. Senator William Proxmire mockingly awarded what he called the Golden Fleece Award to researchers who obtained a grant to study love: his contention was that love could not be studied and no one should want to decrease the mystery of love, anyway! Well, we've come a long way since then, and today we do know some things about love. Given the delights and the problems it can cause us, it is definitely worthy of study.

Love is an emotion, and generally a pleasant one at that. It may contain biological elements, as in sexual desire; cognitive elements, as in thinking and planning about the object of our affections; and a behavioural element, as in acting in ways to bring the person closer to us, from calling or texting a person to sending flowers and giving a back rub. But love comes in a wide variety of types and contexts, so we really can't say there is any one strong definition, nor is there any one "right" way to give and receive love.

Types of Love

Many theorists have described love in various ways, but one of the most comprehensive and widely used descriptions is that of Robert Sternberg (1988). Sternberg has formulated what he calls the Triangular Model of Love in which each side of the triangle represents one of three elements. The first element is **passion**. This is the biological side of love, but also encompasses the emotional and cognitive preoccupation we have with the loved one. The second element is **intimacy**. This is an emotional element that describes the way we feel a need to communicate both our day-to-day feelings and experiences and our deepest, most private feelings to the loved one. We also want our loved one to communicate fully with us. The third element is **commitment**. This is a cognitive element that reveals a decision we have made to stay in the relationship and make it work by allowing ourselves to experience the love and being open about it.

Sternberg further puts these elements together and forms descriptions of the different types of love that might exist:

1. **Nonlove**. If there is no passion, no intimacy, and no commitment, then there is no love. This describes how we might feel about very casual acquaintances.

2. **Infatuation**. When there is only passion, a state of infatuation exists. Since there is no intimacy, we typically know very little about the person (who could be wonderful or could be serial murderer, for all we know). Without the intimacy, there is no chance to make a decision about commitment. Infatuation is the state of love that is experienced by some adolescents who become enamoured of celebrities whom they have never met or a classmate they see once a day across the room.

3. **Liking**. In this state, the only element of love that is present is intimacy. We may feel this for our very close friends for whom there is no passion, but there is a bond of trust and mutual self-disclosure. The commitment felt in this type of relationship is relatively minor. For example, few of us would refuse to move to another city with a life partner or to accept a dream job because it meant leaving our friends, sad as we might feel at this.

4. **Empty Love**. When there is no passion and no intimacy, people might still stay in a relationship because of their feelings of commitment. For some people, for example, marriages might continue even though the couple have felt no passion or connection, nor even talked intimately for years. Their adherence to the belief that their marriage vows were binding for life keeps them together.

5. **Romantic Love**. Romantic love is the Western notion that is portrayed in the media. Passion exists, as does intimacy, but commitment has not yet developed, and it might not ever develop.

6. **Fatuous Love**. When there is passion and commitment (imagine the whirlwind romance in which a couple marry after knowing each other for two weeks), fatuous love exists. There typically has not been a great deal of intimacy, which takes time to build.

7. **Companionate Love**. If there is intimacy and commitment in a relationship, Sternberg says a state of companionate love exists. The passion may not be present any more, or perhaps it was never present, but this kind of love remains, with deep caring and sharing and the commitment to continue in the relationship.

8. **Consummate Love**. Consummate love contains all three elements of Sternberg's model. There is passion between the two people, intimacy, and commitment, and all three elements are strong. This type of love is difficult to achieve and to maintain over the long haul, but is the kind of love that the Western world idealizes and the kind that most Western people assume is what will occur and endure when they make a life commitment to a partner.

Which form of love is best is an individual matter: the important thing is that the two people involved are in agreement about their love. (Have you ever been in the situation in which you feel romantic love for another person, who feels only liking for you? It's hard, isn't it?) The type of love we have in a relationship may change over time.

For example, a couple may start out their relationship with liking, which becomes romantic love, have it turn to consummate love, have children and find that their love is now companionate, but experience consummate love again once the children have grown and left home.

By the way, many young people believe that their parents will be desolated when they leave the nest. Usually this is completely incorrect. Children leaving the nest also means that many of the stresses and the time and money expenditures of raising children are removed from the parents' lives, allowing them the freedom and resources to focus on their own wants and needs. In fact, self-reported measures of marital satisfaction indicate that couples are less satisfied with their relationships when the children are living at home and experience an increase in happiness once the kids leave (Glenn, 1998)! Be comforted, though—almost all couples report that having kids was worth it (Demo, 1992).

Styles of Love

In addition to the different states of love that we may experience, we all have different styles of love. The Hendricks described some of these styles several years ago (1986):

1. **Eros** is the romantic love in which lovers sigh and pine for each other. They want to be in constant contact, even if it just means listening to each other breathe.

2. **Ludus** is a playful love, characterized by teasing, game-playing (such as making the partner jealous), and typically involves a reluctance to commit to the relationship.

3. **Storge** is the style of love, based on a deep friendship, that grows slowly and is based on intimacy.

4. **Pragma** is a practical love style in which the partner's primary concern is for down-to-earth evaluations of such things as what kind of partner or parent the other will be and how much real compatibility and shared beliefs exist between the two. This is a logical style of love that focuses on whether there is real potential for a viable relationship that will continue into the future.

5. **Mania** is, as its name suggests, a crazy style of love, characterized by jealousy, possessiveness, obsession with the partner, and continual turbulence.

6. **Agape** is a selfless love style. The partner focuses all caring and concern on the wants and needs of the other, considering his or her welfare above anything else.

Once more, there is no definite "right" or "good" style of love, but a mismatch of styles between the partners may bring more dissatisfaction than happiness in the relationship. The individual with an agape style may be deeply hurt and worn down over time by a partner whose style is ludic, just as the pragmatic lover may opt out of a relationship with someone whose style is manic.

The Conditions That Give Rise to Falling in Love

Not everyone falls in love in their lifetime. And these people are not abnormal, nor are they "unlucky." Does that surprise you? It's a Western conceit that falling in love is inevitable and uncontrollable. In some cultures, there is no concept of "falling in love" and people in these cultures may not fully comprehend what the drama is all about. If the culture doesn't have the concept of "falling in love," people may not be open to such a possibility, and therefore it may never occur for them. Their relationships may be based on compatibility, family dynamics, and friendship, as often occurs in arranged marriages, which, by the way, are just as likely to be satisfying and enduring as marriages based on falling in love (Weiten, Lloyd, Dunn, & Hammer, 2009). So one condition for falling in love is the expectation that this will occur.

Another condition for falling in love is meeting the right person. Naturally, who the "right" person is remains a completely individual matter. We have all seen couples who seem to be very happy and yet we wonder "What does he/she see in her/him?" We all have ideas about what the perfect life partner would be like. The more closely we believe that an individual embodies these qualities, the more likely it is that we will fall in love with that person. Someone whom we believe (rightly or wrongly) has all the desired qualities may lead us to fall in love very, very quickly. If our ideal is based on appearance alone, "love at first sight" may ensue!

Finally, the importance of biology must not be overlooked. In 1974, a classic study was conducted by Dutton and Aron in which they arranged for male college students to have an interview with an attractive female research assistant either on a rickety suspension bridge or on a solid bridge. Subsequently, the men were asked how romantically attracted they were to the research assistant. The men who were interviewed on the suspension bridge reported being more romantically attracted to the young lady than did men who were interviewed on the solid bridge. Presumably, the men's physiological arousal was increased on the more dangerous suspension bridge. This arousal seemed to have been transferred to feelings of arousal (or interpreted as feelings of arousal) caused by the attractive young lady, to whom they now felt romantically inclined!

This is **misattribution of arousal**, or believing that arousal by one source is actually caused by another source. Biology played its part, not in the more readily understandable sexual arousal, but in arousal caused by danger. This sheds some light on why romances seem to start more readily in war zones or at events such as rock concerts or drag races where emotions, and hence physiological arousal, is increased.

When the Relationship has Problems

Every relationship, romantic or platonic, typically involves some disagreements, and quarrelling is often the result. In fact, it pays to be skeptical of couples who say they never have a disagreement. No matter how many areas of similarity there are between the two people in a relationship, they are still distinct, imperfect human beings who will have their own ideas about behaviour, their own priorities, and their own needs.

Never quarrelling often means that people are swallowing their resentments. This can build up over time, damaging the entire relationship. The inevitable issues that arise in any relationship need to be dealt with promptly. If they can be dealt with in a calm conversation, so much the better. Couples who are most satisfied with their relationships don't avoid talking about their relationship problems (Smith, Heaven, & Ciarrochi, 2008). Quarrelling can be constructive or destructive. If you value the relationship, make your quarrels constructive. The next reflective exercise outlines some ways that we decrease our life satisfaction by damaging our relationships with friends, family, and intimate partners during a quarrel, and some ways we can avoid this.

How to quarrel so that matters get worse

1. View the quarrel as something to win or lose.

   Relationships are not about winning and losing, or keeping score. If there is a disagreement, it indicates that an issue needs to be resolved. If one person wins and the other loses, there is perhaps resolution for one, but not for both. And a relationship is about two people, not just one. Blaming won't help; it will only make the quarrel worse.

2. Shout. Get physical. Punch, slap, shove, or grab a partner. Throw a plate, punch the wall, etc.

   That demonstrates a childish lack of control and/or bullying tactics. It's certainly better to punch a pillow than a person, but neither is a constructive way to deal with a disagreement. It is, however, a wonderful way to frighten someone (the person you're supposed to love) and to ensure that their love and trust for you will decrease. Besides, keeping your voice level and pitch down commands attention.

3. Bring up every issue and resentment from the past. Pile them all on one quarrelling session.

   When we do this, we overwhelm a person and practically demand that they bring up all of our past wrongs. Nothing can be resolved this way. It becomes a contest about which partner has more grievances than the other. And it indicates that none of these issues has been dealt with at the time they arose, but rather they have festered over time. So one issue per quarrel is the rule.

4. Exaggerate. Say things like "You *always* do X" or "You *never* do Y." Or, for example, if your partner says "I'm hurt that you flirted with someone at the party," answer with "So you're accusing me of cheating."

   "Always"? "Never"? Hurt at flirting equals an accusation of cheating? Is that really true, or are you overstating the case? This diminishes your credibility. It's easy for your partner to dismiss or minimize the issue when you make such incredible and unrealistic claims. And it suggests that you're not really listening to your partner. This is not the time for miscommunication!

5. Use the silent treatment. Or end the argument by storming out of the room or slamming down the phone.

   We discussed the silent treatment in Chapter 7 and noted that your partner is not a mind reader and perhaps really doesn't know what the issue is or how deeply it's affecting you. Relationships thrive on open and honest communication, not on unspoken resentments and punishment. If you are too angry to talk calmly, let your partner know that you need a cooling off period and go for a walk. Making angry remarks and then storming out of the room is a "hit-and-run" tactic and not only doesn't resolve the issue, it leaves a wounded, puzzled, and angry person behind.

6. Retaliate. Do the same thing to your partner as he/she has done to you so that they know how it feels.

   This technique doesn't work in the vast majority of cases. All it does is demonstrate that you can do things as wrong as your partner. More resentment occurs. Two wrongs never make a right, so take

(Continued)

REFLECTIVE EXERCISE

How to quarrel so that matters get worse, *continued*

the high road and demonstrate to your partner that your differences can be handled in a more constructive fashion.

7. Use the words "I said I was sorry, what more do you want?"

Some people say "I'm sorry" just to end an argument. Often this motivation is very clear to the other person and of course is not satisfactory since it clearly lacks sincerity. If you were wrong, by all means apologize, but do so by re-stating what your partner has

said in order to make it clear that you know where you went wrong. For example: "I'm really sorry. I realize now that my behaviour made you embarrassed and uncomfortable. That was wrong of me, and I won't do it again." Then make sure you don't. If you have been the wronged partner, look again at the section on forgiveness in Chapter 7. Forgiveness means really moving past the wrong that has been done you, not holding it over the transgressor's head in the future.

Most of us contend that honesty in our romantic relationships is important, and this appears to be the case. Zhang and Stafford (2008) investigated the effects of honest but hurtful messages in a relationship. Sometimes we feel we need to deliver a message to our partners that will hurt them. These messages may be about their behaviour ("Your table manners need a lot of improvement"), about their personalities ("You're too sensitive"), their physical appearance ("You look really out of shape"), or the relationship we have with them ("You need to pay more attention to me"). In all cases, the message hurts and makes our partners feel a little less secure in the relationship and, unless they have a high sense of self-esteem, less secure in themselves, even though our partners recognize the honesty and truth in the message.

Zhang and Stafford (2008) find that messages about the relationship are the most hurtful, a result consistent with Knobloch and Carpenter-Theune's (2004) finding that talking about the relationship is the topic most commonly avoided among dating partners, regardless of their degree of intimacy. The honesty of the message does decrease the hurt that is felt, as does the overall degree of satisfaction already felt within the relationship. This suggests that if the overall relationship is satisfying, without an abundance of hurtful messages, and one stresses the honesty of the message, a single hurtful message may not do much harm to the relationship. But be sensitive! If the hurtful message is about something the other person knows about and is already working on or can't help, why do you feel the need to deliver the message?

A sad truth is that most relationships break up. Even committed relationships such as marriage have a divorce rate of about 40 to 65 percent in North America, depending on the group studied (Carrère, Buehlman, Gottman, Coan, & Ruckstuhl, 2000). The reasons people give for relationship break-ups are varied and may or may not reflect the real reason that the relationship failed. Little research has been done on the personal reasons people give for their relationship break-up since the 1980s (e.g., Gleek & Pearson, 1985, as cited by Weiten, Lloyd, Dunn, & Hammer, 2009) but asking the internet "why do relationships fail?" leads to almost 100 million sites! We can pick up some common themes, however.

Betrayal

One common reason given is that one partner betrayed the other. What constitutes betrayal, however, is another individual judgment. We saw in the example of Abel and Byron in Chapter 7 that a rupture occurred in their long-standing friendship because Abel regarded Byron's acceptance of a date with a woman Abel was interested in as a betrayal, while Byron didn't see it that way at all. In intimate relationships, we most often think of betrayal in terms of fidelity. But even here, the definitions vary. One American president contended that he did not betray his wife since he only engaged in sex play, not actual intercourse, with another woman. Most people did not agree with his definition of betrayal but, of course, only his wife's opinion mattered.

Betrayal can include revealing something that was told in confidence, engaging in intimate discussions with someone other than a life partner, viewing pornography on the internet, engaging in cybersex or telephone sex, or even using a fastidious friend's comb. The list is endless and can sometimes include reactions that most of us would find unreasonable. For example, a student of mine once ended a friendship with a classmate because her friend obtained a higher mark on a test than she did; my student contended that this meant that her friend was studying "secretly," a clear betrayal in her eyes. What constitutes betrayal to you? What could a friend or loved one do that you would find a painful disloyalty? If the betrayer showed genuine remorse for the act, are there any betrayals that would still end a relationship for you?

Abuse

Another reason given for break-ups is abuse. Instances of physical and/or sexual abuse are obviously unacceptable and in most cases should be deal-breakers in relationships. But we often overlook the painful cases of emotional abuse, which can be just as, if not more, damaging, especially over time. It often begins insidiously—the occasional comment or disparaging look—but not constantly or often in front of witnesses who might say "Hey, that's not right." Emotional abuse in adults has been studied very little and is difficult to define (see, for example, Queen, Brackley, & Williams, 2009). We can say, however, that emotional abuse consists of insults, demeaning comments, withdrawal from a person without adequate explanation, or putting someone in a situation in which no matter what they do, they are faulted for it.

A friend of mine has given me permission to tell you of how she ended a relationship with her boyfriend of three months as a cautionary tale of what was, relatively speaking, a mild case of emotional abuse. She applied for her dream job, and her boyfriend told her to call him as soon as she heard whether she got the job or not. She received the call that the job was hers, and she immediately called her boyfriend, whose response was "So you get what you want again. It's all about you." After a brief and unhappy conversation, she hung up the phone and realized that his response was characteristic, that she spent most of her time trying to determine what to say to him and how to say it to make him happy, an endeavour that was continually futile. She realized suddenly that she was being emotionally abused and ended the relationship, immediately experiencing great relief, mixed with the sadness that she had been deceiving herself in the relationship for three months. (Post-note: A wiser and more wary woman, she has been in a committed relationship for several years with a man who is kind and respects her, and they have two children who are learning from their parents what good relationships are all about.)

Emotional abuse can be extremely difficult to overcome because it diminishes a person's sense of self-worth and self-esteem (Queen, Brackley, & Williams, 2009). After a continual period of time of being insulted, demeaned, ignored, and in general told that one is wrong, a person may well come to believe it. After all, it is being said by the one person who is supposed to love and know you best and whose word you have trusted. Did anyone ever tell you that "Sticks and stones can break my bones but names can never hurt me"? They were wrong. Words can be more hurtful and more long-lasting than a black eye. On the other hand, happy couples typically use five times more positive comments and behaviours than negative comments and behaviours to each other (Fincham, 2003).

Lack of Intimacy

Another common reason given for a break-up is that there is a lack of intimacy in the relationship. This can come about for a number of reasons. In some cases, people enter into relationships based on passion without considering intimacy. They find out later, through talking and self-disclosure (the only real ways to develop intimacy), that they have little in common and in fact are quite incompatible. This happens frequently in relationships that are entered into prematurely, before the couple has really had time to form their own identities. Sometimes intimacy exists in the early stages of a relationship, but is not maintained and the couple grows apart, finding that they are now on very separate paths in life.

Unrealistic Expectations

It should come as no surprise that another reason for break-ups is the existence of unrealistic expectations (Blonna, 2007). Many people enter into relationships with the idealized, unrealistic notions that they will always feel passion for each other, that they will always be completely open and honest with each other, that every difficulty will be resolved calmly before bedtime, that they will never feel loneliness again, and so on. They may have expectations that their partner will feel and behave in certain ways, only to be disabused of these notions in disturbing ways.

Let's take the example of Bob and Carol: Before marrying, Bob and Carol agreed that they would budget their money carefully to save for a house. After the marriage, Carol found that Bob's idea of budgeting meant having brown bag lunches at work every day. Her idea of budgeting was buying only two silk blouses a month instead of three. Before marrying, they also agreed that their extended families would be a large part of their lives. Bob thought that meant having Sunday dinner with one or the other set of parents every second week. Carol thought that meant letting her free-loading sister move in with them for months at a time. Before marrying, Bob knew that Carol loved to cook. He thought that would mean she would prepare all meals when she got home from work each night, not what Carol had in mind at all! After a year of marriage, both Bob and Carol were questioning whether this union had been a good idea. Love, they found, was not enough, and both felt that they had not known what they were getting into when they made their commitment to each other.

The Break-up Experience

It takes two people to make a relationship, but it takes only one to break it up. If one partner is determined to leave the relationship, there is really nothing the other partner can do about it. In a perfect world, relationships would happily last forever. If that's not possible and they did end, both partners would say goodbye cheerfully; equitably divide their assets; remain connected, supportive parents to their children, and continue to genuinely value the ex-partner as a person of worth and even as a friend. News flash: the world is not perfect.

Most often the break-up of a relationship entails pain and suffering, including for the person who instigates the break-up. There is grief at the end of a relationship for what used to be and what might have been, as well as for the loss of the ex-partner and other benefits such as the lifestyle of two people sharing accommodations. There is the stress of a changed identity, from one of a couple to now a solitary person. There is often guilt on the part of the person who has instigated the end of the relationship, especially if the ex-partner hasn't committed any unpardonable wrong. There is self-doubt and loss of self-esteem for the partner who has been rejected. In many cases, there is self-blame, feeling that there will never be another relationship, and a host of negative self-statements (Boelen & Reijntjes, 2008). There may be stunned disbelief as well, in particular if the rejected partner has not realized there were problems in the relationship. In many ways, the reactions to the end of a relationship mirror the reactions to the death of a loved one, with disbelief and denial, anger, depression, and eventual acceptance and recovery. Life satisfaction and a subjective sense of well-being decrease, and it takes resilience to deal with this life crisis.

It's often asked whether ex-partners can be friends. Yes, but only when each of them has reached the point that they can truly rejoice in the other's new relationships. Think about this: if your best friend were to meet the person of his/her dreams and plan a wonderful life together, you might feel a little pang of "I wish that could happen to me" but you would still be delighted for your friend and give heartfelt good wishes for a fantastic future. That's what friends do: they metaphorically and literally dance at the wedding. Can you feel that for your ex? If not, you're not ready to be friends.

Sometimes the partner who instigated the break-up continues to call, "just to see how you are" and because "we're still friends." He or she may mean well by this or may be doing this to assuage his/her guilt at the break-up, but these actions are often harmful. They tend to keep a faint hope alive in the rejected partner ("He/she still cares!") who has not yet had time to accept that the relationship is over and may be, even unconsciously, desperately looking for ways to hang on to it. The still-bleeding rejected partner may be so hurt and lost that he/she willingly accepts any crumbs of comfort that are offered. A cut can't heal if someone keeps picking the scab. It's a better idea to have as little contact with the ex as possible until some healing has had time to take place. If there are children involved or legal or financial matters that must be resolved, some contact will be necessary, but it should be kept to a minimum and revolve around only the matters at hand. Months (or even years) later, one can re-evaluate whether the ex is someone who can now be only a friend.

REFLECTIVE EXERCISE

How to Get Over a Break-up

1. Call a moratorium on contact with the ex.

2. Allow yourself to feel the grief emotions.

3. Surround yourself with supportive friends, especially those who have lived through break-ups themselves.

4. Practice Seligman's ABCDE technique when negative self-talk arises. It is unrealistic to tell yourself that you have failed; it's the relationship that has failed, and you can grow from this.

5. Take care of yourself, both physically and emotionally. A little extra pampering won't hurt!

6. Meet new people, but avoid getting involved in a rebound romance. You need a chance to get over your grief and to re-establish your identity outside of your couple status first.

7. Take up a new sport, hobby, course, or activity. Increase your self-efficacy by self improvement and new interests apart from your ex.

8. If you find yourself obsessing about your ex after the initial stages of the break-up or becoming mired in an emotion such as depression or anger, get professional help.

Do these ideas make sense to you? Do you disagree with some of them? Do you have other ideas? If you have been through a break-up, what helped you? What made getting over the break-up worse?

LONELINESS

Loneliness and Solitude

In the scenario at the beginning of the chapter, we saw a mother, Naomi, and her son who were lonely. Loneliness is a state that is defined more by the lack of satisfaction we derive from our relationships than the number of relationships we have (Mellor, Stokes, Firth, Hayashi, & Cummins, 2008). We can and sometimes do feel lonely in a crowd of people whom we know. Most of us feel lonely sometimes, and many of us feel lonely frequently (Rokach & Block, 1997). First, let's distinguish between loneliness and solitude. We all need to be alone sometimes, to work, to reflect, to just "hang out" with ourselves. Solitude is freely chosen, whereas loneliness is not. Solitude refreshes, whereas loneliness hurts. Solitude can be a part of a satisfying life, but loneliness generally is not. While loneliness is not usually considered part of positive psychology, it can impede personal growth and diminish our chances of having a sense of well-being. For that reason, it merits more discussion.

Effects of Loneliness

Loneliness can be very debilitating, increasing our stress and making us more likely to contract physiological disorders and illnesses; it is even associated with earlier death (Cacioppo, Hawkley, & Berntson, 2003). Among the elderly, loneliness and depression may lead to a "giving up," with resultant lack of care to medical regimes and diet, leading to an earlier death (Stek et al., 2005). Loneliness is also highly related to a lack of life satisfaction and sense of subjective well-being (Bramston, Pretty, & Chipuer, 2002; Goodwin, Cook, & Yung, 2001; Mellor, Stokes, Firth, Hayashi, & Cummins, 2008), as well as with psychological disorders including depression and thoughts of suicide (Eisses et al., 2004; Kidd, 2004). But loneliness is not a disorder in itself, and it can be beneficial since it sometimes makes us reflect on ourselves and our lives, and can give rise to creativity and change (Nilsson, Lindström, & Nåden, 2006).

Causes of Loneliness

Ami Rokach, at the Institute for the Study and Treatment of Psychosocial Stress in Toronto, has done a great deal of work in the area of loneliness and finds that the primary reasons cited for being lonely depend to a great extent on the cultural norms we live in. In North America, we prize independence, for example, and may feel less loneliness when people are not with us than people in cultures who prize interdependence more. The causes of our loneliness change over our lifespan, as well (Rokach, 2007; Rokach, Orzeck, Moya, & Expósito, 2002). For example, in adolescence we may feel lonely because we lack social skills, whereas in old age we may feel lonely because most of our friends and family have died. In general, the causes of loneliness are found to be the following (categories by Rokach & Brock, 1996):

1. *Personal inadequacies.* Some people blame their loneliness on their own feelings of being socially inept or anxious, shy, or on having mistrust of others and fear of intimacy. They may also believe that their lack of self-esteem is a large factor in their loneliness. This may lead them to be unwilling to approach other people and to be unassertive. Their social skills may be deficient not only because of their own feelings, but also because of their lack of practice in social interactions.

2. *Developmental deficits.* For some people, loneliness is caused by the conditions of their childhood. They contend that having been brought up in unhappy homes, marked by emotionally distant or rejecting parents, physical and/or emotional abuse, family discord, and so on, they are scarred by this and have problems forming relationships with others because of it. They may also indicate that their families did not encourage social relationships with others.

3. *Unfulfilling intimate relationships.* Some people cite their disappointing and unhappy intimate relationships as causes for their loneliness. The hurt and sometimes abuse they experienced in these relationships have left them feeling very lonely, they say.

4. *Relocation/significant separations.* As in the case of Naomi in the scenario at the beginning of the chapter, moving to a new location means entering a situation in which loneliness may be present because one has not had an opportunity to form relationships with new people. It also means that the relationships one has had are not immediately available anymore. In this category we should also include the loneliness felt when a significant relationship has been lost through death or a break-up of some kind.

5. *Social marginality.* Some people feel loneliness because of their very real isolation from others. People who are housebound because of chronic illnesses may experience this, as may prison inmates and the unemployed. Other situations may lead to feelings of social marginality as well: for example, being the only Muslim family in a

community of Christians and Jews, or the only elderly people in a housing complex made up of young families. Social marginality is sometimes felt by hard workers too; people working sixty-hour weeks and going to school part-time may report feeling lonely due to their lack of time for social interactions.

Naomi is in a difficult situation given that she and her family have moved to a new location. But it may be that Naomi is also shy, has had a dysfunctional childhood, and is in an unhappy marriage. That is, the factors that contribute to loneliness may interact with each other, making Naomi's loneliness more profound and difficult to overcome.

Dealing with loneliness can be difficult if the causes are situations we have no control over. But once we meet people, at work, in community centres, through courses, and so on, we can improve our chances of eliminating most of our loneliness through gaining social skills. There are many courses given on just this, and they include eliminating negative self-statements, having realistic expectations about relationships, learning listening skills, and preparing topics for "small talk." All in all, if we become more positive people, others will be attracted to us, and while we may opt for solitude sometimes, our social lives will be more satisfying and loneliness will cease to be problematic.

EMOTIONAL INTELLIGENCE

At the beginning of this chapter, we met Angela, the centre of a group of parents who were having an enjoyable interaction while their children played. People characterized her as being warm and empathetic, with great social skills. Angela has what has been termed **emotional intelligence** (sometimes referred to as EQ). Having satisfying relationships with other people is highly dependent on emotional intelligence. This is a term coined by Daniel Goleman (1995), and it includes many of the qualities we have discussed in previous chapters, qualities such as self-regulation, optimism, hope, and stress management. It also includes being sensitive to the needs of other people and knowing how to respond to them. Much research has been done on emotional intelligence, and it has been found to be so important in good social functioning in day-to-day life and life satisfaction that we need to pay special attention to it. Some people, such as Bar-On (2010), consider it to be a fundamental part of positive psychology.

The Abilities of Emotional Intelligence

Salovey, Mayer, Caruso, and Yoo (2009) conceive of emotional intelligence as being comprised of a group of four abilities. The first ability is perceiving emotions in ourselves and in others. If we are not able to perceive our own emotions, we can't regulate them, nor can we learn from them. It also makes it very difficult to understand the emotions of others, and without this understanding, we might not respond to others in the way they need. Relationships would lack intimacy and satisfaction. But at the same time, if we assume that everyone else has the same emotions to the same situations that we do, we will miss the unique differences that exist among people, and again we will be at a disadvantage in responding to people according to their needs, as well as our own. Perceiving emotions, then, includes being attentive to signals, verbal or nonverbal, from other people that indicate what they are feeling. It includes being able to discriminate between honest and dishonest emotions and being able to express emotions and needs accurately. Angela, in the scenario at the beginning of the chapter, seems very capable of doing this, as her friends attest.

The second ability of emotional intelligence is that of being able to use emotions to better our cognitive functioning. Since we know that negative emotions can get in the way of clear thinking, problem solving, and decision-making (see Chapter 9, for example) and that positive emotions can make us interpret situations in an optimistic light, sometimes an overly optimistic light (see Chapter 5), it is plain that if we want to maximize our cognitive abilities, we need to regulate these emotions and use them to our benefit. The person with emotional intelligence can use emotions to prioritize what to attend to in a situation and to redirect attention to appropriate areas.

It also becomes possible to use emotions to gain different perspectives on a situation. For example, Angela knows that when she feels sad thinking about the death of her father, she probably isn't as patient with her son's loud play as she usually is. Knowing this about herself, she can decide to let her son stay with his father while she takes time for herself to grieve. Or, if that's not possible, she can put effort into dismissing her feelings about her father until later and concentrate on being more patient with her son. Knowing that the same activity from her son can make her impatient when she is sad, but can amuse her when she isn't sad allows her to see that her son's play may be irritating to other people sometimes and gives her an advantage in recognizing when to curb her son's exuberance and when to permit it. It also gives her more understanding of other people and their feelings. By seeing situations from different perspectives, she increases her creativity in problem solving.

This is also helpful in making her less judgmental when forming a first impression. Recall that when we discussed first impressions, it was noted briefly that Angela might not be likely to jump to conclusions when meeting someone for the first time. Because she can see different perspectives, when Angela glances at Naomi and her son, she is more likely to wonder whether Naomi is shy, or new in town, or isn't feeling well, rather than assuming that Naomi is antisocial and has other negative qualities.

Emotional intelligence includes the third ability of understanding emotions. Emotions are highly complex, often blending together to create another emotion and a different situation. Let's go back to Angela's son and his loud play. Angela knows that her impatience with her son's loud play when she is sad can combine with annoyance and frustration. These emotions, if not checked, can lead to anger and turn the situation of a little boy playing in a happy, normal, loud, childhood fashion into a situation of a little boy being punished for just being a kid. Angela, understanding emotions, won't let that happen. When she interacts with other people, she understands that their emotions can change and can be mixed with other emotions. She knows that her own grief about her father's death is mixed with the relief that his suffering from a long and painful illness is over, emotions that might seem contradictory. But with the understanding of emotions, she knows that she and others are perfectly capable of holding contradictory emotions, making her more capable of supportive responding to both herself and others.

Finally, Salovey, Mayer, Caruso, and Yoo (2009) propose a fourth ability of emotional intelligence: the ability to manage emotions. As we have seen, Angela, using and understanding her emotions, is able to regulate them in herself. She doesn't deny or suppress her feelings, but she handles them effectively (see Chapter 6). She can also handle the emotions of other people, knowing when and how to give a pep talk to another person who might be feeling discouraged or how to persuade her son to let another child play with his highly desirable toy. She doesn't run away from the painful emotions of others, as many people do. She will stay and listen to a friend relate the story of her house burning down, even though she has heard the story several times before because she knows this is part of the way her friend is working through her pain.

We might wonder how Angela would react to Naomi. Having emotional intelligence, she might notice Naomi and her son sitting alone and come by to introduce herself. She would probably listen to Naomi relate the story of her relocation and her subsequent loneliness without interrupting her. She would probably indicate that she understands how difficult relocation is and how hard it can be to make new friends. After talking for a while, she might ask Naomi and her son to join her and her son with their friends, where she would introduce them and include them in group play and small talk. When it was time to leave, Angela would probably indicate to Naomi that she hopes to see her again, perhaps even mentioning when she and her son usually come to the playground. She would tread slowly and carefully, since she doesn't know at this point what Naomi's wants and needs are. If Naomi responded by coming to the playground at the indicated time the next day, Angela would probably greet her enthusiastically and continue to include Naomi as part of the group. Angela and Naomi might become friends as these kinds of interactions continue.

Benefits of Emotional Intelligence

Emotional intelligence certainly contains a complex array of abilities, but the payoff for these abilities is great. People with emotional intelligence are happier and have a greater sense of well-being (Bar-On, 2005; Brackett & Mayer, 2003; Furnham & Petrides, 2008; Gallagher & Vella-Brodrick, 2008). This is hardly surprising, since people with high emotional intelligence, by definition, have qualities that make their lives more pleasurable in many ways. They cope with stress better than those with lower amounts of emotional intelligence (Kluemper, 2008). For one thing, they have a greater sense of self-efficacy which allows them to deal with stress more effectively since they appraise situations as challenge rather than threat (Mikolajczak & Luminet, 2008). They are also more adept at reducing their negative emotions and maintaining their positive emotions (Mikolajczak, Nelis, Hansenne, & Quoidbach, 2008). They feel more control of their own lives and procrastinate less (Deniz, Traş, & Aydoğan, 2009), and there is even some evidence that they have more academic success than equally bright people who have less emotional intelligence (Di Fabio & Palazzeschi, 2009). To top it off, they have better physical health than other people (Martins, Ramalho, & Morin, 2010).

Clearly, having emotional intelligence predicts better individual functioning, but its greatest impact may be seen in its relationship to our social functioning. People with high levels of emotional intelligence report having better, more satisfying relationships with their friends, family, and intimate partners (Brackett, Mayer, & Warner, 2004; Brackett, Warner, & Bosco, 2005; Mestre, Guil, Lopes, Salovey, & Gil-Olarte, 2006). And their friends and family say that they are indeed warmer and more supportive, fostering relationships of intimacy and admiration, as Angela does (Lopes et al., 2004; Lopes, Salovey, Côté, & Beers, 2005). Even objective observers agree that men with high degrees of emotional intelligence are more socially engaged and competent (Brackett, Rivers, Shiffman, Lerner, & Salovey, 2006).

Angela's approach to other people like Naomi is fulfilling to her: she feels good about reaching out to Naomi and she may have made a new friend. This will give her more optimism and hope in her social interactions and more social support if she needs it. She will be more likely to reach out to others again. As Frederickson's broaden-and-build theory would indicate (Frederickson & Joiner, 2002), Angela's emotional intelligence may lead to more positive situations and more positive emotions for her (see Chapter 5).

Given all the benefits that go along with emotional intelligence, it is obvious why many school curricula include training children to increase this quality, and many workplaces have included emotional intelligence training workshops for their employees and managers (see Salovey, Mayer, Caruso, & Yoo, 2009 for a review of interventions to improve emotional intelligence). It's encouraging to note that Nelis, Quoidbach, Mikolajczak, and Hansenne (2009) found in a controlled experiment that participants given only ten hours of emotional intelligence group training showed a significant increase in their emotion identification and emotion management abilities as compared to people who had not undergone this training. The effects persisted at a six-month follow-up as well.

REFLECTIVE EXERCISE

Increasing Emotional Intelligence

Training in emotional intelligence includes many of the skills we have already discussed in this book. For example, learning to be more optimistic and decrease unrealistic and negative self-statements will be helpful (Chapter 5). Learning to regulate emotions and increase self-efficacy (Chapter 6) will be necessary for the development of emotional intelligence. Finding meaning and purpose in life, growing from our adversities (Chapter 8) will make us more sensitive to others as well. Recognizing the potential problems of first impressions and becoming an active listener (this chapter) is useful. You might also consider taking one of the many courses available in the area of emotional intelligence. Given what you have read about emotional intelligence, you may recognize yourself what areas you might need to develop. What are these areas? What can you do to help yourself strengthen these areas?

To take a free test of your own emotional intelligence, go to the website of the Institute for Health and Human Potential at www.ihhp.com/quiz.php

---

Conclusion

Other people can be a huge source of satisfaction in our lives and a huge source of distress. The benefits certainly outweigh the problems in contributing to our satisfaction with our lives. But in order to gain these benefits, we all need to learn how to be a good friend and a supportive person in a relationship. There is an old saying that to have a friend, you must be a friend. True. Quality counts. It's all right to end relationships that are not satisfying to you—just because you have known someone for years doesn't mean that he/she is really a friend. If you find that, despite your best efforts, the relationship is unsatisfying, and worse, is impairing your own growth as a human being, leaving the relationship may be the best idea. Consider carefully.

SPOTLIGHT ON RESEARCH

Emotional Intelligence and Mindfulness

Mindfulness, as we saw in Chapter 6, involves greater awareness of what is happening in the moment. That includes awareness of one's own emotional state and sometimes the emotional state of others in a non-judgmental fashion. This awareness and non-judgmental state seem to fit in well with the concept of emotional intelligence, which also involves awareness and tolerance of emotional states.

Schutte and Malouff (2011) reasoned that since this commonality exists, and since both emotional intelligence and mindfulness are positively related to life satisfaction and a sense of well-being, perhaps mindfulness has a role in the development of emotional intelligence. Specifically, they thought that mindfulness would facilitate emotional intelligence, and emotional intelligence would increase well-being. To determine if this is so, they recruited 125 university students in Australia to fill out questionnaires about their mindfulness, their emotional intelligence, their experience of positive and negative emotions, and their life satisfaction. They discovered that people who had high scores on mindfulness also had high scores on emotional intelligence and life satisfaction, as well as experiencing more positive emotions and fewer negative emotions. Furthermore, their statistical analyses found that their hypothesis was indeed right: mindfulness does lead to increased emotional intelligence, which then leads to more life satisfaction. The route is this:

$$\text{mindfulness} \rightarrow \text{emotional intelligence} \rightarrow \text{life satisfaction}$$

Knowing this, we can speculate that mindfulness has an effect on life satisfaction and well-being because it facilitates emotional intelligence. Mindfulness training, then, might be another way of helping people to increase their emotional intelligence. We must be cautious, however, of the fact that this is preliminary research. Further research, testing a wider range of people than Australian university students, is required to strengthen this argument. An experiment in which people are trained in mindfulness and are compared on emotional intelligence to people who have not had such training will help us to determine whether this is a useful technique in increasing emotional intelligence. We will await more research eagerly.

Summary

- Self-described happy people and those who have high self-esteem report having satisfying relationships with others.
- Physical appearance has been found to be very influential in our assumptions about what other people are like at a first meeting.
- People who are attractive are assumed to have other positive qualities and more success in their relationships, academic performance, and occupations.
- If we are meeting someone about whom we have heard positive statements, we are more inclined to be open to the person, but if we have heard negative statements, it may be that we don't give the individual much chance.
- On first meeting, if the person speaks and acts in what is typically regarded as a societally unacceptable manner, we tend to form a negative opinion of that person.
- Stereotyping a person because of the group he/she belongs to can lead us to mistakes in forming a first impression.
- We also make mistakes because of the fundamental attribution error (not taking account of the situation and concluding that behaviour is caused by personality).
- We also make errors by making global judgments about people, attributing several positive qualities to someone who is observed to have one good quality, or several negative qualities to someone with one negative trait or action.
- Making friends is influenced by propinquity, similarity, and self-disclosure.
- Secure attachment predicts good interpersonal relationships even more than personality factors do.
- In intimate relationships, the response to positive life events may be more important than the response to negative life events.
- Active listening includes focusing on the speaker, paraphrasing what has been said, asking clarifying questions, and summarizing at the end.
- Love may contain biological, cognitive, and behavioural elements.
- The Triangular Model of Love includes passion, intimacy, and commitment. These elements can be combined to form different types of love. The combination in a relationship may change over time.
- If a culture doesn't have the concept of falling in love, people may not be open to such a possibility and therefore it may never occur for them. Meeting the right person and physiological arousal are also important factors in falling in love.
- Couples who are most satisfied talk about their relationship problems.
- Relationships may break up because of perceived betrayal, abuse, lack of intimacy, or unrealistic expectations.
- Relationship break-ups may leave several negative emotions and cognitions.
- Loneliness can increase stress and the likelihood of contracting physiological disorders and illnesses. Loneliness is also related to lower life satisfaction and subjective well-being, as well as to psychological disorders.
- Causes of loneliness include personal inadequacies, developmental deficits, unfulfilling intimate relationships, relocation/significant separations, and social marginality.

- Emotional intelligence is the ability to perceive, understand, handle, and use emotions in a personally and socially constructive manner.
- People with emotional intelligence are happier and have a greater sense of well-being. They cope with stress better and are also more adept at reducing their negative emotions and maintaining their positive emotions. They feel more control of their own lives and procrastinate less, and they have better physical health.
- People with high levels of emotional intelligence report having better, more satisfying relationships with their friends, family, and intimate partners.
- Emotional intelligence can be learned.

Group Discussion Questions

1. Are first impressions justifiable? Would the world be a better place if no one ever made conclusions about people without getting to know them well?
2. Are hermits happy?
3. In some cultures, people don't form committed relationships based on "falling in love." Would this be a good idea? What are the pros and cons of arranged marriages?
4. Is the concept of "emotional intelligence" just another way of saying that people may be sensitive to emotions of themselves and others? Or does it go beyond this?

CHAPTER 11

Work and Leisure

Nick works hard and plays hard. He works as a computer analyst, and he gets so absorbed in his tasks that time seems to fly by. Generally, he needs to be told that it's quitting time. His work contains a variety of tasks, and he looks forward to the new challenges of each working day.

LEARNING OBJECTIVES

In this chapter, students will learn

- ☐ What characteristics of a job make the job more or less satisfying for the individual.
- ☐ What characteristics of the individual make it more likely that he/she will find a job satisfying.
- ☐ How work satisfaction is related to work performance.
- ☐ What attitudes people hold towards leisure.
- ☐ How leisure satisfaction relates to life satisfaction, before and after retirement.
- ☐ The relationship between leisure satisfaction and social interaction.
- ☐ About making the transition from work life to home life.
- ☐ The need for balance in attaining life satisfaction.
- ☐ The benefits of savouring.
- ☐ The components of flow.
- ☐ The benefits of flow.

His employer and his co-workers think he's terrific, always helpful and pleasant to be around. They can count on him. When he gets home, though, he is completely a husband and father, ready to help with housework and play with the kids. He loves the time that he spends making dinner and talking with his wife, but his favourite time is when he reads the kids a story and puts them to bed. When they're asleep, he reads, watches a movie with his wife, and talks with her. On the weekends, the whole family engages in at least one planned activity. Sometimes it's watching a sport, other times it may be something as simple as taking a walk in the park or building a snowman. Whenever possible, Nick includes a child from the Big Brother program in the family outings. His work with this program brings him great satisfaction. He feels that he has so much in his life that sharing some of it is a privilege, and he plans to share even more when he retires someday.

Maybe then he can do more of the activities, like kayaking, that he has always enjoyed. Or maybe he'll go back to school and learn about history, a subject that fascinates him, but one that he has never formally pursued. There's so much he could do! But in the meantime, on Sunday evenings, as he prepares for work the next day, he thinks, "Life is good."

Nick is right—his life is good. He gets enjoyment and fulfillment from both his work and his leisure time, and he brings an attitude of optimism and enthusiasm to everything he does. Nick is lucky, too. It appears that his work is interesting to him, and his co-workers and employer are congenial and supportive. His home life gives him opportunities to interact with the people he loves and to volunteer in a highly meaningful organization. We have already seen that optimism and enthusiasm enhance one's sense of well-being. Now it's time to look specifically at how work and play can do this, as they have for Nick.

WORK

Jobs don't just provide us with money; they also give us social interactions, opportunities to use our skills and learn new ones, and the chance to develop personally with valuable experiences (Emberland & Rundmo, 2010). Most of us are concerned with having, and feel more satisfaction with, jobs that we see as interesting and meaningful (Armstrong-Stassen & Ursel, 2009; Li, Li, & Wang, 2009). But what makes a job satisfying?

Work Characteristics Related to Job Satisfaction

For many years now, Hackman and Oldham's (1976, 1980) Job Characteristics Model has been used to understand engagement and satisfaction in a job. According to this model, five basic characteristics of a job have an impact on a worker's feelings about the job and the behaviour he or she shows on the job. These characteristics are (1) skill variety, (2) task identity, (3) task significance, (4) feedback, and (5) autonomy. Let's look at these characteristics, and others that have been found to be important, in more detail.

Skill Variety

How many skills are needed for the worker to perform the task? In some jobs, tasks require very few skills. For example, working on a product control potato chip assembly line would require the skill of recognizing which chips were below standard and physically plucking them off the conveyor belt. This might become boring before very long and might result in lower satisfaction with the job. Then there are jobs that require several skills. Selling cars, for example, requires the salesperson to have extensive knowledge about cars, friendly and persuasive communication skills, excellent negotiating skills, understanding of financing, knowledge of legal requirements of a sale, the ability to fill out appropriate forms, and so on. The need for such a wide variety of skills is challenging for a worker, but if the skills are present, this may increase satisfaction of the job.

Task Identity

Once upon a time, a cabinet maker would select the wood (maybe even chop down the tree), design the cabinet, and build it from start to finish. In doing this, the cabinet maker saw his or her skills create a unique object—raw wood transformed into a beautiful sideboard, perhaps. The cabinet maker's task had task identity: the requirement that the worker see the project through from start to finish. The satisfaction of seeing a project through in this way spills into overall job satisfaction, Hackman and Oldham (1976, 1980) contended. Contrast this with the way most furniture is made today, with assembly lines that produce one small piece of the furniture, manned by workers who may never see the end product or even know what the end product will be. Workers in this situation may feel little satisfaction and perhaps even a certain alienation from their jobs.

Task Significance

Is the work meaningful? Does it contribute to society in some way or influence the contentment people feel in their lives? Meaningfulness may be found in different occupations by different people. Many people would find making guns to be of inestimable service to the world, seeing firearms as fundamental in the preservation of safety and liberty. Other people would find making guns to be an abomination, seeing firearms as mechanisms of destruction and pain. If the worker believes that the work he or she does is of worth beyond the salary, that it is important to humanity in some way, there is more satisfaction with the job than if the worker believes the job he or she does has no effect or is detrimental to others.

Feedback

According to Hackman and Oldham (1976, 1980), we find more satisfaction in our work if we get feedback about how we're doing or if we can see for ourselves the progress we are making in a task. On the other hand, performing a task without being told whether you're doing a good job or not or how to improve, and not being able to see an end result that would give you some indication of your success or failure, is intuitively demoralizing and would be expected to be related to lower job satisfaction. Imagine enrolling in a university course in which you would be required to write essays, complete projects and reports, and take tests, but after which you would not find out your grade or even whether you passed the course or not. Would you recommend that course to your friends?

Autonomy

We have seen autonomy mentioned in conjunction with satisfaction and feelings of well-being before (see Chapters 1 and 6). In the Job Characteristics Model, autonomy refers to the degree to which workers are able to make their own decisions about their allotment of time to particular tasks and how the tasks will be done. As in other areas of life, autonomy has a major role in job satisfaction; in fact, recent evidence has determined that autonomy is one of the major factors influencing job satisfaction.

We feel more satisfied with a job, as with other facets of our lives, when we feel that we have some control over what we are doing, as we saw in Chapter 6. Control over our time is important to us, at work and at play (e.g., Chen, Zhang, Leung, & Zhou, 2010; Claessens, Eerde, Rutte, & Roe, 2004). At work, several organizations offer workers the opportunity to have flex-time, in which the exact hours they work are determined, within limits, by them. Similarly, the opportunity to work a compressed week, in which employees work longer hours per day but fewer days, may be offered. McNall, Masuda, and Nicklin (2010) found that workers given these opportunities indicated more satisfaction with their jobs, reporting that they felt that their work made them more effective in their home life and family roles because of this. In addition, they felt less likely to want to change jobs. The researchers interpret this as indicating that the opportunities gave the workers the belief that the employer cared about them and their families' welfare.

Golden and Wiens-Tuers (2005) report that 28 percent of workers in the United States are *compelled* to work overtime by their employers. The effect of this on workers is negative (see also Fenwick & Tausig, 2001). Beckers and her colleagues (2008) also found that, when employers take control of their workers' time by forcing them to work overtime, the workers' job satisfaction decreased. This was especially the case when the overtime was not paid, but even when paid, job satisfaction was lower. Money, it seems, cannot completely compensate for the lack of autonomy in scheduling hours of work.

The ability to structure our time during working hours is also an important part of the autonomy that is related to job satisfaction (Boezerman & Ellemers, 2009; Karsh, Beasley, & Brown, 2010). But other forms of autonomy, such as input into how the work should be done and non-interfering supervision, are important as well (Li, Li, & Wang, 2009; Miner, Dowson, & Sterland, 2010; Van den Broeck, Vansteenkiste, De Witte, & Lens, 2008).

Social Relationships

One of the functions of work, as we have seen, is to provide us with social relationships, and self-determination theory indicates that belongingness is a basic psychological need that, if fulfilled, is a component in motivating us to do our work to the best of our ability (Deci & Ryan, 2000; see Chapter 6). The social aspects of a job, therefore, would be expected to have an impact on worker satisfaction as well, and this expectation has been borne out. For example, relationships with their patients is the best predictor of the job satisfaction that family physicians report (Karsh, Beasley, & Brown, 2010).

The social aspect of work is important even when the work is of a voluntary nature. Volunteer workers typically choose to do volunteer work because of intrinsic motivation—after all, as volunteers they are not forced to work by definition, and they have a great deal of autonomy in their working schedules since they can easily leave a situation in which they have little control. Their work, often drudge work well below their skill level, is fuelled by their desire, in most cases, to be of service to others, and this intrinsic motivation is related to their satisfaction with their work (Millette & Gagné, 2008). But in particular, they report, they are most satisfied with their volunteer work because of the social factors involved (Boezerman & Ellemers, 2009).

Supervisors and Team Leaders

A rather different part of the social aspects of a job concerns the relationship between the worker and his/her supervisor. The support of a supervisor can be very significant in a worker's job satisfaction in several ways. The supervisor may give constructive feedback and encouragement to workers, which are important to the job satisfaction of most workers, as we have seen, but especially important to workers with low self-efficacy (Chen & Scannapieco, 2010; Li, Li, & Wang, 2009). In stressful situations at work, supervisors may also be helpful to workers in the self-regulation of their emotions. Since the ability to manage and use emotions appropriately is related to life satisfaction, it is not surprising that supervisors who help with this have workers who are more satisfied with their jobs (Chen, Ku, Shyr, Chen, & Chou, 2009).

Team leaders who encourage and inspire their teams increase the workers' feeling of personal and team efficacy, and the workers feel more satisfied with their jobs (Nielsen, Yarker, Randall, & Munir, 2009). On the other hand, supervisors who are perceived to engage in "office politics" or self-serving and manipulative behaviour have workers who are less satisfied with their jobs and more inclined to contemplate leaving the job (Karadal & Arasli, 2009; Poon, 2003).

Nick, who we met at the beginning of the chapter, seems to have a working situation that includes most, if not all, of these factors. His tasks seem clear, requiring many skills, and feedback is readily gained through the completion of his work. He may be presumed to have a sizable amount of autonomy in allocating his time and deciding how to complete his work. Moreover, he has excellent relations with his co-workers and his employer. We know little about how meaningful he finds his job, but these factors alone set a fine stage for providing workers like Nick with job fulfillment and satisfaction.

The Organization

The organization for which an individual works also can be perceived as supportive of workers. If workers feel that the policies and procedures of their workplace indicate a concern about the welfare of the worker, the worker's job satisfaction is generally increased (Armstrong-Stassen & Ursal, 2009; McNall, Masuda, & Nicklin, 2010). In addition, if the organization provides the worker with perceived job security and adequate resources, such as materials, training, and sufficient personnel to do the job, the worker is more likely to be satisfied (Emberland & Rundmo, 2010; Karadal & Arasli, 2009; Sverke, Hellgren, & Näswall, 2002; Van den Broeck, Vansteenkiste, De Witt, & Lens, 2008). On the other hand, an organization that does not clearly define the role the worker must play (i.e., role ambiguity—"Do I have the responsibility of finding new clients or is that the territory of others?") or one which sometimes places the worker in a conflicted situation (i.e., role conflict—"Is the customer always right or do the interests of the company come first?") tends to have employees that have less commitment to the organization, are less satisfied with their jobs, and have more intention to leave the job (Antón, 2009).

Expectations

When we first take a job, we have certain expectations of what the job will entail, many of which are explicitly given to us by our new employers. Irving and Montes (2009), working with employees in Ontario, Canada, examined some of these expectations and their relationship to job satisfaction. They found that when employees were led to expect employer support (e.g., feedback, supervision, encouragement) and their expectations were met by the organization or even exceeded, job satisfaction was high. Intuitively this makes sense—if our expectations are met, we have the assurance that we are in the employ of an organization that keeps its word and there are few, if any, surprises. If our expectations are exceeded, we can only think "This is even better than I thought it would be!"

But when Irving and Montes (2009) examined expectations about skill development, a somewhat different picture emerged. Often, a potential employer will offer the inducement of providing training and/or opportunities for workers to develop and enhance work-related skills. When this expectation is met, job satisfaction is high. However, when the expectation is *exceeded*, with more opportunities for skill development than promised, job satisfaction decreases! Irving and Montes suggest that this might be because employees become overwhelmed and feel pressured by too many opportunities that they feel they are expected to take advantage of or that they feel coerced into doing so.

Similarly, the researchers found that when the salary received met the employees' expectations, satisfaction with the job tended to be high, but when the salary exceeded expectations, job satisfaction was lower. How strange! Who doesn't want more money? Irving and Montes can only speculate on this result and suggest that it may be that a higher-than-expected salary is accompanied by real or perceived higher-than-expected employer demands and expectations of the employee, a sometimes stressful and psychologically threatening situation.

Personal Characteristics Related to Job Satisfaction

The "Big Five"

So far we have been discussing factors external to the individual that affect job satisfaction. But the individual's own personality can make a difference as well. Research in personality has established that there are five traits that are present to some degree or another in all of us and from which many other traits derive (Goldberg, 1990). The "Big Five," as they are termed, are the following:

1. *Conscientiousness.* This refers to being responsible and reliable. People with high degrees of this trait also tend to be careful, thorough, and organized. They are hardworking generally, with a large amount of ambition, perseverance, and self-discipline.

2. *Extraversion.* Extraverted people are open, optimistic, and sociable. They are people-oriented and talkative, but they are also assertive. They tend to be ambitious and have a higher amount of desire for external rewards such as status, material gain, and recognition.

3. *Agreeableness.* As the term implies, agreeable people are trusting and cooperative. They are flexible, tolerant, soft-hearted, and good-natured. They tend to be forgiving, but they are also often gullible.

4. *Neuroticism.* Neuroticism in this context refers to the inclination to be low in emotional stability. People who are high on this trait are angry, hostile, anxious, and nervous. They may be impulsive, but they generally feel insecure and inadequate and are often embarrassed and self-conscious. They have a tendency to be depressed.

5. *Openness.* This trait refers to openness to experience. People with high degrees of openness are often creative and imaginative. They are curious about the world and they are broad-minded in their approach to it.

In a review and meta-analysis of the research done in the area, Bruk-Lee, Khoury, Nixon, Goh, and Spector (2009) report that, for the most part, the traits of conscientiousness, extraversion, and agreeableness have been found to be related to job satisfaction, and it is not difficult to see why: these traits suggest that people who possess them will make good employees and will be rewarded for their performance. They have the qualities to maximize the positive aspects of any situation, including a job, and to interact well with other people such as co-workers and supervisors. People high on neuroticism, though, typically report low job satisfaction, regardless of the job. Again, it is not difficult to see why: these people seem to put a negative spin on all elements of their world. Openness has not been generally found to be related to job satisfaction in all studies (although one must wonder whether a positive relationship would exist between openness and jobs that demand creativity).

Have you noticed that you are a slightly different person at work than you are at home? While we all have certain core personality traits that are seen in different situations, we use or emphasize different facets of our personalities depending upon the situation we are in. Heller, Ferris, Brown, and Watson (2009) obtained information from

Canadians and Americans that indicates that, at work, we tend to be more conscientious, more open to experience, and less extraverted than we are at home. Moreover, our work personalities predict our job satisfaction better than our overall personalities do. They found that people who are low in neuroticism, but high on extraversion, conscientiousness, openness, and agreeableness are more satisfied with their jobs, but the relationship is even higher if they bring these qualities to work. (Not unexpectedly, our home personalities predict marital satisfaction better than measures of our work personalities or our global personalities.)

We have only a brief description of Nick, but we can surmise that he is agreeable and probably quite extraverted, given his employer's and co-workers' positive evaluations of him. It's a good guess that he is conscientious: his clear enjoyment of his work and his eager anticipation of work challenges speak to that. And Nick's contented statement "Life is good" suggests that he is generally positive in his outlook in life. All in all, Nick seems to have many of the internal qualities that enhance his job satisfaction.

Emotional Intelligence

Given what we know about emotional intelligence (see Chapter 10), we would expect that people who are high in emotional intelligence would function better at work and get more enjoyment from it, at least in terms of getting along with clients/customers/patients, co-workers, and supervisors. We would also expect that since they are high in the ability to manage their own emotions, hence manage their stress levels, they would report a higher level of job satisfaction than people with lower levels of emotional intelligence. Our predictions are correct: the ability to regulate and use emotions and the ability to recognize other people's emotions are related to higher levels of job satisfaction (Güleryüz, Güney, Aydin, & Aşan, 2008; Kafetsios & Zampetakis, 2008; Lopes, Grewal, Kadis, Gall, & Salovey, 2006; Sy, Tram, & O'Hara, 2006). Kafetsios and Zampetakis (2008) also found that this is particularly true when events at work induce good moods, with relatively few events inducing negative emotions.

Group and Self-Efficacy

Along with autonomy and belongingness, self-determination theory contends that the third basic psychological need is for competence (Deci & Ryan, 2000; see Chapter 6). We need to feel that we can be effective in performing our jobs. Certainly this need can, at least in part, be fulfilled by an organization that gives us the resources to do our jobs, and this will typically leave us feeling more satisfied with our jobs (Emberland & Rundmo, 2010; Karadal & Arasli, 2009; Sverke, Hellgren, & Näswall, 2002; Van den Broeck, Vansteenkiste, De Witt, & Lens, 2008). Having competence includes feeling self-efficacy in our abilities to do the job, and this feeling of self-efficacy is positively related to our job satisfaction (Klassen, Usher, & Bong, 2010; Nielsen, Yarker, Randall, & Munir, 2009; Woolfolk & Davis, 2006). If we feel that we can do the job well, the job seems more satisfying to us.

In many cases, group or collective efficacy—the belief that the working group to which we belong is capable and effective in doing the job—is an additional factor in our job satisfaction. Klassen, Usher, and Bong (2010) studied the effect of efficacy on job satisfaction in teachers. Teachers from Canada, the United States, and South Korea who felt that teachers in general are effective in their work reported more individual job satisfaction.

This is particularly noteworthy because the same results were found in individualistic cultures (Canada and the United States) in which emphasis is put on individual achievement, and in a collectivist culture (South Korea) in which emphasis is placed on group achievement. We might expect that group efficacy would be more influential in increasing job satisfaction in a collectivist culture than in an individualistic culture, but such was not the case.

Interestingly, perceived job stress was related to lower job satisfaction in Canada and the United States, but not in South Korea (Klassen, Usher, & Bong, 2010). Perhaps, then, the perceived group efficacy was an ameliorating influence on the effects of stress for teachers in South Korea, and the emphasis on the group did pay off for the collectivist culture in that the teachers' own stress was not as important to them as their feeling that their own group of workers were making a difference.

Other Personality Factors

In addition to their examination of the relationships between the "Big Five" personality factors and job satisfaction, Bruk-Lee, Khoury, Nixon, Goh, and Spector (2009) also report that other personality traits are influential. Specifically, people who have an internal locus of control (believe that they control their own destinies), strive for achievement, and are in general positive in their outlooks report more job satisfaction than people who have low degrees of these qualities. But hostile, angry people and those who have an external locus control (believe that factors outside themselves control their destinies) have lower job satisfaction, as do those who tend to be manipulative and self-serving and, in the main, negative in their outlooks.

This isn't surprising, and these qualities in coworkers can affect our experience of satisfaction in the workplace too. Responsible, positive coworkers are more pleasurable to work with and can increase our satisfaction at work through providing us with enjoyable social relationships, more comfort and constructiveness by their style of giving feedback to us, and by their social skills and work ethic on teams. But sometimes negative people who don't take responsibility can make the workplace a toxic environment, full of discordant relationships, unnecessary harshness in delivering feedback, and resentment from those being supervised and fellow team members.

Increasing Job Satisfaction on an Individual Level

"But I can't change my personality!" some people cry. Perhaps that's not necessary. We have seen throughout this book that we *can* change the way we think about ourselves and the world. Proudfoot, Corr, Guest, and Dunn (2009) instituted a seven-week (21 hours) cognitive–behavioural therapy program for financial service sales agents to train them to recognize and change their negative and faulty work-related thoughts, attitudes, and behaviours.

For example, instead of saying to oneself "The boss ignored me just now. He hates me," the person would be coached to re-think this and recognize that it might be that the boss was preoccupied, felt stressed, or maybe just didn't have a lot of social skills. At the end of the seven weeks, and over the following four and a half months, participants in the program reported higher job satisfaction and showed higher productivity and lower levels of employee turnover. As an added benefit, the participants reported higher self-esteem and general psychological well-being as a result of the program. The same results were found for a second group of people that subsequently participated in the same program (Proudfoot, Corr, Guest, & Dunn, 2009). So maybe we can make our job satisfaction increase just by re-thinking our own behaviour. That sounds pretty hopeful!

Work Satisfaction vs. Work Performance

Naturally, employers want to know if more satisfied workers are actually better workers. That question may seem like an easy one to answer, but it is more complicated than it appears. Certainly we know that students who are satisfied with their academic programs tend to perform better academically (Wefald, & Downey, 2009), so it seems intuitively obvious that this relationship would also be found at the workplace: that people who are satisfied with their jobs also perform their jobs better. But the empirical evidence for this has been mixed (Judge, Thoreson, Bono, & Patton, 2001).

Edwards, Bell, Arthur, and Decuir (2008) suggest that this may be due, at least in part, to the fact that job performance is not a unitary concept and is comprised of two factors. The first factor is "task performance," which refers to the actual work done by the employee (e.g., teaching, road construction, farming, nursing, etc.). The second component is "contextual performance," which refers to worker behaviours that are in support of the effective functioning of the whole organization. These behaviours may include willingness to work overtime, helpful and pleasant attitudes toward co-workers and supervisors, and general defence of the organization's policies and goals.

Edwards and his colleagues found that there is a positive relationship between overall job satisfaction and both task performance and contextual performance, but different elements of job satisfaction are related to them. For example, people who are satisfied with the tasks they perform show better task performance, but not necessarily better contextual performance. Similarly, workers who are satisfied with their supervision show better contextual performance, but not necessarily better task performance. Task performance seems to be more related to how much workers like the tasks they perform, whereas contextual performance seems to be more related to the social interaction aspects surrounding the tasks. Clearly, employers would be wise to be attentive to both components of job performance to maximize their organization's productivity, and we, the workers, need to be aware that multiple facets of our work affect our own satisfaction and productivity.

REFLECTIVE EXERCISE

Job Satisfaction

How satisfied are you with your job or your school program? If you are satisfied, what factors make the job or program satisfying to you? That is, what is it that you like? If you are not satisfied, why not? What factors of the job or program decrease your satisfaction?

What about your internal factors? Do you have traits that might contribute to your job/program satisfaction or dissatisfaction? What conditions of your work or of yourself can you change that might increase your satisfaction? What can you do to make your working life better?

LEISURE

We don't spend all our time working and sleeping. We have some hours during the week when we can indulge in doing what we want. Leisure. Most of us wish we had more of it. There are millions of possibilities for our leisure time, and what we choose to do depends on our opportunities and our individual preferences. For some people, leisure time is used in passive activities such as watching television, listening to music, and sleeping. For others, more active pursuits, such as engaging in hobbies, sports, and exercise are chosen.

Among adolescents, males and females are involved in about the same number of hours of structured leisure activity, but girls are more likely to take part in creative activities while boys are more likely to participate in group physical activities (Fawcett, Garton, & Dandy, 2009). As young adults, males are more likely to engage in sports-related leisure activities while females engage in more social-related activities (Barnett, 2006). But no matter what the age, no category of leisure activity is engaged in by only one gender—we human beings have widely divergent interests.

Attitudes Toward Leisure

It is often taken for granted that attitudes towards leisure are straightforward and positive, but this is a little simplistic. Some people, for example, feel guilty about taking time for leisure activities, and others may find it downright sinful! In constructing a measurement scale for attitudes toward leisure and obtaining information from working people, Neulinger and Breit (2009) reported five relatively independent facets of attitudes toward leisure. The first factor is *affinity for leisure*, which includes indications of how long people believe they could stand living a life of leisure, whether they would want such a life for their children, and whether the individual would feel guilty living a life of leisure. The second factor encompassed *society's role in leisure planning.* This factor reflects people's perceptions of how much society encourages and supports leisure activities. The next factor, *self definition through leisure or work*, pertains to questions such as whether people feel that their leisure activities express their talents better than their jobs do and whether their leisure activities are more satisfying than their jobs. The fourth factor, *amount of perceived leisure,* taps the basic issue of whether people feel that they have enough leisure time, and the fifth factor, *amount of work or vacation desired,* examines how much leisure time people ideally want and how much of their time should be spent working.

Neulinger and Breit (2009) found that younger people had a higher affinity for leisure than older people, and people whose work can be classified as professional had a higher affinity than did non-professional people, such as clerical workers. In examining religion, the researchers found that Catholics indicated the least attraction to leisure, a result that was unexpected if there is indeed a "Protestant work ethic"! Younger rather than older people tend to define themselves through their leisure activities more than through their jobs, and professional people or people in prestigious occupations find their self-definition through work. Being younger may mean that one has not yet had the opportunity to obtain professional training or a professional job, so younger people, like those with less prestigious jobs, may find less meaning and fulfillment in their jobs.

Finding self-definition through leisure activities seems reasonable, then. This may also explain why younger people, as compared to older people, want to work less and play more. Women more than men report not having enough leisure time. Since Neulinger and Breit (2009) investigated working women, this result may reflect the fact that housework and childcare fall predominantly to women, employed or not, even in the twenty-first century. For women more than men, free time (i.e., time away from the job) is spent in domestic activities that should still be classified as "work," even if some of these activities are enjoyable to the individual.

Leisure Satisfaction and Life Satisfaction

That our leisure satisfaction is positively related to our happiness and life satisfaction is well-established. Nick, at the beginning of the chapter, provides an example of that. He loves his work, but he also loves his time at home with his family and the volunteer work he does. He looks forward to retirement, although he doesn't seem to want to rush it! Spiers and Walker (2009) found that both British Canadians and Chinese Canadians who were satisfied with their leisure reported more happiness, peacefulness, and a higher quality of life as indicated by their reports of their standard of living, personal health, achievement in life, personal relationships, personal safety, community connectedness, future security, and spirituality/religion.

In fact, what we do with our leisure time is related to how happy we feel with our lives. Tkach and Lyubomirsky (2006) found that people use leisure time activities deliberately to increase and maintain their happiness. But it seems that only the active pursuits are actually related to self-reported levels of happiness in life. Consistent with this are data obtained by Heo, Lee, McCormack, and Pedersen (2010). These researchers found that "serious leisure" was positively related to subjective well-being. "Serious leisure" refers to leisure activities that we pursue in a committed and systematic fashion. For example, becoming a proficient fly-fisher requires study, skill, and time. It would qualify as serious leisure. The rewards are personal gratification, enrichment, enhancement of self-esteem, and often social interaction and the feeling that one has been of service to others (e.g., as in many kinds of volunteer activities). Contrast this to "non-serious leisure" activities such as watching television, which are only rewarded by some distraction and perhaps some short-lived enjoyment. Couch potatoes don't seem to be increasing their subjective well-being by their choice of actions.

The Leisure of Retirement

Heo, Lee, McCormack, and Pedersen (2010) investigated the leisure time of older adults. Special attention has been paid to older adults because most of them are retired from the working world, and therefore most of their time is leisure. Making the transition from worker to retiree is difficult for many people. We who are still working may glorify the idea of retirement or regard the idea with distaste. As this chapter is being written, newspapers have been reporting massive national strikes and protest demonstrations in France where the age of retirement is being raised from 60 years to 62 years. In Canada, however, there was more pervasive approval when the mandatory age of retirement (65 years in most cases) was abolished and where the average age on retirement is 62 years!

Retirement may be involuntary, with workers forced to retire because of poor health or organizational downsizing. The transition to retirement may involve, then, a change that is unwelcome and brings negative feelings due to physical malaise or to loss of control, self-identity, social interactions, self-worth, and other psychological benefits of a job. The transition may also mean a substantially reduced income.

Or retirement may be voluntary and anticipated with delight. While many of the psychological benefits of a job may be lost and income may be reduced, it is still likely that the benefits, in terms of increased leisure, compensate more than adequately. In a study in Germany in which the researchers followed older adults for nineteen years, both before their retirement and after their retirement, Pinquart and Schindler (2009) found that most of their participants reported a steady moderate increase in their leisure satisfaction that started four years *before* they retired. This suggests that these people had begun to engage in leisure activities that they found enjoyable and meaningful prior to their retirement, perhaps in anticipation of their forthcoming retirement. As expected, their leisure satisfaction was positively related to their global life satisfaction.

Many retirees do not take on several new activities, but devote more time to activities that they enjoyed prior to retirement (Rosenkoetter, Garris, & Engdahl, 2001). Nimrod (2007) calls these people *concentrators.* But there are some people who can be termed *expanders*: they participate in more activities more often. Others are *reducers* who participate in the same or fewer number of activities as before their retirement, at the same or lower frequency, while other people Nimrod has called *diffusers*, those who engage in a larger number of activities at the same frequency or less often. In studying 430 American retirees, Nimrod, Janke, and Kleiber (2009) found that most people were reducers: that is, they continued with their pre-retirement activities at about the same rate even though they had more free time in their retirement. They reported a high sense of well-being in their lives, but not quite as high as concentrators, those people who increase the amount of time they spend on their pre-retirement pleasurable activities. Combining their results with the results of Nimrod's (2007) study of Israelis, the researchers conclude that the amount of change from pre-retirement engagement in leisure activities is not the important factor for retirees' sense of well-being; rather, the important factor is the frequency of participation, whether that includes a change in frequency or not. Noteworthy as well is their finding that there is a significant relationship between volunteering in a worthwhile endeavour and a subjective sense of well-being for these retirees. It seems that participating often in a meaningful activity is most adaptive for feeling satisfied with one's leisure and with one's life in general.

Our friend Nick's plans for his retirement include more time spent in an activity he had enjoyed but spent limited time with (kayaking), taking up formal study in a new interest (history), and increasing his volunteer participation in a meaningful organization (Big Brothers). The chances that he will have a highly satisfying retirement are good.

Leisure and Social Interaction

Much of the satisfaction we feel with our leisure pursuits comes from social interaction. Leisure activities that engage other known people (not necessarily in clubs or associations) seem to be more satisfying to us (Ateca-Amestoy, Serrano-del-Rosal, & Vera-Toscano, 2008). Lloyd and Little (2010) found that women's well-being was higher when engaging in leisure physical activity if social interactions were included.

Volunteering is one way of combining meaningful activity with social interaction, but it is not the only way. Schwartz and Campagna (2008) surveyed 100 men and women between the ages of 60 and 80 years in Brazil. All these people had participated in a once-a-week trekking activity in a forest near São Paulo for 10 weeks as part of an educationally-oriented program for older adults. Ninety-one of the 100 participants reported feeling positive about their experiences, saying that the trekking experiences had made them feel encouraged and excited, had given them a chance to learn new things, make new friends, and feel valued and important. The opportunity to be in contact with nature, they felt, increased their sense of personal worth and opened their minds to new perspectives. Clearly this activity was meaningful for them, and participation in it increased their psychological well-being, as well as, no doubt, their physical well-being. And a large part of the benefit was derived from the social experience of participating in this adventure together with like-minded others.

"The family that plays together, stays together" goes an old saying. Is it true? Yes and no. Decades of research have indicated that family leisure, whether of the everyday kind (e.g., watching movies together, preparing and eating meals together, playing board games, and so on) and of the more exceptional kind (family vacations, excursions to theme parks, special events, and so on) provide opportunities for family bonding, development of problem-solving and other life skills, and general strengthening of the family. It is expected and found that family leisure is related to satisfaction with family life (e.g., Freeman & Zabriskie, 2003; Zabriskie & McCormack, 2003). But simply spending time together in leisure pursuits isn't enough to account for a greater satisfaction with family life.

Agate, Zabriskie, Agate, and Poff (2009) found that parents' and children's *satisfaction* with family leisure was the important predictor of their overall satisfaction with family life. Clearly, spending time together is necessary to promote conditions for satisfaction with family leisure, but insisting that the kids spend time with the parents in a leisure activity they do not enjoy won't do the trick, nor will family satisfaction be increased if the parents spend time with the kids' favoured activities if the parents don't enjoy them. The time together may be there, but the satisfaction with the time isn't. (Note that Nick reports great satisfaction with his leisure time with his wife and children—a better recipe for success.) Similarly, Johnson, Zabriskie, and Hill (2006) found that, among married couples, the amount of time spent together or the type of activity engaged in together did not predict marital satisfaction, but satisfaction with their leisure time together did.

The Transition from Work to Leisure

It's not always easy making the transition from work to home and leisure activities. Some people bring their work home with them in terms of thinking about their work, especially work that needs to be done and problems that must be solved or are anticipated. That is, some people ruminate about their work even when they are at home. For them, the transition is only partial: their bodies may be at home, but their minds are still at work. Not being able to unwind after a working day brings problems: it is associated with sleep disturbances, cardiovascular disease, and mild depression (Cropley, Dijk, & Stanley, 2006; Nylen, Melin, & Laflamme, 2007; Pravettoni, Cropley, Leotta, & Bagnara, 2007). It seems harder to unwind after work if the job is demanding and the amount of control the worker has on the job is low (Cropley, Dijk, & Stanley, 2006). It can be especially difficult to unwind if the worker works from home—separating leisure and work is a real challenge if the home environment and the work environment are one and the same (Dart, 2006).

Cropley and Millward (2009) interviewed high ruminators and low ruminators, that is, people who had difficulty turning off thoughts of work when they came home and people who found the switching off to be easy. The first difference they found between high and low ruminators was their attitudes toward their work. Low ruminators (those who could switch off work-related thoughts easily) viewed their work as what they did to make a living, not as the most important component of their lives. In the researchers' words, they "work-to-live," as opposed to high ruminators (those who cannot switch off readily) who "live-to-work" (p. 338). Low ruminators were more detached from their work, whereas high ruminators were over-committed to it, taking much of their identity from it. In addition, low ruminators showed intrinsic motivation for their jobs, focusing on their internal satisfaction at doing their work well and feeling in control of their work, while high ruminators showed extrinsic motivation, focusing on their salaries and recognition from others.

A second difference that Cropley and Millward (2009) found was in the strategies that high and low ruminators used to cope with their work-related thoughts. Low ruminators drew very distinct lines between work and home, and limited or actively avoided thoughts of work. They interacted with others, such as their families, more and indicated that when they did talk about work they found it beneficial in helping them release work-related thoughts. On the other hand, high ruminators showed very blurred boundaries between work and home and found their work-related thoughts intrusive. They tended to withdraw from social interaction, feeling unable to concentrate on other people.

The third difference between high and low ruminators was the outcomes of their work-related thinking: high ruminators reported unfulfilling, unsatisfying leisure and high work–family conflict, whereas low ruminators found their leisure time to be fulfilling and enjoyable, with no conflict between their work and their home lives. It isn't difficult to see that Nick is a low ruminator.

REFLECTIVE EXERCISE

Leisure

What do you do with your leisure time? Many people find it difficult to answer this question. They may say, in a rather confused fashion, "Well, I don't get much leisure. When I come home from work, there always seems to be so much to do around the house. When I do get an hour or so to spare, I generally watch television." Other people may complain that they don't have enough time for all the work they do, but they spend excessive hours on hobbies, such as video gaming.

For a week or two, keep track of what you do with your leisure time. Do you have as much, less, or more leisure than you thought? Are you spending your leisure time the way you want to? Or does the time just pass by without any real awareness from you?

Do you have a hobby that absorbs you? If not, consider starting one. The internet is a good place to look for ideas. In fact, one website (www.notsoboringlife.com/list-of-hobbies) lists 238 different hobbies, some of which might intrigue you!

BALANCE

One way we can view the differences between the high and low ruminators in Cropley and Millward's (2009) study is in terms of balance. Low ruminators achieved a balance between their home lives and their working lives, while the high ruminators did not. Consistent with this is the study done by Boniwell, Osin, Linley, and Ivanchenko (2010). They found that British and Russian students who balanced their time between work and play had a greater sense of overall well-being. Similar results were found by Sheldon, Cummins, and Khamble (2010) who examined American and Indian students' time allocation. Moreover, these researchers found that when students were encouraged to balance their time allocation in accordance with what they felt would be ideal for their practical and psychological needs, their sense of well-being increased. Nick, the case at the beginning of this chapter, seems to be an expert at balance, a situation that feeds his life satisfaction greatly.

Obviously our feelings about our work and our leisure time have profound effects on our sense of well-being in our lives. "All work and no play makes Jack a dull boy," goes one old adage. On the other hand, the grasshopper who only played and never worked met with a tragic end in the fable that is so often told to children. Balance seems to be required. We hear about balance all the time. Balance is important to life satisfaction, as we have seen, and many people strive to achieve a balance among the different facets of their lives.

When I teach a course in stress management, I always have several students ask about how to achieve balance in their future lives as workers and as family people. There is no easy answer, but perhaps it's notable that, while this question is posed by many female students, I have never had a male student ask the question. Maybe this is because of a traditional gender role stereotype that inhibits men from asking about an area that implies they don't have all the answers (like the stereotypic idea that men never admit they are lost or ask for directions). Or perhaps it's because the idea of women in the workplace is still a non-traditional notion, with women feeling worry about taking on dual roles, while men are accustomed traditionally to one role, that of breadwinner. As we shall see in Chapter 13 of this book, women think more about home matters while at work than men do, one reason that employers who provide onsite daycare promote more satisfaction among their employees.

If we think about balance, we can see that we have already discussed some of the factors that are needed to attain it. We need to be able to regulate our thoughts and stop ruminating about work when we are at home and stop ruminating about home when we are at work. We need to be able to control where our attention is placed. This actually means that we need flexibility as well. Kashdan and Rottenberg (2010) make the point that psychological flexibility underlies our ability to function both at work and at home in an optimal and satisfying way. Change is a constant, in our lives and in society in general. Being psychologically flexible includes switching from one focus of attention to another; choosing our thoughts and behaviours to fit the situation we are in; seeing the world from the perspective of others as well as from our own perspective; interpreting events in a number of ways, not always relying on the interpretations that make us feel negative; and dealing with stress by using a number of strategies, not simply relying on one that may not always be effective. Being able to manage ourselves and our lives in a flexible manner increases our general self-efficacy as well. We feel assured that we can cope with whatever life brings our way, both at work and at home. Such assurance increases our sense of well-being and makes our lives happier and more fulfilling.

REFLECTIVE EXERCISE

Balance

How do you spend your time? How would you like to spend your time? Fill in the following chart to determine whether you have the balance you want in your life and to get an indication of where changes might be made.

Area of life	How you ACTUALLY spend your time	How you WOULD LIKE to spend your time
Sleeping & time in bed		
School (classes & studying)		
Paid work		
Household chores		
Community activities (clubs, groups, volunteering, etc.)		
Recreation (sports, TV, computer, music, etc.)		
Commuting (to and from work & school)		
Personal relationships		
Health and self-maintenance (exercising, eating, washing, etc.)		
Spirituality or religion (meditation, prayer, religious duties such as attendance at a place of worship, etc.)		
Other		
Total Hours	24	24

Source: Adapted from Sheldon, K. M., Cummins, R., & Khamble, S. (2010). Life balance and well-being: Testing a novel conceptual and measurement approach. *Journal of Personality, 78(4)*, p. 1133.

SAVOURING

Do you savour the moment? **Savouring** refers to an experience that includes being aware of what is happening in the moment, but it also includes an awareness of one's own experience and being fully engaged in the moment. It involves being fully present in the moment and examining the sensations and emotions that the moment brings.

On Sunday evenings when Nick says to himself "Life is good," it seems apparent that he is savouring the moment. Mindfulness is a required first step in savouring, that is, becoming completely aware of the experience of the moment. The second step is allowing oneself to feel and to examine all the sensations and emotions that accompany the experience. Savouring is full engagement of the entire mind with the moment. The Western conception of savouring emphasizes positive emotions, but in Chinese philosophy, both positive and negative experiences should be savoured (Bryant & Veroff, 2007; Sundararajan, 2008, 2010). We often don't attend to the moment, whether it's pleasant or unpleasant; our thoughts and our attention are elsewhere (see Kashdan & Rottenberg, 2010).

The broaden-and-build theory of positive emotions suggests that brief experiences of savouring positive experiences and emotions can build into more general positive emotions that in turn lead to other positive emotions and positive experiences. You can also access memories of the savouring positive experiences (mental "time travel"; Quoidbach, Berry, Hansenne, & Mikolajczak, 2010) and almost relive the pleasure, again increasing your positive emotions and making you more likely to experience more positive emotions in the future (Garland et al., 2010). Or you can capitalize on the memories, re-accessing them by telling other people about them. This seems to be the best strategy, as found by Quoidbach, Berry, Hansenne, and Mikolajczak (2010). One's perceived ability to savour the moment has been found to be related to lower levels of psychological and emotional disturbances (Bryant, 2003; Bryant & Veroff, 2007), and it's no wonder. When we learn to savour our positive experiences and emotions, to become more engaged in the moment, we become more attuned to the positives in our lives (Erisman & Roemer, 2010) and we are happier (Quoidbach, Berry, Hansenne, & Mikolajczak, 2010).

REFLECTIVE EXERCISE

Savouring

The next time you eat your favourite food, really taste it. What is the predominant taste? Shrimp? Chocolate? A good wine? Rice? What are the underlying tastes? Salty? Sweet? Spicy? Is there a hint of other flavours? Garlic? Mint? Berries? What does the food feel like in your mouth? Smooth? Crunchy? Creamy? Cold? Hot? How does it make you feel? Nostalgic? Amazed? Content? Discontent? Does it evoke memories? What are the memories? Are they pleasant or unpleasant? How do the memories make you feel? Happy? Sad? Amused?

You can savour many other experiences as well. Perhaps music is important to you, for example. Listen to your favourite music and perform the same exercise, listening to the overall melody, to the words of the song, to the individual contributions of each instrument. What feelings arise? What memories are evoked and how do those memories make you feel?

The experiences you savour need not be only those of a sensory nature. Remember the last time that something wonderful happened to you. A great mark on a test or essay? A kiss from a loved one? A promotion at work? Remember those experiences and how you felt when they occurred. And resolve to savour the next one.

FLOW

> "Wow! That is what it is like…wow! There is nothing that I have ever done in this world that has made me feel this way…You just feel good all over, especially inside…it's an unreal feeling."

> "In the zone is like you are in a different world all together. It's not like you are in this world at all. You just feel away. You feel far away from everything and everyone else…"

> "It's hard to describe, but it's almost like you are so completely wrapped up in what you are doing that your mind shuts itself off from anything else."

The quotations above are from skateboarders in St. John's, Newfoundland who were observed skateboarding and were interviewed about, in their terms, being *in the zone* (Seifert & Hedderson, 2010, pp. 279–285). In the terms of positive psychology, they are describing *flow*. The term *flow* was first coined by Mihaly Csikszentmihalyi (pronounced cheek-SENT-me-high) in 1975 in his book, *Beyond Boredom and Anxiety: Experiencing Flow in Work and Play* and made more popular by his 1990 book, *Flow: The Psychology of Optimal Experience*. **Flow** is a state in which people are intensely involved in an intrinsically motivated activity, losing sight of anything but that activity, and deriving much pleasure from it. When experiencing flow, people often move in and out of this state (Ceja & Navarro, 2009; Pearce, Ainley, & Howard, 2005).

The Components of Flow

Csikszentmihalyi conceptualizes flow as having nine components (Csikszentmihalyi, 1975, 1990; Nakamura & Csikszentmihalyi, 2009):

1. *Challenge–skill balance.* If the task is beyond our capabilities, we will probably experience frustration and anxiety. If the task requires far less than we are capable of, we will probably get bored. In neither case is flow likely to occur. But if the task requires the same level of skill that we have, or maybe just a little bit more that we can aspire to, at a moderate level of difficulty and complexity, balance is achieved, and the conditions for flow to occur are optimized.

2. *Merging of action and awareness.* As the quotations at the beginning of this section suggest, being in a state of flow involves immersing oneself in the activity, with the actions performed becoming spontaneous and automatic.

3. *Clarity of goals.* In a state of flow, we know exactly what it is we want to do. The goal is clear, the pathway to it is open, and we aim ourselves toward the goal surely and definitely.

4. *Unambiguous feedback.* In a flow state, we know exactly how we are doing in our progress toward the goal. Typically, the activity itself gives us feedback: we can see the steps forward that we are making, and we can see the goal coming ever closer.

5. *Concentration on the task at hand.* All our energy and concentration is directed toward the activity when we are "in the zone." We are not bothered by distractions, and, in fact, it may be rather difficult for others to capture our attention when our focus is so completely on the activity we are engaged in.

6. *Paradox of control.* Have you ever paid close attention to something that you normally do automatically, only to find that paying close attention disrupts your performance? People who think nothing of walking downstairs, for example, often fall when they start to pay close attention to the details of their walking (e.g., how they shift their weight, where they place their foot on the stair tread). The paradox is that we feel in control of those automatic actions, such as walking down the stairs, but as soon as we try to deliberately *take* control of the action, trouble ensues. In flow, people feel that they are control of the actions they are taking, but when they try to take control to maintain their flow state, flow vanishes.

7. *Loss of self-consciousness.* As the actions become automatic and spontaneous and the focus of attention becomes the activity itself, the individual in flow loses interest in the self. There is no embarrassment or concern about other people's opinions; there is only the activity. The doing and doer seem to meld into one.

8. *Transformation of time.* People who experience flow commonly lose track of time. Their focus on the activity is so intense that hours may go by without their being aware of it. This was the case with Nick, at the beginning of the chapter: he lost awareness of time at work and his co-workers often had to tell him that it was time to quit.

9. *The autotelic experience. Autotelic* is a word coined by Csikszentmihalyi (1990) from the Greek words for "self" and "goal." The autotelic experience that is a component of flow is intensely pleasurable, so much so that people are motivated to experience it again and again. In this way, the autotelic experience is intrinsically motivated. Csikszentmihalyi (1990; 1999) describes the *autotelic person* as someone who is intrinsically motivated and more likely to engage in activities that will be characterized by flow.

Evidence has been collected that is consistent with the role of many of the hypothesized components of flow. For example, Fullagar and Mills (2008) found that students with intrinsic motivation were more likely to experience flow in their academic work, especially if they also had a high need for autonomy. Similarly, Seifert and Hedderson (2010) concluded from their interviews with skateboarders that intrinsic motivation and autonomy were major factors that related to flow and the willingness to engage in new challenges. The importance of autonomy was also found in the flow experiences of customer service representatives in Taiwan (Kuo & Ho, 2010) and in working students (Fullagar & Kelloway, 2009). Certainly we can conclude that flow is associated with interest in the activity and with a perceived sense of control over what one is doing (Ainley, Enger, & Kennedy, 2008).

Attention has been paid to the challenge–skill balance as well. Generally it is found that when the task difficulty and the individual's skill level are matched, flow is more likely to result (Keller & Blomann, 2008). But there may be a catch: Engeser and Rheinberg (2008) found that when the task was not important, a balance of skill and challenge was more likely to lead to flow, but when the task was important, flow was more likely when skill exceeded challenge. It seems that with unimportant activities, we feel more comfortable and more inclined to experience flow if we feel that the activity will be "right up our alley"; but when the task is important, it may be that we feel a little anxious that our skills will fail us or turn out not to be up to the job. Even in tasks that are low in importance and where there is a balance between skills and challenge, people who have a fear of failure demonstrate a decreased likelihood of flow, while people with hopes of success have an increased likelihood of flow. Clearly the relationship between skills and challenge is a little more complicated than Csikszentmihalyi (1990) had first suggested.

Work resources, such as social support, innovative ideas, and clear goals, facilitate the experience of flow, but work-related flow also has a positive influence on personal and organizational resources. Salanova, Bakker, and Llorens (2006) found that teachers who experienced more flow had more self-efficacy and more work resources at their disposal, but they also created more work resources for others and found their personal resources, such as their feelings of self-efficacy, increased. This is supportive of the broaden-and-build theory we discussed in Chapter 5—the pebble thrown in the pond causes a ripple that spreads out.

In examining what leads to flow, we must attend to the individual's personality as well. While Fullagar and Kelloway (2009) found that the situation was more significant than personality characteristics in predicting flow, personality played a role as well. Csikszentmihalyi (1990, 1999) suggested that there is an **autotelic personality**, referring to traits that might predispose a person to experience more instances of flow than other people. The suggestion was that this person was characterized by persistence, lack of self-centredness, and a general curiosity and interest in life that would make him or her more likely to develop intrinsic motivation (Nakamura & Csikszentmihalyi, 2009).

This suggestion has received support from several studies. For example, Keller and Blomann (2008) demonstrated that people with a strong internal locus of control (i.e., people who believe that they are fully responsible for their destinies) were more likely to experience flow than those whose internal locus of control was weaker. People with an autotelic personality are also more likely to have better time management skills and to be more goal-directed (Ishimura & Kodama, 2009). They have higher self-esteem and lower anxiety than others, and they manage their stress with more active coping skills (Asakawa, 2010). As expected, they also have higher self-efficacy (Basom & Frase, 2004; Salanova, Bakker, & Llorens, 2006). In Taiwan, where meditation is a popular national activity, the amount of experience with meditation is related to the increased experience of flow (Kuo & Ho, 2010). We saw in Chapter 9 that meditation is an excellent technique for managing stress and in Chapter 3 that Eastern belief systems include meditation as a primary means of achieving enlightenment and tranquility. In light of this, it seems likely that the practice of meditation enhances and even develops other qualities, such as self-esteem and lower anxiety, that are related to flow.

The Benefits of Flow

What does flow do for us? Guo, Klein, Ro, and Rossin (2007) found that graduate students who experienced flow in their studies were more likely to have higher scores and more learning satisfaction. Consistent with this, Steele and Fullagar (2009) found that college students are more likely to experience flow when their professors support their autonomy and role clarity, a major component of which is constructive feedback on their work. The flow that these students experience then increases their feelings of psychological well-being, and through this, their physical health as well.

The positive relationship of flow to life satisfaction was found in Japanese college students as well (Asakawa, 2010). In senior adults, too, high quality flow is associated with greater life satisfaction (Collins, Sarkisian, & Winner, 2009). Flow doesn't just increase positive feelings; it decreases negative feelings as well, especially if the quality of the flow experience is high (Collins, Sarkisian, & Winner, 2009; Rogatko, 2009). As well, Ishimura and Kodama (2009) found that Japanese students described their flow experiences as being related to their personal growth and their self-advancement.

Demerouti (2006), Kuo and Ho (2010), and Engeser and Rheinberg (2008) also demonstrated that performance is more likely to be optimal when flow is present. Sometimes this effect is direct and sometimes it is indirect. For example, Schüler and Brunner (2009) found that marathon runners did not run faster when they experienced flow during a race, but flow did increase their motivation to run another race and to train for it. The extra training enhanced their running abilities, making their future performance better. This is undoubtedly the case in many other endeavours in which people experience flow: the flow experience may or may not directly improve their performance, but it acts as a powerful motivator to engage in the activity again and again, thereby improving skills that lead to improved performance. It comes as no surprise that the experience of flow is negatively related to procrastination (Lee, 2005)—we are less likely to procrastinate when we intensely enjoy the task and know that we do it well.

Flow may be experienced at work or at leisure, but a paradox exists: flow is higher at work, but subjective experiences of happiness are higher at leisure (Ceja & Navarro, 2009; Csikszentmihalyi & Lefevre, 1989; Rheinberg, Manig, Reinhold, Engeser, & Vollmeyer, 2007; and Schallberger & Pfiser, 2001, as reported by Nakamura & Csikszentmihalyi, 2009). It's possible that the cultural interpretation of "work" as a generally unenjoyable activity mitigates against people perceiving the happiness they actually have at work, or it may be that work provides the conditions for growth and long-term fulfillment, while leisure is a time of relieved stress and fun that is more likely to be interpreted as happiness (Nakamura & Csikszentmihalyi, 2009). From the description of Nick given earlier, it sounds as if he experiences more flow at work than at home, but there's a good chance he too would describe himself as happier at home.

REFLECTIVE EXERCISE

Flow

Have you ever experienced flow? What were you doing at the time? Was anyone with you? Have you tried to re-create the experience? Are there some activities that are more likely to result in flow for you than others? Keep track of your experiences of flow daily (there may be more than you think!) and determine what conditions are most likely to be present for you when flow occurs. Try to engage in these activities more often, and when you do, practise mindfulness and savouring: let your attention focus on what you are doing and really experience it!

SPOTLIGHT ON RESEARCH

Flow

Many young people spend hours on the internet, losing track of time, barely pausing to eat. Their enjoyment of the activity is surmised from this, and their task absorption suggests that they may be experiencing flow.

Zhao, Lu, Wang, and Huang (2011) were interested in examining factors that motivate adolescents to spend time surfing the internet. They believed that the easy answer ("Because it's fun!") had merit, but thought that other factors would be important as well. To research this, they created a survey that was completed by 3475 high school students in China. Their survey was comprised of selected questions from several previously well-validated surveys created by other researchers. In order to examine the experience of flow, they selected survey questions that focused on concentration on a task, forgetting where one is during the experience, and time distortion during the experience. Since the questions were originally in English, the questions were translated into Chinese and then back to English (by a different translator) to check the accuracy of the Chinese translation.

The researchers hypothesized that both enjoyment and curiosity would be positively related to flow state and to further exploratory behaviour on the internet. Their hypotheses were supported by the data, but interestingly, curiosity was more strongly related to further exploratory behaviour on the internet than enjoyment was.

What can we conclude from this study? First, as the researchers themselves point out, the participants of this study may not be representative of all adolescents in China. Certainly there are differences between these students and students in the West. For one thing, only a minority of Chinese households have computers, and only a small portion of these have access to the internet. It may be that for adolescents for whom the internet is more available (such as those in the West), curiosity is more readily satisfied and enjoyment is more strongly related to exploratory behaviour on the internet and, possibly, to the experience of flow. Also, since enjoyment and curiosity were the only factors assumed to be directly related to the experience of flow, we must wonder whether another factor, such as open-mindedness, might be even more strongly predictive of flow.

Note as well that while the researchers performed sophisticated statistical analyses of their data, the data are based on self-reports, which may not always reveal the true feelings or experiences of the participants. Additionally, as sophisticated as they are, the statistical analyses reveal correlations, and correlations do not imply causality. Thus we cannot rightfully conclude that enjoyment and curiosity cause flow, only that they are predictive of a flow experience.

One other question arises in this study: did the researchers really examine the experience of flow? Their survey questions attended to only some of the components of flow that Csikszentmihalyi (1975, 1990) posited, components that certainly suggest absorption in an activity, but not necessarily flow.

Conclusion

Do you languish or do you flourish? Barbara Frederickson and her colleagues (Frederickson, 1998; Frederickson & Losada, 2005) see **languishing** as feeling hollow and empty in life, with little flexibility of thought or action, and generally having few positive emotions. **Flourishing**, though, is characterized by creativity, social connectedness, resilience, and few negative emotions. Nick, who we met at the beginning of the chapter, is flourishing. Our jobs and our leisure activities, and more importantly, how we feel about them, contribute greatly to whether we languish or flourish in life.

It's reasonable to suppose that we all want to flourish and feel the satisfaction and fulfillment that a job well done and an enjoyable playtime can bring. The responsibility for this is mainly our own, in the attitudes and self-statements we make. But it is not completely our responsibility. Some jobs are almost soul-crushing because of the conditions that are imposed upon workers. Some communities provide little in the way of opportunities for leisure activity. And of course a number of factors, such as a low level of education, low income, and lack of ability to speak the local language, can mean little choice in jobs and little time or money for recreation. In Chapter 13 we will examine some of these problems and how some organizations are working to correct them. When the individual balances life with flexibility in allocating time and resources to work and leisure, and views both with enthusiasm, optimism, and feelings of self-efficacy, *and* when resources and support are provided in the work environment and in society, the chances of flourishing, like Nick, are increased.

Summary

- Jobs provide us with money, social interactions, opportunities to use our skills and learn new ones, and to develop personally with valuable experiences.
- The Job Characteristics Model states that skill variety, task identity, task significance, feedback, and autonomy affect feelings about a job and behaviour on the job.
- Workers who have more autonomy in their work hours and the way they do their work have more job satisfaction.
- Having good social relationships at work adds to job satisfaction. Supervisors who give constructive criticism, encouragement, support, and help in regulating negative emotions enhance workers' job satisfaction, while political, manipulative, and self-serving supervisors decrease workers' satisfaction.
- If workers feel that their workplace indicates a concern about their welfare, the worker's job satisfaction is generally increased. If the organization provides perceived job security and adequate resources, the worker is more likely to be satisfied. But if the organization does not provide role clarity, or provides role conflict, less satisfaction results.
- When employees are led to expect employer support and their expectations are met or exceeded by the organization, job satisfaction is high, but when the expectations for salary or skill development opportunities are exceeded, job satisfaction decreases.
- Both individual self-efficacy and group efficacy are positively related to job satisfaction.
- In general, people who enjoy their tasks at work perform these tasks better.

- People who have higher levels of conscientiousness, extraversion, and agreeableness and low levels of neuroticism are more likely to have job satisfaction, as will those with an internal locus of control and a high degree of emotional intelligence.
- Younger people have a higher affinity for leisure than older people, and professional people have a higher affinity than non-professional people. Younger people tend to define themselves through their leisure activities more than through their jobs, and professional people or people in prestigious occupations find their self-definition through work.
- People who are satisfied with their leisure report more life satisfaction than do others, but only active or serious leisure seems to have this effect.
- For retirees' sense of well-being the important factor is the frequency of leisure activities participation. There is a significant relationship between volunteering and a subjective sense of well-being for retirees.
- Leisure activities that engage other known people seem to be more satisfying.
- Satisfaction with leisure time predicts satisfaction with family and marital life.
- High ruminators find it harder to make the transition from work to home.
- Low ruminators "work-to-live" whereas high ruminators "live-to-work." Low ruminators are more detached from their work, whereas high ruminators are over-committed to it, taking much of their identity from it. Low ruminators show intrinsic motivation for their jobs, while high ruminators show extrinsic motivation. Low ruminators draw clear boundaries between work and home and find their home life more satisfying.
- Subjective well-being is increased when the individual balances work and play. Balance requires regulated thought and emotions and flexibility.
- Savouring refers to an experience that includes being aware of what is happening in the moment, an awareness of one's own experience, and being fully engaged in the moment. Perceived ability to savour the moment has been found to be related to lower levels of psychological and emotional disturbances.
- Flow is a state in which people are intensely involved in an intrinsically motivated activity, losing sight of anything but that activity and deriving pleasure from it.
- Flow has challenge–skill balance, merging of action and awareness, clarity of goals, unambiguous feedback, concentration on the task at hand, paradox of control, loss of self-consciousness, transformation of time, and the autotelic experience.
- Intrinsic motivation and autonomy are major factors contributing to the likelihood of a flow experience. Work resources also contribute.
- The person who is more likely to experience flow typically has a strong internal locus of control, better time management skills, higher self-esteem, and more self-efficacy. This person also has active stress management skills and is more goal-directed than others.
- Flow increases one's sense of well-being, increasing positive emotions and decreasing negative emotions. It directly or indirectly leads to improved performance.
- Flow is higher at work, but subjective experiences of happiness are higher at leisure.
- Jobs and leisure activities, and how we feel about them, contribute greatly to whether we languish or flourish in life.

Group Discussion Questions

1. At present, few employers take note of the happiness or satisfaction of their employees. Why might this be the case? Would it be beneficial for them to do so? If so, how might they be encouraged to allocate resources to improve their employees' job satisfaction? Are there cases in which this can't be done?

2. Vacation time is an important part of most employees' jobs, but the time allotted for vacations is limited. How might a vacation package be structured to allow the maximum benefit of leisure to employees?

3. Are there any disadvantages to achieving flow in one's endeavours? What might they be? Are they disturbing enough to discourage the attainment of flow in some situations?

CHAPTER 12

Community, Milieu, and Culture

Jeyani's parents emigrated to Canada from India when Jeyani was nine years old. They worked very hard to establish a prosperous life for themselves and their children, but it wasn't easy. Their professional credentials were not accepted readily in Canada, and they had to take jobs beneath their educational levels, but today, fourteen years later, they live in an affluent neighbourhood.

They feel partially integrated into a wider Canadian society, but they maintain most of their social ties with the Indian community in the large

city in which they live. They want Jeyani and her younger brother to be part of the Western world, but they don't want them to lose the traditional Indian values that have been so enriching to them, and they fear for Jeyani's well-being in what they see as a very permissive society.

Jeyani loves and admires her parents, but sometimes she chafes under the restrictions they impose on her. As a child, she wasn't permitted the freedom her schoolmates had, and she still wishes she had been allowed to go to sleepovers and, most of all, later, to date. But school was fun and she excelled, especially, she believes, because of caring teachers.

Although she has successfully completed a university degree and holds a professional job, she feels that they still treat her like a child sometimes, and she notes that her brother is given much more freedom and less work than she is. Housework chores fall to her, and she sometimes resentfully thinks that her brother is treated like a prince who expects to be served rather than helping to clean and cook. Yet she knows that the values of her traditional parents mean that her brother will have more responsibility for her family's welfare in the future than she does. She doesn't want to lose the values of her ethnic background, but many times, she feels like a woman who is torn between two worlds.

LEARNING OBJECTIVES

In this chapter, students will learn about

- ☐ Social identity and social identity theory.
- ☐ The role of the neighbourhood in feelings of well-being.
- ☐ What constitutes a good school and its effects on young people.
- ☐ The role of urban vs. rural life in well-being.
- ☐ National factors that have an impact on individual well-being.
- ☐ The stresses of immigration and the factors that increase immigrants' sense of well-being.
- ☐ The role of culture in feelings of well-being.
- ☐ The multicultural personality.

Jeyani's feeling of being torn between two worlds is not unusual. She has been raised in a traditional Indian home, but in Canada where she is exposed to Western values and norms. Her sense of herself is informed by both Indian and Canadian viewpoints, and sometimes they clash. Her parents, as well, experience the clash and worry about their children's ability to negotiate the difficulties of maintaining a balance between the cultures.

Jeyani, like all of us, is affected not only by her parents' values, but also by the values held by the wider culture in which she lives. Her neighbourhood, her schools, her workplaces, and the country she lives in all have an input into her identity and her viewpoints.

We discussed the effects of close relationships in the last chapter, but now we must turn to the effects of the wider community in examining how our life satisfaction is influenced.

SOCIAL IDENTITY THEORY

It is a truism to say that human beings are social creatures. Whether we are introverted or extraverted, the fact still remains that we live in communities of other people, be they family, friends, co-workers, acquaintances, or strangers. We belong to some groups as a matter of our genetic endowments (e.g., male or female, tall people or short people), as a matter of choices made for us by our parents (e.g., raised in suburban Toronto, Canada), and as a matter of the choices we make for ourselves (e.g., a member of the high school swim team). When we describe ourselves, we typically make note of these group memberships. Jeyani might say, for example, "I am an Indian-Canadian woman who was raised in both India and Toronto, and I have a degree from Ryerson University in business." Our group membership forms part of our identity, a **social identity**, which can be defined as both the knowledge of belongingness to and value for certain social groups.

Social identity is important to us because belonging to groups increases our social relationships, a critical part of our life satisfaction, as well as providing us with information and sometimes the means to achieve our goals. Group membership also often has the effect of increasing our self-esteem and helping us create meaning in our lives. **Social identity theory** notes our tendency to define ourselves in terms of the groups we belong to and suggests that our well-being is often dependent on the groups that we define ourselves by. If our defining groups are those that provide us with a sense of groundedness and stability, as well as purpose and direction, they will typically have a beneficial effect on our satisfaction with ourselves and our lives. If, however, they have negative connotations to us and to the rest of society, our feelings of self-worth and fulfillment with life may be diminished.

For Jeyani, belonging to the group of business graduates from Ryerson University may give her a feeling of accomplishment and connection with other Ryerson University graduates and other graduates of business programs. If, on the other hand, she had failed at university and been asked to leave, she might feel that belonging to the group of "failures" (an unjust characterization since there are many valid reasons why a person may fail at university) indicates that she is an inadequate person in some respects.

Social identity theory goes on to state that if the group to which one belongs is seen as having permeable boundaries (i.e., one can escape from it), people may take action to leave it or change it (Haslam, Jetten, Postmes, & Haslam, 2009). Groups such as Jeyani's Indian-Canadian group are both permeable and impermeable: nothing can change her Indian heritage, although she may change the "Canadian" part by emigrating to another country and attaining citizenship there. Jeyani sees her Indian social identity as positive, but if she didn't, she might take action to see it in a more positive light or work within her Canadian society to raise its visibility and value to the wider community.

Such action can be seen in the group of people who have mental disorders: in most communities, these groups have been involved in excellent efforts to educate society in understanding that stereotypes, fears, and ridicule are inaccurate, unjust, and inappropriate. By doing so, social identity theory would postulate that the diminished self-worth that might accompany membership in this group would be alleviated, and this has been found to be the case (see, for example, the documentary *Working Like Crazy*, 1996, about a group of people with psychological disorders who have developed and staffed their own businesses).

Haslam and his colleagues (2009) point out that, when groups are impermeable, it may be that people in these groups take on the characteristics of stereotypes that the wider society has, and this becomes part of their social identity. Thus, a person reaching the age of 65 years, now labelled by society as a "senior citizen," may begin to think of himself/herself as old or elderly and may then begin to act in ways that he/she regards as old, reducing physical activity unnecessarily and to the detriment of health, and deciding that he/she is too old to learn.

In actual fact, of course, the line between middle-aged and old is meaningless, as we see people in their 40s and 50s who may have physical disabilities and rigid thought patterns that have been erroneously associated with old age, and active, lively people in their 70s and 80s (or older!) whose viewpoints and thoughts are fresh and flexible, thought to be more characteristic of the young. It is easy to see that any of us may reduce our life satisfaction and our fulfillment in life if we believe negative stereotypes about the impermeable groups we belong to. We must be aware, then, that social identity has a strong bearing on our ability to cope with stressors and to have a satisfying life.

THE NEIGHBOURHOOD

One of the groups we belong to is the neighbourhood we live in. This is a permeable group for many adults who choose where they want to live, but it may be at least temporarily impermeable for children and for adults who have financial or other limitations. Neighbourhoods can be vital, interactive communities in which neighbours know each other and look out for each other, taking part in activities such as block parties, fairs, and other events. They may have community centres for these activities and many others in which people may gather to socialize, inform, and make decisions together regarding the community. Other neighbourhoods, however, may be characterized by impersonality and mistrust, where violence, vandalism, and other distressing events are commonplace. In the face of disaster, such as Hurricane Katrina, the quality of a neighbourhood may even affect whether and how well a community can recover (Norris, Stevens, Pfefferbaum, Wyche, & Pfefferbaum, 2008).

Defining a Good Neighbourhood

Specifically, what qualities does a "good" neighbourhood have? Burke, O'Campo, Salmon, and Walker (2009) asked this question of people in Toronto and found that people described six distinct clusters of qualities: (1) necessary human and social services (e.g., churches, libraries, fire department); (2) neighbourhood support for each other (e.g., safety, privacy, cleanliness, sense of community); (3) green area and natural environment (air quality, parks, gardens); (4) social makeup of people in the neighbourhood (e.g., average education levels, average income, well-maintained homes); (5) neighbourhood affordability (e.g., good schools, accessible and affordable parking, restaurants, and shopping); (6) negative community factors (e.g., low violence, low noise, few aversive smells).

Burke, O'Campo, Salmon, and Walker (2009) found that people from lower socioeconomic groups felt that necessary human and social services in a neighbourhood were most important to individuals' psychological well-being, while people in higher socioeconomic groups felt that neighbourhood support for each other was the most important factor. It may be that people in higher socioeconomic groups rate access to human and social services lower because, having more money, they can purchase or avail themselves of more of these services without the community providing them (e.g., rehabilitative programs), and because they have less need of some of the services (e.g., employment training programs, public transportation).

Similarly, Sylvie Jutras and Geneviève Lepage (2006) at the Université du Québec à Montréal asked Francophone parents how their neighbourhood contributed to their children's psychological wellness. Their answers revealed their perceptions that a neighbourhood most conducive to their child's psychological well-being was one characterized by child-friendliness (e.g., playgrounds, other children, proximity to parks, recreation centres), environmental amenities (e.g., space, cleanliness, landscape), and the presence of cordial and supportive neighbours, with low social disorder. The researchers were struck by the way the parents' answers reflected how a neighbourhood may contribute to a child's positive self-identity in giving children a feeling of safety and security in which to explore and grow and to develop skills, self-efficacy, and self-esteem.

People's opinions about what makes a good neighbourhood seem to be supported by other research. Farrell, Aubrey, and Coulombe (2004) found that in Winnipeg, Manitoba, people who felt a sense of community in their neighbourhoods had a higher sense of well-being. They also found that a sense of community is mediated by marital status and stability. This means that neighbourhoods that have many people who stay in the neighbourhood for a length of time are more likely to develop a sense of community: people become more attached to their neighbourhoods over time, the neighbourhood becomes a large part of who and what they are, and their social identities become tied to the neighbourhood, at least in part. Another community factor that facilitates community activity and promotes social relationships among neighbours is the presence of trees and grass (Sullivan, Kuo, & DePooter, 2004). Nature, it seems, invites us to see our neighbourhoods as personal communities.

Effects of the Neighbourhood

One relationship that has been studied is between the perceived quality of a neighbourhood and people's physical health. Since feeling physically well is a large component of overall life satisfaction, the impact of a neighbourhood may be seen through this relationship. Bisegger, Cloetta, Ravens-Sieberer, and members of the European KIDSCREEN Group (2008) developed a scale to measure this and found that adolescents who perceived their neighbourhoods as safe, quiet, and clean, with places and opportunities to engage in leisure activities, had a higher health-related quality of life than did adolescents whose neighbourhoods did not have these elements.

Zhang, Chen, McCubbin, McCubbin, and Foley (2011) also found a relationship between neighbourhood and physical health. They surveyed people in Hawaii and found that the average level of education in a neighbourhood is related to physical well-being. The investigators believe that more educated people in a neighbourhood tend to put more effort into making the neighbourhood a safe and pleasant place to engage in leisure activities that may improve their health: for example, when the neighbourhood is safe and clean, people are more likely to go out for walks or to run or jog in the area, thus promoting physical health. This interpretation is supported by evidence obtained by Sugiyama, Leslie, Giles-Corti, and Owen (2009) in Australia, and Stronegger, Titze, and Oja (2010) in Austria.

The effects of the neighbourhood, especially disadvantaged neighbourhoods, on children and adolescents have been of particular concern in research. One examination of positive neighbourhoods is the work of McGrath, Brennan, Dolan, and Barnett (2009), who found that neighbourhood quality of life was positively associated with adolescents' well-being in Ireland, but not in Florida where factors such as father having a job and being bullied in school were more influential. This seems to reflect the socio-logical differences between the two locations: in Ireland, for example, 84 percent of the adolescent participants lived with both parents. In contrast, only 54 percent of the Florida youth lived with both parents.

More research has centred on the effects of lower-quality neighbourhoods on children's mental and physical well-being. Neighbourhoods characterized by economic disadvantage and social disorder increase the likelihood of emotional and behavioural problems in young children (Caspi, Taylor, Moffitt, & Plomin, 2000; Ingoldsby et al., 2006). Such neighbourhoods provide a climate of stress for their inhabitants. Families living in these neighbourhoods are often under individual stress as well, as they cope with financial uncertainty and the conditions that led to this uncertainty (e.g., unemployment, mental or physical disability, substance abuse). Their children are at risk for psychological and behavioural problems partly because the degree of stress on the parents decreases the likelihood that they will parent in a positive manner (De Marco & De Marco, 2010; Kotchick & Forehand, 2002). The children's psychological well-being is therefore impaired.

Lima, Caughy, Nettles, and O'Campo (2010) wondered if elements of the neighbour-hood could affect this; that is, specifically, would neighbourhood negative social climate exacerbate the problems of negative parenting in already-high risk families? Would the negative social climate of the neighbourhood further impair the psychological well-being of the child? They found that in communities where people were afraid of retalia-tion or victimization and where the neighbourhood was characterized by physical and/or social disorder (e.g., trash, graffiti, abandoned cars, gangs, and drug dealers), the psy-chological well-being of children living in high-risk homes was further decreased, beyond the effects of the risks within the family constellation.

Similarly, Leventhal and Brooks-Gunn (2000), in a review of the literature of the effects of neighbourhoods on children and adolescents, concluded that neighbourhoods like Jeyani's—which have resources such as good schools and daycares, opportunities for supervised recreational activities, and involved neighbours who monitor and work to decrease disordered activity in children and the community in general—provide the greatest positive influence on the development and well-being of children.

While most of the research has been done in the United States, Kohen, Brooks-Gunn, Leventhal, and Hertzman (2002) found similar results for young children across Canada: children were more likely to have lower verbal competency and to show more behav-ioural problems in neighbourhoods characterized by few affluent neighbours, high unem-ployment rates, and low social cohesion. In a nutshell, living in a negative, poor-quality neighbourhood is associated with decreased well-being for children and adolescents and even worse problems for a child who is already coming from a high-risk family.

Deleterious effects of a poor-quality neighbourhood are not limited to children. Warr, Feldman, Tacticos, and Kelaher (2009) found that neighbourhoods that are perceived as unsafe and insecure are predictive of decreased feelings of physical health and physical well-being in adults in Australia, for example. Moreover, people living in poor-quality neighbourhoods who feel that other people stigmatize the neighbourhood, giving it a reputation of being dangerous and uncivil, report having poorer physical well-being and lower life satisfaction (Kelaher, Warr, Feldman, & Tacticos, 2010). Kelaher and her colleagues suggest that stigmatization of one's neighbourhood provides a threat to one's social identity, increasing the stress upon an individual, thereby leading to reduced physical and psychological well-being.

In general, then, we can see that the research evidence suggests that when we live in neighbourhoods that are of higher quality, we feel comfortable taking part of our social identity from the neighbourhood, and our general well-being increases. We feel that we belong, and we can enjoy our community and our neighbours who will be positive presences in our lives. But when the neighbourhood is unsafe and unpleasant or is stigmatized by others as being disagreeable, taking our social identities from this may not be so desirable. Then our sense of well-being is diminished—indeed, many residents may actually wish to leave the neighbourhood at the first possible opportunity.

This idea is further strengthened by research done by Pickett and Wilkinson (2008) on ethnic density. These researchers noted that while living in a poor neighbourhood is associated with poorer physical and psychological well-being, this does not seem to be the case in poor neighbourhoods populated by a higher proportion of members of the same minorities. In urban centres in particular, it is often found that people belonging to the same ethnic or racial groups live in the same neighbourhood. Even when the group is considered low status by others (i.e., is stigmatized) and even when the group members are very financially disadvantaged, the neighbourhood provides acceptance and support from others within the same group. The individual's social identity is made up in part by identification with their racial or ethnic group, an impermeable boundary. While this group may meet with harassment, discrimination, condescension, and rejection from other groups, individuals within the neighbourhood are within their own group, a group that will not reject or demean them, a group in which they may feel the comfort of being at home. It is no wonder that there have been calls for positive psychology to join in the effort to promote wellness within communities (Schueller, 2009).

REFLECTIVE EXERCISE

Your Neighbourhood

What kind of neighbourhood did you grow up in? Would you say that it promoted your well-being or diminished it? What factors in particular would you say were beneficial or detrimental to you?

What about the neighbourhood you live in now? Does it contain elements that might be beneficial or detrimental to you? Take a walk around the neighbourhood and note its good and bad factors. What do you think a perfect neighbourhood would be like for you? What elements would be important to you?

SCHOOLS

As we have seen, part of what people consider a good neighbourhood includes the proximity of good schools. Many people select the neighbourhood they will live in on the basis of the availability of a good school for their children. This seems entirely reasonable: after all, children spend a large part of their day for years in schools, and the education they receive there is critical to the quality of the rest of their lives. In today's technological age in particular, education is lifelong. We want our children to not only learn what they will need for a successful life, but we want them to enjoy the learning process and embrace the joy of learning. We also want them to increase their social network and learn to function well in groups, as well as learn the values and expectations of the larger society. These are clearly other aspects of the school situation. As Herman, Reinke, Parkin, Traylor, and Agarwal (2009) point out, school factors greatly influence the child's developing sense of identity. School situations provide chances for a child to develop a sense of competence, autonomy, self-control, and relatedness. Children's adaptation to the school environment and the success or failure experiences therein will greatly affect the way they come to view themselves and the world they live in, determining to a large degree whether a child will feel optimistic and hopeful or pessimistic and despairing, setting the stage for a satisfying or an unsatisfying life.

What Constitutes a "Good" School?

A great deal of attention has been paid in research to what makes a school one in which children will thrive and feel satisfaction with their educational experience and with their lives in general. Saab and Klinger (2010) studied over 9600 Canadian children in grades 6 to 10 and found that children who attended schools with a higher-income population had greater emotional well-being than children from schools in neighbourhoods with lower incomes, even if the income of the child's own family was lower. The researchers concluded that the school culture created by a higher-income neighbourhood was beneficial for children beyond their families' financial situation. Again we see that living in a poor neighbourhood, as reflected by the population of a school and the culture created by it, may have deleterious effects on a child's sense of well-being.

In studying over 400 children in grades 1 to 10 in Norway, Løhre, Lydersen, and Vatten (2010) found that for boys, enjoying school work and knowing that they would receive the help they might need from teachers were the critical factors in their school well-being. For girls, one factor stood out as decreasing their school well-being: being bothered during their lessons. May one also conclude that the girls in this study were not being well-supported by their teachers who did not seem to be addressing the girls' complaints of "being bothered"? In Finland, as well, perceived help and support from teachers were found to be important factors in children's sense of general well-being (Konu, Lintonen, & Rimpelä, 2002).

The factor of teacher support for the student has been found to be overwhelming for a child's or adolescent's feelings of school well-being and overall satisfaction with their lives. Basing their conclusions on a study interviewing students, parents, teachers, and administrators in Scotland, Spratt, Shucksmith, Philip, and Watson (2006) noted that children and adolescents repeatedly referred to the importance of their relationships with teachers in their satisfaction with school, a factor echoed by teachers, many of whom entered the profession in part because they wanted to interact with and support children.

Similarly, social support from teachers was found to increase Norwegian students' self-reported happiness significantly (Natvig, Albrektsen, & Qvarnstrøm, 2003). This result was also found in Australian students who were in the senior years of their schooling (Gray & Hackling, 2009) and in American students for whom well-being was strongly related to perceived support from teachers and other school personnel, a relationship that increased over time (Chu, Saucier, & Hafner, 2010). Jeyani certainly credits her pleasure in school to the presence of caring teachers who, we may assume, supported and encouraged her and helped her achieve academic success.

Another factor in school satisfaction is school connectedness (Frydenberg, Care, Freeman, & Chan, 2009). **School connectedness** refers to the degree to which children feel themselves to be a part of the school community that accepts, values, and supports them. Being a member of this community is part of the individual's social identity and is promoted by the relationships students have with teachers and other school personnel, as well as with their schoolmates. Lack of such connectedness has been found to be related to depression and lack of well-being in high school students (McGraw, Moore, Fuller, & Bates, 2008).

Gray and Hackling (2009) reported on the initial stages of their Australian study regarding senior students' well-being in their final years of high school. Student retention and completion of secondary school is of concern in Australia, as it is in many countries. Gray and Hackling administered surveys and talked with 255 senior students to determine what they perceived as critical to success and completion in secondary school and found a strong relationship with students' feelings of being connected to their school and their academic achievement: students whose identity included their sense of belonging to their school had higher marks and were more likely to complete their secondary school education. Their feelings of connectedness and their satisfaction with school, they felt, were partly determined by the level of respect they felt their school culture gave them.

In fact, for these students, mutual respect was a key factor. This mutual respect, they said, gave them the courage to take the risks in attempting courses and planning their futures. They did not want their courses to be made overly easy because they felt that this would show a lack of respect for their intelligence and their work ethic. They believed that the support of their teachers was vital to their engagement in their school-work and in their ability to learn and succeed. Moreover, they especially valued teachers who gave them responsibility for their own learning and allowed them to be active decision-makers in how they would learn. Gray and Hackling (2009) concluded that senior students value three dimensions as being crucial to a supportive school environment: respect, relationship, and responsibility.

In Chapter 13 we will examine some schools that are trying to provide experiences for their students that will maximize their well-being and academic success, while addressing their social and emotional needs, with the aim of helping them become responsible, purposeful adults who enjoy their lives and contribute to the welfare of society.

CITY

People have different levels of life satisfaction depending on what city they live in as well (Morrison, 2007), but exactly what factors determine this are largely unknown.

It has been hypothesized historically that living in the city may bring greater economic opportunities, but the price of this is increased isolation, alienation, impersonality, and stress (Berry & Okulicz-Kozaryn, 2009), but is this true today? Would Jeyani and her family have been happier living in a smaller centre? Maybe or maybe not, say Berry and Okulicz-Kozaryn (2009). Their research, based on statistical data from the World Values Survey, "a worldwide network of social scientists studying changing values and their impact on social and political life" (www.worldvaluessurvey.org), finds that when 97 societies containing almost 90 percent of the world's population are regarded overall, there is essentially no difference in life satisfaction between city and rural living.

But a more fine-grained analysis indicates that in societies that are more affluent (i.e., the per capita gross domestic product exceeds $10,000), living in more rural regions is positively related to greater life satisfaction. In societies of lower affluence, Berry and Okulicz-Kozaryn (2009) conclude, happiness is dependent on individual factors, not the place of residence in terms of urban versus rural. Canada and the United States, for example, show among the lowest levels of disparity in life satisfaction between people living in urban centres and people living in rural areas. So whether Jeyani and her family would be happier living in a smaller centre than the large centre they presently live in would depend on their own preferences. But if they did decide to move to a "happier" location, they might want to look at Box 12.1, which shows the "happiest" cities.

BOX 12.1

The Happiest Cities

According to data gathered by Statistics Canada and published in the *Edmonton Journal*, the Canadian cities with the most satisfied residents are

1. Saint John, New Brunswick
2. Québec City, Québec
3. Charlottetown, Prince Edward Island
4. Moncton, New Brunswick; Kitchener, Ontario (tie)
5. Saskatoon, Saskatchewan

December 29, 2007,
www.canada.com/edmontonjournal/news/story

In the United States, The Gallup–Healthways Well-Being Index ascertained that the happiest American cities in 2009 were

1. Boulder, Colorado
2. Holland–Grand Haven, Michigan
3. Honolulu, Hawaii
4. Provo–Orem, Utah
5. Santa Rosa–Petaluma, California

www.cnbc.com/id/35522560/America_s_Happiest_Cities?
www.cnbc.com/id/35522560/America_s_Happiest_Cities?

And *Forbes Magazine* reported that the "ten urban centers closely associated with unmitigated joy" in 2009 were

1. Rio de Janeiro, Brazil
2. Sydney, Australia
3. Barcelona, Spain
4. Amsterdam, Netherlands
5. Melbourne, Australia

www.forbes.com/2009/09/02/worlds-happiest-cities-lifestyle-cities

---

Your City

Do you live in an urban or rural setting? Are you happy living there, or do you wish you could live somewhere else? What are the factors about where you live that make you happy or unhappy? Do you plan on moving to another location in the future? If so, why? What factors in a new setting do you think will bring you more satisfaction? Do some research on your own location and the one you would like to live in (if the two are different). What are the pros and cons of each? Did you learn anything that surprised you about these locations? Explore your own location more fully—it probably holds more surprises for you than you realized!

COUNTRY

Some countries, such as Bhutan, Brazil, Italy, and parts of Canada, are paying particular attention to measures of Gross National Happiness (GNH) to evaluate the well-being of their people. The term *gross national happiness* was first coined in 1972 by Jigme Singye Wangchuck, the fourth king of Bhutan, who believed that the happiness of the people rather than the economic measure of the gross national product should be the guiding goal of a country's development (Ura, 2008). The GNH reflects a variety of indicators, such as psychological well-being, cultural well-being, community vitality, physical health, and so on. It is a sign of the times, as well as an indication that the wider environment plays a large part in people's sense of well-being, that the GNH is gaining greater prominence.

National Factors Impacting Well-being

Income

As we saw in Chapter 1, people living in countries of poverty report less life satisfaction than do those in more affluent countries (Biswas-Diener, 2008). This is hardly an unexpected finding: how much life satisfaction can there be when a person must struggle simply to find the means to satisfy basic human needs? Consistent with this is the finding that people living in countries with high rates of unemployment report less life satisfaction than do people in countries where the rate of unemployment is low (Owen, Videras, & Willemsen, 2008). But Suzanne Skevington (2009), in her work with the World Health Organization in studying quality of life, points out that the evidence may indicate that a major factor in people's satisfaction with their lives is not the absolute level of their income, but the psychological gap between their income and their dreams. That is, if people aspire to much but have little, their dissatisfaction is greater than if they aspire to little. In a low-income country, one with high unemployment, people may work very hard in order to achieve a good standard of living, but may be thwarted by the lack of jobs and other resources in their country, thus decreasing their estimation of the quality of their lives. On the other hand, if people expect little, they may be pleased with any small gain in their lives.

Democracy

Another difference among countries is that of the existence of democracy. The question is whether living in a democracy is related to people's sense of well-being. It would make sense if it did: in a democracy, people exert more control over the policies that will govern their lives, increasing the chance that these policies will be favourable to them and increasing their sense of self-efficacy and purpose, as well as their social connectedness to other citizens. Owen, Videras, and Willemsen (2008) surveyed people in 46 countries and found that people living in democracies did indeed report more life satisfaction, even when other cultural and economic factors were controlled. Being able to participate in the political process was a significant factor in people's sense of well-being. But there is a complication: Bjørnskov, Dreher, and Fischer (2010) found that in countries characterized by higher income, democracy is an important factor in perceived well-being, but for countries characterized by lower income, national institutions that provide economic opportunities while safeguarding life and property have a greater impact. This was also found by Helliwell and Huang (2008), who reported that in low-income countries, the presence of democracy was not as important as trust in the government and the government's ability to deliver goods and services efficiently and honestly.

Trust

Trust is an issue that has been explored by John Hudson (2006). His research indicates that trust in national institutions (such as the national government, the nation's justice system, the national media broadcasts as conveying accurate information) is in part dependent on the past performance of these institutions and impacts people's subjective well-being, at least in Europe. When people trust, with good reason, the institutions of their country, their satisfaction with their lives is increased.

Open Economic Market

Another national factor that has been investigated is the openness of the economic market. In an open market, with little or no governmental control placed on trade, measures of subjective well-being are higher than in closed markets in which the government regulates what can be traded, how much, at what price, and with whom. An open market fosters people's sense of control in their lives, as well as provides more opportunities for them to prosper. This effect, however, may be more applicable to people who have ample financial resources to take advantage of the openness of the market; without adequate resources, people with a lower income may feel no effect or may actually be at a disadvantage in acquiring the means to satisfy basic needs (Tsai, 2009).

Climate and Scenery

"Never mind all that," cried a friend of mine when I discussed this with her. "I just know I could be happier if I lived in a tropical paradise!" It's noteworthy that she, a patriotic Canadian who loves her country, made this comment in the midst of an early March snowstorm in Toronto! And looking out the window at the blizzard, I wondered if she had a good point. Research into factors such as weather and scenery are scant, but one study gives us some insight.

Brereton, Clinch, and Ferreira (2008) examined spatial variables and their relationship to self-reported happiness in Ireland. They found that, with other factors controlled, their participants reported more life satisfaction when they lived in areas characterized by warmer Januarys and Julys and increased rainfall overall. They point out that increased rainfall is conducive to the lush green scenery of Ireland, so the positive relationship between rainfall and life satisfaction may actually reflect a positive relationship between scenery and life satisfaction. They also found increased life satisfaction among people living within two kilometres of the coast. Perhaps warmer climate, lush scenery, and easy access to an ocean or sea really do influence our feelings of well-being.

REFLECTIVE EXERCISE

Your Country

What do you like about the country you live in? Are there any elements that you dislike? Have you ever thought about living in another country? Which one? Why? What seems desirable about doing this? Have you explored your own country yet? While travel can be a broadening and wonderful educational experience, consider traveling in your own country first to see the wonders that it offers and to enrich yourself in the experience of getting to know your fellow countrymen. Then consider taking this expanded vision to other countries as you travel to experience their wonders.

At the beginning of the chapter, we saw that Jeyani's parents chose to live in Canada because they wanted more prosperity and opportunity for their children. The economic and political factors of the country made Canada very desirable to them, as it does to many people (it's probably not the climate, although the scenery is often breathtaking). They performed a life-changing and courageous act: they immigrated.

IMMIGRATION

In North America, unless we are a member of an Indigenous People, we or our forebearers were immigrants. We or our parents, grandparents, or more distant ancestors left the homeland to come to North America. For most people, the immigration was in the hopes of finding a new and better life for themselves and their children, as it was for Jeyani's parents, but some, no doubt, left their native countries for the sake of adventure, to be with other family members who had previously immigrated or, perhaps, to flee danger and persecution.

Whatever the reason, what a courageous act that was! Immigration often requires separation from family and friends, perhaps never to see them again. It may require learning a new language, one that might not even be related to the native tongue (e.g., Mandarin and English have almost nothing in common in terms of vocabulary and grammar). It requires finding accommodation that one can afford. In many cases, it requires finding a job when one's training and credentials from the homeland may not be acceptable in the new country, as Jeyani's parents found. It requires learning about and in some way dealing with what may be very different cultural norms and expectations. How do all these transitions and new experiences affect the sense of well-being and life satisfaction of immigrants?

Acculturation

Acculturation refers to the process of change that is undergone in adapting to a new culture. John Berry (2001) contends that when two culturally different groups meet, both groups experience psychological changes, or **psychological acculturation**, although the effects are greater for the nondominant group. Immigrants, then, have decisions to make about how they will deal with the new culture, within the constraints of what the new culture will allow. They may choose **assimilation** if they decide not to retain their own cultural heritage but to merge with the dominant society as much as possible. Or they could choose **separation** if they decide to retain their original cultural identity and to interact with the dominant society as little as possible.

Between these extremes is another possibility. **Integration** is the choice for immigrants who decide that they want to retain their original cultural identity, but also want to participate in the society of the new culture. Immigrants who have little or no interest in maintaining their original heritage and little or no interest in participating in the new culture have chosen **marginalization** (Berry, 2001). Which strategy is related to the highest life satisfaction?

Most of the evidence indicates that integration is the strategy associated with the highest level of life satisfaction in immigrants. For example, adolescents from the former Soviet Union and from Albania who felt connected to both their original cultural heritage and the culture of Greece, where they now lived, had the most psychological and school adjustment (Motti-Stefanidi, Pavlopoulos, Obradović, & Masten, 2008). Similarly, adolescents from the former Soviet Union who immigrated to Israel showed increasing psychological wellness as time went on, an effect the researchers attribute to the adolescents' use of integration in their adaptation to a new homeland (Mirsky, Slonim-Nevo, & Rubinstein, 2007). Also, Abu-Rayya (2009) found that adults who immigrated to France showed better psychological adjustment when their social identity was associated primarily with France as opposed to their country of origin.

Adolescent immigrants from Hong Kong to Canada reported a higher level of life satisfaction if they were able to make friends with Canadians, had good experiences in school, experienced little discrimination, and had moved to Canada for reasons that were not based on financial considerations (Chow, 2007). Lincoln, Taylor, Chae, and Chatters (2010) also found that immigrating at a later age was associated with less life satisfaction than immigrating at an earlier age, possibly because of the reduced time available to adapt to a new country. This is echoed in the research of Jackson, Forsythe-Brown, and Govia (2007) who found that, among black Caribbean immigrants, subjective well-being was less if they had not been in the United States for very long, but that was somewhat ameliorated by close ties to family members and their social support.

As we have indicated, a major reason for immigrating is to improve present life and future opportunities for one's children. This implies an understanding that the children must adapt to a different culture from that of the parents, but it is also reasonable that immigrant parents want their children to maintain their ethnic identity. Inman, Howard, Beaumont, and Walker (2007) found that Indian immigrant parents were aware of and were concerned with the problems their children faced as second generation in the United States and they often modified their parenting styles (i.e., became less authoritarian and strict) with their children, but they still tried to instill traditional Indian values in their children. Thus it seems that they generally fostered integration in their children, with the aim that their children might experience what they saw as the best of both worlds. This seems to be what Jeyani's parents want for her and her brother, and they may well have modified their parenting styles more than Jeyani realizes. But the conflict that Jeyani has in being "a woman of two worlds" points out that this strategy, while beneficial, is difficult sometimes.

Expectations

Jeyani's parents did their homework before immigrating and obtained a great deal of information about what to expect from living in Canada. Because of this, they were able to cope better with the new culture and lifestyle, even though taking jobs below their educational level must have been disappointing for them. The role of expectations is important in determining how we will react to any situation. For example, Lincoln, Taylor, Chae, and Chatters (2010) found that life satisfaction among older Caribbean black adults was less if they felt that their expectations of life in their new home, the United States, had not been met.

The possibility their expectations may not be met, the need to learn a new language and new social norms, the absence of friends and family, the difficulties in finding employment and accommodation, and the chance of encountering prejudice and discrimination provide enormous challenges for immigrants that could well lead to psychological disorders. On the other hand, financial gain for themselves, along with a new ability to help their families, as well as living in a country that might not inflict the same social, economic, and political restrictions on the individual as the home country might lead to improved mental health. Stillman, McKenzie, and Gibson (2009) took advantage of the system in New Zealand in which a limited number of Tongans are allowed to immigrate to New Zealand based on a random draw of the names of applicants. This system allowed the researchers to compare the mental health of successful applicants to unsuccessful applicants. They found that immigration was associated with better mental health, especially for women and for people with poor mental health, an effect that could be cautiously attributed to immigration.

Social Identity

Sometimes integration is not the only productive route to feeling satisfaction in living in a new country. The impact of social identity still must be noted, especially since we choose our social identities to a great extent. Murdie and Ghosh (2010) examined the geographical concentration of different ethnic groups in one city in Canada. Toronto received more immigrants than any other city in Canada from 2001 to 2006; indeed, Toronto is the major city with the world's second-highest proportion of residents who were born outside of the country (Miami is in first place). Murdie and Ghosh report that some ethnic groups have clustered together while others are more widespread in Toronto. Certainly, they say, Toronto and Canadian cities in general do not have ethnic ghettoes as are found in most American cities. The question that Murdie and Ghosh were particularly interested in was whether immigrant groups could successfully integrate into their new country if they lived in an ethnically-concentrated area.

To answer this question Murdie and Ghosh (2010) talked to immigrants from Bangladesh who lived in the Victoria Park area of Toronto. This area, also known as

"Little Bangladesh," is home to the largest concentration of Bangladeshi immigrants, and many of these immigrants indicated that they chose to live here simply because of this high concentration. Their responses to Murdie and Ghosh suggested that the Little Bangladesh enclave was "home" to them, the place they had strong social and familial ties with, and the rest of Toronto was the "outside world." They felt satisfied with their immigration to Canada and felt sure that their children would have more opportunities and a brighter future, but they did not seem to identify with Canada, with Toronto, or even with other ethnic groups living in the same area. Their social identities were of their original national and cultural group, and their integration into Canadian society in general seems to be marginal by their choice, but to their satisfaction. Spatial concentration, say Murdie and Ghosh, does not always mean a lack of integration, but sometimes it does and this is not necessarily a bad thing.

Immigration's Impact on the Community

What impact does a high influx of immigrants have on a community? Sometimes immigrants are perceived negatively in general, termed **migrantophobia** (Badyshtova, 2005). Hombrados-Mendieta, Gomez-Jacinto, and Dominguez-Fuentes (2009) studied this in the city of Malaga in Spain where there has been a recent increase in immigration. They found that the quality of life reported by people living in the same block of apartments as recent immigrants was lower than the quality of life reported by people who did not have recent immigrants living on their block; however, quality of life was positively related to the amount of contact they had with the new residents.

This suggests that increasing the diversity of a community provides challenges and a need to adapt, but the influence of social relationships is again seen. It can be surmised that increased contact with diverse groups lowers the perception of differences and heightens the sense of belonging and common social identity: the perception of "Mrs. Fernandez the immigrant" changes to "Mrs. Fernandez who lives next door" with increased contact.

CULTURE

Looking at differences in subjective well-being across countries is illuminating, but somewhat simplistic. Within the vast majority of countries there are many different cultures, with many different norms and values. What is regarded as well-being often shows differences across cultures (Diener, Oishi, & Lucas, 2003).

Constantine and Sue (2006), for example, point out that among Buddhists, suffering is considered to be the essential quality of life (see Chapter 3). Negative affect might be considered the norm by them, whereas the same emotions might be considered depressed by non-Buddhists. Well-being for Buddhists might consist of a state of enlightenment, a state that is fully reached by very few.

One division that has been made among cultures is that of individualism versus collectivism; that is, the orientation of finding the greatest good for the individual as opposed to finding the greatest good for the group. But this distinction is somewhat vague in many cases. For example, people of colour in the United States live in an individualistic society, yet a major factor in their coping and adjustment to life comes from their commitment to and their bonds with their families and communities, a collectivist orientation (Constantine & Sue, 2006).

Political Violence and Personal Well-Being

When we talk about the effect of living in a particular country upon the individual's well-being, we immediately realize that in many countries there is little peace and stability. Indeed, violence seems to be the order of the day. At this writing, many countries in the Middle East are experiencing revolt against the established government. How does such exposure to danger and upheaval impact on the ordinary person's feelings of satisfaction with life? It is no stretch of the imagination to know that there must be a continual feeling of stress and impending danger for oneself and one's family and friends. Yet research in this area is scant, and it's no wonder. How can research be done when it is all but impossible to find respondents who will feel safe enough to reveal their attitudes and emotions in such conditions, conditions that in themselves render tracking and communicating with potential respondents all but impossible?

Muldoon, Schmid, and Downes (2009), however, have examined some of the impact of violence in one's country on perceived well-being in terms of the social identities of the people. Their location is Ireland, both the Republic of Ireland and Northern Ireland. Both locations have seen violence as a consequence of the political conflict between those leaning toward British rule (typically identified as Protestants, although it would be a mistake to see divisions on purely religious grounds) and those favouring independence (typically identified as Catholics).

"The Troubles," as they are called, have been more pronounced in Northern Ireland where people can choose British or Irish citizenship, although a minority of both Protestants and Catholics identify themselves as "Northern Irish."

Muldoon and her colleagues questioned whether the social identity as British, Irish, or Northern Irish would be important in determining how people's sense of well-being would be affected by their proximity to or experience with political violence. To that end, they took pains to obtain a random sample of respondents in Northern Ireland, where exposure to violence was more likely, and in the border counties of the Republic of Ireland where political violence was far less common. They originally contacted 2000 people in Northern Ireland, but 275 people (13.75 percent) were eliminated from the research because they were either from outside the United Kingdom and Ireland or refused to reveal their nationalities. The researchers do not report how many people fell into each category of elimination. Similarly, 1000 people were contacted in the Republic of Ireland, but now the researchers reveal that 102 respondents, or 10.2 percent, refused to indicate their nationalities. Furthermore, the response rate to the research interviews and surveys was only 49 percent. These numbers suggest that, as meticulous as the researchers had been in trying to obtain a representative sample of people from the regions under study,

(Continued)

Political Violence and Personal Well-Being, *continued*

any results of the research might have limited generalizability. It remains forever unknown whether those people who refused to reveal their nationalities or refused to take part in the study, even with assurances of confidentiality and anonymity, did so because of mistrust of involvement in questioning, which might imply a lessened sense of overall well-being or simply (as is often the case in research of this type) a lack of time or interest in involvement.

When people agreed to identify their nationalities and agreed to participate in the studies, they were interviewed over the telephone by trained interviewers and administered scales determining their exposure to political violence, their national identification, and their psychological well-being. These scales rely on self-report, however, and as has been noted repeatedly in this book, self-reports may or may not reveal the true feelings and affiliations of the respondents. This is especially important in a research situation in which, given the large numbers of people who refused to participate for one reason or another, generalizability is already viewed with caution.

Bearing these limitations in mind, the research by Muldoon and her colleagues indicated that in Northern Ireland, the site of more frequent exposure to political violence, identifying oneself strongly as Irish was related to greater psychological well-being even though these respondents were more likely to have been directly exposed to the violence. The researchers believe their results indicate that if national identity is related to the source of the stress, the identities become consolidated, and the feeling of being part of the minority group in the political conflict provides a buffer against decreased feelings of well-being by ameliorating the stress. The researchers note another caveat: their study employed a cross-section of respondents, meaning that it is impossible to determine whether exposure to political violence increased their sense of national identity and hence their well-being, or their national identity remained constant from before their time of exposure to the time of the research. Indeed, it may be that their sense of well-being determined their strong national identification, or perhaps other factors might have accounted for any or all of the relationships found.

Nonetheless, the results of this study indicate to Muldoon and her colleagues that even in the face of a great deal of exposure to political violence, people with strong national social identities are often psychologically healthy with a sense of well-being and satisfaction in life. This, they note, may be a double-edged sword at the societal level: on one hand, these people are well-placed to be strong advocates for their positions and their communities, but on the other hand, the strength of their national identities may hinder the society's progress toward reconciliation and their nation's healing.

Karen Lincoln and her colleagues studied older African Americans and Caribbean Black adults who had immigrated to the United States. They found that being of African descent by no means placed all of these people within a single cultural group (Lincoln, Taylor, Chae, & Chatters, 2010). Even within a cultural group, individual differences arise in the emphasis that people put on positive and negative events in determining their sense of well-being (Lavee & Ben-Ari, 2008).

With the proviso that differences among people may counteract, confound, or even corrupt the influences of culture on satisfaction with life, it is still instructive to examine the impact of cultures that are very different from those of North America. Traditional Chinese culture, for example, views aging in a very positive light: the elderly are traditionally regarded as wise and knowledgeable and are given heightened respect for this wisdom and for all their contributions to society. These attitudes are reflected in young Chinese today as well (Tan, Zhang, & Fan, 2004). While research has found that satisfaction with life decreases as one grows older in many cultures, this has not been found to be the case in China (Qiao & Suchindran, as reported by Chappell, 2005). This has been attributed to the traditional Chinese reverence for old age that gives the elderly a feeling of positive regard and usefulness, thereby raising their self-esteem and their subsequent satisfaction with their lives.

But consider this: in a discussion with my Chinese-Canadian students who immigrated to Canada in middle childhood, there was disagreement with this interpretation. Their contention was that modern Chinese culture measures success in life by external achievements; that is, accumulation of material goods and financial prosperity for themselves and their children. The elderly, they say, have had more time to achieve this success and this, they believe, accounts for their life satisfaction.

While China has been regarded as a collectivist culture, two of my students (Jenny Liu and Fei Zuo) contend that the modern Chinese view is modified. Rather than an emphasis on the welfare of the entire group, they report, an emphasis is put on the welfare of the family. The elderly, they say, may report more well-being for themselves based on whether their family is doing well. Respect for elders certainly exists, but the "Chinese" values they were taught highlights respect for people of all ages. These are values certainly espoused by Western culture as well. What do we make of this? The first point to note is that China is a vast country encompassing many cultural elements. It is also a country that has gone through many significant changes, changes in the political arena that demanded cultural changes as well. The advent of worldwide technology that has become increasingly available to more and more members of the society has brought about changes in attitudes too.

These factors apply to several other countries and cultures and should make us wary of reading too much into research results that suggest that understanding the subjective sense of well-being is dictated by the individual's country and culture.

Another point that should be noted is that, as my students pointed out, there is a difference between Chinese who choose to immigrate and those who don't, as well as between Chinese living in China and those living in other countries. My students contend that more traditional Chinese people do not typically immigrate unless they are elderly and are joining their families in another country. Traditional Chinese people are more likely to wish to stay in China. That implies that the sample of Chinese people who are living in other countries may be more open to or are already living lives that integrate old and new cultures, thus forming a new and different culture from either the traditional one they left or the new one they entered. How far these differences that my students have observed can be extended beyond the Chinese to other ethnic groups remains to be seen.

Neena L. Chappell (2005) at the University of Victoria in British Columbia examined life satisfaction among elderly Chinese who lived in major Canadian cities (Victoria, Vancouver, Edmonton, Calgary, Winnipeg, Toronto, and Montreal). She reasoned that these people might have more attachment to traditional Chinese culture, and that their participation in elements of this culture might affect their feelings of well-being. This study included almost 2300 people with an average age of around 70 years who had been in Canada an average of about 19 years. Most of these people had immigrated to Canada to join their families who had immigrated previously.

Chappell (2005) found that overall, involvement in elements of traditional Chinese culture was positively related to the life satisfaction that her participants felt, but different elements were related to different domains of well-being. For example, ancestor worship was only related to the domain of well-being in family relationships and not to other domains; making visits to China was related to overall well-being, but not to general attitudes towards life or spiritual well-being. Chappell's conclusions are that Chinese seniors do blend elements of the traditional culture with the culture of their new homes (i.e., integration) and that involvement in traditional culture is important for their well-being. Her feeling, however, is that these results reflect *involvement* in the traditional culture and not necessarily adherence to the *beliefs* of the culture, a wise distinction.

Jeyani, as we have seen, was not altogether happy with the restrictions her parents put upon her. Her Canadian friends had more freedom and less supervision than she. This reflects the difference between the cultural norms of Indian parenting and that of Canadian parenting: by Indian norms, females are seen to need more protection and supervision to keep them safe, while by Canadian norms, safety is still seen as paramount, but some situations are seen as fraught with less danger than would be accepted in India. In addition, in Canada, there is a premium put on encouraging independence in children, while connection to family and tradition may be more important to many Indians. Again, we can see the difficulties inherent in integration. Jeyani feels some resentment and conflict as a result, yet she seems to be well-integrated into both her Indian traditions and her Canadian life. How do you think she will raise her own children?

That country and culture are part of the context of the individual's life and have a role in their life satisfaction is undeniably true, but in our changing world, these factors may be becoming less important than they once were. The major influence may prove in the future to lie in how individuals define themselves and well-being and life satisfaction within their milieu, be it neighbourhood, urban or rural, country, or culture.

The Multicultural Personality

Since we live in a world that is closely connected, we come into contact with people, events, and ideas from other cultures very often. This is even more the case if we live in a large centre with a great deal of diversity. How do we cope with such diversity? As we have seen, in some cases there is stereotyping, discrimination, prejudice, and stigmatization levelled against anyone in a minority group. But many people not only cope well with such diversity, they thrive on it. They have what has been termed a **multicultural personality**. A great deal of the research on the multicultural personality has been done by Joseph G. Ponterotto and his colleagues. He and his fellow researchers define the multicultural personality as someone who

> embraces diversity in his/her life; makes active attempts to learn about other cultures and interact with culturally different people (e.g., friends, colleagues); effectively negotiates and copes within multiple cultural contexts; possesses the ability to live and work effectively among different groups and types of people; understands the biases inherent in his/her own worldview and actively learns about alternative worldviews; and is a social activist, empowered to speak out against all forms of social injustice (e.g., racism, homophobia, sexism, ageism, domestic violence, religious stereotyping).

> *(Ponterotto, Mendelsohn, & Belizaire, 2003, p. 204)*

In order to do this, one would guess that this individual has a positive attitude toward social relationships along with social skills and is able to handle stress effectively. This has been found to be true (Brummett, Wade, Ponterotto, Thombs, & Lewis, 2007). It comes as no surprise to learn that the person with a multicultural personality also has healthy self-esteem and experiences greater psychological and subjective well-being (Brummett, Wade, Ponterotto, Thombs, & Lewis, 2007; Ponterotto et al., 2007; Ponterotto, Mendelowitz, & Collabolletta, 2008). Ponterotto and his colleagues believe that elements of the multicultural personality can be enhanced in the school system by the promotion of individual strengths in children, strengths such as open-mindedness, flexibility, critical thinking skills, spirituality, and humour (Ponterotto, Mendelowitz, & Collabolletta, 2008). By doing this, schools would foster more effective functioning in our diverse world and greater satisfaction in life.

Perhaps Jeyani, with her background of two cultures, will have or even already has a multicultural personality. It surely is something to strive for!

REFLECTIVE EXERCISE

Culture

What is your ethnic background? Does it affect your lifestyle or your attitudes and feelings? Do you know much about your ethnic background? If you don't, talk to family members or others who have immigrated to this country. What were their experiences in immigration? What differences in cultures do they see as most important? What similarities do they see?

What would they like you to know about your ethnic background? What traditions do they want you to keep? How do you feel about this? Are there elements of your background culture that you would like to learn more about? Practices that you might like to start?

Share what you learn with people who have different ethnic backgrounds, and learn about their backgrounds.

Conclusion

Our well-being is not simply a consequence of our own thoughts, feelings, and person-alities. We are affected by our environments, and we, in turn, shape our environments. We have opportunities to engage with our communities to make them more conducive to the life satisfaction of everyone. Even picking up some trash can make a difference. This engagement will have beneficial effects on our own well-being, too, as it increases the meaning and purpose in our lives. All it takes is a commitment to notice our environments and to be ready to do something to make it better.

Look around. Schools may need volunteers to help children with their schoolwork. This would be a chance to form a one-to-one relationship with a child, a relationship that might make all the difference in the world for the child's life. Hospitals and nursing homes may need friendly visitors to brighten the day of people who are incapacitated. Your community may have shut-ins who would appreciate someone willing to pick up some milk for them from the neighbourhood store. And what about fundraisers and block parties and community athletic teams, and … the list can go on and on. And each one contributes to the individual and collective feeling of well-being in the environment. We may not be able to stop the snow in Canada, but maybe we can help shovel it for someone else. Or if we can't, maybe we can teach some neighbourhood kids how to make a really good snowman!

Summary

- Social identity includes both the knowledge of belongingness to and value for certain social groups. Social identity theory notes our tendency to define ourselves in terms of the groups we belong to and suggests that our well-being is often dependent on the groups that we define ourselves by.
- When groups are impermeable, people may take on the characteristics of stereotypes that the wider society has, and this becomes part of their social identity. Social identity has a strong bearing on our ability to cope with stressors and to have a satisfying life.
- A "good" neighbourhood has necessary human and social services, neighbourhood support, green area and natural environment, coherent social makeup of people in the neighbourhood, neighbourhood affordability, and few negative community factors.
- A good neighbourhood contributes to children's positive self-identity in giving them a feeling of safety and security in which to explore and grow and to develop skills, self-efficacy, and self-esteem.
- People who feel a sense of community in their neighbourhoods have greater well-being.
- The presence of trees and grass facilitates community activity and promotes social relationships among neighbours.
- Good neighbourhoods promote physical health.
- Neighbourhoods characterized by economic disadvantage and social disorder increase the likelihood of emotional and behavioural problems in young children. Poor quality neighbourhoods are associated with decreased well-being for children and adolescents and even worse problems for a child who is already coming from a high-risk family.
- Neighbourhoods that are perceived as unsafe and insecure are predictive of decreased feelings of physical health and physical well-being in adults.
- Children who attend schools with a higher-income population have greater emotional well-being than children from schools in neighbourhoods with lower incomes.

- Teacher support for the student has been found to be important for a child's or adolescent's feelings of school well-being and overall satisfaction with their lives.
- School connectedness refers to the degree to which children feel themselves to be a part of the school community that accepts, values, and supports them and is a large factor in school satisfaction.
- In more affluent societies, living in more rural regions is positively related to greater life satisfaction. In societies of lower affluence, happiness is dependent on individual factors, not the place of residence in terms of urban versus rural.
- National factors that influence individual well-being include level of income, the presence of democracy, trust, and an open economic market.
- In the process of adapting to a new culture (acculturation), immigrants may opt for integration, assimilation, separation, or marginalization.
- Integration is most closely associated with immigrants' sense of well-being.
- How well immigrants' expectations of their new home are met and their social identities are related to their feelings of well-being.
- The quality of life in a community may be lowered by an influx of immigrants but this is ameliorated when contact among all the residents is increased.
- What is regarded as well-being often shows differences across cultures.
- Immigrants' involvement in the traditional culture, and not necessarily adherence to the beliefs of the culture, increases their feelings of well-being.
- People with a multicultural personality enjoy and understand cultural diversity and live and work very effectively in multicultural situations. They also have healthy self-esteem and experience greater psychological and subjective well-being.

Group Discussion Questions

1. Realistically, how can good neighbourhoods be developed and fostered?
2. Is an emphasis on developing the psychological well-being of the child endangering the academic training of the child? That is, is time spent nurturing the child's social and emotional welfare decreasing the amount of time available to teach children academic skills? Is this a danger? How can this be balanced?
3. Is emphasis on Gross National Happiness meaningful in a country? Or is it a fad or a political ploy to make people feel that their government cares about their happiness?
4. Is it better for a country to be multicultural or to insist on assimilation of all immigrants into the dominant culture?

CHAPTER 13

Applied Positive Psychology

Roland is twenty-two years old. He was raised by parents who loved each other and laughed together, and they raised him with love and laughter. They guided him and encouraged him in his explorations of the world; they were attentive to his activities and provided him with the opportunity to engage in activities that maximized his strengths and independence, and they taught him how to cope with stress. Best of all, they were role models for optimism, hope, gratitude, and forgiveness, as well as active participation in community service.

LEARNING OBJECTIVES

In this chapter, students will see examples of the applications of positive psychological principles to

- ☐ Individual therapies and interventions.
- ☐ Schools.
- ☐ Universities and colleges.
- ☐ Workplaces.
- ☐ Communities.
- ☐ National policies.

Roland's parents chose schools for him whose philosophy was to develop keen academic minds and enriched personalities and spirits. The teachers in his small classes took the time to know him and support him, guiding his learning and allowing him autonomy in many of his tasks.

He has developed a love of learning, which he knows is lifelong.

Now he is in university, one that again was carefully chosen to have a number of small classes, a chance to get to know instructors and fellow students, and a strong commitment to engagement with the wider community. Roland hopes to find a workplace that will give him the prospect of using his strengths and his training alongside a congenial team of co-workers and a supportive team leader who allows him independence in structuring his work. He also hopes for continued mutually enriching relationships with his friends and maybe even a life partner one day, living in a cohesive community with good neighbours and lots of grass and trees. In the meantime, Roland is happy and confident and is thankful for every day and every new experience.

Roland is indeed a fortunate young man. He has been exposed to caring people who have used principles of positive psychology in raising him and teaching him. His experiences are not very common, but they could be. In previous chapters, we have noted how the empirical findings and principles of positive psychology can be used to enrich our lives and increase our life satisfaction. In this chapter, we will take a closer look at areas and places that have used some positive psychological practices and principles in an attempt to make the wonderful life of Roland a reality for many more people.

THERAPY AND INTERVENTIONS

We don't know if any of Roland's family members needed or wanted interventions to help them psychologically grow and thrive in their lives, but they might have. In the past and often today, people visit mental health workers in order to deal with a psychological disorder. The idea has been that mental health professionals work with people who can be diagnosed with a verifiable psychological ailment.

In the past and often today, as well, the role of the mental health worker has been to "cure" people of their psychological disorders or at least teach them strategies to deal with their problems. (We won't include the role of the medical profession whose answer to psychological disorders or problems is frequently dispensing medications.) But increasingly, people who don't have psychological disorders are seeking the help of mental health professionals because their lives, they feel, are not as personally satisfying to them as they would like them to be.

These people aren't necessarily unhappy, but they aren't flourishing either. The office of the mental health worker is now being seen as a place to grow and learn to thrive. What better place to use the principles of positive psychology? Instead of concentrating on people's problems, why not concentrate on their strengths and how they use these strengths and teach new techniques to make their lives better? We have already seen some personal techniques for increasing our life satisfaction in previous chapters of this book, so why shouldn't mental health workers use the positive approach for everyone, whether they have a diagnosable psychological disorder or not?

Several psychologists and other mental health professionals have thought along these lines and devised therapies that are based on elements of positive psychology.

Positive Psychotherapy

If building on positive emotions and strengths and endowing life with meaning and purpose can increase life satisfaction, then these strategies should alleviate psychological distress as well. This was the reasoning of Seligman, Rashid, and Parks (2006), who devised **positive psychotherapy**. As a pilot test, these researchers administered some positive psychological strategies to volunteers online and measured their self-reported depressive symptoms and happiness before and after the exercises.

Some of the exercises include taking the Values in Action (VIA) strengths questionnaire (online at www.authentichappiness.sas.upenn.edu), writing down each day for a week three good things that happened during the day and why the person thought they happened, and composing a letter of gratitude and reading it out loud it to someone the person is grateful to but has never thanked. The results indicated that people who did the exercises subsequently showed fewer or reduced depressive symptoms and increased happiness. Later research, they reported, indicated that positive psychotherapy was effective in reducing the symptoms of people with severe depression. From results such as these, Seligman and his colleagues have devised what they call "an idealized session-by-session description of positive psychotherapy" for the treatment of depression (2006, p. 782). Each session includes instruction and homework for the client, as follows:

1. *Orientation.* The importance of positive emotions, character strengths, and meaning in having a satisfying life and experiencing psychological well-being is discussed. Clients are assigned the homework of writing a 300-word essay on an episode that displayed them using their character strengths.

2. *Engagement.* Identification of signature character strengths and a discussion of situations in which these strengths have been helpful. The role of pleasure, engagement,

and meaning as factors in creating a satisfying life are discussed. Clients are required to complete the VIA questionnaire online.

3. *Engagement/Pleasure.* Specific ways to use strengths are discussed and developed. At this point, clients begin keeping a journal of three good things that happened during the day (the Blessings Journal). This will be an ongoing activity.

4. *Pleasure.* The focus is on bad memories and how they maintain depressive symptoms. Clients are required to write about three of their bad memories, expressing their anger and bitterness, as well as how these memories maintain their depression.

5. *Pleasure/Engagement.* Forgiveness is discussed as a means of dispelling anger and bitterness. Clients write a letter of forgiveness to someone who hurt them, describing the episode, how they felt, and promising to forgive at some time. The clients do not have to deliver the letter at this point.

6. *Pleasure/Engagement.* Gratitude is discussed as a positive emotion that highlights good memories and militates against depression. Clients write a letter of gratitude to someone they have never thanked.

7. *Pleasure/Engagement.* Consolidation and follow-up of previous sessions, discussions, and activities. The client's opinion of the efficacy of the sessions so far is solicited.

8. *Meaning/Engagement.* Learning to be satisfied with "good enough" instead of demanding the "best." (e.g., "I can never be happy with a Honda Civic. I have to have a BMW or else life is meaningless.") This is termed **satisficing**. Clients develop strategies to increase their own satisficing.

9. *Pleasure.* Discussion centres on optimism and hope. Clients discuss disappointments and failures they have experienced and they are asked to consider the possibility that these doors closing may have led to other doors opening. Clients write about three times when, for them, a door closed only to have another door open.

10. *Engagement/Meaning.* The emphasis is put on social relationships and the appropriate and constructive ways to respond to other people. Clients practise this kind of responding and arrange a date to celebrate their own strengths and the strengths of a meaningful person in their lives.

11. *Meaning.* Discussion surrounds recognizing and valuing the signature strengths of family members. Clients ask their family members to complete the VIA questionnaire online, and they construct a family tree displaying the strengths of each family member. Clients then arrange a family gathering to discuss these strengths.

12. *Pleasure.* Clients learn to savour enjoyable events and activities. They then plan and carry out their own pleasurable activities using savouring techniques.

13. *Meaning.* At this session, the discussion is about how one can use one's signature strengths to benefit others. Clients are required to find a way to do this, taking a significant amount of time and using their own strengths.

14. *Integration.* A discussion of the full life that includes pleasure, engagement, and meaning. A final measure of the client's depressive symptoms is taken, progress is reviewed, and follow-up plans for maintenance of gains are devised.

Undoubtedly individual mental health professionals are using some of these exercises in their individual practices, but further research on the efficacy of the "idealized sessions" remains to be done.

Hope Therapy

Hope theory, as we saw in Chapter 5, regards hope as being goal directed and as having two components, agency and pathways. *Agency* is the motivational factor that leads the hopeful person to say "I can do this" and *pathways* refers to formulating strategies and plans for achieving the goal. Cheavens, Feldman, Gum, Michael, and Snyder (2006) devised a psychotherapy based on the idea that increasing hopeful thinking and fostering goal-directed activity could decrease symptoms of depression and increase people's satisfaction with their lives.

Hope therapy, as they call it, teaches people to set reasonable and measurable goals and to develop a number of strategies for approaching and achieving the goals. This therapy also addresses the importance of motivation and helps people to identify situations that might decrease their motivation and combat these. It monitors the individual's progress toward the goal and helps the individual modify the goal and the strategies if necessary along the way. Thus, hope therapy focuses on positive goals rather than removing symptoms or dealing with problems. For example, a lonely, depressed person would work on making new friends rather than dealing with loneliness. Cheavens and her colleagues found that after an eight-week intervention using hope therapy, anxiety and depressive symptoms were decreased in participants, and life meaning and self-esteem were enhanced.

Goal-setting and planning techniques have also been found to be effective in increasing the feelings of well-being in mentally disordered imprisoned offenders (Ferguson, Conway, Endersby, & MacLeod, 2009), results also found among non-clinically disordered people by a methodology that actually suggests that "goal-setting and planning skills have a causal link to subjective well-being" (MacLeod, Coates, & Hetherton, 2008, p. 185).

Well-Being Therapy

In Chapter 1, we briefly discussed psychological well-being as seen by Carol Ryff and her associates (e.g. Ryff, & Singer, 2008). They see a satisfying life as being comprised of an individual's autonomy, environmental mastery, personal growth, positive relations with others, purpose in life, and self-acceptance.

Giovanni Fava and his colleagues (e.g., Fava & Tomba, 2009; Ruini & Fava, 2009; Tomba et al., 2010) have developed a short-term therapeutic intervention they call *well-being therapy* based on these dimensions. The therapy is designed to help the individual move from an impaired level of functioning to an optimal level of functioning in these six areas. For example, people who feel stagnant in life and unable to move forward or to change their behaviour or attitudes would be helped to see themselves as growing and developing their not-inconsiderable potential. Well-being therapy runs for eight to twelve 30- to 50-minute sessions.

In the initial sessions of well-being therapy, the individual identifies episodes in which he or she felt a sense of well-being, rating the episode on a scale of 1 to 100.

During the intermediate sessions, the person notes the negative thoughts and self-statements that interrupt episodes of well-being. The therapist can now determine which episodes of well-being are allowed to occur and which are being sabotaged by negativity.

The therapist can then challenge the negative thoughts ("Is there any real evidence that you're right in this?") and encourage the activities that result in well-being but are not plagued by negative thinking. By the time the final sessions occur, the individual should be quite competent at self-observation and able to identify moments of well-being and the negative thoughts that banish this well-being. Techniques of cognitive behaviour therapy may be used to counteract negativity and irrational thoughts (a form of this is seen in the ABCDE technique described in Chapter 5), and other techniques such as assertiveness training, goal-setting and planning, and problem-solving may be used, depending on the dimension of well-being that requires it.

Well-being therapy has been found to be effective in the treatment of mood disorders and generalized anxiety disorder and, in general, decreases the risk of anxiety and depression in groups of people at high risk for such problems (Fava & Tomba, 2009; Ruini & Fava, 2009; Tomba et al., 2010).

Family-Centred Interventions

Positive psychology has been recognized as useful in dealing with entire families as well as with individuals (e.g., Conoley & Conoley, 2009; Lee et al., 2009). One form that the application of positive psychology to family therapy has taken is that of **family-centred positive psychology** (FCPP), which focuses on the family's strengths and assets, identifying them, developing them, and building on them (Sheridan, Warnes, Cowan, Schemm, & Clarke, 2004). One of the key principles of this approach includes empowering the family. The family identifies its own needs and sets the goals, and the mental health professional assists the family members in acquiring skills and building on their already-evident competencies that will help them meet their needs and achieve their goals.

This includes problem-solving skills to help family members meet challenges on their own in the future and increasing their access to social networks that will be able to provide further help and support. This is a radical change from a traditional form of family therapy in which the mental health professional decides what the family needs and what goals should be met, an approach that may be met with resentment and the family's diminished sense of adequacy. It is evident that the FCPP approach is more likely to gain cooperation from families and to increase their sense of control and confidence in coping with any problems they may presently have and any that may arise in the future.

Sheridan and her colleagues (2004) report a case study of a family whose four-year-old had severe tantrums, along with physical fragility, developmental delay, and speech impairment. The child's mother reported that her greatest need was to reduce the number and severity of the tantrums, and she set her goal at gaining behavioural control of the child to the point that tantrums would last no longer than three minutes. The mother demonstrated expertise in the understanding and management of her child's other physical and psychological problems and willingly undertook to learn new behavioural techniques for managing the tantrums (ignoring tantrums and rewarding behaviour other than tantrums when in high-risk situations for the child). The child's preschool teacher joined in the plan along with the mother, and the two began to meet to plan strategies for the child's further educational success. The goal was met, and both the mother and the teacher felt that the intervention used had been highly acceptable and effective. A satisfying ending for the mother, the teacher and, most of all, for the child, was achieved by the empowerment of the mother, building on her skills and expertise in dealing with her child's problems, and facilitating a partnership between the mother and teacher.

Certainly there are other therapies that utilize many of the principles of positive psychology, and no doubt many more will develop in the future. In concluding this section, however, it is encouraging to note that research suggests that strengthening the positive side of ourselves and our lives can often outweigh the debilitation of the negative side of ourselves and our lives.

REFLECTIVE EXERCISE

Your Own Growth

Would you consider consulting a mental health professional to assist you in your own personal growth? If not, why not? If so, what form of therapy would you prefer? Why?

Would you consider becoming a mental health worker using positive psychology yourself? What facet of positive psychology would you concentrate on if you were a professional in the field? Why?

SCHOOLS

Roland's parents chose schools very carefully for him. They were concerned that the values they were teaching him be maintained and fostered and that his character development be regarded as just as important as his academic development. In previous chapters, we have seen that many of the strengths highlighted by positive psychology are associated with school achievement. For example, optimism is correlated with higher academic scores (Ruthig, Hanson, & Marino, 2009), as are self-regulation (Obradović, 2010), resilience (Kwok, Hughes, & Luo, 2007), and emotional intelligence (Di Fabio & Palazzeschi, 2009). We have also seen that satisfaction with one's program of studies (Wefald & Downey, 2009), school connectedness, and supportive relationships with teachers were related to academic success as well (Gray & Hackling, 2009).

But scholastic success is not the only aim of the school. The governments of Canada, the United States, and the United Kingdom, as well as those of many other countries, have specified that the mandate of schools is to promote both student success and student well-being. The goal in educating children is not only to give them the academic skills (such as reading and mathematics) to allow them to function well in the world, but also to help them acquire decision-making skills, responsibility, cooperativeness, self-discipline, and eagerness and optimism about learning.

The values of honesty, conscientiousness, compassion, and courage, values that parents have typically been emphasizing in the home, should be fostered in the school as well. Considering that school is usually one of the first places that a child encounters the world beyond the family and that children in the Western world spend about six hours a day in school, five days of the week for a nine- or ten-month school year for perhaps twelve years, the role of the school in the child's well-being and present and subsequent life satisfaction cannot be overestimated.

Interventions and school programs based on positive psychological research and principles seem uniquely appropriate to aid schools in their onerous tasks (Gomez & Ang, 2007). Such approaches to education have been explored and instituted in many elementary and high schools around the world, and we now turn our attention to these positive schools.

What characteristics would it take for a school to use the findings of positive psychology to maximize the well-being of children? Huebner, Gilman, Reschly, and Hall (2009) highlight four characteristics of positive schools. First, schools would have to appreciate the fact that students' well-being is strongly related to their academic success. Academically successful children tend to be those who are emotionally healthy, and so the school must be prepared to monitor their students' well-being, including their emotional well-being and school satisfaction on a continual basis.

Second, positive schools recognize the individual differences and needs of their students, and they are prepared to work with these individual differences, adapting to their students' unique talents, strengths, and abilities to ensure that there is a good fit between the school and its curriculum and the individual student's personality.

Third, since the relationship between the teacher and student has been found to be so important for the student's school satisfaction, a positive school must facilitate supportive relationships between the teachers and students, arranging settings where positive interactions among all members of the school community can be enhanced.

Finally, positive schools need curricula that include tasks to challenge and engage students at the appropriate level for each child. Voluntary challenging and engaging tasks should also be provided to encourage the children's development of autonomy and to promote healthy social interactions with others.

Seligman, a staunch proponent of positive schools, has been investigating two particular well-being programs in schools (Seligman, Ernst, Gillham, Reivich, & Linkins, 2009). One, the Penn Resiliency Program (PRP), was designed to prevent depression in children and adolescents by increasing students' ability to handle stressors in day-to-day life. This program aims to increase optimism in young people by teaching creativity, flexibility, assertiveness, decision-making, and problem-solving skills. Its hope is that, by doing so, young people will gain in realistic optimism, thereby decreasing the chances of becoming depressed and increasing the chances of experiencing well-being and satisfaction in their life within and beyond the school setting. Seligman and his colleagues report that studies have found that this program does indeed decrease symptoms of depression, as well as hopelessness, anxiety, and behavioural problems. Teachers and group leaders of this program need to be well trained, however, for maximal effects to be seen.

The second program reviewed by Seligman, Ernst, Gillham, Reivich, and Linkins (2009) is the Positive Psychology Programme (PPP), a positive psychology curriculum for adolescents. This program concentrates on identifying students' character strengths and helping them use these strengths in daily life. The program is comprised of 20 to 25 80-minute sessions in Language Arts classes, spread over the Grade 9 school year, in which character strengths are discussed, followed by an in-class activity, a real-world homework activity, and finally a journal reflection.

An example of one of the activities was writing down three good things, big or small, that happen to a student each day for a week. The students were then asked to write a reflection on why they believed the good thing happened, what it means to them, and how they can increase the chances of such an event happening in the future. It is not difficult to see that this exercise requires the child to focus on positive events rather than negative events and to recognize how they can control the occurrence of such events. In this way, the aim would seem to be that the child's optimism, hope, self-efficacy, and resilience will be promoted. Seligman and his research team have done preliminary research, comparing the results of this program to those of similar students who were not in the program. They report that students in the program stated that they had greater enjoyment and engagement in school than did students not in the program. As well, the students showed some academic improvement through the following eighteen months, and their parents and teachers indicated that their skills in areas such as empathy, cooperation, assertiveness, and self-control were enhanced.

These results are very encouraging, but the program was limited to sessions within one course that the students took. What would happen if a whole school adopted such a program? Seligman and his colleagues got a chance to find out when the Geelong Grammar School in Australia asked them to train about 100 members of their faculty in positive psychology techniques and to act as resources for their teachers throughout the academic year.

In the program developed for this school, students have explicit courses and units within other courses to teach positive skills such as resilience, gratitude, and the use of character strengths. They were also taught techniques such as the ABCDE method of discovering false beliefs and changing self-statements (see Chapter 5) and keeping a "blessings journal" in which the positive occurrences of the day are recorded. Seligman, Ernst, Gillham, Reivich, and Linkins (2009) report that teachers are now embedding positive psychology elements into regular academic classes, as well as in sports, counselling, music, and in the chapel. For example, say the researchers, a question asked of students who are studying *Macbeth* might be to suggest what character strengths the characters might have and how these character strengths might have both good and bad sides attached to them. Another example, given by geography teachers, is questioning how the concept of happiness and well-being might differ in the various countries that are studied. Seligman and his colleagues have only first impressions to go on at this point, but so far, it looks good—the children seem to be approaching their learning with more eagerness, and they seem to be experiencing more positive events. We keenly await more research on the outcomes of this project.

Other school programs exist which include at least elements of positive psychology. The Canadian Association for Stress-Free Schools, for example, supports "programs that promote the health, happiness and full development of every child. Improving academic achievement. Preventing and treating stress, anxiety, depression and learning disabilities. Creating a peaceful school that prevents school violence and produces peace in society" (www.stressfreeschools.ca). A major technique this association advocates is teaching Transcendental Meditation in schools.

Daniel Goleman (who coined the term *emotional intelligence*, see Chapter 10) helped to establish the Collaborative for Academic, Social, and Emotional Learning (CASEL) in order to foster the inclusion of curricula and techniques of social and emotional learning in schools (www.casel.org). The belief of this organization is that

"Social and emotional learning is a process for helping children and even adults develop the fundamental skills for life effectiveness. These are the skills we all need to handle ourselves, our relationships, and our work, effectively and ethically" (CASEL, 2011, www.casel.org).

The Unique Minds School Program emphasizes skills such as self-efficacy, problem-solving, and social–emotional competence along with academic competence. Linares et al. (2005) describe some components of this program and report on its outcomes in Grade 4 and 5 classes. One particularly interesting technique that is used is externalization, in which children are introduced to the character of the "Can'tasaurus" (p. 406). The Can'tasaurus tells children that they can't perform certain tasks, and the children learn how to combat the evil effects of this creature, thus enhancing their self-efficacy beliefs. Compared to children not in this program, the children in the program demonstrated better problem-solving skills, increases in self-efficacy, more social competence (e.g., empathy and compassion), and they were more attentive and less disruptive in class. In addition, their academic grades were higher by the second year of the program.

Another program to examine is the Responsive Classroom Approach®, designed to integrate social and academic learning (Northeast Foundation for Children, 2011). The principles guiding this approach are as follows:

- The social curriculum is as important as the academic curriculum.
- How children learn is as important as what they learn: process and content go hand in hand.
- The greatest cognitive growth occurs through social interaction.
- To be successful academically and socially, children need a set of social skills: cooperation, assertion, responsibility, empathy, and self-control.
- Knowing the children we teach—individually, culturally, and developmentally—is as important as knowing the content we teach.
- Knowing the families of the children we teach and working with them as partners is essential to children's education.
- How the adults at school work together is as important as their individual competence: Lasting change begins with the adult community

Source: www.responsiveclassroom.org/sites/default/files/pdf_files/rc_fact_sheet.pdf

The program uses ten specific practices as a part of normal classroom routine:

1. *Morning Meeting.* The whole class gathers to start the day by greeting one another and by discussing new events in the students' lives. This sets a positive tone for the day and promotes the idea of group sharing and cooperation. At this time, students may also discuss ways to improve their achievement.

2. *Rule Creation.* The rules for the classroom are discussed and decided upon by the students and teachers together. These rules encompass anything that aids in the students' accomplishing their learning goals. The students are then more invested in the rules, more likely to comply, and feel a sense of belongingness and efficacy in their environment.

3. *Interactive Modelling.* Teachers are specially trained to model desired and expected behaviours for the students and engage students in this activity. This provides a more skills-based learning and practice in the behaviours.

4. *Positive Teacher Language.* Teachers comment on specifics of student activities, encouraging them rather than praising them. Praise may be given in an offhand manner and the child may not realize exactly what aspects of the child's behaviour the praise refers to. For example, "I see you're working very hard on your social studies workbook" rather than "Good work" is more effective because it leaves no ambiguity for the student and emphasizes the teacher's attentiveness to the child's activity.

5. *Logical Consequences.* When misbehaviour occurs, teachers do not punish, but allow students to experience the consequences of their actions and to rectify and make amends if possible. This is designed to promote responsibility in the students while maintaining their dignity.

6. *Guided Discovery.* Students are taught using materials that encourage them to take responsibility for their own learning and to be creative in their use of materials.

7. *Academic Choice.* Intrinsic motivation, autonomy, and responsibility are increased in students by allowing them a choice in their approach to learning. This is accomplished by providing children with different teacher-structured formats of learning.

8. *Classroom Organization.* The classroom itself is set up physically to encourage independence, cooperation, and productivity in the children.

9. *Working with Families.* This program involves parents in their children's learning. Their insights and observations about their children are actively sought to assist in the teachers' approach to each individual child, and parents are educated about the principles and reasoning behind the program.

10. *Collaborative Problem Solving.* Strategies such as conferencing and role playing are used to engage students in problem-solving activities to foster their autonomy, responsibility, cooperation, and their problem-solving skills.

Source: The Northeast Foundation for Children, Inc.

Sara Rimm-Kaufman and her colleagues at the Curry School of Education at the University of Virginia are presently conducting a multi-year controlled study of the efficacy of this program. A preliminary set of findings examined the reading and mathematics achievement of children in Grades 2, 3, and 4 (i.e., those who had been in the program for 1, 2, or 3 years, respectively). Their data show higher scores in reading and especially mathematics for children in the program compared to children not in the program. This effect increases with the length of time the students are in the program; that is, compared to children not in the program, children who had been in the program for three years showed greater reading and mathematics achievement than did children who had been in the program for two years, who in turn showed more reading and mathematics achievement than did children who had been in the program for only one year (Rimm-Kaufman, Fan, Chiu, & You, 2007). In fact, these researchers conclude that one year in the program is not sufficient for meaningful gains to be obtained, a finding consistent with other research on different intervention programs (e.g., Greenberg et al., 2003; Wandersman & Florin, 2003).

There is a great deal of research on the effects of many programs, much like the ones described and those more limited in scope, addressing limited facets of children's and adolescents' well-being (e.g., Allen, 2010; Horowitz & Garber, 2007). To clarify the results of some of the research, Durlak, Weissberg, Dymnicki, Taylor, and Schellinger (2011) performed a meta-analysis of research involving 213 school-based and school-wide programs including social and emotional learning. They concluded that the effects of these programs are positive: children and adolescents in these programs show enhanced social-emotional competencies and attitudes about school, themselves, and other people, and a substantially higher academic achievement.

Further, they find that these programs are effective at all levels of school and that social–emotional teaching practices can be integrated into a regular classroom curriculum. The most successful programs are those that are interactive and include coaching and role-playing as well as structured activities to help students attain their goals. They believe that, when well-designed programs have had less than optimal success, the problem has been with the implementation of the programs rather than with the programs themselves, highlighting the need for all school personnel to be on board and trained in the procedures of the program.

Lest they be forgotten, Terjesen, Jacofsky, Froh, and DiGiuseppe (2004) have pointed out that school counsellors can also use positive psychology with good effect. School counsellors often only see students who have problems with academics or with behaviour; that is, they seek to intervene in negative situations. Terjesen and colleagues advocate a wider role for counsellors who may, in the use of positive psychology, stave off many of the problems that might otherwise arise by developing programs to increase students' positive success experiences. These experiences would increase students' optimism by taking a lead role in discovering and promoting individual students' strengths.

REFLECTIVE EXERCISE

Your School

What was your elementary school like? Can you remember any teachers who used positive psychological principles in teaching? Were there any programs in your elementary school that seemed to use these principles? What about in your high school?

Are there any techniques described above that you wish had been included in your elementary or high school experiences? Which ones? Why did you select those? What difference do you think the inclusion of these techniques might have made to you and to other students?

COLLEGES AND UNIVERSITIES

College and university students are often readily available participants for many psychological research studies, and positive psychological research has obtained a great deal of useful information from their participation. One might wonder, then, if positive psychological interventions have been used to aid students in a postsecondary institution in their life satisfaction as well. This is generally not the case, however. More attention has been paid to bringing the techniques of positive psychology into play at elementary and high schools, rather than at the college and university level.

This might be so for a number of reasons. First, college and university students are regarded as adults whose personalities and habits are formed and who are capable of regulating their own lives. It seems intuitively obvious to many people that these adults, who are paying a great deal of money and making many sacrifices for their education, would be eager on their own to benefit from the education and services provided by institutions of higher learning. (A glance around a lecture hall where laptops are used more to check email than to take notes by many students puts the lie to this notion.)

Almost all colleges and universities have medical and psychological services available to the students, so as adults they can readily access these services as needed. This presupposes, though, that adults at this stage have more insight and emotional maturity than may be the case—clearly they will not access services if they are unaware that they need them, a state many young adults experience. Second, most colleges and universities have grown substantially larger in student enrolment and number of faculty, yet the number of counsellors available to students tends to remain low. For this reason, counsellors are often seriously overworked and can only manage to counsel those students who are in the greatest academic and/or emotional need, i.e., when a student has a crisis. A student who is doing fairly well academically and is unhappy but not clinically depressed may be put on a long waiting list to see a counsellor, or may never see a counsellor at all.

Another reason may be related to the fact that for a widespread or even universal positive psychology program to be put in place, all the faculty and staff need to be trained and supportive of the program. The large size of most colleges and universities militates against this, with faculty and staff numbers often reaching several hundreds. The probability of this many people being on board with the program and the practical problems of training and supervising such a large population makes the idea of instituting a positive psychology program infeasible to many administrators.

Another headache the administrators must continually contend with is the lack of funding; they regularly find that they do not have a big enough budget to fund upgraded tools and materials for courses and enough faculty to teach students (it is not uncommon for college and university students to spend many of their classroom hours in classes of 200 or more). Where, then, can they find the money to train and supervise instructors in implementing a new way of teaching and interacting with students? And won't they need many, many more instructors, who must be paid, to bring the instructor:student ratio down to a level where the instructor really can form relationships with students and implement a positive psychology program effectively? Should a new positive psychology program be a priority for the budget that is already under intense strain?

Many people say yes and that these problems are not insurmountable (e.g., Shults, 2008). Programs utilizing positive psychological principles are already being used in the area of counselling, for example, as college and university counsellors and researchers have begun to test and include techniques of determining and enhancing students' strengths (e.g., Jones, 2009; Shearer, 2009; Sullivan-Vance, 2008) and training mindfulness and meditation to improve their psychological and academic well-being (e.g., Caldwell, Harrison, Adams, Quin, & Greeson, 2010; Delgado et al., 2010; Oman, Shapiro, Thoreson, Plante, & Flinders, 2008; Weinstein, Brown, & Ryan, 2009).

In other cases, the principles of positive psychology have been utilized and examined in specific courses such as university outdoor adventure courses, and their positive effects on hardiness and personal growth have been noted (Passarelli, Hall, & Anderson, 2010; Sheard & Golby, 2006). Sometimes positive psychological principles have been recommended for entire courses of study, such as in the graduate training of counselling students (Greason & Cashwell, 2009), and the training of social work students (Turner, 2009; Ying, 2009) and medical students (Cottingham et al., 2008).

Braskamp, Trautvetter, and Ward (2008) strongly advocate for total campus environments that aid students in finding meaning and purpose in their lives. To this end, they propose what they call a "4C framework (culture, curriculum, cocurriculum, community)" (p. 26) and they illustrate this with some examples. The first C, culture, refers to the vision that the leaders of the post-secondary institution need to have, along with the norms of conducting day-to-day life at the institution. The vision must be one of commitment to helping students develop academically as well as develop their self-awareness and their obligations as moral individuals and citizens. Creighton University, a Catholic university in Omaha, Nebraska with about 7000 students, states its mission as "form[ing] women and men of competence, conscience and compassion who have learned from reflecting upon their experiences of being for and with others" (www.creighton.edu/about/).

The second C, curriculum, refers to the content and manner of teaching academic subjects. The curriculum, say these authors, must reflect the developmental stages of the student (first year, second year, third year, fourth year), with an emphasis on integrating what is being taught into the student's own worldview and applying the information to their lives. Hope College, a private Christian college in Holland, Michigan, with just over 3000 students, provides curricula designed to enhance the total development of the student as a human being (Hope College, 2010, www.hope.edu). It encourages classes in which students reflect on the information they receive from a variety of sources and report on what they have learned from these sources that makes an impact on their own lives, their goals, and their general worldviews. One senior seminar, for example, requires a "life view paper" in which students answer questions about what is important in their lives, what their goals are, how they plan on reaching these goals, and what their moral principles are.

The third C, cocurriculum, addresses the availability and type of extracurricular activities that the institution offers. These activities, say Breskamp, Trautvetter, and Ward (2008), should be located all over the campus and beyond it and should include opportunities for students to integrate what they learn academically with their private lives. At the University of Dayton, a large Catholic university in Ohio, the philosophy includes an emphasis on service in one's life and the belief that learning takes place best in communities. Their website states

> Hallmates are classmates. First-year students are members of living-learning communities, united in class and in residence halls around common themes or areas of interest. You might walk down the hall from your room in Marianist Hall to attend history class, or step off your front porch in ArtStreet into a gallery or performance space. Perhaps you'll learn a thing or two about teamwork while climbing the rock wall at RecPlex. And then there are the front porches. We own hundreds of single-family homes in neighborhoods that our students call home. They play competitive games of cornhole, gather on each other's porches—and share

meals and prayers with the Marianist brothers and priests who live right there with them. At the University of Dayton, lessons take place in the classroom. Or on the front porch.

(University of Dayton, 2010, www.udayton.edu/main/living_learning_environment.php)

The University of Dayton has over 170 clubs and organizations situated around the campus, and the physical environment allows for classes, activities, discussions, and so on to take place in a wide variety of settings apart from traditional classrooms. In this way, integration of learning into daily life is fostered and furthered by having many of the instructors live in the same residence as the students. This also expands the students' relationships, a meaningful component of a satisfying life.

Community is the fourth C in Braskamp, Trautvetter, and Ward's framework (2008). Community, they believe, refers to cohesive and cooperative relationships within the structure of the post-secondary institution and with the world outside the institution. The world is wider than a post-secondary campus, and what is learned in a classroom and in students' own growth processes needs to encompass the larger world. By interacting with the community at large, students can learn cooperation, compassion, and responsibility and give added purpose and meaning to their lives. At Union University in Jackson, Tennessee, there are 4200 students, a student:instructor ratio of 12:1, clearly allowing individual students to connect with faculty and for faculty to know them, their interests, their needs, and their thoughts. But beyond this, Union University, a Christian university, holds a Day of Remembrance each November when classes are cancelled to allow students and faculty to engage in community service projects such as building structures, gardening, and cleaning parks. The hope is that by formalizing such service to the community, students will be inspired to continue their service throughout the year (Union University, 2010, www.uu.edu/events/dayofremembrance/).

Shushok and Hulme (2006) state that colleges and universities that attempt to use positive psychology on campus will first examine the successful students on campus to find out the qualities and factors that make them successful, establish a campus-wide philosophy that fosters students' discovery and understanding of their individual strengths, and aid students in finding groups, organizations, and activities in which they can use their signature strengths. Some universities, they note, may conduct strengths assessments of their students during their first-year orientation, and make information available to them online about how these strengths can be used to maximize the students' learning and satisfaction with their lives. Universities can go even farther in helping students by introducing them to groups and organizations in which their strengths are valuable and will be enhanced and encouraged. This may even expose students to different ideas about possible careers that will utilize their strengths and increase their life satisfaction.

WORKPLACES

An online search of "positive workplaces" produces over 3.5 million hits. Many, if not most, of these are in some way advocating the introduction of positive psychological principles into the workplace, and there are a number of consulting firms that offer their services to accomplish this. It seems very clear that the message of positive psychology about job satisfaction and its benefits for industries, organizations, institutions, and other workplaces has spread. Certainly our friend Roland from the case at the beginning of the chapter wants to enter a workplace that encompasses positive psychology principles, as do most of us.

In Canada, there is an annual competition for Canada's Top 100 Employers in which various workplaces are rated on (1) physical workplace; (2) work and social atmosphere; (3) health, financial, and family benefits; (4) vacation and time off; (5) employee communications; (6) performance management; (7) training and skills development; and (8) community involvement (Canada's Top 100 Employers, 2011).

As one example of a top workplace, let us consider Alberta–Pacific Forest Industries, Inc., a producer of kraft pulp used in the manufacture of various paper products. Al-Pac, located northeast of Edmonton, Alberta, is set on grounds that include a baseball diamond, a 40-acre trout pond, hiking trails, and a beach volleyball court. The company also provides onsite fitness facilities, cafeterias with free snacks, and an indoor and outdoor employee lounge. Financial planning and assistance for retirement and upgrading education is provided, along with a profit-sharing plan for all employees. The benefits package includes coverage of fertility treatments, extended parental leave, and a generous number of paid sick days and personal paid days off, as well as vacation periods of at least four weeks. Employees have the autonomy to choose flexible working hours, telecommuting, a shortened or compressed work week, or even job-sharing.

Relationships among all workers at all levels at Al-Pac are fostered by social gatherings such as picnics, golf tournaments, barbeques, sports teams, a company newsletter, and special celebrations (e.g., National Aboriginal Day). Every day, employees can listen to music at work and, if necessary, bring their pets to work. Managers are trained in giving performance reviews, and work groups meet every month to discuss group and individual performance with the aim of solving any problems that may arise. Outstanding performance by an individual employee is recognized with rewards of tickets to sports and performance events, social events, and company merchandise. Al-Pac supports a number of charities, selected by employees who are also given paid time off to volunteer for the charities of their choice. It seems clear that this company strives to enhance its employees' autonomy, competence, and social relationships, the basic psychological needs that are highly related to satisfaction. The message sent to employees of Al-Pac is that the company cares about their welfare, the welfare of their families, and of the community at large.

In the United States, SAS, a privately owned software company employing 5629 workers, was named the best company to work for by *Fortune* magazine in 2011 for the second year in a row, appearing on the list for the fourteenth time, based on employee surveys (Great Place to Work Institute, 2011). What makes SAS such a great place to work? The CEO, Jim Goodnight, says "Treat employees like they make a difference and they will" (SAS, 2011).

The SAS philosophy is that, to be good workers, people must balance their work and family life obligations, and SAS profits by helping them to do that. To that end, the SAS benefits package is extensive, including workers, family members of workers, and retirees. These benefits range from medical, dental, vision, and drug plans, to assistance for families wishing to adopt a child, paid paternity leave, and, at the North Carolina headquarters, onsite daycare, summer camp, health care services, recreation and fitness centre, and even amenities such as dry cleaning, massage therapy, skin and nail care, a book exchange, and even a car washing service. Employees and their families have access to a number of support groups, workshops, and courses on topics such as parenting, eldercare, separation and divorce, financial planning, and stress management. Benefits such as these combined with opportunities for challenge, professional growth, and learning on the job make turnover very low and make the satisfaction of the employees very high indeed.

A great deal of research has been done on the workplace environments of nurses, stemming from the high turnover of nursing personnel due to the stress levels of the job itself and the institutional practices and problems of the workplace. According to the research, nurses, who are often overworked because of understaffing, face significant job-related problems beyond those of caring for seriously ill or injured people who may be in physical and emotional pain or even in a terminal condition.

Some of the major problems for nurses include bullying and incivility from colleagues and others (Hutchinson, Vickers, Jackson, & Wilkes, 2010; Luparell, 2011), and violence (Gates, Gillespie, & Succop, 2011; Hegney, Tuckett, Parker, & Eley, 2010). Lavoie-Tremblay and her colleagues found that over 43 percent of young nurses in Québec experienced psychological distress in their jobs, particularly concerning low social support from colleagues and superiors, and low autonomy (Lavoie-Tremblay et al., 2008). Additionally, both younger and older nurses report being negatively affected by the workplace climate that would be improved by an absence of conflict, enhanced warmer relationships, and increased job-skill challenge (Lavoie-Tremblay et al., 2010). It is evident that particular concentration should be placed on finding ways to make the workplace more positive for nurses, for both their sakes and that of their patients.

It may be that, in the ideal world our friend Roland seems to inhabit, there are ample opportunities, exceptional financial resources, and universal concern and good will that give rise to positive psychological principles underpinning work conditions at every health care facility. But in reality, lack of funding and lack of understanding and commitment to providing a positive workplace have often left nurses and other healthcare personnel in high-stress, burnout-prone working conditions. In some cases, with more or less institutional help, health care personnel have created better workplace conditions on their own. For example, the North Carolina Nurses Association began a program called Hallmarks of Healthy Workplaces Program in 2003. This program recognizes health care settings that

- Actively respond to employee concerns and promote a culture that views employees as powerful, skilful, knowledgeable, competent, and solution-oriented.
- Provide opportunities for nurses to expand knowledge, skills, and competencies.
- Maintain an employee skill mix appropriate for patient needs.
- Promote employee health and well-being.
- Initiate innovations to improve service and the work environment.
- Provide orientation for new employees, support for mentors and preceptors, and skill-building for managers to ensure they are effective.

(Trossman, 2009, p. 8)

One recipient of this recognition in 2009 was the Durham Regional Hospital's Endoscopy Services unit, known throughout the hospital as the "sunshine unit" because people are happy to come in to work and happy when they leave work. What makes this such a happy place to work? Trossman (2009) reports that interviews with the personnel who work on the unit make it apparent that the individual worker is greatly valued and respected. Workers take part in decision-making, both on the unit and on hospital committees. Their managers reward their hard work and support their pursuit of additional education and their involvement with wider hospital committees. They create programs and motivational aids for patients, a challenging enterprise, but one fraught with meaning and the opportunity to use their skills. They feel strongly that teamwork is valuable and necessary, and they help each other without being asked. The patients comment that the medical personnel seem to genuinely like each other. In short, even though understaffing is a problem and the job is sometimes heart-wrenching, many of the conditions for job satisfaction are being fulfilled.

REFLECTIVE EXERCISE

Your Business

Imagine that you are creating your own business. Money is limited, but there is some available for you to make your employees feel satisfied with their jobs. You want to use some positive psychological principles in this endeavour.

What would you do? What do you think the most important first step in creating job satisfaction would be? What would be the second step? Make a list of the top five priority steps that you believe an employer should take to maximize worker satisfaction.

COMMUNITY

Community improvement programs are taking place all over the world. Their aim is to improve the lives of people by making the impact of the environment on them more beneficial. Some programs are focused on goals such as managing HIV (e.g., Rhodes, Malow, & Jolly, 2010), preventing suicide (Hegerl, 2009), reducing crime and addiction rates (Lasnier, Brochu, Boyd, & Fischer, 2010), or reducing obesity (Samuels et al., 2010). Programs typically include consultants from a wide variety of disciplines, such as health care, social work, education, environmental studies, and construction. Often there is no measurement of the outcome at all, but when there is, it focuses on the specific aim of the program.

One program, the Better Beginnings, Better Futures project, in Ontario, Canada, has had a broader scope (Peters, Petrunka, & Arnold, 2003). This program is aimed at promoting the general development of young children, preventing behavioural and psychological problems, and improving family and neighbourhood characteristics. Three communities with economic disadvantage were selected as target areas, and programs differed somewhat at each location to meet local needs.

Two of the communities received school-based programs, which might include activities for children and parents, home visits, a breakfast (or three-meal) plan, parent–child drop-in centres, parent relief, toy libraries, and activities involving the whole community. The third location included even more community involvement. The Native Friendship Centre served as its base, and before- and after-school care programs were instituted, along with holiday outings and activities for the children and their parents.

There were also community kitchens, community gardens, and other projects to beautify the community. Other projects included programs to maintain peaceful playgrounds and to enhance cultural awareness. Over a five-year period, the outcomes of this program were found to be very encouraging, with improvements seen in children's academic, emotional, social, and behavioural functioning, as well as their physical health. Parental health, stress management, family functioning, and social support also improved, especially at one location.

A review of programs aimed at various aspects of youth development finds that there are generally positive results when programs seek to improve a school's social climate, enhance family functioning often through modifying parental practices, providing role models and mentors for children, and establishing connections between families, schools, and community-based programs (Durlak et al., 2007). These positive findings depend not only on the program offered, but also on the effective implementation of the program (Durlak & DuPre, 2008).

While these results give one reason to be optimistic about community programs, they focus on group data gathered from all the participants. What of the individual, though? Does community development actually increase the individual's sense of well-being? This was the question asked by Blunsdon and Davern (2007). They asked this question of two groups of people in Australia. One group lived in a community that received extensive community development initiatives, while the other group lived nearby in a community that did not receive such initiatives. The researchers found that residents of the community that received the initiatives reported feeling more satisfied with their neighbourhood, more connectedness to their community, and an enhanced sense of personal well-being as compared to both the residents of the community that did not receive the initiatives and to Australians overall.

It seems that if a government is seriously concerned about the well-being of its citizens, allocating funds to community programs and community development is a wise action. But money, as we all know, is scarce. How can a government determine which communities will receive funding for program initiatives and development? Given all the worthwhile demands for government funding, such decisions are difficult to make, but they can be made easier by the active participation of people in grassroots programs, some of which have spurred governments to fund the programs further (see, for example, Moore, 2005).

NATIONAL POLICY

As I write this, another national election is under way in Canada. Canada is a parliamentary democracy, and as we saw in Chapter 12, people are generally happy under such a system. Whichever political party wins, it's a fair bet that the Prime Minister will not have a Minister of Happiness in his cabinet. Yet clearly there are concerns about the public happiness. Electioneering speeches have stressed preserving democracy, increasing our financial security through job creation and pensions, and improving health care, as well as community development, special programs for families—children and the elderly in particular—and so on. All the promises are aimed at making the populace happier. Indeed, we should already be pretty happy (and we are, as we saw in Chapters 1 and 12) since we have many programs in place, and more continue to be funded on the national and provincial levels. The Better Beginnings, Better Futures program discussed previously is an example of a program initiated by the Ontario government.

So perhaps the government's concern for our sense of well-being isn't just political posturing. The happiness of its people is enshrined or at least implied in the constitutions and mandates of many countries, and as we have seen, many countries are actively measuring their people's happiness as the Gross National Happiness. Yet even the country that started this movement, Bhutan, has committed acts on some of its people that many would call flagrant violations of civil rights.

Veenhoven (2004) feels that the subjective well-being of people could be raised if governments enacted public policies based on what research has told us contributes to well-being. This could be done in several areas that the government exerts some control over, such as the rule of law. The question is, *should* this be done?

Duncan (2010) points out some practical and ethical problems with this viewpoint. First, what is happiness? It differs from person to person, and policies that make one person happy may make others miserable. Take, for example, the legalization of same-sex marriages. For many people, this is a right that has been denied them, and the legalization of same-sex marriage now gives them the same rights as other people have enjoyed. They are happy with the government's action, and many heterosexual people agree with them wholeheartedly. Yet other people contend that this is a violation of the country's traditional values and makes a mockery of the institution of marriage. They are unhappy and frustrated that their government did not listen to them in enacting this law. This emphasizes the point that what makes perhaps a majority of people happy may make the minority disgruntled. There seems to be no way that everybody can be pleased.

This is a substantial problem in a multicultural society wherein both individual differences in what makes people happy and cultural differences in the definition of happiness combine. In Canada, a bilingual country, Québec Francophones registered great unhappiness at the lip service given to bilingualism, contending that Anglophones neither spoke French nor wanted to and even looked down on those who spoke French. Subsequent laws making the French language more visible and mandating that French be taught to Anglophone children starting in elementary school may have pleased many Francophones, but they made several Anglophones resentful. This resentment has faded in many people over the years since the laws were enacted, but it still exists among some who say that the government has placed the rights of Francophones over the rights of Anglophones.

Another problem stems from the possibility that enacting laws may actually infringe on people's autonomy, even if it is "for their own good." An eighteen-year-old acquaintance of mine is offended by high schools banning the sale of soft drinks on the premises. "I can join the army and maybe get killed for my country, but I can't buy a can of pop in school? What gives? " he says. And my neighbour expounded to me this morning that everyone eligible to vote should be compelled to do so by law. Such a mystery! Can we maintain the freedom of a democracy if we are forced to vote? Yet if enough of us don't vote, where is democracy then? Should we have the right *not* to vote? In this election (as in many elections in many places), there are citizens who don't feel that they can endorse any of the political parties. But Canada does not have the option of "I decline to support any party" on the ballot. Defacing the ballot means that it is simply thrown out. For some people, not voting at all, reflected in a lower voter turnout, is the only way of registering a protest. In the final analysis, should we or should we not be free to make our own decisions, even if they are mistakes that will make us unhappy? If this seems like an obvious question to answer yes to, consider this: should people have the right to commit suicide, or should we intervene to stop them?

Another potential problem is that of the "slippery slope." If the government makes public policy in some areas that have been found to be conducive to a sense of well-being, where does it end? For example, we know that people who engage in some physical activity experience a higher sense of well-being than those who don't. So should there be a law that we all have to exercise? (Note that children have compulsory physical education classes in elementary school and for at least the first years of high school.) And if we all have to exercise, will the next law tell us how long and what kind of exercise we should be engaging in? Who would monitor this? Will there be "exercise police"? And will there fines or jail time for infractions? Slippery slopes may seem absurd and the automatic reaction tends to be "Oh, that would never happen," and that may be true. But then again, history tells us that they *can* occur and, contrariwise, liberty may be mistaken for license.

Diener and Seligman (2004) suggest that a Gross National Happiness rating in countries should be used by governments as indicators of how well national policies are working, a more conservative argument. That, however, would tell us only that national policies may be related to greater or lesser well-being, a correlation, and would give us no proof that the policies actually caused a change in reported well-being. And, of course, this would be based on group data, indicating only how some of the population feels. There would still be people, perhaps a significant number, who would feel differently.

Let's go back to our friend Roland, whom we met at the beginning of the chapter. He is a happy young man who has been exposed to the principles of positive psychology by his parents and his schools. If he were to become Prime Minister one day, could he relate to the problems and anxieties of people who have not had such a fortunate upbringing? Or would he be better equipped to bring a sense of well-being to the people?

Given the problems that national policy has in making people happy, perhaps for the moment it is best if positive psychological principles were used in more limited programs and were included in extra opportunities that people may avail themselves of. For instance, giving people incentives to save for their retirement (registered retirement savings plans in which contributions are not taxed) might be a better idea than enacting a law which says that we all must put a certain portion of our net income into a retirement fund. But maybe research and creative thinking will find more and better ways for governments to use positive psychological principles for our happiness in the future. And maybe people like Roland can help.

REFLECTIVE EXERCISE

Rule the World

Imagine for a few minutes that you are the ultimate ruler of the world. Undoubtedly you would concentrate on ending world hunger and bringing peace to all, but what else would you do? What policies would you enact that would contribute to the well-being of your people? Would you concentrate on maximizing happiness or on maximizing autonomy? How would you balance these? (Imagine whatever you want, money is no object, and the sky's the limit!)

Conclusion

Positive psychology has made many inroads into programs and interventions to help us increase our sense of well-being and will undoubtedly make many more in the years to come. For a very young area of psychology, it has expanded in an unprecedented fashion. Perhaps this indicates an idea whose time has come: we have paid so much attention to what has been wrong with ourselves, others, and our world (and justifiably so) that we need to hear about what's right with us as well. We need to be reminded of our strengths and how to use them, for our own happiness and for the promotion of a satisfying life for us all.

Summary

- Positive therapy builds on positive emotions and strengths, endowing life with meaning and purpose to increase life satisfaction.
- Hope therapy teaches people to set reasonable and measurable goals and to develop a number of strategies for approaching and achieving them. This therapy also addresses the importance of motivation and helps people to identify situations that might decrease their motivation and combat these.
- Well-being therapy is designed to help the individual move from an impaired to an optimal level of functioning in the areas of autonomy, environmental mastery, personal growth, positive relations with others, purpose in life, and self-acceptance. Well-being therapy is effective in the treatment of mood disorders and generalized anxiety disorder and decreases the risk of anxiety and depression in high risk groups.
- Family-centred positive psychology (FCPP) focuses on the family's strengths and assets, identifying them, developing them, and building on them.
- Positive schools appreciate the fact that students' well-being is strongly related to their academic success. They recognize the individual differences and needs of their students, facilitate supportive relationships between the teachers and students, and develop curricula that include tasks that challenge and engage students at appropriate levels.
- Children and adolescents in positive psychology programs in schools show enhanced social–emotional competencies and attitudes about school, themselves, and other people, and a substantially higher academic achievement.
- A positive college or university must have commitment to helping students develop academically as well as developing their self-awareness and their obligations as moral individuals and citizens. The curriculum must reflect the developmental stages of the student, with an emphasis on integrating what is being taught into the students' own worldviews and applying the information to their lives. Extracurricular activities should be located all over the campus and beyond it and should include opportunities for students to integrate what they learn academically with their private lives. The institution should also have cohesive and cooperative relationships within the structure of the post-secondary institution and with the world outside the institution.
- The best workplaces enhance their employees' autonomy, competence, and social relationships with their benefits, social gatherings, encouragement of upgrading

competency, and provision of various amenities that make balancing work and family easier for the employee.

- If community development initiatives are specific to the needs of the community and are implemented well, they can increase the collective and individual well-being.
- Enacting national policies to enhance the well-being of the people is already occurring, but in some cases, enacting policies runs into practical and ethical problems. These problems include the individual differences found among people in what makes them happy, the possible curtailment of autonomy, and the potential of a slippery slope.

Group Discussion Questions

1. Suggestions have been made that therapies using positive psychology can take the place of more traditional therapies for various psychological disorders. Is this true?

2. Positive schools take on the responsibility of raising children, say some people. Do you think the schools described in this chapter do this? Where is the dividing line between school responsibility and parental responsibility?

3. Community programs often concentrate on interventions for children and adolescents, and sometimes for disadvantaged, infirm, or ill adults. Design a grassroots community program to increase the well-being of adults who face only the ordinary challenges of living.

4. What *one* national policy to increase the well-being of the nation would you like to see enacted? What do you think is the most important area for the application of positive psychology?

Glossary

ABCDE technique Seligman's technique for increasing one's explanatory optimism

accusatory nafs in Sufism, second stage of nafs in which the individual feels self-recrimination and guilt

active procrastinator a person who delays a task in order to do tasks that are deemed more urgent and who seems to thrive on last-minute work that the active procrastinator seems to do well

actualizing tendency Carl Rogers's term for the human being's innate potential to grow and develop, to become the best that they can possibly be

affective forecasting predicting how we will react emotionally in given situations

affiliative humour humour that is often used for social purposes, to build relationships, without demeaning the self or others

agape a selfless style of love

agency according to Snyder's definition, the motivational component of hope

aggressive humour humour that is demeaning to others

alarm reaction the first stage of the general adaptation syndrome in which the body mobilizes to flee a threat or to fight it

alienation from self Karen Horney's term for becoming farther and farther removed from the person we really are and can be

amotivation lack of any kind of motivation

animal nafs in Sufism, irrational tendencies that respond only to base wants and needs

antecedent-focused strategies emotion-regulating strategies that are used to manage an emotion before it is fully activated

anxiety Fritz Perls's term for discomfort produced by not living in the present; Rollo May's term for the feeling we experience in our fight to maintain our being against the threat of nonbeing

arhat in the Theravada school of Buddhism, the person who withdraws from the world, becoming a monk or nun, spending his or her life in meditation on the path to enlightenment

Ashtanga- (Raja-) Yoga eight-limbed, classical yoga

assimilation abandonment of one's original cultural heritage and adoption of the new culture

atman in yoga, Brahman within the human being

attentional deployment an antecedent-focused strategy for regulating emotions in which we shift our attention to something else within a situation

authenticity Rollo May's term for being true to oneself and living by one's own values

autotelic personality referring to traits that might predispose a person to experience more instances of flow than other people

autonomy free will, individual volition

basic anxiety Karen Horney's term for a feeling that the whole world cannot be trusted, that there is no real safety anywhere in the world

basic evil Karen Horney's term for parental behaviour that denies the child the feeling of complete trust in the caregivers and safety and security in the world

basic hostility Karen Horney's term for the resentment and anger against the caregivers who are supposed to make the child feel safe and secure and valued and loved, but do not do this

beautiful-is-good phenomenon the tendency to attribute many positive qualities to someone who is physically attractive

Bhakti-Yoga the yoga of love and devotion

bodhisattva in the Mahayana school of Buddhism, the enlightened individual who stays in the world and helps others on their path to enlightenment

bottom-up model of subjective well-being pleasure from different areas of life provide a global sensation of happiness

Brahman yogic term for the complete unity of the universe

broaden-and-build theory Fredrickson's theory that positive emotions broaden attention and experience and pave the way to build strategies to increase positive emotions in the future

burnout a debilitating psychological condition resulting from prolonged exposure to a stressful, uncontrollable, usually work, environment

caring Rollo May's term for the source of will

catastrophic expectations Fritz Perls's term for the deliberate or unwitting message to the child that failure to live up to expectations will result in loss of parental love

character strengths a subset of personality traits that are morally valued in most cultures

cognitive change an antecedent-focused strategy for regulating emotions in which we change our perceptions and interpretations of a situation

commanding nafs in Sufism, personality traits and tendencies that incite one to evil

commitment part of Sternberg's Triangular Model of Love, the cognitive element

companionate love in Sternberg's Triangular Model of Love, a relationship containing only intimacy and commitment, but not passion

compassion fatigue a condition in which a caregiver feels overwhelmed by his/her exposure to the needs of others

competence the need to feel that one can be effective in performing a task

consummate love in Sternberg's Triangular Model of Love, a relationship containing passion, intimacy, and commitment

contented nafs in Sufism, stage in which the person has surmounted the difficulties posed by the previous nafs and feels great peace

coping efficacy how well we believe we can handle a situation

defensive pessimism a type of negative thinking that directs anxiety about possible failure into productive action

deficiency needs the bottom four needs of Maslow's hierarchy of needs, termed so because in fulfilling these needs we attempt to gain that which we lack

depressive realism the tendency for mildly depressed people to be more realistic and accurate in their judgments of themselves and life in general than are people who are not depressed

desacralization Abraham Maslow's term for the loss of wonder and awe in the face of the unknown

devil effect assuming that if a person has one negative quality, they have many other negative qualities

diseases of adaptation Selye's term for illness that results from the body's prolonged exposure to stress; psychosomatic disorders

dispositional optimism a personality trait that disposes people to see the positives in life more than the negatives. Dispositional optimism is general; it affects all or most aspects of our lives with the tendency to look for the good

ego depletion the amount of self-control exerted on a second task is reduced if self-control has been exerted on a first task

Eightfold Path Buddha's prescription for living

emotional intelligence the ability to perceive, understand, handle, and use emotions in a personally and socially constructive manner

emotion-focused coping coping with feelings about a situation or task; coping with the feelings engendered by a stressful situation

emotion regulation the processes by which people maintain or change their flow of their emotions

empathy Carl Rogers's term for the ability to see the world through another person's perspective

empty love in Sternberg's Triangular Model of Love, a relationship containing only commitment

eros a romantic style of love

esteem needs Abraham Maslow's term for the fourth basic human need, to be respected by others and by ourselves

eudaimonia a philosophical concept that views happiness as living a virtuous life, or one in which the individual's best characteristics are fulfilled

eudaimonic well-being the extent to which an individual experiences and functions in a eudaimonic way in life, pursuing goals that optimize the individual's personal growth and are motivated by internal interest and desire rather than by external gain

exhaustion stage the third stage of the general adaptation syndrome in which, with prolonged stress, bodily resources are depleted and illness may follow

experience sampling methods (ESM) methods of studying feelings in real time

explanatory optimism the tendency to explain life's events within a positive framework of expecting life to work out in a constructive way

external regulation a form of extrinsic motivation in which the only reason for performing a task comes from outside rewarding or punishing forces

extrinsic motivation refers to performing an action because of outside rewarding or punitive influences

extrinsic religiosity following religious practices because of societal or familial expectations rather than personal belief

fatuous love in Sternberg's Triangular Model of Love, a relationship containing only passion and commitment, but not intimacy

flourishing characterized by creativity, social connectedness, resilience, and few negative emotions

flow a state in which people are intensely involved in an intrinsically motivated activity, losing sight of anything but that activity, and deriving much pleasure from it

focalism attending to the specific situation and disregarding the outcomes and the context of the situation

forgiveness acknowledging and accepting the hurt that has been done to us and finding a way to move past it

Four Noble Truths the revelation of Buddha's enlightenment

fully functioning person Carl Rogers's term for the individual who uses the actualizing tendency to direct and motivate life in all its facets, leading to happiness and satisfaction in life

fundamental attribution error concluding that people's behaviour is a result of their personalities without taking the context of the behaviour into account

general adaptation syndrome Selye's term for the body's reaction to stress

general courage performing actions that the majority of people would find risky and would avoid

general wisdom wisdom applied to other people and life in general

gestalt Fritz Perls's term for the complete cycle of an individual experiencing a need and satisfying it

global causes causes that affect every area of a person's life

global judgments assuming that if a person has one positive/negative quality, they have many other positive/negative qualities

global meaning the meaning found in life in general, the world, the Cosmos; also known as *cosmic meaning*

golden mean Aristotle's term for a moderate approach to life in which one has enough of what one needs and wants but not too much

gratitude a positive emotion that arises when we feel that someone has voluntarily and intentionally done something (or tried to do something) that benefited us, especially if it cost the benefactor to do so

growth need Abraham Maslow's term for the final human need, so termed because it can never be fully satisfied since there is no limit to how much one can grow

guru a yoga teacher

halo effect assuming that if a person has one positive quality, they have many other positive qualities

haqiqa third stage of Sufism in which the person fully understands the previous stages

Hatha-Yoga yoga using physical techniques

hedonic treadmill we have fluctuations of positive emotions, episodes of happiness, but in the long run, we simply drift back to where we were, with no overall progress

hedonic well-being often used synonymously with *subjective well-being*, but could be seen as referring to experiencing several events that give generally sensual pleasure

hedonism a philosophical concept which views happiness in terms of acquiring objects and experiences that give pleasure

hierarchy of needs Abraham Maslow's pyramidal arrangement of human needs with the most basic, life-sustaining needs at the base

hope a pattern of thinking in which a person has both the capacities to find routes to desired goals and the motivation to use those routes

HPA axis the hypothalamus, the pituitary gland, and the adrenal glands, in their response to stress

human nafs in Sufism, personality traits and tendencies that are concerned with reason and rationality

hypercompetitiveness Karen Horney's term for the excessive competitiveness often found in American culture

idealized self Karen Horney's term for the person's dream of what they could be or should be

identified regulation a form of extrinsic motivation in which the reason for performing a task comes from a belief that it will further other external goals

immune neglect underestimation of people's own resilience and ability to cope with the trials of life

impact bias overestimation of the intensity and the duration of the emotions people believe they will experience in future situations

impasse Fritz Perls's term for the state a child is placed in when parents have expectations that the child is not ready to fulfill

infatuation in Sternberg's Triangular Model of Love, a relationship containing only passion

inspired nafs in Sufism, a stage in which people have real motivation to make changes in their lives

integrated regulation a form of extrinsic motivation in which the reason for performing a task comes from beliefs that the task is valuable in itself

integration retaining one's cultural heritage while participating in the culture of the present society

intentionality Rollo May's term for the meaning which we give to experience or elements of our environment; the orientation to and the perspective we take in viewing the world

internal causes causes stemming from the individual's personality traits

intimacy part of Sternberg's Triangular Model of Love, the emotional element

intrinsic motivation refers to performing an action because of internal factors such as interest, curiosity, and satisfaction, without the necessity of any external reward or coercion

intrinsic religiosity following the practices of a particular faith because of profound belief in the truth of the teachings of the faith

introjected regulation a form of extrinsic motivation in which the reason for doing a task comes from feelings of guilt or lowered self-esteem for not performing the task, or feelings of self-enhancement for successful completion

Jnana-Yoga the yoga of wisdom

John Henryism a belief that one can achieve anything if one works hard enough and long enough

Jonah complex Abraham Maslow's term for fear of our own potential for greatness

karma the moral law of cause and effect that is inherent in everything

Karma-Yoga the yoga of acting selflessly

koan Zen nonsensical sentences and riddles used for meditation

languishing feeling hollow and empty in life, with little flexibility of thought or action and generally having few positive emotions

liking in Sternberg's Triangular Model of Love, a relationship containing only intimacy

ludus a playful style of love

mania a crazy style of love

mantra a spiritually meaningful phrase or sound that is repeated over and over; in Transcendental Meditation, a sound or word used as the focus of concentration

Mantra-Yoga yoga involving the repetition of a spiritually meaningful phrase or sound

marginalization abandoning one's cultural heritage yet not participating in the culture of the present society

marifa the final stage of Sufism in which the person has the definitive knowing of the truth, the union with the Divine, and the ultimate goal of Sufism

maya delusion; Fritz Perls's term for a level of thinking or illusion that is mainly rehearsal for future roles and situations

meaning-making the extent to which people comprehend, make sense of, or see significance in their lives, accompanied by the degree to which they perceive themselves to have a purpose, mission, or over-arching aim in life; the imposition of structure, coherence, and significance on events in our lives

mental toughness the ability to cope with stress by having control, commitment, confidence, and seeing change as challenge

migrantophobia fear, aversion, and negative stereotyping of anyone who immigrates

misattribution of arousal believing that arousal by one source is actually caused by another source

moral courage performing actions in which a person stands up for what he/she believes in, even in the face of possible disapproval, rejection, or other negative consequences

motivation the activation toward doing a task

moving against people Karen Horney's term for coping with anxiety by demonstrating superiority to others; also known as *hostile*

moving away from other people Karen Horney's term for coping with anxiety by avoiding any emotional commitments to others; also known as *detached*

moving toward other people Karen Horney's term for coping with anxiety by developing positive or dependent relationships with others; also known as *compliant* or *self-effacing*

multicultural personality a personality that includes flexibility, open-mindedness, social initiative, and the ability to function well in culturally diverse situations

nafs in Sufism, ego traits and tendencies

nafs pleasing to God in Sufism, a stage in which the individual recognizes the omnipotence of the Divine

need for love and belongingness Abraham Maslow's term for the third most basic human need, to be cared for and accepted by others

need for safety and security Abraham Maslow's term for the second most basic human need, to feel safe in body and secure in mind and emotion

near-death experience (NDE) the reported memory of impressions during a special state of consciousness, including a number of special elements such as out-of-body experience, pleasant feelings, seeing a tunnel, a light, deceased relatives, or a life review

nirvana in Buddhism, a state in which the boundary between self and all the rest of the Cosmos is extinguished

nonlove in Sternberg's Triangular Model of Love, the state when passion, intimacy, and commitment are all lacking

nonspecific action tendencies part of the broaden-and-build theory; positive emotions lead to tendencies to approach situations in life rather than avoid them, to explore rather than to remain static, to interact rather than remain isolated

openness Carl Rogers's term for the chance to be honest and true to the self

optimism a positive orientation that focuses concentration on the pluses of life instead of the negatives

overindulgence Fritz Perls's term for parental overconcern with making the child's life pleasant

overjustification effect providing rewards (extrinsic motivation) decreases the intrinsic pleasure derived from an activity

paradox of affluence the wealthier the nation becomes, the less its populace seems satisfied with their lives

passion part of Sternberg's Triangular Model of Love, the biological element

pathways according to Snyder's definition, the cognitive and active component of hope

peak-end rule the maximum intensity and the final intensity of emotion have a disproportionate effect on our evaluations of an experience

peak experiences Abraham Maslow's term for a situation which seems to take us out of ourselves, giving us a feeling of experiencing life with greater intensity and awareness than normal

personal wisdom wisdom applied to the self and one's own life

phenomenal field Carl Rogers's term for the unique way each individual views the world

physiological needs Abraham Maslow's term for needs that are necessary for life (e.g., food, water)

physical courage performing actions in which an action may result in the person's bodily harm or even death

plateau experience Abraham Maslow's term for a situation or event that triggers a changed perception of the world and a greater appreciation of life

pleased nafs in Sufism, a stage in which the individual accepts and appreciates both the good and the bad in life

positive illusions seeing ourselves in a more positive light than is realistically warranted

positive psychology the scientific study of the personal qualities, life choices and circumstances, and sociocultural conditions that promote a life well-lived, defined by criteria of happiness, physical and mental health, meaningfulness, and virtue

post-traumatic growth (PTG) positive changes that people may report after having had aversive experiences

posttraumatic stress disorder (PTSD) a major psychological disorder that may arise after someone has been involved in an incident in which stress has been extreme

pragma a practical style of love

primary appraisal determination of whether an event is threatening or not

problem-focused coping coping with the actual situation that engenders stress; coping with a situation or task by concentrating on ways to approach and solve the problem

procrastination the tendency to delay a task to the point of discomfort

propinquity geographical closeness; a factor in forming a friendship

psychological acculturation psychological changes that come about when two cultural groups meet and interact

psychological courage performing an action that may threaten one's psychological well-being

psychological well-being refers to happiness in terms of flourishing in life, comprised of individual characteristics of autonomy, environmental mastery, personal growth, positive relations with others, purpose in life, and self-acceptance

psychosomatic disorders real physical problems that are believed to be caused, at least in part, by stress and other psychological factors

pure nafs final level in Sufism, in which the ego is completely transcended and the person is in complete union with the Divine

real self Karen Horney's term for what we think we really are

reappraisal an antecedent-focused strategy for regulating emotions using cognitive change in which we change our interpretation of a situation to enhance positive feelings

religion a search for significance in ways related to the sacred, usually within an organized structure of belief

resilience the ability to handle stress and bounce back from stressful situations

resistance stage the second stage of the general adaptation syndrome in which, with prolonged stress, physiological responses decrease but still remain above resting level

response-focused strategies emotion-regulating strategies that are used to manage an emotion that is already activated

response modulation a response-focused strategy for regulating emotions in which we attempt to change an emotion that is already activated

romantic love in Sternberg's Triangular Model of Love, a relationship containing only passion and intimacy, but not commitment

roshi a Zen practitioner who has progressed to the point where he/she can be called a master and is permitted to teach

samadhi yoga enlightenment; a state of unimaginable bliss

sanzen Zen consultation about meditation

satori Zen enlightenment

savouring an experience that includes being aware of what is happening in the moment and examining the sensations and emotions that the moment brings

school connectedness the degree to which children feel themselves to be a part of the school community that accepts, values, and supports them

search for glory Karen Horney's term for the attempt to surmount the gap between the real self and the idealized self

secondary appraisal determination of whether one has the resources to cope with a stressful situation

self-actualization Abraham Maslow's term for the final human need to reach the state of optimal human functioning

self-compassion kindness toward oneself in the face of failure and disappointment

self-control voluntary and conscious self-regulation

self-defeating humour humour that is generally intended to build relationships, but demeans the self

self-disclosure revealing personal and private thoughts, feelings, and events to another person

self-enhancing humour humour with the primary purpose of protecting one's own ego by reframing a potentially threatening situation into one that is not so threatening

self-realization Karen Horney's term for the innate tendency for people to develop their own unique and special gifts, become attuned to their own thoughts and feelings, express these thoughts and feelings spontaneously, and relate to other people in a free and open manner

self-reports measurements using what people say about themselves, as revealed through asking them to answer open-ended questions or to fill out a questionnaire

separation retaining one's original cultural heritage and not participating in the culture of the present society

setpoint theory people have a stable point of happiness from which they may temporarily stray but to which they return in the long run

sharia the Sufi moral code that people should live by

sheikh Sufi spiritual leader or teacher

similarity shared values and worldviews; a factor in forming a friendship

situational meaning meaning found in the various events and episodes of day-to-day life

situation modification an antecedent-focused strategy for regulating emotions in which we change the situation

situation selection an antecedent-focused strategy for regulating emotions in which we choose the situation we want to be in to enhance or regulate our emotions

social comparison evaluating oneself and one's acquisitions by comparing oneself to other people who are similar

social desirability the tendency to make ourselves and our behaviour seem a little better than reality indicates

social identity both the knowledge of belongingness to and value for certain social groups

social identity theory our tendency to define ourselves in terms of the groups we belong to, which affects our sense of well-being

spirituality a search for the sacred, which may or may not be in conjunction with an organized religion

stable causes causes that remain at all times and will not change in the future

stress any circumstances that threaten or are perceived to threaten one's well-being and thereby tax one's coping abilities

storge a friendship style of love

subjective well-being often used as a synonym for happiness, examines whether the individual has more positive than negative emotions, and whether the individual feels satisfied with his or her life

suppression a response-focused strategy in which we hide our emotions within the situation

top-down model of subjective well-being innate predispositions for happiness affect perceptions of the different areas of our lives

tyranny of should Karen Horney's term for oppressive feelings about what one should be and do

unconditional positive regard Carl Rogers's term for the value we are (should) be given by others because of our being members of the human race

undoing hypothesis Fredrickson's theory that positive emotions aid in the psychological and physical process of recovering from negative emotions

tariqa stage of Sufism in which the person practises Sufism specifically

thought-action tendencies part of the broaden-and-build theory; learned strategies to use in the future to increase positive emotions

validity a measurement scale is valid if it measures what we think it's supposed to measure

vital courage a form of psychological courage in which a person lives and thrives in the face of physical or mental illness

will Rollo May's term for the capacity to organize our actions and feelings so that we can actually move toward our goal and fulfill our wish

wisdom the competence in, intention to, and application of critical life experiences to facilitate the optimal development of self and others (Webster, 2010)

zazen in Zen, seated meditation

References

Abele, A. E., & Gendolla, G. H. E. (2007). Individual differences in optimism predict the recall of personally relevant information. *Personality and Individual Differences, 43,* 1125–1135.

Ablett, J. R., & Jones, R. S. P. (2007). Resilience and well-being in palliative care staff: A qualitative study of hospice nurses' experience of work. *Psycho-Oncology, 16,* 733–740.

Abu-Rayya, H. M. (2009). Acculturation and its determinants among adult immigrants in France. *International Journal of Psychology*, 44(3), 195–203.

Ad-Dab'bagh, Y. (2008). The transformative effect of seeking the eternal: A sampling of the perspectives of two great Muslim intellectuals—Ibn-Ĥazm and Al-Ghazāli. *Psycholanalytic Inquiry, 28,* 550–559.

Adler, M. G., & Fagley, N. S. (2005). Appreciation: Individual differences in finding value and meaning as a unique predictor of subjective well-being. *Journal of Personality, 73(1),* 79–114.

Agate, J. R., Zabriskie, R. B., Agate, S. T., & Poff, R. (2009). Family leisure satisfaction and satisfaction with family life. *Journal of Leisure Research, 41(2),* 205–223.

Ai, A. L., Peterson, C., Bolling, S. F., & Rodgers, W. (2006). Depression, faith-based coping, and short-term post-operative global functioning in adult and older patients undergoing cardiac surgery. *Journal of Psychosomatic Research, 60,* 21–28.

Ainley, M., Enger, L., & Kennedy, G. (2008). The elusive experience of 'flow': Qualitative and quantitative indicators. *International Journal of Educational Research, 47,* 109–121.

Ainsworth, M. D. S. (1979). Infant–mother attachment, *American Psychologist, 34(10),* 932–937.

Ainsworth, M. D. S., Blehar, M. C., Waters, E., & Wall, S. (1978). *Patterns of attachment: A psychological study of the strange situation.* Hillsdale, NJ: Erlbaum.

Aldao, A., Nolen-Hoeksema, S., & Schweizer, S. (2010). Emotion-regulation strategies across psychopathology. *Clinical Psychology Review, 30,* 217–237.

Alexander, E. S., & Onwuegbuzie, A. J. (2007). Academic procrastination and the role of hope as a coping strategy. *Personality and Individual Differences, 42,* 1301–1310.

Ali, Z. I. (2007). Al-Ghazali and Schopenhauer on knowledge and suffering. *Philosophy East and West, 57,* 409–419.

Allan, L. G., Siegel, S., & Hannah, S. (2007). The sad truth about depressive realism. *The Quarterly Journal of Experimental Psychology, 60(3),* 482–495.

Allemand, M., Job, V., Christen, S., & Keller, M. (2008). Forgiveness and action orientation. *Personality and Individual Differences, 45,* 762–766.

Allen, K. P. (2010). A bullying system intervention in high school: A two-year school-wide follow-up. *Studies in Educational Evaluation, 36,* 83–92.

Allport, G. W. (1950). *The individual and his religion.* New York, NY: Macmillan.

Almedom, A. M., & Glandon, D. (2007). Resilience is not the absence of PTSD any more than health is the absence of disease. *Journal of Loss and Trauma, 12,* 127–143.

Alvarez, J., & Hunt, M. (2005). Risk and resilience in canine search and rescue handlers after 9-11. *Journal of Traumatic Stress, 133,* 584–600.

Antón, C. (2009). The impact of role stress on workers' behaviour through job satisfaction and organizational commitment. *International Journal of Psychology, 44(3),* 187–194.

Archer, J., Cantwell, R., & Bourke, S. (1999). Coping at university: An examination of achievement, motivation, self-regulation, confidence, and method of entry. *Higher Education Research & Development, 18(1),* 31–54.

Ardelt, M. (2005). How wise people cope with crises and obstacles in life. *ReVision, 28(1),* 7–19.

Argyle, M. (1987). *The psychology of happiness.* London, UK: Methuen.

Argyle, M. (1999). Causes and correlates of happiness. In D. Kahneman, E. Diener, & N. Schwartz, (Eds.) *Well-being: The foundation of hedonic psychology* (pp. 353–373), New York, NY: Russell Sage Foundation.

Aristotle, (4th century BCE/2003). *Ethics.* trans. J. A. K. Thomson. London, UK: The Folio Society.

Armata, P. M., & Baldwin, D. R. (2008). Stress, optimism, resiliency, and cortisol with relation to digestive symptoms or diagnosis. *Individual Differences Research, 6(2),* 123–138.

Armor, D. A., Massey, C., & Sackett, A. M. (2008). Prescribed optimism: Is it right to be wrong about the future? *Psychological Science, 19(4),* 329–331.

Armstrong-Stassen, M., & Ursel, N. D. (2009). Perceived organizational support, career satisfaction, and the retention of older workers. *Journal of Occupational and Organizational Psychology, 82,* 201–220.

Asante, M. K., & Nwadiora, E. (2007). *Spear masters.* Latham, MD: University Press of America.

Asakawa, K. (2010). Flow experience, culture, and well-being: How do autotelic Japanese college students feel, behave, and think in their daily lives? *Journal of Happiness Studies, 11,* 205–223.

Ateca-Amestoy, V., Serrano-del-Rosal, R., & Vera-Toscano, E. (2008). The leisure experience. *The Journal of Socio-Economics, 37,* 64–78.

Augustine, A. A., & Hemenover, S. H. (2009). On the relative effectiveness of affect regulation strategies: A meta-analysis. *Cognition and Emotion, 23(6),* 1181–1220.

Baca-Garcia, E., Parra, C. P., Perez-Rodriguez, M. M., Sastre, C. D., Torres, R. R., Saiz-Ruiz, J., & de Leon, J. (2007). Psychosocial stressors may be strongly associated with suicide attempts. *Stress and Health, 23,* 191–198.

Badyshtova, I. M. (2005). Attitudes of the local population towards migrants. *Sociological Research, 44(1),* 26–46.

Bagwell, C. L., Bender, S. E., Andreassi, C. L., Kinoshita, T. L., Montarello, S. A., & Muller, J. G. (2005). Friendship quality and perceived relationship changes predict psychosocial adjustment in early adulthood. *Journal of Social and Personal Relationships, 22(2),* 235–254.

Bailey, T. C., & Snyder, C. R. (2007). Satisfaction with life and hope: A look at age and marital status. *The Psychological Record, 57,* 233–240.

Baker, S. R. (2007). Dispositional optimism and health status, symptoms and behaviours: Assessing idiothetic relationships using a prospective daily diary approach. *Psychology and Health, 22(4),* 431–455.

Bakker, A. B. (2009). The crossover of burnout and its relation to partner health. *Stress and Health, 25,* 343–353.

Baldwin, D. R., Kennedy, D. L., & Armata, P. (2008a). Short communication: De-stressing mommy: Ameliorative association with dispositional optimism and resiliency. *Stress and Health, 24,* 393–400.

Baldwin, D. R., Kennedy, D. L., & Armata, P. (2008b). De-stressing mommy: Ameliorative association with dispositional optimism and resiliency. *Stress and Health, 24,* 393–400.

Baltes, P. B., & Smith, J. (2008). The fascination of wisdom: Its nature, ontogeny, and function. *Perspectives on Psychological Science, 3,* 56–64.

Bandura, A. (1977). Self-efficacy: Toward a unifying theory of behavioral change. *Psychological Review, 84,* 191–215.

Bandura, A. (1997). *Self-efficacy: The exercise of control.* New York, NY: Freeman.

Barlow, P. J., Tobin, D. J., & Schmidt, M. M. (2009). Social interest and positive psychology: Positively aligned. *The Journal of Individual Psychology, 65(3),* 191–202.

Barnett, L. A. (2006). Accounting for leisure preferences from within: The relative contributions of gender, race or ethnicity, personality, affective style, and motivational orientation. *Journal of Leisure Research, 38(4),* 445–474.

Bar-On, R. (2005). The impact of emotional intelligence on subjective well-being. *Perspectives in Education, 23,* 41–61.

Bar-On, R. (2010). Emotional intelligence: An integral part of positive psychology. *South African Journal of Psychology, 40(1),* 54–62.

Barskova, T., & Oesterreich, R. (2009). Post-traumatic growth in people living with a serious medical condition and its relations to physical and mental health: An overview. *Disability and Rehabilitation, 31(21),* 1709–1733.

Bartlett, M. Y., & DeSteno, D. (2006). Gratitude and prosocial behavior: Helping when it costs you. *Psychological Science, 17(4),* 319–325.

Basom, M. R., & Frase, L. (2004). Creating optimal work environments: Exploring teacher flow experiences. *Mentoring and Tutoring, 12(2),* 241–258.

Basso, K. H. (1996). *Wisdom sits in places: Landscape and language among the western Apache.* Albuquerque, NM: University of New Mexico Press.

Batool, S. S., & Khalid, R. (2009). Role of emotional intelligence in marital relationship. *Pakistan Journal of Psychological Research, 24,* 43–62.

Battista, J., & Almond, R. (1973). The development of meaning in life. *Psychiatry, 36,* 409–427.

Baum, L. F. (1944). *The wizard of Oz.* New York, NY: Gross & Dunlop, Inc.

Baumeister, R. F. (2002). Ego depletion and self-control failure: An energy model of the self's executive function. *Self and Identity, 1,* 129–136.

Baumeister, R. F. (2008). Free will in scientific psychology. *Perspectives on Psychological Science, 3(1),* 14–19.

Baumeister, R. F., Campbell, J. D., Krueger, J. I., & Vohs, K. D. (2003). Does high self-esteem cause better performance, interpersonal success, happiness, or

healthier lifestyles? *Psychological Science in the Public Interest, 4,* 1–44.

Baumeister, R. F., Gailliot, M., DeWall, C. N., & Oaten, M. (2006). Self-Regulation and personality: How interventions increase regulatory success, and how depletion moderates the effects of traits on behavior. *Journal of Personality, 74 (6),* 1773–1801.

Baumeister, R. F., Vohs, K. D., & Tice, D. M. (2007). The strength model of self-control. *Current Directions in Psychological Science, 16(6),* 351–355.

Baumgardner, S. R., & Crothers, M. K. (2009). *Positive psychology.* Upper Saddle River, NJ: Prentice Hall.

Baumrind, D. (1971). Harmonious parents and their preschool children. *Developmental Psychology, 41(1),* 99–102.

Baumrind, D., & Black, A. E. (1967). Socialization practices associated with dimensions of competence in preschool boys and girls. *Child Development, 38(2),* 291–327.

Bayer, U. C., Gollwitzer, P. M., & Achtziger, A. (2010). Staying on track: Planned goal striving is protected from disruptive internal states. *Journal of Experimental Social Psychology, 46,* 505–514.

Bayram, N., & Bilgel, N. (2008). The prevalence and socio-demographic correlations of depression, anxiety and stress among a group of university students. *Social Psychiatry & Psychiatric Epidemiology, 43,* 667–672.

Beaumont, S. L. (2009). Identity processing and personal wisdom: An information-oriented identity style predicts self-actualization and self-transcendence. *Identity: An International Journal of Theory and Research, 9,* 95–115.

Beckers, D. G. J., van der Linden, D., Smulders, P. G. W., Kompier, M. A. J., Taris, T. W., & Geurts, S. A. E. (2008). Voluntary or involuntary? Control over overtime and rewards for overtime in relation to fatigue and work satisfaction. *Work & Stress, 22(1),* 33–50.

Bembenutty, H. (2009). Self-regulation of homework completion. *Psychology Journal, 6(4),* 138–153.

Benzies, K., & Mychasiuk, R. (2009). Fostering family resilience: A review of the key protective factors. *Child & Family Social Work, 14,* 103–114.

Bergsma, A. (2008). Do self-help books help? *Journal of Happiness Studies, 9,* 341–360.

Berry, B. J. L., & Okulicz-Kozaryn, A. (2009). Dissatisfaction with city life: A new look at some old questions. *Cities, 26,* 117–124.

Berry, J. W. (2001). A psychology of immigration. *Journal of Social Issues, 57(3),* 615–631.

Beydoun, H., & Saftlas, A. F. (2008). Physical and mental health outcomes of prenatal maternal stress in human and animal studies: A review of recent evidence. *Paediatric and Perinatal Epidemiology, 22,* 438–466.

Bisegger, C., Cloetta, B., Ravens-Sieberer, U., & The European KIDSCREEN Group. (2008). The CANEP Scale: Preliminary psychometric findings of a measure of youths' perception of their neighborhood environment. *Journal of Community Psychology, 36(1),* 81–95.

Biswas-Diener, R. M. (2008). Material wealth and subjective well-being. In M. Eid & R. J. Larsen (Eds.), *The science of subjective well-being* (pp. 307–322), New York, NY: Guilford Press.

Bjørnskov, C., Dreher, A., & Fischer, J. A. V. (2010). Formal institutions and subjective well-being: Revisiting the cross-country evidence. *European Journal of Political Economy, 26,* 419–430.

Blanco, F., Matute, H., & Vadillo, M. A. (2009). Depressive realism: Wiser or quieter? *The Psychological Record, 59,* 551–562.

Blonna, R. (2007). *Coping with stress in a changing world* (4th ed.), Boston, MA: McGraw-Hill.

Blunsdon, B., & Davern, M. (2007). Measuring wellness through interdisciplinary community development: Linking the physical, economic and social environment. *Journal of Community Practice, 15(1/2),* 217–238.

Bodian, S. (2006). *Meditation for dummies* (2nd ed.). Hoboken, NJ: Wiley Publishing, Inc.

Boelen, P. A., & Reijntjes, A. (2008). Negative cognitions in emotional problems following romantic relationship break-ups. *Stress and Health, 25,* 11–19.

Boezerman, E. J., & Ellemers, N. (2009). Intrinsic need satisfaction and job attitudes of volunteers versus employees working in a charitable volunteer organization. *Journal of Occupational and Organizational Psychology, 82,* 897–914.

Bonebright, C. A., Clay, D. L., & Ankenmann, R. D. (2000). The relationship of workaholism with work-life conflict, life satisfaction, and purpose in life. *Journal of Counseling Psychology, 47,* 469–477.

Boniwell, I., Osin, E., Linley, P. A., & Ivanchenko, G. V. (2010). A question of balance: Time perspective and well-being in British and Russian samples. *Journal of Positive Psychology, 5,* 24–40.

Bono, G., & McCullough, M. E. (2006). Positive responses to benefit and harm: Bringing forgiveness and gratitude into cognitive psychotherapy. *Journal of Cognitive Psychotherapy, 20,* 147–158.

Booth-Butterfield, M., Booth-Butterfield, S., & Wanzer, M. (2007). Funny students cope better: Patterns of humor enactment and coping effectiveness. *Communication Quarterly, 55(3),* 299–315.

Bopp, J., Bopp, M., Brown, L., & Lane Jr., P. (1984). *The sacred tree: Reflections on Native American spirituality.* Twin Lakes, WS: Lotus Light Publications.

Bosticco, C., & Thompson, T. L. (2005). Narratives and story telling in coping with grief and bereavement. *Omega, 51(1),* 1–16.

Bourke, C. (2006). Economics: Independence or welfare. In C. Bourke, E. Bourke, & B. Edwards (Eds.), *Aboriginal Australia* (2nd ed.) (pp. 219–244), St. Lucia, Australia: University of Queensland Press.

Bouteyre, E., Maurel, M., & Bernaud, J-L. (2007). Daily hassles and depressive symptoms among first year psychology students in France: The role of coping and social support. *Stress and Health, 23,* 93–99.

Brackett, M. A., & Mayer, J. D. (2003). Convergent, discriminant. and incremental validity of competing measures of emotional intelligence. *Personality and Social Psychology Bulletin, 29,* 1147–1158.

Brackett, M. A., Mayer, J. D., & Warner, R. M. (2004). Emotional intelligence and its relations to everyday behaviour. *Personality and Individual Differences, 36,* 1387–1402.

Brackett, M. A., Rivers, S. E., Shiffman, S., Lerner, N., & Salovey, P. (2006). Relating emotional abilities to social functioning: A comparison of self-report and performance measures of emotional intelligence. *Journal of Personality and Social Psychology, 91,* 780–795.

Brackett, M. A., Warner, R. M., & Bosco, J. S. (2005). Emotional intelligence and relationship quality among couples. *Personal Relationships, 12,* 197–212.

Bramston, P., Pretty, G., & Chipuer, H. (2002). Unravelling subjective quality of life: An investigation of individual and community determinants. *Social Indicator Research, 59,* 261–274.

Braskamp, L., Trautvetter, L. C., & Ward, K. (2008). Putting students first: Promoting lives of purpose and meaning. *About Campus, 13(1),* 26–32.

Brdar, I., Rijavec, M., & Miljković, D. (2010). Life goals and well-being: Are extrinsic aspirations always detrimental to well-being? *Psychological Topics, 18(2),* 317–334.

Brennan, M. A. (2008). Conceptualizing resiliency: An interactional perspective for community and youth development. *Child Care in Practice, 14(1),* 55–64.

Brereton, F., Clinch, P., & Ferreira, S. (2008). Happiness, geography and the environment. *Ecological Economics, 65,* 386–396.

Bresó, E., Salanova, M., & Schaufeli, W. B. (2007). In search of the "third dimension" of burnout: Efficacy or inefficacy? *Applied Psychology: An International Review, 56(3),* 460–478.

Brickman, P., & Campbell, D. (1971). Hedonic relativism and planning the good society. In M. H. Appley (Ed.), *Adaptation-level theory: A symposium* (pp. 287–302), New York, NY: Academic Press.

Brickman, P., Coates, D., & Janoff-Bulman, R. (1978). Lottery winners and accident victims: Is happiness relative? *Journal of Personality and Social Psychology, 36,* 917–927.

Brodhagen, A., & Wise, D. (2008). Optimism as a mediator between the experience of child abuse, other traumatic events, and distress. *Journal of Family Violence, 23,* 403–411.

Bruk-Lee, V., Khoury, H. A., Nixon, A. E., Goh, A., & Spector, P. E. (2009). Replicating and extending past personality/job satisfaction meta-analyses. *Human Performance, 22,* 156–189.

Brummett, B. H., Helms, M. J., Dahlstrom, G., & Siegler, I. C. (2006). Prediction of all-cause mortality by the Minnesota Multiphasic Personality Inventory Optimism-Pessimism Scale scores: Study of a college sample during a 40-year follow-up period. *Mayo Clinic Proceedings, 81(12),* 1541–1544.

Brummett, B. R., Wade, J. C., Ponterotto, J. G., Thombs, B., & Lewis, C. (2007). Psychosocial well-being and a multicultural personality disposition. *Journal of Counseling & Development, 85,* 73–81.

Bryant, F. B. (2003). Savoring beliefs inventory (SBI): A scale for measuring beliefs about savoring. *Journal of Mental Health, 12,* 175–196.

Bryant, F. B., & Veroff, J. (2007). *Savoring: A new model of positive experience.* Mahwah, NJ: Erlbaum.

Brydon, L., Walker, C., Wawrzyniak, A. J., Chart, H., & Steptoe, A. (2009). Dispositional optimism and stress-induced changes in immunity and negative mood. *Brain, Behavior, and Immunity, 23,* 810–816.

Burka, J. B., & Yuen, L. M. (2008). *Procrastination: Why you do it, what to do about it now* (2nd ed.), Cambridge, MA: Da Capo Press.

Burke, J., O'Campo, P., Salmon, C., & Walker, R. (2009). Pathways connecting neighborhood influences and mental well-being: Socioeconomic position and gender differences. *Social Science & Medicine, 68,* 1294–1304.

Burnette, J. L., Davis, D. E., Green, J. D., Worthington Jr., E. L., & Bradfield, E. (2009). Insecure attachment and depressive symptoms: The mediating role of rumination, empathy, and forgiveness. *Personality and Individual Differences, 46,* 276–280.

Burns, A. B., Brown, J. S., Sachs-Ericsson, N., Plant, A., Curtis, J. T., Fredrickson, B. L., & Joiner, T. E. (2008). Upward spirals of positive emotion and coping: Replication, extension, and initial exploration of neurochemical substrates. *Personality and Individual Differences, 44(2),* 360–370.

Burris, J. L., Brechting, E. H., Salsman, J., & Carlson, C. R. (2009). Factors associated with the psychological well-being and distress of university students. *Journal of American College Health, 57,* 536–543.

Bushman, B. J. (2002). Does venting anger feed or extinguish the flame? Catharsis, rumination, distraction, anger, and aggressive responding. *Personality and Social Psychology Bulletin, 28(6),* 724–731.

Buss, D. M., Shackelford, T. K., Kirkpatrick, L. A., & Larsen, R. J. (2001). A half century of mate preferences: The cultural evolution of values. *Marriage and Family, 63,* 491–503.

Byrne, D. G., & Espnes, G. A. (2008). Occupational stress and cardiovascular disease. *Stress and Health, 24,* 231–238.

Byron, K., & Miller-Perrin, C. (2009). The value of life purpose: Purpose as a mediator of faith and well-being. *The Journal of Positive Psychology, 4(1),* 64–70.

Cacioppo, J. T., Hawkley, L. C., & Berntson, G. C. (2003). The anatomy of loneliness. *Current Directions in Psychological Science, 12(3),* 71–74.

Caldwell, K., Harrison, M., Adams, M., Quin, R. H., & Greeson, J. (2010). Developing mindfulness in college students through movement-based courses: Effects on self-regulatory self-efficacy, mood, stress, and sleep quality. *Journal of American College Health, 58(5),* 433–442.

Campbell-Sills, L., Cohan, S. L., & Stein, M. B. (2006). Relationship of resilience to personality, coping, and psychiatric symptoms in young adults. *Behavior Research and Therapy, 44,* 585–599.

Campbell-Sills, L., Forde, D. R., & Stein, M. B. (2009). Demographic and childhood environmental predictors of resilience in a community sample. *Journal of Psychiatric Research, 43,* 1007–1012.

Canada's Top 100 Employers. (2011). www.canadastop100.com

Canadian Association for Stress-Free Schools. (2011). www.stressfreeschools.ca

Canli, T., Ferri, J., & Duman, E. A. (2009). Genetics of emotion regulation. *Neuroscience, 164,* 43–54.

Cann, A., & Etzel, K. C. (2008). Remembering and anticipating stressors: Positive personality mediates the relationship with sense of humor. *Humor, 21(2),* 157–178.

Capps, D. (2006). The psychological benefits of humor. *Pastoral Psychology, 54(5),* 393–411.

Carleton, R. A., Esparza, P., Thaxter, P. J., & Grant, K. E. (2008). Stress, religious coping resources, and depressive symptoms in an urban adolescent sample. *Journal for the Scientific Study of Religion, 47(1),* 113–121.

Carmody, D. L., & Carmody, J. T. (1993). *Native American religions: An introduction.* New York, NY: Paulist Press.

Carr, A. (2007). *Positive psychology: The science of happiness and human strengths.* New York, NY: Routledge.

Carrère, S., Buehlman, K. T., Gottman, J. M., Coan, J. A., & Ruckstuhl, L. (2000). Predicting marital stability and divorce in newlywed couples. *Journal of Family Psychology, 14(1),* 42–58.

Caspi, A., Taylor, A., Moffitt, T. E., & Plomin, R. (2000). Neighborhood deprivation affects children's mental health: Environmental risks identified in a genetic design. *Psychological Science, 11(4),* 338–342.

Ceja, L., & Navarro, J. (2009). Dynamics of flow: A nonlinear perspective. *Journal of Happiness Studies, 10,* 665–684.

Chambers, R., Gullone, E., & Allen, N. B. (2009). Mindful emotion regulation: An integrative review. *Clinical Psychology Review, 29,* 560–572.

Chan, W. (1963). *A source book in Chinese philosophy.* San Francisco, CA: Harper-Collins.

Chaplin, L. N. (2009). Please may I have a bike? Better yet, may I have a hug? An examination of children's and adolescents' happiness. *Journal of Happiness Studies, 10,* 541–562.

Chappell, N. L. (2005). Perceived change in quality of life among Chinese Canadian seniors: The role of involvement in Chinese culture. *Journal of Happiness Studies, 6,* 69–91.

Cheavens, J. S., Feldman, D. B., Gum, A., Michael, S. T., & Snyder, C. R. (2006). Hope therapy in a community sample: A pilot investigation. *Social Indicators Research, 77,* 61–78.

Chen, F-C., Ku, E. C. S., Shyr, Y-H., Chen, F-H., & Chou, S-S. (2009). Job demand, emotional awareness, and job satisfaction in internships: The moderating effect of social support. *Social Behavior and Personality, 37(10),* 1429–1440.

Chen, S-Y., & Scannapieco, M. (2010). The influence of job satisfaction on child welfare worker's [sic] desire to stay: An examination of the interaction effect of self-efficacy and supportive supervision. *Child and Youth Services Review, 32,* 482–486.

Chen, W-Q., Siu, O-L., Lu, J-F., Cooper, C. L., & Phillips, D. R. (2009). Work stress and depression: The direct and moderating effects of informal social support and coping. *Stress and Health, 25,* 431–443.

Chen, Z., Zhang, X., Leung, K., & Zhou, F. (2010). Exploring interactive effect of time control and justice perception on job attitudes. *The Journal of Social Psychology, 150(2),* 181–197.

Chida, Y., & Hamer, M. (2008). Chronic psychosocial factors and acute physiological responses to laboratory-induced stress in healthy populations: A quantitative review of 30 years of investigation. *Psychological Bulletin, 134(6),* 829–885.

Chiesa, A. (2009). Zen meditation: An integration of current evidence. *The Journal of Alternative and Complementary Medicine, 15(5),* 585–592.

Chiesa, A., & Serretti, A. (2009). Mindfulness-based stress reduction for stress management in healthy people: A review and meta-analysis. *The Journal of Alternative and Complementary Medicine, 15(5),* 593–600.

Chopko, B. A., & Schwartz, R. C. (2009). The relation between mindfulness and posttraumatic growth: A study of first responders to trauma-inducing incidents. *Journal of Mental Health Counseling, 31(4),* 363–376.

Chow, H. P. H. (2007). Sense of belonging and life satisfaction among Hong Kong adolescent immigrants in Canada. *Journal of Ethnic and Migration Studies, 33(3),* 511–520.

Chow, R. M., & Lowery, B. S. (2010). Thanks, but no thanks: The role of personal responsibility in the experience of gratitude. *Journal of Experimental Social Psychology, 46,* 487–493.

Chu, A. H. C., & Choi, J. N. (2005). Rethinking procrastination: Positive effects of "active" procrastination behaviour on attitudes and performance. *The Journal of Social Psychology, 145(3),* 245–264.

Chu, P S., Saucier, D. A., & Hafner, E. (2010). Meta-analysis of the relationships between social support and well-being in children and adolescents. *Journal of Social and Clinical Psychology, 29(6),* 624–645.

Ciarrocchi, J. W., Dy-Liacco, G. S., & Deneke, E. (2008). Gods or rituals? Relational faith, spiritual discontent, and religious practices as predictors of hope and optimism. *The Journal of Positive Psychology, 3(2),* 120–136.

Claessens, B. J. C., Eerde, W. V., Rutte, C. G., & Roe, R. A. (2004). Planning behavior and perceived control of time at work. *Journal of Organizational Behavior, 25,* 937–950.

Clauss-Ehler, C. S. (2008). Sociocultural factors, resilience, and coping: Support for a culturally sensitive measure of resilience. *Journal of Applied Developmental Psychology, 29,* 197–212.

Clinton, J. (2008). Resilience and recovery. *International Journal of Children's Spirituality, 13(3),* 213–222.

Clough, P., Earle, K., & Sewell, D. (2002). Mental toughness: The concept and its measurement. In I. Cockerill (Ed.), *Solution in sport psychology* (pp. 32–45), London, UK: Thomson.

Collaborative for Academic, Social and Emotional Learning. (2011). www.casel.org

Collins, A. L., Sarkisian, N., & Winner, E. (2009). Flow and happiness in later life: An investigation into the roles of daily and weekly flow experiences. *Journal of Happiness Studies, 10,* 703–719.

Colville, G., & Cream, P. (2009). Post-traumatic growth in parents after a child's admission to intensive care: Maybe Nietzsche was right? *Intensive Care Medicine, 35,* 919–923.

Compton, R. J., Robinson, M. D., Ode, S., Quandt, L. C., Fineman, S. L., & Carp, J. (2008). Error-monitoring ability predicts daily stress regulation. *Psychological Science, 19(7),* 702–708.

Compton, W. C. (2005). *An introduction to positive psychology.* Belmont, CA: Wadsworth.

Confucius. (2008). *The analects.* London, UK: The Folio Society.

Connor, K. M., & Davidson, J. R. T. (2003). Development of a new resilience scale: The Connor-Davidson Resilience Scale (CD-RISC). *Depression and Anxiety, 18,* 76–82.

Conoley, C. W., & Conoley, J. C. (2009). *Positive psychology and family therapy: Creative techniques and practical tools for guiding change and enhancing growth.* Hoboken, NJ: John Wiley & Sons.

Constantine, M. G., & Sue, D. W. (2006). Factors contributing to optimal human functioning in people of color in the United States. *The Counseling Psychologist, 34(2),* 228–244.

Coppola, F., & Spector, D. (2009). Natural stress relief meditation as a tool for reducing anxiety and increasing self-actualization. *Social Behavior and Personality, 37(3),* 307–312.

Cottingham, A. H., Suchman, A. L., Litzelman, D. K., Frankel, R. M., Mossbarger, D. L., Williamson, P. R., Baldwin, D. C., & Inui, T. S. (2008). Enhancing the informal curriculum of a medical school: A case study in organizational culture change. *Journal of General Internal Medicine, 23(6),* 715–722.

Cox, L. (2009). Queensland Aborigines, multiple realities and the social sources of suffering: Psychiatry and moral regions of being. *Oceania, 79(2),* 97–120.

Coyhis, D., & Simonelli, R. (1999). The Native American healing experience. *Substance Use & Misuse, 43,* 1927–1949.

Creighton University. (2011). The mission and identity of Creighton University. www.creighton.edu/about/

Cropley, M., Dijk, D. J., & Stanley, N. (2006). Job strain, work rumination, and sleep in school teachers. *European Journal of Work and Organizational Psychology, 15(2),* 181–196.

Cropley, M., & Millward, L. J. (2009). How do individuals "switch-off" from work during leisure? A qualitative description of the unwinding process in high and low ruminators. *Leisure Studies, 28(3),* 333–347.

Csikszentmihalyi, M. (1975). *Beyond boredom and anxiety: Experiencing flow in work and play.* New York, NY: Harper & Row.

Csikszentmihalyi, M. (1990). *Flow: The psychology of optimal experience.* New York, NY: Harper Collins.

Csikszentmihalyi, M. (1999). If we are so rich, why aren't we happy? *American Psychologist, 54,* 821–827.

Csikszentmihalyi, M., & Lefevre, J. (1989). Optimal experience in work and leisure. *Journal of Personality and Social Psychology, 56(5),* 815–822.

Darling, C. A., McWey, L. M., Howard, S. N., & Olmstead, S. B. (2007). College student stress: The influence of interpersonal relationships on sense of coherence. *Stress and Health, 23,* 215–229.

Dart, J. (2006). Home-based work and leisure spaces: Settee or work station? *Leisure Studies, 25(3),* 313–328.

Davydov, D. M., Stewart, R., Ritchie, K., & Chaudieu, I. (2010). Resilience and mental health. *Clinical Psychology Review, 30,* 479–495.

Day, A. (2009). Offender emotion and self-regulation: Implications for offender rehabilitation programming. *Psychology, Crime & Law, 15(2&3),* 119–130.

De Marco, A., & De Marco, M. (2010). Conceptualization and measurement of the neighborhood in rural settings: A systematic review of the literature. *Journal of Community Psychology, 38(1),* 99–114.

Debats, D. L., van der Lubbe, P. M., & Wezeman, F. R. A. (1993). On the psychometric properties of the Life Regard Index (LRI): A measure of meaningful life. *Personality and Individual Differences, 14,* 337–345.

Deci, E. L., & Ryan, R. M. (1995). Human autonomy: The basis for true self-esteem. In M. Kernis (Ed.), *Efficacy, agency, and self-esteem* (pp. 31–49), New York, NY: Plenum Press.

Deci, E. L., & Ryan, R. M. (2000). The "what" and "why" of goal pursuits: Human needs and the self-determination of behavior. *Psychological Inquiry, 11,* 319–338.

del Valle, C. H. C., & Mateos, P. M. (2008). Dispositional pessimism, defensive pessimism and optimism: The effect of induced mood on prefactual and counterfactual thinking and performance. *Cognition and Emotion, 22(8),* 1600–1612.

Delgado, L. C., Guerra, P., Perakakis, P., Vera, M. N., del Paso, G. R., & Vila, J. (2010). Treating chronic worry: Psychological and physiological effects of a training programme based on mindfulness. *Behaviour Research and Therapy, 48(9),* 873–882.

Deloria Jr., V. (1994). *God is red: A native view of religion.* Golden, CO: Fulcrum Publishing.

Deloria Jr., V. (1999). *For this land: Writings on religion in America.* New York, NY: Routledge.

Demerouti, E. (2006). Job characteristics, flow, and performance: The moderating role of conscientiousness. *Journal of Occupational Health Psychology, 11,* 266–280.

Demo, D. H. (1992). Parent-child relations: Assessing recent changes. *Journal of Marriage and the Family, 54,* 104–117.

Denham, S. A., & Kachanoff, A. T. (2002). Parental contributions to preschoolers' understanding of emotion. *Marriage and Family Review, 34,* 311–343.

Deniz, M. E., Traş, Z., & Aydoğan, D. (2009). An investigation of academic procrastination, locus of control, and emotional intelligence. *Educational Sciences: Theory & Practice, 9(2),* 623–632.

Denson, T. F., Spanovic, M., & Miller, N. (2009). Cognitive appraisals and emotions predict cortisol and immune responses: A meta-analysis of acute laboratory social stressors and emotion inductions. *Psychological Bulletin, 135(6),* 823–853.

De Souza, M., & Rymarz, R. (2007). The role of cultural and spiritual expressions in affirming a sense of self, place, and purpose among young urban, Indigenous Australians. *International Journal of Children's Spirituality, 12(3),* 277–288.

Devereux, G. (1994). *The elements of Yoga.* Shaftesbury, UK: Element Books.

Diener, E. (1984). Subjective well-being. *Psychological Bulletin, 95,* 542–575.

Diener, E. (2000). Subjective well-being: The science of happiness and a proposal for a national index. *American Psychologist, 55,* 34–43.

Diener, E. (2008). Myths in the science of happiness, and directions for future research. In M. Eid & R. J. Larsen (Eds.), *The science of subjective well-being* (pp. 493–514), New York, NY: Guilford Press.

Diener, E., & Biswas-Diener, R. (2002). Will money increase subjective well-being? A literature review and guide to needed research. *Social Indicators Research, 57,* 119–169.

Diener, E., Emmons, R. A., Larson, R. J., & Griffin, S. (1985). The satisfaction with life scale. *Journal of Personality Assessment, 49,* 71–75.

Diener, E., Horowitz, J., & Emmons, R. (1985). Happiness of the very wealthy. *Journal of Personality Assessment, 49,* 71–75.

Diener, E., Oishi, S., & Lucas, R. (2003). Personality, culture, and subjective well-being: Emotional and cognitive evaluations of life. *Annual Review of Psychology, 54,* 403–425.

Diener, E., & Ryan, K. (2009). Subjective well-being: A general overview. *South African Journal of Psychology, 39(4),* 391–406.

Diener, E., & Seligman, M. E. P. (2004). Beyond money: Toward an economy of well-being. *Psychological Science in the Public Interest, 5(1),* 1–31.

Di Fabio, A., & Palazzeschi, L. (2009). An in-depth look at scholastic success: Fluid intelligence, personality traits or emotional *Differences, 46,* 581–585.

Dittmar, H., & Halliwell, E. (2008). *Consumer society, identity, and well-being: The search for the 'good life' and the 'body perfect'.* London, UK: Psychology Press.

Dolan, P. (2008). Prospective possibilities for building resilience in children, their families and communities. *Child Care in Practice, 14(1),* 83–91.

Domes, G., Schulze, L., & Herpertz, S. C. (2009). Emotion recognition in borderline personality disorder: A review of the literature. *Journal of Personality Disorders, 23(1),* 6–19.

Drakopoulos, S. A. (2008). The paradox of happiness: Towards an alternative explanation. *Journal of Happiness Studies, 9,* 303–315.

Duckworth, A. L., & Seligman, M. E. P. (2005). Self-discipline outdoes IQ in predicting academic performance of adolescents. *Psychological Science, 16(12),* 939–944.

Duffy, K. G., Kirsh, S. J., & Atwater, E. (2011). *Psychology for living: Adjustment, growth, and behavior today* (10th ed.). Upper Saddle River, NJ: Prentice-Hall.

Duncan, G. (2010). Should happiness-maximization be the goal of government? *Journal of Happiness Studies, 11,* 163–178.

Durand, V. M., Barlow, D. H., & Stewart, S. H. (2007). *Essentials of Abnormal Psychology,* 1st Canadian Edition. Toronto, ON: Thomson-Nelson.

Durkin, J., & Joseph, S. (2009). Growth following adversity and its relation with subjective well-being and psychological well-being. *Journal of Loss and Trauma, 14,* 228–234.

Durlak, J. A., & DuPre, E. P. (2008). Implementation matters: A review of research on the influence of implementation on program outcomes and the factors affecting implementation. *American Journal of Community Psychology, 41,* 327–350.

Durlak, J. A., Taylor, R. D., Kawashima, K., Pachan, M. K., DuPre, E. P., Celio, C. I., Berger, S. R., Dymnicki, A. B., & Weissberg, R. P. (2007). Effects of positive youth development programs on school, family, and community systems. *American Journal of Community Psychology, 39,* 269–286.

Durlak, J. A., Weissberg, R. P., Dymnicki, A. B., Taylor, R. D., & Schellinger, K. B. (2011). The impact of enhancing students' social and emotional learning: A meta-analysis of school-based universal interventions. *Child Development, 82(1),* 405–432.

Dutton, D. G., & Aron, A. P. (1974). Some evidence for heightened sexual attraction under conditions of high anxiety. *Journal of Personality and Social Psychology, 30,* 510–517.

Eaton, J., & Struthers, C. W. (2006). The reduction of psychological aggression across varied interpersonal contexts through repentance and forgiveness. *Aggressive Behavior, 32,* 195–206.

Edwards, B. (2006). Living the Dreaming. In C. Bourke, E. Bourke, & B. Edwards (Eds.) *Aboriginal Australia* (2nd ed.) (pp. 77–99), St. Lucia, Australia: University of Queensland Press.

Edwards, B. D., Bell, S. T., Arthur Jr., W., & Decuir, A. D. (2008). Relationships between facets of job satisfaction and task and contextual performance. *Applied Psychology: An International Review, 57(3),* 441–465.

Eisses, A. M. H., Kluiter, H., Jongenelis, K., Pot, A. M., Beekman, A. T., Ormel, J. (2004). Risk indicators of depression in residential homes. *International Journal of Geriatric Psychiatry, 19,* 634–640.

Eliade, M. (1969). *Yoga: Immortality and freedom.* Princeton, NJ: Princeton University Press.

Ellison, C. G., Burdette, A. M., & Hill, T. D. (2009). Blessed assurance: Religion, anxiety, and tranquility among US adults. *Social Science Research, (38),* 656–667.

Emberland, J. S., & Rundmo, T. (2010). Implications of job insecurity perceptions and job insecurity responses for psychological well-being, turnover intentions and reported risk behavior. *Safety Science, 48,* 452–459.

Emerson, R. W. (1912). Borrowing. In T. R. Lounsby (Ed.), *Yale book of American verse.* New Haven, CT: Yale University Press, retrieved from Bartleby.com, 1999. www.bartleby.com/102/.

Emmons, R. A. (2005). Striving for the sacred: Personal goals, life meaning, and religion. *Journal of Social Issues, 61(4),* 731–745.

Emmons, R. A., Cheung, C., & Tehrani, K. (1998). Assessing spirituality through personal goals: Implications for research on religion and SWB. *Social Indicators Research, 45,* 391–422.

Emmons, R. A., & Kneezel, T. T. (2005). Giving thanks: Spiritual and religious correlates of gratitude. *Journal of Psychology and Christianity, 24(2),* 140–148.

Emmons, R. A., & McCullough, M. E. (2003). Counting blessings versus burdens: An experimental investigation of gratitude and subjective well-being in daily life. *Journal of Personality and Social Psychology, 84(2),* 377–389.

Enseger, S., & Rheinberg, F (2008). Flow, performance and moderators of challenge–skill balance. *Motivation and Emotion, 32,* 158–172.

Erickson, S. J., & Feldstein, S. W. (2007). Adolescent humor and its relationship to

coping, defense strategies, psychological distress, and well-being. *Child Psychiatry and Human Development, 37,* 255–271.

Erisman, S. M., & Roemer, L. (2010). A preliminary investigation of the effects of experimentally induced mindfulness on emotional responding to film clips. *Emotion, 10(1),* 72–82.

Esler, M., Schwarz, R., & Alvarenga, M. (2008a). Mental stress is a cause of cardiovascular diseases: From scepticism to certainty. *Stress and Health, 24,* 175–180.

Esler, M., Schwarz, R., & Alvarenga, M. (2008b). Acute mental stress responses: Neural mechanisms of adverse cardiac consequences. *Stress and Health, 24,* 196–202.

Exline, J. J., & Zell, A. L. (2009). Empathy, self-affirmation, and forgiveness: The moderating roles of gender and entitlement. *Journal of Social and Clinical Psychology, 28(9),* 1071–1099.

Fadiman, J., & Frager, R.. (Eds.) (1997). *Essential Sufism.* San Francisco, CA: Harper-Collins.

Faris, N. A. (trans.) (2009). *The book of knowledge.* Retrieved from www.ghazali.org/books/knowledge.pdf.

Farrell, S. J., Aubry, T., & Coulombe, D. (2004). Neighborhoods and neighbors: Do they contribute to personal well-being? *Journal of Community Psychology, 32(1),* 9–25.

Fava, G. A., & Tomba, E. (2009). Increasing psychological well-being and resilience by psychotherapeutic methods. *Journal of Personality, 77(6),* 1903–1934.

Fawcett, L. M., Garton, A. F., & Dandy, J. (2009). Role of motivation, self-efficacy and parent support in adolescent-structured leisure activity participation. *Australian Journal of Psychology, 61(3),* 175–182.

Feeney, B. C. (2004). A secure base: Responsive support of goal strivings and exploration in adult intimate relationships. *Journal of Personality and Social Psychology, 87(5),* 631–648.

Feeney, J. A. (2006). Parental attachment and conflict behavior: Implications for offspring's attachment, loneliness, and relationship satisfaction. *Personal Relationships, 13,* 19–36.

Ferguson, G., Conway, C., Endersby, L., & MacLeod, A. (2009). Increasing subjective well-being in long-term forensic rehabilitation: Evaluation of well-being therapy. *The Journal of Forensic Psychiatry & Psychology, 20(6),* 906–918.

Feltman, R., Robinson, M. D., & Ode, S. (2009). Mindfulness as a moderator of neuroticism-outcome relations: A self-regulation perspective. *Journal of Research in Personality, 43,* 953–961.

Fenwick, R., & Tausig, M. (2001). Scheduling stress. Family and health outcomes of shift work and schedule control. *American Behavioral Scientist, 44,* 1179–1198.

Fetterman, A. K., Robinson, M. D., Ode, S., & Gordon, K. H. (2010). Neuroticism as a risk factor for behavioral dysregulation: A mindfulness meditation perspective. *Journal of Social and Clinical Psychology, 29(3),* 301–321.

Feurstein, G. (1996). *The Shambhala guide to Yoga.* Boston, MA: Shambhala Publications, Inc.

Feurstein, G. (1998). *The Yoga tradition.* Prescott, AZ: Hohm Press.

Fincham, F. D. (2003). Marital conflict: Correlates, structure, and context. *Current Directions in Psychological Science, 12,* 23–27.

Fischer, R., & Chalmers, A. (2008). Is optimism universal? A meta-analytical investigation of optimism levels across 22 nations. *Personality and Individual Differences, 45,* 378–382.

Flood, J. (2006). *The original Australians: Story of the Aboriginal people.* Crows Nest, Australia: Allen & Unwin.

Flynn, C. P. (1986). *After the beyond: Human transformation and the near-death experience.* Englewood Cliffs, NJ: Prentice-Hall.

Forbes, J. D. (2001). Indigenous Americans: Spirituality and Ecos, *Daedalus, 130(4),* 283–300.

Fortey, R. (2008). *Life: An unauthorized biography.* London, UK: The Folio Society.

Fortmann, A. L., Gallo, L. C., Walker, C., & Philis-Tsimikas, A. (2010). Support for disease management, depression, self-care, and clinical indicators among Hispanics with type 2 diabetes in San Diego County, United States of America. *Revista Panamericana de Salud Pública, 28(3),* 230–234.

Frager, R., & Fadiman, J. (1998). *Personality & personal growth* (4th ed.). New York, NY: Longman.

Frankl, V. (1984). *Man's search for meaning.* New York, NY: Washington Square Press.

Franklin, S. S. (2010). *The psychology of happiness.* New York, NY: Cambridge University Press.

Frantz, C. M., & Bennigson, C. (2005). Better late than early: The influence of timing on apology effectiveness. *Journal of Experimental Social Psychology, 41,* 201–207.

Fraley, B., & Aron, A. (2004). The effect of a shared humorous experience on closeness in initial encounters. *Personal Relationships, 11,* 61–78.

Fraley, R. C., Fazzari, D. A., Bonanno, G. A., & Dekel, S. (2006). Attachment and psychological adaptation in high exposure survivors of the September 11th attack on the World Trade Center. *Personality and Social Psychology Bulletin, 32(4),* 538–551.

Frederickson, B. L. (1998). What good are positive emotions? *Review of General Psychology, 2,* 300–319.

Frederickson, B. L. (2001). The role of positive emotions in positive psychology: The broaden-and-build theory of positive emotions. *American Psychologist, 56,* 218–226.

Fredrickson, B. L., & Branigan, C. (2005). Positive emotions broaden the scope of attention and thought-action repertoire. *Cognition and Emotion, 19(3),* 313–332.

Fredrickson, B. L., & Joiner, T. (2002). Positive emotions trigger upward spirals toward emotional well-being. *Psychological Science, 13(2),* 172–175.

Frederickson, B. L., & Losada, M. (2005). Positive affect and the complex dynamics of human flourishing. *American Psychologist, 60,* 678–686.

Fredrickson, B. L., Mancuso, R. A., Branigan, C., & Tugade, M. M. (2000). The undoing effect of positive emotions. *Motivation and Emotion, 24(4),* 237–254.

Freeman, P., & Zabriskie, R. B. (2003). Leisure and family functioning in adoptive families: Implications for therapeutic recreation. *Therapeutic Recreation Journal, 37(1),* 73–93.

Frodi, A., Bridges, L., & Grolnick, W. S. (1985). Correlates of mastery-related behavior: A short-term longitudinal study of infants in their second year. *Child Development, 56,* 1291–1298.

Froh, J. J., Sefick, W. J., & Emmons, R. A. (2008). Counting blessings in early adolescents: An experimental study of gratitude and subjective well-being. *Journal of School Psychology, 46,* 213–233.

Froh, J. J., Yurkewicz, C., & Kashdan, T. B. (2009). Gratitude and subjective well-being in early adolescence: Examining gender differences. *Journal of Adolescence, 32,* 633–650.

Frydenberg, E., Care, E., Freeman, E., & Chan, E. (2009). Interrelationships between coping, school connectedness and wellbeing. *Australian Journal of Education, 53(3),* 261–276.

Fullagar, C. J., & Kelloway, E. K. (2009). 'Flow' at work: An experience sampling approach. *Journal of Occupational and Organizational Psychology, 82,* 595–615.

Fullagar, C. J., & Mills, M. J. (2008). Motivation and flow: Toward an understanding of the dynamics of the relation in architecture students. *The Journal of Psychology, 142(5),* 533–553.

Furnham, A., & Petrides, K. V. (2008). Trait emotional intelligence and happiness. In J. C. Cassady, & M. A. Eissa (Eds.), *Emotional intelligence: Perspectives on educational and positive psychology* (pp. 121–129). New York, NY: Peter Lang.

Gable, S. L., Gonzaga, G. C., & Strachman, A. (2006). Will you be there for me when things go right? Supportive responses to positive event disclosures. *Journal of Personality and Social Psychology, 91(5),* 904–917.

Galek, K., Krause, N., Ellison, C. G., Kudler, T., & Flannelly, K. J. (2007). Religious doubt and mental health across the lifespan. *Journal of Adult Development, 14,* 16–25.

Gallagher, E. N., & Vella-Brodrick, D. A. (2008). Social support and emotional intelligence as predictors of subjective well-being. *Personality and Individual Differences, 44,* 1551–1561.

Gardarsdóttir, R. B., Dittmar, H., & Aspinall, C. (2009). It's not the money, it's the quest for a happier self: The role of happiness and success motives in the link between financial goals and subjective well-being. *Journal of Social and Clinical Psychology, 28 (9),* 1100–1127.

Garland, E. L., Fredrickson, B., Kring, A. M., Johnson, D. P., Meyer, P. S., & Penn, D. L. (2010). Upward spirals of positive emotions counter downward spiral of negativity: Insights from the broaden-and-build theory and affective neuroscience on the treatment of emotional dysfunctions and deficits in psychopathology. *Clinical Psychology Review, 30,* 849–864.

Gates, D. M., Gillespie, G. L., & Succop, P. (2011). Violence against nurses and its impact on stress and productivity. *Nursing Economics, 29(2),* 59–67.

Gatti, M. E., Jacobson, K. L., Gazmararian, J. A., Schmotzer, & Kripalani, S. (2009). Relationships between beliefs about medications and adherence. *American Journal of Health-Systems Pharmacy, 66,* 657–664.

Gauthier, K. I., Christopher, A. N., Walter, M. I., Mourad, R., & Marek, P. (2006). Religiosity, religious doubt, and the need for cognition: Their interactive relationship with life satisfaction. *Journal of Happiness Studies, 7,* 139–154.

Geers, A. L., Wellman, J. A., Helfer, S. G., Fowler, S. L., & France, C. R. (2008). Dispositional optimism and thoughts of well-being determine sensitivity to an experimental pain task. *Annals of Behavioral Medicine, 36,* 304–313.

Gerrish, N., Dyck, M. J., & Marsh, A. (2009). Post-traumatic growth and bereavement. *Mortality, 14(3),* 226–244.

Gillham, J., Adams-Deutsch, Z., Werner, J., Reivich, K., Coulter-Heindl, V., Linkins, M., et al. (2011). Character strengths predict subjective well-being during adolescence. *The Journal of Positive Psychology, 6(10,* 31–44.

Glenn, N. D. (1998). The course of marital success and failure in five American 10-year marriage cohorts. *Journal of Marriage and the Family, 60,* 569–576.

Glück, J., & Baltes, P. B. (2006). Using the concept of wisdom to enhance the expression of wisdom knowledge: Not the philosopher's dream but differential effects of developmental preparedness. *Psychology and Aging, 21(4),* 679–690.

Glück, J., Bluck, S., & Baron, J. (2005). The wisdom of experience: Autobiographical narratives across adulthood. *International Journal of Behavioral Development, 29(3),* 197–208.

Goei, R., & Boster, F. J. (2005). The roles of obligation and gratitude in explaining the effect of favors on compliance. *Communication Monographs, 72(3),* 284–300.

Gold, R. S. (2008). Unrealistic optimism and event threat. *Psychology, Health & Medicine, 13(2),* 193–201.

Goldberg, L. R. (1990). An alternative "description of personality": The big-five factor structure. *Journal of Personality and Social Psychology, 59,* 1216–1229.

Golden, L., & Wiens-Tuer, B. (2006). To your happiness? Extra hours of labor supply and worker well-being. *The Journal of Socio-Economics, 35,* 382–397.

Goleman, D. (1995). *Emotional intelligence: Why it can matter more than IQ.* Toronto, ON: Bantam Books.

Gomez, B. J., & Ang, P. M-M. (2007). Promoting positive youth development in schools. *Theory Into Practice, 46(2),* 97–104.

Gomez, V., Krings, F., Bangerter, A., & Grob, A. (2009). The influence of personality and life events on subjective well-being from a life span perspective. *Journal of Research in Personality, 43,* 345–354.

Goodwin, R., Cook, O., & Yung, Y. (2001). Loneliness and life satisfaction among three cultural groups. *Personal Relationships, 8,* 225–230.

Goosen, G. C. (1999). Christian and Aboriginal interface in Australia. *Theological Studies, 60,* 72–94.

Gordon, R. A. (2008). Attributional style and athletic performance: Strategic optimism and defensive pessimism. *Psychology of Sport and Exercise, 9,* 336–350.

Gostin, O., & Chong, A. (2006). Living Wisdom: Aborigines and the environment. In C. Bourke, E. Bourke, & B. Edwards (Eds.), *Aboriginal Australia* (2nd ed.) (pp. 147–167), St. Lucia, Australia: University of Queensland Press.

Goud, N. H. (2005). Courage: Its nature and development. *Journal of Humanistic Counseling, Education, and Development, 44,* 102–116.

Gray, J., & Hackling, M. (2009). Wellbeing and retention: A senior secondary school perspective. *The Australian Educational Researcher, 36(2),* 119–145.

Greason, P. B., & Cashwell, C. S. (2009). Mindfulness and counselling self-efficacy: The mediating role of attention and empathy. *Counselor Education & Supervision, 49,* 2–19.

Great Place to Work Institute. (2011). www.greatplacetowork.com

Greenberg, M. T., Weissberg, R. P., O'Brien, M. U., Zins, J. E., Fredericks, L., Resnik, H., & Elias, M. J. (2003). Enhancing school-based prevention and youth development through coordinated social, emotional, and academic learning. *American Psychologist, 58(6–7),* 466–474.

Greyson, B. (2006). Near-death experiences and spirituality. *Zygon, 41(2),* 393–414.

Greyson, B. (2007). Consistency of near-death experience accounts over two decades: Are reports embellished over time? *Resuscitation, 73,* 407–411.

Grolnick, W. S., & Ryan, R. M. (1987). Autonomy in children's learning: An experimental and individual difference investigation. *Journal of Personality and Social Psychology, 52,* 890–898.

Gross, J. J. (1998). The emerging field of emotion regulation: An integrative review. *Review of General Psychology, 2(3)*, 271–299.

Gross, J. J. (1999). Emotion regulation: Past, present, future. *Cognition and Emotion, 13(5)*, 551–573.

Gross, J. J. (2001). Emotion regulation in adulthood: Timing is everything. *Current Directions in Psychological Science, 10(6)*, 214–219.

Gross, J. J. (2002). Emotion regulation: Affective, cognitive, and social consequences. *Psychophysiology, 39*, 281–291.

Gross, J. J., & Munoz, R. F. (1995). Emotion regulation and mental health. *Clinical Psychology: Science & Practice, 2*, 95–103.

Grote, N. K., Bledsoe, S. E., Larkin, J., Lemay Jr., E. P., & Brown, C. (2007). Stress exposure and depression in disadvantaged women: The protective effects of optimism and perceived control. *Social Work Research, 31(1)*, 19–32.

Güleryüz, G., Güney, S., Aydin, E. M., & Aşan, Ö. (2008). The mediating effect of job satisfaction between emotional intelligence and organisational commitment of nurses: A questionnaire survey. *International Journal of Nursing Studies, 45*, 1625–1635.

Guo, Y., Klein, B., Ro, Y., & Rossin, D. (2007). The impact of flow on learning outcomes in a graduate-level information management course. *Journal of Global Business Issues, 1(2)*, 31–39.

Hackman, J. R., & Oldham, G. R. (1976). Motivation through the design of work: Test of a theory. *Organizational Behaviour and Human Performance, 16*, 250–279.

Hackman, J. R., & Oldham, G. R. (1980). *Work redesign.* Reading, MA: Addison-Wesley.

Hadad, M. (2009). *The ultimate challenge: Coping with death, dying, and bereavement.* Toronto, ON: Nelson Education.

Hadad, M., & Reed, M., J. (2007). *The postsecondary learning experience.* Toronto, ON: Nelson Education.

Hafen, M., & Crane, D. R. (2003). When marital interaction and intervention researchers arrive at different points of view: The active listening controversy. *Journal of Family Therapy, 25*, 4–14.

Hannah S. T., Sweeney, P. J., & Lester, P. B. (2007). Toward a courageous mindset: The subjective act and experience of courage. *Journal of Positive Psychology, 2(2)*, 129–135.

Harker L., & Keltner, D. (2001). Expressions of positive emotion in women's college yearbook pictures and their relationship to personality and life outcomes across adulthood. *Journal of Personality and Social Psychology, 80*, 112–124.

Harlow, L. L., Newcomb, M. D., & Bentler, P. M. (1986). Depression, self-derogation, substance use, and suicide ideation: Lack of purpose in life as a mediational factor. *Journal of Clinical Psychology, 42*, 5–21.

Harris, G. E., & Larsen, D. (2007). HIV peer counseling and the development of hope: Perspectives from peer counselors and peer counseling recipients. *AIDS Patient Care and STDs, 21(11)*, 843–859.

Harris, J. I., Erbes, C. R., Engdahl, B. E., Tedeschi, R. G., Olson, R. H., Winskowski, A. M. M., & McMahill, J. (2010). Coping functions of prayer and posttraumatic growth. *The International Journal for the Psychology of Religion, 20*, 26–38.

Harrison, A., Sullivan, S., Tchanturia, K., & Treasure, J. (2009). Emotion recognition and regulation in anorexia nervosa. *Clinical Psychology and Psychotherapy, 16*, 348–356.

Hart, J., Shaver, P. R., & Goldenberg, J. L. (2005). Attachment, self-esteem, worldviews, and terror management: Evidence for a tripartite security system. *Journal of Personality and Social Psychology, 88(6)*, 999–1013.

Haslam, S. A., Jetten, J., Postmes, T., & Haslam, C. (2009). Social identity, health and well-being: An emerging agenda for applied psychology. *Applied Psychology: An International Review, 58(1)*, 1–23.

Haslam, S. A., Jetten, J., & Waghorn, C. (2009). Social identification, stress and citizenship in teams: A five-phase longitudinal study. *Stress and Health, 25*, 21–30.

Headey, B., & Wearing, A. (1992). *Understanding happiness: A theory of subjective well-being.* Melbourne, Australia: Longman Cheshire.

Heaven, P., & Ciarrochi, J. (2008). Parental styles, gender and the development of hope and self-esteem. *European Journal of Personality, 22,* 707–724.

Heaven, P. C. L., Ciarrochi, J., & Leeson, P. (2010). Parental styles and religious values among teenagers: A 3-year prospective analysis. *The Journal of Genetic Psychology, 171(1),* 93–99.

Hefferon, K., Grealy, M., & Mutrie, N. (2009). Post-traumatic growth and life-threatening physical illness: A systematic review of the qualitative literature. *British Journal of Health Psychology, 14,* 343–378.

Hegerl, U. (2009). CS05-04 Symposium: Suicide across Europe: The European Alliance Against Depression (EAAD): Evidence base for cost efficiency. *European Psychiatry, 24, Supplement 1,* S66.

Hegney, D., Tuckett, A., Parker, D., & Eley, R. M. (2010). Workplace violence: Differences in perceptions between those exposed and those not exposed: A cross-sector analysis. *International Journal of Nursing Practice, 16(2),* 188–202.

Heller, D., Ferris, D. L., Brown, D., & Watson, D. (2009). The influence of work personality on job satisfaction: Incremental validity and mediation effects. *Journal of Personality, 77(4),* 1051–1084.

Helliwell, J. F., & Huang, H. (2008). How's your government? International evidence linking good government and well-being. *British Journal of Political Science, 38,* 595–619.

Hendrick, C., & Hendrick, S. (1986). A theory and method of love. *Journal of Personality and Social Psychology, 50,* 392–402.

Heo, J., Lee, Y., McCormack, B. P., & Pedersen, P. M. (2010). Daily experiences of serious leisure, flow and subjective well-being of older adults. *Leisure Studies, 29(2),* 207–225.

Herek, G. M., Janis, I. L., & Huth, P. (1987). Decision making during international crises. *Journal of Conflict Resolution, 31(2),* 203–226.

Herek, G. M., Janis, I. L., & Huth, P. (1989). Quality of U. S. decision making during the Cuban missile crisis. *Journal of Conflict Resolution, 33(3),* 446–459.

Herman, K. C., Reinke, W. M., Parkin, J., Traylor, K. B., & Agarwal, G. (2009). Childhood depression: Rethinking the role of the school. *Psychology in the Schools, 46(5),* 433–446.

Herwig, U., Kaffenberger, T., Jänke, L., & Brühl, A. B. (2010). Self-related awareness and emotion regulation. *NeuroImage, 50,* 734–741.

Highwater, J. (1982). *The primal mind: Vision and reality in Indian America.* New York, NY: Meridian.

Hill, P. C., Pargament, K. I., Hood Jr., R. W., McCullough, M. E., Swyers, J. P., Larson, D. B., & Zinnbauer, B. J. (2000). Conceptualizing religion and spirituality: Points of commonality, points of departure. *Journal for the Theory of Social Behaviour, 30(1),* 51–77.

Hill, P. L., & Allemand, M. (2010). Forgivingness and adult patterns of individual differences in environmental mastery and personal growth. *Journal of Research in Personality, 44,* 245–250.

Hirsch, J. K., Wolford, K., LaLonde, S. M., Brunk, L., & Morris, A. P. (2007). Dispositional optimism as a moderator of the relationship between negative life events and suicide ideation and attempts. *Cognitive Therapy Research, 31,* 533–546.

Ho, M. Y., Cheung, F. M., & Cheung, S. F. (2010). The role of meaning in life and optimism in promoting well-being. *Personality and Individual Differences, 48,* 658–663.

Ho, S. M. Y., Chu, K. W., & Yiu, J. (2008). The relationship between explanatory style and posttraumatic growth after bereavement in a non-clinical sample. *Death Studies, 32,* 461–478.

Hofmann, S. G., Heering, S., Sawyer, A. T., Asnaani, A. (2009). How to handle anxiety: The effects of reappraisal, acceptance, and suppression strategies on anxiety arousal. *Behaviour Research and Therapy, 47,* 389–394.

Höge, T. (2009). When work strain transcends psychological boundaries: An inquiry into the relationship between time pressure, irritation, work-family conflict and psychosomatic complaints. *Stress and Health, 25,* 41–51.

Holder, M. D., & Coleman, B. (2008). The contribution of temperament, popularity, and physical appearance to children's happiness. *Journal of Happiness Studies, 9,* 279–302.

Holt, S., Buckley, H., & Whelan, S. (2008). The impact of exposure to domestic violence on children and young people: A review of the literature. *Child Abuse & Neglect, 32,* 797–810.

Hombrados-Mendieta, I., Gomez-Jacinto, L., and Dominguez-Fuentes, J. M. (2009). The impact of immigrants on the sense of community. *Journal of Community Psychology, 37(6),* 671–683.

Hoorens, V., Smits, T., & Shepperd, J. A. (2008). Comparative optimism in the spontaneous generation of future life-events. *British Journal of Social Psychology, 47,* 441–451.

Hope College (2010). Overview. www.hope.edu/about/#overview

Horan, S. M., Martin, M. M., Smith, N., Schoo, M., Eidsness, M., & Johnson, A. (2009). Can we talk? How learning of an invisible illness impacts forecasted relational outcomes. *Communication Studies, 60(1),* 66–81.

Horney, K. (1937). *The neurotic personality of our time.* New York, NY: Norton.

Horney, K. (1945). *Our inner conflicts.* New York, NY: Norton.

Horney, K. (1950). *Neurosis and human growth.* New York, NY: Norton.

Horney, K. (1967). *Feminine psychology.* New York, NY: Norton.

Horowitz, J. L., & Garber, J. (2007). The prevention of depressive symptoms in children and adolescents. *Journal of Consulting and Clinical Psychology, 74,* 401–415.

Horsburgh, A. A., Schermer, J. A., Veselka, L., & Vernon, P. A. (2009). A behavioural genetic study of mental toughness and personality. *Personality and Individual Differences, 46,* 100–105.

Howell, A. J., Watson, D. C., Powell, R. A., & Buro, K. (2006). Academic procrastination: The pattern and correlates of behavioural postponement. *Personality and Individual Differences, 40,* 1519–1530.

Hudson, J. (2006). Institutional trust and subjective well-being across the EU. *Kyklos, 59(1),* 43–62.

Huebner, E. S., Gilman, R., Reschly, A. L., & Hall, R. (2009). Positive schools. In S. J. Lopez, & C. R. Snyder (Eds.), *Oxford Handbook of Positive Psychology* (2nd ed.) (pp. 561–568), New York, NY: Oxford University Press.

Hughes, B. M. (2007). Individual differences in hostility and habituation of cardiovascular reactivity to stress. *Stress and Health, 23,* 37–42.

Hultkrantz, Å. (1967). *The religions of the American Indians.* Berkeley, CA: University of California Press.

Hutchinson, M., Vickers, M. H., Jackson, D., & Wilkes, L. (2010). Bullying as circuits of power: An Australian nursing perspective. *Administrative Theory & Praxis, 32(1),* 25–47.

Huxley, A. (1955). *Brave new world: A novel.* Harmondsworth, UK: Penguin.

Hwang, G., Kim, S-K., Kim, J-H., Kim, H-R., Park, S-H, & Kim, S-H. (2008). Influence of psychological stress on physical pain. *Stress and Health, 24,* 159–164.

Ingoldsby, E. M., Shaw, D. S., Winslow, E., Schonberg, M., Gilliom, M., & Criss, M. M. (2006). Neighborhood disadvantage, parent-child conflict, neighborhood peer relationships, and early antisocial behavior problem trajectories. *Journal of Abnormal Child Psychology, 34(3),* 303–319.

Inman, A. G., Howard, E. E., Beaumont, R. L., & Walker, J. A. (2007). Cultural transmission: Influence of contextual factors in Asian Indian immigrant parents' experiences. *Journal of Counseling Psychology, 54(1),* 93–100.

Irving, P. G., & Montes, S. D. (2009). Met expectations: The effects of expected and delivered inducements on employee satisfaction. *Journal of Occupational and Organizational Psychology, 82,* 431–451.

Isen, A. M. (2005). A role for neuropsychology in understanding the facilitating influence of positive affect on social behavior and cognitive processes. In C. R. Snyder, & S. J. Lopez (Eds.), *Handbook of positive psychology* (pp. 528–540), New York, NY: Oxford University Press.

Ishimura, I., & Kodama, M. (2009). Flow experiences in everyday activities of Japanese college students: Autotelic people and time management. *Japanese Psychological research, 51(1),* 47–54.

Iwaiec, D., Larkin, E., & Higgins, S. (2006). Research review: Risk and resilience in cases of emotional abuse. *Child and Family Social Work, 11,* 73–82.

Jackson, J. S., Forsythe-Brown, I., & Govia, I. O. (2007). Age cohort, ancestry, and immigrant generation influences in family relations and psychological well-being among black Caribbean family members. *Journal of Social Issues, 63(4),* 729–743.

Jackson, L. M., Pratt, M. W., Hunsberger, B., & Pancer, S. M. (2005). Optimism as a mediator of the relation between perceived parental authoritativeness and adjustment among adolescents: Finding the sunny side of the street. *Social Development, 14(2),* 273–304.

Jacobs, S., Thomas, W., & Lang, S. (Eds.). (1997). *Two-spirit people: Native American gender identity, sexuality, and spirituality.* Chicago, IL: University of Illinois Press.

Jamal, M. (2007). Short communication: Burnout and self-employment: A cross-cultural empirical study. *Stress and Health, 23,* 249–256.

Janis, I. L., & Mann, L. (1977). *Decision making: A psychological analysis of conflict, choice and commitment.* New York, NY: Free Press.

Jason, L. A., Reichler, A., King, C., Madsen, D., Camacho, J., & Marchese, W. (2001). The measurement of wisdom: A preliminary report. *Journal of Community Psychology, 29(5),* 585–598.

Jennings, P. A., Aldwin, C. M., Levenson, M. R., Spiro III, A., & Mroczek, D. K. (2006). Combat exposure, perceived benefits of military service, and wisdom in later life: Findings from the Normative Aging Study. *Research on Aging, 28(1),* 115–134.

Johnson, J., Gooding, P. A., Wood, A. M., & Tarrier, N. (2010). Resilience as positive coping appraisal: Testing the schematic appraisals model of suicide (SAMS). *Behavior Research and Therapy, 48,* 179–186.

Johnson, H. A., Zabriskie, R. B., & Hill, B. (2006). The contribution of couple leisure involvement, leisure time, and leisure satisfaction to marital satisfaction. *Marriage and Family Review, 40(1),* 69–91.

Jones, L. V. (2009). Claiming your connections: A psychosocial group intervention study of black college women. *Social Work Research, 33(3),* 159–171.

Jonker, L., & Greeff, A. P. (2009). Resilience factors in families living with people with mental illness. *Journal of Community Psychology, 37(7),* 859–873.

Joseph, S. (2004). Client-centred therapy, post-traumatic stress, and post-traumatic growth: Theoretical perspectives and practical implications. *Psychology and Psychotherapy: Theory, Research and Practice, 77,* 101–120.

Joseph, S. (2009). Growth following adversity: Positive psychological perspectives on posttraumatic stress. *Psychological Topics, 8,* 335–344.

Judge, T. A., Thoresen, C. J., Bono, J. E., & Patton, G. K. (2001). The job satisfaction-job performance relationship: A qualitative and quantitative review. *Psychological Bulletin, 127,* 376–407.

Judkins, S., Arris, L., & Keener, E. (2005). Program evaluation in graduate nursing education: Hardiness as a predictor of success among nursing administration students. *Journal of Professional Nursing, 21,* 314–321.

Jung, Y-H., Kang, D-H., Jang, J. H., Park, H. Y., Byun, M. S., Kwon, S. J., Jang, G-E., Lee, U, S., An, S. C., & Kwon, J. S. (2010). The effects of mind–body training on stress reduction, positive affect, and plasma catecholamines. *Neuroscience Letters, 479,* 138–142.

Jutras, S., & Lepage, G. (2006). Parental perceptions of contributions of schools and neighborhood to children's psychological wellness. *Journal of Community Psychology, 34(3),* 305–325.

Kafetsios, K., & Zampetakis, L. A. (2008). Emotional intelligence and job satisfaction: Testing the mediatory role of positive and negative affect at work. *Personality and Individual Differences, 44,* 712–722.

Kaiseler, M., Polman, R., & Nicholls, A. (2009). Mental toughness, stress, stress appraisal, coping and coping effectiveness in sport. *Personality and Individual Differences, 47,* 728–733.

Kanner, A. D., Coyne, J. C., Schaefer, C., & Lazarus, R. S. (1981). Comparison of two modes of stress measurement: Daily hassles and uplifts versus major life events. *Journal of Behavioral Medicine, 4(1),* 1–37.

Kapleau, P. (1989). *The three pillars of Zen.* New York, NY: Doubleday.

Karadal, H., & Arasli, H. (2009). The impacts of superior politics on frontline employees' behavioral and psychological outcomes. *Social Behavior and Personality, 37(2),* 175–190.

Karademas, E. C., Kafetsios, K., & Sideridis, G. D. (2007). Optimism, self-efficacy and information-processing of threat- and well-being-related stimuli. *Stress and Health, 23,* 285–294.

Karremen, A, van Tuijl, C., van Aken, M. A. G., & Dcković, M. (2006). Parenting and self-regulation in preschoolers: A meta-analysis. *Infant and Child Development, 15,* 561–579.

Karsh, B-T., Beasley, J. W., & Brown, R. L. (2010). Employed family physician satisfaction and commitment to their practice, work group, and health care organization. *HSR: Health Services Research, 45(2),* 457–475.

Kashdan, T. B., & Rottenberg, J. (2010). Psychological flexibility as a fundamental aspect of health. *Clinical Psychology Review, 30,* 865–878.

Kasser, T., Ryan, R. M., Zax, M., & Sameroff, A. J. (1995). The relations of maternal and social environments to late adolescents' materialistic and prosocial values. *Developmental Psychology, 31,* 907–914.

Kastenbaum, R. J. (2009). *Death, society, and the human experience* (10th ed.). New York, NY: Allyn & Bacon.

Kelaher, M., Warr, D. J., Feldman, P., & Tacticos, T. (2010). Living in 'Birdsville': Exploring the impact of neighbourhood stigma on health. *Health & Place, 16,* 381–388.

Keller, J., & Blomann, F. (2008). Locus of control and the flow experience: An experimental analysis. *European Journal of Personality, 22,* 589–607.

Kidd, S. A. (2004). "The walls are closing in, and we were trapped": A qualitative analysis of street youth suicide. *Youth and Society, 36,* 30–55.

Kiecolt-Glaser, J. K., McGuire, L., Robles, T. F., & Glaser, R. (2002). Emotions, morbidity, and morality: New perspectives from psychoneuroimmunology. *Annual Review of Psychology, 53,* 83–107.

Kim, Y. (2005). Emotional and cognitive consequences of adult attachment: The mediating effect of the self. *Personality and Individual Differences, 39,* 913–923.

Kit, W. K. (1998). *The complete book of Zen.* Boston, MA: Element Books.

Klassen, R. M., Krawchuk, L. L., Lynch, S. L., & Rajani, S. (2008). Procrastination and motivation of undergraduates with learning disabilities: A mixed methods inquiry. *Learning Disabilities Research & Practice, 23(3),* 137–147.

Klassen, R. M., Usher, E. L., & Bong, M. (2010). Teachers' collective efficacy, job satisfaction, and job stress in cross-cultural context. *The Journal of Experimental Education, 78,* 464–486.

Kluemper, D. H. (2008). Trait emotional intelligence: The impact of core-self evaluations and social desirability. *Personality and Individual Differences, 44,* 1402–1412.

Knobloch, L. K., & Carpenter-Theune, K. E. (2004). Topic avoidance in developing romantic relationships: Association with intimacy and relational uncertainty. *Communication Research, 31,* 173–205

Knowles, E. (1999). *The Oxford dictionary of quotations* (5th ed.). New York, NY: Oxford University Press.

Koenen, K. C. (2007). Genetics of posttraumatic stress disorder: Review and recommendations for future studies. *Journal of Traumatic Stress, 20(5),* 737–750.

Koenig, H. G., McCullough, M. E., & Larson, D. B. (2001). *Handbook of religion and health.* New York, NY: Oxford University Press.

Kohen, D. E., Brooks-Gunn, J., Leventhal, T., & Hertzman, C. (2002). Neighborhood income and physical and social disorder in Canada: Associations with young children's competencies. *Child Development, 73(6),* 1844–1860.

Konu, A. I., Lintonen, T. P., & Rimpelä, M. K. (2002). Factors associated with schoolchildren's general subjective well-being. *Health Education Research, 17(2),* 155–165.

Koole, S. L. (2009). The psychology of emotion regulation: an integrative review. *Cognition and Emotion, 23(1),* 4–41.

Korb, M. P., Gorrell, J., & Van De Riet, V. (1989). *Gestalt therapy: Practice and theory,* (2nd ed.). Needham Hts., MA: Allyn and Bacon.

Kotchick, B. A., & Forehand, R. (2002). Putting parenting in perspective: A discussion of the contextual factors that shape parenting practices. *Journal of Child and Family Studies, 11(3),* 255–269.

Krause, N. (2006). Religious doubt and psychological well-being: A longitudinal investigation. *Review of Religious Research, 47(3),* 287–302.

Kubitschek, W. N., & Hallinan, M. T. (1998). Tracking students' friendships. *Social Psychology Quarterly, 61(1),* 1–15.

Kuiper, N. A., & Borowicz-Sibenik, M. (2005). A good sense of humor doesn't always help: Agency and communion as moderators of psychological well-being. *Personality and Individual Differences, 38,* 365–377.

Kuiper, N. A., & McHale, N. (2009). Humor styles as mediators between self-evaluative standards and psychological well-being. *The Journal of Psychology, 143(4),* 359–376.

Kunzmann, U., & Baltes, P. B. (2003). Wisdom-related knowledge: Affective, motivational, and interpersonal correlates. *Personality and Social Psychology Bulletin, 29,* 1104–1119.

Kuo, T-H., & Ho, L-A. (2010). Individual difference and job performance: The relationships among personal factors, job characteristics, flow experience, and service quality. *Social Behavior and Personality, 38(4),* 531–552.

Kwok, O., Hughes, J. N., & Luo, W. (2007). Role of resilient personality on lower achieving first grade students' current and future achievements. *Journal of School Psychology, 45,* 61–82.

Lai, J. C. L. (2009). Dispositional optimism buffers the impact of daily hassles on mental health in Chinese adolescents. *Personality and Individual Differences, 47,* 247–249.

Lam, C. B., & McBride-Chang, C. A. (2007). Resilience in young adulthood: The moderating influences of gender-related personality traits and coping flexibility. *Sex Roles, 56,* 159–172.

Lambert, N. M., Fincham, F. D., Stillman, T. F., & Dean, L. R. (2009). More gratitude, less materialism: The mediating role of life satisfaction. *The Journal of Positive Psychology, 4(1),* 32–42.

Lambert, N. M., Graham, S. M., Fincham, F. D., & Stillman, T. F. (2009). A changed perspective: How gratitude can affect sense of coherence through positive reframing. *The Journal of Positive Psychology, 4(6),* 461–470.

Lamkin, D. M., Bloom, C. M., Michaels, Z. J., Hunter, E., Aguilar, M., Venard, J., & Barnett, J. K. (2007). Short communication: Performance may predict natural killer cell activity after an acute time-limited stressor. *Stress and Health, 23,* 169–173.

Langlois, J. H., Kalakanis, L., Rubenstein, A. J., Larson, A., Hallam, M., & Smoot, M. (2000). Maxims or myths of beauty? A meta-analytic and theoretical review. *Psychological Bulletin, 126,* 390–423.

Lao Tzu, (1988). *Tao te ching.* London, UK: Penguin Books.

Lasnier, B., Brochu, S., Boyd, N., & Fischer, B. (2010). A heroin prescription trial: Case studies from Montreal and Vancouver on crime and disorder in the surrounding neighbourhoods. *International Journal of Drug Policy, 21(1),* 28–35.

Laufer, A., RazHamama, Y., Levine, S. Z., & Solomon, Z. (2009). Posttraumatic growth in adolescence: The role of religiosity, distress, and forgiveness. *Journal of Social and Clinical Psychology, 28(7),* 862–880.

Laurencelle, R. M., Abell, S. C., & Schwartz, D. J. (2002). The relation between intrinsic religious faith and psychological wellbeing. *The International Journal for the Psychology of Religion, 12(2),* 109–123.

Lavee, Y., & Ben-Ari, A. (2008). The association of daily hassles and uplifts within family and life satisfaction: Does cultural orientation make a difference? *American Journal of Community Psychology, 41,* 89–98.

Lavoie-Tremblay, M., Paquet, M., Duchesne, M-A., Santo, A., Gavrancic, A., Courcy, F., & Gagnon, S. (2010). Retaining nurses and other hospital workers: An intergenerational perspective of the work climate. *Journal of Nursing Scholarship, 42(4),* 414–422.

Lavoie-Tremblay, M., Wright, D., Desforges, N., Gélinas, C., Marchionni, C., & Drevniok, U. (2008). Creating a healthy workplace for new-generation nurses. *Journal of Nursing Scholarship, 40(3),* 290–297.

Lavy, S., & Littman-Ovadia, H. (2011). All you need is love? Strengths mediate the negative associations between attachment orientations and life satisfaction. *Personality and Individual Differences, 50,* 1050–1055.

Lawler, K. A., Younger, J. W., Piferi, R. L., Jobe, R. L., Edmondson, K. A., & Jones, W. H. (2005). The unique effects of forgiveness on health: An exploration of pathways. *Journal of Behavioral Medicine, 28(2),* 157–167.

Lawler-Row, K. A., & Piferi, R. L. (2006). The forgiving personality: Describing a life well-lived? *Personality and Individual Differences, 41,* 1009–1020.

Lawler-Row, K. A., Karremans, J. C., Scott, C. A., Edlis-Matityahou, M., & Edwards, L. (2008). Forgiveness, physiological reactivity and health: The role of anger. *International Journal of Psychophysiology, 68,* 51–58.

Lawler-Row, K. A., Scott, C. A., Raines, R. L., Edlis-Matityahou, M., & Moore, E. W. (2007). The varieties of forgiveness experience: Working toward a comprehensive definition of forgiveness. *Journal of Religion and Health, 46(2),* 233–248.

Lay, C. H., Knish, S., & Zanatta, R. (1992). Self-handicappers and procrastinators: A comparison of their practice behaviour prior to an evaluation. *Journal of Research in Personality, 26,* 242–257.

Lazarus, R. S. (1990). Theory-based stress measurement. *Psychological Inquiry, 1(1),* 3–13.

Lazarus, R. S., & Folkman, S. (1984). *Stress, appraisal and coping.* New York, NY: Springer.

Le, T. N., & Levenson, M. R. (2005). Wisdom as self-transcendence: What's love (& individualism) got to do with it? *Journal of Research in Personality, 39,* 443–457.

Lee, E. (2005). The relationship of motivation and flow experience to academic procrastination in university students. *Journal of Genetic Psychology, 166,* 1322–1325.

Lee, M. Y., Greene, G. J., Hsu, K. S., Solovey, A., Grove, D., Fraser, J. S., Washburn, P., & Teater, B. (2009). Utilizing family strengths and resilience: Integrative family and systems treatment with children and adolescents with severe emotional and behavioural problems. *Family Process, 48(3),* 395–416.

Lench, H. C., & Ditto, P. H. (2008). Automatic optimism: Biased use of base rate information for positive and negative events. *Journal of Experimental Social Psychology, 44,* 631–639.

Leondari, A., & Gialamas, V. (2009). Religiosity and psychological well-being. *International Journal of Psychology, 44(4)*, 241–248.

Lepper, M., & Greene, D. (1978). *The hidden costs of reward*. Hillsdale, NJ: Lawrence Erlbaum Associates.

Lepper, M., Greene, D., & Nisbett, R. (1973). Undermining children's intrinsic interest with extrinsic rewards: A test of the "over-justification" hypothesis. *Journal of Personality and Social Psychology, 28*, 129–137.

Leventhal, T., & Brooks-Gunn, J. (2000). The neighborhoods they live in: The effects of neighborhood residence on child and adolescent outcomes. *Psychological Bulletin, 126(2)*, 309–337.

Levine, S. Z., Laufer, A., Hamama-Raz, Y., Stein, E., & Solomon, Z. (2008). Posttraumatic growth in adolescence: Its components and relationship with PTSD. *Journal of Traumatic Stress, 21(5)*, 492–496.

Li, F., Li, Y., & Wang, E. (2009). Task characteristics and team performance: The mediating effect of team member satisfaction. *Social Behavior and Personality, 37(10)*, 1373–1382.

Lim, B. S. C., & Wang, C. K. J. (2009). Perceived autonomy support, behavioural regulations in physical education and physical activity intention. *Psychology of Sport and Exercise, 10*, 52–60.

Lim, L. (2009). A two-factor model of defensive pessimism and its relations with achievement motives. *The Journal of Psychology, 143(3)*, 318–336.

Lima, J., Caughy, M., Nettles, S. M., & O'Campo, P. J. (2010). Effects of cumulative risk on behavioral and psychological well-being in first grade: Moderation by neighborhood context. *Social Science & Medicine, 71*, 1447–1454.

Linares, L. O., Rosbruch, N., Stern, M. B., Edwards, M. E., Walker, G., Abikoff, H. B., & Alvir, J. M. J. (2005). Developing cognitive-social-emotional competencies to enhance academic learning. *Psychology in the Schools, 42(4)*, 405–417.

Lincoln, K. D., Taylor, R. J., Chae, D. H., & Chatters, L. M. (2010). Demographic correlates of psychological well-being and distress among older African Americans and Caribbean Black adults. *Best Practices in Mental Health, 6(1)*, 103–126.

Lings, M. (1975). *What is Sufism?* London, UK: George Allen & Unwin Ltd.

Linley, P. A., & Joseph, S. (2004). Positive change following trauma and adversity. *Journal of Traumatic Stress, 17*, 11–21.

Liu, R. T., & Alloy, L. B. (2010). Stress generation in depression: A systematic review of the empirical literature and recommendations for future study. *Clinical Psychology Review, 30*, 582–593.

Löckenhoff, C. E., De Fruyt, F., Terracciano, A., McCrae, R. R., De Bolle, M. et al. (2009). Perceptions of aging across 26 cultures and their culture-level associates. *Psychology and Aging, 24(4)*, 941–954.

Loftus, E. F. (2003). Make-believe memories. *American Psychologist, 58*, 867–873.

Løhre, A., Lydersen, S., & Vatten, L. J. (2010). School wellbeing among children in grades 1–10. *BMC Public Health, 10*, 526–532.

Lopes, P. N., Brackett, M. A., Nezlek, J. B., Schutz, A., Sellin, I., & Salovey, P. (2004). Emotional intelligence and social interaction. *Personality and Social Psychology Bulletin, 30*, 1018–1034.

Lopes, P. N., Salovey, P., Côté, S., & Beers, M. (2005). Emotion regulation abilities and the quality of social interaction. *Emotion, 5*, 113–118.

Lopez, S. J., O'Byrne, K. K., & Peterson, S. (2003). Profiling courage. In S. J. Lopez, & C. R. Snyder (Eds.), *Positive psychological assessment: A handbook of models and measures* (pp. 185–197), Washington, DC: American Psychological Association.

Lounsbury, J. W., Fisher, L. A., Levy, J. J., & Welsh, D. P. (2009). An investigation of character strengths in relation to the academic success of college students. *Individual Differences Research, 7(1)*, 52–69.

Lloyd, K., & Little, D. E. (2010). Self-determination theory as a framework for understanding women's psychological well-being outcomes from leisure-time physical activity. *Leisure Sciences, 32,* 369–385.

Lopes P. N., Grewal, D., Kadis, J., Gall, M., & Salovey, P. (2006). Evidence that emotional intelligence is related to job performance and affect and attitudes at work. *Psicothema, 18(1),* 132–138.

Lucas, R. E. (2008). Personality and subjective well-being. In M. Eid, & R. J. Larsen (Eds.), *The science of subjective well-being* (pp. 171–194), New York, NY: Guilford Press.

Lucas, R. E., & Diener, E. (2009). Personality and subjective well-being. In E. Diener (Ed.), *The science of well-being: The collected works of Ed Diener* (pp. 75–102), New York, NY: Springer-Verlag.

Lucas, R. E., & Dyrenforth, P. S. (2006). Does the existence of social relationships matter for subjective well-being? In E. J. Finkel & K. D. Vohs (Eds.), *Self and relationships: Connecting intrapersonal and interpersonal processes* (pp. 254–273), New York, NY: Guilford Press.

Lucas, R. E., & Schimmack, U. (2009). Income and well-being: How big is the gap between the rich and the poor? *Journal of Research in Personality, 43,* 75–78.

Lunkenheimer, E. S., Shields, A. M., & Cortina, K. S. (2007). Parental emotion coaching and dismissing in family interaction. *Social Development, 16(2),* 232–248.

Luparell, S. (2011). Academic Education. Incivility in nursing: The connection between academia and clinical settings. *Critical Care Nurse, 31(2),* 92–95.

Määttä, S., Nurmi, J-E., & Stattin, H. (2007). Achievement orientations, school adjustment, and well-being: A longitudinal study. *Journal of Research on Adolescence, 17(4),* 789–812.

Macaskill, A., & Denovan, A. (2011). Developing autonomous learning in first-year university students using perspectives from positive psychology. *Studies in Higher Education, 35(3),* 1–19.

Macavei, B., & Miclea, M. (2008). An empirical investigation of the relationship between religious beliefs, irrational beliefs, and negative emotions. *The Journal of*

Cognitive and Behavioral Psychotherapies, 8(1), 1–16.

MacLeod, A. K., Coates, E., & Hetherton, J. (2008). Increasing well-being through teaching goal-setting and planning skills: Results of a brief intervention. *Journal of Happiness Studies, 9,* 185–196.

Maddi, S. R. (2002). The story of hardiness: Twenty years of theorizing, research, and practice. *Consulting Psychology Journal: Practice and Research, 54(3),* 175–185.

Maddi, S. R. (2006). Hardiness: The courage to grow from stresses. *Journal of Positive Psychology, 1(3),* 160–168.

Maddux, J. E. (1993). Social cognitive models of health and exercise behavior: An introduction and review of conceptual issues. *Journal of Applied Sport Psychology, 5,* 116–140.

Maddux, J. E. (2009). Self-efficacy: The power of believing you can. In S. J. Lopez, & C. R. Snyder (Eds.), *Oxford handbook of positive psychology* (2nd.ed.) (pp. 335–343), New York, NY: Oxford University Press.

Maher, P. (1999). A review of 'traditional' aboriginal health beliefs. *Australian Journal of Rural Health, 7,* 229–236.

Manzeske, D. P., & Stright, A. D. (2009). Parenting styles and emotion regulation: The role of behavioural and psychological control during young adulthood. *Journal of Adult Development, 16,* 223–229.

Marcus, S. (2008). *The Sufi experience.* Toronto, ON: The Sufi Press.

Martin, A. J., & Marsh, H. W. (2008). Academic buoyancy: Toward an understanding of students' everyday academic resilience. *Journal of School Psychology, 46,* 53–83.

Martin, M. W. (2008). Paradoxes of happiness. *Journal of Happiness Studies, 9,* 171–184.

Martin, R. A., Puhlik-Doris, P., Larson, G., Gray, J., & Weir, K. (2003). Individual differences in use of humor and their relation to psychological well-being: Development of the Humor Styles Questionnaire. *Journal of Research in Personality, 37,* 48–75.

Martins, A., Ramalho, N., & Morin, E. (2010). A comprehensive meta-analysis of the relationship between emotional intelligence and health. *Personality and Individual Differences, 49,* 554–564.

Marziali, E., McDonald, L., & Donahue, P. (2008). The role of coping humor in the physical and mental health of older adults. *Aging & Mental Health, 12(6),* 713–718.

Mascaro, J. (trans.) (1962). *The Bhagavad Gita.* Middlesex, UK: Penguin Books.

Maslach, C. (2003). Job burnout: New directions in research and intervention. *Current Directions in Psychological Science, 12(5),* 189–192.

Maslow, A. (1964). *Religions, values and peak experiences.* Columbus, OH: State University Press.

Maslow, A. (1968). *Toward a psychology of being* (2nd ed.). New York, NY: Van Nostrand.

Maslow, A. (1970). *Motivation and personality* (2nd ed.). New York, NY: Harper & Row.

Maslow, A. H. (1971). *The farther reaches of human nature.* New York, NY: Viking Press.

Masten, A. S., Cutuli, J. J., Herbers, J. E., & Reed, M-G. J. (2009). Resilience in development. In S. J. Lopez, & C. R. Snyder (Eds.), *Oxford handbook of positive psychology* (2nd ed.) (pp. 117–131), New York, NY: Oxford University Press.

Matthews, E. E., & Cook, P. F. (2009). Relationships among optimism, well-being, self-transcendence, coping, and social support in women during treatment for breast cancer. *Psycho-Oncology, 18,* 716–726.

Matthews, M. D., Eid, J., Kelly, D., Bailey, J. K. S., Peterson, C. (2006). Character strengths and virtues of developing military leaders: An international comparison. *Military Psychology, 18(Suppl.),* S57–S68.

May, Rollo. (1953). *Man's search for himself.* New York, NY: W.W. Norton and Co.

May, Rollo. (1967). *Psychology and the human dilemma.* New York, NY: W.W. Norton and Co.

May, Rollo. (1969). *Love and Will.* New York, NY: Dell Publishing.

May, Rollo. (1972). *Power and innocence.* New York, NY: W.W. Norton and Co.

May, Rollo. (1975). *The courage to create.* New York, NY: W.W. Norton and Co.

May, Rollo. (1977). *The meaning of anxiety.* New York, NY: W.W. Norton and Co.

May, Rollo. (1981). *Freedom and destiny.* New York, NY: W.W. Norton and Co.

May, Rollo. (1983). *The discovery of being: Writings in existential psychology.* New York, NY: W.W. Norton and Co.

May, R., Angel, E., & Ellenberger, H. F. (Eds.). (1958). *Existence: A new dimension in psychiatry and psychology.* New York, NY: Simon & Schuster.

Mbiti, J. S. (1989). *African religions and philosophy* (2nd ed.). Oxford, UK: Heineman Educational Publishers.

Mbon, F. M. (1991). Socio-religious ethics and national development. In J. K. Olupona (Ed.), *African traditional religions in contemporary society* (pp. 101–109), St. Paul, MN: Paragon House.

McCullough, M. E., Kilpatrick, S. D., Emmons, R. A., & Larson, D. B. (2001). Is gratitude a moral affect? *Psychological Bulletin, 127(2),* 249–266.

McCullough, M. E., Emmons, R. A., & Tsang, J. (2002). The grateful disposition: A conceptual and empirical topography. *Journal of Personality and Social Psychology, 82(1),* 112–127.

McCullough, M. E., Kimeldorf, M. B., & Cohen, A. D. (2008). An adaptation for altruism? The social causes, social effects, and social evolution of gratitude. *Current Directions in Psychological Science, 17(4),* 281–285.

McEwen, B, S., & Wingfield, J. C. (2010). What is in a name? Integrating homeostasis, allostasis and stress. *Hormones and Behavior, 57,* 105–111.

McGaa, Ed, Eagle Man. (1990). *Mother Earth spirituality: Native American paths to healing ourselves and our world.* New York, NY: HarperCollins.

McGrath, B., Brennan, M. A., Dolan, P., & Barnett, R. (2009). Adolescent well-being and supporting contexts: A comparison of adolescents in Ireland and Florida. *Journal of Community & Applied Social Psychology, 19,* 299–320.

McGrath, R. E., Rashid, T., Park, N., & Peterson, C. (2010). Is optimal functioning a distinct state? *The Humanistic Psychologist, 38,* 159–169.

McGraw, K., Moore, S., Fuller, A., & Bates, G. (2008). Family, peer and school connectedness in final year secondary school students. *Australian Psychologist, 43(1),* 27–37.

McGregor, B. A., Antoni, M. H., Ceballos, R., & Blonberg, B. B. (2008). Short communication: Very low CD19+ B-lymphocyte percentage is associated with high levels of academic stress among healthy graduate students. *Stress and Health, 24,* 413–418.

McIntyre, K. P., Korn, J. H., & Matsuo, H. (2008). Sweating the small stuff: How different types of hassles result in the experience of stress. *Stress and Health, 24,* 383–392.

McKee, P., & Barber, C. (1999). On defining wisdom. *International Journal of Aging and Human Development, 49,* 149–164.

McLaughlin, S. A., & Malony, H. N. (1984). Near-death experiences and religion: A further investigation. *Journal of Religion and Health, 23(2),* 149–159.

McNall, L. A., Masuda, A. D., & Nicklin, J. M. (2010). Flexible work arrangements, job satisfaction, and turnover intentions: The mediating role of work-to-family enrichment. *The Journal of Psychology, 144(1),* 61–81.

McPherson, M., Smith-Lovin, L., & Cook, J. M. (2001). Birds of a feather: Homophily in social networks. *Annual Review of Sociology, 27,* 415–444.

Melamed, S., Shirom, A., Toker, S., Berminer, S., & Shapira, I. (2006). Burnout and risk of cardiovascular disease: Evidence, possible causal paths, and promising research directions. *Psychological Bulletin, 132(3),* 327–353.

Mellor, D., Stokes, M., Firth, L., Hayashi, Y., & Cummins, R. (2008). Need for belonging, relationship satisfaction, loneliness, and life satisfaction. *Personality and Individual Differences, 45,* 213–218.

Mestre, J. M., Guil, R., Lopes, P. N., Salovey, P., & Gil-Olarte, P. (2006). Emotional intelligence and social and academic adaptation to school. *Psicothema, 18,* 112–117.

Mickler, C., & Staudinger, U. M. (2008). Personal wisdom: Validation and age-related differences of a performance measure. *Psychology and Aging, 23(4),* 787–799.

Miczo, N. (2004). Humor ability, unwillingness to communicate, loneliness, and perceived stress: Testing a security theory. *Communication Studies, 55(2),* 209–226.

Mikolajczak, M., & Luminet, O. (2008). Trait emotional intelligence and the cognitive appraisal of stressful events: An exploratory study. *Personality and Individual Differences, 44,* 1445–1453.

Mikolajczak, M., Nelis, D., Hansenne, M., & Quoidbach, J. (2008). If you can regulate sadness, you can probably regulate shame: Associations between trait emotional intelligence, emotion regulation and coping efficiency across discrete emotions. *Personality and Individual Differences, 44,* 1356–1368.

Mikulincer, M., Shaver, P. R., Gillath, O., & Nitzberg, R. A. (2005). Attachment, caregiving, and altruism: Boosting attachment security increases compassion and helping. *Journal of Personality and Social Psychology, 89(5),* 817–839.

Miller, A. J., Worthington Jr., E. L., & McDaniel, M. A. (2008). Gender and forgiveness: A meta-analytic review and research agenda. *Journal of Social and Clinical Psychology, 27(8),* 843–876.

Miller, G. E., Chen, E., & Zhou, E. S. (2007). If it goes up, must it come down? Chronic stress and the hypothalamus-pituitary-adrenal axis in humans. *Psychological Bulletin, 133(1),* 25–45.

Millette, V., & Gagné, M. (2008). Designing volunteers' tasks to maximize motivation, satisfaction and performance: The impact of job characteristics on volunteer engagement. *Motivation and Emotion, 2,* 11–22.

Mimura, C., Murrells, T., & Griffiths, P. (2009). The association between stress, self-esteem and childhood acceptance in nursing and pharmacy students: A comparative cross-cultural analysis. *Stress and Health, 25,* 209–220.

Mirsky, J., Slomin-Nevo, V., & Rubinstein, L. (2007). Psychological wellness and distress among recent immigrants: A four-year longitudinal study in Israel and Germany. *International Migration, 45(1)*, 151–175.

Moore, K. S. (2005). What's class got to do with it? Community development and racial identity. *Journal of Urban Affairs, 27(4)*, 437–451.

Moos, R. H. (2008). Active ingredients of substance use-focused self-help groups. *Addiction, 103,* 387–396.

Moreall, J. (2010). Comic vices and comic virtues. *Humor, 23(1),* 1–26.

Morrill, E. F., Brewer, N. T., O'Neill, S. C., Lillie, S. E., Dees, E. C., Carey, L. A., & Rimer, B. K. (2008). The interaction of post-traumatic growth and post-traumatic stress symptoms in predicting depressive symptoms and quality of life. *Psycho-oncology, 17,* 948–953.

Morris, A. S., Silk, J. S., Steinberg, L., Myers, S. S., & Robinson, L. R. (2007). The role of the family context in the development of emotion regulation. *Social Development, 16(2),* 361–388.

Morris, B. (2006). *Religion and anthropology: A critical introduction.* Cambridge, UK: Cambridge University Press.

Morrison, P. S. (2007). Subjective wellbeing and the city. *Social Policy of New Zealand, 31,* 74–103.

Motti-Stefanidi, F., Pavlopoulos, V., Obradovic, J., & Masten, A. M. (2008). Acculturation and adaptation of immigrant adolescents in Greek urban schools. *International Journal of Psychology, 43(1)*, 45–58.

Mulago, V. (1991). Traditional African religion and Christianity. In J. K. Olupona (Ed.), *African traditional religions in contemporary society* (pp. 119–134), St. Paul, MN: Paragon House.

Muldoon, O. T., Schmid, K., & Downes, C. (2009). Political violence and psychological well-being: The role of social identity. *Applied Psychology: An International Review, 58(1),* 129–145.

Murdie, R., & Ghosh, S. (2010). Does spatial concentration always mean a lack of integration? Exploring ethnic concentration and integration in Toronto. *Journal of Ethnic and Migration Studies, 36(2),* 293–311.

Murphy, K. A., Blustein, D. L., Bohlig, A. J., & Platt, M. G. (2010). The college-to-career transition: An exploration of emerging adulthood. *Journal of Counseling & Development, 88,* 174–181.

Murray, K., & Ciarrocchi, J. W. (2007). The dark side of religion, spirituality and the moral emotions: Shame, guilt, and negative religiosity as markers for life dissatisfaction. *Journal of Pastoral Counseling, 42,* 22–41.

Murray, S. L. (2005). Regulating the risks of closeness. *Current Directions in Psychological Science, 14(2),* 74–78.

Musgrave, C. (1997). The near-death experience: A study of spiritual transformation. *Journal of Near-Death Studies, 15(3),* 187–201.

Myers, D. G. (2000). *The paradox of affluence: Spiritual hunger in an age of plenty.* New Haven, CT: Yale University Press.

Nakamura, J., & Csikszentmihalyi, M. (2009). Flow theory and research. In S. J. Lopez, & C. R. Snyder (Eds.), *Oxford handbook of positive psychology* (2nd. ed.) (pp. 195–206), New York, NY: Oxford University Press.

Natvig, G. K., Albrektsen, & Qvarnstrøm, U. (2003). Associations between psychosocial factors and happiness among school adolescents. *International Journal of Nursing Practice, 9,* 166–175.

Neff, K. D. (2003a). Self-compassion: An alternative conceptualization of a healthy attitude toward oneself. *Self and Identity, 2,* 85–102.

Neff, K. D. (2003b). The development and validation of a scale to measure self-compassion. *Self and Identity, 2,* 223–250.

Neff, K. D. (2009). The role of self-compassion in development: A healthier way to relate to oneself. *Human Development, 52,* 211–214.

Neff, K. D., Hsieh, Y-P., & Dejitterat, K. (2005). Self-compassion, achievement goals, and coping with academic failure. *Self and Identity, 4,* 263–287.

Neff, K. D., Kirkpatrick, K. L., & Rude, S. S. (2007). Self –compassion and adaptive psychological functioning. *Journal of Research in Personality, 41(1),* 139–154.

Neff, K. D., Rude, S. S., & Kirkpatrick, K. L. (2007). An examination of self-compassion in relation to positive psychological functioning and personality traits, *Journal of Research in Personality, 41,* 908–916.

Neff, K. D., & Vonk, R. (2009). Self-compassion versus global self-esteem: Two different ways of relating to oneself. *Journal of Personality, 77(1),* 23–50.

Nelis, D., Quoidbach, J., Mikolajczak, M., & Hansenne, M. (2009). Increasing emotional intelligence: (How) is it possible? *Personality and Individual Differences, 47,* 36–41.

Nelms, L. W., Hutchins, E., Hutchins, D., & Pursley, R. J. (2007). Spirituality and the health of college students. *Journal of Religion and Health, 46(2),* 249–265.

Neulinger, J., & Breit, M. (2009). Attitude dimensions of leisure: A replication study. *Journal of Leisure Research, 41(3),* 361–368.

Nevid, J. S., & Rathus, S. A. (2007). *Psychology and the challenge of life: Adjustment in the new millennium* (10th ed.). Hoboken NJ: Wiley.

Nevid, J. S., & Rathus, S. A. (2010). *Psychology and the challenges of life: Adjustment and growth* (11th ed.). Hoboken, NJ: John Wiley & Sons, Inc.

Nicholls, A. R., Polman, R. C. J., Levy, A. R., & Backhouse, S. H. (2008). Mental toughness, optimism, pessimism, and coping among athletes. *Personality and Individual Differences, 44,* 1182–1192.

Nielsen, A. M., & Hansson, K. (2007). Associations between adolescents' health, stress and sense of coherence. *Stress and Health, 23,* 331–341.

Nielsen, K., Yarker, J., Randall, R., & Munir, F. (2009). The mediating effects of team and self-efficacy on the relationship between transformational leadership, and job satisfaction and psychological well-being in healthcare professionals: A cross

sectional questionnaire survey. *International Journal of Nursing Studies, 46,* 1236–1244.

Nikhilananda. (1953). *Vivekananda: The Yogas and other works.* New York, NY: Ramakrishna-Vivekananda Center.

Nilsson, B., Lindström, U. Å., & Nåden, D. (2006). Is loneliness a psychological dysfunction? A literary study of the phenomenon of loneliness. *Scandinavian Journal of Caring Sciences, 20,* 93–101.

Nimrod, G. (2007). Expanding, reducing, concentrating and diffusing: Post retirement leisure behavior and life satisfaction. *Leisure Sciences, 29(1),* 91–111.

Nimrod, G., Janke, M. C., & Kleiber, D. A. (2009). Expanding, reducing, concentrating and diffusing: Activity patterns of recent retirees in the United States. *Leisure Sciences, 31,* 37–52.

Nix, G., Ryan, R. M., Manly, J. B., & Deci, E. L. (1999). Revitalization through self-regulation: The effects of autonomous and controlled motivation on happiness and vitality. *Journal of Experimental Social Psychology, 35,* 266–284.

Noftle, E. E., & Shaver, P. R. (2006). Attachment dimensions and the big five personality traits: Associations and comparative ability to predict relationship quality. *Journal of Research in Personality, 40,* 179–208.

Norem, J. K., & Chang, E. C. (2002). The positive psychology of negative thinking. *Journal of Clinical Psychology, 58(9),* 993–1001.

Norris, F. H., Stevens, S. P., Pfefferbaum, B., Wyche, K. F., & Pfefferbaum, R. L. (2008). Community resilience as a metaphor, theory, set of capacities, and strategy for disaster readiness. *American Journal of Community Psychology, 41,* 127–150.

Northeast Foundation for Children. (2011). Responsive Classroom®. www.responsiveclassroom.org

Noyes, R. (1980). Attitude change following near-death experiences. *Psychiatry, 43,* 234–242.

Nylen, L., Melin, B., & Laflamme, L. (2007). Interference between work and outside-work demands relative to health: Unwinding possibilities among full-time and part-time employees. *International Journal of Behavioral Medicine, 14(4),* 229–236.

Obradović, J. (2010). Effortful control and adaptive functioning of homeless children: Variable-focused and person-focused analysis. *Journal of Applied Developmental Psychology, 31,* 109–117.

O'Connor, M. (2002–2003). Making meaning of life events: Theory, evidence, and research directions for an alternative model. *Omega, 46(1),* 51–75.

O'Connor, R. C., & Cassidy, C. (2007). Predicting hopelessness: The interaction between optimism/pessimism and specific future expectancies. *Cognition and Emotion, 21(3),* 596–613.

O'Rourke, J. J. F., Tallman, B. A., & Altmaier, E. M. (2008). Measuring post-traumatic changes in spirituality/religiosity. *Mental Health, Religion & Culture, 11(7),* 719–728.

Öhman, L., Bergdahl, J., Nyberg, L., & Nilsson, L-G. (2007). Longitudinal analysis of the relation between moderate long-term stress and health. *Stress and Health, 23,* 131–138.

Oishi, S., Diener, E., & Lucas, R. E. (2009). The optimal level of well-being: Can people be too happy? In E. Diener (Ed.), *The science of well-being: The collected works of Ed Diener* (pp. 175–200), New York, NY: Springer-Verlag.

Oishi, S., & Koo, M. (2008). Two new questions about happiness: "Is happiness good?" and "Is happier better?" In M. Eid & R. J. Larsen (Eds.), *The science of subjective well-being* (pp. 290–306), New York, NY: Guilford Press.

Okulicz-Kozaryn, A. (2010). Religiosity and life satisfaction across nations. *Mental Health, Religion & Culture, 13(2),* 155–169.

Olson, I. R., & Marshuetz, C. (2005). Facial attractiveness is appraised in a glance. *Emotion, 5,* 498–502.

Oman, D., Shapiro, S. L., Throeson, C. E., Plante, T. G., & Flinders, T. (2008). Meditation lowers stress and supports forgiveness among college students: A randomized controlled trial. *Journal of American College Health, 56(5),* 569–578.

Ong, A. D., Bergeman, C. S., Bisconti, T. L., & Wallace, K. A. (2006). Psychological resilience, positive emotions, and successful adaptation to stress in later life. *Journal of Personality and Social Psychology, 91,* 730–749.

Oosthuizen, G. C. (1991). Traditional religion in contemporary South Africa. In J. K. Olupona (Ed.), *African traditional religions in contemporary society* (pp. 35–50), St. Paul, MN: Paragon House.

Orth, U., Berking, M., Walker, N., Meier, L. L., & Znoj, H. (2008). Forgiveness and psychological adjustment following interpersonal transgressions: A longitudinal analysis. *Journal of Research in Personality, 42,* 365–385.

Osis, K., & Haraldsson, E. (1977). *At the hour of death.* New York, NY: Avon.

Otake, K., Shimai, S., Tanaka-Matsumi, J., Otsui, K., & Frederickson, B. L. (2006). Happy people become happier through kindness: A counting of kindnesses intervention. *Journal of Happiness Studies, 7,* 361–375.

Owen, A. L., Videras, J., & Willemsen, C. (2008). Democracy, participation, and life satisfaction. *Social Science Quarterly, 89(4),* 987–1005.

Özer, B. U., Demir, A., & Ferrari, J. R. (2009). Exploring academic procrastination among Turkish students: Possible gender differences in prevalence and reasons. *The Journal of Social Psychology, 149(2),* 241–257.

Palmer, J. K., & Loveland, J. M. (2008). The influence of group discussion on performance judgments: Rating accuracy, contrast effects, and halo. *Journal of Psychology: Interdisciplinary and Applied, 142,* 117–130.

Pargament, K. I. (2002). The bitter and the sweet: An evaluation of the costs and benefits of religiousness. *Psychological Inquiry, 13(3),* 168–181.

Pargament, K. I., Koenig, H. G., & Perez, L. M. (2000). The many methods of religious coping: Development and initial validation of the RCOPE. *Journal of Clinical Psychology, 56,* 519–543.

Pargament, K. I., Magyar-Russell, G. M., & Murray-Swank, N. A. (2005). The sacred and the search for significance: Religion as a unique process. *Journal of Social Issues, 61(4),* 665–687.

Park, C. L. (2005). Religion as a meaning-making framework in coping with life stress. *Journal of Social Issues, 61(4),* 707–729.

Park, C. L. (2006). Exploring relations among religiousness, meaning, and adjustment to lifetime and current stressful encounters in later life. *Anxiety, Stress, and Coping, 19(1),* 33–45.

Park, C. L. (2010). Making sense of the meaning literature: An integrative review of meaning making and its effects on adjustment to stressful life events. *Psychological Bulletin, 36(2),* 257–301.

Park, C. L., & Folkman, S. (1997). Meaning in the context of stress and coping. *Review of General Psychology, 30,* 115–144.

Park, L. E., Crocker, J., & Mickelson, K. D. (2004). Attachment styles and contingencies of self-worth. *Personality and Social Psychology Bulletin, 30(10),* 1243–1254.

Park, N., & Peterson, C. (2006). Character strengths and happiness among young children: Content analysis of parental descriptions. *Journal of Happiness Studies, 7,* 323–341.

Park, N., Peterson, C., & Seligman, M. E. P. (2004). Strengths of character and well-being. *Journal of Social and Clinical Psychology, 23,* 603–619.

Passarelli, A., Hall, E., & Anderson, M. (2010). A strengths-based approach to outdoor and adventure education: Possibilities for personal growth. *Journal of Experiential Education, 33(2),* 120–135.

Pat-Horenczyk, R., & Brom, D. (2007). The multiple faces of post-traumatic growth. *Applied Psychology: An International Review, 56(3),* 379–385.

Pavey, L. J., & Sparks, P. (2008). Threats to autonomy: Motivational responses to risk information. *European Journal of Social Psychology, 38,* 852–865.

Pearce, J., Ainley, M., & Howard, S. (2005). The ebb and flow of online learning. *Computers in Human Behavior, 21,* 745–771.

Peng, W. (2008). The mediational role of identification in the relationship between experience mode and self-efficacy: Enactive role-playing versus passive observation. *CyberPsychology & Behavior, 11(6),* 649–652.

Perls, F. S. (1947). *Ego, hunger, and aggression: The beginning of Gestalt therapy.* New York, NY: Random House.

Perls, F. S. (1969). *Gestalt therapy verbatim.* Highland, NY: The Gestalt Journal Press.

Perls, F. S. (1992). *In and out the garbage pail.* Highland, NY: The Gestalt Journal Press.

Perls, F. S. (1973). *The Gestalt approach and eyewitness to therapy.* Palo Alto, CA: Science and Behavior Books.

Perls, F. S., Hefferline, R., & Goodman, P. (1994). *Gestalt therapy: Excitement and growth in the human personality.* Highland, NY: The Gestalt Journal Press.

Peterson, C. (2006). *A primer in positive psychology.* New York, NY: Oxford University Press.

Peterson, C., Park, N., & Seligman, M. E. P. (2006). Greater strengths of character and recovery from illness. *The Journal of Positive Psychology, 1(1),* 17–26.

Peterson, C., Ruch, W., Beermann, U., Park, N., & Seligman, M. E. P. (2007). Strengths of character, orientations to happiness, and life satisfaction. *Journal of Positive Psychology, 2,* 149–156.

Peterson, C., & Seligman, M. E. P. (2004). *Character strengths and virtues.* New York, NY: Oxford University Press.

Peterson, C., & Steen, T. A. (2009). Optimistic explanatory style. In S. J. Lopez, & C. R. Snyder (Eds.), *Oxford handbook of positive psychology* (2nd ed.) (pp. 313–321), New York, NY: Oxford University Press.

Philippe, F. L., Lecours, S., & Beaulieu-Pelletier, G. (2009). Resilience and positive emotions: Examining the role of emotional memories. *Journal of Personality, 77(1),* 139–175.

Phillips, A. C., Der, G., & Carroll, D. (2008). Stressful life-events exposure is associated with 17-year mortality, but it is health-related events that prove predictive. *British Journal of Health Psychology, 13,* 647–657.

Pickett, K. E., & Wilkinson, R. G. (2008). People like us: Ethnic group density effects on health. *Ethnicity & Health, 13(4),* 321–334.

Pinquart, M., & Fröhlich, C. (2009). Psychosocial resources and subjective well-being of cancer patients. *Psychology and Health, 24 (4),* 407–421.

Pinquart, M., & Schindler, I. (2009). Change of leisure in the transition to retirement: A latent-class analysis. *Leisure Sciences, 31,* 311–329.

Polak, E. L., & McCullough, M. E. (2006). Is gratitude an alternative to materialism? *Journal of Happiness Studies, 7,* 343–360.

Pollard, C., & Kennedy, P. (2007). A longitudinal analysis of emotional impact, coping strategies and post-traumatic psychological growth following spinal cord injury: A 10-year review. *British Journal of Health Psychology, 12,* 347–362.

Polster, E., & Polster, M. (1973). *Gestalt therapy integrated: Contours of theory and practice.* New York, NY: Vintage Books.

Ponterotto, J. G., Costa-Wofford, C. I., Brobst, K. E., Spelliscy, D., Kacanski, J. M., Scheinholtz, J., & Martines, D. (2007). Multicultural personality dispositions and psychological well-being. *The Journal of Social Psychology, 147(2),* 119–135.

Ponterotto, J. G., Mendelowitz, D. E., & Collabolletta, E. A. (2008). Promoting multicultural personality development: A strengths-based, positive psychology worldview for schools. *Professional School Counseling, 12(2),* 93–99.

Ponterotto, J. G., Medelsohn, J., & Belizaire, L. (2003). Assessing teacher multicultural competence: Self-report scales, observer-report evaluations, and a portfolio assessment. In D. B. Pope-Davis, H. L. K. Coleman, R. Toporek, & W. Liu (Eds.), *Handbook of multicultural competencies* (pp. 191–210), Thousand Oaks, CA: Sage.

Poon, J. M. L. (2003). Situational antecedents and outcomes of organizational politics perception. *Journal of Managerial Psychology, 18,* 138–155.

Powdthavee, N. (2008). Putting a price tag on friends, relatives, and neighbours: Using surveys of life satisfaction to value social relationships. *The Journal of Socio-Economics, 37,* 1459–1480.

Powers, R. (2009). *Generosity: An enhancement.* New York, NY: Farrar, Straus and Giroux.

Proudfoot, J. G., Corr, P. J., Guest, D. E., & Dunn, G. (2009). Cognitive-behavioural training to change attributional style improves employee well-being, job satisfaction, productivity, and turnover. *Personality and Individual Differences, 46,* 147–153.

Pury, C. L. S., & Kowalski, R. M. (2007). Human strengths, courageous actions, and general and personal courage. *Journal of Positive Psychology, 2(2),* 120–128.

Pury, C. L. S., Kowalski, R. M., & Spearman, J. (2007). Distinctions between general and personal courage. *Journal of Positive Psychology, 2(2),* 99–114.

Putnam, D. (1997). Psychological courage. *Philosophy, Psychiatry, and Psychology, 4,* 1–11.

Puzziferro, M. (2008). Online technologies, self-efficacy and self-regulated learning as predictors of final grade and satisfaction in college-level online courses. *The American Journal of Distance Education, 22,* 72–89.

Queen, J., Brackley, M. H., & Williams, G. B. (2009). Being emotionally abused: a phenomenological study of adult women's experiences of emotionally abusive intimate partner relationships. *Issues in Mental Health Nursing, 30,* 237–245.

Quoidbach, J., Berry, E. V., Hansenne, M., & Mikolajczak, M. (2010). Positive emotion regulation and well-being: Comparing the impact of eight savoring and dampening strategies. *Personality and Individual Differences, 43,* 368–373.

Rand, K. L. (2009). Hope and optimism: Latent structures and influences on grade expectancy and academic performance. *Journal of Personality, 77(1),* 231–260.

Rand, K. L., & Cheavens, J. S. (2009). Hope theory. In S. J. Lopez & C. R. Snyder (Eds.), *Oxford handbook of positive psychology* (2nd ed.) (pp. 323–333), New York, NY: Oxford University Press.

Rangganadhan, A. R., & Todorow, N. (2010). Personality and self-forgiveness: The roles of shame, guilt, empathy and conciliatory behavior. *Journal of Social and Clinical Psychology, 29(1),* 1–22.

Rate, C. R., Clarke, J. A., Lindsay, D. R., & Sternberg, R. J. (2007). Implicit theories of courage. *Journal of Positive Psychology, 2(2),* 80–98.

Reeve, J. (2002). Handbook of self-determination research. In E. L. Deci & R. M. Ryan (Eds.), *Self-determination theory applied to educational settings* (pp. 183–203), Rochester, NY: University of Rochester Press.

Renault, D. (Wa'na'nee'che') & Freke, T. (1996). *Native American spirituality.* London, UK: Thorsons.

Resnick, S., Warmoth, A., & Serlin, I. A. (2001). The humanistic psychology and positive psychology connection: Implications for psychotherapy, *Journal of Humanistic Psychology, 41(1),* 73–101.

Rhodes, S. D., Malow, R. M., & Jolly, C. (2010). Community-based participatory research: A new and not-so-new approach to HIV/AIDS prevention, care, and treatment. *AIDS Education and Prevention, 22(3),* 173–183.

Rimm-Kaufman, S. E., Fan, X., Chiu, Y-J., & You, W. (2007). The contribution of the Responsive Classroom Approach on children's academic achievement: Results from a three year longitudinal study. *Journal of School Psychology, 45,* 401–421.

Ring, K. (1980). Religiousness and the near-death experience: An empirical study. *Theta, 8(3),* 3–5.

Robinson, E., Dilorio, C., DePadilla, L., McCarty, F., Yeager, K., Henry, T., Schomer, D., & Shafer, P. (2008). Psychosocial predictors of lifestyle management in adults with epilepsy. *Epilepsy & Behavior, 13,* 523–528.

Rogatko, T. P. (2009). The influence of flow on positive affect in college students. *Journal of Happiness Studies, 10,* 133–148.

Rogers, C. R. (1951). *Client-centered therapy.* Boston, MA: Houghton-Mifflin.

Rogers, C. R. (1961). *On becoming a person: A therapist's view of psychotherapy.* Boston, MA: Houghton Miflin.

Rokach, A. (2007). The effects of age and culture on the causes of loneliness. *Social Behavior and Personality, 35(2),* 169–186.

Rokach, A., & Brock, H. (1996). The causes of loneliness. *Psychology: A Journal of Human Behavior, 33(3),* 1–11.

Rokach, A., & Brock, H. (1997). Loneliness: A multidimensional experience. *Psychology: A Journal of Human Behavior, 34(1),* 1–9.

Rokach, A., Orzeck, T., Moya, M. C., & Expósito, F. (2002). Causes of loneliness in North America and Spain. *European Psychologist, 7(1),* 70–79.

Roohafza, H., Sadeghi, M., Sarraf-Zadegan, N., Baghaei, A., Kelishadi, R., Mahvash, M., Sajjadi, F., Toghianifar, N., & Talaei, M. (2007). Short communication: Relation between stress and other life style factors. *Stress and Health, 23,* 23–29.

Rosenberger, P. H., Kerns, R., Jokl, P., & Ickovics, J. R. (2009). Mood and attitude predict pain outcomes following arthroscopic knee surgery. *Annals of Behavioral Medicine, 37,* 70–76.

Rosenkoetter, M. M., Garris, J. M., & Engdahl, R. A. (2001). Postretirement use of time: Implications for pre-retirement planning and post-retirement management. *Activities, Adaptation & Aging, 25(3/4),* 1–18.

Ross, R. (1992). *Dancing with a ghost: Exploring Indian reality.* Toronto, ON: Reed Books.

Ross, R. (1996). *Returning to the teachings: Exploring aboriginal justice.* Toronto, ON: Penguin Books.

Ruini, C., & Fava, G. A. (2009). Well-being therapy for generalized anxiety disorder. *Journal of Clinical Psychology, 65(5),* 510–519.

Rust, T., Diessner, R., & Reade, L. (2009). Strengths only or strengths and relative weaknesses? A preliminary study. *The Journal of Psychology, 143(5),* 465–476.

Ruthig, J. C., Hanson, B. L., & Marino, J. M. (2009). A three-phase examination of academic comparative optimism and perceived academic control. *Learning and Individual Differences, 19,* 435–439.

Ryan, R. M., & Connell, J. P. (1989). Perceived locus of causality and internalization: Examining reasons for acting in two domains. *Journal of Personality and Social Psychology, 57,* 749–761.

Ryan, R. M., & Deci, E. L. (2000a). Intrinsic and extrinsic motivation: Classic definitions and new directions. *Contemporary Educational Psychology, 25,* 54–67.

Ryan, R. M., & Deci, E. L. (2000b). Self-determination theory and the facilitation of intrinsic motivation, social development, and well-being. *American Psychologist, 55(1),* 68–78.

Ryan, R. M., Deci, E. L., & Grolnick, W. S. (1995). Autonomy, relatedness, and the self: Their relationship to development and psychopathology. In D. Cicchetti & D. J. Cohen (Eds.), *Developmental psychopathology: Theory and methods* (pp. 618–655), New York, NY: Wiley.

Ryan, R. M., Huta, V., & Deci, E. L. (2008). Living well: A self-determination theory perspective on eudaimonia. *Journal of Happiness Studies, 9,* 139–170.

Ryff, C. D. (1989). Happiness is everything, or is it? Explorations of the meaning of psychological well-being. *Journal of Personality and Social Psychology, 57,* 1069–1081.

Ryff, C. D., & Singer, B. H. (2008). Know thyself and become what you are: A eudaimonic approach to psychological well-being. *Journal of Happiness Studies, 9,* 13–39.

Saab, H., & Klinger, D. (2010). School differences in adolescent health and wellbeing: Findings from the Canadian Health Behaviour in School-aged Children Study. *Social Science & Medicine, 70,* 850–858.

Salanova, M., Bakker, A. B., & Llorens, S. (2006). Flow at work: Evidence for an upward spiral of personal and organizational resources. *Journal of Happiness Studies, 7,* 1–22.

Salovey, P., Mayer, J. D., Caruso, D., & Yoo, S. H. (2009). The positive psychology of emotional intelligence. In S. J. Lopez & C. R. Snyder (Eds.), *Oxford handbook of positive psychology* (2nd ed.) (pp. 237–248), New York, NY: Oxford University Press.

Salsman, J. M., Brown, T. L., Brechting, E. H., & Carlson, C. R. (2005). The link between religion and spirituality and psychological adjustment: The mediating role of optimism and social support. *Personality and Social Psychology Bulletin, 31(4),* 522–535.

Sams, J. (1999). *Dancing the dream.* San Francisco, CA: HarperCollins.

Samuels, S. E., Craypo, L., Boyle, M., Crawford, P. B., Yancey, A., & Flores, G. (2010). The California Endowment's Healthy Eating, Active Communities program: A midpoint review. *American Journal of Public Health, 100(11),* 2114–2123.

Saroglou, V., Buxant, C., & Tilquin, J. (2008). Positive emotion as leading to religion and spirituality. *The Journal of Positive Psychology, 3(3),* 165–173.

SAS (2011). www.sas.com/news/fortune2011.html

Scheibe, S., Kunzmann, U., & Baltes, P. B. (2009). New territories of positive life-span development: Wisdom and life-longings. In S. J. Lopez & C. R. Snyder (Eds.), *Oxford handbook of positive psychology* (2nd ed.) (pp. 171–183), New York, NY: Oxford University Press.

Scheier, M. F., Carver, C. S., & Bridges, M. W. (1994). Distinguishing optimism from neuroticism (and trait anxiety, self-mastery, and self-esteem): A reevaluation of the Life Orientation Test. *Journal of Personality and Social Psychology, 67(6),* 1063–1078.

Scheier, M. F., Carver, C. S., & Bridges, M. W. (2002). Optimism, pessimism, and psychological well-being. In E. C. Chang (Ed.), *Optimism and pessimism: Implications for theory, research and practice* (pp. 189–216), Washington DC: American Psychological Association.

Schmidt, S., Tinti, C., Levine, L. J., & Testa, S. (2010). Appraisals, emotions and emotion regulation: An integrative approach. *Motivation and Emotion, 34,* 63–72.

Schouwenburg, H. C. (1995). Academic procrastination: Theoretical notions, measurement, and research. In J. R. Ferrari *Procrastination and task avoidance: Theory, research, and treatment* (pp. 71–96), New York, NY: Plenum Press.

Schouwenburg, H. C., & Groenewoud, J. T. (2001). Study motivation under social temptation: Effects of trait procrastination. *Personality and Individual Differences, 30,* 229–240.

Schueller, S. M. (2008). Promoting wellness: Integrating community and positive psychology. *Journal of Community Psychology, 37(7),* 922–937.

Schüler, J., & Brunner, S. (2009). The rewarding effect of flow experience on performance in a marathon race. *Psychology of Sport and Exercise, 10,* 168–174.

Schüler, J., Job, V., Fröhlich, S. M., & Brandstätter, V. (2009). Dealing with a 'hidden stressor': Emotional disclosure as a coping strategy to overcome the negative effects of motive incongruence on health. *Stress and Health, 25,* 221–233.

Schulman, P., Keith, D., & Seligman, M. E. P. (1993). Is optimism heritable? A study of twins. *Behaviour Research and Therapy, 31(6),* 569–574.

Schunk, D. H. (1984). The self-efficacy perspective on academic behavior. *Education Psychologist, 19,* 48–58.

Schunk, D. H. (1989). Self-efficacy and cognitive achievement: Implications for students with learning problems. *Journal of Learning Disabilities, 22,* 14–22.

Schutte, N., & Malouff, J. M. (2011). Emotional intelligence mediates the relationship between mindfulness and subjective well-being. *Personality and Individual Differences, 50(7),* 1116–1119.

Schwartz, B., & Sharpe, K. E. (2006). Practical wisdom: Aristotle meets positive psychology. *Journal of Happiness Studies, 7,* 377–395.

Schwartz, G. M., & Campagna, J. (2008). New meaning for the emotional state of the

elderly, from a leisure standpoint. *Leisure Studies, 27(2),* 207–211.

Seifert, T., & Hedderson, C. (2010). Intrinsic motivation and flow in skateboarding: An ethnographic study. *Journal of Happiness Studies, 11,* 277–292.

Seery, M. D., West, T. V., Weisbuch, M., & Blascovick, J. (2008). The effects of negative reflection for defensive pessimists: Dissipation or harnessing of threat? *Personality and Individual Differences, (45),* 515–520.

Segerstrom, S. C. (2007). Optimism and resources: Effects on each other and on health over 10 years. *Journal of Research in Personality, 41,* 772–786.

Segerstrom, S. C., & Miller, G. E. (2004). Psychological stress and the human immune system: A meta-analytic study of 30 years of inquiry. *Psychological Bulletin, 130,* 601–630.

Seligman, M. E. P. (2002). *Authentic happiness: Using the new positive psychology to realize your potential for lasting fulfillment.* New York, NY: The Free Press.

Seligman, M. E. P. (2006). *Learned optimism: How to change your mind and your life.* New York, NY: Knopf Doubleday Publishing Group.

Seligman, M. E. P. (2011). *Flourish: A visionary new view of happiness and well-being.* New York, NY: Simon & Schuster.

Seligman, M. E. P., with K. Reivich, L. Jaycox, J. Gillham, & K. Reivich. (2007). *The Optimistic Child.* New York, NY: Houghton Mifflin Harcourt.

Seligman, M. E. P., Ernst, R. M., Gillham, J., Reivich, K., & Linkins, M. (2009). Positive education: Positive psychology and classroom interventions. *Oxford Review of Education, 35(3),* 293–311.

Seligman, M. E. P., Rashid, T., & Parks, A. C. (2006). Positive psychotherapy. *American Psychologist, 61,* 774–788.

Seligman, M. E. P., Steen, T. A., Park, N., & Peterson, C. (2005). Positive psychology progress: Empirical validation of interventions. *American Psychologist, 60,* 410–421.

Sellers, D., Dochen, C. W., & Hodges, R. (2011). *Academic transformation: The road to college success* (2nd ed.). New York, NY: Pearson.

Selye, H. (1956). *The stress of life.* New York, NY: McGraw-Hill.

Serida, J., Almeida, D. M., & Wethington, E. (2004). Chronic stressors and daily hassles: Unique and interactive relationships with psychological distress. *Journal of Health and Social Behavior, 45,* 17–33.

Shah, I. (1964). *The Sufis.* New York, NY: Anchor Books.

Shaku, S. (1993). *Zen for Americans.* New York, NY: Barnes and Noble.

Shaw, A., Joseph, S., & Linley, P. A. (2005). Religion, spirituality, and posttraumatic growth: A systematic review. *Mental Health, Religion & Culture, 8(1),* 1–11.

Sheard, M., & Globy, J. (2006). The efficacy of an outdoor adventure education curriculum on selected aspects of positive psychological development. *Journal of Experiential Education, 29(2),* 187–209.

Shearer, C. B. (2009). Exploring the relationship between intrapersonal intelligence and university students' career confusion: Implications for counseling, academic success, and school-to-career transition. *Journal of Employment Counseling, 46,* 52–61.

Sheldon, K. M., Cummins, R., & Khamble, S. (2010). Life balance and well-being: Testing a novel conceptual and measurement approach. *Journal of Personality, 78(4),* 1093–1133.

Sheldon, K. M., & Houser-Marko, L. (2001). Self-concordance, goal attainment, and the pursuit of happiness: Can there be an upward spiral? *Journal of Personality and Social Psychology, 80,* 152–165.

Sheldon, K. M., Ryan, R. M., Rawsthorne, L., & Ilardi, B. (1997). Trait self and true self: Cross-role variation in the Big Five traits and its relations with authenticity and subjective well-being. *Journal of Personality and Social Psychology, 73,* 1380–1393.

Shen, Y. E. (2009). Relationships between self-efficacy, social support and stress coping strategies in Chinese primary and secondary school teachers. *Stress and Health, 25,* 129–138.

Sheridan, S. M., Warnes, E. D., Cowan, R. J., Schemm, A. V., & Clarke, B. L. (2004). Family-centered positive psychology: Focusing on strengths to build student success. *Psychology in the Schools, 41(1),* 7–17.

Shorey, H. S., Snyder, C. R., Yang, X., & Lewin, M. R. (2003). The role of hope as a mediator in recollected parenting, adult attachment, and mental health. *Journal of Social and Clinical Psychology, 22(6),* 685–715.

Shults, C. (2008). Making the case for a positive approach to improving organizational performance in higher education institutions. *Community College Review, 36(2),* 133–159.

Shushok, F., & Hulme, E. (2006). What's right with you: Helping students find and use their personal strengths. *About Campus, 11(4),* 2–8.

Silberman, I. (2005). Religion as a meaning system: Implications for the New Millennium. *Journal of Social Issues, 61(4),* 641–663.

Simpson, D. B., Newman, J. L., & Fuqua, D. R. (2007). Spirituality and personality: Accumulating evidence. *Journal of Psychology and Christianity, 26(1),* 33–44.

Skevington, S. M. (2009). Conceptualising dimensions of quality of life in poverty. *Journal of Community & Applied Social Psychology, 19,* 33–50.

Sleebos, E., Ellemers, N., & de Gilder, D. (2006). The carrot and the stick: Affective commitment and acceptance anxiety as motives for discretionary group efforts by respected and disrespected group members. *Personality and Social Psychology Bulletin, 32,* 244–255.

Smith, A. P. (20019a). Effects of chewing gum on mood, learning, memory and performance of an intelligence task. *Nutritional Neuroscience, 12,* 81–88.

Smith, A. P. (2009b). Chewing gum, stress and health. *Stress and Health, 25,* 445–451.

Smith, B. W., Dalen, J., Wiggins, K., Tooley, E., Christopher, P., & Bernard, J. (2008). The Brief Resilience Scale: Assessing the ability to bounce back. *International Journal of Behavioral Medicine, 15,* 194–200.

Smith, L., Heaven, P. C. L., & Ciarrochi, J. (2008). Trait emotional intelligence, conflict communication patterns, and relationship satisfaction. *Personality and Individual Differences, 44,* 1314–1325.

Snyder, C. R. (1998). Hope. In H. S. Friedman (Ed.), *Encyclopedia of mental health* (pp. 421–431), San Diego, CA: Academic Press.

Snyder, C. R. (2002). Hope theory: Rainbows in the mind. *Psychological Inquiry, 13(4),* 249–275.

Soenens, B., & Vansteenkiste, M. (2010). A theoretical upgrade of the concept of parental psychological control: Proposing new insights on the basis of self-determination theory. *Developmental Review, 30,* 74–99.

Sogyal, R. (1994). *The Tibetan book of living and dying.* San Francisco, CA: Harper-Collins.

Sohl, S. J., & Moyer, A. (2009). Refining the conceptualization of a future-oriented self-regulatory behavior: Proactive coping. *Personality and Individual Differences, 47,* 139–144.

Solomon, L. J., & Rothblum, E. D. (1984). Academic procrastination: Frequency and cognitive-behavioral correlates. *Journal of Counseling Psychology, 31(4),* 503–509.

Souza, G. G. L., Mendonca-De-Souza, A. C. F., Barros, E. M., Coutinho, E. F. S., Oliviera, L., Mendlowicz, M. V., Figueira, I., & Volchan, E. (2007). Resilience and vagal tone predict cardiac recovery from acute social stress. *Stress, 10(4),* 368–374.

Spiers, A., & Walker, G. J. (2009). The effects of ethnicity and leisure satisfaction on happiness, peacefulness, and quality of life. *Leisure Sciences, 31,* 84–99.

Spilka, B., Hood Jr., R. W., Hunsberger, B., & Gorsuch, R. (2003). *The psychology of religion: An empirical approach.* New York, NY: Guilford Press.

Sprang, G., Clark, J. J., & Whitt-Woosley, A. (2007). Compassion fatigue, compassion satisfaction, and burnout: Impacting a professional's quality of life. *Journal of Loss and Trauma, 12,* 259–280.

Spratt, J., Shucksmith, J., Philip, K., & Watson, C. (2006). 'Part of who we are as a school should include responsibility for well-being': Links between the school environment, mental health and behavior. *Pastoral Care, 24(3),* 14–21.

Staats, S., Hupp, J. M., & Hagley, A. M. (2008). Honesty and heroes: A positive psychology view of heroism and academic honesty. *The Journal of Psychology, 142(4),* 357–372.

Staats, S., Hupp, J. M., Wallace, H., & Gresley, J. (2009). Heroes don't cheat: An examination of academic dishonesty and students' views on why professors don't report cheating. *Ethics & Behavior, 19(3),* 171–183.

Stanley, R. O., & Burrows, G. D. (2008). Psychogenic heart disease—Stress and the heart: historical perspective. *Stress and Health, 24,* 181–187.

Statistics Canada (2001). Selected Religions, for Canada, Provinces and Territories. www.statscan.gc.ca

Stavrou, N. A. (2008). Intrinsic motivation, extrinsic motivation and amotivation: Examining self-determination theory from flow theory perspective. In F. M. Olsson (Ed.), *New developments in the psychology of motivation* (pp. 1–24), New York, NY: Nova Science Publishers.

Steel, P. (2007). The nature of procrastination: A meta-analytic and theoretical review of the quintessential self-regulatory failure. *Psychological Bulletin, 133(1),* 65–94.

Steel, P., Brothen, T., & Wambach, C. (2001). Procrastination and personality, performance, and mood. *Personality and Individual Differences, 30,* 95–106.

Steffen, P. R., & Fearing, M. (2007). Does defensiveness account for the relationship between religiosity and psychosocial adjustment? *The International Journal for the Psychology of Religion, 17(3),* 233–244.

Steger, M. F. (2009). Meaning in life. In S. J. Lopez, & C. R. Snyder (Eds.), *Oxford*

Handbook of Positive Psychology (2nd ed.) (pp. 679–687), New York, NY: Oxford University Press.

Steger, M. F., Frazier, P., & Zacchanini, J. L. (2008). Terrorism in two cultures: Traumatization and existential protective factors following the September 11th attacks and the Madrid train bombings. *Journal of Trauma and Loss, 13,* 511–527.

Steger, M. F., & Kashdan, T. B. (2007). Stability and specificity of meaning in life and life satisfaction over one year. *Journal of Happiness Studies, 8,* 161–179.

Steger, M. F., Oishi, S., & Kashdan, T. B. (2009). Meaning in life across the life span: Levels and correlates of meaning in life from emerging adulthood to older adulthood. *Journal of Positive Psychology, 4(1),* 43–52.

Steinhardt, M., & Dolbier, C. (2008). Evaluation of a resilience intervention to enhance coping strategies and protective factors and decrease symptomatology. *Journal of American College Health, 56(4),* 445–453.

Stek, M. L., Vinkers, D. J., Gussekloo, J., Beekman, A. T., Van der Mast, R., & Westendorp, R. G. (2005). Is depression in old age fatal only when people feel lonely? *American Journal of Psychiatry, 162(1),* 178–180.

Steptoe, A., O'Donnell, K., Marmot, M., & Wardle, J. (2008). Positive affect and psychosocial processes related to health. *British Journal of Psychology, 99,* 211–227.

Sternberg, R. J. (1988). *The triangle of love: Intimacy, passion, commitment.* New York, NY: Basic Books.

Sternberg, R. J. (1998). A balance theory of wisdom. *Review of General Psychology, 2,* 347–365.

Sternberg, R. J. (2001). Why schools should teach for wisdom: The balance theory of wisdom in educational settings. *Educational Psychologist, 36(4),* 227–245.

Stillman, S., McKenzie, D., & Gibson, J. (2009). Migration and mental health: Evidence from a natural experiment. *Journal of Health Economics, 28,* 677–687.

Strawbridge, W. J., Cohen, R. D., Shema, S. J., & Kaplan, G. A. (1997). Frequent attendance at religious services and mortality over 28 years. *American Journal of Public Health, 87,* 957–961.

Stronegger, W. J., Titze, S., & Oja, P. (2010). Perceived characteristics of the neighborhood and its association with physical activity behavior and self-rated health. *Health & Place, 16,* 736–743.

Strongman K. T., & Burt, C. D. B. (2000). Taking breaks from work: An exploratory inquiry. *Journal of Psychology, 134,* 229–242.

Strümpfer, D. J. W. (2005). Standing on the shoulders of giants: Notes on early positive psychology (Psychofortology). *South African Journal of Psychology, 35(1),* 21–45.

Struthers, C. W., Eaton, J., Santelli, A. G., Uchiyama, M., & Shirvani, N. (2008). The effects of attributions of intent and apology on forgiveness: When saying sorry may not help the story. *Journal of Experimental Social Psychology, 44,* 983–992.

Struthers, C. W., Eaton, J., Shirvani, N., Georghiou, M., & Edell, E. (2008). The effect of preemptive forgiveness and a transgressor's responsibility on shame: Motivation to reconcile, and repentance. *Basic and Applied Social Psychology, 30,* 130–141.

Sugiyama, T., Leslie, E., Giles-Corti, B., & Owen, N. (2009). Physical activity for recreation or exercise on neighbourhood streets: Associations with perceived environmental attributes. *Health & Place, 15,* 1058–1063.

Sullivan, W. C., Kuo, F. E., & DePooter, S. E. (2004). The fruit of urban nature: Vital neighborhood spaces. *Environment and Behavior, 36(5),* 678–700.

Sundararajan, L. (2008). Toward a reflexive positive psychology. *Theory & Psychology, 18(5),* 655–674.

Sullivan-Vance, K. (2008). Reenvisioning and revitalising academic advising at Western Oregon University. *Peer Review, 10(1),* 15–17.

Sundararajan, L. (2010). Two flavors of aesthetic tasting: *Rasa* and Savoring, A cross-cultural study with implications for psychology of emotion. *Review of General Psychology, 14(1),* 22–30.

Sutherland, C. (1990). Changes in religious beliefs, attitudes, and practices following near-death experiences: An Australian study. *Journal of Near-Death Studies, 9(1),* 21–31.

Sverke, M., Hellgren, J., & Näswall, K. (2002). No security: A meta-analysis and review of job insecurity and its consequences. *Journal of Occupational Health Psychology, 7(3),* 242–264.

Swain, T. (2006). Part 1: Australia. In T. Swain & G. Trompf (1995), *The religions of Oceania,* New York, NY: Routledge.

Swendeman, D., Ingram, B. L., & Rotheram-Borus, M. J. (2009). Common elements in self-management of HIV and other chronic illnesses: An integrative framework. *AIDS Care, 21(10),* 1321–1334.

Sy, T., Tram, S., & O'Hara, L. A. (2006). Relation of employee and manager emotional intelligence to job satisfaction and performance. *Journal of Vocational Behavior, 68,* 461–473.

Szalma, J. L. (2009). Individual differences in performance, workload, and stress in sustained attention: Optimism and pessimism. *Personality and Individual Differences, 47,* 444–451.

Tal-Or, N., & Papirman, Y. (2007). The fundamental attribution error in attributing fictional figures' characteristics to the actors. *Media Psychology, 9,* 331–345.

Tamir, M. (2009). What do people feel and why? Pleasure and utility in emotion regulation. *Current Directions in Psychological Science, 18(2),* 101–105.

Tan, P. P., Zhang, N., & Fan, L. (2004). Students' attitudes towards the elderly in the People's Republic of China. *Educational Gerontology, 30,* 305–314.

Tangney, J. P., Baumeister, R. F., & Boone, A. L. (2004). High self-control predicts good adjustment, less pathology, better grades, and interpersonal success. *Journal of Personality, 72(2),* 271–324.

Taylor, S. E., Dickerson, S. S., & Klein, L. C. (2005). Toward a biology of social support. In C. R. Snyder, & S. J. Lopez (Eds.), *Handbook of positive psychology* (pp. 556–569), New York, NY: Oxford University Press.

Tedeschi, R. G., & Calhoun, L. G. (1995). *Trauma and transformation: Growing in the aftermath of suffering.* Newbury Park, CA; Sage.

Tedeschi, R. G., & Calhoun, L. G. (2004). A clinical approach to posttraumatic growth. In P. A. Linley & S. Joseph (Eds.), *Positive psychology in practice* (pp. 405–419), Hoboken, NJ: Wiley.

Telfer, E. (1990). *Happiness.* New York, NY: St. Martin's Press.

Tehrani, N. (2007). The cost of caring—The impact of secondary trauma on assumptions, values and beliefs. *Counselling Psychology Quarterly, 20(4),* 325–339.

Terjesen, M. D., Jacofsky, M., Froh, J., & DiGiuseppe, R. (2004). Integrating positive psychology into schools: Implications for practice. *Psychology in the Schools, 41(1),* 163–172.

Thomas, D. E. (2005). *African traditional religion in the modern world.* London, UK: McFarland & Company, Inc, Publishers.

Tice, D. M., & Baumeister, R. F. (1997). Longitudinal study of procrastination, performance, stress, and health: The costs and benefits of dawdling. *Psychological Science, 8(6),* 454–458.

Tillich, P. (1952). *The courage to be.* New Haven, CT: Yale University Press.

Tkach, C., & Lyubomirsky, S. (2006). How do people pursue happiness?: Relating personality, happiness-increasing strategies, and well-being. *Journal of Happiness Studies, 7,* 183–225.

Tomba, E., Belaise, C., Ottolini, F., Ruini, C., Bravi, A., Albieri, E., Rafanelli, C., Caffo, E., & Fava, G. A. (2010). Differential effects of well-being promoting and anxiety-management strategies in a non-clinical school setting. *Journal of Anxiety Disorders, 24,* 326–333.

Toppinen-Tanner, S., Ahola, K., Koskinen, A., & Väänänen, A. (2009). Burnout predicts hospitalization for mental and cardiovascular disorders: 10-year prospective results for industrial sector. *Stress and Health, 25,* 287–296.

Toussaint, L., & Friedman, P. (2009). Forgiveness, gratitude, and well-being: The mediating role of affect and beliefs. *Journal of Happiness Studies, 10,* 635–654.

Trossman, S. (2009). Creating healthy workplaces and getting recognized for it. *The American Nurse, 41(4),* 8.

Tsai, M-C. (2009). Market openness, transition economies and subjective wellbeing. *Journal of Happiness Studies, 10,* 523–539.

Tsang, J. (2006a). Gratitude and prosocial behaviour: An experimental test of gratitude. *Cognition and Emotion, 20(1),* 138–148.

Tsang, J. (2006b). The effects of helper intention on gratitude and indebtedness. *Motivation and Emotion, 30,* 199–205.

Tse, S., Lloyd, C., Petchkovsky, L., & Manaia, W. (2005). Exploration of Australian and New Zealand indigenous peoples spirituality and mental health. *Australian Occupational Therapy Journal, 52,* 181–187.

Tse, W. S., & Yip, T. H. J. (2009). Relationship among dispositional forgiveness of others, interpersonal adjustment and psychological well-being: Implication for interpersonal theory of depression. *Personality and Individual Differences, 46,* 365–368.

Tugade, M. M., & Fredrickson, B. L. (2004). Resilient individuals use positive emotions to bounce back from negative emotional experiences. *Journal of Personality and Social Psychology, 86(2),* 320–333.

Tugade, M. M., & Fredrickson, B. L. (2007). Regulation of positive emotions: Emotion regulation strategies that promote resilience. *Journal of Happiness Studies, 8,* 311–333.

Turner, K. (2009). Mindfulness: The present moment in clinical social work. *Clinical Social Work Journal, 37(2),* 95–103.

Tusaie, K., Puskar, K., & Sereika, S. M. (2007). A predictive and moderating model of psychosocial resilience in adolescents. *Journal of Nursing Scholarship, 39(1),* 54–60.

Ungar, M., Brown, M., Liebenberg, L., Othman, R., Kwong, W. M., Armstrong, M, & Gilgun, J. (2007). Unique pathways to resilience across cultures. *Adolescence, 42(166),* 287–310.

Union University (2010). Campus and community: A day of remembrance and service. www.uu.edu/events/dayofremembrance/

University of Dayton (2010). Living-learning environment. www.udayton.edu/main/ living_learning_environment.php

Ura, K. (2008). Explanation of GNH index. *The Centre for Bhutan Studies: Gross National Happiness,* www.grossnationalhappiness.com/gnhIndex/ intruductionGNH.aspx

Ursano, R. J., Fullerton, C. S., Vance, K., & Kao, T. C. (1999). Posttraumatic stress disorder and identification in disaster workers. *American Journal of Psychiatry, 156,* 353–359.

Vaillant, G., Templeton, J., Ardelt, M., & Meyer, S. E. (2008). The natural history of male mental health: Health and religious involvement. *Social Science & Medicine (66),* 221–231.

Valle, M. F., Huebner, E. S., & Suldo, S. M. (2006). An analysis of hope as a psychological strength. *Journal of School Psychology, 44,* 393–406.

Van Cleef, G. A. (2009). How emotions regulate social life: The emotions as social information (EASI) model. *Current Directions in Psychological Science, 18(3),* 184–188.

Van den Broeck, A., Vansteenkiste, M., De Witte, H., & Lens, W. (2008). Explaining the relationships between job characteristics, burnout, and engagement: The role of basic psychological need satisfaction. *Work & Stress, 22(3),* 277–294.

Vanderbilt-Adriance, E., & Shaw, D. S. (2008). Conceptualizing and re-evaluating resilience across levels of risk, time, and domains of competence. *Clinical Child and Family Psychological Review, 11,* 30–58.

Van Dijk, W. W. (2009). How do you feel? Affective forecasting and the impact bias in track athletics. *The Journal of Social Psychology, 149(3),* 243–248.

Van Dyke, C. J., & Elias, M. J. (2007). How forgiveness, purpose, and religiosity are related to the mental health and well-being of youth: A review of the literature. *Mental Health, Religion, & Culture, 10(4),* 395–415.

Van Lommel, P. (2006). Near-death experience, consciousness, and the brain: A new concept about the continuity of our consciousness based on recent scientific research on near-death experience in survivors of cardiac arrest. *World Futures, 62,* 134–151.

Van Lommel, P., Van Wees, R., Meyers, V., & Elfferich, I. (2001). Near-death experience in survivors of cardiac arrest: A prospective study in the Netherlands. *Lancet, 358,* 2039–2045.

Varenne, J. (1976). *Yoga and the Hindu tradition.* Chicago, IL: University of Chicago Press.

Veenhoven, R. (2004). Happiness as a public policy aim: The greatest happiness principle. In P. A. Linley & S. Joseph (Eds.), *Positive psychology in practice* (pp. 658–678), Hoboken, NJ.: Wiley.

Verderber, R. F., Verderber, K. S., & Berryman-Fink, C. (2008). *Communicate.* Belmont, CA: Wadsworth.

Vernon, L. L., Dillon, J. M., & Steiner, A. R. W. (2009). Proactive coping, gratitude, and posttraumatic stress disorder in college women. *Anxiety, Stress & Coping, 22(1),* 117–127.

Versluis, A. (1997). *The elements of Native American traditions.* Boston, MA: Element Books, Inc.

Volling, B. L., Blandon, A. Y., Kolak, A. M. (2006). Marriage, parenting, and the emergence of early self-regulation in the family system. *Journal of Child and Family Studies, 15(4),* 493–506.

Volokhov, R. N., & Demaree, H. A. (2010). Spontaneous emotion regulation to positive and negative stimuli. *Brain and Cognition, 73,* 1–6.

Wagnild, G. M., & Young, H. M. (2009). The Resilience Scale™. www.resiliencescale.com

Wandersman, A., & Florin, P. (2003). Community interventions and community

prevention. *American Psychologist, 58(6–7),* 441–448.

Wanzer, M. B., Sparks, L., & Frymier, A. B. (2009). Humorous communication within the lives of older adults: The relationships among humor, coping efficacy, age, and life satisfaction. *Health Communication, 24,* 128–136.

Warr, D., Feldman, P., Tacticos, T., & Kelaher, M. (2009). Sources of stress in impoverished neighbourhoods: Insights into links between neighbourhood environments and health. *Australian and New Zealand Journal of Public Health, 33(1),* 25–33.

Waschull, S. B. (2005). Predicting success in online psychology courses: Self–discipline and motivation. *Teaching of Psychology, 32(3),* 190–192.

Waterman, A. S. (2008). Reconsidering happiness: A eudaimonist's perspective. *The Journal of Positive Psychology, 3(4),* 234–252.

Waterman, A. S., Schwartz, S. J., & Conti, R. (2008). The implications of two conceptions of happiness (hedonic enjoyment and eudaimonia) for the understanding of intrinsic motivation. *Journal of Happiness Studies, 9,* 41–79.

Watkins, P. C., Scheer, J., Ovnicek, M., & Kolts, R. (2006). The debt of gratitude: Dissociating gratitude and indebtedness. *Cognition and Emotion, 20(2),* 217–241.

Watkins, P. C., Van Gelder, M., & Frias, A. (2009). Furthering the science of gratitude. In S. J. Lopez & C. R. Snyder (Eds.), *Oxford handbook of positive psychology* (2nd ed.) (pp. 437–445), New York, NY: Oxford University Press.

Watson, D. L., & Tharp, R. G. (2007). *Self– directed behavior* (9th ed.). Belmont, CA: Wadsworth.

Waugh, C. E., Fredrickson, B. L., & Taylor, S. F. (2008). Adapting to life's slings and arrows: Individual differences in resilience when recovering from an anticipated threat. *Journal of Research in Personality, 42,* 1031–1046.

Weber, H., Vollman, M., & Renner, B. (2007). The spirited, the observant, and the disheartened: Social concepts of optimism, realism, and pessimism. *Journal of Personality, 75(1),* 169–197.

Weber, M. (1968). *The religion of China.* London, UK: The Free Press.

Webster, J. D. (2010). Wisdom and positive psychosocial values in young adulthood. *Journal of Adult Development, 17,* 70–80.

Wefald, A. J., & Downey, R. G. (2009). Construct dimensionality of engagement and its relation with satisfaction. *The Journal of Psychology, 143(1),* 91–111.

Weger, H., Castle, G. R., & Emmett, M. C. (2010). Active listening in peer interviews: The influence of message paraphrasing on perceptions of listening skill. *The International Journal of Listening, 24,* 34–49.

Weinstein, N., Brown, K. W., & Ryan, R. M. (2009). A multi-method examination of the effects of mindfulness on stress attribution, coping, and emotional well-being. *Journal of Research in Personality, 43,* 374–385.

Weiss, A., Bates, T. C., & Luciano, M. (2008). Happiness is a personal(ity) thing: The genetics of personality and well-being in a representative sample. *Psychological Science, 19(3),* 205–210.

Weiten, W., Lloyd, M. A., Dunn, D. S., & Hammer, E. Y. (2009). *Psychology applied to modern life: Adjustment in the 21st century* (9th ed.). Belmont, CA: Wadsworth.

Whittington, B. L., & Scher, S. J. (2010). Prayer and subjective well-being: An examination of six different types of prayer. *The International Journal for the Psychology of Religion, 20,* 59–68.

Whitton, S. W., Larson, J. J., & Hauser, S. T. (2008). Depressive symptoms and bias in perceived social competence among young adults. *Journal of Clinical Psychology, 64(7),* 791–805.

Williams, E. F., Gilovich, T. (2008). Do people really believe they are above average? *Journal of Experimental Social Psychology, 44,* 1121–1128.

Williams, G. C., Cox, E. M., Hedberg, V., & Deci, E. L. (2000). Extrinsic life goals and health risk behaviors in adolescents. *Journal of Applied Social Psychology, 30,* 1756–1771.

Williams, G. C., Rodin, G. C., Ryan, R. M., Grolnick, W. S., & Deci, E. L. (1998). Autonomous regulation and long-term medication adherence in adult outpatients. *Health Psychology, 17,* 269–276.

Williams, P. G., & Moroz, T. L. (2009). Personality vulnerability to stress-related sleep disruption: Pathways to adverse mental and physical health outcomes. *Personality and Individual Differences, 46,* 598–603.

Williams, P. G., Rau, H. K., Cribbet, M. R., & Gunn, H. E. (2009). Openness to experience and stress regulation. *Journal of Research in Personality, 43,* 777–784.

Williams, P. G., Suchy, Y., & Rau, H. K. (2009). Individual differences in executive functioning: Implications for stress regulation. *Annals of Behavioral Medicine, 37,* 126–140.

Wilson, J. (1996). *The earth shall weep: A history of Native America.* New York, NY: Atlantic Monthly Press.

Wilson, T. D., & Gilbert, D. T. (2005). Affective forecasting: Knowing what to want. *Current Directions in Psychological Science, 14(3),* 131–134.

Windle, G., Markland, D. A., & Woods, R. T. (2008). Examination of a theoretical model of psychological resilience in older age. *Aging & Mental Health, 12(3),* 285–292.

Wohl, M. J. A., Pychyl, T. A., & Bennett, S. H. (2010). I forgive myself, now I can study: How self-forgiveness for procrastinating can reduce further procrastination. *Personality and Individual Differences, 48,* 803–808.

Wolfe, R. N., & Johnson, S. D. (1995). Personality as a predictor of college performance. *Educational and Psychological Measurement, 55,* 177–185.

Wolters, C. A. (2003). Understanding procrastination from a self-regulated learning perspective. *Journal of Educational Psychology, 95(1),* 179–187.

Wong, J. G. W. S., Cheung, E. P. T., Chan, K. K. C., Ma, K. K. M., & Tang, S. W. (2006). Web-based survey of depression, anxiety, and stress in first-year tertiary education students in Hong Kong. *Australia and New Zealand Journal of Psychiatry, 40(9),* 777–782.

Wong, E. (1997). *The Shambhala guide to Taoism*. Boston, MA: Shambhala Publications.

Wong, S. S., & Lim, T. (2009). Hope versus optimism in Singaporean adolescents: Contributions to depression and life satisfaction. *Personality and Individual Differences, 46*, 648–652.

Wood, A. M., Joseph, S., & Linley, P. A. (2007). Coping style as a psychological resource of grateful people. *Journal of Social and Clinical Psychology, 26(9)*, 1076–1093.

Wood, A. M., Joseph, S., Lloyd, J., & Atkins, S. (2009). Gratitude influences sleep through the mechanism of pre-sleep cognitions. *Journal of Psychosomatic Research, 66*, 43–48.

Wood, A. M., Joseph, S., & Maltby, J. (2008). Gratitude uniquely predicts satisfaction with life: Incremental validity above the domains and facets of the five factor model. *Personality and Individual Differences, 45*, 49–54.

Wood, A. M., Joseph, S., & Maltby, J. (2009). Gratitude predicts psychological well-being above the Big Five facets. *Personality and Individual Differences, 46*, 443–447.

Wood, A. M., Maltby, J., Gillett, R., Linley, P. A., & Joseph, S. (2008). The role of gratitude in the development of social support, stress, and depression: Two longitudinal studies. *Journal of Research in Personality, 42*, 854–871.

Wood, A. M., Maltby, J., Stewart, N., & Linley, P. A. (2008). A social-cognitive model of trait and state levels of gratitude. *Emotion, 8(2)*, 281–290.

Woodard, C. R., & Pury, C. L. S. (2007). The construct of courage: Categorization and measurement. *Counseling Psychology Journal: Practice and Research, 59(2)*, 135–147.

Woolfolk, H. A., & Davis, H. A. (2006). Teacher self-efficacy and its influence on the achievement of adolescents. In F. Pajares & T. Urdan (Eds.), *Adolescence and education, Vol. 5: Self-efficacy and adolescence* (pp. 117–137), Greenwich, CT: Information Age Publishing.

World Values Survey. (2011). www.worldvaluessurvey.org/index_html

Worthington Jr., E. L. (2005). *Handbook of forgiveness*. New York, NY: Routledge.

Worthington, E. L., & Scherer, M. (2004). Forgiveness is an emotion-focused coping strategy that can reduce health risks and promote health resilience: Theory, review, and hypothesis. *Psychology and Health, 19(3)*, 385–405.

Yalom, I. D. (1980). *Existential psychotherapy*. New York, NY: Basic Books.

Yang, K-P., Su, W-M., & Huang, C-K. (2009). The effect of meditation on physical and mental health in junior college students: A quasi-experimental study. *Journal of Nursing Research, 17(4)*, 261–268.

Yap, M. B. H., Allen, N. B., & Ladouceur, C. D. (2008). Maternal socialization of positive affect: The impact of invalidation on adolescent emotion regulation and depressive symptomatology. *Child Development, 79(5)*, 1415–1431.

Yeh, Z-T., & Liu, S-I. (2007). Depressive realism: Evidence from false interpersonal perception. *Psychiatry and Clinical Neurosciences, 61*, 135–141.

Ying, Y-W. (2009). Contribution of self-compassion to competence and mental health in social work students. *Journal of Social Work Education, 45(2)*, 309–323.

Ysseldyk, R., Matheson, K., & Anisman, H. (2009). Forgiveness and the appraisal-coping process in response to relationship conflicts: Implications for depressive symptoms. *Stress, 12(2)*, 152–166.

Zabriskie, R. B., & McCormack, B. P. (2003). Parent and child perspectives of family leisure involvement and satisfaction with family life. *Journal of Leisure Research, 35(2)*, 163–189.

Zhang, S., & Stafford, L. (2008). Perceived face threat of honest but hurtful evaluative messages in romantic relationships. *Western Journal of Communication, 72(1)*, 19–39.

Zhang, W., Chen, Q., McCubbin, H., McCubbin, L., & Foley, S. (2011). Predictors of mental and physical health: Individual and neighborhood levels of education, social well-being, and ethnicity. *Health & Place, 17,* 238–247.

Zhang, Y., Fishbach, A., & Dhar, R. (2007). When thinking beats doing: The role of optimistic expectations in goal-based choice. *Journal of Consumer Research, 34,* 567–578.

Zhao, L., Lu, Y., Wang, B., & Huang, W. (2011). What makes them happy and curious online? An empirical study on high school students' Internet use from a self-determination theory perspective. *Computers & Education, 56,* 346–356.

Zinnbauer, B. J., Pargament, K. I., & Scott, A. B. (1999). The emerging meanings of religiousness and spirituality: Problems and prospects. *Journal of Personality, 67(6),* 889–919.

Zinnbauer, B. J., Pargament, K. I., Cole, B., Rye, M. S., Butter, E. M., Belavich, T. G.,

Hipp, K. M., Scott, A. B., & Kadar, J. L. (1997). Religion and spirituality: Unfuzzing the fuzzy. *Journal for the Scientific Study of Religion, 36(4),* 549–564.

Zoellner, T., & Maercker, A. (2006). Posttraumatic growth in clinical psychology: A critical review and introduction of a two component model. *Clinical Psychology Review, 26(5),* 626–653.

Zuesse, E. M. (1991). Perseverance and transmutation in African traditional religions. In J. K. Olupona (Ed.), *African traditional religions in contemporary society* (pp. 167–184), St. Paul, MN: Paragon House.

Zyphur, M. J., Warren, C. R., Landis, R. S., & Thoreson, C. J. (2007). Self-Regulation and performance in high-fidelity simulations: An extension of ego-depletion research. *Human Performance, 20(2),* 103–118.

Index